KT-502-436

PAGES 80–93
Street Finder
maps 3–4

PAGES 60–79
Street Finder
maps 3–4

PAGES 142–157
Street Finder
maps 3–6

Jewish Quarter
JOSEFOV

Old Town
STARÉ MĚSTO

New Town
NOVÉ MĚSTO

0 metres   500

0 yards   500

EYEWITNESS TRAVEL
PRAGUE

EYEWITNESS TRAVEL
PRAGUE

MAIN CONTRIBUTOR: VLADIMÍR SOUKUP

DK

LONDON, NEW YORK,
MELBOURNE, MUNICH AND DELHI
www.dk.com

PROJECT EDITOR Heather Jones
ART EDITOR Lisa Kosky
EDITORS Ferdie McDonald, Carey Combe
DESIGNERS Louise Parsons, Nicki Rawson

CONTRIBUTORS
Petr David, Vladimír Dobrovodský, Nicholas Lowry,
Polly Phillimore, Joy Turner-Kadečková, Craig Turp

PHOTOGRAPHERS
Jiří Doležal, Jiří Kopřiva, Vladimír Kozlík, František Přeučil,
Milan Posselt, Stanislav Tereba, Peter Wilson

ILLUSTRATORS
Gillie Newman, Chris Orr, Otakar Pok, Jaroslav Staněk

This book was produced with the assistance of
Olympia Publishing House, Prague.

Reproduced by Colourscan, Singapore
Printed and bound by South China Printing Co. Ltd., China

First published in Great Britain in 1994
by Dorling Kindersley Limited
80 Strand, London, WC2R 0RL

Reprinted with revisions 1994, 1995, 1996, 1997,
1998, 1999, 2000, 2001, 2002, 2003, 2004, 2005, 2006, 2008, 2009

Copyright 1994, 2009 © Dorling Kindersley Limited, London
A Penguin Company

ALL RIGHTS RESERVED. NO PART OF THIS PUBLICATION MAY BE
REPRODUCED, STORED IN A RETRIEVAL SYSTEM, OR TRANSMITTED IN ANY
FORM OR BY ANY MEANS, ELECTRONIC, MECHANICAL, PHOTOCOPYING,
RECORDING OR OTHERWISE, WITHOUT THE PRIOR WRITTEN PERMISSION
OF THE COPYRIGHT OWNER.

A CIP CATALOGUE RECORD IS AVAILABLE FROM THE BRITISH LIBRARY.

ISBN 978-1-40533-387-0

FLOORS ARE REFERRED TO THROUGHOUT IN ACCORDANCE WITH EUROPEAN USAGE;
IE THE "FIRST FLOOR" IS THE FLOOR ABOVE GROUND LEVEL.

*Front cover main image: the Church of Our Lady before Týn towers above
the houses of Staré Město*

We're trying to be cleaner and greener:

- we recycle waste and switch things off
- we use paper from responsibly managed forests whenever possible
- we ask our printers to actively reduce water and energy consumption
- we check out our suppliers' working conditions – they never use child labour

Find out more about our values and best practices at www.dk.com

The information in this
Dorling Kindersley Travel Guide is checked annually.

Every effort has been made to ensure that this book is as up-to-date
as possible at the time of going to press. Some details, however,
such as telephone numbers, opening hours, prices, gallery hanging
arrangements and travel information, are liable to change.
The publishers cannot accept responsibility for any consequences
arising from the use of this book, nor for any material on third-party
websites, and cannot guarantee that any website address in this
book will be a suitable source of travel information.
We value the views and suggestions of our readers very highly.
Please write to: Publisher, DK Eyewitness Travel Guides,
Dorling Kindersley, 80 Strand, London WC2R 0RL, Great Britain.

◁ **View over the rooftops to Prague Castle**

CONTENTS

Rudolph II (1576–1612)

INTRODUCING
PRAGUE

Outdoor café tables

Wallenstein Palace and Garden in the Little Quarter

Church of Our Lady before Týn

Czech beer-bottle cap

Fiacre, Old Town Square

Baroque façades
of houses at the
southern end of
Old Town Square

HOW TO USE THIS GUIDE

This Eyewitness Travel Guide helps you get the most from your stay in Prague with the minimum of difficulty. The opening section, *Introducing Prague*, locates the city geographically, sets modern Prague in its historical context and describes events through the entire year. *Prague at a Glance* is an overview of the city's main attractions, including a feature on the River Vltava. Section two, *Prague Area by Area*, starts on page 58. This is the main sightseeing

Planning the day's itinerary in Prague

section, which covers all the important sights, with photographs, maps and drawings. It also includes day trips from Prague and four guided walks around the city. Carefully researched tips for hotels, restaurants, shops and markets, cafés and bars, enter- tainment and sports are found in *Travellers' Needs*. The last section, the *Survival Guide*, contains useful practical advice on all you need to know, from making a telephone call to using the public transport system.

FINDING YOUR WAY AROUND THE SIGHTSEEING SECTION

Each of the five sightseeing areas in the city is colour-coded for easy reference. Every chapter opens with an introduction to the part of Prague it covers, describing its history and character, followed by a Street-by-Street

map illustrating the heart of the area. Finding your way around each chapter is made simple by the numbering system used throughout. The most important sights are covered in detail in two or more full pages.

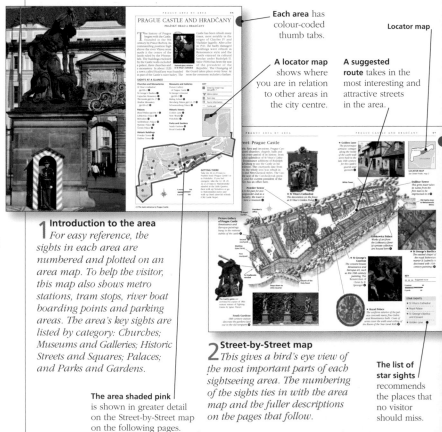

Each area has colour-coded thumb tabs.

A locator map shows where you are in relation to other areas in the city centre.

Locator map

A suggested route takes in the most interesting and attractive streets in the area.

1 Introduction to the area
For easy reference, the sights in each area are numbered and plotted on an area map. To help the visitor, this map also shows metro stations, tram stops, river boat boarding points and parking areas. The area's key sights are listed by category: Churches; Museums and Galleries; Historic Streets and Squares; Palaces; and Parks and Gardens.

The area shaded pink
is shown in greater detail on the Street-by-Street map on the following pages.

2 Street-by-Street map
This gives a bird's eye view of the most important parts of each sightseeing area. The numbering of the sights ties in with the area map and the fuller descriptions on the pages that follow.

The list of star sights
recommends the places that no visitor should miss.

PRAGUE AREA MAP

The coloured areas shown on this map *(see inside front cover)* are the five main sightseeing areas of Prague – each covered in a full chapter in *Prague Area by Area (pp58–157)*. They are highlighted on other maps throughout the book. In *Prague at a Glance (pp36–57)*, for example, they help locate the top sights. They are also used plot the routes of the river trip *(pp56–7)* and the four guided walks *(p172)*.

Numbers refer to each sight's position on the area map and its place in the chapter.

Practical information lists all the information you need to visit every sight, including a map reference to the *Street Finder (pp252–7)*.

Façades of important buildings are often shown to help you recognize them quickly.

The visitors' checklist provides all the practical information needed to plan your visit.

3 Detailed information on each sight

All the important sights in Prague are described individually. They are listed in order, following the numbering on the area map. Practical information on opening hours, telephone numbers, admission charges and facilities available is given for each sight. The key to the symbols used can be found on the back flap.

4 Prague's major sights

Historic buildings are dissected to reveal their interiors; and museums and galleries have colour-coded floorplans to help you find important exhibits.

A timeline charts the key events in the history of the building.

Stars indicate the features no visitor should miss.

INTRODUCING
PRAGUE

FOUR GREAT DAYS IN PRAGUE

Few cities have as much to offer as Prague, so it can be difficult to decide how best to spend your time. The Old Town is a joy in itself, and you could amble around here admiring its old houses for days. Yet, with some planning you can see much more of

Astronomical clock

what makes this historic city special. Here are four distinct days packed with the best that Prague has to offer. Feel free to mix and match: leaving out a museum or sight will not alter the overall effect. The price guides include cost of travel, food and admission fees.

NATIONAL TREASURES

- Hradčany Square guards
- Lunch in the Little Quarter
- Cross the Charles Bridge
- Watch the Town Hall clock
- Majestic art or church

TWO ADULTS allow at least Kč2,400

Morning
Starting at **Hradčany Square**, admire the guards in their elaborate costumes then walk through První nádvoří to **St Vitus's Cathedral** *(see pp100–3)*, the soul of the Castle. Take a short tour around here before moving on to look at the Baroque art collection in **St George's Convent** *(see pp106–7)*. If you fancy some souvenir shopping, go for the artisans' cottages on **Golden Lane** *(see p99)*. Alternatively, head to **Lobkowicz Palace**, and tour the exhibition

The sumptuous interior of the Spanish synagogue

inside *(see p99)*. Take the easy route along Nerudova to **Little Quarter Square**. Here, enjoy a late lunch and admire the architectural gems of the **Little Quarter** *(see pp124–5)*.

Afternoon
It is a short walk from here to **Charles Bridge** *(see pp136–9)*, and on to Old Town Square. Time your arrival on the hour to see the **Old Town Square's Astronomical Clock** *(see pp72–4)* in action. The **Old Town Hall Tower** *(see p73)* is well worth a visit for amazing views of Prague Castle and the Little Quarter. Next, choose between seeing the art in the Rococo **Kinský Palace** *(see p70)* or the bare majesty of **St Nicholas' Church** *(see pp70–1)*. The narrow streets and shops of the Týn courtyard now await exploration. Enjoy dinner at the **Staroměstská** restaurant, which serves traditional Czech food in elegant surroundings *(see p203)*.

A little respite for visitors at an outdoor café in Old Town Square

LITERARY, ART AND RELIGIOUS LANDMARKS

- Kafka's home
- The Jewish Quarter
- Decorative and Medieval Art collections
- Quality shopping

TWO ADULTS allow at least Kč4,560

Morning
Jewish Prague and Franz Kafka are inseparable, so you may want to start the day with a coffee at **Café Grand Praha** *(see p209)* in Old Town Square. Kafka lived above here and the café was once named after his journalist girlfriend, Milena. Refreshed, head along Pařížská into the **Jewish Quarter** *(see pp80–9)*. Stop at the **Maisel Synagogue** *(see p90)*, then cross the road to the historic **Old Jewish Cemetery** *(see pp86–7)*. A good walk around here, as well as a look inside the **Klausen Synagogue** *(see p85)* will set you up for lunch. Try one of the local Jewish restaurants or the non-Jewish **Les Moules** *(see p204)*.

Afternoon

Admire the Gobelin tapestries at the **Museum of Decorative Arts** *(see p84)*. Stroll along to the **Jewish Town Hall** *(see p85)*, and the **Old-New Synagogue** *(see pp88–9)*. The eastern side of the Jewish Quarter is home to two must-see sights: the glorious **Spanish Synagogue** *(see p90)* and the medieval art in **St Agnes of Bohemia Convent** *(see pp92–3)*. After a day of high cultural input, it's time for a little quality shopping on Pařížská – a large thoroughfare in the Jewish Quarter. Eat at **King Solomon,** one of Prague's best Jewish restaurants *(see p204)*.

FAMILY DAY

- Funicular ride and tower
- Mirror Maze
- Peacocks and caves
- Church of St James

FAMILY OF 4 allow at least Kč2,900

Morning

Take the funicular railway up **Petřín Hill** *(see p141)*, to see Prague's mini-Eiffel Tower – the **Observation Tower** *(see p140)* which has it has a spiral staircase to the top. The Mirror Maze *(see p140)*, a short walk away, will keep youngsters happy for hours, as will the nearby **Observatory** *(see p140)*. Take the funicular halfway back down the hill for lunch at the **Nebozízek** *(see p205)* with its outdoor patio and panoramic views.

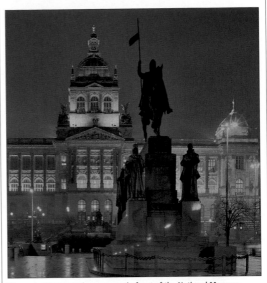
Wenceslas Square and monument in front of the National Museum

The Mirror Maze, great fun for young and old alike

Afternoon

Take a stroll on Střelecký Ostrov, where the swans await the remnants of your lunchtime bread. There's more wildlife to be seen at the **Wallenstein Palace** *(see p126)*, home to peacocks and a bizarre replica of a limestone cave. Walk or take the metro over the river to catch the Old Town Square's **Astronomical Clock** *(see pp72–4)* in action. Eat at one of the cafés on the square. Then on to the **Church of St. James** *(see p65)*. Children will be intrigued by the mummified arm, which has been hanging above the church entrance for 400 years.

HISTORY AND HEROES

- Wenceslas Square – the rise and fall of Communism
- Lunch in splendid style
- Wartime history
- Shopping for antiques

TWO ADULTS allow at least Kč3,060

Morning

Start the day with a walk along **Wenceslas Square** *(see pp144–5)* to see where the

communist regime was toppled. Walk the length of the square and imagine it lined with people as it was for weeks in 1989. Pay your respects at the **Monument to the Victims of Communism** *(see p145)*, and to Jan Palach, who set himself alight here in 1969 in protest at the Soviet invasion. Just off the Square is the former Gestapo HQ on Politických vězňů (now the national trade office) where thousands of Czechs were imprisoned during WWII. Stop for lunch at the Art Nouveau **Evropa Hotel** *(see p206)* on Wenceslas Square.

Afternoon

Walk to the Baroque **Church of St Cyril and St Methodius** *(see p152)*, where Czech resistance fighters took their own lives in 1942. Bullet holes can still be seen on the wall of the crypt, where a fascinating museum chronicles the events. End the day with a bit of antique browsing. **Military Antiques** in Charvátova *(see p214)*, is a treasure trove of relics from the Nazi and Soviet occupations, as well as military bric-a-brac from all periods.

Putting Prague on the Map

Prague has a population of just over 1 million and covers 500 sq km (200 sq miles) at its outer limits. It is the capital of the recently-formed Czech Republic and head of the region of Bohemia. Prague's geographical position at the centre of Europe makes it a convenient base from which to visit both the Bohemian countryside and many other major cities, such as Nuremberg, Vienna, Bratislava and Budapest.

GERMANY

Berlin

Dresden

Terezín

Praha (PRAGUE)

Karlovy Vary (Karlsbad)

Karlštejn (Karlstein)

Kutná Hora

View looking southwest over the Vltava

Nuremberg

Paris

Plzeň (Pilsen)

Vltava

Elbe

Elbe

Bóbr

EUROPE

NORWAY
FINLAND
SWEDEN
ESTONIA
RUSSIAN FEDERATION
UNITED KINGDOM
DENMARK
LATVIA
REP. OF IRELAND
LITHUANIA
NETHERLANDS
POLAND
BELORUSSIA
BELGIUM
GERMANY
Prague
CZECH REPUBLIC
UKRAINE
FRANCE
SWITZ.
AUSTRIA
SLOVAKIA
MOLDOVA
SLOVENIA
HUNGARY
CROATIA
ROMANIA
BOSNIA HERZ.
SERBIA
SPAIN
MONTENEGRO
BULGARIA
ITALY
ALBANIA
MACEDONIA
GREECE
TURKEY

České Budějovice (Budweis)

Danube

Linz

Salzburg

AUSTRIA

Europe
The Czech Republic, right at the heart of continental Europe, is completely landlocked. Prague, the capital, has one airport and road and rail links to neighbouring countries.

ITALY

Verona

Drava

Graz

PRAGUE AND ENVIRONS

Veltrusy
Neratovice
Lysá n. Labem
Slaný
Kralupy n. Vltavou
Brandýs n. Labem-Stará Boleslav
Čakovice
Čelákovice
Švermov
Roztoky
Horní Počernice
Kladno
Ruzyně
Úvaly
Český Brod
Unhošt
Rudná
Říčany
Beroun
Zbraslav
Karlštejn
Berounka
Jílové u Prahy
Řevnice
Vltava
Sázava

0 km 10
0 miles 5

Prague and Environs

*Most sights are in the central, historic area of Prague.
These are covered in detail on pages 58–157.
Important sights outside the centre and day
trips can be found on pages 159–71. For
road and rail networks, see pages 238–9.*

P O L A N D

Oder
Warsaw
Breslau

Elbe

C Z E C H
R E P U B L I C

Cracow

Ostrava

Brno

Morava

Aerial view of Greater Prague

VIENNA

S L O V A K I A

BRATISLAVA

Váh

H U N G A R Y

BUDAPEST

Lake Balaton

0 kilometres 50
0 miles 30

Zagreb

KEY

☐ Greater Prague
✈ Airport
▬ Motorway
▬ Major road
— Railway line
–·– Country boundary

Central Prague

PRAŽSKÝ HRAD A HRADČANY

PRAGUE CASTLE AND HRADČANY

Šternberský palác
Sternberg Palace

Chrám sv. Víta
St Vitus's Cathedral

Královský palác
Royal Palace

Klášter sv. Jiří
St George's Convent

Malostranská

Loreta
The Loreto

Kostel sv. Mikuláše
Church of St Nicholas

Strahovský klášter
Strahov Monastery

MALÁ STRANA

LITTLE QUARTER

České Muzeum Hudby
Museum of Music

Orb and Cross
An important part of the royal coronation regalia, this orb is now kept at St.Vitus's Cathedral (see pp100–3).

KEY

▪	Major sight
M	Metro station
🚌	Bus stop
🚊	Tram stop
🚋	Funicular railway
⛴	River boat boarding point
P	Parking
ℹ	Tourist information
✚	Hospital
👮	Police station
✝	Church
✡	Synagogue
---	City wall

View of the Church of St Lawrence
Petřín Park offers outstanding views of Prague (see p141 and Four Guided Walks, pp176–7).

Painted House Façade
The Old Town has many Renaissance and Baroque houses. Some have colourful mural paintings like this one in Old Town Square (see pp66–9).

Art Nouveau Statue
The New Town has many examples of Art Nouveau architecture (see pp148–9).

0 metres   200
0 yards   200

THE HISTORY OF PRAGUE

Prague's position at the crossroads of Europe has made it a magnet for foreign traders since prehistoric times. By the early 10th century Prague had become a thriving town with a large market place, the Old Town Square, and two citadels, Prague Castle and Vyšehrad, from where its first rulers, the Přemyslids, conducted their many family feuds. These were often bloody: in 935, Prince Wenceslas was murdered by his brother Boleslav. Wenceslas was later canonized and became Bohemia's best-known patron saint.

Prague coat of arms

During the Middle Ages Prague enjoyed a golden age, especially during the reign of the Holy Roman Emperor, Charles IV. Under the government of this wise and cultured king, Prague grew into a magnificent city, larger than Paris or London. Charles instigated the founding and building of many institutions in Prague, including the first University of Central Europe in Prague. The University's first Czech rector was Jan Hus, the reforming preacher whose execution for alleged heresy in 1415 led to the Hussite wars. The radical wing of the Hussites, the Taborites, were finally defeated at the Battle of Lipany in 1434. During the 16th century, after a succession of weak kings, the Habsburgs gained control, beginning a rule that would last for almost 400 years. One of the more enlightened of all the Habsburg Emperors was Rudolph II. He brought the spirit of the Renaissance to Prague through his love of the arts and sciences. Soon after his death, in 1618, Prague was the setting for the Protestant revolt which led to the Thirty Years' War. The war's aftermath caused a serious decline in the fortunes of the city that would revive only in the 18th century. Prague's many fine Baroque churches and palaces date from this time.

The 19th century saw a period of national revival and the burgeoning of civic pride. The great public monuments – the National Museum, the National Theatre and Rudolfinum – were built. But a foreign power still ruled the city, and it was not until 1918 that Prague became the capital of an independent Republic. World War II brought occupation by the German army, followed by four decades of Communism. After the "Velvet Revolution" of 1989, Prague is today on the threshold of a new era.

View of Prague Castle and Little Quarter, 1493

◁ *St Wenceslas and St Vitus*, by Bartholomaeus Spränger, about 1600

Rulers of Prague

Three great dynasties have shaped the history of Prague: the Přemyslids, the Luxemburgs and the Habsburgs. According to Slavic legend, the Přemyslids were founded by Princess Libuše *(see p21)*. Her line included St Wenceslas and Přemysl Otakar II, whose death in battle at Marchfeld paved the way for the Luxemburgs. This family produced one of the city's greatest rulers, Charles IV, who was King of Bohemia and Holy Roman Emperor *(see pp24–5)*. In 1526, Prague came under the control of the Austrian House of Habsburg whose rule lasted 400 years, until after World War I, when the newly formed Czechoslovakia gained its independence. Since then there has been a succession of presidents.

The mythical Princess Libuše

1346–78 Charles IV

1453–7 Ladislav Posthumus

1310–46 John of Luxemburg

1140–72 Vladislav I

935–72 Boleslav I

1230–53 Wenceslas I

1305–6 Wenceslas III

1278–1305 Wenceslas II

1034–55 Břetislav I

900	1000	1100	1200	1300	1400

PŘEMYSLIDS   **LUXEMBURGS**

900	1000	1100	1200	1300	1400

972–99 Boleslav II

1061–92 Vratislav II

921–35 St Wenceslas

1173–9 Soběslav II

1197–1230 Přemysl Otakar I

1253–78 Přemysl Otakar II

1378–1419 Wenceslas IV

1419–37 Sigismund

1935–8 and 1945–8 Edvard Beneš

1938–9 and 1939–45 Emil Hacha

1948–53 Klement Gottwald

1953–7 Antonín Zápotocký

1740–80 Maria Theresa

1790–92 Leopold II

1918–35 Tomáš Garrigue Masaryk

1957–68 Antonín Novotný

1526–64 Ferdinand I

1564–76 Maxmilian II

1657–1705 Leopold I

1792–1835 Franz II

1458–71 George of Poděbrady

1637–57 Ferdinand III

1711–40 Charles VI

1835–48 Ferdinand V

1968–75 Ludvík Svoboda

1500 1600 1700 1800 1900

JAGIELLOS HABSBURGS PRESIDENTS

1500 1600 1700 1800 1900

1619–37 Ferdinand II

1516–26 Ludvíc II

1705–11 Josef I

1916–18 Charles I

1471–1516 Vladislav Jagiello

1848–1916 Franz Josef

1611–19 Matthias

1975–89 Gustáv Husák

1576–1611 Rudolph II

1780–90 Josef II

1989–92 and 1993–2003 Václav Havel (below) 2003– Václav Klaus

Prague under the Přemyslids

Early Celtic tribes, from 500 BC, were the first inhabitants of the area around the Vltava valley. The Germanic Marcomans arrived in 9–6 BC, and gradually the Celts left. The first Slavic tribes came to Bohemia in about 500 AD. Struggles for supremacy led to the emergence of a ruling dynasty, the Přemyslids, around 800 AD.

9th-century earring

They built two fortified settlements: the first at Prague Castle *(see pp94–111)*, the second at Vyšehrad, a rocky headland on the right bank of the Vltava *(see pp180–1)*. These remained the seats of Czech princes for hundreds of years. One prince crucial to the emerging Czech State was the pious Wenceslas. He enjoyed only a brief reign but left an important legacy in the founding of St Vitus's rotunda *(see p102)*.

EXTENT OF THE CITY

☐ 1000 AD   ☐ Today

Boleslav's henchman raises his sword to strike the fatal blow.

St Cyril and St Methodius
Originally Greeks from Salonica, these two brothers brought Christianity to Moravia in about 863. They baptized early Přemyslid, Bořivoj, and his wife Ludmilla, grandmother of St Wenceslas.

Second assassin grapples with the Prince's companion.

Early Coin
Silver coins like this denar were minted in the royal mint of Vyšehrad during Boleslav II's reign from 967–99.

Wild Boar Figurine
Celtic tribes made small talismans of the wild animals that they hunted for food in the forested areas around Prague.

TIMELINE

Bronze head of a Celtic goddess

623–658 Bohemia is part of an empire formed by Frankish merchant, Samo

600 AD		700

500 BC Celts in Bohemia. Joined by Germanic Marcomans in 1st century AD

6th century Slavs settle alongside Germanic tribes in Bohemia

8th century Tribe of Czechs settle in central Bohemia

Vyšehrad acropolis – first Czech settlement on the right bank of the Vltava

Sword and Helmet
St Wenceslas was buried in the southern apse of the rotunda of St Vitus. His sword and helmet were preserved as relics and today form part of the Cathedral's treasure.

Wenceslas seeks sanctuary.

A monk closes the door against Wenceslas.

PRINCESS LIBUŠE
The legendary founder of the Přemyslids was Princess Libuše, head of a West Slavic tribe. She took notice of the discord among her clansmen, and succeeded her father to become the first woman ruler. Choosing a humble plough-man (*Přemysl-Oráč*) as consort and ruler, she began a dynasty that was to last 400 years.

Princess Libuše foresaw the glory of Prague in a vision

Rotunda of St Vitus
Founded by Wenceslas in the early 10th century, the rotunda became a place of pilgrimage after the saint's death in 929. It stood where St Wenceslas Chapel is today.

Roman-arched windows

Curving stone walls

ASSASSINATION OF PRINCE WENCESLAS
In 935, the young Wenceslas was murdered on the orders of his brother, Boleslav. This manuscript illustration of 1006 shows the moment when the assassins caught up with the prince as he was about to enter the church for the morning mass.

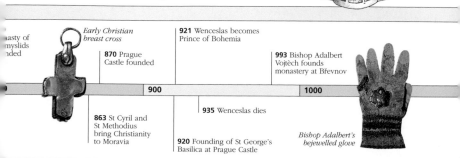

...asty of ...myslids ...nded

Early Christian breast cross

870 Prague Castle founded

921 Wenceslas becomes Prince of Bohemia

993 Bishop Adalbert Vojtěch founds monastery at Břevnov

900

1000

863 St Cyril and St Methodius bring Christianity to Moravia

935 Wenceslas dies

920 Founding of St George's Basilica at Prague Castle

Bishop Adalbert's bejewelled glove

Early Medieval Prague

Prague Castle steadily grew in importance from the beginning of the 9th century onwards. Prone to frequent fires, its wooden buildings were gradually replaced by stone and the area developed into a sturdy Romanesque fortress with a palace and religious buildings. Clustered around the original outer bailey was an area inhabited by skilled craftsmen and German merchants, encouraged to come and stay in Prague by Vladislav II and, later, Přemysl Otakar II. This came to be known as the "Little Quarter" and achieved town status in 1257. It was joined to the Old Town by a bridge, known as the Judith Bridge.

Initial letter D from the Vyšehrad Codex

EXTENT OF THE CITY

▨ 1230   ☐ Today

St George's Convent and Basilica (see pp106–9 and p98)

PRAGUE CASTLE IN 1230

Sited on a high ridge, the Romanesque fortress had protective stone walls and easily-guarded gates.

The Prince's Palace grew into the Royal Palace (see pp104–5).

Entrance from Old Town

The White Tower gave access from the west.

Decorative Comb
This ornate, bone, fine-toothed comb was one of the relics of St Adalbert.

Site of Hradčany Square

External staircase

Living room

Vaulted ceiling

Romanesque Stone House
These three-storeyed houses were based around a very simple floor plan.

Ground floor

St Vitus's Basilica and Chapter House (see pp100–3)

Stone houses were built on what is now Nerudova Street in the Little Quarter (see p130).

TIMELINE

1040 St Adalbert's remains brought to Prague

1092–1110 Reign of Bretislav II

1091 Old Town marketplace first mentioned by travellers

1110 Small German settlement in Prague

1140 Strahov Monastery founded

1050

1100

1

1070 Vyšehrad becomes temporary seat of Czech princes

1091 Great fire at Prague Castle

1110–20 Reign of Bořivoj II

St Adalbert with a martyr's palm frond

1085 Vratislav I becomes first King of Bohemia

1135 Seat of Czech princes moves from Vyšehrad to Prague Castle

Romanesque stone head from Judith Bridge Tower

St Agnes of Bohemia
Sister of Wenceslas I, this devout woman built a convent for the order of the Poor Clares (the female counterparts of the Franciscans) (see pp92–3). She was not canonized until 1989.

WHERE TO SEE ROMANESQUE PRAGUE

Remains can be seen in the crypt of St Vitus's *(pp100–3)*, the basements of the Palace of the Lords of Kunštát *(p78)* and the Royal Palace *(pp104–5).*

St George's Basilica
The vaulting in the crypt dates from the 12th century (p98).

Vratislav II
The Vyšehrad Codex, an illuminated selection from the gospels, was made to mark Vratislav's coronation in 1061.

The Black Tower was the exit to Bohemia's second town, Kutná Hora *(see p168).*

Little Quarter Square

St Martin's Rotunda
This well-preserved building is in Vyšehrad (p180).

Little Quarter Coat of Arms
Vladislav II's portrait was incorporated into this 16th-century miniature painting.

Přemysl Otakar II
The last great Přemyslid king was killed in battle after trying to carve out a huge empire.

1233 Founding of St Agnes's Convent

1182 Romanesque construction of Prague Castle completed

1257 Little Quarter receives town status

1258–68 Strahov Monastery rebuilt in Gothic style after fire

1200   **1250**   **1290**

1212 Přemysl Otakar I receives the Sicilian Golden Bull, confirming the sovereignty of Bohemian kings

Sicilian Golden Bull

1278 Přemysl Otakar II dies at Marchfeld

1158 Judith Bridge built *(see pp136–9)*

Prague's Golden Age

In the late Middle Ages, Prague attained the height of its glory. The Holy Roman Emperor Charles IV chose Prague as his Imperial residence and set out to make the city the most magnificent in Europe. He founded a university (the Carolinum) and built many fine churches and monasteries in the Gothic style. Of major importance were his town-planning schemes, such as the reconstruction of Prague Castle, the building of a new stone bridge to replace the Judith Bridge, and the foundation of a new quarter, the New Town. A devout Catholic, he owned a large collection of relics which were kept, along with the Crown Jewels, at Karlstein Castle *(see pp168–9).*

Gift from Pope Urban V in 1368

EXTENT OF THE CITY

| ☐ 1350 | ☐ *Today* |

Charles IV wears the Imperial crown, set with sapphires, rubies and pearls.

St Wenceslas Chapel
Proud of his direct descent from the Přemyslids, Charles had this shrine to St Wenceslas built in St Vitus's Cathedral (see pp100–3).

The Emperor places the piece of the cross in its reliquary.

St Wenceslas Crown
Worn by Charles at his coronation in 1347, the Bohemian crown was based on early Přemyslid insignia.

TIMELINE

1280 Old-New Synagogue completed in Gothic style

1344 Elevation of Prague bishopric to archbishopric

Town Hall, Old Town Square

1333 Charles IV makes Prague his home

| 1305 | 1320 | 1335 |

1306 Přemyslid dynasty ends

1338 John of Luxemburg gives permission to Old Town to build a town hall

Portal of Old-New Synagogue

1310 John of Luxemburg occupies Prague

Votive panel showing Charles, Archbishop Jan Očko and Bohemia's patron saints

St Vitus by Master Theodoric
This is one of a series of paintings of saints by the great Bohemian artist for the Holy Rood Chapel at Karlstein Castle (c1365).

A jewelled reliquary cross was made to house the new relic.

University Seal, 1348
The seal depicts the Emperor offering the foundation documents to St Wenceslas.

WHERE TO SEE GOTHIC PRAGUE

Prague's rich Gothic legacy includes three of its best-known sights – St Vitus's Cathedral (pp100–3), Charles Bridge (pp136–9) and the Old-New Synagogue (pp88–9). Another very important building from Charles IV's reign is the Carolinum (p65). Churches that have retained most of their original Gothic features include the Church of Our Lady before Týn (p70).

Carolinum
This fine oriel window was part of the university (p65).

Building the New Town
This manuscript records Charles IV supervising the building of the New Town during the 14th century.

Old Town Bridge Tower
The sculptural decoration is by Peter Parler (p139).

CHARLES IV AND HIS RELICS

Charles collected holy relics from all over the Empire. In about 1357 he received a part of Christ's cross from the Dauphin. This mural in Karlstein Castle is thought to be the best likeness of the Emperor.

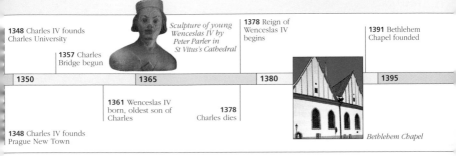

1348 Charles IV founds Charles University

1357 Charles Bridge begun

Sculpture of young Wenceslas IV by Peter Parler in St Vitus's Cathedral

1378 Reign of Wenceslas IV begins

1391 Bethlehem Chapel founded

| 1350 | 1365 | 1380 | 1395 |

1348 Charles IV founds Prague New Town

1361 Wenceslas IV born, oldest son of Charles

1378 Charles dies

Bethlehem Chapel

Hussite Prague

In the early 15th century, Europe shook in fear of an incredible fighting force – the Hussites, followers of the reformist cleric, Jan Hus. Despite simple weapons, they achieved legendary military successes against the Emperor's Catholic crusades, due largely to their religious fervour and to the discipline of their brilliant leader, Jan Žižka, who

George of Poděbrady invented mobile artillery. The Hussites split into two camps, the moderate "Utraquists" (see p75) and the radical "Taborites" who were finally defeated at the Battle of Lipany in 1434, paving the way for the moderate Hussite king, George of Poděbrady.

EXTENT OF THE CITY

■ 1500   □ Today

Nobles' Letter of Protest
Several hundred seals of the Bohemian nobility were affixed to a letter protesting about the execution of Jan Hus.

GOD'S WARRIORS
The early-16th-century Codex of Jena illustrated the Hussite successes. Here the Hussites, who included artisans and barons, are shown singing their hymn, with their blind leader, Jan Žižka.

Jan Žižka

The priest held a gilded monstrance.

War Machine
For maximum effect, farm waggons were tied together to form a shield. A chilling array of weapons were unleashed including crossbows, flails and an early form of howitzer.

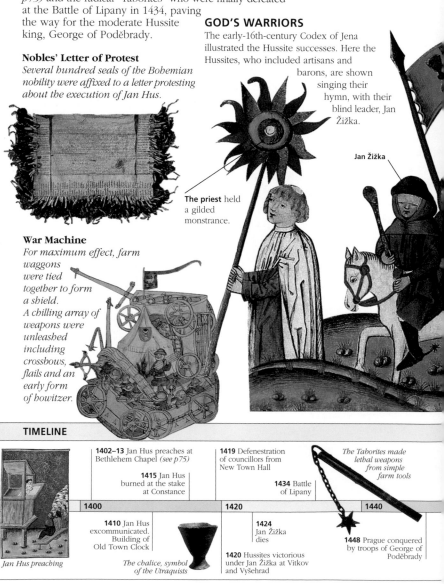

TIMELINE

1402–13 Jan Hus preaches at Bethlehem Chapel (see p75)

1415 Jan Hus burned at the stake at Constance

1419 Defenestration of councillors from New Town Hall

The Taborites made lethal weapons from simple farm tools

1434 Battle of Lipany

1400	1420	1440

1410 Jan Hus excommunicated. Building of Old Town Clock

The chalice, symbol of the Utraquists

1424 Jan Žižka dies

1420 Hussites victorious under Jan Žižka at Vitkov and Vyšehrad

1448 Prague conquered by troops of George of Poděbrady

Jan Hus preaching

Satan Dressed as the Pope
Lurid images satirizing the corruption of the church were painted on placards and carried through the streets.

The banner was decorated with the Hussite chalice.

A variety of farm implements were used as makeshift weapons by the peasants.

Hussite Shield
Wooden shields like this one that bears the arms of the city of Prague, were used to fill any gaps in the waggon fortress's tight formation.

The peasant army marched behind Jan Žižka.

REFORMER, JAN HUS
Born to poor parents in a small Bohemian town, Jan Hus became one of the most important religious thinkers of his day. His objections to the Catholic Church's corrupt practices, opulent style and wealth were shared by many Czechs – nobles and peasants alike. His reformist preaching in Prague's Bethlehem Chapel earned him a huge following, noticed by the Roman Papacy, and Hus was excommunicated. In 1412 Wenceslas IV, brother of the Emperor Sigismund, asked him to leave Prague. In October 1414, Hus decided to defend his teaching at the Council of Constance. Even though he had the Emperor's safe conduct, he was put in prison. The following year he was declared a heretic and burned at the stake.

Jan Hus at the Stake in 1415
After suffering death at the hands of the Church on 6 July 1415, Jan Hus became a revered martyr of the Czech people.

1458 Coronation of George of Poděbrady *(see p19)*

1485 Hussite uprising in Prague

1492–1502 Vladislav Hall built

1460 | **1480** | **1500**

Chalice on the outside of the Týn Church denotes the Hussite cause

1487 First book printed in Prague

1485 King Vladislav Jagiello begins to rebuild Royal Palace at Prague Castle

Vladislav Jagiello

The Renaissance and Rudolph II

With the accession of the Habsburgs, the Renaissance reached Prague. Art and architecture were dominated by the Italians who enjoyed the patronage of the Imperial court, especially that of Rudolph II. The eccentric Rudolph often neglected politics, preferring to indulge his passions for collecting and science. His court was a haven for artists, astrologers, astronomers and alchemists, but his erratic rule led to revolts and an attempt by his brother Matthias to usurp him. In the course of the Thirty Years' War *(see pp30–31)* many works of art from Rudolph's collection were looted.

Renaissance tankard

EXTENT OF THE CITY

▨ 1550   ▢ Today

Fish pond

Dalibor Tower

Belvedere

Pergola

Rudolph II
A connoisseur of the bizarre, Rudolph was delighted by this vegetable portrait by Giuseppe Arcimboldo (1590).

Orchard

Formal flower beds

Lion House

Rabbi Löw
A revered Jewish sage, he was said to have invented an artificial man (see pp88–9).

Mosaic Desk Top
Renaissance table tops with Florentine themes of fountains and gardens were made at Rudolph's court in semi-precious stones.

TIMELINE

1502 Vladislav Hall built

1526 Habsburg rule begins with Ferdinand I

1541 Great fire in Little Quarter, the Castle and Hradiany

1556 Ferdinand I invites Jesuits to Prague

1520   1540   1560

Ferdinand I

1538–63 Belvedere built

1547 Unsuccessful uprising of towns of Prague against Ferdinand I

Vladislav Hall

Charter for manglers and dyers

Sense of Sight
Jan Brueghel's allegorical painting shows the extent of Rudolph II's huge collection – from globes to paintings, jewels and scientific instruments.

Ball Game Hall

Tycho Brahe
The Danish astronomer spent his last years living in Prague.

A covered bridge connected the Palace to the garden.

ROYAL PALACE GARDENS
No longer a medieval fortress, Prague Castle and its gardens were given over to the pleasure of the King. Here Rudolph enjoyed ball games, exotic plants and his menagerie.

WHERE TO SEE RENAISSANCE PRAGUE
The Royal Garden (*p111*) preserves much of the spirit of Renaissance Prague. Paintings and objects from Rudolph's collections can be seen in the Sternberg Palace (*pp112–15*), the Picture Gallery of Prague Castle (*p98*) and the Museum of Decorative Arts (*p84*).

At the Two Golden Bears
Built in 1590, the house is famous for its symmetrical, carved doorway, one of the most graceful in Prague (p71).

Belvedere
The palace is decorated with stone reliefs by Italian architect, Paolo della Stella (p110).

Ball Game Hall
Beautiful Renaissance sgraffito covers the façade of this building in the Royal Garden, but it has been heavily restored (p111).

1583 Prague becomes seat of Imperial court of Rudolph II; great art collection begun

1614 Matthias Gate at Prague Castle built

1618 Defenestration of two royal governors from Royal Palace (*see p105*)

1580

1600

1620

A ten-ducat coin (1603)

1609 Publication of Rudolph's Imperial Charter on religious freedom

1612 Rudolph II dies

Baroque Prague

In 1619 the Czech nobles deposed Habsburg Emperor Ferdinand II as King of Bohemia and elected instead Frederick of the Palatinate. The following year they paid for their defiance at the Battle of the White Mountain, the beginning of the Thirty Years' War. There followed a period of persecution of all non-Catholics, accompanied by the Germanization of the country's institutions. The leaders in the fight against Protestantism were the Jesuits and one of their most powerful weapons was the restoration of their churches in Prague in the Baroque style. Many new churches also adopted this style.

EXTENT OF THE CITY

■ 1750   □ Today

A sculpture of Atlas (1722) adorns the top of the tower.

Mirror Chapel

Church of St Nicholas
This outstanding High Baroque church in the Little Quarter was the work of the great Dientzenhofers (see pp128–9).

Grape Courtyard

Measuring the World
Some monasteries were seats of learning. Strahov (see pp120–21) had two libraries built, decorated with Baroque painting. This fresco detail is in the Philosophical Hall.

Holy Saviour Church

TIMELINE

1620 Battle of the White Mountain	*Old Town coat of arms – embellished with the Imperial eagle and 12 flags in recognition of the defence of the city against the Swedes*		**1706–14** Decoration of Charles Bridge with statues
1627 Beginning of Counter-Reformation committee in Prague			

1625	1645	1665	1685	1705

1621 Execution in Old Town Square of 27 Protestant leaders	**1634** Wallenstein killed by Irish mercenaries	**1648** Swedes occupy Prague Castle. Treaty of Westphalia and end of Thirty Years' War		**1704–53** Building of Church of St Nicholas in the Little Quarter
	1631 Saxon occupation of Prague		**1676–8** New bastions built to fortify Vyšehrad	

Battle of the White Mountain
In 1620 the Czech army was defeated by Habsburg troops at Bílá Hora (White Mountain), a hill northwest of Prague (see p163). After the battle, Bohemia became a de facto province of Austria.

Observatory
Tower

St Clement's Church
gave its name to the
whole complex.

Italian
Chapel

Monstrance
*Baroque
monstrances –
used to display the
communion host –
became increasingly
elaborate and ornate
(see pp116–17).*

CLEMENTINUM

The Jesuits exercised enormous power over
education. Between 1653 and 1723 they built this
College. It was the largest complex of buildings after
Prague Castle and included three churches, smaller
chapels, libraries, lecture halls and an observatory.

WHERE TO SEE BAROQUE PRAGUE

The Baroque is everywhere
in Prague. Almost all the
churches were built or
remodelled in Baroque style,
the finest being St Nicholas
(pp128–9). There are also
the grand palaces and smaller
houses of the Little Quarter
(pp122–41), the façades in
the Old Town *(pp60–79)*, and
statues on churches, street
corners and along the
parapets of Charles Bridge.

Nerudova Street
*At the Golden Cup, No. 16, has
preserved its typical Baroque
house sign (p130).*

Charles Bridge
*This statue of St Francis Borgia
by Ferdinand Brokof was
added in 1710 (pp136–9).*

1740 Accession of
Empress Maria
Theresa

Maria Theresa

1748 Bohemian
Chancellery loses last
vestiges of power

1773 Jesuit Order
dissolved

1784 Four towns of
Prague united to form
a single city

Mozart at Bertramka (p160)

1725	1745	1765	1785

1757 Prague
besieged by
Prussians

1782 Convents and
monasteries closed

1787 Mozart stays at Bertramka
preparing for the premiere of
Don Giovanni at the Estates
Theatre *(see p65)*

The National Revival in Prague

Emperor Franz Josef

The 19th century was one of the most glorious periods in the history of Prague. Austrian rule relaxed, allowing the Czech nation to rediscover its own history and culture. Silent for so long, Czech was re-established as an official language. Civic pride was rekindled with the building of the capital's great showpieces, such as the National Theatre, which utilized the talents of Czech architects and artists. The Jewish Quarter and New Town underwent extensive redevelopment and, with the introduction of public transport, Prague grew beyond its ancient limits.

EXTENT OF THE CITY

☐ 1890   ☐ Today

Days of the year

Smetana's Libuše
Written for the scheduled opening of the National Theatre in 1881, the opera drew on early Czech legend (see pp20–21).

Months and zodiac signs revolve around the centre.

Old Town coat of arms

Rudolfinum
A major concert venue beside the Vltava, the building (see p84) is richly decorated with symbols of the art of music.

OLD TOWN CLOCK TOWER CALENDAR
In 1866, the revolving dial on Prague's most enduring landmark was replaced by a new one by celebrated artist, Josef Mánes. His studies of Bohemian peasant life are incorporated into pictures symbolizing the months of the year.

TIMELINE

1805 Czechs, Austrians and Russians defeated by Napoleon at Battle of Slavkov (Austerlitz)

1833 Englishman Edward Thomas begins production of steam engines

1818 National Museum founded

Restored clock from the east face of the Town Hall Tower

1848 Uprising of people of Prague against Austrian troops

1800	1820	1840	186

1815 First public demonstration of a vehicle driven by a steam engine

The battle of Slavkov

1838–45 Old Town Hall undergoes reconstruction

1845 First train arrives in Prague

1868 Foundation stone for National Theatre laid

Expo 95 Poster
Vojtěch Hynais designed this poster for the ethnographic exhibition of folk culture in 1895. In the Art Nouveau style, it reflected the new appreciation of regional traditions.

WHERE TO SEE THE NATIONAL REVIVAL

Many of Prague's remarkable monuments, the National Museum for example, were built around this period. One fine example of Art Nouveau architecture is the Municipal House (p64), where the Mayor's Room has murals by Mucha. The Rudolfinum (p84) and the National Theatre (pp156–7) have gloriously-decorated interiors by great artists of the day. The Prague Museum has many objects from the late 19th and early 20th centuries as well as the original painting for Mánes' Old Town Clock.

December   Sagittarius

Municipal House
Allegories of civic virtues painted by Alfons Mucha adorn this Art Nouveau interior.

Jewish Quarter
From 1897 onwards, the slum housing of the ghetto was replaced with new apartment blocks.

National Museum
The Neo-Renaissance façade dominates the skyline (p147).

National Theatre
The décor has murals by Czech artists, including Aleš (pp156–7).

National Theatre

1883 Re-opening of the National Theatre

1896 Proper city transport of electric trams starts

1914 World War I begins

1891 Jubilee Exhibition

1912 Municipal House opens

1916 Emperor Franz Josef dies

1880   **1900**

1884–91 Building of the National Museum

1897–1917 Slums of Jewish Ghetto cleared

1881 Newly opened National Theatre destroyed by fire, then rebuilt

1883 First public lighting with electric lamps

Early electric trams

The satirical novel Good Soldier Švejk (see p154) explored the futility of war and the inept Austrian military

Prague after Independence

Just 20 years after its foundation, the Czechoslovak Republic was helplessly caught up in the political manoeuvring that preceded Nazi domination of Europe. Prague emerged from World War II almost unscathed by bombings, no longer part of a Nazi protectorate but of a Socialist republic. Any resistance was brutally suppressed. Ultimately, the intellectuals spoke out, demanding observance of civil rights. Denial of such rights led these dissidents to unite and prepare for the "Velvet Revolution". In the end, it was a playwright, Václav Havel, who stepped onto the balcony of Prague Castle to lead the country at the start of a long and often difficult return to independence.

Letná Park metronome

1945 Soviet Red Army enter Prague on 9 May to rapturous welcome, following four days of uprisings. In October, provisional National Assembly set up under Beneš

1935 Edvard Beneš succeeds Masaryk as President. Nazi-funded Sudeten German Party, led by Konrad Henlein, makes election gains

1920 Avantgarde left-wing artists form Devětsil movement in Prague's Union Café

1938 Munich Agreement hands over parts of Republic to Hitler. Beneš flees country

1952 Most famous of many show trials under Gottwald, Slánský Trial sends 11 senior politicians to gallows as Trotskyites and traitors

Edvard Beneš

1918	1930	1940	1950

1918	1930	1940	1950

1924 Death of Franz Kafka, author of *The Trial*

1932 Traditional gymnastic rally or *slet* takes place at Strahov stadium

1942 Tyrannical "Protector" for only eight months, Reinhard Heydrich assassinated by Czech resistance

1955 Largest statue of Stalin in the world unveiled in Letná Park, overlooking city

1958 Premiere of innovative animated film, *The Invention of Destruction* directed by Karel Zeman

1948 Communist Party assumes power under Klement Gottwald; announces 89% support in May elections

PRAHA 1932

IX·SLET VŠESOKOLSKÝ
NA OSLAVU STÝCH NAROZENIN DR.MIROSLAVA TYRŠE
ZA UČASTI SVAZU · SLOVANSKÉ SOKOLSTVO

1918 Foundation of Czechoslovak Republic. Tomáš Masaryk first democratically-elected President

1939 German troops march into Prague; city declared capital of Nazi Protectorate of Bohemia and Moravia. Emil Hácha president under the German protectorate

VYNÁLEZ ZKÁZY

POZDRAV

TOMÁŠI G. MASARYKOVI

Welcome Home poster, to mark the president's return on 21 December 1918

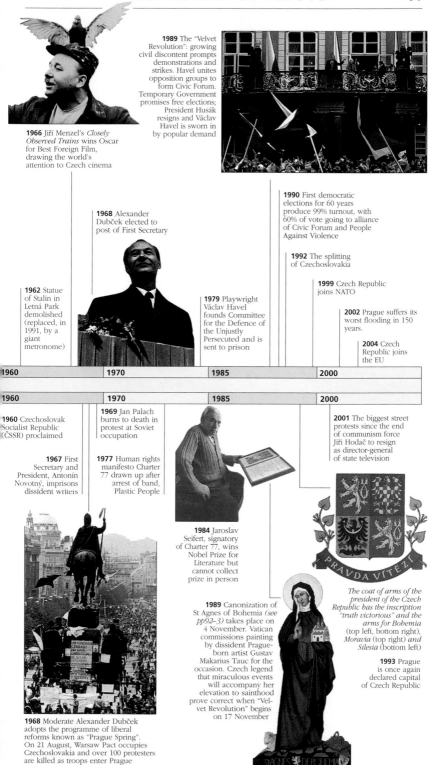

1966 Jiří Menzel's *Closely Observed Trains* wins Oscar for Best Foreign Film, drawing the world's attention to Czech cinema

1989 The "Velvet Revolution": growing civil discontent prompts demonstrations and strikes. Havel unites opposition groups to form Civic Forum. Temporary Government promises free elections; President Husák resigns and Václav Havel is sworn in by popular demand

1968 Alexander Dubček elected to post of First Secretary

1990 First democratic elections for 60 years produce 99% turnout, with 60% of vote going to alliance of Civic Forum and People Against Violence

1992 The splitting of Czechoslovakia

1999 Czech Republic joins NATO

1962 Statue of Stalin in Letná Park demolished (replaced, in 1991, by a giant metronome)

1979 Playwright Václav Havel founds Committee for the Defence of the Unjustly Persecuted and is sent to prison

2002 Prague suffers its worst flooding in 150 years.

2004 Czech Republic joins the EU

1960	1970	1985	2000

1960	1970	1985	2000

1960 Czechoslovak Socialist Republic (ČSSR) proclaimed

1969 Jan Palach burns to death in protest at Soviet occupation

2001 The biggest street protests since the end of communism force Jiří Hodač to resign as director-general of state television

1967 First Secretary and President, Antonín Novotný, imprisons dissident writers

1977 Human rights manifesto Charter 77 drawn up after arrest of band, Plastic People

1984 Jaroslav Seifert, signatory of Charter 77, wins Nobel Prize for Literature but cannot collect prize in person

1989 Canonization of St Agnes of Bohemia (see pp92–3) takes place on 4 November. Vatican commissions painting by dissident Prague-born artist Gustav Makarius Tauc for the occasion. Czech legend that miraculous events will accompany her elevation to sainthood prove correct when "Velvet Revolution" begins on 17 November

The coat of arms of the president of the Czech Republic has the inscription "truth victorious" and the arms for Bohemia (top left, bottom right), Moravia (top right) and Silesia (bottom left)

1993 Prague is once again declared capital of Czech Republic

1968 Moderate Alexander Dubček adopts the programme of liberal reforms known as "Prague Spring". On 21 August, Warsaw Pact occupies Czechoslovakia and over 100 protesters are killed as troops enter Prague

PRAGUE AT A GLANCE

There are almost 150 places of interest described in the *Area by Area* section of this book. A broad range of sights is covered: from the ancient Royal Palace, which was the site of the Defenestration of 1618 *(see p105)*, to cubist houses built in the Jewish Quarter in the 1920s *(see p91)*; from the peaceful oasis of Petřín Park *(see p141)*, to the bustle of Wenceslas Square *(see pp144–5)*. To help you make the most of your stay, the following 12 pages are a time-saving guide to the best Prague has to offer visitors. Museums and galleries, churches and synagogues, palaces and gardens all have their own sections. Each sight has a cross reference to its own full entry. Below are the attractions that no visitor should miss.

PRAGUE'S TOP TEN SIGHTS

Old Town Square
See pp66–9.

National Theatre
See pp156–7.

Church of St Nicholas
See pp128–9.

Charles Bridge
See pp136–9.

Old Town Hall
See pp72–4.

Wallenstein Palace and Garden *See p126.*

Old Jewish Cemetery
See pp86–7.

St Vitus's Cathedral
See pp100–3.

Prague Castle
See p96–7.

St Agnes's Convent
See pp92–3.

◁ Mucha's allegory of Vigilance in the Mayor's Room in the Municipal House *(see p64)*

Prague's Best: Museums and Galleries

With more than 20 museums and almost 100 galleries and exhibition halls, Prague is a city of unexpected and rare delights. Here, religious masterpieces of the Middle Ages vie with the more recent opulence of Art Nouveau and the giants of modern art. New galleries have opened since 1989 with many more temporary exhibitions. There are museums devoted to the history of the state, the city of Prague and its people, many of them housed in buildings that are historical landmarks and works of art in themselves. This map gives some of the highlights, with a detailed overview on pages 40–41.

St George's Convent
Among the 19th-century art on display is the historical painting of King George of Poděbrady and Matthias Corvinus of Hungary by Czech artist Mikoláš Aleš.

Sternberg Palace
The collection of European art here is outstanding, represented in works such as The Feast of the Rosary by Albrecht Dürer (1506).

Prague Castle and Hradčany

The Loreto
The offerings of devout local aristocrats form the basis of this collection of religious decorative art. In 1721 this jewel-encrusted, tree-shaped monstrance was given to the treasury by Countess Wallenstein.

Little Quarter

VLTAVA

Smetana Museum
The life and work of this 19th-century Czech composer are remembered beside the river that inspired one of his most famous pieces – the Vltava.

Schwarzenberg Palace
The ornate Renaissance palace, formerly the home of the Museum of Military History, is now a gallery exhibiting Renaissance art.

Museum of Decorative Arts
Five centuries of arts and crafts are represented here, with particularly impressive collections of Bohemian glass, graphic art and furniture. This carved and painted chest dates from 1612.

St Agnes of Bohemia Convent
This collection includes the 14th-century Resurrection of Christ by the Master of the Třeboň Altar.

Maisel Synagogue
One of the most important collections of Judaica in the world is housed in the Maisel Synagogue and other buildings of the State Jewish Museum. The displays include religious artefacts, furnishings and books. This illuminated page is from the manuscript of the Pesach Haggadah of 1728.

Jewish Quarter

Old Town

0 metres   500

0 yards   500

National Museum
The vast skeleton of a whale dominates the other exhibits in one of seven grand halls devoted to zoology. The museum's other displays include fine collections of minerals and meteorites.

New Town

Dvořák Museum
This viola, which belonged to the influential 19th-century Czech composer, is among the personal effects and musical scores on display in the charming Michna Summer Palace.

Exploring the Museums and Galleries

The city's museums give a fascinating insight into the history of the Czechs and of Prague's Jewish population. Also a revelation to visitors unfamiliar with the culture is the art of the Gothic and Baroque periods and of the 19th-century Czech National Revival. The major museums and galleries are cramped for space, but plans are under way to put more of their collections on show in the near future.

Carved figure on façade of the Museum of Decorative Arts

14th-century *Madonna Aracoeli*, St Vitus Treasure, Prague Castle

CZECH PAINTING AND SCULPTURE

The most important and wide-ranging collection in Prague is that of the National Gallery. Its holdings of Czech art are shown at three venues: medieval art at **St Agnes's Convent**; works dating from the 19th century at **St George's Convent**; and 19th to 20th-century art at the Trades Fair Palace.

The **Picture Gallery of Prague Castle** is a reminder of Emperor Rudolph II's once-great collection. Alongside the paintings are documents

Commerce by
Otto Gutfreund (1923), Trades Fair Palace

and other evidence of just how splendid the original collection must have been.

For the best of the Castle's Bohemian art, you must visit the Baroque works at St George's Convent. These include examples by Baroque masters Karel Škréta and Petr Brandl. Also within the Castle but currently without a permanent display space is the St Vitus Treasure, a collection of religious pieces including a Madonna from the School of Master Theodoric.

Centuries of Czech sculpture are housed in the Lapidarium at the **Exhibition Ground**. Among its exhibits is statuary formerly found on the Charles Bridge, and the Marian pillar that used to stand in the Old Town Square.

The collection at the **St Agnes of Bohemia Convent** includes Bohemian and central European Gothic painting and sculpture, including panels painted for Charles IV by Master Theodoric. Works by 19th- and 20th-century Prague artists can be seen at the Prague Gallery. Its branches include the Baroque **Troja Palace**, where the architecture makes a great backdrop. Exhibitions are drawn from the gallery's collection of 3,000 paintings, 1,000 statues and 4,000 prints. The superb Centre for Modern and Contemporary Art at **Trades Fair Palace** represents almost every 19th- and 20th-century artistic movement. Romanticism and Art Nouveau are both represented, as are the understandably popular 1920s figures of Otto Gutfreund. The

development of such ground-breaking groups as Osma, Devětsil, Skupina 42 and the 12.15 group is also strikingly well documented.

EUROPEAN PAINTING AND SCULPTURE

On view at **Sternberg Palace** is an exceptional range of masterpieces by Europe's finest artists from antiquity to the 18th century.

The most treasured work in the collection is the *Feast of the Rosary* by Albrecht Dürer. Works by 17th-century Dutch masters such as Rubens and Rembrandt also feature.

The Centre for Modern and Contemporary Art at **Trades Fair Palace** has a fine collection of Picassos and Rodin bronzes, as well as works from almost every Impressionist, Post-Impressionist and Fauvist. Three notable self-portraits are those of Paul Gauguin (*Bonjour Monsieur Gauguin*, 1889), Henri Rousseau (1890) and Pablo Picasso (1907). Modern German and Austrian painting is also on show, with works by Gustav Klimt and Egon Schiele. The *Dance of Life*, by Norwegian Edvard Munch, is considered greatly influential upon Czech avant-garde art.

The other main venue for European art is the **Picture Gallery of Prague Castle**, which focuses on European painters of the 16th to 18th centuries. As well as Titian's superb *The Toilet of a Young Lady*, there are also works in the collection by Rubens and Tintoretto. The exquisite building of **Schwarzenberg Palace** is due to house a new gallery of Renaissance art.

MUSIC

Two Czech composers merit their own museums, as does Prague's much-loved visitor, Mozart. The **Smetana Museum**, **Dvořák Museum** and **Mozart Museum** all contain personal memorabilia, musical scores and correspond-ence. In the summer, concerts are held on the terrace of the Mozart Museum.

The Museum of Musical Instruments, at Újezd 40, Prague 1 (257 53 34 59), has many rare and historic instruments, and a number of scores by composers such as Josef Haydn.

HISTORY

The historical collections of the **National Museum** are held at the main Wenceslas Square building. The **Prague Museum** centres on the history of the city, with period rooms, historical prints and a model of Prague in the 19th century, made of paper and wood by the litho-grapher Antonín Langweil.

Bohemian Baroque glass goblet (1730), Museum of Decorative Arts

A branch of the museum at Výtoň, on the banks of the Vltava, depicts the way of life of a former settlement. Another at Vyšehrad records the history of this royal seat.

The Museum of Military History, housed in the Schwarzenberg Palace since 1945 but now on U Památníku 3, displays battle charts, weaponry, uniforms and other military regalia. The Lobkowicz Collection, to be housed in the 16th century **Lobkowicz Palace**, includes rare books and manuscripts.

The Jewish Museum is made up of various sites in the Jewish Quarter, including the **High Synagogue, Maisel Synagogue** and the **Old Jewish Cemetery**. Among its collections are holy artefacts taken from other Jewish communities and brought to Prague by the Nazis as part of a chilling plan for a museum of "an extinct race". Another moving display is of drawings made by children who were imprisoned in the Terezín concentration camp.

DECORATIVE ARTS

With glassware spanning centuries, from medieval to modern, porcelain and pewterware, furniture and textiles, books and posters, the **Museum of Decorative Arts** in the Jewish Quarter is one of Prague's best, but only a small selection of its holdings is on show. Look out for specialized temporary exhibitions mounted either at the museum itself or at other venues in Prague.

Many other museums have examples of the decorative arts, ranging from grandiose monstrances – including one with 6,222 diamonds – in the treasury of **The Loreto** to simple everyday furnishings in the **Prague Museum**. There is also a fascinating collection of pre-Columbian artefacts from Central America in the **Náprstek Museum**.

16th-century astrolabe from the National Technical Museum

SCIENCE AND TECHNOLOGY

A vast exhibition hall holds the transport section of the **National Technical Museum**. Ranks of vintage cars, motorcycles and steam engines fill the space, and over them hang examples of early flying machines. Other sections in the museum trace the progress of sciences such as electronics. Visitors even have the opportunity to tour a reconstruction of a coal mine. There is also a fascina-ting astronomy exhibition.

Prague's Best: Churches and Synagogues

The religious buildings of Prague vividly record the
city's changing architectural styles, and many are
treasure houses of religious art. But they
also reflect Prague's times of religious
and political strife, the lives of its
people, its setbacks and growth as a
city. This map features highlights of
their architecture and art, with a more
detailed overview on pages 44–5.

St George's Basilica
*St George, sword raised to slay the
dragon, is portrayed in this late-Gothic
relief, set above the doorway of the magnificent early Renaissance south portal.*

St Vitus's Cathedral
*The jewel of the cathedral is the
Chapel of St Wenceslas. Its walls
are decorated with semi-precious
stones, gilding and frescoes. Elizabeth of Pomerania, the fourth
and last wife of Charles IV, is
shown at prayer in the fresco
above the Gothic altar.*

*Prague Castle
and Hradčany*

The Loreto
*This shrine to the
Virgin Mary
has been a
place of
pilgrimage
since 1626.
Each hour,
its Baroque
clock tower
chimes a
hymn on the
carillon of 27 bells.*

Little Quarter

Church of St Thomas
*The skeleton of the martyr St Just rests
in a glass coffin below a
Crucifixion by
Antonín Stevens,
one of several
superb works of
religious art in
this church.*

**Church of
St Nicholas**
*In the heart of the
Little Quarter, this
is Prague's finest
example of High
Baroque. The dome
over the high altar
is so lofty that early
worshippers feared
it would collapse.*

VLTAVA

Church of Our Lady before Týn
Set back behind a row of arcaded buildings, the many-spired twin towers of the church dominate the eastern end of Old Town Square. The Gothic, Renaissance and Baroque features of the interior create striking contrasts.

Old-New Synagogue
Prague's oldest synagogue dates from the 13th century. Its Gothic main portal is carved with a vine which bears twelve bunches of grapes symbolizing the tribes of Israel.

Jewish
Quarter

Old Town

Church of St James
Consecrated in 1374, this church was restored to new Baroque glory after a fire in 1689. Typical of its grandeur is this 18th-century monument to chancellor Jan Vratislav of Mitrovice. Fine acoustics and a superb organ make the church a popular venue for concerts.

Slavonic Monastery Emauzy
These cloisters hold a series of precious frescoes from three Gothic masters depicting scenes from the Old and New Testaments.

New Town

0 metres	500
0 yards	500

Church of St Peter and St Paul
Remodelled many times since the 11th century, the design of this church is now 1890s Neo-Gothic. This striking relief of the Last Judgment marks the main entrance.

Exploring Churches and Synagogues

Religious building began in Prague in the 9th century, reaching its zenith during the reign of Charles IV

(see pp24–5). The remains of an 11th-century synagogue have been found, but during the 19th-century clearance of the overcrowded Jewish ghetto three synagogues were lost. Many churches were damaged during the Hussite rebellions *(see pp26–7)*. The political regime of the 20th century also took its toll, but now churches and synagogues have been reclaimed and restored, with many open to visitors.

Altar, Capuchin Monastery

High, Gothic windows at the east end of St Vitus's Cathedral

ROMANESQUE

Three reasonably well-preserved Romanesque rotundas, dating from the 11th and 12th centuries, still exist in Prague. The oldest is the **St Martin's Rotunda**; the others are the rotundas of the Holy Rood and of St Longinus. All three are tiny, with naves only 6 m (20 ft) in diameter.

By far the best-preserved and most important Romanesque church is **St George's Basilica**, founded in 920 by

11th-century Romanesque Rotunda of St Martin in Vyšehrad

Prince Vratislav I. Extensive reconstruction was carried out after a fire in 1142, but its chancel, with some exquisite frescoes on its vaulting, is a Late-Romanesque gem.

The **Strahov Monastery**, founded in 1142 by Prince Vladislav II *(see pp22–3)*, has retained its Romanesque core in spite of fire, wars and extensive renovation.

GOTHIC

Gothic architecture, with its ribbed vaulting, flying buttresses and pointed arches, reached Bohemia in about 1230 and was soon adopted into religious architecture.

The first religious building in Gothic style was the **St Agnes of Bohemia Convent**, founded in 1233 by Wenceslas I's sister, Agnes. Prague's oldest synagogue, the **Old-New Synagogue**, built in 1270, is rather different in style to the churches but is still a superb example of Early-Gothic.

The best example of Prague Gothic is **St Vitus's Cathedral**. Its fine tracery and towering

nave epitomize the style. Other notable Gothic churches are **Our Lady before Týn** and **Our Lady of the Snows**.

Important for its historical significance is the reconstructed Gothic **Bethlehem Chapel** where Jan Hus *(see p27)* preached for 10 years.

The superb Gothic frescoes found in abundance at the **Slavonic Monastery Emauzy**, were badly damaged in World War II, but have been restored.

RENAISSANCE

In the 1530s the influence of Italian artists living in Prague sparked the city's Renaissance movement. The style is more clearly seen in secular than religious building. The Late-Renaissance period, under Rudolph II (1576–1611), offers the best remaining examples.

DOMES AND SPIRES

The domes and spires of Prague's churches are the city's main landmarks, as the view from the many vantage points will confirm. You will see a variety of spires, towers and domes: Gothic and Neo-Gothic soar skywards, while Baroque often have rounded cupolas and onion domes. The modern top of the 14th-century Slavonic Monastery, added after the church was struck in a World War II air raid, is a rare example of modernist religious architecture in Prague. Its sweeping, intersecting twin spires are a bold reinterpretation of Gothic themes, and a striking addition to the city's skyline.

Gothic

Church of Our Lady before Týn (1350–1511)

Baroque

Church of St Nicholas in the Little Quarter (1750)

The **High Synagogue** and the **Pinkas Synagogue** retain strong elements of the style: the former in its 1586 exterior, the latter in the reworking of an original Gothic building.

The Church of St Roch in the **Strahov Monastery** is probably the best example of Late-Renaissance "Mannerism".

Renaissance-influenced vaulting, Pinkas Synagogue (1535)

BAROQUE

The Counter-Reformation *(see pp30–31)* inspired the building of new churches and the revamping of existing ones for a period of 150 years. Prague's first Baroque church

was **Our Lady Victorious**, built in 1611–13. **St Nicholas** in the Little Quarter took almost 60 years to build. Its lush interior and frescoed vault make it Prague's most important Baroque building, followed by **The Loreto** (1626–1750), adjoining the **Capuchin Monastery**. The father-and-son team, Christoph and Kilian Ignaz Dientzenhofer designed both buildings, and **St John on the Rock** and **St Nicholas** in the Old Town.

A special place in Prague's history was occupied by the Jesuit **Clementinum**. This influential university's church was the **Holy Saviour**. The Baroque style is closely linked with Jesuit teachings: Kilian Ignaz Dientzenhofer was educated here.

Klausen Synagogue (now the Jewish Museum) was built in 1689 with Baroque stuccoed barrel vaults.

Many early buildings were given Baroque facelifts. The Gothic nave of **St Thomas** has Baroque vaulting, and the once-Gothic **St James** went Baroque after a fire in 1689.

19th-century Neo-Gothic portal, Church of St Peter and St Paul

NEO-GOTHIC

During the height of the 19th-century Gothic Revival *(see pp32–3)*, **St Vitus's Cathedral** was completed, in accordance with the original Gothic plan. Work by Josef Mocker, the movement's leader, aroused controversy but his **St Peter and St Paul** at Vyšehrad is a well-loved landmark. The triple-naved basilica of **St Ludmilla** in Náměstí Míru was also designed by Mocker.

Nave ceiling of the Church of St Nicholas in the Little Quarter

Baroque   *Neo-Gothic*   *Modernist*

Loreto (1725)   St Peter and St Paul (1903)   Slavonic Monastery Emauzy (1967)

Prague's Best: Palaces and Gardens

Prague's palaces and gardens are among the most important historical and architectural monuments in the city. Many palaces house museums or galleries *(see pp38–41)*, and some are concert venues.

The gardens range from formal, walled oases with fountains and grand statuary, to open spaces beyond the city centre. This map features some of the best palaces and gardens, with a detailed overview on pages 48–9.

Belvedere
The Singing Fountain (1568) stand in front of the exquisite Renaissance summer palace.

Royal Garden
Though redesigned in the 19th century, the Renaissance garden preserves much of its original character. Historic statues still in place include a pair of Baroque lions (1730) guarding the entrance.

Prague Castle and Hradčany

| 0 metres | 500 |
| 0 yards | 500 |

Little Quarter

South Gardens
Starting life as the Castle's defensive bastions, these gardens afford a wonderful view of Prague. First laid out as a park in 1891, their present design was landscaped by Josip Plečnik 40 years later.

Wallenstein Palace
Built in 1624–30 for Duke Albrecht of Wallenstein, this vast Baroque palace was intended to outshine Prague Castle. Over 20 houses and a town gate were demolished to make room for the palace and garden. This Fountain of Venus (1599), stands in front of the arches of the sala terrena.

Wallenstein Garden
The garden statues are copies of 17th-century bronzes. The originals were plundered by the Swedes in 1648.

Kolowrat-Černín Garden
In the Baroque period, several palace gardens with spectacular terraces were laid out on the hillside below Prague Castle.

Kinský Palace
The Kinský coat of arms adorns the pink and white stuccoed façade designed by Kilian Ignaz Dientzenhofer. The Rococo palace is now part of the National Gallery.

Jewish Quarter

Old Town

VLTAVA

Clam-Gallas Palace
Four giant statues of Hercules (c1715) by Matthias Bernard Braun show the hero straining to support the weight of the massive Baroque front portals of the palace.

Michna Summer Palace
This charming villa was designed by Kilian Ignaz Dientzenhofer in 1712. It now houses the Dvořák Museum. The garden's sculptural decorations are from the workshop of Antonín Braun.

New Town

Kampa Island
A tranquil waterside park was created on the island after the destruction of its original gardens in World War II.

Exploring the Palaces and Gardens

Prague boasts an amazing number of palaces and gardens, spanning centuries. Comparatively few palaces were lost to the ravages of war. Instead, they tended to evolve in style during restoration or enlargement. Palace gardens became fashionable in the 17th century, but could only be laid out where there was space, such as below Prague Castle. More vulnerable to change, most have been relandscaped several times. In the 19th century, and again after 1989, many of the larger parks and private gardens were opened up to the public.

Statue on Kampa Island

MEDIEVAL PALACES

The oldest palace in Prague is the **Royal Palace** at Prague Castle. In the basement is the Romanesque ground floor, started in about 1135. It has been rebuilt many times, particularly between the 14th and 16th centuries. The heart of the Palace, Vladislav Hall, dates from the 1490s and is late Gothic in structure. Less well known is the **Palace of the Lords of Kunštát**. Here,

the vaulted ground floor of the 13th-century building survives as the basement of a later Gothic structure.

RENAISSANCE PALACES

One of the most beautiful Renaissance buildings in Prague is the 16th-century **Schwarzenberg Palace**. The work of Italian architects, its façade is entirely covered with geometric, two-tone *sgraffito* designs. Italians also

Bronze Singing Fountain in the Royal Garden by the Belvedere

worked on the **Belvedere**. Its graceful arcades and columns, all covered with rich reliefs, make this one of the finest Renaissance buildings north of the Alps. The **Martinic Palace**, built in 1563, was the first example of late-Renaissance building in Prague. Soon after came the **Lobkowicz Palace**. Its terracotta relief-decorated windows and plaster *sgraffito* have survived later Baroque modifications. The huge **Archbishop's Palace** was given a later Rococo façade over its Renaissance structure.

BAROQUE PALACES

Many palaces were built in the Baroque style, and examples of all its phases still exist in Prague. A handsome, if ostentatious, early Baroque

Southern façade of Troja Palace and its formal gardens

DECORATIVE PORTALS AND GATES

The elaborate gates and portals of Prague's palaces are among the most beautiful and impressive architectural features in the city. Gothic and Renaissance portals have often survived, even where the buildings themselves have been destroyed or modified by renovations in a later architectural style. The period of most prolific building was the Baroque, and distinctive portals from this time can be seen framing many a grand entrance around the city. Statues of giants, heroes and mythological figures are often depicted holding up the doorways. These were not merely decorative but acted as an integral element of support.

Gateway to Court of Honour of Prague Castle (1768)

example is the **Wallenstein Palace**. Similar ostentation is evident in the **Černín Palace**, one of Prague's most monumental buildings. The mid-Baroque had two strands, one opulent and Italianate, the other formal and French or Viennese in influence. **Troja Palace** and **Michna Summer Palace** are in Italian villa style while the **Sternberg Palace** on Hradčanské náměstí is more Viennese in style. Troja was designed in 1679 by Jean-Baptiste Mathey, who, like the Dientzenhofers *(see p129)*, was a master of the Baroque. The pairs of giants on the portals of the **Clam-Gallas Palace**, and the **Morzin Palace** in Nerudova Street, are a popular Baroque motif. The **Kinský Palace** is a superb Rococo design by Kilian Ignaz Dientzenhofer.

GARDENS

The finest of Prague's palace gardens, such as the **Wallenstein Garden**, are in the Little Quarter. Though the style of Wallenstein Palace is Early Baroque, the garden still displays the geometric formality of the Renaissance, also preserved in the **Royal Garden** behind Prague Castle. The **South Gardens** on the Castle's old ramparts were redesigned in the 1920s.

Many more gardens were laid out in the 17th and 18th centuries, when noble families vied with each other to have fine winter residences in the Little Quarter below the Castle. Many are now the grounds of embassies, but others have been opened to the public. The **Ledebour Garden** has been combined with two neighbouring gardens. Laid out on a steep hillside, the **Kolowrat-Černín Garden**, in particular, makes ingenious use of pavilions, stairs and terraces from which there are wonderful views of the city. The **Vrtba Garden**, landscaped on the site of former vineyards, is a similar Baroque creation with statues and splendid views. Former palace gardens were also used to create a park on **Kampa Island**.

The many old gardens and orchards on Petřín Hill have

Ancient trees in Stromovka

been transformed into the large public area of **Petřín Park**. Another former orchard is **Vojan Park**, laid out by archbishops in the 13th century. The **Botanical Gardens** are one of the few areas of green open to the public in the New Town.

Generally, the larger parks are situated further out of the city. **Stromovka** was a royal deer park, while **Letná Park** was developed in 1858 on the open space of Letná Plain.

WHERE TO FIND THE PALACES AND GARDENS

The Royal Garden of Prague Castle, planted with spring flowers

Troja Palace (c1703)

Clam-Gallas Palace (c1714)

PRAGUE THROUGH THE YEAR

Springtime in Prague sees the city burst into colour as its gardens start to bloom. Celebrations begin with the Prague Spring Music Festival. In summer, visitors are entertained by street performers and the city's glorious gardens come into their own. When the weather begins to turn cooler, Prague hosts the International Jazz Festival.

Painted Easter egg

The year often draws to a close with snow on the streets. The ball season starts in December, and in the coldest months, most events are held indoors. At Prague Castle, an all-year-round attraction is the changing of the guard around midday. For details of activities, check the listings magazines *(see p219)* or the Prague Information Service *(see p218)*.

Concert at Wallenstein Palace during the Prague Spring Music Festival

SPRING

As Prague sees its first rays of spring sunshine, the city comes alive. A mass of colours, blooms and cultural events makes this one of the most exciting times of the year to visit. The city's blossoming parks and gardens open their gates again, after the colder months of winter. During April the temperatures rise and an entertainment programme begins – dominated by the Prague Spring Music Festival.

EASTER

Easter Monday *(dates vary)* is a public holiday. Easter is observed as a religious holiday but it is also associated with a bizarre pagan ritual in which Czech men beat their women with willow sticks in order to keep them fertile during the coming year. The women retaliate by throwing water over their male tormentors. Peace is finally restored when the women present the men with a painted egg. Church services are held during the entire Easter period *(see p235)*.

MARCH

The Prague-Prčice March *(third Saturday of March)*. Thousands of people walk to the small town of Prčice in celebration of spring.

APRIL

Boat trips *(1 April)*. A number of boats begin trips up and down the Vltava.
Witch-burning *(30 April)*, at the Exhibition Ground *(see p162)*. Concerts accompany this 500-year-old tradition where old brooms are burnt on bonfires, in a symbolic act to rid nature of evil spirits.

MAY

Labour Day *(1 May)*. Public holiday celebrated with numerous cultural events.
Opening day of Prague's gardens *(1 May)*. Regular summer concerts are held in many parks and gardens.
Anniversary of Prague Uprising *(5 May)*. At noon sirens are sounded for one minute. Flowers are laid at the commemorative plaques of those who died *(see p34)*.
Day of Liberation from Fascism *(8 May)*. Public holiday for VE day. Wreaths are laid on the graves of soldiers at Olšany cemeteries.
Prague International Book Fair *(second week in May)*, Palace of Culture *(see p176)*. The best of Czech and international authors.
Prague International Marathon *(third week in May)*.

THE PRAGUE SPRING MUSIC FESTIVAL

This international festival presents a busy programme of concerts, ballet and opera from 12 May to 3 June. Music lovers can hear a huge selection of music played by some of the best musicians in the world. The main venue is the Rudolfinum *(see p84)* but others include churches and palaces – some of which are only open to the public on these occasions. The festival begins on the anniversary of Bedřich Smetana's death *(see p79)*. A service is held at his grave in Vyšehrad *(see p180)*, and in the evening there is a concert at the Municipal House *(see p64)* where musicians perform his most famous work, *Má Vlast* (My Country). Municipal House is also where the festival ends.

Bedřich Smetana

AVERAGE DAILY HOURS OF SUNSHINE

Hours

| | Jan | Feb | Mar | Apr | May | Jun | Jul | Aug | Sep | Oct | Nov | Dec |

Sunshine Chart
*Prague's longest and
hottest days fall
between May and
August. At the height
of summer, daylight
starts at 5am. The
snow-covered city
looks stunning on a
sunny winter's day.
But sunny days can
be spoiled by thick
smog (see p53).*

Czechs and tourists enjoying the beauty of
Vyšehrad Park on a sunny afternoon

SUMMER

Summer arrives with high
temperatures, frequent, sometimes heavy, showers and
thousands of visitors. This is a
beautiful, if busy, time to visit.
Every weekend, Czechs set out
for the country to go hiking
in the surrounding hills or stay
in country cottages. Those
remaining in Prague visit the
reservoirs and lakes *(see
p213)*, just outside the city to
try and escape the heat. There
is a wealth of entertainment
on offer as culture moves into
the open air taking over the
squares, streets and gardens.
Street performers, buskers
and classical orchestras all help
to keep visitors entertained.
Many cafés have tables outside
allowing you to quench your
thirst while watching the fun.

JUNE

Mayoral Boat Race *(first
weekend in June)*. Rowing
races are held on the river
Vltava, just below Vyšehrad.

Summer Concerts
*(throughout the
summer)*. Prague's
gardens *(see pp46–9)*
are the attractive and
popular setting for a
large number of free
classical and brass-
band concerts. One of
the most famous, and
spectacular, outdoor
classical concerts is
held by Křižík Fountain
at the Exhibition
Ground *(see p162)*. Full
orchestras play to the
stunning backdrop of
coloured lights and
water, synchronized to
the music by computer.
**Anniversary of the Murder of
Reinhard Heydrich's
Assassins** *(18 June)*. A mass
is held in remembrance at
the Church of St Cyril and
St Methodius *(see p152)* for
those who died there.
Golden Prague *(first week of
June)*, Kaiserstein Palace.
International TV festival of
prize-winning programmes.

Battle Re-enactments
(throughout summer), held in
Prague's palaces and gardens.
Mozart's Prague *(mid-June to
first week in July)*. Celebration
of Mozart. International
orchestras perform his works
at Bertramka *(see p160)* and
Lichtenstein Palace.
Dance Prague *(last week in
June)*. An international festival
of contemporary dance at the
National Theatre *(see p156)*.

JULY

**Remembrance of the
Slavonic Missionaries**
(5 July). Public holiday in
honour of St Cyril and St
Methodius *(see p152)*.
**Anniversary of Jan Hus's
Death** *(6 July)*. A public
holiday when flowers are laid
on his memorial *(see pp26–7)*.

AUGUST

Theatre Island *(all of August)*,
Střelecký Island. Czech
theatre and puppet festival.

Changing of the Guard at Prague Castle

AVERAGE MONTHLY RAINFALL

Rainfall Chart
Prague has plenty of rain throughout the year. The wettest months are October and November, but there are frequent light showers in the summer months as well. Winter snowfalls can be quite heavy, but they are rarely severe.

AUTUMN

When the gardens below Prague Castle take on the shades of red and gold, and visitors start to leave, the city gets ready for the cold winter months. This is also the traditional mushroom-gathering season when you encounter people with baskets full of freshly-picked mushrooms. Market places are flooded with fruit and vegetables. The tree-lined slopes above the Vltava take on the beautiful colours of autumn. September and October still have a fair number of warm and sunny days, although November often sees the first snowfalls. Football fans fill the stadiums and the popular steeplechase course at Pardubice reverberates to the cheers of fans.

A view of St Vitus's Cathedral through autumn trees

SEPTEMBER

Prague Autumn *(early September)*, at the Rudolfinum *(see p84)*. An international classical music festival.
The Autumn Fair *(dates vary)*, at the Exhibition Ground *(see p162)*. Fairground, food stalls, puppet shows and theatrical and musical performances.
Kite competitions *(third Sunday in September)*, on Letná Plain in front of Sparta Stadium. Very popular competition for children but open to anyone with a kite.
St Wenceslas *(28 September)*. A sacred music festival is held for the feast of the patron saint.
Bohemia Championship *(last Sunday in September)*. This 10-km (6-mile) road race has been run since 1887. Starts from Běchovice, a suburb of Prague, and ends in Žižkov.

Jazz musicians playing at the International Jazz Festival

OCTOBER

The Great Pardubice Steeplechase *(second Sunday in October)*, held at Pardubice, east of Prague. This horse race has been run since 1874 and is considered to be the most difficult in Europe.
The Locking of the Vltava *(early October)*. Symbolic conclusion of the water sports season, during which the Vltava is locked with a key until the arrival of spring.
International Jazz Festival *(date varies)*, Lucerna Palace. A famous jazz festival, held since 1964, attracts musicians from around the world.
The Day of the Republic *(28 October)*. Despite the splitting up of Czechoslovakia into two separate republics, the founding of the country in 1918 is still a public holiday.

NOVEMBER

Velká Kunratická *(second Sunday in November)*. Popular, but gruelling, cross-country race in Kunratice forest. Anyone can enter.
Celebration of the Velvet Revolution *(17 November)*. Peaceful demonstrations take place around Wenceslas Square *(see pp144–5)*.

AVERAGE MONTHLY TEMPERATURE

Temperature Chart
The chart shows the average minimum and maximum temperatures for each month in Prague. The summer usually remains comfortably warm, while the winter months can get bitterly cold and temperatures often drop below freezing.

WINTER

If you are lucky enough to catch Prague the morning after a snowfall with the sun shining, the effect is magical. The view over the Little Quarter rooftops with their pristine white covering is a memorable sight. Unfortunately Prague is rarely at its best during the winter months. The weather is changeable. Foggy days with temperatures just above freezing can quickly go down to -5° C (23° F). Pollution and Prague's geographical position in the Vltava basin, lead to smog being trapped just above the city.

As if to try and make up for the winter weather's shortcomings, the theatre season reaches its climax and there are a number of premieres. Balls and dances are held in these cold months. Just before Christmas Eve large barrels containing live carp – which is the traditional Czech Christmas delicacy – appear on the streets. Christmas trees adorn the city, and carol singers can be heard on street

View of the Little Quarter rooftops covered in snow

corners. Christmas mass is held in most churches and New Year's Eve is celebrated, in time-honoured style, throughout the entire city.

DECEMBER

Christmas markets
(throughout December), Můstek metro station, 28. října, Na příkopě, Old Town Square. Stalls sell Christmas decorations, gifts, hot wine, punch and the traditional Czech carp *(see p213).*
Christmas Eve, Christmas Day and Boxing Day *(24, 25 and 26 December).* Public holidays. Mass is held in churches throughout the city.
Swimming competitions in the Vltava *(26 December).* Hundreds of hardened and determined swimmers gather together at the Vltava to swim in temperatures of around 3° C (37° F).
New Year celebrations *(31 December).* Thousands of people congregate around Wenceslas Square.

Barrels of the traditional Christmas delicacy, carp, on sale in Prague

JANUARY

New Year's Day
(1 January). Public holiday.

FEBRUARY

Dances and Balls
(early February).
Matthew Fair *(end of February to beginning of April),* the Exhibition Ground *(see p176).* Fairground, stalls and various entertainments.

PUBLIC HOLIDAYS

New Year's Day (1 Jan); **Easter Monday**; **Labour Day** (1 May); **Day of Liberation from Fascism** (8 May); **Remembrance of the Slavonic Missionaries** (5 July); **Anniversary of Jan Hus's death** (6 July); **St Wenceslas** (28 Sep); **Foundation of Czechoslovakia** (28 Oct); **Fall of Communism** (17 Nov); **Christmas Eve, Christmas Day, Boxing Day** (24–26 Dec).

A RIVER VIEW OF PRAGUE

The Vltava river has played a vital part in the city's history (see pp20 –21) and has provided inspiration for artists, poets and musicians throughout the centuries.

Up until the 19th century, parts of the city were exposed to the danger of heavy flooding. To try and alleviate the problem, the river's embankments have been strengthened and raised many times, in order to try to prevent the water penetrating too far (the foundations of today's embankments are made of stone or concrete). During the Middle Ages, year after year of disastrous flooding led to the decision to bury the areas affected under 2 m (6 ft) of earth to try to minimize the damage. Although this strategy was only partially effective, it meant that the ground floors of many Romanesque and Gothic buildings were preserved and can still be seen today *(see*

Statues on the wrought-iron Čechův Bridge

pp78–9). In 2002 however, a state of emergency was declared as flooding devastated large parts of the city. Despite its destructive side, the Vltava has provided a vital method of transport for the city, as well as a source of income. As technology improved, the river became increasingly important; water mills, weirs and water towers were built. In 1912 a large hydroelectric power plant was built on Štvanice Island, supplying almost a third of Prague's electricity. To make the river navigable, eight dams, a large canal and weirs were constructed along the Slapy-Prague-Mělník stretch, where the Vltava flows into the river Elbe. For the visitor, an excursion on one of the many boats and paddle steamers that travel up and down the river, is well worth it. There are trips to Troja *(see pp166– 7)* and as far as Slapy Lake. Catching a boat from one of the piers on the river is one of the best ways of seeing the city.

A view of the steamboat landing stage (přístaviště parníků) on Rašínovo nábřeží

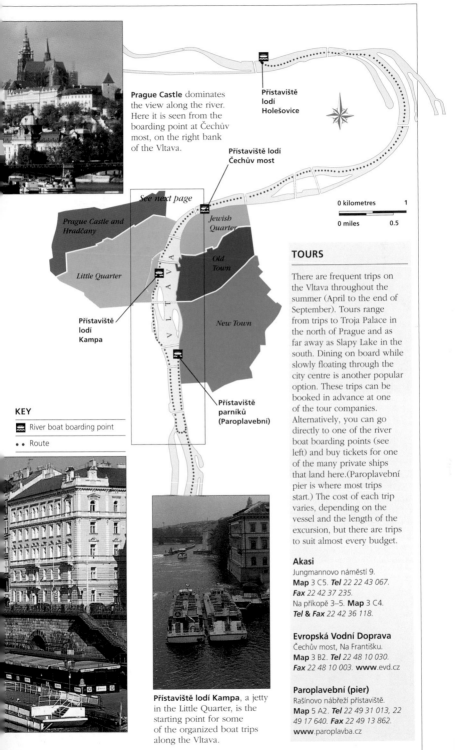

Prague Castle dominates the view along the river. Here it is seen from the boarding point at Čechův most, on the right bank of the Vltava.

Přístaviště lodí Holešovice

Přístaviště lodí Čechův most

See next page

Prague Castle and Hradčany

Little Quarter

Jewish Quarter

Old Town

New Town

Přístaviště lodí Kampa

Přístaviště parníků (Paroplavebni)

0 kilometres 1
0 miles 0.5

KEY

River boat boarding point

•• Route

TOURS

There are frequent trips on the Vltava throughout the summer (April to the end of September). Tours range from trips to Troja Palace in the north of Prague and as far away as Slapy Lake in the south. Dining on board while slowly floating through the city centre is another popular option. These trips can be booked in advance at one of the tour companies. Alternatively, you can go directly to one of the river boat boarding points (see left) and buy tickets for one of the many private ships that land here.(Paroplavební pier is where most trips start.) The cost of each trip varies, depending on the vessel and the length of the excursion, but there are trips to suit almost every budget.

Akasi
Jungmannovo náměstí 9.
Map 3 C5. **Tel** 22 22 43 067.
Fax 22 42 37 235.
Na příkopě 3–5. **Map** 3 C4.
Tel & Fax 22 42 36 118.

Evropská Vodní Doprava
Čechův most, Na Františku.
Map 3 B2. **Tel** 22 48 10 030.
Fax 22 48 10 003. **www**.evd.cz

Paroplavební (pier)
Rašínovo nábřeží přístaviště.
Map 5 A2. **Tel** 22 49 31 013, 22 49 17 640. **Fax** 22 49 13 862.
www.paroplavba.cz

Přístaviště lodí Kampa, a jetty in the Little Quarter, is the starting point for some of the organized boat trips along the Vltava.

Prague River Trip

Taking a trip on the Vltava gives you a unique view of many of the city's historic monuments. Although the left bank was the site of the first Slavonic settlement in the 9th century, it was the right bank, heavily populated by merchants and traders, that developed into a thriving and bustling commercial centre, and the tradition continues today. The left bank was never developed as intensively and much of it is still an oasis of parks and gardens. The river's beauty is enhanced by the numbers of swans which have made it their home.

Hanavský Pavilion
This flamboyant cast-iron staircase is part of a pavilion built for the Jubilee Exhibition of 1891.

Little Quarter Bridge Towers
The smaller tower was built in 1158 to guard the entrance to the original Judith Bridge, while the larger one was built on the site of an old Romanesque tower in 1464 (see p136).

Vltava Weir
The thickly-wooded slopes of Petřín Hill tower above one of several weirs on the Vltava. During the 19th century this weir, along with others on this stretch, were built to make the river navigable to ships.

The Vltava Statue on the northern tip of Children's Island is where, every year, wreaths are placed in memory of the drowned.

Little Quarter Water Tower
Built in 1560, the tower supplied river water to 57 fountains throughout the Little Quarter.

Karlův

Kampa

Přístaviště lodí Kampa

Grand Priory Mill

most Legii

Střelecký ostrov

Plavební kanál

Jiráskův most

Palackého most

Apartment buildings of Art Nouveau design

Železniční most

0 metres		500
0 yards		500

KEY

🚋 Tram

⛴ River boat boarding point

• • Boat trip

To
Troja

Čechův
most

Přístaviště
lodí

Mánesův

Rudolfinum
*This allegorical statue of music
by Antonín Wagner is one of two
which decorate the imposing
entrance to the Neo-Renaissance
concert hall (see p84).*

The Clementinum,
a former Jesuit college, is
one of the largest buildings
in the city *(see p79).*

**The Old Town Bridge
Tower** was built as part
of the city's 14th-century
fortifications *(see p139).*

Smetana
Museum

Weir

National Theatre
*This symbol of the Czech revival, with
its spectacularly-decorated roof, has
dominated the skyline of the right
bank since the 1860s (see pp156–7).*

The Šítka Tower, with its
late-18th-century Baroque
roof, was originally built
in 1495 and pumped
water to the New Town.

Slovanskýo
strov

"Ginger and Fred" Building
*This charming, quirky office
building is home to the stylish
Perle de Prague restaurant
(see p207).*

**The Memorial to
František Palacký**
commemorates the
life of this eminent
19th-century Czech
historian and was
built in 1905.

Přístaviště
parníků

**Výtoň
Excise House**
*The coat of arms on this
16th-century house – built
to collect duty on timber transpored along
the river – is of the New Town from 1671.*

**The Na Slovanech
Monastery** was built in
1347 by Charles IV. Its
two modern steeples
are easily recognizable
from the river.

Church of St Peter and St Paul
*The Neo-Gothic steeples
on this much-rebuilt church were
designed by František Mikeš
and erected in 1903. They are
the dominant feature of
Vyšehrad rock (see pp180–1).*

PRAGUE AREA BY AREA

OLD TOWN

STARÉ MĚSTO

The heart of the city is the Old Town and its central square. In the 11th century the settlements around the Castle spread to the right bank of the Vltava. A marketplace in what is now Old Town Square (Staroměstské náměstí) was mentioned for the first time in 1091. Houses and churches sprang up

Physician, Jan
Marek (1595–1667)

around the square, determining the random network of streets, many of which survive. The area gained the privileges of a town in the 13th century, and, in 1338, a Town Hall. This and other great buildings, such as Clam-Gallas Palace and the Municipal House, reflect the importance of the Old Town.

SIGHTS AT A GLANCE

Churches
Church of St James ❹
Church of Our Lady
   before Týn ❽
Church of St Nicholas ⓫
Church of St Gall ⓮
Church of St Martin
   in the Wall ⓯
Church of St Giles ⓱
Bethlehem Chapel ⓲

Museums and Galleries
Náprstek Museum ⓰
Smetana Museum ㉔

Historic Streets and Squares
Celetná Street ❸
Old Town Square
   pp66–9 ❼
Mariánské Square ⓴
Charles Street ㉑
Knights of the Cross Square ㉕

Historic Monuments and Buildings
Powder Gate ❶
Municipal House ❷
Carolinum ❻
Jan Hus Monument ❿
Old Town Hall pp72–4 ⓬
House at the Two Golden
   Bears ⓭
Clementinum ㉓

Theatres
Estates Theatre ❺

Palaces
Clam-Gallas Palace ⓳
Kinský Palace ❾
Palace of the Lords
   of Kunštát ㉒

GETTING THERE
Můstek on metro lines A and B and Staroměstská on line A are both handy for the area. Trams do not cross the Old Town, but from Charles Bridge or Náměstí Republiky it is only a short walk to Old Town Square and the other sights.

KEY

Street-by-Street map
See pp62–3

Street-by-Street map
See pp76–7

Ⓜ Metro station

Tram stop

0 metres   250

0 yards   250

◁ Café tables and strolling pedestrians in Old Town Square

Street-by-Street: Old Town (East)

Free of traffic (except for a few horse-drawn
carriages) and ringed with historic buildings,
Prague's Old Town Square (Staroměstské
náměstí) ranks among the finest public spaces
in any city. Streets like Celetná and Ovocný trh
are also pedestrianized. In summer, café tables
spill out onto the cobbles, and though the area
draws tourists by the thousands, the unique
atmosphere has not yet been destroyed.

Kinský Palace
*This stunning Rococo
palace now serves as
an art gallery* ❾

Church of St Nicholas
*The imposing façade of
this Baroque church
dominates one corner
of Old Town Square* ⓫

STAROMĚSTSKÉ
NÁMĚSTÍ

★ **Old Town Square**
*This late-19th-century
watercolour by Václav Jansa
shows how little the Square
has changed in 100 years* ❼

MALÉ
NÁMĚSTÍ

ŽELEZNÁ

**Jan Hus
Monument**
*Religious reformer
Hus is a symbol
of integrity, and
the monument
brings together the
highest and lowest
points in Czech
history* ❿

U Rotta, now Hotel Rott, is a
former ironmonger's shop,
decorated with colourful
paintings by the 19th-century
artist Mikuláš Aleš.

**House at the Two
Golden Bears**
*The carved Renaissance
portal is the finest of
its kind in Prague* ⓭

★ **Old Town Hall**
*The famous astronomical
clock draws a crowd of
visitors every hour* ⓬

The Štorch house has painted
decoration based on designs
by Mikuláš Aleš showing
St Wenceslas on horseback.

| 0 metres | 100 |
| 0 yards | 100 |

KEY

– – – Suggested route

Church of Our Lady before Týn
The church's Gothic steeples are the Old Town's most distinctive landmark **8**

LOCATOR MAP
See Street Finder, maps 3–4

Church of St James
This wooden Pietà, on the main altar, was made in the 15th century **4**

★ **Municipal House**
This Art Nouveau building is a popular concert venue **2**

Týn courtyard

JAKUBSKÁ

ŠTUPARTSKÁ

CELETNÁ

UPRAŠNÉ BRÁNY

Powder Gate
This much-restored Gothic gate is a relic of when there was a royal palace here at the entrance to the Old Town **1**

OVOCNÝ TRH

House at the
Black Madonna

Estates Theatre
The theatre featured in director Miloš Forman's film Amadeus **5**

Ovocný trh was
Prague's fruit market.

Celetná Street
This ornamental Baroque plaque is the sign of the House at the Black Sun **3**

Carolinum
A magnificently carved Oriel window projects from the oldest surviving part of the Carolinum university – founded by Charles IV in the 14th century **6**

STAR SIGHTS

★ Old Town Square

★ Old Town Hall

★ Municipal House

Powder Gate ●
PRAŠNÁ BRÁNA

Náměstí Republiky. **Map** 4 D3.
Tel 72 40 63 723. ⓂNáměstí
Republiky. 🚋 5, 8, 14. **Open**
Apr–Oct: 10am–6pm daily.

There has been a gate here
since the 11th century, when
it formed one of the 13
entrances to the Old Town.
In 1475, King Vladislav II laid
the foundation stone of the
New Tower, as it was to be
known. A coronation gift
from the city council, the
gate was modelled on Peter
Parler's Old Town bridge
tower built a century earlier.
The gate had little defensive
value; its rich sculptural
decoration was intended to
add prestige to the adjacent
palace of the Royal Court.
Building was halted eight
years later when the king
had to flee because of riots.
On his return in 1485 he
opted for the safety of the
Castle. Kings never again
occupied the Royal Court.

The gate acquired its
present name when it was
used to store gunpowder in
the 17th century. The
sculptural decoration, badly
damaged during the Prussian
occupation in 1757 and mostly
removed soon afterwards,
was replaced in 1876.

**The Powder Gate viewed from
outside the Old Town**

Karel Špillar's mosaic *Homage to Prague* on Municipal House's façade

Municipal House ●
OBECNÍ DŮM

Náměstí Republiky 5. **Map** 4 D3.
Tel 22 20 02 111. ⓂNáměstí
Republiky. 🚋 5, 8, 14. **Gallery
open** for exhibitions only, 10am–
6pm daily. 🎧 by arrangement. ♿
www.obecnidum.cz

Prague's most prominent Art
Nouveau building stands on
the site of the former Royal
Court palace, the King's residence between 1383 and 1485.
Abandoned for centuries, what
remained was used as a seminary and later as a military
college. It was demolished in
the early 1900s to be replaced
by the present cultural centre
(1905–11) with its exhibition
halls and auditorium, designed
by Antonín Balšánek assisted
by Osvald Polívka.

The exterior is embellished
with stucco and allegorical
statuary. Above the main
entrance there is a huge semicircular mosaic entitled
Homage to Prague by Karel
Špillar. Inside, topped by an
impressive glass dome, is
Prague's principal concert
venue and the core of the
entire building, the
Smetana Hall, sometimes

also used as a ballroom. The
interior of the building is
decorated with works by
leading Czech artists of the
first decade of the century,
including Alfons Mucha
(see p149).

There are numerous smaller
halls, conference rooms and
offices, as well as cafés and
restaurants where visitors can
relax and enjoy the centre's
flamboyant Art Nouveau
decoration at
their leisure.
On 28 October,
1918, Prague's
Municipal
House was the
scene of the
momentous
proclamation
of the new
independent
state of
Czechoslovakia.

**Decorative detail
by Alfons Mucha**

Hollar
Hall

Foyer

Mayor's Salon
with paintings by
Alfons Mucha

Entrance hall

Entrance to Art
Nouveau café

Restaurants

Celetná Street ❸
CELETNÁ ULICE

Map 3 C3. ᴹ *Náměstí Republiky, Můstek.* **House of the Black Madonna** *Tel 22 42 11 732.* *Open* 10am–6pm Tue–Fri. ♿ ▢ www.ngprague.cz

One of the oldest streets in Prague, Celetná follows an old trading route from eastern Bohemia. Its name comes from the plaited bread rolls that were first baked here in the Middle Ages. It gained prestige in the 14th century as a section of the Royal Route *(see p172)* used for coronation processions. Foundations of Romanesque and Gothic buildings can be seen in some of the cellars, but most of the houses with their picturesque signs are Baroque remodellings.

At No. 34, the House of the Black Madonna is home to a small collection of Czech Cubism, including paintings, sculpture, furniture, architectural plans and applied arts.

Church of St James ❹
KOSTEL SV. JAKUBA

Malá Štupartská. **Map** 3 C3. ᴹ *Můstek, Náměstí Republiky.* *Open in the season,* 9:30am–noon, 2–3:45pm Mon–Sat. ⛪ 📷

This attractive Baroque church was originally the Gothic presbytery of a Minorite monastery. The order (a branch of the Franciscans) was invited to Prague by King Wenceslas I in 1232. It was

Baroque organ loft in the Church of St James

rebuilt in the Baroque style after a fire in 1689, allegedly started by agents of Louis XIV. Over 20 side altars were added, decorated with works by painters such as Jan Jiří Heinsch, Petr Brandl and Václav Vavřinec Reiner. The tomb of Count Vratislav of Mitrovice (1714–16), designed by Johann Bernhard Fischer von Erlach and executed by sculptor Ferdinand Brokof, is the most beautiful Baroque tomb in Bohemia. The count is said to have been accidentally buried alive – his corpse was later found sitting up in the tomb. Hanging on the right of the entrance is a mummified forearm. It has been there for over 400 years, ever since a thief tried to steal the jewels from the Madonna on the high altar. But the Virgin grabbed his arm and held on so tightly it had to be cut off.

Because of its long nave, the church's acoustics are excellent and many concerts and recitals are given here. There is also a magnificent organ built in 1702.

Estates Theatre ❺
STAVOVSKÉ DIVADLO

Ovocný trh 1. **Map** 3 C4. *Tel 22 42 28 503.* ᴹ *Můstek.* *Foyer open* for performances only. www.narodni-divadlo.cz

Built by Count Nostitz in 1783, the theatre is one of the finest examples of Neo-Classical elegance in Prague. It is a mecca for Mozart fans *(see p220)*. On 29 October 1787, Mozart's opera, *Don Giovanni* had its debut here with Mozart at the piano conducting the orchestra. In 1834 the musical *Fidlovačka* premiered here. One of the songs, *Kde domov můj?* (Where is my Home?), became the Czech national anthem.

Carolinum ❻
KAROLINUM

Ovocný trh 3. **Map** 3 C4. *Tel 22 44 91 111.* ᴹ *Můstek.* **Closed** to the public. *Open* for special exhibitions.

At the core of the university-founded by Charles IV in 1348 is the Carolinum. The chapel, arcade and walls still survive, together with a fine oriel window, but in 1945 the courtyard was reconstructed in Gothic style. In the 15th and 16th centuries the university played a leading role in the movement to reform the church. After the Battle of the White Mountain *(see pp30–31)*, the university was taken over by the Jesuits.

Old Town Square ❼
STAROMĚSTSKÉ NÁMĚSTÍ

See pp66–9.

Smetana Hall

Old Town Square: East and North Sides ➐

STAROMĚSTSKÉ NÁMĚSTÍ

Some of Prague's colourful history is preserved around the Old Town Square in the form of its buildings. On the north side of the Square, the Pauline Monastery is the only surviving piece of original architecture. The east side boasts two superb examples of the architecture of their times: the House at the Stone Bell, restored to its former appearance as a Gothic town palace, and the Rococo Kinský Palace. An array of pastel-coloured buildings completes the Square.

★ House at the Stone Bell
At the corner of the building, the bell is the sign of this medieval town palace.

**Statues by
Ignaz Platzer
from 1760–65**

Kinský Palace
C G Bossi created the elaborate stucco decoration on the façade of this Rococo palace (see p70).

EAST SIDE

Rococo
stucco work

NORTH SIDE

**★ Church of
St Nicholas**
Besides its original purpose as a parish church and, later, a Benedictine monastery church, this has served as a garrison church and a concert hall (see p70).

STAR SIGHTS

★ Church of Our Lady before Týn

★ House at the Stone Bell

★ Church of St Nicholas

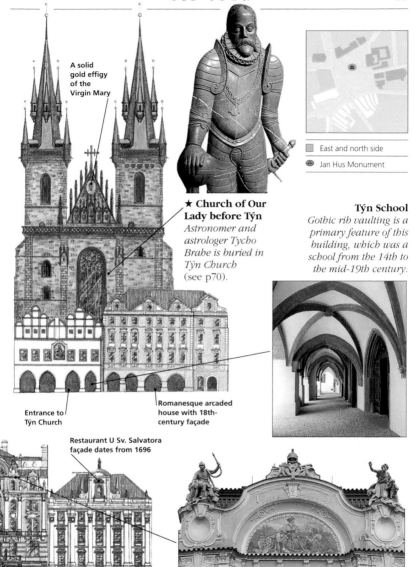

A solid gold effigy of the Virgin Mary

East and north side

Jan Hus Monument

★ Church of Our Lady before Týn
Astronomer and astrologer Tycho Brahe is buried in Týn Church (see p70).

Týn School
Gothic rib vaulting is a primary feature of this building, which was a school from the 14th to the mid-19th century.

Entrance to Týn Church

Romanesque arcaded house with 18th-century façade

Restaurant U Sv. Salvatora façade dates from 1696

Ministerstvo pro místní rozvoj
Architect Osvald Polívka designed this Art Nouveau building in 1898, with figures of firefighters on the upper façade. It houses the Ministry of Local Development.

Staroměstské náměstí, 1793
The engraving by Filip and František Heger shows the Old Town Square teeming with people and carriages. The Old Town Hall is on the left.

Old Town Square: South Side ⑦
STAROMĚSTSKÉ NÁMĚSTÍ

A colourful array of houses of Romanesque or Gothic origin, with fascinating house signs, graces the south side of the Old Town Square. The block between Celetná Street and Železná Street is especially attractive. The Square has always been a busy focal point, and today offers visitors a tourist information centre, as well as a number of restaurants, cafés, shops, and galleries.

FRANZ KAFKA (1883–1924)

The author of two of the most influential novels of the 20th century, *The Trial* and *The Castle*, Kafka spent most of his short life in the Old Town. From 1893 to 1901 he studied in the Golz-Kinský Palace *(see p70)*, where his father later had a shop. He worked as an insurance clerk, but frequented Berta Fanta's literary salon at the Stone Ram, Old Town Square, along with others who wrote in German. Hardly any of his work was published in his lifetime.

U Lazara (At Lazarus's)
Romanesque barrel vaulting testifies to the house's early origins, though it was rebuilt during the Renaissance. The ground floor houses the Staroměstská restaurace.

At the Stone Table

At the Golden Unicorn

Železná Street

SOUTH SIDE

★ **At the Stone Ram**
The early-16th-century house sign shows a young maiden with a ram. The house has been referred to as At the Unicorn due to the similarity between the one-horned ram and a unicorn.

★ **Štorch House**
The late-19th-century painting of St Wenceslas on horseback by Mikuláš Aleš appears on this ornate Neo-Renaissance building, also known as At the Stone Madonna.

STAR SIGHTS

★ Štorch House

★ At the Stone Ram

Melantrichova Passage
*Václav Jansa's painting (1898)
shows the narrow passageway
leading to the Old Town Square.*

☐ South side

⚉ Jan Hus Monument

At the Red Fox
*A golden Madonna and Child
look down from the Baroque
façade of an originally
Romanesque building.*

At The Ox
*Named after its
15th-century owner,
the burgher Ochs,
this house features an
early-18th-century
stone statue of
St Anthony of Padua.*

At the
Blue Star

At the Storks

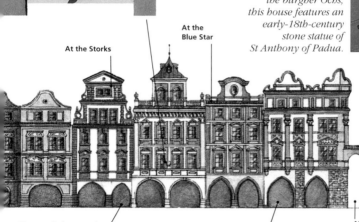

The arcade houses the
Grand Café Praha.

**U Orloje
restaurant**

Melantrichova
Passage

TIMELINE					
1338 Old Town becomes municipality	*Leopold II's Royal Procession through the Old Town Square in 1791*	**1735** Church of St Nicholas completed		**1948** Klement Gottwald proclaims Communist state from balcony of Golz-Kinský Palace	
1300	**1450**	**1600**	**1750**	**1900**	
1200 Square is meeting point of trade routes and important market	**1365** Building of present Týn Church	**1621** Execution of 27 anti-Habsburg leaders in square *(see p31)*	**1784** Unification of Prague towns		
		1689 Fire destroys large part of Old Town	**1915** Unveiling of Jan Hus Monument		
			Hus Monument (detail)		

Statue of the Madonna on Our Lady before Týn

Church of Our Lady before Týn ⑧

KOSTEL MATKY BOŽÍ PŘED TÝNEM

Týnská, Štupartská. **Map** 3 C3. *Tel 60 22 04 213.* ⁛Mᵀ *Staroměstská, Můstek.* **Open** *10am–1pm, 3–5pm Tue–Sun.* **Closed** *in winter.* 🔔 *6pm Wed–Thu, 8am Sat, 9:30am & 9pm Sun.* 🚫

Dominating the Old Town Square are the magnificent multiple steeples of this historic church. The present Gothic church was started in 1365 and soon became associated with the reform movement in Bohemia. From the early 15th century until 1620 Týn was the main Hussite church in Prague. The Hussite king, George of Poděbrady, took Utraquist communion *(see Church of St Martin in the Wall p73)* here and had a gold chalice – the Utraquist symbol – mounted on the façade. After 1621 the chalice was melted down to become part of the statue of the Madonna that replaced it.

On the northern side of the church is a beautiful entrance portal (1390) decorated with scenes of Christ's passion. The dark interior has some notable features, including Gothic sculptures of *Calvary*, a pewter font (1414) and a 15th-century Gothic pulpit. Behind the church is the Týn Courtyard, with its numerous architectural styles.

Kinský arms on Golz-Kinský Palace

Kinský Palace ⑨

PALÁC KINSKÝCH

Staroměstské náměstí 12. **Map** 3 C3. *Tel 22 48 10 758.* ⁛Mᵀ *Staroměstská.* **Open** *10am–6pm Tue–Sun.* 📷 🚫 🍴 www.ngprague.cz

This lovely Rococo palace, designed by Kilian Ignaz Dientzenhofer, has a pretty pink and white stucco façade crowned with statues of the four elements by Ignaz Franz Platzer. It was bought from the Golz family in 1768 by Štěpán Kinský, an Imperial diplomat. In 1948 Communist leader, Klement Gottwald, used the balcony to address a huge crowd of party members – a key event in the crisis that led up to his *coup d'état.* The National Gallery now uses the Kinský Palace for art exhibitions.

Jan Hus Monument ⑩

POMNÍK JANA HUSA

Staroměstské náměstí. **Map** 3 B3. ⁛Mᵀ *Staroměstská.*

At one end of the Old Town Square stands the massive monument to the religious reformer and Czech hero, Jan Hus *(see pp26–7).* Hus was burnt at the stake after being pronounced a heretic by the Council of Constance in 1415. The monument by Ladislav Šaloun was unveiled in 1915 on the 500th anniversary of his death. It shows two groups of people, one of victorious Hussite warriors, the other of Protestants forced into exile 200 years later, and a young mother symbolizing national rebirth. The dominant figure of Hus emphasizes the moral authority of the man who gave up life rather than his beliefs.

Church of St Nicholas ⑪

KOSTEL SV. MIKULÁŠE

Staroměstské náměstí. **Map** 3 B3. *Tel 22 41 90 991.* ⁛Mᵀ *Staroměstská.* **Open** *10am–4pm daily and for evening concerts Apr–Nov.* 🔔 *10:30am Sun.* www.svmikulas.cz

There has been a church here since the 12th century. It was the Old Town's parish church and meeting place until Týn Church was completed in the 14th century. After the Battle of the White Mountain in 1620 *(see pp30–31)* the church became part of a Benedictine monastery. The present church by Kilian Ignaz Dientzenhofer, was completed in 1735. Its dramatic white façade is studded with statues by Antonín Braun.

Defiant Hussites on the Jan Hus Monument in Old Town Square

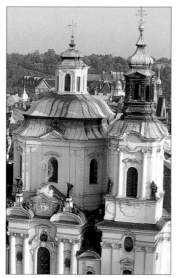

Church of St Nicholas in the Old Town

When in 1781 Emperor Joseph II closed all monasteries not engaged in socially useful activities, the church was stripped bare. In World War I the church was used by the troops of Prague's garrison. The colonel in charge took the opportunity to restore the church with the help of artists who might otherwise have been sent to the front. The dome has frescoes of the lives of St Nicholas and St Benedict by Kosmas Damian Asam. In the nave is a huge crown-shaped chandelier. At the end of the war, the church of St Nicholas was given to the Czechoslovak Hussite Church. Concerts are given now in the church during the summer.

Old Town Hall ⓬
STAROMĚSTSKÁ RADNICE

See pp72–3.

House at the Two Golden Bears ⓭
DŮM U DVOU ZLATÝCH MEDVĚDŮ

Kožná 1. **Map** 3 B4. Ⓜ *Můstek.* **Closed** to the public.

If you leave the Old Town Square by the narrow Melantrichova Street, make a point of turning into the first alleyway on the left to see the portal of the house called "At the Two Golden Bears". The present Renaissance building was constructed from two earlier houses in 1567. The portal was added in 1590, when a wealthy merchant, Lorenc Štork, secured the services of court architect Bonifaz Wohlmut, who had designed the spire on the tower of St Vitus's Cathedral *(see pp100–3)*. His ornate portal with reliefs of two bears is one of the most beautiful Renaissance portals in Prague. Magnificent arcades, also dating from the 16th century, have been preserved in the inner courtyard. In 1885 Egon Erwin Kisch, known as the "Furious Reporter", was born here. He was a German-speaking Jewish writer and journalist, feared for the force of his left-wing rhetoric.

Church of St Gall ⓮
KOSTEL SV. HAVLA

Havelská. **Map** 3 C4. Ⓜ *Můstek.* **Tel** *22 42 13 475.* **Open** *only for services.* 🕐 *12:15pm Mon–Fri, 8am Sun.* 🚫

Dating from around 1280, this church was built to serve an autonomous German community in the area known as Gall's Town (Havelské Město). In the 14th century this was merged with the Old Town. In the 18th century the church was given a Baroque facelift by Giovanni Santini-Aichel, who created a bold façade decorated with statues of saints by Ferdinand Brokof. Rich interior furnishings include paintings by the leading Baroque artist Karel Škréta, who is buried here. Prague's best-known market has been held in Havelská Street since the middle ages, selling flowers, vegetables, toys, and clothes.

One of nine statues on façade of St Gall's

Carved Renaissance portal of the House at the Two Golden Bears

Old Town Hall ⑫

STAROMĚSTSKÁ RADNICE

One of the most striking buildings in Prague is the
Old Town Hall, established in 1338 after King John of
Luxemburg agreed to set up a town council. Over the
centuries a number of old houses were knocked
together as the Old Town Hall expanded, and it now
consists of a row of colourful Gothic and Renaissance
buildings, most of which have been carefully restored
after heavy damage inflicted by the Nazis in the 1945
Prague Uprising. The
tower is 69.5 m (228
ft) high and offers a
spectacular view
of the city.

Old Council Hall
*This 19th-century engraving
features the well-preserved
15th-century ceiling.*

Old Town Coat of Arms
*Above the inscription, "Prague,
Head of the Kingdom", is the
coat of arms of the Old Town,
which was adopted in 1784 for the
whole city.*

Tourist
information
and entrance
to Tower

Temporary
art exhibitions

EXECUTIONS IN THE OLD TOWN SQUARE

A bronze tablet below the Old Town Hall
chapel records the names of the 27 Protestant
leaders executed here by order of the Catholic
Emperor Ferdinand on 21 June 1621. This was
the humiliating aftermath of the Battle of the
White Mountain *(see pp30–31)*. This defeat led
to the emigration of Protestants unwilling to
give up their faith, a Counter-Reformation drive
and Germanization.

★ Old Town Hall Tower
In 1364 the tower was added to what was the private house of Volflin of Kamen. Its gallery provides a fine city view.

Viewing gallery

VISITORS' CHECKLIST

Staroměstské náměstí 1. **Map** 3
C3. **Tel** 72 45 08 584. ⓶
Staroměstská (line A), Můstek
(A & B). ⓶ 17, 18. **Open** Apr–Oct:
9am–6pm daily (from 11am Mon);
Nov–Mar: 9am–5pm daily (from
11am Mon). ⓶ ⓶ ⓶ ⓶

Oriel Chapel
The original stained-glass windows on the five-sided chapel were destroyed in the last days of World War II, but were replaced in 1987.

Former house of Volflin of Kamen

Steps to gallery

Oriel Chapel Ceiling
The chapel, which was built on the first floor of the tower in 1381, has an ornate, recently restored ceiling.

★ Astronomical Clock
Mechanical figures perform above the zodiac signs in the upper section (see p74); the lower section is a calendar.

Calendar *(see pp32–3)*

Entrance hall decorated with mosaics

Gothic Door
This late Gothic main entrance to the Town Hall and Tower was carved by Matthias Rejsek. The entrance hall is filled with wall mosaics after designs by the Czech painter Mikuláš Aleš.

STAR FEATURES

★ Astronomical Clock

★ Old Town Hall Tower

Town Hall Clock

ORLOJ

Jan Táborský

The Town Hall acquired its first clock at the beginning of the 15th century. According to legend, in 1490, when it was rebuilt by a master clockmaker called Hanuš (real name Jan Z Růže), the councillors were so anxious to prevent him from re-creating his masterpiece elsewhere, that they blinded the poor man. Though the clock has been repaired many times since, the mechanism was perfected by Jan Táborský between 1552 and 1572.

The Apostles

APOSTLES

The centrepiece of the show that draws a crowd of spectators every time the clock strikes the hour is the procession of the 12

Vanity and Greed

Vojtěch Sucharda's Apostles, sculpted after the last set was burnt in 1945

Arabic numerals 1–24

Astronomical Clock with the sun in Aries

Death

Blue, representing the daylight hours

Calendar by Josef Mánes (see pp32–3)

The Turk, a symbol of lust

Apostles. First the figure of Death, the skeleton on the right of the clock, gives a pull on the rope that he holds in his right hand. In his left hand is an hourglass, which he raises and inverts. Two windows then open and the clockwork Apostles (or to be precise 11 of the Apostles plus St Paul) move slowly round, led by St Peter.

At the end of this part of the display, a cock crows and the clock chimes the hour. The other moving figures are a Turk, who shakes his head from side to side, Vanity, who looks at himself in a mirror and Greed, adapted from the original medieval stereotype of a Jewish moneylender.

ASTRONOMICAL CLOCK

The clockmaker's view of the universe had the Earth fixed firmly at the centre. The purpose of the clock was not to tell you the exact time but to imitate the supposed orbits of the sun and moon about the Earth. The hand with the sun, which points to the hour, in fact records three different kinds of time. The outer ring of medieval Arabic numerals measures Old Bohemian time, in which a day of 24 hours was reckoned from the setting of the sun. The ring of Roman numerals indicates time as we know it. The blue part of the dial represents the

visible part of the sky. This is divided into 12 parts. In so-called Babylonian time, the period of daylight was divided into 12 hours, which would vary in length from summer to winter.

The clock also shows the movement of the sun and moon through the 12 signs of the zodiac, which were of great importance in 16th-century Prague.

The figures of Death and the Turk

Church of St Martin in the Wall **⑮**

KOSTEL SV. MARTINA VE ZDI

Martinská. **Map** 3 B5. ⓂＮ Národní třída, Můstek. 🚊 6, 9, 17, 18, 22. **Open** for concerts.

This 12th-century church became part of the newly erected town wall during the fortification of the Old Town in the 13th century, hence its name. It was the first church where blessed wine, usually reserved for the clergy, was offered to the congregation as well as bread. This was a basic tenet of belief of the moderate Hussites (see pp26–7), the Utraquists, who took their name from the Latin sub utraque specie, "in both kinds". In 1787 the church was converted into workshops, but rebuilt in its original form in the early years of this century.

Náprstek Museum **⑯**

NÁPRSTKOVO MUZEUM

Betlémské náměstí. **Map** 3 B4. **Tel** 22 44 97 511. ⓂＮ Národní třída, Staroměstská. 🚊 6, 9, 17, 18, 22. **Open** 10am–6pm Tue–Sun. 📷 www.aconet.cz/npm

Vojta Náprstek, art patron and philanthropist, created this museum as a tribute to modern industry following a decade of exile in America after the 1848 revolution (see pp32–3). On his return in 1862, inspired by London's Victorian museums, he began his collection. He created the Czech Industrial Museum by joining five older buildings together, and in the process virtually destroyed the family brewery and home – an 18th-century house called At the Haláneks (U Halánků). He later turned to ethnography and the collection now consists of artefacts from Asian, African and Native American cultures, including weapons and ritual objects from the Aztecs, Toltecs and Mayas. The museum is part of the National Museum.

Nearby, on Smetanovo nábřeží is Neo-Gothic Kranners Fountain erected in 1850.

Ceiling fresco by Václav Vavřinec Reiner in Church of St Giles

Church of St Giles **⑰**

KOSTEL SV. JILJÍ

Husova. **Map** 3 B4. **Tel** 22 42 20 235. ⓂＮ Národní třída. 🚊 6, 9, 17, 18, 22. **Open** for services only. ✝ 7am & 6:30pm Mon–Fri, 6:30pm Sat, 9:30am, 6:30pm Sun. 📷 www.jilji.op.cz

Despite a beautiful Gothic portal on the southern side, the inside of this church is essentially Baroque. Founded in 1371 on the site of an old Romanesque church, it became a Hussite parish church in 1420. Following the Protestant defeat in 1620 (see pp30–31), Ferdinand II presented the church to the Dominicans, who built a huge friary on its southern side. It has now been returned to the Dominicans, religious orders having been abolished under the Communists.

The vaults of the church are decorated with frescoes by the painter Václav Vavřinec Reiner, who is buried in the nave before the altar of St Vincent. The main fresco, a glorification of the Dominicans, shows St Dominic and his friars helping the pope defend the Catholic Church from non-believers.

Bethlehem Chapel **⑱**

BETLÉMSKÁ KAPLE

Betlémské náměstí. **Map** 3 B4. ⓂＮ Národní třída, Staroměstská. 🚊 6, 9, 17, 18, 22. **Open** Apr–Oct: 10am–6:30pm Tue–Sun; Nov-Mar: 10am–5:30pm Tue–Sun. 📷 organized by the Prague Information Service (see p227).

The present "chapel" is a reconstruction of a hall built by the followers of the radical preacher Jan Milíč z Kroměříže in 1391–4. The hall was used for preaching in Czech. Between 1402 and 1413 Jan Hus (see pp26–7) preached in the Chapel. Influenced by the teachings of the English religious reformer John Wycliffe, Hus condemned the corrupt practices of the Church, arguing that the Scriptures should be the sole source of doctrine. After the Battle of the White Mountain in 1620 (see pp30–31), when Protestant worship was outlawed, the building was handed over to the Jesuits, who rebuilt it with six naves. In 1786 it was almost demolished. After World War II the chapel was reconstructed following old illustrations.

16th-century illustration showing Jan Hus preaching in Bethlehem Chapel

Street-by-Street: Old Town (West)

The narrow streets near Charles Bridge follow
Prague's medieval street plan. For centuries Charles
Street (Karlova) was the main route across the Old
Town. The picturesque, twisting street is lined with
shops and houses displaying Renaissance and Baroque
façades. In the 17th century the Jesuits bought up a
vast area of land to the north of the street to house
the complex of the Clementinum university.

★ Clementinum
*This plaque records the
founding in 1783 of a state-
supervised seminary in place
of the old Jesuit university* ㉓

**Knights of the
Cross Square**
*From the façade of
the Church of the
Holy Saviour, black-
ened statues overlook
the small square* ㉕

**Church of
St Francis**

★ Smetana Museum
*A museum devoted to the life
and work of composer Bedřich
Smetana is housed in this Neo-
Renaissance building set on the
riverfront, which was once
an old waterworks* ㉔

A N E N S K Á

St Anne's Convent
was abolished in 1782.
Some of its buildings
are now used by the
National Theatre
(see pp156–7).

The Old Town Bridge Tower
*dates from 1380. The Gothic
sculptural decoration on the
eastern façade was from Peter
Parler's workshop. The kingfisher
was the favourite personal symbol
of Wenceslas IV (son of Charles
IV) in whose reign the tower was
completed (see p139).*

Charles Street
*Among the many decorated houses
along the ancient street, be sure to
look out for this Art Nouveau
statue of the legendary Princess
Libuše (see p21) surrounded by
roses at No. 22/24* ㉑

Mariánské Square
The square used to be flooded so often, it was called "the puddle". The Art Nouveau sculptures on the balcony of the New Town Hall, built here in 1911, are by Stanislav Sucharda **20**

Observatory tower

MARIÁNSKÉ NÁMĚSTÍ

LOCATOR MAP
See Street Finder, map 3

JEWISH QUARTER
OLD TOWN
NEW TOWN
Vltava

Clam-Gallas Palace
One of Prague's grandest Baroque palaces and full of wonderful statuary, the Clam-Gallas has been restored and is open for concerts **19**

KARLOVA

LILIOVÁ

ŘETĚZOVÁ

HUSOVA

To Old Town Square

Church of St Giles
Much of the Baroque sculpture, like this angel on the altar (1738), is by František Weiss **17**

Palace of the Lords of Kunštát
George of Poděbrady lived here before he became King in 1458 **22**

Bethlehem Chapel
In this spacious chapel, rebuilt in the 1950s, Hus and other reformers preached to huge congregations **18**

| 0 metres | 100 |
| 0 yards | 100 |

KEY
--- Suggested route

STAR SIGHTS

★ Clementinum

★ Smetana Museum

Clam-Gallas Palace ⑲
CLAM-GALLASŮV PALÁC

Husova 20. **Map** 3 B4. **Tel** 23 60
02 019. ᴹ Staroměstská.
Open for concerts and temporary
exhibitions only. **www**.ahmp.cz

The interior of this magnificent
Baroque palace had suffered
during its use as a store for the
city archives, but has now
been lovingly restored. The
palace, designed by Viennese
court architect Johann
Bernhard Fischer von Erlach,
was built in 1713–30 for the
Supreme Marshal of Bohemia,
Jan Gallas de Campo. Its grand
portals, each flanked by two
pairs of Hercules sculpted
by Matthias Braun, give a taste
of what lies within. The main
staircase is also decorated with
Braun statues, set off by a
ceiling fresco, *The Triumph of*

Apollo by Carlo Carlone. The
palace has a theatre, where
Beethoven performed some
of his works.

Mariánské Square ⑳
MARIÁNSKÉ NÁMĚSTÍ

Map 3 B3. ᴹ Staroměstská, Můstek.

Two statues dominate the
square from the corners
of the forbidding Town Hall,
built in 1912. One illustrates
the story of the long-lived
Rabbi Löw *(see p88)* finally
being caught by the Angel of
Death. The other is the Iron
Man, a local ghost condemned
to roam the Old Town after
murdering his mistress. A
niche in the garden wall of the
Clam-Gallas Palace houses a
statue of the River Vltava,
depicted as a nymph pouring
water from a jug. There is a
story that an old soldier once
made the nymph sole
beneficiary of
his will.

Matthias Braun's statues on a portal of the Clam-Gallas Palace (c.1714)

Charles Street ㉑
KARLOVA ULICE

Map 3 A4. ᴹ Staroměstská.

A 19th-century sign on the House at the Golden Snake

Dating back to the 12th
century, this narrow, winding
street was part of the Royal
Route *(see pp174–5)*, along
which coronation processions
passed on the way to Prague
Castle. Many original Gothic
and Renaissance houses
remain, most converted into
shops to attract tourists.

A café at the House at the
Golden Snake (No. 18) was
established in 1714 by an
Armenian, Deodatus Damajan,
who handed out slanderous
pamphlets from here. It is
now a restaurant. Look out
for At the Golden Well (No.
3), which has a magnificent
Baroque façade and stucco
reliefs of saints including
St Roch and St Sebastian,
who are believed to offer
protection against plagues.

Palace of the Lords of Kunštát ㉒
DŮM PÁNŮ Z KUNŠTÁTU

Řetězová 3. **Map** 3 B4. **Tel** 22 22 21
240. ᴹ Národní třída, Staroměstská.
6, 9, 17, 18, 22. **Open** Apr–Oct:
11am–9pm daily.

The basement of the palace,
dating from around 1200,
contains three of the best-
preserved Romanesque rooms
in Prague. It was originally
the ground floor, but over the
years the surrounding ground
level was raised by 3m (10 ft)
to prevent flooding. In the
15th century the house was
enlarged in Gothic style by its
owners, the Lords of Kunštát
and Poděbrady. The palace

houses a historical exhibition devoted to Bohemia's only Hussite king, George of Poděbrady (see pp26–7), who lived here for a time.

Clementinum ㉓
KLEMENTINUM

Křižovnické náměstí 4, Mariánské náměstí 5, Seminářská 1. **Map** 3 A4. **Tel** 60 22 59 314. 🚇 Staroměstská. 🚊 17, 18. **Library open** 9am–10pm Mon–Fri, 8am–2pm Sat. **Church open** only for services. 🕐 7pm Tue, 2pm & 8pm Sun. 🎫 ♿ 📷 Mar–Oct: every hour from 10am–4pm daily. **Tel** 22 22 21 339.

Former Jesuit Church of the Holy Saviour in the Clementinum

In 1556 Emperor Ferdinand I invited the Jesuits to Prague to help bring the Czechs back into the Catholic fold. They established their headquarters in the former Dominican monastery of St Clement, hence the name Clementinum. This soon became an effective rival to the Carolinum (see p65), the Utraquist university. Prague's first Jesuit church, the Church of the Holy Saviour (Kostel sv. Salvátora) was built here in 1601. Its façade, with seven large statues of saints by Jan Bendl (1659), is dramatically lit at night.

Expelled in 1618, the Jesuits were back two years later more determined than ever to stamp out heresy. In 1622 the two universities were merged, resulting in the Jesuits gaining a virtual monopoly on higher education in Prague. They believed two-thirds of the population were secret heretics, searched for books in Czech and then burnt them by the thousand. Between 1653 and 1723 the Clementinum expanded eastwards. Over 30 houses and three churches were pulled down to make way for the new complex.

When in 1773 the pope dissolved their order, the Jesuits had to leave Prague and education was secularized. The Clementinum became the Prague University library, today the National Library. Look out for any classical concerts performed in the beautiful Chapel of Mirrors (Zrcadlová kaple).

Smetana Museum ㉔
MUZEUM BEDŘICHA SMETANY

Novotného lávka 1. **Map** 3 A4. **Tel** 22 22 20 082. 🚇 Staroměstská. 🚊 17, 18. **Open** 10am–noon, 12:30–5pm Wed–Mon. 📷 🎫 www.nm.cz

On a spit of land beside the Vltava, a former Neo-Renaissance waterworks has been turned into a memorial to Bedřich Smetana, the father of Czech music. The museum contains documents, letters, scores and musical instruments detailing the composer's life and work. Smetana was a fervent patriot and his music helped inspire the Czech national revival. Deaf towards the end of his life, he never heard his cycle of symphonic poems Má Vlast (My Country), being performed.

Statue of Charles IV(1848) in Knights of the Cross Square

Knights of the Cross Square ㉕
KŘIŽOVNICKÉ NÁMĚSTÍ

Map 3 A4. **Tel** 23 60 33 680. 🚇 Staroměstská. 🚊 17, 18. 🚌 133. **Church of St Francis open** for services and concerts. 🕐 7am Mon–Fri, 9am Sun. 🎫 ♿

This small square in front of the Old Town Bridge Tower offers fine views across the Vltava. On the north side is the Church of St Francis (kostel sv. Františka), once part of the monastery of the crusading Knights of the Cross with the Red Star. In summer, concerts of popular Classical and Baroque music take place in this beautiful Baroque church most evenings at 8pm. To the east is the Church of the Holy Saviour, part of the huge Clementinum complex. In the square stands a large bronze Neo-Gothic statue of Charles IV.

Sgraffitoed façade of the Smetana Museum

JEWISH QUARTER
JOSEFOV

I n the Middle Ages there were two distinct Jewish communities in Prague's Old Town: Jews from the west had settled around the Old-New Synagogue, Jews from the Byzantine Empire around the Old Shul (on the site of today's Spanish Synagogue). The two settlements gradually merged and were confined in an enclosed ghetto. For centuries Prague's Jews suffered from oppressive laws – in the 16th century they had to wear a yellow circle as a mark of shame. Christians

Art Nouveau detail on house in Kaprova

often accused them of starting fires and poisoning wells – any pretext for a pogrom. Discrimination was partially relaxed in 1784 by Joseph II, and the Jewish Quarter was named Josefov after him. In 1850 the area was officially incorporated as part of Prague. In the 1890s the city authorities decided to raze the ghetto slums because the area's complete lack of sanitation made it a health hazard. However, the Town Hall, a number of synagogues and the Old Jewish Cemetery were saved.

SIGHTS AT A GLANCE

Synagogues and Churches
Pinkas Synagogue ❹
Klausen Synagogue ❺
Old-New Synagogue pp88–9 ❻
High Synagogue ❼
Maisel Synagogue ❾
Church of the Holy Ghost ❿
Spanish Synagogue ⓫
Church of St Simon and St Jude ⓭
Church of St Castullus ⓮

Concert Hall
Rudolfinum ❶

Museums and Galleries
Museum of Decorative Arts ❷
St Agnes of Bohemia Convent pp92–3 ⓯

Historic Buildings
Jewish Town Hall ❽
Cubist Houses ⓬

Cemeteries
Old Jewish Cemetery pp86–7 ❸

GETTING THERE
Staroměstská station on metro line A is close to all the major sights in the Jewish Quarter. The alternative is to take tram 17 or 18 to Náměstí Jana Palacha. For St Agnes of Bohemia Convent, bus 207 is convenient.

0 metres 250
0 yards 250

KEY

Street-by-Street map
See pp82–83

Ｍ Metro station

Tram stop

River boat boarding point

◁ Densely-packed gravestones in the Old Jewish Cemetery

Street-by-Street: Jewish Quarter

Though the old ghetto has disappeared, much of
the area's fascinating history is preserved in the
synagogues around the Old Jewish Cemetery, while
the newer streets are lined with many delightful Art
Nouveau buildings. The old lanes
to the east of the former
ghetto lead to the quiet
haven of St Agnes's
Convent, beautifully
restored as a branch of
the National Gallery.

Cubist Houses
*One of the new architectural
styles used in the rebuilding
of the old Jewish Quarter was
based on the ideas of Cubism* ⑫

★ Old Jewish Cemetery
*Thousands of gravestones
are crammed into the
ancient cemetery* ❸

★ Old-New Synagogue
*The Gothic hall with its distinctive
crenelled gable has been a house
of prayer for over 700 years* ❻

**Klausen
Synagogue**
*The exhibits of
the Jewish
Museum include
this alms box, dating
from about 1800* ❺

High Synagogue
*The interior has splendid
Renaissance vaulting* ❼

**★ Museum of
Decorative Arts**
*Stained glass panels
on the staircase depict
the crafts represented
in the museum's wide-
ranging collection* ❷

Pinkas Synagogue
*The walls are now a
moving memorial to
the Czech Jews killed
in the Holocaust* ❹

To Metro
Staroměstská

Jewish Town Hall
*The 16th-century building
still serves the Czech
Jewish community* ❽

**Maisel
Synagogue**
*The original synagogue
was built for Mayor
Mordechai Maisel
in 1591* ❾

★ **St Agnes of Bohemia Convent**
Christ on Clouds, by the Czech Master, is one of the Medieval and Gothic works on show in the converted convent ⑮

Na Františku Hospital

LOCATOR MAP
See Street Finder, map 3

Former Charnel House

Church of St Castullus
Some fine mid-14th-century Gothic vaulting has been preserved in this restored parish church ⑭

Parsonage of St Castullus

Church of St Simon and St Jude
Part of the Na Františku Hospital since the 17th century, the church is now a popular venue for concerts ⑬

Spanish Synagogue
The newest of the synagogues in this part of Prague, it was built in flamboyant imitation Moorish style in 1868 ⑪

Church of the Holy Ghost
This Baroque statue of St John Nepomuk by Ferdinand Brokof (1727) stands in front of the church ⑩

| 0 metres | 50 |
| 0 yards | 50 |

KEY

- - - Suggested route

STAR SIGHTS

★ Museum of Decorative Arts

★ Old Jewish Cemetery

★ Old-New Synagogue

★ St Agnes's Convent

Stage of the Dvořák Hall in the Rudolfinum

Rudolfinum ❶

Alšovo nábřeží 12. **Map** 3 A3. 〰
Staroměstská. 🚋 *17, 18.* 🚌 *133.*
Philharmonic *Tel 22 70 59 352.*
***Galerie* Rudolphinum** *Tel 22 70 59
204.* **Open** *10am–6pm Tue–Sun.*
📷 *by appointment – call 22 17 14
151.* Ø 🅴 ♿ 🖥 www.rudolfinum.cz

Now the home of the Czech
Philharmonic Orchestra, the
Rudolfinum is one of the most
impressive landmarks on the
Old Town bank of the Vltava.
Many of the major concerts of
the Prague Spring music festival *(see p50)* are held here.
There are several concert halls,
the sumptuous Dvořák Hall is
one of the finest creations of
19th-century Czech architecture.
The Rudolfinum was built
between 1876 and 1884 to a
design by Josef Zítek and Josef
Schulz and named in honour
of Crown Prince Rudolph of
Habsburg. Like the National
Theatre *(see pp156–7)*, it is an
outstanding example of Czech
Neo-Renaissance style. The
curving balustrade is decorated
with statues of distinguished
Czech, Austrian and German
composers and artists.
Also known as the House of
Artists (Dům umělců), the
building houses the Gallerie

Rudolphinum, a collection of
modern art. Between 1918
and 1939, and for a brief
period after World War II, the
Rudolfinum was the seat of
the Czechoslovak parliament.

Museum of
Decorative Arts ❷

UMĚLECKOPRŮMYSLOVÉ
MUZEUM

17. listopadu 2. **Map** 3 B3. *Tel 25 10
93 111.* 〰 *Staroměstská.* 🚋 *17,
18.* 🚌 *133.* **Open** *10am–6pm Tue–
Sun.* 📷 Ø 🖥 www.upm.cz

For some years after its
foundation in 1885, the
museum's collections were
housed in the Rudolfinum.
The present building, designed
by Josef Schulz in French
Neo-Renaissance style, was
completed in 1901.

The museum's glass collection
is one of the largest in the
world, but only a fraction
of it is ever on display.
Pride of place goes to the
Bohemian glass, of which
there are many fine Baroque
and 19th- and 20th-century
pieces. Medieval and Venetian
Renaissance glass are also
well represented.
Among the permanent
exhibitions of other crafts are
Meissen porcelain, the Gobelin
tapestries and displays
covering fashion, textiles,
photography and printing.
The furniture collection has
exquisitely carved escritoires
and bureaux from the Renaissance. On the mezzanine
floor are halls for temporary
exhibitions and an extensive
art library housing more than
100,000 publications.

Old Jewish
Cemetery ❸

STARÝ ŽIDOVSKÝ HŘBITOV

See pp86–7.

Pinkas
Synagogue ❹

PINKASOVA SYNAGÓGA

Široká 3. **Map** 3 B3. *Tel 22 23 26
660.* 〰 *Staroměstská.* 🚋 *17, 18.*
🚌 *133.* **Open** *Apr–Oct:
9am–6pm Sun–Fri; Nov–Mar:
9am–4:30pm.* 📷 Ø ♿
www.jewishmuseum.cz

The synagogue was founded
in 1479 by Rabbi Pinkas and
enlarged in 1535 by his great-
nephew Aaron Meshulam
Horowitz. It has been rebuilt
many times over the centuries.
Excavations have turned up
fascinating relics of life in the
medieval ghetto, including a
mikva or ritual bath. The
core of the

Names of Holocaust victims on Pinkas Synagogue wall

present building is a hall with Gothic vaulting. The gallery for women was added in the early 17th century.

The synagogue now serves as a memorial to all the Jewish Czechoslovak citizens who were imprisoned in Terezín concentration camp and later deported to various Nazi extermination camps. The names of the 77,297 who did not return are inscribed on the synagogue walls. The building now houses an exhibition of children's drawings from the Terezín concentration camp.

Klausen Synagogue **5**
KLAUSOVÁ SYNAGÓGA

U starého hřbitova 3a. **Map** 3 B3. **Tel** *22 23 10 302.* Ⓜ *Staroměstská.* ⚡ *17, 18.* 🚌 *133.* **Open** *Apr–Oct: 9am–6pm daily; Nov–Mar: 9am–4:30pm.* 📷 📄 **www.**jewishmuseum.cz

Before the fire of 1689, this site was occupied by a number of small Jewish schools and prayer houses known as *klausen*. The name was preserved in the Klausen Synagogue, built on the ruins and completed in 1694.

The High Baroque structure has a fine barrel-vaulted interior with rich stucco decorations. It now houses Hebrew prints and manuscripts and an exhibition of Jewish tradi-

19th-century Torah pointer in Klausen Synagogue

tions and customs, tracing the history of the Jews in Central Europe back to the early Middle Ages. Many exhibits relate to famous figures in the city's Jewish community including the 16th-century Rabbi Löw *(see p88)*, who, according to legend, created an artificial man out of clay.

Adjoining the synagogue is a building that looks like a tiny medieval castle. It was built in 1906 as the ceremonial hall of the Jewish Burial

18th-century silver-gilt Torah shield in the High Synagogue

Society. In 1944 an exhibition was put on here detailing the history of the Prague ghetto.

Old-New Synagogue **6**
STARONOVÁ SYNAGÓGA

See pp88–9.

High Synagogue **7**
VYSOKÁ SYNAGÓGA

Červená 4. **Map** 3 B3. **Tel** *22 23 19 002.* Ⓜ *Staroměstská.* ⚡ *17, 18.* 🚌 *133.* **Open** *for services only: 8am & 2pm Sun–Fri, 9am & 12:45pm Sat.* **www.**kehila.cz

Like the Jewish Town Hall, the building of the High Synagogue was financed by Mordechai Maisel, mayor of the Jewish Town, in the 1570s. Originally the two buildings formed a single complex and to facilitate communication with the Town Hall, the main hall of the synagogue was on the first floor. It was not until the 19th century that the two buildings were separated and the synagogue was given a staircase and street entrance. You can still see the original Renaissance vaulting and stucco decoration.

Jewish Town Hall **8**
ŽIDOVSKÁ RADNICE

Maislova 18. **Map** 3 B3. **Tel** & **Fax** *22 23 19 002.* Ⓜ *Staroměstská.* ⚡ *17, 18.* 🚌 *133.* **Closed** *to the public.*

The core of this attractive pink and white building is the original Jewish Town Hall, built in 1570–77 by architect Panacius Roder at the expense of the immensely rich mayor, Mordechai Maisel. In 1763 it acquired a new appearance in the flowery style of the Late Baroque. The last alterations date from 1908, when the southern wing was enlarged.

The building is one of the few monuments that survived far-reaching sanitation of this medieval part of Prague at the beginning of the 20th century. On the roof stands a small wooden clock tower with a distinctive green steeple. The right to build the tower was originally granted to the Jewish community after their part in the defence of Charles Bridge against the Swedes in 1648 *(see pp30–31)*. On one of the gables there is another clock. This one has Hebrew figures and, because Hebrew reads from right to left, hands that turn in an anti-clockwise direction. The Town Hall is now the seat of the Council of Jewish Religious Communities in the Czech Republic.

Façade and clock tower of the Jewish Town Hall

Old Jewish Cemetery ➌

STARÝ ŽIDOVSKÝ HŘBITOV

This remarkable site was, for over 300 years, the only burial ground permitted to Jews. Founded in 1478, it was slightly enlarged over the years but still basically corresponds to its medieval size. Because of the lack of space people had to be buried on top of each other, up to 12 layers deep. Today you can see over 12,000 gravestones crammed into the tiny space, but an estimated 100,000 people are thought to have been buried here. The last burial was of Moses Beck in 1787.

View across the cemetery towards the western wall of the Klausen Synagogue

Jewish printers, Mordechai Zemach (d 1592) and his son Bezalel (d 1589), are buried under this square gravestone.

The Pinkas Synagogue is the second-oldest in Prague *(see p84)*.

David Gans' Tombstone
The tomb of the writer and astronomer (1541–1613) is decorated with the symbols of his name – a star of David and a goose (Gans in German).

The oldest tomb is that of the writer Rabbi Avigdor Kara (1439).

Rabbi David Oppenheim (1664–1736)
The chief rabbi of Prague owned the largest collection of old Hebrew manuscripts and prints in the city.

Klausen Synagogue *(see p85)*

The gravestone of Moses Beck

Main entrance

The Nephele Mound was where infants who died under a year old were buried.

★ 14th-Century Tombstones
Embedded in the wall are fragments of Gothic tombstones brought here from an older Jewish cemetery discovered in 1866 in Vladislavova Street in the New Town.

VISITORS' CHECKLIST

Široká 3 (main entrance). **Map** 3
B3. **Tel** 22 23 17 191 (bookings),
22 48 10 099, 22 48 19 456
(Jewish Museum). Staroměstská. 17, 18 to
Staroměstská. **Open** Apr–Oct:
9am–6pm Sun–Fri; Nov–Mar:
9–4:30pm Sun–Fri (last admission
30 mins before closing).
www.jewishmuseum.cz

Prague Burial Society
Founded in 1564, the group carried out ritual burials and performed charitable work in the community. Members of the society wash their hands after leaving the cemetery.

The Museum of Decorative Arts (see p84)

★ **Tombstone of Rabbi Löw**
The most visited grave in the cemetery is that of Rabbi Löw (1520–1609). Visitors place hundreds of pebbles and wishes on his grave as a mark of respect.

The Neo-Romanesque Ceremonial Hall

Mordechai Maisel (1528–1601) was Mayor of Prague's Jewish Town and a philanthropist.

★ **Tombstone of Hendela Bassevi**
The highly-decorated tomb (1628) was built for the beautiful wife of Prague's first Jewish nobleman.

UNDERSTANDING THE GRAVESTONES

From the late 16th century onwards, tombstones in the Jewish cemetery were decorated with symbols denoting the background, family name or profession of the deceased person.

 Blessing hands: Cohen family

 A pair of scissors: tailor

A stag: Hirsch or Zvi family

 Grapes: blessing or abundance

Old-New Synagogue ⑥

STARONOVÁ SYNAGOGA

Star of David in Červená Street

Built around 1270, this is the oldest synagogue in Europe and one of the earliest Gothic buildings in Prague. The synagogue has survived fires, the slum clearances of the 19th century and many Jewish pogroms. Residents of the Jewish Quarter have often had to seek refuge within its walls and today it is still the religious centre for Prague's Jews. It was originally called the New Synagogue until another synagogue was built nearby – this was later destroyed.

The synagogue's eastern side

The 14th-century stepped brick gable

★ **Jewish Standard**
The historic banner of Prague's Jews is decorated with a Star of David and within it the hat that had to be worn by Jews in the 14th century.

These windows formed part of the 18th-century extensions built to allow women a view of the service.

RABBI LÖW AND THE GOLEM

The scholar and philosophical writer Rabbi Löw, director of the Talmudic school (which studied the Torah) in the late 16th century, was also thought to possess magical powers. He was supposed to have created a figure, the Golem, from clay and then brought it to life by placing a magic stone tablet in its mouth. The Golem went berserk and the Rabbi had to remove the tablet. He hid the creature among the Old-New Synagogue's rafters.

Rabbi Löw and the Golem

Candlestick holder

★ **Five-rib Vaulting**
Two massive octagonal pillars inside the hall support the five-rib vaults.

Right-hand Nave
The glow from the bronze chandeliers provides light for worshippers using the seats lining the walls.

VISITORS' CHECKLIST

Pařížská and Červená. **Map** 3 B2.
Tel 22 23 17 191. ⓂStaroměstská. 🚋 17, 18 to Staroměstská, 17 to Law Faculty (Právnická fakulta). **Open** 9:30am–6pm Sun–Fri (to 5pm Nov–Mar).
Closed Jewish holidays. 🚫 📷
✡ 8am Mon–Fri, 9am Sat.
www.jewishmuseum.cz

The tympanum above the Ark is decorated with 13th-century leaf carvings.

★ Rabbi Löw's Chair
A star of David marks the chair of the Chief Rabbi, placed where the distinguished 16th-century scholar used to sit.

The cantor's platform and its lectern is surrounded by a wrought-iron Gothic grille.

Entrance to the Synagogue in Červená Street

The Ark
This shrine is the holiest place in the synagogue and holds the sacred scrolls of the Torah.

Entrance Portal
The tympanum above the door in the south vestibule is decorated with clusters of grapes and vine leaves growing on twisted branches.

STAR FEATURES

★ Rabbi Löw's Chair

★ Five-rib Vaulting

★ Jewish Standard

18th-century silver Torah crown in the Maisel Synagogue

Maisel Synagogue **9**
MAISELOVA SYNAGÓGA

Maiselova 10. **Map** 3 B3. **Tel** 22 48 19 456. Ⓜ Staroměstská. 🚊 17, 18. 🚌 133. **Open** Apr–Oct: 9am–6pm Sun–Fri; Nov–Mar: 9am–4.30pm Sun–Fri. 📷 🚫
♿ www.jewishmuseum.cz

When it was first built, at the end of the 16th century, this was a private house of prayer for the use of mayor Mordechai Maisel and his family. Maisel had made a fortune lending money to Emperor Rudolph II to finance wars against the Turks, and his synagogue was the most richly decorated in the city. The original building was a victim of the fire that devastated the Jewish Town in 1689 and a new synagogue was built in its place. Its present crenellated, Gothic appearance dates from the start of the 20th century. Since the 1960s the Maisel Synagogue has housed a fascinating collection of Jewish silver and other metalwork dating from Renaissance times to the 20th century. It includes many Torah crowns, shields and finials. Crowns and finials were used to decorate the rollers on which the text of the Torah (the five books of Moses) was kept. The shields were hung over the mantle that was draped over the

Torah and the pointers were used to follow the text so that it was not touched by readers' hands. There are also objects such as wedding plates, lamps and candlesticks. By a tragic irony, nearly all these Jewish treasures were brought to Prague by the Nazis from synagogues throughout Bohemia and Moravia with the intention of founding a museum of a vanished people.

Church of the Holy Ghost **10**
KOSTEL SV. DUCHA

Dušní, Široká. **Map** 3 B3. Ⓜ Staroměstská. 🚊 17. 🚌 133. **Open** only for services. ✝ 9:30am Sun.
🚫 ♿

This church stands on the narrow strip of Christian soil which once separated the two Jewish communities of the Middle Ages – the Jews of the eastern and western rites. Built in the mid-14th century, the single-naved Gothic church was originally part of a convent of Benedictine nuns. The convent was destroyed in 1420 during the Hussite Wars (see pp26–7) and not rebuilt.

The church was badly damaged in the Old Town fire of 1689. The exterior preserves the original Gothic buttresses and high windows, but the vault of the nave was rebuilt in Baroque style after the fire. The furnishings too

are mainly Baroque. The high altar dates from 1760, and there is an altar painting of St Joseph by Jan Jiří Heintsch (c1647–1712). In front of the church stands a stone statue of St John Nepomuk (see p83) distributing alms (1727) by the prolific sculptor of the Czech Baroque Ferdinand Maximilian Brokof. Inside the church there are a few earlier statues, including a 14th-century Pietà (the heads of the figures are later, dating from 1628), a Late Gothic statue of St Ann and busts of St Wenceslas and St Adalbert from the early 16th century.

Church of the Holy Ghost

Spanish Synagogue **11**
ŠPANĚLSKÁ SYNAGÓGA

Vězeňská 1. **Map** 3 B2. **Tel** 22 48 19 464. Ⓜ Staroměstská. 🚊 17, 18. 🚌 133. **Open** Apr–Oct: 9am–6pm Sun–Fri; Nov–Mar: 9am–4.30pm Sun–Fri. 📷 ♿
www.jewishmuseum.cz

Prague's first synagogue, known as the Old School (Stará škola), once stood on this site. In the 11th century the Old School was the centre of the community of Jews of the eastern rite, who lived strictly apart from Jews of the western rite, who were concentrated round the Old-New Synagogue. The present building dates from the second half of the 19th century. The exterior and interior are both pseudo-Moorish in

Motif of the Ten Commandments on the Spanish Synagogue's façade

appearance. The rich stucco decorations on the walls and vaults are reminiscent of the Alhambra in Spain, hence the name. Once closed to the public, the Spanish Synagogue now houses a permanent exhibition dedicated to the history of the Jews of Bohemia.

Cubist Houses ⑫
KUBISTICKÉ DOMY

Elišky Krásnohorské, 10–14. **Map** 3 B2. **Ⓜ** *Staroměstská*. **🚋** *17, 18.* **Closed** *to the public.*

The rebuilding of the old Jewish Quarter at the turn of the 20th century gave Prague's architects scope to experiment with many new styles. Most of the blocks in this area are covered with flowing Art Nouveau decoration, but on the corner of Bílkova and Elišky Krásnohorské there is a plain façade with a few simple repeated geometrical shapes. This is an example of Cubist architecture, a fashion that did not really catch on in the rest of Europe, but was very popular with the avant-garde in Bohemia and Austria before and after World War I. This block was built for a cooperative of teachers in 1919–21.

At No. 7 Elišky Krásnohorské you can see the influence of Cubism in the curiously flattened atlantes supporting the windows. Another interesting Cubist building is the House of the Black Mother of God in Celetná *(see pp174–5).*

Church of St Simon and St Jude ⑬
KOSTEL SV. ŠIMONA A JUDY

U milosrdných. **Map** 3 B2. **Ⓜ** *Staroměstská*. **🚋** *17, 18.* **🚌** *133.* **Open** *for concerts.* **www**.fok.cz

Members of the Bohemia Brethren built this church with high Late Gothic windows in 1615–20. The Brethren, founded in the mid-15th century, agreed with the Utraquists *(see p75)* in directing the congregation to receive both bread and wine

Cubist-style atlantes framing a window in Elišky Krásnohorské Street

at Holy Communion. In other respects they were more conservative than other Protestant sects, continuing to practise celibacy and Catholic sacraments such as confession. After the Battle of the White Mountain *(see pp30–31)*, the Brethren were expelled from the Empire.

The church was then given to a Catholic order, the Brothers of Mercy, becoming part of a monastery and hospital. Tradition has it that the monastery's wooden steps were built from the scaffold on which 27 Czechs were executed in 1621 *(see p72)*. In the 18th century the city's first anatomy lecture hall was established here and the complex continues to serve as a hospital – the Na Františku. The church is now used as a venue for concerts.

Detail of Baroque façade of Church of St Simon and St Jude

Church of St Castullus ⑭
KOSTEL SV. HAŠTALA

Haštalské náměstí. **Map** 3 C2. **🚋** *5, 8, 14.* **🚌** *133.* **Open** *irregularly.* **✝** *5pm Sun.* **🚫 ♿**

This peaceful little corner of Prague takes its name – Haštal – from the parish church of St Castullus. One of the finest Gothic buildings in Prague, the church was erected on the site of an older Romanesque structure in the second quarter of the 14th century. Much of the church had to be rebuilt after the fire of 1689, but fortunately the double nave on the north side survived. It has beautiful slender pillars supporting a delicate ribbed vault.

The interior furnishings are mainly Baroque, though there are remains of wall paintings of about 1375 in the sacristy and a metal font decorated with figures dating from about 1550. Standing in the Gothic nave is an impressive sculptural group depicting *Calvary* (1716) from the workshop of Ferdinand Maximilian Brokof.

St Agnes of Bohemia Convent ⑮
KLÁŠTER SV. ANEŽKY ČESKÉ

See pp92–3.

St Agnes of Bohemia Convent ⑮

KLÁŠTER SV. ANEŽKY ČESKÉ

In 1234 a convent of the Poor Clares was founded here by Agnes, sister of King Wenceslas I. She was not canonized until 1989. The convent, one of the very first Gothic buildings in Bohemia, was abolished in 1782 and fell into disrepair. Following painstaking restoration in the 1960s, it has recovered much of its original appearance and is now used by the National Gallery to display a collection of medieval art from Bohemia and Central Europe. The recent enlargement of the exhibition space, has enabled these to be shown in a much broader Central European context.

Head of statue of St Agnes by Josef Myslbek

First floor

★ **Votive panel of Archbishop Jan Očko of Vlašim**
This detailed panel, painted around 1370 by an anonymous artist, shows Charles IV kneeling before the Virgin in Heaven.

Ground floor

Steps to first-floor gallery

★ **The Annunciation of Our Lady**
Painted around 1350 by the renowned Master of the Vyšší Brod Altar, this panel is one of the oldest and finest works in the museum.

STAR EXHIBITS

★ The Annunciation by the Master of the Vyšší Brod Altarpiece

★ Strakonice Madonna

★ Votive panel of Archbishop Jan Očko of Vlašim

Terrace café

Cloister
The Gothic vaulting around the cloister of the convent dates from the 14th century.

GALLERY GUIDE

The permanent exhibition is housed on the first floor of the old convent in a long gallery and smaller rooms around the cloister. The works are arranged chronologically.

VISITORS' CHECKLIST

U Milosrdných 17. **Map** 3 C2.
Tel 22 48 10 628. Náměstí Republiky, Staroměstská. 17 to Law faculty, 5, 8, 14 to Dlouhá třída. 133 to Řásnovka.
Open 10am–6pm Tue–Sun (last guided tour:5pm). www.ngprague.cz

Upper part of Church of the Holy Saviour

Steps down to cloister

Upper part of concert hall

Chapel of St Mary Magdalene

Variant of the Krumlov Madonna
Dating from around 1400, this touching image of mother and child was crafted by an unknown sculptor, a follower of the Master of the Krumlov Madonna.

Church of the Holy Saviour
This capital decorated with heads of five Bohemian queens is matched by one with five Přemyslid kings.

Church of St Francis and concert hall

★ Strakonice Madonna
This 700-year-old statue evokes the Classical French sculpture found in such places as Reims Cathedral.

Entrance to Convent from Anežská

KEY

- ▨ Medieval and early Renaissance Art
- ☐ Cloister
- ☐ Churches
- ☐ Concert hall
- ▨ Special exhibitions
- ▨ Non-exhibition space

PRAGUE CASTLE AND HRADČANY

PRAŽSKÝ HRAD A HRADČANY

The history of Prague begins with the Castle, founded in the 9th century by Prince Bořivoj. Its commanding position high above the river Vltava soon made it the centre of the lands ruled by the Přemyslids. The buildings enclosed by the Castle walls included a palace, three churches and a monastery. In about 1320 a town called Hradčany was founded in part of the Castle's outer bailey. The

Stained-glass window in St Vitus's Cathedral

Castle has been rebuilt many times, most notably in the reigns of Charles IV and Vladislav Jagiello. After a fire in 1541, the badly damaged buildings were rebuilt in Renaissance style and the Castle enjoyed its cultural heyday under Rudolph II. Since 1918 it has been the seat of the president of the Republic. The Changing of the Guard takes place every hour. At noon the ceremony includes a fanfare.

SIGHTS AT A GLANCE

Churches and Monasteries
St Vitus's Cathedral pp100–3 ❷
St George's Basilica ❺
Capuchin Monastery ⓳
The Loreto pp116–17 ⓴
Strahov Monastery pp120–21 ㉓

Palaces
Royal Palace pp104–5 ❹
Lobkowicz Palace ❽
Belvedere ⓫
Archbishop's Palace ⓮
Martinic Palace ⓰
Černín Palace ㉑

Historic Buildings
Powder Tower ❸
Dalibor Tower ❾

Museums and Galleries
Picture Gallery of Prague Castle ❶
St George's Convent pp106–9 ❻
Riding School ⓭
Sternberg Palace pp112–15 ⓯
Schwarzenberg Palace ⓱

Historic Streets
Golden Lane ❼
New World ⓲
Pohořelec ㉒

Parks and Gardens
South Gardens ⓾
Royal Garden ⓬

KEY

▮	Street-by-Street map See pp96–7
Ⓜ	Metro station
🚊	Tram stop
🅸	Tourist Information
—	Castle wall

GETTING THERE
Take the 22 or 23 tram to Pražský hrad (Prague Castle) or to Pohořelec. If you feel energetic, take the 12, 18, 20, 22 or 23 tram to Malostranské náměstí in the Little Quarter, then walk up Nerudova or go to Malostranská metro and walk up Staré zámecké schody (Old Castle Steps).

0 metres	500
0 yards	500

◁ **The main entrance to Prague Castle**

Street-by-Street: Prague Castle

Despite periodic fires and invasions, Prague
Castle has retained churches, chapels, halls
and towers from every period of its history,
from the the Gothic splendour of St Vitus's
Cathedral to the Renaissance additions of
Rudolph II, the last Habsburg to use the Castle
as his principal residence. The courtyards date
from 1753–75 when the whole area was rebuilt
in Late Baroque and Neo-Classical styles. The
Castle became the seat of the Czechoslovak
president in 1918, and the current president
of the Czech Republic has an office here.

★ St Vitus's Cathedral
*The decoration on the fence
at St Vitus's Golden Portal* ❷

Powder Tower
*Used in the past for
storing gunpowder and as
a bell foundry, the tower
is now a museum* ❸

**Gothic reliquary of
St George's arm in
St Vitus's Cathedral**

To Royal
Garden

President's
office

**Picture Gallery
of Prague Castle**
*Renaissance and
Baroque paintings
hang in the restored
stables of the castle* ❶

Second
courtyard

Matthias
Gate (1614)

First
courtyard

To Hradčanské
náměstí

Steps down to
Little Quarter

Church of the
Holy Rood

The Castle gates are
crowned by copies of 18th-
century statues of Fighting
Giants by Ignaz Platzer.

South Gardens
*18th-century statues
decorate the gardens laid
out in the old ramparts* ❿

★ Golden Lane
The picturesque artisans' cottages along the inside of the castle wall were built in the late 16th century for the Castle's guards and gunners **7**

LOCATOR MAP
See Street Finder, map 2

White Tower

Dalibor Tower
This grim tower takes its name from the first man to be imprisoned in it **9**

Old Castle steps to Malostranská Metro

JIŘSKÁ

Lobkowicz Palace
Works of art from the Lobkowicz family's private collection are housed here **8**

★ St George's Basilica
The vaulted chapel of the royal Bohemian martyr St Ludmilla is decorated with 16th-century paintings **5**

KEY

– – – Suggested route

| 0 metres | 60 |
| 0 yards | 60 |

★ St George's Convent
The convent houses 19th-century Czech art such as this piece titled Summer Countryside with Chapel *by Adolf Kosárek* **6**

STAR SIGHTS

★ St Vitus's Cathedral

★ Royal Palace

★ St George's Basilica and Convent

★ Golden Lane

★ Royal Palace
The uniform exterior of the palace conceals many fine Gothic and Renaissance halls. Coats of arms cover the walls and ceiling of the Room of the New Land Rolls **4**

Picture Gallery of Prague Castle ❶
OBRAZÁRNA PRAŽSKÉHO HRADU

Prague Castle, the second courtyard.
Map 2 D2. **Tel** 22 43 73 531.
🚊 Malostranská, Hradčanská.
🚋 22, 23 **Open** 9am–4pm daily in winter, 9am–6pm daily in summer.
🖼 ♿ www.obrazarna-hradu.cz

The gallery was created in 1965 to hold works of art collected since the reign of Rudolph II (see pp28–9). Though most of the collection was looted by the Swedes in 1648, many interesting paintings remain. Paintings from the 16th–18th centuries form the bulk of the collection, but there are also sculptures, among them a copy of a bust of Rudolph by Adriaen de Vries. Highlights include Titian's *The Toilet of a Young Lady*, Rubens' *The Assembly of the Olympic Gods* and Guido Reni's *The Centaur Nessus Abducting Deianeira*. Master Theodoric, Paolo Veronese, Tintoretto and the Czech Baroque artists Jan Kupecký and Petr Brandl are among other artists represented. The Picture Gallery houses many of Rudolph's best paintings.

You can also see the remains of the Castle's first church, the 9th-century Church of our Lady, thought to have been built by Prince Bořivoj, the first Přemyslid prince to be baptized a Christian (see pp20–21). The site was discovered during reconstruction.

St Vitus's Cathedral ❷
CHRÁM SV. VÍTA

See pp100–3.

Powder Tower ❸
PRAŠNÁ VĚŽ

Prague Castle, Vikářská.
Map 2 D2. **Tel** 22 43 73 434.
🚊 Malostranská, Hradčanská.
🚋 22, 23. **Open** Apr–Oct: 9am–6pm; Nov–Mar: 9am–4pm daily.
🖼 🚫 🍴

A tower was built here in about 1496 by the King Vladislav II's architect Benedikt Ried as a cannon bastion overlooking the Stag Moat. The original was destroyed in the fire of 1541, but it was rebuilt as the home and workshop of gunsmith and bell founder Tomáš Jaroš. In 1549 he made Prague's largest bell, the 18-tonne Sigismund, for the bell tower of St Vitus's Cathedral.

During Rudolph II's reign (1576–1612), the tower became a laboratory for

View of the Powder Tower from across the Stag Moat

alchemists. It was here that adventurers such as Edward Kelley performed experiments that convinced the emperor they could turn lead into gold.

In 1649, when the Swedish army was occupying the Castle, gunpowder exploded in the tower, causing serious damage. Nevertheless it was used as a gunpowder store until 1754, when it was converted into flats for the sacristans of St Vitus's Cathedral. Today, the tower houses a permanent exhibition of Czech military history.

Royal Palace ❹
KRÁLOVSKÝ PALÁC

See pp104–5.

St George's Basilica ❺
BAZILIKA SV. JIŘÍ

Jiřské náměstí. **Map** 2 E2. **Tel** 22 43 73 368. 🚊 Malostranská, Hradčanská.
🚋 22, 23. **Open** Apr–Oct: 9am–6pm daily; Nov–Mar: 9am–4pm daily.
🖼 🚫 ♿ www.hrad.cz

Founded by Prince Vratislav (915–21), the basilica predates St Vitus's Cathedral

Titian's *The Toilet of a Young Lady* in the Castle Picture Gallery

and is the best-preserved Romanesque church in Prague. It was enlarged in 973 when the adjoining St George's Convent was established here, and rebuilt following a fire in 1142. The massive twin towers and austere interior have been scrupulously restored to give a good idea of the church's original appearance. However, the rusty red façade was a 17th-century Baroque addition.

Buried in the church is St Ludmilla, widow of the 9th-century ruler Prince Bořivoj *(see pp20–21)*. She became Bohemia's first female Christian martyr when she was strangled on the orders of Drahomíra, her daughter-in-law, as she knelt at prayer. Other members of the Přemyslid dynasty buried here include Vratislav. His austere tomb stands on the right-hand side of the nave at the foot of the curving steps that lead up to the choir. The impressive Baroque grille opposite encloses the tomb of Boleslav II (973–99).

Façade and towers of St George's Basilica

St George's Convent ❻
KLÁŠTER SV. JIŘÍ

See pp106–9.

Golden Lane ❼
ZLATÁ ULIČKA

Map 2 E2. **ᴹ** *Malostranská, Hradčanská.* ⛾ *22, 23.* 📷

Named after the goldsmiths who lived here in the 17th century, this short, narrow street is one of the most picturesque in Prague. One side of the lane is lined with tiny, brightly

One of the tiny houses in Golden Lane

painted houses which were built right into the arches of the Castle walls. They were constructed in the late 1500s for Rudolph II's 24 Castle guards. A century later the goldsmiths moved in and modified the buildings. But by the 19th century the area had degenerated into a slum and was populated by Prague's poor and the criminal community. In the 1950s all the remaining tenants were moved and the area restored to something like its original state. Most of the houses were converted into shops selling books, Bohemian glass and other souvenirs for tourists, who flock to the narrow lane.

Golden Lane has been home to some well-known writers, including the Nobel prize-winning poet, Jaroslav Seifert, and Franz Kafka *(see p68)* who stayed at No. 22 with his sister for a few months in 1916–17. Because of its name, legends have spread about the street being filled with alchemists huddled over their bubbling alembics trying to produce gold for Rudolph II. In fact the alchemists had laboratories in Vikářská, the lane between St Vitus's Cathedral and the Powder Tower.

Lobkowicz Palace ❽
LOBKOVICKÝ PALÁC

Jiřská 3. **Map** 2 E2. **Tel** 23 33 12 925. **ᴹ** *Hradčanská.* ⛾ *22, 23.* **Open** 10:30am–6pm daily. ♿ 🅿 **www**.lobkowiczevents.cz **Toy Museum Tel** 22 43 72 294. **Open** 9:30am–5:30pm daily. **www**.barbiemuseum.cz

Detail of 16th-century sgraffito on façade of Lobkowicz Palace

This is one of the palaces that sprang up after the fire of 1541, when Hradčany was almost totally destroyed. It dates from 1570, and some original *sgraffito* on the façade has been preserved, but most of the present palace is Carlo Lurago's 17th-century reconstruction for the Lobkowicz family, who had inherited it in 1627. The most splendid room is the 17th-century banqueting hall with mythological frescoes by Fabian Harovník.

The palace once formed part of Prague's National Museum but has since been returned to the Lobkowicz family. It now houses the Princely Collections, a permanent exhibition of paintings, decorative arts, original music scores and instruments. The palace restaurant has fine views from its terrace and opposite the palace, at No. 6, is a delightful toy museum claiming to be the world's second largest, with toys from ancient Greece to the present.

St Vitus's Cathedral ➋

KATEDRÁLA SV. VÍTA, VÁCLAVA A VOJTĚCHA

Work began on the city's most distinctive landmark in 1344 on the orders of John of Luxembourg. The first architect was the French Matthew of Arras. After his death, Swabian Peter Parler took over. His masons' lodge continued to work on the building until the Hussite Wars. Finally completed by 19th- and 20th-century architects and artists, the cathedral houses the crown jewels and the tomb of "Good King" Wenceslas (pp20–21).

St Vitus's Cathedral
This 19th-century engraving shows how the cathedral looked before the additions made in 1872–1929.

Twin west spires

Triforium

Rose Window
Designed by František Kysela in 1925–7, the window above the portals depicts scenes from the biblical story of the creation.

Gargoyles
On the ornate west front, gutter spouts are given their traditional disguise.

West front

Main entrance

Nave

TIMELINE

c925 Rotunda of St Vitus built by St Wenceslas	**1356** Masterbuilder Peter Parler summoned to continue work on the cathedral		**1619** Calvinists take over cathedral as house of prayer	**1929** Consecration of completed cathedral, nearly 1,000 years after death of St Wenceslas	

Bust of Peter Parler on triforium

1000	1200	1400	1600	1800

| **1060** Building of triple-naved basilica begins on orders of Prince Spytihněv | *Tomb of Přemysl Otakar II* | **1421** Hussites occupy St Vitus's | **1589** Royal tomb completed | **1872** Joseph Mocker begins work on west nave |
| | | **1344** King John of Luxembourg founds Gothic cathedral. French architect Matthew of Arras begins work | | **1770** New steeple added to tower after fire |

★ Flying Buttresses
The slender buttresses that surround the exterior of the nave and chancel, supporting the vaulted interior, are richly decorated like the rest of the cathedral.

The **Renaissance bell tower** is capped with a Baroque "helmet".

Chancel

★ Chapel of St Wenceslas
The bronze ring on the chapel's north portal was thought to be the one to which St Wenceslas clung as he was murdered by his brother Boleslav (see pp20–21).

To Royal Palace
(See pp104–5)

The tomb of
St Wenceslas is
connected to an altar,
decorated with semi-
precious stones.

★ Golden Portal
Until the 19th century this was the main cathedral entrance, and it is still used on special occasions. Above it is a mosaic of The Last Judgment *by 14th-century Venetian craftsmen.*

Gothic Vaulting
The skills of architect Peter Parler are never more clearly seen than in the delicate fans of ribbing that support the three Gothic arches of the Golden Portal.

STAR FEATURES

★ Chapel of
St Wenceslas

★ Golden Portal

★ Flying Buttresses

A Guided Tour of St Vitus's Cathedral

West door: St Wenceslas' murder

A walk around St Vitus's takes you back through a thousand years of history. Go in through the west portal to see some of the best elements of the modern, Neo-Gothic style and continue past a succession of side chapels to catch glimpses of religious artefacts such as saintly relics, and works of art from Renaissance paintings to modern statuary. Allow plenty of time to gaze at the richly decorated, jewel-encrusted St Wenceslas Chapel before you leave.

② Chancel
The chancel was built by Peter Parler from 1372. It is remarkable for the soaring height of its vault, counterpointed by the intricacy of the webbed Gothic tracery.

Cathedral organ (1757)

New sacristy

① Alfons Mucha Window
The cathedral contains many superb examples of 20th-century Czech stained glass, notably St Cyril and St Methodius.

Main entrance (West Portal)

Thun Chapel

Chapel of St Ludmilla

THE FOUR ERAS OF ST VITUS'S

Excavations have revealed sections of the northern apse of St Wenceslas's original rotunda, and architectural and sculptural remains of the later basilica, beneath the existing cathedral. The western, Neo-Gothic end is a faithful completion of the 14th-century plan.

KEY

☐ Rotunda, 10th century

☐ Basilica, 11th century

☐ Gothic cathedral, 14th century

☐ 19th- and 20th-century additions to cathedral

Leopold II is shown in a contemporary engraving being crowned King of Bohemia at the cathedral in September 1791. Mozart composed an opera, *La Clemenza di Tito*, in honour of the occasion.

③ **Flight of Frederick of the Palatinate**
In depicting the sad aftermath of the Battle of the White Mountain in 1620 (see p31), this carved wooden panel shows 17th-century Prague in fascinating detail.

Chapel of St John the Baptist

Pulpit (1618)

Chapel of the Holy Relics

Chapel of the Holy Rood

Stairs to crypt

Golden Portal

Exit from crypt

④ **Tomb of St John Nepomuk**
Crafted from solid silver in 1736, this elaborate tomb honours the saint who became the focus of a Counter-Reformation cult (see p137).

⑤ **Royal Oratory**
The vault of the 15th-century Late-Gothic oratory is carved with branches instead of ribs.

⑥ **Crypt**
Steps lead down to the royal tombs, including those of Charles IV and his four wives, as well as vestiges of the early rotunda and basilica.

⑧ **St Wenceslas Chapel**
Gothic frescoes with scenes from the Bible and the life of the saint cover the walls, interspersed with a patchwork of polished gemstones and fine gilding. Every object is a work of art – this golden steeple held the wafers and wine for Holy Communion.

⑦ **Royal Mausoleum**
Ferdinand I died in 1564. His beloved wife and son, Maximilian II, are buried alongside him in the mausoleum.

KEY

– – – Tour route

Royal Palace ❹

KRÁLOVSKÝ PALÁC

From the time Prague Castle was first fortified in stone in the 11th century *(see pp22–3)*, the palace was the seat of Bohemian princes. The building consists of three different architectural layers. A Romanesque palace built by Soběslav I around 1135 forms the cellars of the present building. Přemysl Otakar II and Charles IV then added their own palaces above this, while the top floor, built for Vladislav Jagiello, contains the massive Gothic Vladislav Hall. During the period of Habsburg rule the palace housed government offices, courts and the old Bohemian Diet (parliament). In 1924 it was extensively restored.

Riders' Staircase
These wide and gently sloping steps, with their Gothic rib vault, were used by knights on horse-back to get to Vladislav Hall for indoor jousting competitions.

The Diet, the medieval parliament, was also the throne room. Destroyed by fire in 1541, it was rebuilt by Bonifaz Wohlmut in 1563.

An overhead passage from the palace leads to the Royal Oratory in St Vitus's Cathedral *(see p103)*.

14

4

3

6

2

5

Vladislav Hall
The 17th-century painting by Aegidius Sadeler shows that the Royal Court was very like a public market. The hall's magnificent rib vaulting was designed by Benedikt Ried in the 1490s.

Entrance

1

TIMELINE

Přemysl Otakar II, 1230–78

1253 Palace reconstructed by Přemysl Otakar II

1618 Defenestration from Bohemian Chancellery

1041 Castle besieged and palace burnt

1541 Fire destroys large part of Castle

1766–8 Building of Theresian Wing

900	1100	1300	1500	1700	1900

Late 9th century Founding of Prague Castle by Prince Bořivoj

1340 Charles IV rebuilds palace

1370s Peter Parler rebuilds All Saints' Chapel

Decorated door of office in Royal Palace

1135 Rebuilding undertaken by Soběslav I

1502 Completion of Vladislav Hall by Benedikt Ried after nine years

1924 Palace undergoes extensive restoration

PLAN AND CROSS SECTION OF ROYAL PALACE

The cross section of the palace shows the three distinct levels of the building, all constructed at different times. The plan shows how Vladislav Hall dominates the entire palace structure.

Upper floor
Ground level
Lower floor

VISITORS' CHECKLIST

Prague Castle, third courtyard. **Map** 2 D2. **Tel** 22 43 73 102. Hradčanská, up K Brusce, then through the Royal Garden; Malostranská, left up Klárov, then up Old Castle Steps. 22, 23 to Prague Castle (Pražský hrad). **Open** Apr–Oct: 9am–6pm daily; Nov–Mar: 9am–4pm daily; last adm: 1hr before closing.

All Saints' Chapel was built by Peter Parler for Charles IV. After the 1541 fire, its vault had to be rebuilt and it was redecorated in the Baroque style.

KEY TO ROYAL PALACE

☐ Romanesque and Early Gothic

☐ Late Gothic

☐ Rebuilt after 1541 fire

☐ Baroque and later

1 Eagle Fountain
2 Vestibule
3 Green Chamber
4 King's Bedchamber
5 Romanesque tower
6 Vladislav Hall
7 Bohemian Chancellery
8 Imperial Council Room steps
9 Terrace
10 All Saints' Chapel
11 Diet Hall
12 Ride staircase
13 Court of Appeal
14 Palace courtyard
15 Hall of the Romanesque palace
16 Old Land Rolls
17 Palace of Charles IV
18 New Land Rolls

The Theresian Way was built to house the office registers.

Bohemian Chancellery
This 17th-century Dutch-style stove decorates the former royal offices of the Habsburgs. The chancellery is the site of the 1618 defenestration.

DEFENESTRATION OF 1618

Painting by Václav Brožík, 1889

On 23 May, 1618, more than 100 Protestant nobles, led by Count Thurn, marched into the palace to protest against the succession to the throne of the intolerant Habsburg Archduke Ferdinand. The two Catholic Governors appointed by Ferdinand, Jaroslav Martinic and Vilém Slavata, were confronted and, after a row, the Protestants threw both the Governors and their secretary, Philipp Fabricius, out of the eastern window. Falling some 15 m (50 ft), they survived by landing in a dung heap. This event signalled the beginning of the Thirty Years' War. The Catholics attributed the survival of the Governors to the intervention of angels.

The New Land Rolls
These rooms are decorated with the crests of clerks who worked here from 1561 to 1774.

St George's Convent ❻

KLÁŠTER SV. JIŘÍ

The first convent in Bohemia was founded here close to the Royal Palace in 973 by Prince Boleslav II. His sister Mlada was its first abbess. Rebuilt over the centuries, the convent was finally abolished in 1782 and converted into barracks. In 1962–74 it was reconstructed and today it houses the National Gallery's collection of 19th-century Czech art. The collection, chosen as an artistic mirror to 19th-century Bohemian society, features paintings from luminaries such as Josef Navrátil, the Mánes family and Jakub Schikaneder plus sculpture from Josef Václav Myslbek. The collection is interspersed with pieces of decorative art from the period.

★ **George of Poděbrady and Matthius Corvinus**
Mikoláš Aleš painted many patriotic historical scenes. Here, Corvinus King of Hungary, signs a treaty with King George in 1469.

Winter Evening in the Town
Jakub Schikaneder is renowned for his atmospheric, soft compositions and this dusky painting (1907–1909) is a fine example. The chill of winter is artfully rendered.

Chapel of St Anne

Stairs down to exit

Ground floor

St George's Basilica
(see pp98–9)

Entrance to Gallery from Jiřské náměstí

STAR EXHIBITS

★ George of Poděbrady with Matthius Corvinus by Mikoláš Aleš

★ Stallion, Ardo by Josef Václav Myslbek

Summer Country with a Chapel
One of Adolf Kosárek's final paintings before his untimely death in 1859, the Romantic motif is a composite of landscape views.

VISITORS' CHECKLIST

Prague Castle, Jiřské náměstí 33.
Map 2 E2. *Tel* 25 75 31 644.
Ⓜ Hradčanská or Malostranská, then 10 mins up steep steps. 22, 23 to Prague Castle (Pražský hrad) **Open** 10am–6pm daily.
www.ngprague.cz

Upper floor

Josefina
Josef Mánes's evocative portrait (1855) asks the eternal question: who is Josefina? Was she the mother of Mánes's daughter or an actress?

★ Stallion, Ardo
Perfectionist Josef Václav Myslbek created many drafts of the iconic mounted statue of St Wenceslas (see p146). As with the others, this bronze (1898–99) was modeled on a seven-year-old Oldenburg stallion named Ardo.

Fox Hunt
This striking landscape from the 1850s illustrates the aesthetic traits of the Romantic movement. Josef Navrátil highlights the gloom with one hunter's red scarf and glowing cigarette.

KEY

▨	Late Baroque, Neo-Classicism and Early Romanticism
☐	Onset of Romanticism
▨	The Mánes family
☐	Romanticism: Hausofer & landscape
☐	Romanticism: Ruben & history painting
☐	The Realists
☐	Generation of the National Theatre
☐	Neo-Romanticism, Symbolism and Naturalism
▨	St George's Basilica
▨	Special exhibitions
▨	Non-exhibition space

GALLERY GUIDE
The permanent exhibition is located on both the upper and lower floors of the convent. The collection is laid out chronologically and thematically and spans the years 1790–1910. The 350 paintings and 54 sculptures show the progression of Czech art and illustrate the changes occurring in Bohemian society through this period. There are also examples of religious art in the Chapel of St Anne.

Exploring the St George's Collection

This fine collection of 19th-century Czech art is produced in collaboration with the Museum of Decorative
Art in Prague, which has interspersed the artworks with
various items of furniture, jewellery and clothing from
the day. The collection spans the period from 1790 to
1910, when Prague witnessed a renewed interest in art
and a growth in communication between artists and the
public. The burgeoning influence of the middle classes
is evident in portraits of artistic patrons, members of the
intelligentsia and, latterly, the National Revival movement. The cultural climate of Bohemia and specifically
Prague has been beautifully mapped by this collection
of paintings, sculptures, sketches and monuments.

Detail from *Goldsmith* (1861) by
Quido Mánes

THE MÁNES FAMILY

Unsurprisingly, the influential
Mánes family of painters take
up a whole section. Father
Antonín Mánes was a forerun-
ner of Romantic Czech landscape painting, even though
he took much of his inspiration from western Europe.
Landscape with Church Ruins
(1827–28), for example, was
sketched, fairly accurately,
from literary discriptions of
Kelso Abbey in Scotland.
   Antonín's son Quido's ability
grew with experience and his
Goldsmith (1861) is exemplary
of his evocative paintings of
workers and peasants.
It is Quido's brother Josef
who is undoubtedly the most
successful of the family and
his cabinet-sized *Red Umbrella* (1855) is one of the more
familiar exhibits in the collection. Josef Václav Mylsbek was
much inspired by Josef and a
draft (1916) of his monument
to the artist is on show here.

ONSET OF ROMANTICISM

The aesthetic experience and
emphasis on high emotions
and untamed nature that epit-
omises Romanticism is beautifully demonstrated by this
vast collection of landscapes,
portraits and even shop signs
by master painter Josef
Navrátil. The contemporane-
ous lure of western Europe is
evident in his Alpine landscapes, but it is Navrátil's
dedication to homespun subjects that truly delights; an
example is the beloved,
relaxed nature of *In Chum-
lecký's Wine Cellar* (1850s).
   Other artists here include
Jenny Salmová who couples
the exotic and the mundane
in *Still Life with Lizard and
Flowers* (1826) and Charlotta
Piepenhagenová who is
appropriately rugged in, *A
Lake in the Mountains* (1870s).

Still Life with Lizard and Flowers
(1826) by Jenny Salmová

LATE BAROQUE, NEO-
CLASSICISM AND EARLY
ROMANTICISM

The drama and exuberant
religious motifs of the Late-
Baroque period are evident in
the masterful compositional
style of *St Bernard's Dream*
(c. 1830) by Josef Führich as
well as *St Wenceslas and St
Ludmila at Mass* (1837) by
František Tkadlík.
   Antonín Machek was a key
artist of this genre as illustrated by his whimsical labour of
love, *Cycle of Rulers* (1828–
35). His portraits also interest-
ingly demonstrate the societal
emergence of the middle
class as patrons of the arts.
   Elsewhere in this section
are Romantic pastorals by
master landscape painter Norbert Grund and Neo-Classical
scenes from Ludvík Kohl and
Kryštof Seckel. Also of note
are some religious sculpture
by Václav Prachner and
Václav Levý.

Landscape With Church Ruins (1827–28) by Antonín Mánes

Deserted Countryside (1858) by Adolf Kosárek

ROMANTICISM: HAUSOFER & LANDSCAPE

The 19th century is often considered the golden age of landscape painting in Prague, with Romanticism being the principal style. Master painters such as Josef Navrátil and Antonín Mánes made names for themselves but it was Max Haushofer, professor of landscape painting at the Prague Academy of Fine Arts from 1845 to 1866, who influenced many painters of the time. Here, the legacy of his mammoth landscape, *A Lake in the Alps* (1860), for example, is evident in Alois Bubák's *Summer Afternoon* (1863). Other students of his include Bedřich Havránek, Václav Prachner and Adolf Kosárek. Note the typically Romantic stormy landscape in the latter's *Deserted Countryside* (1858).

ROMANTICISM: RUBEN & HISTORY PAINTING

Christian Ruben was appointed director of the Prague Academy of Fine Arts in 1841 and his monumental visions of a brave new world formed the basis of his teachings. The human quest and trepidation is palpable in his *Columbus Discovering America* (1846) and also resonates in *Kriemhild's Accusation* (1879) by his student Emil Jan Lauffer.

Early Christian scenes and Bohemia's past are the predominant subjects within this genre. Another student of Ruben, Jaroslav Čermák, however, found much inspiration from the history and people, particularly women, of Montenegro, as displayed in the atmospheric *Captives* (1870).

THE REALISTS

Jaroslav Čermák's talent crossed genres into the Realist style as illustrated by *Still Life with Fish* (1873). However, it is the prolific Karel Purkyně who dominates this section. Faithful to the Realist aesthetic, his *Snowy Owl* (1862), actually records where the owl was killed. Purkyně's portraits are typically peopled with ordinary folk at work; a blacksmith and woodcarver for instance.

Elsewhere look out for Soběslav Hippolyt Pinkas's compositional skills in *Vine* (1856–7) and landscapes by Antonín Chittussi. Note how the latter's *Bohemian Moravian Highlands* (1882) contains almost Impressionistic touches.

Captives (1870) by Jaroslav Čermák

GENERATION OF THE NATIONAL THEATRE

The Czech nation acquired some of its most exceptional buildings during the period of the National Revival *(see pp32–3)*, including the National Theatre and National Museum, which were embellished by many of the great painters, sculptors and architects of the day. Here, sketches of the interior and exterior decorations to the National Theatre are on display as well as other works by the artists involved. The spirit of the time is particularly captured in portraits of contemporary cultural personalities by J V Myslbek.

Master academic painter Václav Brožík is represented by some excellent snapshots of country life as well as a study for the 7 m- (23 ft-) long painting *Tu, Felix Austria, Nube* (1897), commissioned by the Emperor Franz Josef I. The Chapel of St Anne contains drafts of the four saints that flank Myslbek's St Wenceslas Monument *(see p146)* and Emanuel Max's sublime *Christ on the Cross* (1843).

J V Myslbek's Music (c.1895)

NEO-ROMANTICISM, SYMBOLISM AND NATURALISM

The end of the 19th century saw artistic style veer toward the heightened emotional traits of Neo-Romanticism, here beautifully illustrated by Lev Lerch's *Will-o'-the-Wisp* (before 1890) and Maximilían Pirner's emotive *Frenzy, Hatred and Death* (1886–93). Beneš Knüpfer more subtly symbolises the despair and remorse felt by Judas in his eponymous painting (c.1906).

Also in this section are some interesting Naturalistic street scenes from Jakub Schikaneder and Vojtěch Bartonek among others, displayed opposite the other-worldly *Water Sprite* (1886) by Hanuš Schwaiger, who was credited with making fantasy look real.

Old prison in the Dalibor Tower

Dalibor Tower ❾
DALIBORKA

Prague Castle, Zlatá ulička. **Map** 2 E2. Ⓜ *Malostranská.* 🚋 *18, 20, 22, 23.* **Open** *9am–5pm daily (to 4pm Nov–Mar).* 🈺 🚫

This 15th-century tower with a conical roof was part of the fortifications built by King Vladislav Jagiello *(see p26–7).* His coat of arms can be seen on the outer wall. The tower also served as a prison and is named after its first inmate, Dalibor of Kozojedy, a young knight sentenced to death for harbouring some outlawed serfs. While awaiting execution, he was kept in an underground dungeon, into which he had to be lowered through a hole in the floor.

According to legend, while in prison he learnt to play the violin. People sympathetic to his plight came to listen to his playing and provided him with food and drink, which they lowered on a rope from a window – prisoners were often left to starve to death. The story was used by Bedřich Smetana in his opera *Dalibor.* The tower ceased to serve as a prison in 1781. Visitors can see part of the old prison.

South Gardens ❿
JIŽNÍ ZAHRADY

Prague Castle (access from Hradčanské náměstí). **Map** 2 D3. Ⓜ *Malostranská, Hradčanská.* 🚋 *18, 20, 22, 23.* **Open** *Apr–Oct: 10am–6pm daily (to 7pm May & Sep, 9pm Jun, Jul & Aug).* 📷 **www**.hrad.cz

The gardens occupy the long narrow band of land below the Castle overlooking the Little Quarter. Several small gardens have been linked to form what is now known as the South Gardens. The oldest, the Paradise Garden (Rajská zahrada), laid out in 1562, contains a circular pavilion built for Emperor Matthias in 1617. Its carved wooden ceiling shows the coloured emblems of the 39 countries of the Habsburg Empire. The Garden on the Ramparts (Zahrada Na valech) dates from the 19th century. It occupies a former vegetable patch and is famous as the site of the defenestration of 1618 *(see p105),* when two Imperial governors were thrown from a first-floor window. Two obelisks were subsequently erected by Ferdinand II to mark the spots where they landed. Modifications were carried out in the 1920s by Josip Plečnik, who built the Bull Staircase leading to the Paradise Garden and the observation terrace. Below the terrace, in the former Hartig Garden, is a Baroque music pavilion designed by Giovanni Battista Alliprandi. Beside it stand four statues of Classical gods by Antonín Braun.

Alliprandi's music pavilion in the South Gardens

Belvedere ⓫
BELVEDÉR

Prague Castle, Royal Garden. **Map** 2 E1. Ⓜ *Malostranská, Hradčanská.* 🚋 *18, 20, 22, 23.* **Open** *10am–6pm Tue–Sun during exhibitions only.* 🈺 ♿ **www**.hrad.cz

Built by Ferdinand I for his beloved wife Anne, the Belvedere is one of the finest Italian Renaissance buildings north of the Alps. Also known as the Royal Summer Palace

The Belvedere, Emperor Ferdinand I's summer palace in the Royal Garden beside Prague Castle

Antonín Braun's statue of *The Allegory of Night* in front of the *sgraffito* decoration of the Ball Game Hall in the Royal Garden

Riding School ⑬
JÍZDÁRNA

Prague Castle. **Map** 2 D2. *Tel 22 43 73 368.* Malostranská, Hradčanská. 22, 23. **Open** 10am–6pm during exhibitions.

The 17th-century Riding School forms one side of U Prašného mostu, a road which runs to the northern side of Prague Castle via Deer Moat. In the 1920s it was converted into an exhibition hall, which now holds important exhibitions of painting and sculpture. A garden provides excellent views of St. Vitus's Cathedral and the northern fortifications of the castle.

Archbishop's Palace ⑭
ARCIBISKUPSKÝ PALÁC

Hradčanské náměstí 16. **Map** 2 D3. *Tel 22 03 92 111.* Malostranská, Hradčanská. 22, 23. **Not open** to the public.

Ferdinand I bought this sumptuous palace in 1562 for the first Catholic Archbishop since the Hussite Wars *(see pp26–7)*. It replaced the old Archbishop's Palace in the Little Quarter, which had been destroyed during the wars, and has remained the Archbishop's seat in Prague ever since. In the period after the Battle of the White Mountain *(see p30–31)*, it was a powerful symbol of Catholic domination of the city and the Czech lands. Its spectacular cream-coloured Rococo façade was designed by Johann Joseph Wirch in the 1760s for Archbishop Antonín Příchovský, whose coat of arms sits proudly above the portal.

Příchovský coat of arms

Royal Garden ⑫
KRÁLOVSKÁ ZAHRADA

Prague Castle, U Prašného mostu. **Map** 2 D2. Malostranská, Hradčanská. 22, 23. **Open** May–Oct: 10am–6pm daily (to 7pm May & Sep, 9pm Jun, Jul & Aug). www.hrad.cz

The garden was created in 1535 for Ferdinand I. Its appearance has been altered over time, but some examples of 16th-century garden architecture have survived, notably the Belvedere and the Ball Game Hall (Míčovna), built by Bonifaz Wohlmut in 1569. The building is covered in beautiful, though much re-stored, Renaissance *sgraffito*, a form of decoration created by cutting a design through the wet top layer of plaster on to a contrasting undercoat. The garden is beautiful in spring when thousands of tulips bloom. This is where tulips were first acclimatized to Europe.

(Královský letohrádek), it is an arcaded summerhouse with slender Ionic columns topped by a roof shaped like an inverted ship's hull clad in blue-green copper. The main architect was Paolo della Stella, who was also responsible for the ornate reliefs inside the arcade. Work began in 1538, but was interrupted by the great Castle fire of 1541. The Belvedere was eventually completed in 1564.

In the middle of the small geometrical garden in front of the palace stands the Singing Fountain. Dating from 1568, it owes its name to the musical sound the water makes as it hits the bronze bowl, though you have to listen closely to appreciate the effect. The fountain was cast by Tomáš Jaroš, the famous bell founder, who lived and worked in the Powder Tower *(see p98)*.

Many of the Belvedere's works of art were plundered by the occupying Swedish army in 1648. The statues stolen included Adriaen de Vries's 16th-century bronze of *Mercury and Psyche*, which is now in the Louvre in Paris. The Belvedere is now used as an art gallery.

Sternberg Palace ⑮
ŠTERNBERSKÝ PALÁC

See pp112–15.

Sternberg Palace ⑮

ŠTERNBERSKÝ PALÁC

Franz Josef Sternberg founded the Society of Patriotic
Friends of the Arts in Bohemia in 1796. Fellow noble-
men would lend their finest pictures and sculpture to
the society, which had its headquarters in the early-
18th-century Sternberg Palace. Since 1949, the fine
Baroque building has been used to house the
National Gallery's collection of European art, with
its superb range of Old Masters.

The Lamentation of Christ
*The frozen, sculptural
figures make this one of the
finest paintings by Lorenzo
Monaco (1408).*

Cardinal Cesi's Garden in Rome
*Henrick van Cleve's painting (1548) provides
a valuable image of a Renaissance collections of
antiquities. The garden was later destroyed.*

First
floor

Garden
Room

Stairs to
second
floor

Ground
floor

Stairs to
first floor

Ticket
office

Passageway
to Hradčanské
náměstí

STAR SIGHTS

★ Head of Christ by
El Greco

★ Scholar in his Study
by Rembrandt

★ The Martyrdom of
St Thomas by Rubens

★ Scholar in his Study
In this painting from 1634 Rembrandt used keenly observed detail to convey wisdom in the face of the old scholar.

VISITORS' CHECKLIST

Hradčanské náměstí 15.
Map 1 C2. **Tel** 23 33 50 068.
🚇 *Hradčanská, Malostranská.*
🚋 22, 23 to Prague Castle
(Pražský hrad) or Pohořelec.
Open *10am– 6pm Tue–Sun*
(last tour: 5pm). **www**.
ngprague.cz 📷 🚫 🎫 📶
45 minutes' walk from centre
(old town).

Chinese Cabinet

Eden *(1618)*
Roelandt Savery studied models of exotic animals, brought to Prague by Persian nobles, at the court of Emperor Rudolf II. He was then able to paint real animals.

Second floor

GALLERY GUIDE
The gallery is arranged on three floors around the central courtyard of the palace. The ground floor, reached from the courtyard, houses German and Austrian art from the 15th to 19th centuries. The stairs to the collections on the upper floors are opposite the ticket office at the main entrance.

Stairs down to other floors and exit

★ Head of Christ
Painted by El Greco in the 1590s, this portrait emphasizes the humanity of Christ. At the same time the curious square halo framing the head gives the painting the qualities of an ancient icon.

KEY

▢	German and Austrian Art 1400–1800
▢	Flemish and Dutch Art 1400–1600
▢	Italian Art 1400–1500
▢	Roman Art
▢	Flemish and Dutch Art 1600–1800
▢	French Art 1600–1800
▢	Icons, Classical and Ancient Art
▢	Venice 1700–1800 and Goya
▢	Spanish Art 1600–1800
▢	Naples and Venice 1600–1700
▢	Italian Art 1500–1600
▢	Non-exhibition space

★ The Martyrdom of St Thomas
This magnificent work is by Peter Paul Rubens, the foremost Flemish painter of the 17th century.

Exploring the Sternberg Collections

The National Gallery's collection of European art ranks among the countries best collections. Since the transfer of the outstanding 19th- and 20th-century exhibits to Veletržní Palace in 1996 *(see pp164–5)* the Sternberg has expanded its permanent exhibition, with especially strong representations from Italian medieval art, Neapolitan artists of the 17th and 18th centuries, Dutch and Flemish works, and German art of the 15th to 17th centuries. There is also a fine collection of Renaissance bronzes. The fascinating Chinese Cabinet is on display after a restoration lasting several years. The exhibition covers the Classical Era to the close of the Baroque.

ICONS, CLASSICAL AND ANCIENT ART

Two small rooms in the gallery are occupied by an odd assortment of paintings that do not quite fit in with the rest of the collection. These include a *Portrait of a Young Woman* dating from the 2nd century AD, discovered during excavations at Fayoum in Egypt in the 19th century.

The majority of the exhibits, however, are icons of the Orthodox church – some are Byzantine, some Italo-Greek and some Russian. The finest examples on show here are two of the later 16th-century works, *The Lamentation of Christ* from Crete and *Christ's Entry Into Jerusalem* from Russia. The icons on display offer examples from a variety of the most important Mediterranean and Eastern European centres.

Christ's Entry into Jerusalem, a 16th-century Russian icon

GERMAN AND AUSTRIAN ART (1400–1800)

One of the most celebrated paintings in the Sternberg's collection is Albrecht Dürer's *The Feast of the Rosary*, painted during the artist's stay in Venice in 1506. The work has a particular significance for Prague since it was bought by Emperor Rudolph II. The two figures

seen in front of the Virgin and Child are Maximilian I (Rudolph's great-great-grandfather) and Pope Julius II.

The collection also includes works by several other important German painters of the Renaissance, including Hans Holbein the Elder and the Younger and Lucas Cranach the Elder. Cranach is represented by works including a striking *Adam and Eve* whose nudes show the spirit of the Renaissance, tempered by Lutheran Reform.

ITALIAN ART (1300–1800)

When you enter the Italian galleries, you are greeted by a splendid array of early diptychs, triptychs and other richly gilded panel paintings from the churches of Tuscany and northern Italy. Most came originally from the d'Este collection at Konopiště Castle *(see p169)*. Of particularly high quality are the two triangular panels of saints by the 14th-century Sienese painter Pietro Lorenzetti and a moving *Lamentation of Christ* by Lorenzo Monaco.

A fascinating element of the collection is the display of Renaissance bronze statuettes. Fashionable amongst Italian nobility of the 15th century, these little bronzes were at first cast from famous or newly-discovered works of antiquity. Later, sculptors began to use the medium more freely – Padua, for example, specialized in the depiction of small animals – and producers also adapted items for use as decorative household goods such as oil lamps, ink pots and door knockers. This small collection has representative works from all the major Italian producers except Mantua and, while many variations can be found in other museums throughout the world, there are some pieces here that are both unique and outstanding examples of the craft.

The Feast of the Rosary by Dürer (1506)

Don Miguel de Lardizábal (1815), by Francisco Goya

Among the 16th-century Italian works on display, there are some delightful surprises. These include *St Jerome* by the Venetian painter, Tintoretto, and *The Flagellation of Christ* and *Portrait of an Elderly Man* by another Venetian, Jacopo Bassano. There is also an expressive portrait by the Florentine mannerist, Bronzino, of *Eleanor of Toledo*, the wife of Cosimo de' Medici.

FLEMISH AND DUTCH ART (1400–1800)

The collections of Flemish and Dutch art are rich and varied, ranging from rural scenes by Pieter Brueghel the Elder to portraits by Rubens and Rembrandt.

Highlights of the former include an altarpiece showing the *Adoration of the Magi* by Geertgen tot Sint Jans. Other early works of great interest include *St Luke Drawing the Virgin* by Jan Gossaert (c1515), one of the first works of art from the Netherlands to show the clear influence of the

Italian Renaissance. The collection from the 17th century includes several major works, notably by Peter Paul Rubens who, in 1639, sent two paintings to the Augustinians of the Church of St Thomas (*see p127*) in the Little Quarter. The originals were lent to the gallery in 1896 and replaced by copies. The violence and drama of *The Martyrdom of St Thomas* is in complete

***Eleanor of Toledo* (1540s) by the Florentine Mannerist painter Agnolo Bronzino**

contrast to the spiritual calm of *St Augustine*. Two other fine portraits are those of Rembrandt's *Scholar in His Study* and Frans Hals' *Portrait of Jasper Schade*.

Also on display is a wide assortment of paintings by other, less-prominent, artists who nonetheless represent the enormous range and quality of this period.

SPANISH, FRENCH AND ENGLISH ART (1400–1800)

French art is represented chiefly by the 17th-century painters Simon Vouet (*The Suicide of Lucretia*), Sébastien Bourdon and Charles Le Brun. Spanish painting is even less well represented, but two of the collection's finest works are a haunting *Head of Christ* by El Greco – the only work by the artist on display in the Czech Republic – and a noble half-length portrait of the politician *Don Miguel de Lardizábal* by Goya.

THE CHINESE CABINET

After several years of difficult restoration work, this curiosity is once again open to the public. The richly-decorated little chamber was part of the original furnishings of the Sternberg Palace, and was designed as an intimate withdrawing room away from the bustle of the grand state rooms. In its plethora of decorative styles, Baroque mingles with Far Eastern motifs and techniques, which were fashionable at the turn of the 18th century. The vaulted ceiling features the Star of the Sternbergs among its geometric decorations. Black lacquered walls are embellished with cobalt blue and white medallions in golden frames, while gilded shelves once held rare Oriental porcelain.

The Loreto ⑳

LORETA

Ever since its construction in 1626, the Loreto has been an important place of pilgrimage. It was commissioned by Kateřina of Lobkowicz, a Czech aristocrat who was very keen to promote the legend of the Santa Casa of Loreto *(see opposite)*. The heart of the complex is a copy of the house believed to be the Virgin Mary's. The Santa Casa was enclosed by cloisters in 1661, and a Baroque façade 60 years later by Christoph and Kilian Ignaz Dientzenhofer. The grandiose design and miraculous stories about the Loreto were part of Ferdinand II's campaign to recatholicize the Czechs *(see pp30–31)*.

Kateřina Lobkowicz, founder of the Santa Casa

Bell Tower
Enclosed in this large Baroque tower, is a set of 30 bells cast 1691–94 in Amsterdam by Claudy Fremy.

Chapel of St Joseph

Fountain decorated with a sculpture of the Resurrection

Chapel of St Francis Seraphim

Chapel of St Ann

Entrance from Loretánské náměstí

★ **Loreto Treasury**
This gold-plated, diamond-encrusted monstrance, for displaying the host, is one of the valuable liturgical items in the Loreto treasury, most of which originated in the 16th–18th centuries.

STAR SIGHTS

★ Loreto Treasury

★ Santa Casa

★ Church of the Nativity

Baroque Entrance
The balustrade above the Loreto's front entrance is decorated with statues of St Joseph and St John the Baptist by Ondřej Quitainer.

★ Santa Casa
Stucco figures of many of the Old Testament prophets and reliefs from the life of the Virgin Mary by Italian artists decorate the chapel.

VISITORS' CHECKLIST

Loretánské náměstí, Hradčany.
Map 1C3 **Tel** 22 05 16 740.
22, 23 to Pohořelec. **Open**
9am–12:15pm, 1–4:30pm
Tue–Sun. 7:30am
Sat, 5pm Sun. www.loreta.cz

★ Church of the Nativity
Gruesome relics, including fully-clothed skeletons with death masks made of wax, line the walls of this 18th-century church. The frescoes are by Václav Vavřinec Reiner.

Chapel of
the Holy
Rood

17th-Century Cloister
Built originally as a shelter for the many pilgrims who visited the shrine, the cloister is covered with frescoes.

Chapel of
St Anthony
of Padua

Chapel of Our
Lady of Sorrows

Fountain Sculpture
This copy of The Ascension of the Virgin *Mary is taken from Jan Brüderle's 1739 sandstone statue, now in the Lapidarium (see p162).*

LEGEND OF THE SANTA CASA

The original house, said to be where the Archangel Gabriel told Mary about the future birth of Jesus, is in the small Italian town of Loreto. It was believed that angels transported the house from Nazareth to Loreto in 1278 following threats by infidels. After the Protestants' defeat in 1620 *(see pp30–31)*, Catholics promoted the legend, and 50 replicas of the Loreto were built in Bohemia and Moravia. This, the grandest, became the most important in Bohemia, and received many visitors.

The stuccoed Santa Casa

Martinic Palace ⑯
MARTINICKÝ PALÁC

Hradčanské náměstí 8. **Map** 1 C2.
Tel 23 33 26 722. **ᴹ**
Malostranská, Hradčanská. 🚋 22,
23. **Open** 10am–6pm daily. 🕮
www.martinickypalac.cz

In the course of the palace's
restoration in the early 1970s,
workmen uncovered the
original 16th-century façade
decorated with ornate cream
and brown sgraffito (see p111).
It depicts Old Testament
scenes, including the story of
Joseph and Potiphar's wife.
More sgraffito in the courtyard
shows the story of Samson
and the Labours of Hercules.
Martinic Palace was enlarged
by Jaroslav Bořita of Martinice,
who was one of the imperial
governors thrown from a
window of the Royal Palace
in 1618 (see p105).
According to an old legend,
between 11pm and midnight
the ghost of a fiery black dog
appears at the palace and
accompanies walkers as far
as the Loreto (see pp116–17),
where it disappears again.
Today the palace houses the
city architecture department.

Schwarzenberg Palace ⑰
SCHWARZENBERSKÝ PALÁC

Hradčanské náměstí 2. **Map** 2 D3.
Tel 23 30 81 720. **ᴹ**
Malostranská, Hradčanská
🚋 22, 23. **Open** 10am–6pm
Tue–Sun. 🕮 🎫 www.ngprague.cz

From a distance, the façade of
this grand Renaissance palace
appears to be clad in project-
ing pyramid-shaped stone-
work. On closer inspection,
this turns out to be an
illusion created
by sgraffito
patterns incised

on a flat wall. Built
originally for the
Lobkowicz family by
the Italian architect
Agostino Galli in
1545–76, the gabled
palace is Florentine
rather than Bohemian
in style. It passed
through several hands
before the Schwarzen-
bergs, a leading family
in the Habsburg
Empire, bought it in
1719. Much of the
interior decoration has
survived, including
four painted ceilings
on the second floor
dating from 1580. The
palace once housed
the Museum of Military
History, now at U Pamatniku
3. Following renovation, the
palace has become home to
the National Gallery's
collection of Renaissance art.
In the square outside is the
statue of Tomáš G Masaryk,
Czechoslovakia's first president.

New World ⑱
NOVÝ SVĚT

Map 1 B2. 🚋 22, 23.

Now a charming street of
small cottages, Nový Svět
(New World) used to be the
name of this area of Hradčany.
Developed in the mid-14th
century to provide houses for
the castle workers, the area
was twice destroyed by fire,
the last time being in 1541.
Most of the cottages date from
the 17th century. They have
been spruced up, but are
otherwise unspoilt and very
different in character from the

Tycho Brahe, Rudolph II's astronomer

rest of Hradčany. In defiance
of their poverty, the inhabitants
chose golden house signs to
identify their modest houses –
you will see a Golden Pear,
a Grape, a Foot, a Bush and
an Acorn. Plaques identify
No. 1 as the former home of
Rudolph II's brilliant court
astronomer, Tycho Brahe, and
No. 25 as the 1857 birthplace
of the great Czech violinist
František Ondříček.

Capuchin Monastery ⑲
KAPUCÍNSKÝ KLÁŠTER

Loretánské náměstí 6. **Map** 1 B3
🚋 22, 23. **Closed** to the public
except the church.

Bohemia's first Capuchin
monastery was founded here
in 1600. It is connected to the
neighbouring Loreto (see
pp116–17) by an overhead
roofed passage. Attached to the
monastery is the Church of
Our Lady Queen of Angels, a
single-naved building with
plain furnishings, typical of
the ascetic Capuchin order.
The church is famous for
its miraculous statue of the
Madonna and Child. Emperor
Rudolph II liked the statue so
much he asked the Capuchins
to give it to him to place in
his private chapel. The monks
agreed, but then the statue
somehow found its way back
to the church. Three times
Rudolph had the Madonna
brought back but each time

The Carmelite monastery next to the Schwarzenberg Palace

she returned to her original position. The Emperor eventually gave up, left her where she was and presented her with a gold crown and a robe. Each year at Christmas the church attracts crowds of visitors to see its delightful Baroque nativity scene of life-sized figures dressed in costumes from the period.

Church of the Capuchin Monastery

The Loreto @

LORETA

See pp116–17.

Černín Palace @

ČERNÍNSKÝ PALÁC

Loretánské náměstí 5. **Map** 1 B3.
Tel 22 41 81 111 [22, 23].
Closed to the public. www.mzv.cz

Built in 1668 for Count Černín of Chudenice, the Imperial Ambassador to Venice, the Černín Palace is 150 m (500 ft) long with a row of 30 massive Corinthian half-columns running the length of its upper storeys. The palace towers over the attractive, small, grassy square that lies between it and the Loreto.

The huge building suffered as a result of its prominent position on one of Prague's highest hills. It was looted by the French in 1742 and badly damaged in the Prussian bombardment of the city in 1757. In 1851 the impoverished Černín family sold the palace to the state and it became a

barracks. After the creation of Czechoslovakia in 1918 the palace was restored to its original design and became the Ministry of Foreign Affairs. A few days after the Communist Coup in 1948 the Foreign Minister, Jan Masaryk, the popular son of Czechoslovakia's first President, Tomáš Masaryk, died as the result of a fall from a top-floor window of the Palace. He was the only non-Communist in the government that had just been formed. No-one really knows whether he was pushed or jumped, but he is still widely mourned.

Capital on Černín Palace

Pohořelec @

Map 1 B3. [22, 23].

First settled in 1375, this is one of the oldest parts of Prague. The name is of more recent origin: Pohořelec

means "place destroyed by fire", a fate the area has suffered three times in the course of its history – the last time being in 1741. It is now a large open square on a hill high over the city and part of the main access route to Prague Castle. In the centre stands a large monument to St John Nepomuk (1752) *(see p137)*, thought to be by Johann Anton Quitainer. The houses around the square are mainly Baroque and Rococo. In front of the Jan Kepler grammar school stands a monument to Kepler and his predecessor as astronomer at the court of Rudolph II, Tycho Brahe, who died in a house on the school site in 1601.

Strahov Monastery @

STRAHOVSKÝ KLÁŠTER

See pp120–21.

Kučera Palace, a Rococo building in Pohořelec

Strahov Monastery ㉓

STRAHOVSKÝ KLÁŠTER

When it was founded in 1140 by an austere religious order, the Premonstratensians, Strahov rivalled the seat of the Czech sovereign in size. Destroyed by fire in 1258, it was rebuilt in the Gothic style, with later Baroque additions. Its famous library, in the theological and philosophical halls, is over 800 years old and despite being ransacked by many invading armies, is one of the finest in Bohemia. Strahov also escaped Joseph II's 1783 dissolution of the monasteries by changing its library into a research institute. It is now a working monastery and museum.

The bust of Joseph II over entrance gate

Statue of St John
A Late-Gothic, painted statue of St John the Evangelist situated in the Theological Hall, has the saint's prayer book held in a small pouch.

Baroque tower

The Museum of National Literature is devoted to Czech literature.

Refectory

Entrance to main courtyard of the monastery

Baroque organ on which Mozart played

★ **Church of Our Lady**
The interior of this Baroque church is highly decorated. Above the arcades of the side naves, there are 12 paintings with scenes from the life of St Norbert, founder of the Premonstratensian order, by Jiří Neunhertz.

Entrance to Church of Our Lady

Church Façade
The elaborate statues, by Johann Anton Quitainer, were added to the western façade of the church when it was remodelled by the architect Anselmo Lurago in the 1750s.

STAR FEATURES

★ Church of Our Lady

★ Philosophical Hall

★ Theological Hall

VISITORS' CHECKLIST

Královská Kanonie Premonstrátů
na Strahově. Strahovské nádvoří 1.
Map 1 B4. **Tel** *22 05 16 671.*
🚊 *22, 23 to Pohořelec* **Open**
*9am–noon, 12:30–5pm
Tue–Sun. **Philosophical Hall,
Theological Hall, Church of Our
Lady, Picture Gallery open** 9am–
noon, 1–5pm daily,* **closed** *Easter
Sun, 25 Dec.* 📷 🚻

View from Petřín Hill
*A gate at the eastern end of the first
courtyard leads to Petřín Hill, part of
which was once the monastery's orchards.*

★ Theological Hall
*One of the 17th-century
astronomical globes by
William Blaeu that line the
hall. The stucco and wall
paintings relate to
librarianship.*

The façade of the
Philosophical
Hall is decorated
with vases and a
gilded medallion
of Joseph II by
Ignaz Platzer.

★ Philosophical Hall
*The ceiling fresco depicts
the* Struggle of Mankind to
Know Real History *by
Franz Maulbertsch. It was
built in 1782 to hold the
Baroque bookcases and
their valuable books from
a dissolved monastery
near Louka, in Moravia.*

Entrance
to libraries

Strahov Gospel Book
*A facsimile of this superb
and precious 9th-century
volume, is now on display
in the Theological Hall.*

LITTLE QUARTER

MALÁ STRANA

The Little Quarter is the part of Prague least affected by recent history. Hardly any new building has taken place here since the late 18th century and the quarter is rich in splendid Baroque palaces and old houses with attractive signs. Founded in 1257, it is built on the slopes below the Castle hill with magnificent views across the river to the Old Town.

Sign from At the Golden Horseshoe in Nerudova

The centre of the Little Quarter has always been Little Quarter Square (Malostranské náměstí), dominated by the Church of St Nicholas. The Grand Prior's millwheel at Kampa Island still turns, pilgrims still kneel before the Holy Infant of Prague in the Church of Our Lady Victorious, and music rings out from churches and palaces as it did when Mozart stayed here.

SIGHTS AT A GLANCE

Churches
Church of St Thomas ❸
Church of St Nicholas
 pp128–9 ❺
Church of Our Lady
 Victorious ❾
Church of Our Lady beneath
 the Chain ⓭
Church of St Lawrence ㉒

Parks and Gardens
Vrtba Garden ❽
Vojan Park ⓱
Ledebour Garden ⓳
Observation Tower ⓴
Mirror Maze ㉑
Observatory ㉓
Petřín Park ㉕
Funicular Railway ㉖

Museums
Kampa Museum of
 Modern Art ⓲
Museum of Music ㉗

Historic Monuments
Hunger Wall ㉔

Historic Restaurants and Beer Halls
At St Thomas's ❷
At the Three Ostriches ⓯

Historic Streets and Squares
Little Quarter Square ❹
Nerudova Street ❻
Italian Street ❼
Maltese Square ❿
Grand Priory Square ⓬
Bridge Street ⓰

Bridges and Islands
Kampa Island ⓫
Charles Bridge
 pp136–9 ⓮

Palaces
Wallenstein Palace
 and Garden ❶
Michna
 Palace ㉘

KEY

▬	Street-by-Street map See pp124–5
▬	Street-by-Street map See pp132–3
Ⓜ	Metro station
🚋	Tram stop
🚋	Funicular railway
⛴	River boat boarding point
ℹ	Tourist information
—	City wall

0 metres   250
0 yards   250

GETTING THERE

The area has little public transport, but Malostranská metro on line A is close to most of the sights. Trams 12, 20, 22 and 23 go to Malostranské náměstí and along Újezd to the funicular railway that takes you up Petřín Hill.

◁ **Charles Bridge and the Little Quarter Bridge Towers**

Street-by-Street: Around Little Quarter Square

The Little Quarter, most of whose grand Baroque palaces now house embassies, has preserved much of its traditional character. The steep, narrow streets and steps have an air of romantic mystery and you will find fascinating buildings decorated with statues and house signs at every turn. Some smart new restaurants have been established in the old buildings.

At the Three Little Fiddles, now a restaurant, acquired its house sign when it was the home of a family of violin makers around 1700.

Thun-Hohenstein Palace (1721–6) has a doorway crowned with two sculpted eagles by Matthias Braun. The palace is now the seat of the Italian embassy.

★ Nerudova Street
This historic street leading up to Prague Castle is named after the 19th-century writer Jan Neruda ❻

Morzin Palace has a striking Baroque façade with a pair of sculpted moors.

Italian Street
From the 16th to the 18th century, houses in the street, like the House at the Golden Scales, were occupied by Italian craftsmen ❼

STAR SIGHTS

* ★ Wallenstein Palace
* ★ Church of St Nicholas
* ★ Nerudova Street

Vrtba Garden
Laid out in about 1725 by František Maximilián Kaňka, these fine Baroque terraces provide good views over the rooftops of the Little Quarter ❽

★ Wallenstein Palace
On the main hall ceiling, Albrecht von Wallenstein, the great general of the 30 Years' War, appears as the god Mars ❶

Czech National Assembly

Plague Column

To Malostranská Metro

T O M Á Š S K Á

Wallenstein Gardens

Little Quarter Town Hall

N Á M Ě S T Í

S T R A N S K É

LOCATOR MAP
See Street Finder, map 2

PRAGUE CASTLE & HRADČANY

LITTLE QUARTER

Vltava

At St Thomas's
This traditional beer hall occupies the cellars of a medieval monastery brewery ❷

Church of St Thomas
A statue of St Augustine by Hieronymus Kohl (1684) decorates the church's dramatic Baroque façade ❸

Little Quarter Square
This 18th-century view shows the lower half of the square between the church of St Nicholas and the Town Hall ❹

★ Church of St Nicholas
The cupola and bell tower of this Baroque church are the best-known landmarks of the Little Quarter ❺

Schönborn Palace, now the American Embassy, is decorated with caryatids from the 17th century.

0 metres	100
0 yards	100

KEY

– – – Suggested route

Wallenstein Palace and Garden ❶

VALDŠTEJNSKÝ PALÁC

Valdštejnské náměstí 4. **Map** 2 E3.
🚇 *Malostranská.* **Tel** 25 70 71
111. 🚋 *12, 18, 20, 22, 23.* **Palace
open** *10am–4pm Sat & Sun
(to 5pm Apr–Oct).* **Riding school
open** *for exhibitions 10am–6pm
Tue–Sun.* 🚫 ♿ *from Valdštejnská.*
Garden open *Apr–Oct: 10am–6pm
daily (to 8pm in Aug).* 📷 ♿ *from
Valdštejnské náměstí.* 💻
www.senat.cz

The first large secular
building of the Baroque era
in Prague, the palace stands
as a monument to the fatal
ambition of imperial military
commander Albrecht von
Wallenstein (1581–1634). His
string of victories over the
Protestants in the 30 Years'
War *(see pp30–31)* made him
vital to Emperor Ferdinand II.
Already showered with titles,
Wallenstein soon started to
covet the crown of
Bohemia. Finally
he dared to begin
to negotiate inde-
pendently with the
enemy, and he
was killed on the
emperor's orders
by mercenaries
in 1634.

Wallenstein

The main hall of Wallenstein Palace

Wallenstein's intention was to
overshadow even Prague Castle with his palace, built
between 1624 and 1630. To
obtain a suitable site, he had
to purchase 23 houses, three
gardens and the municipal
brick kiln. The magnificent
main hall rises to a height of
two storeys with a ceiling
fresco of Wallenstein himself
portrayed as Mars, the god of
war, riding in a triumphal
chariot. The architect,
Andrea Spezza, and
nearly all the artists
employed in the
decoration of the
palace were Italians.
    Today the palace is
used as the home of
the Czech Senate, and
following restoration
is now open to the
public. The gardens
are laid out as they

were when Wallenstein dined
in the huge *sala terrena*
(garden pavilion) that looks
out over a fountain and rows
of bronze statues. These are
copies of works by Adriaen
de Vries that were stolen
by the Swedes in 1648 *(see
pp30–31).* There is also a
pavilion with fine frescoes
showing scenes from the
legend of the Argonauts
and the Golden Fleece.
    Wallenstein was a holder
of the Order of the
Golden Fleece, the
highest order of
chivalry of the Holy
Roman Empire. At the
far end of the garden
is a large ornamental
pond with a central
statue. Behind this
stands the old Riding
School, now used
to house special
exhibitions by the
National Gallery.
Both gardens and
riding school have
undergone sub-
stantial restoration.

**Copy of a bronze statue of
Eros by Adriaen de Vries**

Palace

**Sala
terrena**

Avenue of sculptures

Riding School

**Valdštejnská
Street
entrance**

The grotesquery is a curious imitation
of the walls of a limestone cave,
covered in stalactites.

**Letenská
Street
entrance**

**Statue of
Hercules**

Klárov entrance

At St Thomas's ❷
U SV. TOMÁŠE

Letenská 12. **Map** 2 E3. **Tel** 25 75 33 466. Ⓜ Malostranská. 🚋 12, 20, 22, 23. **Closed** for renovation. 📷

No other beer hall in Prague can match the antiquity of At St Thomas's. Beer was first brewed here in 1352 by Augustinian monks. The brewery gained such renown that it was appointed sole purveyor of beer to Prague Castle. It remained in operation until 1951. Since then a special dark beer from the Braník brewery has been sold here. The basement of the old brewery has three beer halls, the most spectacular being the so-called "Cave", furnished in mock medieval style.

Church of St Thomas ❸
KOSTEL SV. TOMÁŠE

Josefská 8. **Map** 2 E3. **Tel** 25 53 26 75. Ⓜ Malostranská. 🚋 12, 20, 22, 23. **Open** for services. ✝ 6:45am, 12:15pm Mon–Sat, 9:30am, 11am (in English), 12:30pm Sun. 🚫 ♿

Founded by Wenceslas II in 1285 as the monastery church of the Augustinians, the original Gothic church was completed in 1379. In the Hussite period (see pp26–7) this was one of the few churches to remain Catholic. As a result it suffered serious fire damage. During the reign of Rudolph II (see pp28–9), St Thomas's developed strong links with the Imperial court. Several prominent members of Rudolph's entourage were buried here, including court architect Ottavio Aostalli and the sculptor Adriaen de Vries.

In 1723 the church was struck by lightning and Kilian Ignaz Dientzenhofer was called in to rebuild it. The shape of the original church was preserved in the Baroque reconstruction but, apart from the spire, the church today betrays little of its Gothic origins. The interior of the dome and the curving ceiling frescoes in the nave were painted by

Václav Vavřinec Reiner. Above the altar are copies of paintings by Rubens – *The Martyrdom of St Thomas* and a picture of St Augustine. The originals are in the Sternberg Palace (see pp112–15). The English-speaking Catholic community of Prague meets in this church.

Baroque ceiling in the nave of the Church of St Thomas

Little Quarter Square ❹
MALOSTRANSKÉ NÁMĚSTÍ

Map 2 E3. Ⓜ Malostranská. 🚋 12, 20, 22, 23.

The square has been the centre of life in the Little Quarter since its foundation in 1257. It had started life as a large marketplace in the outer bailey of Prague Castle. Buildings sprang up in the middle of the square dividing

it in half – a gallows and pillory stood in its lower part.

Most of the houses around the square have a medieval core, but all were rebuilt in the Renaissance and Baroque periods. The centre of the square is dominated by the splendid Baroque church of St Nicholas. The large building beside it was a Jesuit college. Along the upper side of the square, facing the church, runs the vast Neo-Classical façade of Lichtenstein Palace. In front of it stands a column raised in honour of the Holy Trinity to mark the end of a plague epidemic in 1713.

Other important buildings include the Little Quarter Town Hall with its splendid Renaissance façade and the Sternberg Palace, built on the site of the outbreak of the fire of 1541, which destroyed most of the Little Quarter. Beside it stands the Smiřický; Palace. Its turrets and hexagonal towers make it an unmistakable landmark on the northern side of the lower square. The Baroque Kaiserstein Palace is situated at the eastern side. On the façade is a bust of the great Czech soprano Emmy Destinn, who lived there between 1908 and 1914. She often sang with the famous Italian tenor Enrico Caruso.

Church of St Nicholas ❺
KOSTEL SV. MIKULÁŠE

See pp128–9.

Arcade in front of buildings on the north side of Little Quarter Square

Church of St Nicholas ⑤

KOSTEL SV. MIKULÁŠE

The Church of St Nicholas divides and dominates the two sections of Little Quarter Square. Building began in 1703, and the last touches were put to the glorious frescoed nave in 1761. It is the acknowledged masterpiece of father-and-son architects Christoph and Kilian Ignaz Dientzenhofer, Prague's greatest exponents of High Baroque *(see opposite)*, although neither lived to see the completion of the church. The statues, frescoes and paintings inside the church are by leading artists of the day, and include a fine *Crucifixion* of 1646 by Karel Škréta. Extensive renovation in the 1950s reversed the damage caused by 200 years of leaky cladding and condensation.

Altar Paintings
The side chapels hold many works of art. This painting of St Michael is by Francesco Solimena.

★ Pulpit
Dating from 1765, the ornate pulpit is by Richard and Peter Prachner. It is lavishly adorned with golden cherubs.

Baroque Organ
A fresco of St Cecilia, patron saint of music, watches over the superb organ. Built in 1746, the instrument was played by Mozart in 1787.

Entrance from west side of Little Quarter Square

Chapel of St Ann

Chapel of St Catherine

STAR FEATURES

- ★ Dome Fresco
- ★ Pulpit
- ★ Statues of the Church Fathers

Façade
St Paul, by John Frederick Kohl, is one of the statues that grace the curving façade. It was completed in 1710 by Christoph Dientzenhofer, who was influenced by Italian architects Borromini and Guarini.

The dome was completed by Kilian Ignaz Dientzenhofer in 1751, shortly before his death.

The belfry, added in 1751–6, was the last part to be built. It houses a small museum of musical instruments.

VISITORS' CHECKLIST

Malostranské náměstí. **Map** 2 E3. ᴹ Malostranská. **Tel** 25 75 34 215. 12, 20, 22, 23 to Malostranské náměstí. **Open** Apr–Oct: 9am–5pm daily; Nov–Mar: 9am–4pm daily. **Concerts**. www.psalterium.cz

★ Dome Fresco
Franz Palko's fresco, The Celebration of the Holy Trinity *(1752–3), fills the 70 m (230 ft) high dome.*

High Altar
A copper statue of St Nicholas by Ignaz Platzer surmounts the high altar. Below it, the painting of St Joseph is by Johann Lukas Kracker, who also painted the nave fresco.

Entrance to Belfry

★ Statues of the Church Fathers
The great teachers by Ignaz Platzer stand at the four corners of the crossing. St Cyril dispatches the devil with his crozier.

Chapel of St Francis Xavier

THE DIENTZENHOFER FAMILY

Christoph Dientzenhofer (1655–1722) came from a family of Bavarian master builders. His son Kilian Ignaz (1689–1751) was born in Prague and educated at the Jesuit Clementinum *(see p79)*. They were responsible for the greatest treasures of Jesuit-influenced Prague Baroque architecture. The Church of St Nicholas, their last work, was completed by Kilian's son-in-law, Anselmo Lurago.

Kilian Ignaz Dientzenhofer

Nerudova Street 6
NERUDOVA ULICE

Map 2 D3. Ⓜ *Malostranská.*
🚋 *12, 20, 22, 23.*

A picturesque narrow street
leading up to Prague Castle,
Nerudova is named after the
poet and journalist Jan
Neruda, who wrote many
short stories set in
this part of Prague. He lived
in the house called At the
Two Suns (No. 47) between
1845 and 1857.

Up until the introduction
of numbers in 1770, Prague's
houses were distinguished
by signs. Nerudova's houses
have a splendid selection of
heraldic beasts and emblems.
As you make your way up
Nerudova's steep slope, look
out in particular for the Red
Eagle (No. 6), the Three
Fiddles (No. 12), the Golden
Horseshoe (No. 34), the
Green Lobster (No. 43) and
the White Swan (No. 49) as
well as the Old Pharmacy
museum (No. 32).

There are also a number
of grand Baroque buildings
in the street, including the
Thun-Hohenstein Palace (No.
20, now the Italian embassy)
and the Morzin Palace (No. 5,
the Rumanian embassy).
The latter has a façade with
two massive statues of moors
(a pun on the name Morzin)
supporting the semicircular
balcony on the first floor.
Another impressive façade is
that of the Church of Our
Lady of Unceasing Succour,
the church of the Theatines,
an order founded during the
Counter-Reformation.

Italian Street, heart of the former
colony of Italian craftsmen

Italian Street 7
VLAŠSKÁ ULICE

Map 1 C4 Ⓜ *Malostranská.*
🚋 *12, 20, 22, 23.*

Italian immigrants started to
settle here in the 16th
century. Many were artists or
craftsmen employed to rebuild
and redecorate the Castle. If
you approach the street from
Petřín, on the left you will see
the former Italian Hospital, a
Baroque building with an
arcaded courtyard. Today it
maintains its traditional
allegiance as the cultural
section of the Italian embassy.

The grandest building in the
street is the former Lobkowicz
Palace, now the German
embassy. One of the finest
Baroque palaces in Prague, it
has a large oval hall on the
ground floor leading out onto
a magnificent garden. Look
out too for the pretty stucco
sign on the house called At
the Three Red Roses, dating
from the early 18th century.

Vrtba Garden 8
VRTBOVSKÁ ZAHRADA

Karmelitská 25. **Map** 2 D4. **Tel** 25
75 31 480. Ⓜ *Malostranská.* 🚋 *12,
20, 22, 23.* **Open** *Apr–Oct: 10am–6pm
daily.* 📷 ♿ www.vrtbovska.cz

Behind Vrtba Palace lies a
beautiful Baroque garden
with balustraded terraces.
From the highest part of the
garden there are magnificent
views of Prague Castle and
the Little Quarter. The Vrtba
Garden was designed by
František Maximilián Kaňka in
about 1720. The statues of
Classical gods and stone vases
are the work of Matthias Braun
and the paintings in the *sala
terrena* (garden pavilion) in
the lower part of the garden
are by Václav Vavřinec Reiner.

View of the Little Quarter from the
terrace of the Vrtba Garden

Church of Our Lady Victorious 9
KOSTEL PANNY MARIE VÍTĚZNÉ

Karmelitská. **Map** 2 E4. **Tel** 25 75 33
646. 🚋 *12, 20, 22, 23.* **Open** *9am–
7pm daily.* ✝ *9am, 6pm Mon–Fri,
9am, 6pm Sat, 10am, noon (English),
5pm (French), 6pm (Italian), 7pm Sun.*
www.pragjesu.info

The first Baroque building in
Prague was the Church of the
Holy Trinity, built for the
German Lutherans by Giovanni
Maria Filippi. It was finished in
1613 but after the Battle of the
White Mountain *(see p31)* the
Catholic authorities gave the
church to the Carmelites, who
rebuilt it and renamed it in

Sign of Jan Neruda's house, At the Two Suns, 47 Nerudova Street honour of the victory. The fabric has survived including the portal. Enshrined on a marble altar in the right aisle is a glass case containing the Holy Infant of Prague (better-known by its Italian name – il Bambino di Praga). This wax effigy has a record of miracle cures and is one of the most revered images in the Catholic world. It was brought from Spain and presented to the Carmelites in 1628 by Polyxena of Lobkowicz. A small museum adjacent to the church traces its history.

Maltese Square ⑩
MALTÉZSKÉ NÁMĚSTÍ

Map 2 E4. 🚋 12, 20, 22, 23.

The square takes its name from the Priory of the Knights of Malta, which used to occupy this part of the Little Quarter. At the northern end stands a group of sculptures featuring St John the Baptist by Ferdinand Brokof – part of a fountain erected in 1715 to mark the end of a plague epidemic.

Most of the buildings were originally Renaissance houses belonging to prosperous townspeople, but in the 17th and 18th centuries the Little Quarter was taken over by the Catholic nobility and many were converted to flamboyant Baroque palaces. The largest, Nostitz Palace, stands on the southern side. It was built in the mid-17th century, then in about 1720 a balustrade was added with Classical vases and statues of emperors. The palace now houses the Ministry of Culture and in summer, concerts are held here. The Japanese embassy is housed in the Turba Palace (1767), an attractive pink Rococo building designed by Joseph Jäger.

Čertovka (the Devil's Stream) with Kampa Island on the right

Ferdinand Brokof's statue of John the Baptist in Maltese Square

Kampa Island ⑪
KAMPA

Map 2 F4. 🚋 6, 9, 12, 20, 22, 23.

Kampa, an island formed by a branch of the Vltava known as the Devil's Stream (Čertovka), is a delightfully peaceful corner of the Little Quarter. The stream got its name in the 19th century, allegedly after the diabolical temper of a lady who owned a house nearby in Maltese Square. For centuries the stream was used as a millrace and from Kampa you can see the remains of three old mills. Beyond the Grand Prior's Mill the stream disappears under a small bridge below the piers of Charles Bridge. From here it flows between rows of houses. Predictably, the area has become known as "the Venice of Prague", but instead of gondolas you will see canoes.

For most of the Middle Ages there were only gardens on Kampa, though the island was also used for washing clothes and bleaching linen. In the 17th century the island became well-known for its pottery markets. There are some enchanting houses from this period around Na Kampě Square. Most of the land from here to the southern tip of the island is a park, created from several old palace gardens.

The island all but vanished beneath the Vltava during the floods of 2002, which caused widespread devastation to homes, businesses and historic buildings, many of which are still being rebuilt and restored.

Grand Priory Square ⑫
VELKOPŘEVORSKÉ NÁMĚSTÍ

Map 2 F4. Ⓜ Malostranská. 🚋 12, 20, 22, 23.

On the northern side of this small leafy square stands the former seat of the Grand Prior of the Knights of Malta. In its present form the palace dates from the 1720s. The doorways, windows and decorative vases were made at the workshop of Matthias Braun. On the opposite side of the square is the Buquoy Palace, now the French embassy, a delightful Baroque building roughly contemporary with the Grand Prior's Palace.

The only incongruous features are a painting of John Lennon and graffiti exhorting the world to "give peace a chance". These have decorated the wall of the Grand Prior's garden since Lennon's death.

Street-by-Street: Little Quarter Riverside

On either side of Bridge Street lies a delightful half-hidden world of gently decaying squares, picturesque palaces, churches and gardens. When you have run the gauntlet of the trinket-sellers on Charles Bridge, escape to Kampa Island to enjoy a stroll in its informal park, the views across the Vltava weir to the Old Town and the flocks of swans gliding along the river.

The Church of St Joseph dates from the late 17th century. The painting of *The Holy Family* (1702) on the gilded high altar is by the leading Baroque artist Petr Brandl.

The House at the Golden Unicorn in Lázeňská Street has a plaque commemorating the fact that Beethoven stayed here in 1796.

Bridge Street
A major thoroughfare for 750 years, the narrow street leads to Little Quarter Square **16**

To Little Quarter Square

Grand Priory Square
The Grand Prior's Palace is the former seat of the Knights of Malta and dates from the 1720s. Its street wall features colourful murals and graffitti **12**

MOSTECKÁ

LÁZEŇSKÁ

Church of Our Lady beneath the Chain
Two massive towers survive from when this was a fortified priory **13**

Museum of Music
This museum houses a vast collection of beautifully hand-crafted musical instruments **27**

KARMELITSKÁ

NEBOVIDSKÁ

Church of Our Lady Victorious
This Baroque church houses the famous effigy, the Holy Infant of Prague **9**

Maltese Square
Grand palaces surround the oddly-shaped square. This coat of arms decorates the 17th-century Nostitz Palace, a popular venue for concerts **10**

0 metres	100
0 yards	100

KEY

- - - Suggested route

Vojan Park
Quiet shady paths have been laid out under the apple trees of this former monastery garden **17**

At the Three Ostriches
A restaurant and hotel have kept the sign of a seller of ostrich plumes **15**

LOCATOR MAP
See Street Finder, map 2

★ **Charles Bridge**
The approach to this magnificent 14th-century bridge, with its files of Baroque statues, passes under an arch below a Gothic tower **14**

U LUŽICKÉHO SEMINÁŘE

Čertovka (the Devil's Stream)

NA KAMPĚ

The Grand Priory Mill has had its wheel meticulously restored, though it now turns very slowly in the sluggish water of the Čertovka, the former millrace.

Lichtenstein Palace

★ **Kampa Island**
This 19th-century painting by Soběslav Pinkas shows boys playing on Kampa. The island's park is still a popular place for children **11**

STAR SIGHTS

★ Charles Bridge

★ Kampa Island

Church of Our Lady beneath the Chain ⓭

KOSTEL PANNY MARIE POD ŘETĚZEM

Lázeňská. **Map** 2 E4. **Tel** 25 75 30 876. ᴹ Malostranská. 🚋 12, 20, 22, 23. **Open** for concerts and services. 🕘 9:30am Sat & Sun.

This church, the oldest in the Little Quarter, was founded in the 12th century. King Vladislav II presented it to the Knights of St John, the order which later became known as the Knights of Malta. It stood in the centre of the Knights' heavily fortified monastery that guarded the approach to the old Judith Bridge. The church's name refers to the chain used in the Middle Ages to close the monastery gatehouse.

A Gothic presbytery was added in the 13th century, but in the following century the original Romanesque church was demolished. A new portico was built with a pair of massive square towers, but work was then abandoned and the old nave became a courtyard between the towers and the church. This was given a Baroque facelift in 1640 by Carlo Lurago. The painting by Karel Škréta on the high altar shows the Virgin Mary and John the Baptist coming to the aid of the Knights of Malta in the famous naval victory over the Turks at Lepanto in 1571.

Charles Bridge ⓮

KARLŮV MOST

See pp136–9.

Fresco that gave At the Three Ostriches its name

View along Bridge Street through the tower on Charles Bridge

At the Three Ostriches ⓯

U TŘÍ PŠTROŮ

Dražického náměstí 12. **Map** 2 F3. **Tel** 25 75 32 410. ᴹ Malostranská. 🚋 12, 20, 22, 23. See **Where to Stay** pp182–9, **Restaurants** pp198–209. **www**.utripstrosu.cz

Many of Prague's colourful house signs indicated the trade carried on in the premises. In 1597 Jan Fux, an ostrich-feather merchant, bought this house by Charles Bridge. At the time ostrich plumes were very fashionable as decoration for hats among courtiers and officers at Prague Castle. Fux even supplied feathers to foreign armies. So successful was his business, that in 1606 he had the house rebuilt and decorated with a large fresco of ostriches. The building is now an expensive hotel and restaurant.

Bridge Street ⓰

MOSTECKÁ ULICE

Map 2 E3. ᴹ Malostranská. 🚋 12, 20, 22, 23.

Since the Middle Ages this street has linked Charles Bridge with the Little Quarter Square. Crossing the bridge from the Old Town you can see the doorway of the old customs house built in 1591 in front of the Judith Tower. On the first floor of the tower there is a 12th-century relief of a king and a kneeling man.

Throughout the 13th and 14th centuries the area to the north of the street was the Court of the Bishop of Prague. This was destroyed during the Hussite Wars (see pp26–7), but one of its Gothic towers is preserved in the courtyard of the house called At the Three Golden Bells. It can be seen from the higher of the two bridge towers. The street is lined with a mixture of Renaissance and Baroque houses. As you walk up to Little Quarter Square, look out for the house called At the Black Eagle on the left. It has rich sculptural decoration and a splendid Baroque wrought-iron grille. Kaunic Palace, also on the left, was built in the 1770s. Its Rococo façade has striking stucco decoration and sculptures by Ignaz Platzer.

Vojan Park
VOJANOVY SADY

U lužického semináře. **Map** 2 F3.
🚇 Malostranská. 🚊 12, 18, 20,
22, 23. **Open** 8am–5pm daily (to
7pm in summer).

A tranquil spot hidden behind
high white walls, the park
dates back to the 17th century,
when it was the garden of the
Convent of Barefooted Carmelites. Two chapels erected
by the Order have survived
among the park's lawns and
fruit trees. One is the Chapel
of Elijah, who, because of his
Old Testament associations
with Mount Carmel, is regarded
as the founder of the Order.
His chapel takes the form of a
stalagmite and stalactite cave.
The other chapel, dedicated
to St Theresa, was built in the
18th century as an expression
of gratitude for the convent's
preservation during the Prussian siege of Prague in 1757.

Kampa Museum of Modern Art ⓲
MUZEUM KAMPA

U Sovových mlýnů2. **Map** 2 F4.
Tel 25 72 86 147. 🚊 6, 9, 22, 23.
Open 10am–6pm daily. 🚻 📷 ♿
www.museumkampa.cz

Housed in the historic Sova
mill in the heart of the city, the
Kampa Museum of Modern Art
boasts an impressive collection
of Central European art. The
museum was founded by the
Czech-American couple Jan
and Meda Mládek to house
their private collection of
drawings, paintings and
sculptures. Among the artists
on display are abstract painter
Frantisek Kupka and Czech
cubist sculptor Otto Gutfreund.

Ledebour Garden ⓳
LEDEBURSKÁ ZAHRADA

Valdštejnská. **Map** 2 F2. **Tel** 25 70 10
401. 🚇 Malostranská. 🚊 12, 18, 20,
22, 23. **Open** Apr & Oct: 10am–6pm;
May & Sep: 9am–7pm; Jun& Jul:
9am–9pm; Aug: 9am–8pm daily. ♿
📷 www.palacovezahrady.cz

The steep southern slope
below Prague Castle was
covered with vineyards and
gardens during the Middle
Ages. But in the 16th century,
when nobles started building
palaces here, they laid out
larger formal terraced gardens
based on Italian Renaissance
models. Most of these gardens
were rebuilt during the 18th
century and decorated with
Baroque garden statuary and
fountains. Three of the
gardens – those belonging to
the former Ledebour, Černín
and Pálffy Palaces – have
been linked together. They
have recently undergone a
much-needed programme of
restoration work, and they
again are delighting visitors
with their elegant landscaping
and attractive plants.

From their terraces, the gardens boast magnificent views
of Prague. The Ledebour Garden, designed in the early
18th century, has a fine *sala
terrena* (garden pavilion) by
Giovanni Battista Alliprandi.
The Pálffy Garden was laid
out in the mid-18th century
with terraces (the second still
has its original sundial) and
loggias. The most beautiful of
the three and architecturally the
richest is the Kolowrat-Černín
Garden, created in 1784 by
Ignaz Palliardi. The highest
terrace has a *sala terrena*
decorated with statues and
Classical urns. Below this there
is a wonderful assortment of
staircases, archways and balu-
strades, and the remains of
Classical statuary and fountains.

**18th-century statue of Hercules
located in the Ledebour Garden**

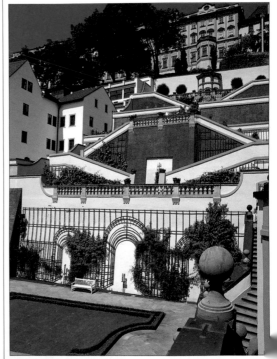

The foot of the Ledebour Garden

Charles Bridge (Little Quarter Side) 🄴

KARLŮV MOST

Prague's most familiar monument, connects the Old
Town with the Little Quarter. Although it is now
pedestrianized, at one time it could take four carriages
abreast. Today, due to wear and tear, many of the
statues on the bridge are copies; the originals are kept
in the Lapidarium of the National Museum *(see p162)*
and at Vyšehrad *(see p181)*. The Gothic Old Town
Bridge Tower *(see p139)*
is one of the finest
buildings of its kind
in existence.

★ **View from Little Quarter
Bridge Tower**
*The tall pinnacled wedge tower,
gives a superb view of the city
of 100 spires. The shorter tower
is the remains of Judith Bridge.*

**Little Quarter
Bridge Tower**

**Tower
entrance**

St Adalbert, 1709
*Adalbert, Bishop of Prague, founded
the Church of St Lawrence (see p140)
on Petřín Hill in 991. He is known
to the Czechs as Vojtěch.*

**St Wenceslas,
1858**

**St Philip
Benizi, 171**

**Judith Bridge
Tower, 1158**

**Steps to
Saská Street**

**Christ between
St Cosmas and
St Damian, 1709**

**St John de Matha, St Felix de Valois
and the Blessed Ivan, 1714**
*These saints, sculpted by Ferdinand
Brokof, founded the Trinitarian Order
of mendicants to collect money to
buy the freedom of Christians
enslaved by the infidels (represented
at the foot of the sculpture).*

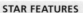

STAR FEATURES

★ Little Quarter Bridge
   Tower and View

★ St John Nepomuk

★ St Luitgard

St Vitus, 1714
*This engraving of the
statue shows the 3rd-
century martyr with the
lions which were supposed
to maul him, but licked
him instead. St Vitus is the
patron saint of dancers
and often invoked against
convulsive disorders.*

★ **St Luitgard, 1710**
This statue, regarded as the most artistically remarkable on the bridge, was sculpted by Matthias Braun when he was only 26. It is based on the blind Cistercian nun's celebrated vision when Christ appeared and she kissed his wounds.

VISITORS' CHECKLIST

Map 2 F4. 🚋 *12, 22, 23 to Malostranské náměstí, then walk down Mostecká.* **Little Quarter Bridge Tower open** *Apr-Oct 10am–6pm daily* 📷 🅾

★ **St John Nepomuk, 1683**
Reliefs on the bridge depict the martyrdom of St John Nepomuk. Here the saint is polished bright from people touching it for good luck.

St Cajetan, 1709

St Augustine, 1708

St Jude Thaddaeus, 1708

St Anthony of Padua, 1707

Steps to Kampa Island

St Nicholas Tolentino, 1708

St Francis of Assisi, with two angels, 1855

St Ludmilla, 1710

St Vincent Ferrer and St Procopius, 1712
This detail shows a rabbi saddened by St Vincent's success in converting many Jews to Christianity. St Procopius is one of Bohemia's patron saints.

ST JOHN NEPOMUK

The cult of St John Nepomuk, canonized in 1729, was promoted by the Jesuits to rival the revered Jan Hus *(see p27)*. Jan Nepomucký, vicar-general of the Archdiocese of Prague, was arrested in 1393 by Wenceslas IV along with the archbishop and others who had displeased the king over the election of an abbot. The archbishop escaped, but John died under torture. The body was bound and thrown off Charles Bridge. Statues modelled on the one placed here in 1683 can be seen throughout central Europe, especially on bridges.

Charles Bridge (Old Town Side) ⑭

KARLŮV MOST

Until 1741, Charles Bridge was the only crossing over the Vltava. It is 520 m (1,706 ft) long and is built of sandstone blocks, rumoured to be strengthened by mixing mortar with eggs. The bridge was commissioned by Charles IV in 1357 to replace the Judith Bridge and built by Peter Parler. The bridge's original decoration was a simple cross. The first statue – of St John Nepomuk – was added in 1683, inspired by Bernini's sculptures on Rome's Ponte Sant'Angelo.

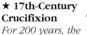

★ 17th-Century Crucifixion

For 200 years, the wooden crucifix stood alone on the bridge. The gilded Christ dates from 1629 and the Hebrew words "Holy, Holy, Holy Lord", were paid for by a Jew as punishment for blasphemy.

St Francis Xavier, 1711

The Jesuit missionary is supported by three Moorish and two Oriental converts. The sculptor Brokof is seated on the saint's left.

St Norbert, St Wenceslas and St Sigismund, 1853

St Francis Borgia, 1710

St John the Baptist, 1857

St Christopher, 1857

St Cyril and St Methodius, 1938

St Ann, 1707

St Joseph, 1854

Thirty Years' War

In the last hours of this war, the Old Town was saved from the Swedish army. The truce was signed in the middle of the bridge in 1648.

STAR FEATURES

★ Old Town Bridge Tower

★ 17th-Century Crucifixion

TIMELINE

1357 Charles IV commissions new bridge

1342 Judith Bridge destroyed by floods

1621 Heads of ten Protestant nobles exhibited on the Old Town Bridge Tower

1648 Swedes damage part of the bridge and Old Town Bridge Tower

1890 flood damage

1100	1300	1500	1700	1900

1158 Europe's second medieval stone bridge, Judith Bridge, is built

1393 St John Nepomuk thrown off Bridge on the orders of Wenceslas IV

Sculptor Matthias Braun (1684–1738)

1890 Three arches destroyed by flood

1713 Bridge decorated with 21 statues by Braun, Brokof and others

1938 Karel Dvořák's sculpture of St Cyril and St Methodius

The Madonna, St Dominic and St Thomas, 1708
The Dominicans, (known in a Latin pun as Domini canes, the dogs of God), are shown with the Madonna and their emblem, a dog.

VISITORS' CHECKLIST

Map 3 A4. 🚊 *17, 18 to Křižovnické náměstí.* **Old Town Bridge Tower open** *10am–5pm daily (Mar: to 6pm; Apr & Oct–Nov: to 7pm; May–Sep: to 10pm).* ♿ 📷

Madonna and St Bernard, 1709
Cherubs and symbols of the Passion, including the dice, the cock and the centurion's gauntlet, form part of the statue.

Old Town Bridge Tower

Tower entrance

Pietà, 1859

St Barbara, St Margaret and St Elizabeth, 1707

★ OLD TOWN BRIDGE TOWER

This magnificent Gothic tower, designed by Peter Parler, was built at the end of the 14th century. A fitting ornament to the new Charles Bridge, it was also an integral part of the Old Town's fortifications.

Bridge Tower sculptures by Peter Parler include St Vitus, the bridge's patron saint, Charles IV (left) and Wenceslas IV.

Pinnacled wedge spire

Roof viewing point

The viewing gallery is a rib-vaulted room, on the tower's first floor. It provides a wonderful view of Prague Castle and the Little Quarter.

Observation Tower ⑳

PETŘÍNSKÁ ROZHLEDNA

Petřín. **Map** 1 C4. 🚋 6, 9, 12, 20, 22, 23, then take funicular railway. 🚌 143, 149, 176, 217. **Open** May–Aug: 10am–10pm daily; Apr & Sep: 10am–7pm daily; Oct: 10am–6pm daily; Jan–Mar & Nov–Dec: 10am–5pm Sat & Sun. 🖼 🖥 🖷 www.pis.cz

The most conspicuous landmark in Petřín Park is an imitation Eiffel Tower, built for the Jubilee Exhibition of 1891. The octagonal tower is only 60 m (200 ft), a quarter the height of the Eiffel Tower. A spiral staircase of 299 steps leads up to the viewing platform. A lift is also available. On a clear day, you can see as far as Bohemia's highest peak, Sněžka in the Krkonoše (Giant) Mountains, 150 km (100 miles) to the northeast.

Mirror Maze ㉑

ZRCADLOVÉ BLUDIŠTĚ

Petřín. **Map** 1 C4. **Tel** 25 73 15 212. 🚋 6, 9, 12, 20, 22, 23, then take funicular railway. 🚌 143, 149, 176, 217. **Open** May–Aug: 10am–10pm daily; Apr & Sep: 10am–7pm daily; Oct: 10am–6pm daily; Jan–Mar & Nov–Dec:10am–5pm Sat & Sun. 🖼 🚫 ♿

Like the Observation Tower, the maze, which has walls lined with distorting mirrors, is a relic of the Exhibition of 1891. It is in a wooden pavilion in the shape of the old Špička Gate, part of the Gothic fortifications of Vyšehrad

The 100-year-old Observation Tower overlooking the city

(see pp180–81). This amusement house moved to Petřín at the end of the exhibition.

When you have navigated your way through the maze and laughed at your reflection, your reward is to view the vivid diorama of *The Defence of Prague against the Swedes*, which took place on Charles Bridge *(see p138)* in 1648.

Church of St Lawrence ㉒

KOSTEL SV. VAVŘINCE

Petřín. **Map** 1 C5. 🚋 6, 9, 12, 20, 22, 23, then take funicular railway. 🚌 143, 149, 176, 217. **Closed** to the public.

According to legend, the church was founded in the 10th century by the pious Prince Boleslav II and St Adalbert on the site of a pagan shrine. The ceiling of the sacristy is decorated with a painting illustrating this legend. The painting dates from the 18th century when the Romanesque church was swallowed up by a large new Baroque structure, featuring a cupola flanked by two onion-domed towers. The small Calvary Chapel, which dates from 1735, is situated to the left of the church entrance.

Observatory ㉓

HVĚZDÁRNA

Petřín 205. **Map** 2 D5. **Tel** 25 73 20 540. 🚋 6, 9, 12, 20, 22, 23, then funicular. **Open** Tue–Sun year-round; opening hours vary monthly, so phone ahead. 🖼 🚫 www.observatory.cz

Since 1930, Prague's amateur astronomers have been able to enjoy the facilities of this observatory on Petřín Hill. You can use its telescopes to view anything from the craters of the moon to unfamiliar distant galaxies. There is an exhibition of old astronomical instruments and special events for children are held on Saturdays and Sundays.

Hunger Wall ㉔

HLADOVÁ ZEĎ

Újezd, Petřín, Strahovská. **Map** 2 D5. 🚋 6, 9, 12, 20, 22, 23, then take funicular railway. 🚌 143, 149, 176, 217.

The fortifications built around the southern edge of the Little Quarter on the orders of Charles IV in 1360–62 have been known for centuries as the Hunger Wall. Nearly 1,200 m (1,300 yards) of the wall have survived, complete with crenellated battlements and a platform for marksmen on its inner side. It runs from Újezd across Petřín Park to Strahov. The story behind the name is that Charles commissioned its construction with the aim of giving employment to the poor during a period of famine. It is true that a great famine did break out in Bohemia in the 1360s and the two events, the famine and the building of the wall, became permanently linked in the people's memory.

Diorama of *The Defence of Prague against the Swedes* in the Mirror Maze

Nebozízek, the station halfway up Petřín's funicular railway

Petřín Park 25
PETŘÍNSKÉ SADY

Map 2 D5. 🚋 6, 9, 12, 20, 22, 23,
then take funicular railway. See **Three
Guided Walks** *pp176–7.*

To the west of the Little
Quarter, Petřín hill
rises above the city to
a height of 318 m
(960 ft). The name derives
either from the Slavonic
god Perun, to whom
sacrifices were made on
the hill or from the Latin
name Mons Petrinus,
meaning "rocky hill".
A forest used to stretch
from here as far as the
White Mountain *(see
p31)*. In the 12th
century the southern
side of the hill was
planted with vineyards, but
by the 18th century most of
these had been transformed
into gardens and orchards.
   Today a path winds up the
slopes of Petřín, offering fine
views of Prague. In the park
is the *Monument to the Victims
of Communism* (2002) by the
sculptor Olbram Zoubek and
a monument to Romantic poet
Karel Hynek Mácha.

Funicular Railway 26
LANOVÁ DRÁHA

Újezd. **Map** 2 D5. 🚋 6, 9, 12, 20,
22, 23. **In operation** *summer: 9am–
11:30pm daily; winter: 9am–
11:20pm daily.* 🖥 📷 ♿

Built to carry visitors to the
1891 Jubilee Exhibition up to
the Observation Tower at the
top of Petřín hill, the

**Statue of Karel
Hynek Mácha in
Petřín Park**

funicular was originally
powered by water. In this
form, it remained in operation
until 1914, then between the
wars was converted to
electricity. In 1965 it had
to be shut down because
part of the hillside
collapsed – coal had
been mined here during
the 19th century. Shoring
up the slope and
rebuilding the railway
took 20 years, but since
its reopening in 1985 it
has proved a reliable
way of getting up Petřín
Hill. At the halfway
station, Nebozízek,
there is a restaurant
(see p205) with fine
views of the Castle
and the city.

Museum of Music 27
ČESKÉ MUZEUM HUDBY

Karmelitská 2, Praha 1, Malá Strana.
Map 2 E4. **Tel** 25 73 27 285. Ⓜ
Malostranská. 🚋 12, 20, 22, 23.
Open *10am–6pm Mon, Wed–Sun.*
🖥 ♿ www.nm.cz

Housed in the former 17th
century Baroque Church of St
Magdalene, the Museum of
Music seeks to present musical
instruments not only as fine
specimens of craftsmanship
and artistry but also as media-
tors between man and music.
   The museum is run by the
National Museum *(see p147)*
and boasts a magnificent
atrium. Exhibits include a look
at the diversity of popular 20th
century music as preserved in
film, television, photographs
and sound recordings. Also
examined is the production of
handcrafted instruments, the

history of musical notation
and the social occasions
linked to certain instruments.
Earphones offer high-quality
sound reproduction of original recordings made on the
instruments displayed. The
museum's collections can be
accessed via the study room
and there is a listening studio
for the library of recordings.

Michna Palace 28
MICHNŮV PALÁC

Újezd 40. **Map** 2 E4. **Tel** 25 73 11
831. 🚋 12, 20, 22, 23.

In about 1580 Ottavio Aostalli
built a summer palace here
for the Kinský family on the
site of an old Dominican
convent. In 1623 the
building was bought by Pavel
Michna of Vacínov, a supply
officer in the Imperial Army,
who had grown rich after the
Battle of the White Mountain.
He commissioned a new
Baroque building that he
hoped would rival the palace
of his late commander,
Wallenstein *(see p126)*.
   In 1767 the Michna Palace
was sold to the army and
over the years it became a
crumbling ruin. After 1918 it
was bought by Sokol (a
physical culture association)
and converted into a gym and
sports centre with a training
ground in the old palace
garden. The restored palace
was renamed Tyrš House in
honour of Sokol's founder.

**Restored Baroque façade of the
Michna Palace (Tyrš House)**

NEW TOWN
NOVE MĚSTO

The New Town, founded in 1348 by Charles IV, was carefully planned and laid out around three large central market-places: the Hay Market (Senovážné Square), the Cattle Market (Charles Square) and the Horse Market (Wenceslas Square). Twice as large as

Art Nouveau decoration on No. 12 Wenceslas Square

the Old Town, the area was mainly inhabited by tradesmen and craftsmen such as blacksmiths, wheelwrights and brewers. During the late 19th century, much of the New Town was demolished and completely redeveloped, giving it the appearance it has today.

SIGHTS AT A GLANCE

Churches and Monasteries
Church of Our Lady of the Snows **2**
Church of St Ignatius **8**
Church of St Cyril and St Methodius **11**
Church of St John on the Rock **13**
Slavonic Monastery Emauzy **14**
Church of St Catherine **16**
Church of St Stephen **19**
Church of St Ursula **22**

Historic Buildings
Hotel Europa **4**
Jesuit College **9**
Faust House **12**
New Town Hall **20**

Theatres and Opera Houses
State Opera **6**
National Theatre pp156–7 **23**

Historic Squares
Wenceslas Square **1**
Charles Square **10**

Museums and Galleries
National Museum **5**
Mucha Museum **7**
Dvořák Museum **18**

Historic Restaurants and Beer Halls
Chalice Restaurant **17**
U Fleků **21**

Parks and Gardens
Franciscan Garden **3**
Botanical Gardens **15**

GETTING THERE
The entire area is well served by the metro with two main stations, Můstek and Muzeum in Wenceslas Square, and others at Karlovo náměstí and Národní třída. Tram routes from most parts of the city pass through Karlovo náměstí.

KEY

■	Street-by-Street map *See pp144–5*
■	Street-by-Street map *See pp150–51*
M	Metro station
⬛	Tram stop
i	Tourist information
⛴	River boat boarding point

◁ **Art Nouveau sculptures on the Hlahol Choir Building (1905) on Masarykovo nábřeží**

Street-by-Street: Wenceslas Square

Hotels and restaurants occupy many of the buildings around Wenceslas Square, though it remains an important commercial centre – the square began life as a medieval horse market. As you walk along, look up at the buildings, most of which date from the turn of last century, when the square was redeveloped. There are fine examples of the decorative styles used by Czech architects of the period. Many blocks have dark covered arcades leading to shops, clubs, theatres and cinemas.

Statue of St Lawrence at U Pinkasů

U Pinkasů became one of Prague's most popular beer halls when it started serving Pilsner Urquell (*see pp200–1*) in 1843.

Koruna Palace (1914) is an ornate block of shops and offices. Its corner turret is topped with a crown (*koruna*).

To Powder Gate

NA PŘÍKOPĚ

Můstek

Church of Our Lady of the Snows
The towering Gothic building is only part of a vast church planned during the 14th century ②

Můstek

Můstek

VODIČKOVA

Jungmann Square is named after Josef Jungmann (1773–1847), an influential scholar of language and lexicographer, and there is a statue of him in the middle. The Adria Palace (1925) used to be the Laterna Magika Theatre (*see p220*), which was where Václav Havel's Civic Forum worked in the early days of the 1989 Velvet Revolution.

Franciscan Garden
An old monastery garden has been laid out as a small park with this fountain, rose-beds, trellises and a children's playground ③

Lucerna Palace

Wiehl House, named after its architect Antonín Wiehl, was completed in 1896. The five-storey building is in striking Neo-Renaissance style, with a loggia and colourful *sgraffito*. Mikuláš Aleš designed some of the Art Nouveau figures.

STAR SIGHTS

★ Wenceslas Square

★ Hotel Europa

★ National Museum

★ **Wenceslas Square**
*The dominant features of
the square are the bronze,
equestrian statue of St
Wenceslas (1912) and the
National Museum behind
it. St Wenceslas, a former
prince who was murdered
by his brother Boleslav, is the
patron saint of Bohemia* ❶

LOCATOR MAP
See Street Finder, maps 3, 4 & 6

**The Assicurazioni Generali
Building** was where Franz
Kafka *(see p68)* worked
as an insurance clerk for
10 months in 1906–7.

**The Monument to the
Victims of Communism**
is on the spot where Jan
Palach staged his protest.
Since the Velvet Revolution
in 1989 an unofficial shrine
has been maintained here.

★ **Hotel Europa**
*Both the façade and the
interior of the hotel
(1906) preserve most
of their original
Art Nouveau
features* ❹

Café
Tramvaj 11

St Wenceslas
Monument

State Opera
*Meticulously refurbished in the
1980s, the interior retains the
luxurious red plush, crystal
chandeliers and gilded
stucco of the original
late-19th-century
theatre* ❻

Muzeum

Fénix
Palace

Muzeum

Memorial to
Jan Palach, who
died in protest
against
communism.

| 0 metres | 100 |
| 0 yards | 100 |

★ **National Museum**
*The grand building with its
monumental staircase was
completed in 1890 as a
symbol of national prestige* ❺

KEY

– – – Suggested route

Wenceslas Monument in Wenceslas Square

Wenceslas Square ❶

VÁCLAVSKÉ NÁMĚSTÍ

Map 3 C5. Ⓜ *Můstek, Muzeum.*
🚋 *3, 9, 14, 24.*

The square has witnessed
many key events in recent
Czech history. It was here that
the student Jan Palach burnt
himself to death in 1969, and
in November 1989 a protest
rally in the square against
police brutality led to the
Velvet Revolution and the
overthrow of Communism.
Wenceslas "Square" is
something of a misnomer,
for it is some 750 m (825 yd)
long and only 60 m (65 yd)
wide. Originally a horse
market, today it is lined with
hotels, restaurants, clubs and
shops, reflecting the seamier
side of global consumerism.
The huge equestrian statue
of St Wenceslas that looks
the length of the square
from in front of the National
Museum was erected in
1912. Cast in bronze, it is the
work of Josef Myslbek, the
leading Czech sculptor of
the late 19th century. At the
foot of the pedestal there
are several other statues of
Czech patron saints. A
memorial near the statue
commemorates the victims
of the former regime.

Church of Our Lady of the Snows ❷

KOSTEL PANNY MARIE SNĚŽNÉ

Jungmannovo náměstí 18. **Map** 3
C5. **Tel** 22 44 90 350. Ⓜ *Můstek.*
Open 9am–7pm daily. **Closed** last
Sat of month. ✝ 7am, 8am, 6pm
Mon–Fri, 9am, 10:15am, 11:30am,
6pm Sun. 📷 ♿ www.pms.ofm.cz

Charles IV founded this church
to mark his coronation in
1347. The name refers to a
4th-century miracle in
Rome, when the
Virgin Mary appeared
to the pope in a dream
telling him to build a
church to her on the
spot where snow fell
in August. Charles's
church was to have
been over 100 m (330
ft) long, but was
never completed. The
towering building we
see today was just
the presbytery of the projected
church. Over 33 m (110 ft)
high, it was finished in 1397,
and was originally part of a
Carmelite monastery. On the
northern side there is a gateway with a 14th-century pediment that marked the entrance
to the monastery graveyard.
In the early 15th century a
steeple was added, but further
building was halted by the
Hussite Wars *(see pp26–7)*. The
Hussite firebrand Jan Želivský
preached at the church and
was buried here after his execution in 1422. The church
suffered considerable damage
in the wars and in 1434 the
steeple was destroyed. For a
long time the church was left
to decay. In 1603 Franciscans

restored the building. The
intricate net vaulting of the
ceiling dates from this period,
the original roof having
collapsed. Most of the interior
decoration, apart from the
1450s pewter font, is
Baroque. The monumental
three-tiered altar is crowded
with statues of saints, and is
crowned with a crucifix.

Franciscan Garden ❸

FRANTIŠKÁNSKÁ ZAHRADA

Jungmannovo náměstí 18. **Map** 3 C5.
Ⓜ *Můstek.* **Open** Apr–Sep: 7am–
10pm (to 8pm Oct, 7pm Nov–Mar). ♿

Originally the physic garden
of a Franciscan monastery, the
area was opened to the
public in 1950 as a tranquil
oasis close to Wenceslas
Square. By the entrance is a
Gothic portal leading down to
a cellar restaurant – U
františkánů (At the Franciscans). In the 1980s several of
the beds were replanted with
herbs, cultivated by the
Franciscans in the 17th century.

Hotel Europa ❹

HOTEL EVROPA

Václavské náměstí 29. **Map** 4 D5.
Tel 22 42 28 117. Ⓜ *Můstek.*
🚋 3, 9, 14, 24. 🍽 ♿ See **Where
to Stay** pp184–95, **Restaurants,
Pubs and Cafés** pp202–11.
www.evropahotel.cz

Though a trifle shabby in
places, the Europa Hotel is
a wonderfully preserved
reminder of the golden age

Art Nouveau decoration on façade of the Hotel Europa

Façade of the State Opera, formerly the New German Theatre

of hotels. It was built in highly decorated Art Nouveau style between 1903 and 1906. Not only has its splendid façade crowned with gilded nymphs survived, but many of the interiors on the ground floor have remained virtually intact, including all the original bars, large mirrors, panelling and light fittings.

National Museum ❺
NÁRODNÍ MUZEUM

Václavské náměstí 68. **Map** 6 E1. *Tel 22 44 97 111.* Muzeum. *Open Oct–Apr: 9am–5pm daily; May–Sep: 10am–6pm (but closed first Tue of month).* for a fee. www.nm.cz

The vast Neo-Renaissance building at one end of Wenceslas Square houses the National Museum. Designed by Josef Schulz as a triumphal affirmation of the Czech national revival, the museum was completed in 1890. The entrance is reached by a ramp decorated with allegorical statues. Seated by the door are History and Natural History.

Inside, the rich marbled decoration is impressive, but overwhelms the collections devoted mainly to mineralogy, archaeology, anthropology, numismatics and natural history. The museum also has a Pantheon containing busts and statues of Czech scholars, writers and artists. It is deco-rated with many paintings by František Ženíšek, Václav Brožík and Vojtěch Hy nais.

State Opera ❻
STÁTNÍ OPERA

Wilsonova 4. **Map** 4 E5. *Tel 22 42 27 266 (box office).* Muzeum. *Open for performances only. See Entertainment p220 & p222.* www.opera.cz

The first theatre built here, the New Town Theatre, was pulled down in 1885 to make way for the present building. This was originally known as the New German Theatre, built to rival the Czechs' National Theatre

(see pp156–7). A Neo-Classical frieze decorates the pediment above the columned loggia at the front of the theatre. The figures include Dionysus and Thalia, the muse of comedy. The interior is stuccoed and original paintings in the auditorium and on the curtain have been preserved. In 1945 the theatre became the city's main opera house.

Mucha Museum ❼
MUCHOVO MUZEUM

Panská 7. **Map** 4 D4. *Tel 22 14 51 333.* Můstek, Náměsti Republiky. *3, 5, 9, 14, 24, 26. Open 10am–6pm daily.* www.mucha.cz

The 18th-century Kaunicky Palace is home to the first museum dedicated to this Czech master of Art Nouveau. A selection of more than 100 exhibits include paintings and drawings, sculptures, photographs and personal memorabilia. The central courtyard becomes a terrace for the café in the summer, and there is a museum shop offering exclusive gifts with Mucha motifs.

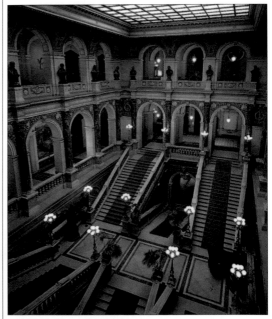

Main staircase of the National Museum

Art Nouveau in Prague

Façade detail,
10 Masaryk
Embankment

The decorative style known as Art Nouveau originated in Paris in the 1890s. It quickly became international as most of the major European cities quickly responded to its graceful, flowing forms. In Prague it was called "Secese" and at its height in the first decade of the 20th century but died out during World War I, when it seemed frivolous and even decadent. There is a wealth of Art Nouveau in Prague, both in the fine and decorative arts and in architecture. In the New Town and the Jewish Quarter *(see pp80–93)*, entire streets were demolished at the turn of the century and built in the new style.

Praha House
This house was built in 1903 for the Prague Insurance Company. Its name is in gilt Art Nouveau letters at the top.

ARCHITECTURE

Art Nouveau made its first appearance in Prague at the Jubilee exhibition of 1891. Architecturally, the new style was a deliberate attempt to break with the 19th-century tradition of monumental buildings. In Art Nouveau the important aspect was ornament, either painted or sculpted, often in the form of a female figure, applied to a fairly plain surface. This technique was ideally suited to wrought iron and glass, popular at the turn of the century. These materials were light but strong. The effect of this, together with Art Nouveau decoration, created buildings of lasting beauty.

Hotel Central
Built by Alois Dryák and Bedřich Bendelmayer in 1900, the façade of this hotel has plasterwork shaped like tree branches.

Hlahol Choir Building, 1905
The architect Josef Fanta embellished this building with mosaics and sculptures by Karl Mottl and Josef Pekárek (see also p142).

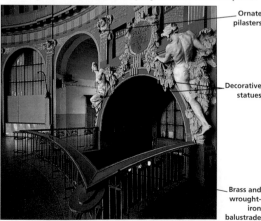

Ornate
pilasters

Decorative
statues

Brass and
wrought-
iron
balustrade

Hotel Meran
Finished in 1904, this grand Art Nouveau building is notable for its fine detailing inside and out.

Hlavní nádraží
Prague's main railway station was completed in 1901. With its huge interior glazed dome and elegant sculptural decoration, it shows many Art Nouveau features.

DECORATIVE AND FINE ARTS

Many painters, sculptors and graphic artists were influenced by Art Nouveau. One of the most successful exponents of the style was the artist Alfons Mucha (1860–1939). He is celebrated chiefly for his posters. Yet he designed stained glass (see p102), furniture, jewellery, even postage stamps. It is perhaps here, in the decorative and applied arts, that Art Nouveau had its fullest expression in Prague. Artists adorned every type of object – doorknobs, curtain ornaments, vases and cutlery – with tentacle- and plant-like forms in imitation of the natural world from which they drew their inspiration.

Postage Stamp, 1918
A bold stamp design by Alfons Mucha marked the founding of the Czechoslovak Republic.

Poster for Sokol Movement
Mucha's colour lithograph for the sixth national meeting of the Sokol gymnastic movement (1912) is in Tyrš's Museum (Physical Culture and Sports).

Záboj and Slavoj
These mythical figures (invented by a forger of old legends) were carved by Josef Myslbek for Palacký Bridge in 1895. They are now in Vyšehrad.

Glass Vase
This iridescent green vase made of Bohemian glass has relief decoration of intertwined threads. It is in the Museum of Decorative Arts.

Curtain Ornament and Candlestick
The silver and silk ornament adorns the Mayor's room of the Municipal House. The candlestick by Emanuel Novák with fine leaf design is in the Museum of Decorative Arts.

WHERE TO SEE ART NOUVEAU IN PRAGUE

Detail of doorway, Široká 9, Jewish Quarter

ARCHITECTURE
Apartment Building, Na příkopě 7
Hanavský Pavilion *p161*
Hlahol Choir Building, Masarykovo nábřeží 10
Hlavní nádraží, Wilsonova
Hotel Central, Hybernská 10
Hotel Evropa *p146*
Industrial Palace *p162* and Four Guided Walks *pp178–9*
Ministerstvo pro místní rozvoj *p67*
Municipal House *p64*
Palacký Bridge (Palackého most)
Praha House, Národní třída 7
Wiehl House *p144*

PAINTING
Trades Fair Palace *pp164–5*

SCULPTURE
Jan Hus Monument *p70*
Vyšehrad Garden and Cemetery *p160* and Four Guided Walks *pp180–1*
Zbraslav Monastery *p163*

DECORATIVE ARTS
Mucha Museum *p147*
Museum of Decorative Arts *p84*
Prague Museum *p161*

Street-by-Street: Charles Square

The southern part of the New Town resounds to the rattle of trams, as many routes converge in this part of Prague. Fortunately, the park in Charles Square (Karlovo náměstí) offers a peaceful and welcome retreat. Some of the buildings around the Square belong to the University and the statues in the centre represent writers and scientists, reflecting the academic environment. There are several Baroque buildings and towards the river stands the historic 14th-century Slavonic Monastery.

Detail of house in Charles Square

The Czech Technical University was founded here in 1867 in a grand Neo-Renaissance building.

Charles Square Centre

Church of St Wenceslas

RESSLOVA

To the river

VÁCLAVSKÁ

NA MORÁNI

KARLOVO N...

To metro Karlovo náměstí

★ Church of St Cyril and St Methodius
A plaque and a bullet-scarred wall are reminders of the siege of the church in 1942, when German troops mounted an assault on the Czech and Slovak agents who were hiding there ⑪

★ Charles Square
The centre of the square is a pleasant 19th-century park with lawns, formal flowerbeds, fountains and statues ⑩

Church of St Cosmas and St Damian

POD SLOVANY

VYŠEHRADSKÁ

Slavonic Monastery Emauzy
In 1965 a pair of modern concrete spires by František Černý were added to the church of the 14th-century monastery ⑭

TROJICKÁ

Church of St John on the Rock
This view of the organ and ceiling shows the dynamic Baroque design of Kilian Ignaz Dientzenhofer ⑬

STAR SIGHTS

★ Charles Square

★ Church of St Cyril and St Methodius

Church of St Ignatius
The sun rays and gilded cherubs on the side altars are typical of the gaudy decoration in this Baroque church built for the Jesuits **8**

Eliška Krásnohorská was a 19th-century poet who wrote the libretti for Smetana's operas. A statue of her was put up here in 1931.

LOCATOR MAP
See Street Finder, map 5

A statue of Jan Purkyně *(1787–1869),* an eminent physiologist and pioneer of cell theory, was erected in 1961. It is the most recent of the many memorials in the square.

Jesuit College
Founded in the mid-17th century, this imposing building has been a hospital since the suppression of the Jesuits in 1773 (see pp30–31) **9**

18th-century Institute of Gentlewomen (now a hospital)

Faust House
In the 18th century this house was owned by Count Ferdinand Mladota of Solopysky. The chemical experiments he performed reinforced the associations that gave the building its name **12**

Botanical Gardens
Though part of the Charles University, the gardens are open to the public and are known for their profusion of rare plants. This is an agreeable place to relax **15**

0 metres 100
0 yards 100

KEY

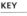

– – – Suggested route

Sculptures on the façade of the Jesuit College by Tomasso Soldati

Church of St Ignatius ❽

KOSTEL SV. IGNÁCE

Ječná 2. **Map** 5 C2. *Tel 22 49 21 254.* ⛔ *Karlovo náměstí.* 🚋 *3, 4, 6, 10, 14, 18, 22, 23, 24.* **Open** *6am–6:30pm daily.* ✝ *frequent.* 📷

With its wealth of gilding and flamboyant stucco decoration, St Ignatius is typical of the Baroque churches built by the Jesuits to impress people with the power and glamour of their faith. The architects were the same two men responsible for the adjoining Jesuit College, Carlo Lurago, who started work on the church in 1665, and Paul Ignaz Bayer, who added the tower in 1687.

The painting on the high altar of *The Glory of St Ignatius* (St Ignatius Loyola, the founder of the Jesuit order) is by Jan Jiří Heinsch.

The Jesuits continued to embellish the interior right up until the suppression of their order in 1773, adding stuccowork and statues of Jesuit and Czech saints.

Jesuit College ❾

JEZUITSKÁ KOLEJ

Karlovo náměstí 36. **Map** 5 B2. ⛔ *Karlovo náměstí.* 🚋 *3, 4, 6, 10, 14, 16, 18, 22, 23, 24.* **Closed** *to the public.*

Half the eastern side of Charles Square is occupied by the former college of the Jesuit order in the New Town. As in other parts of Prague, the Jesuits were able to demolish huge swathes of

the city to put up another bastion of their formidable education system. The college was built between 1656 and 1702 by Carlo Lurago and Paul Ignaz Bayer. The two sculptured portals are the work of Johann Georg Wirch who extended the building in 1770. After the suppression of the Jesuit order in 1773 the college was converted into a military hospital. It is now a teaching hospital and part of Charles University.

Charles Square ❿

KARLOVO NÁMĚSTÍ

Map 5 B2. ⛔ *Karlovo náměstí.* 🚋 *3, 4, 6, 10, 14, 16, 18, 22, 23, 24.*

Since the mid-19th century the square has been a park. Though surrounded by busy roads, it is a pleasant place to sit and read or watch people exercising their dachshunds.

The square began life as a vast cattle market, when Charles IV founded the New Town in 1348. Other goods sold in the square included firewood, coal and pickled herrings from barrels.

In the centre of the market Charles had a wooden tower built, where the coronation jewels were put on display once a year. In 1382 the tower was replaced by a chapel, from which, in 1437, concessions made to the Hussites by the pope at the Council of Basle were read out to the populace.

Church of St Cyril and St Methodius ⓫

KOSTEL SV. CYRILA A METODĚJE

Resslova 9. **Map** 5 B2. *Tel 22 49 16 100.* ⛔ *Karlovo náměstí.* 🚋 *3, 4, 6, 10, 14, 16, 18, 22, 23, 24.* **Open** *Oct–Apr: 10am–4pm Tue–Sun; May–Sep: 10am–5pm Tue–Sun.* 🎦 ⌀ ♿

This Baroque church, with a pilastered façade and a small central tower, was built in the 1730s. It was dedicated to St Charles Borromeo and served as the church of a community of retired priests, but both were closed in 1783. In the 1930s the church was restored and given to the Czechoslovak Orthodox Church, and rededicated to St Cyril and St Methodius, the 9th-century "Apostles to the Slavs" *(see pp20–21).* In May 1942 parachutists who had assassinated Reinhard Heydrich, the Nazi governor of Czechoslovakia, hid in the crypt along with members of the Czech Resistance. Surrounded by German troops, they took their own lives rather than surrender. Bullet holes made by the German machine guns during the siege can still be seen below the memorial plaque on the outer wall of the crypt, which now houses a museum of these times.

Main altar in the Church of St Cyril and St Methodius

Faust House ⓬
FAUSTŮV DŮM

Karlovo náměstí 40, 41. **Map** 5 B3.
Ⓜ Karlovo náměstí. 🚋 3, 4, 14,
16, 18. **Closed** to the public.

Prague thrives on legends of
alchemy and pacts with the
devil, and this Baroque
mansion has attracted many.
There has been a house here
since the 14th century when it
belonged to Prince Václav of
Opava, an alchemist and natural historian. In the 16th century it was owned by the
alchemist Edward Kelley. The
chemical experiments of
Count Ferdinand Mladota of
Solopysky, who owned the
house in the mid-18th century,
gave rise to its association
with the legend of Faust.

Baroque façade of Faust House

Church of St John on the Rock ⓭
KOSTEL SV. JANA NA SKALCE

Vyšehradská 49. **Map** 5 B3.
Tel 22 49 15 371. 🚋 3, 4, 14, 16,
18, 24. **Open** for services only.
🕆 8am Sun. 🚻

One of Prague's smaller
Baroque churches, St John
on the Rock is one of Kilian
Ignaz Dientzenhofer's most
daring designs. Its twin
square towers are set at a
sharp angle to the church's
narrow façade and the
interior is based on an
octagonal floorplan. The
church was completed in

1738, but the double staircase
leading up to the west front
was not added until the
1770s. On the high altar there
is a wooden version of Jan
Brokof's statue of St John
Nepomuk (see p137) which
stands on the Charles Bridge.

Slavonic Monastery Emauzy ⓮
KLÁŠTER NA SLOVANECH-EMAUZY

Vyšehradská 49. **Map** 5 B3.
Tel 221 979 296. 🚋 3, 4, 14, 18, 24.
Monastery church open 9am–4pm
Mon–Fri. **Cloisters open** by appoint-
ment. 🕆 10am, 6pm daily. 🚻 🚫
🚻 www.emauzy.cz

Both the monastery and its
church were almost destroyed
in an American air raid in
1945. During their
reconstruction, the church
was given a pair of modern
reinforced concrete spires.
The monastery was founded
in 1347 for the Croatian
Benedictines, whose services
were held in the Old Slavonic
language, hence its name
"Na Slovanech". In the course
of Prague's tumultuous
religious history it has since
changed hands many times.
In 1446 a Hussite order was
formed here, then in 1635 the
monastery was acquired by
Spanish Benedictines. In the
18th century the complex was
given a thorough Baroque
treatment, but in 1880 it was
taken over by some German
Benedictines, who rebuilt
almost everything in Neo-
Gothic style. The monastery
has managed to preserve some
historically important 14th-
century wall paintings in the
cloister, though many were
damaged in World War II.

**Remains of 14th-century wall
paintings in the Slavonic Monastery**

Botanical Gardens ⓯
BOTANICKÁ ZAHRADA

Na slupi 16. **Map** 5 B3. **Tel** 22 49 18
970. 🚋 18, 24. 🚌 148.
Glasshouses open 10am–4pm daily.
Gardens open Jan–Feb: 10am–5pm
daily; Mar–Oct: 10am–6pm daily;
Nov–Dec: 10am–4pm daily. 🚻 🚫 🚻

Charles IV founded Prague's
first botanical garden in the
14th century. This is a much
later institution. The university
garden was founded in the
Smíchov district in 1775, but
in 1897 it was moved to its
present site. The huge
greenhouses date from 1938.
Special botanical exhibitions
and shows of exotic birds and
tropical fish are often held
here. One star attraction of the
gardens is the giant water lily,
Victoria cruziana, whose huge
leaves can support a small
child. During the summer it
produces dozens of flowers
which only survive for a day.

Entrance to the university's Botanical Gardens

Octagonal steeple of St Catherine's

Church of
St Catherine 🔟

KOSTEL SV. KATEŘINY

Kateřinská. **Map** 5 C3. 🚊 *4, 6, 10, 16, 22, 23.* **Closed** *to the public.*

St Catherine's stands in the garden of a former convent, founded in 1354 by Charles IV to commemorate his victory at the Battle of San Felice in Italy in 1332. In 1420, during the Hussite revolution *(see pp26–7)*, the convent was demolished, but in the following century it was rebuilt by Kilian Ignáz Dientzenhofer as an Augustinian monastery. The monks remained here until 1787, when the monastery closed. Since 1822 it has been used as a hospital. In 1737 a new Baroque church was built, but the slender steeple of the old Gothic church was retained. Its octagonal shape has gained it the nickname of "the Prague minaret".

Chalice
Restaurant 🔟

RESTAURACE U KALICHA

Na bojišti 14. **Map** 6 D3. **Tel** *29 61 89 600.* 🚇 *IP Pavlova.* 🚊 *4, 6, 10, 16, 22, 23.* **Open** *11am–11pm daily (book ahead).* 📷 🛗 *See* **Restaurants** *pp202–9.* **www**.ukalicha.cz

This Pilsner Urquell beer hall owes its fame to the novel *The Good Soldier Švejk* by Jaroslav Hašek. It was Švejk's favourite drinking place and

the establishment trades on the popularity of the best-loved character in 20th-century Czech literature. The staff dress in period costume from World War I, the era of this novel.

Dvořák Museum 🔟

MUZEUM ANTONÍNA DVOŘÁKA

Ke Karlovu 20. **Map** 6 D2. **Tel** *22 49 23 363.* 🚇 *I.P. Pavlova.* 🚌 *148.* **Open** *10am–1:30pm, 2–5pm Tue–Sun and for concerts.* 🎧 📷 🛗 **www**.nm.cz

One of the most enchanting secular buildings of the Prague Baroque now houses the Antonín Dvořák Museum. On display are Dvořák scores and editions of his works, plus photographs and memorabilia of the great 19th-century Czech composer, including his piano, viola and desk.

The building is by the great Baroque architect Kilian Ignaz Dientzenhofer *(see p129)*. Just two storeys high with an elegant tiered mansard roof, the house was completed in 1720, for the Michnas of Vacínov and was originally known as the Michna Summer Palace. It later became known as Villa Amerika, after a nearby inn called Amerika. Between the two pavilions flanking the house is a fine iron

gateway, a replica of the Baroque original. In the 19th century the villa and garden fell into decay. The garden statues and vases, from the workshop of Matthias Braun, date from about 1735. They are original but heavily restored, as is the interior of the palace. The ceiling and walls of the large room on the first floor are decorated with 18th-century frescoes by Jan Ferdinand Schor.

Church of
St Stephen 🔟

KOSTEL SV. ŠTĚPÁNA

Štěpánská. **Map** 5 C2. 🚊 *4, 6, 10, 16, 22, 23.* **Open** *only for services.* ✝ *11am Sun.* 📷

Founded by Charles IV in 1351 as the parish church of the upper New Town, St Stephen's was finished in 1401 with the completion of the multi-spired steeple. In the late 17th century the Branberg Chapel was built on to the north side of the church. It contains the tomb of the prolific Baroque sculptor Matthias Braun.

Most of the subsequent Baroque additions were removed when the church was scrupulously re-Gothicized in the 1870s by Josef Mocker. There are several fine Baroque paintings,

The Michna Summer Palace, home of the Dvořák Museum

Renaissance painted ceiling in the New Town Hall

however, including *The Baptism of Christ* by Karel Škréta at the end of the left hand aisle and a picture of St John Nepomuk *(see p137)* by Jan Jiři Heinsch to the left of the 15th-century pulpit. The church's greatest treasure is undoubtedly a beautiful Gothic panel painting of the Madonna, known as *Our Lady of St Stephen's*, which dates from 1472.

Gothic pulpit in St Stephen's

New Town Hall ⑳
NOVOMĚSTSKÁ RADNICE

Karlovo náměstí 23. **Map** 5 B1. Ⓜ *Karlovo náměstí.* 🚊 *3, 4, 6, 10, 14, 16, 18, 22, 24.* **Tel** *22 49 48 229.* **Tower open** *May–Sep: 10am–6pm Tue–Sun.*

In 1960 a statue of Hussite preacher Jan Želivský was unveiled at the New Town Hall. It commemorates the first and bloodiest of many defenestrations. On 30 July 1419 Želivský led a crowd of demonstrators to the Town Hall to demand the release of some prisoners. When they were refused, they stormed the building and threw the Catholic councillors

out of the windows. Those who survived the fall were finished off with pikes.

The Town Hall already existed in the 14th century, the Gothic tower was added in the mid-15th century and contains an 18th century chapel. In the 16th century it acquired an arcaded courtyard. After the joining-up of the four towns of Prague in 1784 the Town Hall ceased to be the seat of the municipal administration and became a courthouse and a prison. It is now used for cultural and social events, and its splendid Gothic hall can be hired for wedding receptions.

U Fleků ㉑

Křemencova 11. **Map** 5 B1. **Tel** *22 49 34 019.* Ⓜ *Národní třída, Karlovo náměstí.* 🚊 *6, 9, 17, 18, 22.* **Museum open** *10am–4pm Mon–Fri.* See **Restaurants** *pp202–9.* **www.**ufleku.cz

Records indicate that beer was brewed here as early as 1459. This archetypal Prague beer hall has been fortunate in its owners, who have kept up the tradition of brewing as

an art rather than just a means of making money. In 1762 the brewery was purchased by Jakub Flekovský, who named it U Fleků (At the Fleks). The present brewery, the smallest in Prague, makes a special strong, dark beer, sold only here. The restaurant now also features a small museum of Czech brewing history.

Church of St Ursula ㉒
KOSTEL SV. VORŠILY

Ostrovní 18. **Map** 3 A5. **Tel** *22 49 30 502.* Ⓜ *Národní třída.* 🚊 *6, 9, 18, 22, 23.* 🕐 *5pm daily. For visits at any other time, contact Prague Information Service (see p227).* 🚫

The delightful Baroque church of St Ursula was built as part of an Ursuline convent founded in 1672. The original sculptures still decorate the façade and in front of the church stands a group of statues featuring St John Nepomuk (1747) by Ignaz Platzer the Elder. The light airy interior has a frescoed, stuccoed ceiling and on the various altars there are lively Baroque paintings. The main altar has one of St Ursula.

The adjoining convent has been returned to the Ursuline order and is now a Catholic school. One part of the ground floor is still used for secular purposes – the Klášterní Vinárna (Convent Restaurant).

National Theatre ㉓
NÁRODNÍ DIVADLO

See pp156–7.

U Fleků, Prague's best-known beer hall

National Theatre ㉓

NÁRODNÍ DIVADLO

This gold-crested theatre has always been an important symbol of the Czech cultural revival. Work started in 1868, funded largely by voluntary contributions. The original Neo-Renaissance design was by the Czech architect Josef Zítek. After its destruction by fire *(see opposite)*, Josef Schulz was given the job of rebuilding the theatre and all the best Czech artists of the period contributed towards its lavish and spectacular decoration. During the late 1970s and early 80s the theatre was restored and the New Stage was built by architect Karel Prager.

A bronze sculpture in the foyer

The theatre from Marksmen's Island

A bronze three-horse chariot, designed by Bohuslav Schnirch, carries the Goddess of Victory.

Laterna Magika

The New Stage auditorium

★ Auditorium
The elaborately-painted ceiling is adorned with allegorical figures representing the arts by František Ženíšek.

The five arcades of the loggia are decorated with lunette paintings by Josef Tulka, entitled *Five Songs.*

STAR FEATURES

★ Auditorium

★ Lobby Ceiling

★ Stage Curtain

★ Lobby Ceiling
This ceiling fresco is the final part of a triptych painted by František Ženíšek in 1878 depicting the Golden Age of Czech Art.

★ **Stage Curtain**
This sumptuous gold and red stage curtain, showing the origin of the theatre, is the work of Vojtěch Hynais.

VISITORS' CHECKLIST

Národní 2, Nové Město. **Map** 3 A5. **Tel** 22 49 12 673. Národní třída, line B. 17, 18, 22, 23 to Národní třída. **Auditorium open** only during performances. 8:30–11am Sat & Sun. **Tel** 22 17 14 152.

Façade Decoration
This standing figure on the attic of the western façade is one of many figures representing the Arts sculpted by Antonín Wagner in 1883.

The startling sky-blue roof covered with stars, is said to symbolize the summit all artists should aim for.

The President's Box
The former royal box, lined in red velvet, is decorated with famous historical figures from Czech history by Václav Brožík.

NATIONAL THEATRE FIRE

On 12 August, 1881, just days before the official opening, the National Theatre was completely gutted by fire. It was thought to have been started by metalworkers on the roof. But just six weeks later, enough money had been collected to rebuild the theatre. It was finally opened two years late in 1883 with a performance of Czech composer Bedřich Smetana's opera *Libuše* (see p79).

FURTHER AFIELD

Visitors to Prague, finding the old centre packed with sights, tend to ignore the suburbs. It is true that once you start exploring away from the centre, the language can become more of a problem. However, it is well worth the effort, firstly to escape the crowds of tourists milling around the Castle and the Old Town Square, secondly to realize that Prague is a living city as well as a picturesque time capsule. Most of the museums and other sights in the first part of this section are easily reached by Metro, tram or even on foot. If you are prepared to venture a little further, do not miss the grand palace at Troja or the former monastery at Zbraslav, which houses the Asian Art collection of the National Gallery. The Day Trips *(pp168–71)* include visits to castles close to Prague and the historic spa towns of Marienbad and Karlsbad, which attracted the first tourists to Bohemia during the 19th century.

Vaulting in Church of St Barbara, Kutná Hora

SIGHTS AT A GLANCE

Museums and Galleries
Mozart Museum ❶
Prague Museum ❻
National Technical Museum ❽
Trades Fair Palace pp164–5 ❾
Zbraslav Monastery ❺

Monasteries
Břevnov Monastery ❸

Historic Districts
Vyšehrad ❷
Žižkov ❹
Náměstí Míru ❺

Cemeteries
Olšany Cemeteries ❸

Historic Sites
White Mountain and
   Star Hunting Lodge ❹

Historic Buildings
Troja Palace pp166–7 ❶

Parks and Gardens
Letná Park ❼
Exhibition Ground and
   Stromovka Park ❿
Zoo ❿

KEY

- ▮ Central Prague
- ▯ Greater Prague
- ✈ Airport
- ▬ Major road
- ═ Minor road

15 km = 10 miles

◁ **Part of the garden staircase at the 17th-century Troja Palace**

Bertramka, the villa that houses the Mozart Museum

Mozart Museum ❶

BERTRAMKA

Mozartova 169. **Tel** 25 73 17 465.
🚇 Anděl. 🚊 4, 7, 9, 10. **Open**
Apr–Oct: 9:30am–6pm daily; Nov–
Mar: 9:30am–4pm daily. 📷 🖅
www.bertramka.com

Though slightly off the beaten track, the museum is well signposted because of Prague's reverence for Mozart. Bertramka is a 17th-century farmhouse, enlarged in the second half of the 18th century into a comfortable suburban villa. Mozart and his wife Constanze stayed here as the guests of the composer František Dušek and his wife Josefina in 1787, when Mozart was working on *Don Giovanni*. He composed the overture to the opera in the garden pavilion just a few hours before its premiere at the Nostitz (now the Estates) Theatre *(see p65)*. The house, with a small exhibition on Mozart, is at its best in the late afternoon when it is quietest. In summer, recitals take place on the terrace.

Vyšehrad ❷

Map 5 B5. 🚇 Vyšehrad. 🚊 3, 7, 16, 17, 18, 24.

A rocky outcrop above the Vltava, Vyšehrad means "castle on the heights" *(see pp180–1)*. It was fortified in the 10th century and, at times, used as the seat of the Přemyslid princes. The area has great historical and mythological significance, and in the 1870s it became the site of a national cemetery.

Olšany Cemeteries ❸

OLŠANSKÉ HŘBITOVY

Vinohradská 153, Jana Želivského.
🚇 Želivského. **Tel** 26 73 10 652. 🚊
5, 6, 10, 11, 16, 19, 26. **Open** Mar–
Sep: 8am–7pm; Oct–Feb: 8am–6pm.

Well-tended grave in the eastern part of the Olšany Cemeteries

At the northwest corner of the main cemetery stands the small Church of St Roch (1682), protector against the plague – the first cemetery was founded here in 1679 specifically for the burial of plague victims. In the course of the 19th century, the old cemetery was enlarged and new ones developed, including a Russian cemetery, distinguished by its old-fashioned Orthodox church (1924–5), and a Jewish one, where Franz Kafka *(see p68)* is buried. Tombs include those of painter Josef Mánes (1820–71) who worked during the Czech Revival movement *(see pp32–3)*, and Josef Jungmann (1773–1847), compiler of a five-volume Czech-German dictionary.

Žižkov ❹

🚇 Jiřího z Poděbrad, Želivského, Flóra. **National Monument**, Vítkov, U památníku. 🚌 133, 207.
For visits contact Prague Information Service (see p227).

Equestrian statue of Jan Žižka

This quarter of Prague was the scene of a historic victory for the Hussites *(see pp26–7)* over Crusaders sent by the Emperor Sigismund to destroy them. On 14 July 1420 on Vítkov hill, a tiny force of Hussites defeated an army of several thousand well-armed men. The determined, hymn-singing Hussites were led by the one-eyed Jan Žižka.

In 1877 the area around Vítkov was renamed Žižkov in honour of Žižka's victory, and in 1950 a bronze equestrian statue of Žižka by Bohumil Kafka was erected on the hill. About 9m (30 ft) high, this is the largest equestrian statue in the world. It stands in front of the National Monument (1927–32), built as a symbol of the struggle for independence of the Czechoslovak people. The Monument later served as a mausoleum for Klement Gottwald and other Communist leaders. Their remains have since been removed and the building given to the National Museum *(see p147)* which

Relief by Josef Myslbek on portal of St Ludmilla in Náměstí Míru

plans to open a permanent exhibition on modern Czech history in 2009.

Nearby is a giant television transmitter, 260 m (850 ft) high. Locals are suspicious of the rays emanating from this great tube of reinforced concrete, built in 1984–8.

Náměstí Míru ❺

Map 6 F2. ⓂNáměstí Míru. 🚊 4, 6, 10, 16, 22, 23. 🚌 135. **Church of St Ludmila open** only for services.

This attractive square, with a well-kept central garden, is the focal point of the Vinohrady quarter. At the top of its sloping lawns stands the attractive, brick Neo-Gothic Church of St Ludmila (1888–93), designed by Josef Mocker, architect of the west end of St Vitus's Cathedral (see pp100–3). Its twin octagonal spires are 60 m (200 ft) high. On the tympanum of the main portal is a relief of Christ with St Wenceslas and St Ludmila by the great 19th-century sculptor Josef Myslbek. Leading artists also contributed designs for the stained-glass windows and the colourful interior.

The outside of the square is lined with attractive buildings, the most conspicuous being the Vinohrady Theatre, a spirited Art Nouveau building completed in 1907. The façade is crowned by two huge winged figures sculpted by Milan Havlíček, symbolizing Drama and Opera.

Prague Museum ❻

MUZEUM HLAVNÍHO MĚSTA PRAHY

Na Poříčí 52. **Map** 4 F3. **Tel** 22 48 16 772/22 48 16 773. ⓂFlorenc. 🚊 3, 8, 24, 26. **Open** 9am–6pm Tue–Sun (9am–8pm first Thu of every month). 🖼 🅿 **www.**muzeumprahy.cz

The collection records the history of Prague from primeval times. A new museum was built to house the exhibits in the 1890s. Its Neo-Renaissance façade is rich with stucco and sculptures, and the interior walls are painted with historic views of the city. On display are examples of Prague china and furniture, relics of the medieval guilds and paintings of Prague through the ages.

The most remarkable exhibit is the paper and wood model of Prague by Antonín Langweil. Completed in 1834, it covers 20 sq m (25 sq yards). The scale of the extraordinarily accurate model is 1:500.

Letná Park ❼

LETENSKÉ SADY

Map 3 A1. ⓂMalostranská, Hradčanská. 🚊 1, 8, 12, 14, 17, 18, 20, 22, 23, 25, 26.

Across the river from the Jewish Quarter, a large plateau overlooks the city. It was here that armies gathered before attacking Prague Castle. Since the mid-19th century it has been a wooded park.

On the terrace at the top of the granite steps that lead up from the embankment stands a curious monument – a giant metronome built in 1991. It was installed after the Velvet Revolution on the pedestal formerly occupied by the gigantic stone statue of Stalin leading the people, which was blown up in 1962. Nobody likes the metronome any more than they did Stalin and it may soon be replaced. A far more durable monument is the Hanavský Pavilion, a Neo-Baroque cast iron structure, built for the 1891 Exhibition. It was later dismantled and erected on its present site in the park, where it houses a popular restaurant and café.

View of the Vltava and bridges from Letná Park

National Technical Museum ⑧

NÁRODNÍ TECHNICKÉ MUZEUM

Kostelní 42. *Tel 22 03 99 111.* 🚋 *1, 8, 25, 26.* **Open** *call ahead for opening times.* 🖼 🚫 📷 ♿
www.ntm.cz

Though it tries to keep abreast of all scientific developments, the museum's strength is its collection of machines from the Industrial Revolution to the present day, the largest of its kind in Europe. The section that attracts the most visitors is the History of Transportation in the vast central hall. This is filled with locomotives, railway carriages, bicycles, veteran motorcars and motorcycles, with aeroplanes and a hot-air balloon suspended overhead.

The photography and cinematography section is well worth a visit, as is the collection of astronomical instruments. The section on measuring time is also popular, especially on the hour when everything starts to chime at once. In the basement there is a huge reconstruction of a coal mine, with an assortment of tools tracing the development of mining from the 15th to the 19th century.

Trades Fair Palace ⑨

VELETRŽNÍ PALÁC

See pp164–5.

Exhibition Ground and Stromovka Park ⑩

VÝSTAVIŠTĚ A STROMOVKA

🚋 *1, 14, 17, 25.* **Exhibition Ground** *open 10am–11pm daily.* 🖼 **Stromovka Park** *open 24hrs daily.* **Lapidarium** *Tel 23 33 75 636.* **Open** *noon–5pm Tue–Fri, 10am–5pm Sat, Sun.* ♿ www.nm.cz

Laid out for the Jubilee of 1891, the Exhibition Ground has been used for trade fairs, sports and artistic events ever since. With its lively funfair, it is great for a day out with the children. All kinds of exhibitions, sporting events, spectacles and concerts are

The Industrial Palace, centrepiece of the 1891 Exhibition Ground

staged throughout the summer. The large park to the west was the former royal hunting enclosure and deer park, first established in the late 16th century. The name Stromovka means "place of trees", a reminder that a large area of the park was once a flourishing tree nursery. Opened to the public in 1804, the park is still a pleasant wooded area and an ideal place for a walk. The Lapidarium holds an exhibition of 11th–19th century sculpture, including some originals from the Charles Bridge *(see pp136–9).*

Troja Palace ⑪

TROJSKÝ ZÁMEK

See pp166–7.

Zoo ⑫

ZOOLOGICKÁ ZAHRADA

U trojského zámku 3. *Tel 29 61 12 111.* Ⓜ *Holešovice, then* 🚌 *112.* **Open** *Jun–Aug: 9am–7pm daily; Apr, May, Sep, Oct: 9am–6pm daily; Nov–Feb: 9am–4pm daily; Mar: 9am–5pm daily.* 🖼 📷 ♿ 🚻 www.zoopraha.cz

Attractively situated on a rocky slope overlooking the

right bank of the Vltava, the zoo was founded in 1924. It now covers an area of 64 hectares (160 acres) and there is a chair lift to take visitors to the upper part. To travel on the lift, you can use an ordinary metro/tram ticket.

The zoo's 2,500 animals represent 500 species, 50 of them extremely rare in the wild. It is best known for its breeding programme of Przewalski's horses, the only species of wild horse in the world. It has also enjoyed success in breeding big cats, gorillas and orang-utans. In addition there are two pavilions, one for lions, tigers and other beasts of prey and one for elephants.

Red panda, relative of the famous giant panda, in Prague Zoo

Břevnov Monastery ⑬

BŘEVNOVSKÝ KLÁŠTER

Markétská 28. **Tel** 22 04 06 111.
🚋 15, 22, 25. 🅿 only, Sat & Sun;
tour times vary. 📷 🚫
www.brevnov.cz

From the surrounding sub-
urban housing, you would
never guess that Břevnov is
one of the oldest inhabited
parts of Prague. A flourishing
community grew up here
around the Benedictine abbey
founded in 993 by Prince
Boleslav II *(see p20)* and
Bishop Adalbert (Vojtěch) –
the first monastery in Bohemia.
An ancient well called Vojtěška
marks the spot where prince
and bishop are supposed to
have met and decided to
found the monastery.

The gateway, courtyard and
most of the present monastery
buildings are by the great
Baroque architects Christoph
and Kilian Ignaz Dientzenhofer
(see p129). The monastery
Church of St Margaret is the
work of Christoph. Completed
in 1715, it is based on a floorplan of overlapping ovals, as
ingenious as any of Bernini's
churches in Rome. In 1964
the crypt of the original 10th-
century church was discovered below the choir and is
open to the public. Of the
other buildings, the most
interesting is the Theresian
Hall, with a painted ceiling
dating from 1727.

White Mountain and Star Hunting Lodge ⑭

BÍLÁ HORA A HVĚZDA

🚋 22 (White Mountain), 1, 18
(Star Hunting Lodge).
**White Mountain enclosure
open** 24hrs daily. **Star Hunting
Lodge Tel** 23 53 57 938.
Open Apr, Oct: 10am–5pm Tue–
Sun (to 6pm May–Sep). 📷 🚫

The Battle of the White
Mountain *(see p31)*, fought
on 8 November 1620, had a
very different impact for the
two main communities of
Prague. For the Protestants

Star Hunting Lodge

it was a disaster that led
to 300 years of Habsburg
domination; for the Catholic
supporters of the Habsburgs
it was a triumph, so they
built a memorial chapel on
the hill. In the early 1700s
this chapel was converted
into the grander Church of
Our Lady Victorious and
decorated by leading
Baroque artists, including
Václav Vavřinec Reiner.

In the 16th century the
woodland around the battle
site had been a royal game
park. The hunting lodge,
completed in 1556, survives
today. This fascinating
building is shaped as a
six-pointed star – *hvězda*
means star. On site is a
small exhibition about the
building and its history.

Also on show are exhibits
relating to the Battle of
the White Mountain and
temporary exhibitions about
Czech culture.

Zbraslav Monastery ⑮

ZBRASLAVSKÝ KLÁŠTER

Zámek Zbraslav. **Tel** 25 79 21 638.
🚌 129, 241, 243, 255, 360. **Open**
10am–6pm Tue–Sun.
📷 🚫 ♿ www.ngprague.cz

In 1279 Wenceslas II founded
a monastery to serve as the
burial place for the royal
family, though only he and
Wenceslas IV were ever
buried here. Destroyed during
the Hussite Wars *(see pp26–7)*,
the monastery was rebuilt
in 1709–39, only to be
abolished in 1785 and made
into a factory. Earlier this
century it was restored and
in 1941 was given to the
National Gallery. It now houses
a unique collection of Asian
art with exhibits including art
and artefacts from China,
Japan, India, South East Asia
and Tibet. A collection of
Japanese sculpture is featured
which visually impaired
visitors are encouraged to
touch. The exhibition also
includes a section dedicated
to Islamic art. Informative
guided tours are available.

Zbraslav Monastery, home to the National Gallery's Asian Art Collection

Trades Fair Palace ❾
VELETRŽNÍ PALAC

The National Gallery in Prague opened its Centre for Modern and Contemporary Art in 1995, housed in a reconstruction of a former Trades Fair building of 1929. Its vast, skylit spaces make an ideal backdrop for the collection, which ranges from French 19th-century art through superb examples of Impressionist and Post-Impressionist painting, to works by Munch, Klimt, Picasso and Miró, and a splendid collection of Czech modern art.

★ **The Virgin** (1913)
This colourful work epitomizes the distinctive, erotic Art Nouveau style of painter Gustav Klimt.

Screening Room

The Blind (1926)
This intriguing work by František Bílek is one of the sculptures on display.

Fourth Floor

Third Floor

★ **Evening in Hradčany** (1909-13)
This incredibly atmospheric painting by Jakub Schikaneder, typically captures the magic and nostalgia of the city of Prague at dusk.

Pomona (1910)
Aristide Maillol was a pupil of Rodin. This work is part of an exceptional collection of bronzes.

Cleopatra (1942-57)
This painting by Jan Zrzavý, took the artist 45 years to complete and is his best-known piece; making him a major representative of Czech modern art.

STAR SIGHTS

★ The Virgin by Gustav Klimt

★ Evening in Hradčany by Schikaneder

★ Torso by Pešánek

Grand Meal
(1951–55)
Mikuláš Medek's
works range from
post-war Surrealism
to 1960s Abstraction.

VISITORS' CHECKLIST

Veletržní Palác, Dukelských
hrdinů 47. *Tel* 22 23 21 459.
Vltavská. 5, 12, 17
to Veletržní; 1, 8, 14, 25, 26
to Strossmayerovo náměsti.
Open 10am–6pm Tue–Sun (last
adm 30 mins before closing).
www.ngprague.cz

★ **Torso** *(1936)*
Zdeněk Pešánek was a
pioneer of kinetic art, here
combining an organic form
with neon lighting.

Egg Object *(1976)*
Crafted by sculptor
Jiří Kolář, this
form is one of
the late 20th-
century
works on
display in
the museum.

Stairs to
all floors

Second
Floor

Stairs to
all floors

First
Floor

Mezzanine
Floor

Ground
Floor

Main
entrance

The fascia's
concrete and glass
bands are typical of
1920s Functionalism.

KEY

- 19th- and 20th-century European Art
- Czech Art 1900 –1930
- 19th- and 20th-century French Art
- Czech Art 1930 – present day
- Non-Czech Modern Art
- Temporary exhibition space
- Non-exhibition space

Troja Palace ⓫

TROJSKÝ ZÁMEK

One of the most striking summer palaces in Prague, Troja was built in the late 17th century by Jean-Baptiste Mathey for Count Sternberg, a member of a leading Bohemian aristocratic family. Situated at the foot of the Vltava Heights, the exterior of the palace was modelled on a Classical Italian villa, while its garden was laid out in formal French style. The magnificent interior took over 20 years to complete and is full of extravagant frescoes expressing the Sternberg family's loyalty to the Habsburg dynasty. Troja houses a good collection of 19th-century art.

Terracotta urn on the garden balustrade

Defeat of the Turks
This turbaned figure, tumbling from the Grand Hall ceiling, symbolizes Leopold I's triumph over the Turks.

Belvedere turret

Statue of Olympian God

Statues of sons of Mother Earth

Personification of Justice
Abraham Godyn's image of Justice gazes from the lower east wall of the Grand Hall.

★ **Garden Staircase**
The two sons of Mother Earth which adorn the sweeping oval staircase (1685–1703) are part of a group of sculptures by Johann Georg Heermann and his nephew Paul, depicting the struggle of the Olympian Gods with the Titans.

VISITORS' CHECKLIST

U trojského zámku 1, Prague 7. *Tel*
283 851614. 🚊 *see p55.* 🚌 *112*
from Holešovice metro station.
Open *Apr–Oct: 10am–6pm Tue–*
Sun; Nov–Mar: 10am–5pm Sat &
Sun. 📷 🚫 🖥 www.ghmp.cz

★ Grand Hall Fresco
The frescoes in the Grand
Hall (1691–7), by Abraham
Godyn, depict the story of the
first Habsburg Emperor,
Rudolph I, and the victories of
Leopold I over the archenemy
of Christianity, the Sublime
Porte (Ottoman Empire).

Stucco
decoration

★ LANDSCAPED GARDENS

To the
maze

Palace
entrance

Main
entrance

Café

Grand
fountain

Orangery

STAR FEATURES

★ Grand Hall Fresco

★ Landscaped
Gardens

★ Garden Staircase

Chinese Rooms
Several rooms feature 18th-century murals
of Chinese scenes. This room makes a
perfect backdrop for a ceramics display.

Sloping vineyards were levelled, hill-
sides excavated and terraces built to
fulfil the elaborate and grandiose plans
of French architect, Jean-Baptiste
Mathey, for the first Baroque French-
style formal gardens in Bohemia. The
palace and its geometric network of
paths, terracing, fountains, statuary
and beautiful terracotta vases, is best
viewed from the south of the garden
between the two orangeries. The
gardens have been carefully restored
according to Mathey's original plans.

Day Trips from Prague

The sights that attract most visitors away from the city are Bohemia's picturesque medieval castles. Karlstein, for example, stands in splendid isolation above wooded valleys that have changed little since the Emperor Charles IV hunted there in the 14th century. We have chosen four castles, very varied in character. There are regular organized tours *(see p227)* to the major sights around Prague, to the historic mining town of Kutná Hora and, if you have more time to spare, to the famous spa towns of Karlsbad and Marienbad in western Bohemia.

St George and Dragon, Konopiště

SIGHTS AT A GLANCE

Castles	Historic Towns
Veltrusy ❶	Kutná Hora ❺
Karlstein ❷	Karlsbad ❻
Konopiště ❸	Marienbad ❼
Křivoklát ❹	

KEY

■	Central Prague
□	Greater Prague
✈	Airport
═	Motorway
▬	Major road
═	Minor road

25 km = 16 miles

Veltrusy Château ❶

VELTRUSKÝ ZÁMEK

20 km (12 miles) north of Prague. **Tel** *31 57 81 144/146.* 🚆 *from Masarykovo nádraží to Kralupy nad Vltavou, then local bus.* **Open** *May– Sep: 9–11am, 1–4pm Tue–Sun.* 🅿 📷 🚻 *(park only).* **Nelahozeves Castle Tel** *31 57 09 121.* 🚆 *from Masarykovo to Nelahozeves – zastávka.* **Open** *9am–noon, 1–5pm Tue–Sun (last adm: 4pm).* 🅿 🍴 📷 🚻

Veltrusy is a small town beside the Vltava, famous for the 18th-century château built by the aristocratic Chotek family. The building is in the shape of a cross, with a central dome and a grand staircase adorned with statues representing the months of the year and the seasons.

The estate was laid out as an English-style landscaped deer park, covering an area of 300 hectares (750 acres). Near the entrance there is still an enclosure with a herd of deer. The Vltava flows along one side and dotted around the grounds are summer houses.

The Doric and Maria Theresa pavilions, the orangery and the grotto date from the late 18th century. The park is planted with some 100 different kinds of tree. The castle was damaged by floods in 2002 and ongoing repairs mean that some rooms will remain closed to the public until 2008.

Across the river, and accessible from Veltrusy by bus or train, is **Nelahozeves Castle**. This Renaissance castle houses part of one of the finest private collections of art in Europe, the Lobkowicz Collection, which includes works by Veronese, Rubens, Canaletto and Velásquez, as well as rare books and manuscripts. The highlight of the collection is *Haymaking*, a painting by Brueghel the Elder. Part of the collection has moved to Lobkowicz Palace *(see p99)*. The birthplace of Czech composer Antonín Dvořák is nearby.

Karlstein Castle, built by Emperor Charles IV in the 14th century

Karlstein Castle **❷**
KARLŠTEJN

25 km (16 miles) southwest of Prague. *Tel 27 40 08 154.* 🚊 *from Smíchov or Hlavní nádraží to Karlštejn (1.5 km/ 1 mile from castle. The uphill walk takes around 40 minutes).* **Open** *9am–noon, 1–3pm Tue–Sun (to 5pm May, Jun & Sep; to 6pm Jul & Aug).* 📷 🎫 *compulsory (book in advance).* 🚫 www.hradkarlstejn.cz

The castle was founded by Charles IV as a country retreat, a treasury for the crown jewels and a symbol of his divine right to rule the Holy Roman Empire. It stands on a crag above the River Berounka. The castle is largely a 19th-century reconstruction by Josef Mocker. The original building work (1348–67) was supervised by French master mason Matthew of Arras, and then by Peter Parler. You can still see the audience hall and the bed-chamber of Charles IV in the Royal Palace. On the third floor, the Emperor's quarters are below those of the Empress.

The central tower houses the Church of Our Lady, decorated with faded 14th-century wall paintings. A narrow passage leads to the tiny Chapel of St Catherine, the walls of which are adorned with semiprecious stones set into the plaster.

Konopiště Castle **❸**

40 km (25 miles) southeast of Prague. *Tel 31 77 21 366.* 🚊 *from Hlavní nádraží to Benešov, then local bus.* **Open** *Apr & Oct: 9am–12:30pm, 1–3pm Tue–Sun (to 4pm Sat & Sun); May–Sep: 9am–12:30pm, 1–5pm Tue–Sun; Nov: 9am–3pm Sat & Sun (by appointment Tue–Fri).* 📷 🚫 🍴 💻 www.zamek-konopiste.cz

Though it dates back to the 13th century, this moated castle is essentially a late 19th-century creation. In between, Konopiště had been rebuilt by Baroque architect František Kaňka and in front of the bridge across the moat is a splendid gate (1725) by Kaňka and sculptor Matthias Braun.

In 1887 Konopiště was bought by Archduke Franz Ferdinand, who later became heir to the Austrian throne. It

was his assassination in 1914 in Sarajevo that triggered off World War I. To escape the Habsburg court's harsh disapproval of his wife, Ferdinand spent much of his time at Konopiště. He amassed arms, armour and Meissen porcelain, all on display in the fine furnished interiors. However, the abiding memory of the castle is of the hundreds of stags' heads lining the walls.

Hunting trophies at Konopiště

Křivoklát Castle **❹**

45 km (28 miles) west of Prague. *Tel 31 35 58 440.* 🚊 *from Smíchov to Křivoklát (1 km /0.6 miles) from castle).* 🚌 *from Zličín.* **Open** *Mar, Nov, Dec: 9am–noon, 1–3pm Sat, Sun; Apr, Oct: 9am–noon, 1–3pm Tue–Sun; May, Sep: 9am–noon, 1–4pm Tue–Sun; Jun–Aug: 9am–noon, 1–5pm Tue–Sun.* 📷 🚫 🚫

This castle, like Karlstein, owes its appearance to the

View of the castle at Křivoklát, dominated by the Great Tower

restoration work of Josef Mocker. It was originally a hunting lodge belonging to the early Přemyslid princes and the seat of the royal master of hounds. In the 13th century King Wenceslas I built a stone castle here, which remained in the hands of Bohemia's kings and the Habsburg emperors until the 17th century.

Charles IV spent some of his childhood here and returned from France in 1334 with his first wife Blanche de Valois. Their daughter Margaret was born in the castle. To amuse his queen and young princess, Charles ordered the local villagers to trap nightingales and set them free in a wooded area just below the castle. Today you can still walk along the "Nightingale Path".

The royal palace is on the eastern side of the triangular castle. This corner is dominated by the Great Tower, 42 m (130 ft) high. You can still see some 13th-century stonework, but most of the palace dates from the reign of Vladislav Jagiello. On the first floor there is a vaulted Gothic hall, reminiscent of the Vladislav Hall in the Royal Palace at Prague Castle *(see pp104–5).* It has an oriel window and a beautiful loggia that was used by sentries. Also of interest is the chapel, which has a fine Gothic altar carving. Below the chapel lies the Augusta Prison, so-called because Bishop Jan Augusta of the Bohemian Brethren was imprisoned here for 16 years in the mid-16th century. The dungeon now houses a grim assortment of instruments of torture.

Kutná Hora ❺

70 km (45 miles) east of Prague.
Tel 32 75 12 378 (tourist information).
🚊 *from Hlavní nádraží, Masarykovo
nádraží to Kutná Hora, then bus 1 to
Kutná Hora-Město.* 🚌 *from Florenc.*
Church of St Barbara open *Nov–
Mar: 10–noon, 1–4pm Tue–Sun; Apr
& Oct: 9–noon, 1–4:30pm Tue–Sun;
May–Sep: 9am–6pm (last adm 30 mins
before closing).* 🖼 **Italian Court
open** *10am–4pm daily (to 5pm Mar &
Oct; to 6pm Apr–Sep).* 🖼 **Hrádek
open** *Apr & Oct: 9am–5pm Tue–Sun
(to 6pm May, Jun & Sep); Jul–Aug:
10am–6pm Tue–Sun.* 🖼 **Stone
House open** *as Hrádek.* **www.**
kutnahora.cz

The town originated as a
small mining community in
the second half of the 13th
century. When rich deposits
of silver were found, the king
took over the licensing of the
mines and Kutná Hora became
the second most important
town in Bohemia.

In the 14th century five to
six tonnes of pure silver were
extracted here each year, making the king the richest ruler
in Central Europe. The Prague
groschen, a silver coin that
circulated all over Europe, was
minted here in the Italian Court
(Vlašský; dvůr), so-called because Florentine experts were
employed to set up the mint.
Strongly fortified, it was also
the ruler's seat in the
town.
In the late 14th century a
superb palace was con-
structed with reception
halls and the Chapel
of St Wenceslas and St
Ladislav, below which lay
the royal treasury.

When the silver started
to run out in the 16th
century, the town began
to lose its importance;
the mint finally closed in
1727. The Italian Court
later became the town
hall. On the ground floor
you can still see a row
of forges. Since 1947 a
mining museum has
been housed in another
building, the Hrádek,
which was originally a
fort. A visit includes a
tour of a medieval mine.
There is museum in the Stone
House (Kamenný dům), a
restored Gothic building of
the late 15th century.

To the southwest of the
town stands the Church of St
Barbara, begun in 1380 by the
workshop of Peter Parler, also
the architect of St Vitus's
Cathedral *(see pp100–3)*. The
presbytery (1499) has a fine
net vault and windows with
intricate tracery. The slightly
later nave vault is by royal
architect Benedikt Ried. The
murals show mining scenes.

The Italian Court, Kutná Hora's first mint

The cathedral, with its three
massive and tent-shaped spires
rising above a forest of flying

Karlsbad ❻

KARLOVY VARY

140 km (85 miles) west of Prague.
🚊 *from Holešovice.* 🚌 *from
Florenc.* ℹ️ *Lázeňská 1
(35 53 21 176).*

Legend has it that Charles IV
(see pp24–5) discovered one of
the sources of mineral water
that would make the town's
fortune when one of his
staghounds fell into a hot
spring. In 1522 a medical
description of the springs was
published and by the end of
the 16th century over 200 spa
buildings had been built there.
Today there are 12 hot mineral
springs – *vary* means hot
springs. The best-known is the
Vřídlo (Sprudel), which rises to
a height of 12 m (40 ft). At
72°C, it is also the hottest. The
water is good for digestive
disorders, but you do not have
to drink it; you can take the
minerals in the form of salts.

The town is also known for
its Karlovy Vary china and
Moser glass, and for summer
concerts and other cultural
events. The race course is
popular with the more sporting
invalids taking the waters.

Outstanding among the
local historic monuments is
the Baroque parish church of

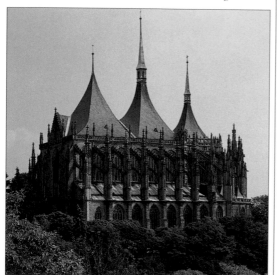

The three steeples of Kutná Hora's great Church of St Barbara

Mary Magdalene by Kilian Ignaz Dientzenhofer (1732–6). More modern churches built for foreign visitors include a Russian church (1896) and an Anglican one (1877). The 19th-century Mill Colonnade (Mlýnská kolonáda) is by Josef Zítek, architect of the National Theatre *(see pp156–7)* in Prague. There have been many royal visitors over the centuries – from Peter the Great of Russia in 1711 to England's Edward VII in 1907.

Marienbad ⑦

MARIÁNSKÉ LÁZNĚ

170 km (105 miles) west of Prague.
🚉 *from Hlavní nádraží.* 🚌 *from Florenc.* 🅸 Hlvaní 47 *(35 46 22 474).*
www.marienbad.cz

The elegance of Marienbad's hotels, parks and gardens has faded considerably since it was the playground of kings and princes at the turn of the century. The area's health-giving waters – *lázně* means bath (or spa) – have been known since the 16th century, but the spa was not founded until the beginning of the last century. The waters are used to treat all kinds of disorders; mud baths are also popular.

Most of the spa buildings date from the latter half of the 19th century. The great cast-iron colonnade with frescoes by Josef Vylětěl is still an impressive sight. In front of it is a "singing fountain", its jets of water now controlled by computer. Churches were

Bronze statue of a chamois at Jeleni skok (Stag's Leap), with a view across the valley to the Imperial Sanatorium, Karlsbad

provided for visitors of all denominations, including an Evangelical church (1857), an Anglican church (1879) and the Russian Orthodox church of St Vladimír (1902). Visitors can learn the history of the spa in the house called At the Golden Grape (U zlatého hroznu), where the German poet Johann Wolfgang von Goethe stayed in 1823. Musical visitors during the 19th century included the composers Weber, Wagner and Bruckner, while writers such as Ibsen, Gogol, Mark Twain and Rudyard Kipling also found its treatments beneficial. King Edward VII also came here and in 1905 he agreed to open the golf course (Bohemia's first), despite hating the game.

There are many pleasant walks in the countryside around Marienbad, especially in the protected Slavkov Forest.

The cast-iron colonnade at Marienbad, completed in 1889

FOUR GUIDED WALKS

Prague offers some good opportunities for walking. In the centre of the city, many streets are pedestrianized and the most important sights are confined to quite a small area *(see pp14–15)*. Here are four guided walks of varied character. The first passes through a main artery of the city, from the Powder Gate on the outskirts of the Old Town to St Vitus's Cathedral in Prague Castle, crossing Charles Bridge at its mid-point. This is the Royal Coronation Route, followed for

House sign in Celetná Street
(See Royal Route Walk pp174–5)

centuries by Bohemian kings. Away from the busy centre, the second and third of the walks takes in the peace and tranquility of two of Prague's loveliest parks – Petřín and the Royal Enclosure. Petřín Park is rewarding for its spectacular views of the city. The Royal Enclosure is outside the centre in the old royal hunting park. The final walk is in Vyšehrad – an ancient fortress which is steeped in history and atmosphere. The views from Vyšehrad of the Vltava and Prague Castle are unparalleled.

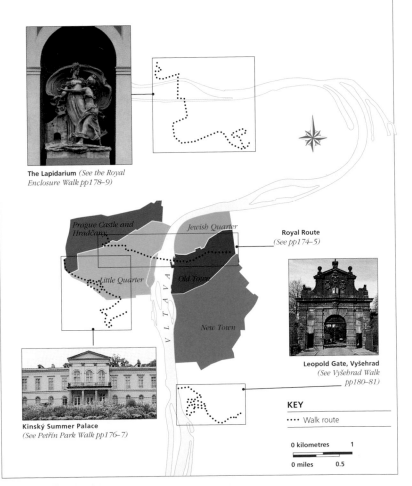

The Lapidarium *(See the Royal Enclosure Walk pp178–9)*

Prague Castle and Hradčany

Jewish Quarter

Little Quarter

Old Town

New Town

V L T A V A

Royal Route
(See pp174–5)

Leopold Gate, Vyšehrad
(See Vyšehrad Walk pp180–81)

Kinský Summer Palace
(See Petřín Park Walk pp176–7)

KEY

•••• Walk route

| 0 kilometres | 1 |
| 0 miles | 0.5 |

◁ **View of the New Town from Petřín Park with the Church of St Lawrence in the foreground**

A 90-Minute Walk along the Royal Route

The Royal Roue originally linked two important royal seats; the Royal Court – situated on the site of the Municipal House and where the walk starts – and Prague Castle, where the walk finishes. The name of this walk derives from the coronation processions of the Bohemian kings and queens who passed along it. Today, these narrow streets offer a wealth of historical and architecturally interesting sights, shops and cafés, making the walk one of Prague's most enjoyable. For more details on the Old Town, the Little Quarter and Hradčany turn to pages 60–79; 122–41 and 94–121 respectively.

Figural *sgraffito* covers the façade of the Renaissance House at the Minute

History of the Royal Route

The first major coronation procession to travel along this route was for George of Poděbrady *(see p26)* in 1458. The next large procession took place in 1743, when Maria Theresa was crowned with great pomp – three Turkish pavilions were erected just outside the Powder Gate. September 1791 saw the coronation of Leopold II. This procession was led by cavalry, followed by mounted drummers, trumpeters and soldiers and Bohemian lords. Some 80 carriages came next, carrying princes and bishops. The most splendid were each drawn by six pairs of horses, flanked by servants with red coats and white leather trousers, and carried the ladies-in-waiting.

The last great coronation procession along the Royal Route – for Ferdinand V – was in 1836 with over 3,391 horses and four camels.

From the Powder Gate to Old Town Square

At Náměstí Republiky turn towards the Municipal House *(see p64)* and walk under the Gothic Powder Gate ① *(see p64)*. Here, at the city gates, the monarch and a large retinue of church dignitaries, aristocrats, and foreign ambassadors were warmly welcomed by leading city represen-tatives. The gate leads into one of Prague's oldest streets, Celetná *(see p65)*. It was here the Jewish community and the crafts guilds, carrying their insignia, greeted their king.

The street is lined with Baroque and Rococo houses. At house No. 36 was the Mint ②. It moved here after the mint at Kutná Hora *(see p170)* was occupied

by Catholic troops in the Hussite Wars *(see pp26–7)*. It minted coins from 1420 to 1784. The House of the Black Madonna ③ contains a museum of Czech Cubist art *(see p65)*. Revellers would watch processions from the taverns At the Spider ④ and At the Vulture ⑤.

At the end of Celetná Street is the Old Town Square ⑥ *(see pp66–9)*. Here, the pro-cessions halted beside Týn Church ⑦ *(see p70)* for pledges of loyalty from the university. Keep to the left of the square, past No. 17, At the Unicorn ⑧, then No. 20, Smetana House, where the composer began a music school in 1848. Proceed to the Old Town Hall ⑨ *(see pp72–4)*.

House at the Black Madonna ③

The distinct Baroque façade of the House at the Golden Well in Karlova Street ⑪

Here, the municipal guard and a band waited for the royal procession and city dignitaries cheered from the temporary balcony around the hall.

Along Karlova Street and across Charles Bridge

Walk past the sgraffitoed façade of the House at the Minute and into Malé náměstí ⑩, where merchants waited with members of the various religious orders. Bear left off the square, then turn right into

good omen. But only a few months later he died. Walk under the Old Town Bridge Tower ⑫ and over Charles Bridge ⑬ and then under the Little Quarter Towers ⑭ *(see pp136–9)*.

The Little Quarter

The walk now follows Mostecká Street. On entering the Little Quarter the mayor handed the city keys to the king and the artillery fired a salute. At the end of this street is Little Quarter Square ⑮ *(see p124)* and the Baroque

Sculpture of Moor by Ferdinand Brokof on Morzin Palace

turn sharp right and walk up the Castle ramp, which leads you to Hradčanské Square. The route ends at the Castle's Matthias Gate *(see p48)* ⑲. The procession ended with the coronation held at St Vitus's Cathedral.

The Old Town from Charles Bridge ⑬

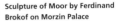

gallery-filled Karlova Street. Beyond Husova Street is an attractive Baroque house, At the Golden Well ⑪. Further on is the 16th-century Clementinum *(see p79)*, where the clergy stood. You then pass into Knights of the Cross Square *(see p79)*. When Leopold II's procession passed through here the clouds lifted, which was considered to be a

church St Nicholas's ⑯ *(see pp128–9)*. The procession passed the church to the sound of its bells ringing.

Leave this picturesque square by Nerudova Street ⑰ *(see p130)*. Poet and writer Jan Neruda, who immortalized hundreds of Little Quarter characters in books like *Mala Strana Tales*, grew up and worked at No. 47, The Two Suns ⑱. Cross the street,

KEY

- ••• Walk route
- Good viewing point
- Metro station
- Tram stop
- City wall

| 0 metres | 300 |
| 0 yards | 300 |

TIPS FOR WALKERS

Starting point: Náměstí Republiky.
Length: 2.4 km (1.5 miles).
Getting there: Line B goes to Náměstí Republiky metro station. At Hradčany you can get tram 22 back into town.
Stopping-off points: Rest beneath the sunshades of the outdoor cafés on Old Town Square or Karlova Street in the summer. On Malostranské náměstí you can enjoy the restaurant Square and in Karlova the café Clementin (at Hotel Clementin).

Coronation procession passing through the Knights of the Cross Square

A Two-Hour Walk through Petřín Park

Part of the charm of this walk around this large and peaceful hillside park are the many spectacular views over the different areas of Prague. The Little Quarter, Hradčany and the Old Town all take on a totally different aspect when viewed from above. The tree-covered gardens are dotted with châteaux, pavilions and statues and crisscrossed by winding paths leading you to secret and unexpected corners. For more on the sights of Petřín Hill see pages 140–41.

One of the gateways in the Hunger Wall ⑤

Actress Hana Kvapilová's statue, near Kinský Summer Palace ①

Kinský Square to Hunger Wall

The walk starts at náměstí Kinských in Smíchov. Enter Kinský Garden through a large enclosed gateway. This English-style garden was founded in 1827 and named after the wealthy Kinský family, supporters of Czech culture in the 19th century.

Take the wide cobbled and asphalt path on your left to the Kinský Summer Palace ①. This 1830s pseudo-classical building was designed by Jindřich Koch and its façade features Ionic columns terminating in a triangular tympanum. Inside the building is a large hall of columns with a triple-branched staircase beautifully decorated with statues. The Ethno-graphical Museum, housed here, holds a permanent exhibition of folk art.

Next to the museum is a 1913 statue of the actress Hana Kvapilová.

About 50 m (150 ft) above the palace is the lower lake ②, where a small waterfall trickles into a man-made pond. Keep going up the hill until you reach the Church of St Michael ③, on your left. This 18th-century wooden folk church was moved here from a village in the Ukraine.

Follow the path up the hill for about 20 m (60 ft), then go to the top of the steps to a wide asphalt path known as the Observation Path for its beautiful views of the city. Turn right and further on your left is the small upper lake ④ with a 1950s bronze statue of a seal at its centre. Keep following the Observation Path; ahead of you stands a Neo-Gothic gate. This allows you to pass through the city's old Baroque fortifications.

Hunger Wall to Observation Tower

Continue along the path to the Hunger Wall ⑤ (see pp140–41). This was a major part of the Little Quarter's fortifica-tions; the wall still runs from Újezd

Church of St Michael ③

Street across Petřín Hill and up to Strahov Monastery. Passing through the gate in the wall brings you to Petřín Park. Take the wide path to the left below the wall and walk up the hill beside the wall until you cross the bridge which spans the funicular railway *(see p141)*. Below on your right you can see the

Sunbathers on Petřín Hill

Nebozízek restaurant *(see p205)* famed for its views. On either side of the path are small sandstone rockeries. Most are entrances to reservoirs, built in the 18th and 19th centuries, to bring water to Strahov Monastery; others are left over from the unsuccessful attempts at mining the area. Walk up to the summit of the hill. On your right is the Mirror Maze ⑥ *(see p140)*. Facing the maze is the 12th-century St Lawrence's Church ⑦ *(see p140)*, renovated in 1740 in the Baroque style.

KEY

- ••• Walk route
- ✷ Good viewing point
- 🚊 Tram stop
- 🚊 Funicular railway
- — Hunger wall

| 0 metres | 300 |
| 0 yards | 300 |

Observation Tower to Strahov Monastery

A little further on stands the Observation Tower ⑧ *(see p140)*. This steel replica of the Eiffel Tower in Paris is 60 m (200 ft) high. Opposite the tower is the main gate of the Hunger Wall. Pass through, turn left and follow the path to the Rose Garden ⑨.

The garden was planted by the city of Prague in 1932, and features a number of attractive sculptures. When you look down to the far end of the garden you can see The Observatory *(see p140)*. This was rebuilt from a municipal building in 1928 by the Czech Astronomical Society and was then modernized in the 1970s. It now houses a huge telescope and is open in the evenings to the public.

Returning to the Observation Tower, follow the wall on the left, passing some chapels of the Stations of the Cross dating from 1834. Then pass through a gap in the Hunger Wall, turn right, and walk past a charming Baroque house. About 50 m (150 ft) beyond this, you pass through another gap in the Hunger Wall on your right. Turn left into a large orchard above Strahov Monastery ⑩ *(see pp120–21)* for spectacular views of the city. Leave by the same hole in the wall that you came in by, turn right, and walk downhill along the wall, through the orchard and past tennis courts

Sgraffitoed façade of the Calvary Chapel next to the Church of St Lawrence ⑦

to the Strahov Monastery courtyard. You can catch tram 22 from here, or linger in the peaceful monastery grounds. If you feel energetic you can walk back down the hill.

TIPS FOR WALKERS

Starting point: *náměstí Kinských in Smíchov.*
Length: *2.7 km (1.7 miles). The walk includes steep hills.*
Getting there: *The nearest metro station to the starting point is Anděl. Trams 6, 9 and 12 go to náměstí Kinských (Kinský Square).*
Stopping-off points: *There is a restaurant, Nebozízek, half way up Petřín Hill and during the summer a few snack bars are open at the summit of the Hill near the Observation Tower.*

Hradčany and the Little Quarter from the summit of Petřín Hill

A 90-Minute Walk in the Royal Enclosure

The royal enclosure, more popularly called Stromovka, is one of the largest parks in Prague. It was created around 1266 during the reign of Přemysl Otakar II, who fenced the area in and built a small hunting château in the grounds. In 1804 it was opened to the public and became Prague's most popular recreational area. The large park of Troja Palace and the zoological garden are on the opposite river bank.

A bust on the Academy of Fine Arts ⑥

The Exhibition Ground (Výstaviště)

From U Výstaviště ① pass through the gate to the old Exhibition Ground. This was created for the 1891 Jubilee Exhibition. Since the late 19th century it has been used for exhibitions and entertainment.

The large Lapidarium of the National Museum ② is on your right. This Neo-Renaissance exhibition pavilion was rebuilt in 1907 in the Art Nouveau style, and decorated with reliefs of figures from Czech history. Many architectural monuments and sculptures from the 11th to the 19th centuries are also housed here.

Facing you is the Industrial Palace ③, a vast Neo-Renaissance building constructed of iron. It is now only open for concerts and events. Walk to the right of the building and you will come to Křižík's Fountain ④. This was restored in 1991 in honour of the Czechoslovakia Exhibition. It

The Art Nouveau Lapidarium ②

was designed by the great inventor František Křižík (1847–1941), who established Prague's first public electric lighting system. From March to September the fountain is illuminated at night by computer-controlled lights which synchronize with the music (see p51).

Behind the fountain there is a permanent fairground. On the left of the Industrial Palace is a circular building which houses Marold's Panorama ⑤. This was painted by Luděk Marold in 1898 and depicts the Battle of Lipany. As you walk back to the Exhibition Ground entrance, you pass the Academy of Fine Arts ⑥, decorated with 18 busts of artists. On leaving the

The summer palace created from a medieval Hunting Château ⑩

KEY

- •••   Walk route
- ⅍   Good viewing point
- ⌷   Tram stop
- ═   Railway line

Exhibition Ground, turn sharp right. Following the outer edge of the Ground you will pass the Planetarium ⑦ on your left; walk straight ahead, then take the road down the slope until you can turn left into a wide avenue of chestnut trees.

The Royal Enclosure

Continue for some way along the avenue until you reach a simple building among trees, on your left. Behind this is the Rudolph Water Tunnel ⑧,

The grand facade of Troja Palace (see pp166–167) ⑭

Statue of lovers in the 16th century gardens of the Enclosure ⑪

a grand monument of the age of Rudolph II (see pp28–9). Hewn into rock, the aqueduct is over 1,000 m (3,000 ft) long. It was built in 1584 to carry water from the Vltava to Rudolph's newly constructed lakes in the Royal Park.

Continue along the path until you reach the derelict Royal Hall ⑨. Built in the late 17th century, it was converted into a restaurant, then rebuilt in 1855 in Neo-Gothic style.

Beyond the Royal Hall, at the bend in the main path, take a steep left fork up through woods to the former Hunting Château ⑩. This medieval building was built for the Bohemian kings who used the park as a hunting reserve. The Château was then later enlarged, and in 1805 was changed again by Jiří Fischer into a Neo-Gothic summer palace. Until 1918, this was a residence of the Governor of Bohemia. Today it is used to house the extensive library of newspapers and magazines of the National Museum.

Retrace your steps to the main path, walk ahead and take the first small path on the right into a late-16th-century formal garden with a modern statue of lovers ⑪.

Return to the main path and turn right. At the fork, take the path which bends to the right along the railway embankment. Continue for a short way then turn left under the railway line to a canal ⑫.

Walk over the bridge, turn left along the canal, then right across the island. Cross the Vltava ⑬ and turn left into Povltavská Street where a wall marks the boundary of Troja Park. Carry along to the south entrance of the gardens of Troja Palace ⑭ (see pp166–7), and then wander through them up to the palace itself.

TIPS FOR WALKERS

Starting point: U Výstaviště in Holešovice.

Length: 5 km (3 miles). The walk goes up a very steep inc line to the former Hunting Château.

Getting there: Trams 5, 12, 14 and 17 run to the starting point. The nearest metro stations are Vltavská or Nádraží Holešovice on line C, ten minutes walk away. At the end of the walk you can get on bus No. 112 at Troja to Nádraží Holešovice metro station.

Stopping-off points: There are a number of restaurants and kiosks in the Exhibition Ground. All the gardens are tranquil spots in which to rest. If you feel like a boat trip down the Vltava, there are often trips starting from the bridge over the canal to Palacký Bridge (see p55).

Industrial Palace

④
⑤
③
⑦
⑥
②
①

Disused entrance to the Rudolph Water Tunnel ⑧

A 60-Minute Walk in Vyšehrad

According to ancient legend, Vyšehrad was the first seat of Czech royalty. It was from this spot that Princess Libuše is said to have prophesied the future glory of the city of Prague (see pp20–21). However, archaeological research indicates that the first castle on Vyšehrad was not built until the 10th century. The fortress suffered a turbulent history and was rebuilt many times. Today, it is above all a peaceful place with parks and unrivalled views of the Vltava valley and Prague. The fascinating cemetery is the last resting place of many famous Czech writers, actors, artists and musicians.

Decorative sculpture on the Baroque Leopold Gate ⑤

The ruin of Libuše's Baths on the cliff face of Vyšehrad Rock ⑩

V Pevnosti

From Vyšehrad metro ①, take the exit for the Congress Centre Prague ②, walk up the steps and continue straight ahead with views of Prague Castle to your right. Go down the incline and straight ahead into the quiet street Na Bučance. Cross the road, turn right at the end, and you find yourself on V Pevnosti, facing the brick walls of the original Vyšehrad Citadel. Ahead of you is the west entrance to the fortress, the mid-17th-century Tábor Gate ③. Through the gate on the right are the ruins

of the 14th-century fortifications built by Charles IV. Further on are the ruins of the original Gothic gate, Špička ④. Past that is the sculpture-adorned Leopold Gate ⑤, one of the most impressive parts of these 17th-century fortifications. It adjoins the brick walls ⑥ that were widened during the French occupation of 1742.

K rotundě to Soběslavova Street

Turn right out of the gate and just after St Martin's Rotunda, turn left into K rotundě. A few metres on your left, almost concealed behind high walls, is the New Deanery ⑦. Situated at the corner of K rotundě and Soběslavova streets is the Canon's House ⑧. Turn left down Soběslavova to see the excavations of the foundations of the

Basilica of St Lawrence ⑨. This was built by Vratislav II, the first Bohemian king, in the late 11th century, but was destroyed by the Hussites (see pp26–7) in 1420. About 20 m (65 ft) past the basilica, turn right on to the fortified walls for a stunning view of Prague.

KEY

- ••• Walk route
- ✼ Good viewing point
- Ⓜ Metro station
- 🚊 Tram stop
- — Castle wall

0 metres	200
0 yards	200

18th-century engraving by I G Ringle, showing Vyšehrad and the Vltava

Vyšehrad Rock

The wooded outcrop of rock on which Vyšehrad was built drops in the west to form a steep rock wall to the river – a vital defensive position. On the summit of the rock are the Gothic ruins of the so-called Libuše's Baths ⑩. This was a defence bastion of the medieval castle. To the left of the bastion is a grassy patch where the remains of a 14th-century Gothic palace ⑪ have been found.

The elaborate memorial to the composer Antonín Dvořák in Vyšehrad Cemetery ⑭

Vyšehrad Park

The western part of Vyšehrad has been transformed into a park. Standing on the lawn south of the Church of St Peter and St Paul (see pp20–21) are four groups of statues ⑫ by the 19th-century sculptor Josef Myslbek. The works represent figures from early Czech history – including the legendary Přemysl and Libuše (see pp20–21). The statues were originally on Palacký Bridge, but were damaged during the US bombardment of February 1945. After being restored, they were taken to Vyšehrad Park. The park was the site of a Romanesque palace, which was connected to the neighbouring church by a bridge. Another palace was built here in the reign of Charles IV (see pp24–5).

The Church of St Peter and St Paul

This twin-spired church ⑬ dominates Vyšehrad. It was founded in the latter half of the 11th century by Vratislav II and was enlarged in 1129. In the mid-13th century it burned down and was replaced by an Early Gothic church. Since then it has been redecorated and restored many times in a variety of styles. In 1885, it was finally rebuilt in Neo-Gothic style, the twin steeples being added in 1902. Note the early-12th-century stone coffin, thought to be of St Longinus, and a mid-14th-century Gothic panel painting *Our Lady of the Rains* on the altar in the third chapel on the right.

Statue of Přemysl and Princess Libuše by Josef Myslbek in Vyšehrad Park ⑫

Vyšehrad Cemetery and the Pantheon

The cemetery ⑭ was founded in 1869 as the burial place for some of the country's most famous figures, such as Bedřich Smetana (see p79). Access is through a gate at the front. On the east side of the cemetery is the Slavín (Pantheon) – built in 1890 for the most honoured citizens of the Czech nation, including the sculptor Josef Myslbek.

Leave the cemetery by the same gate and return down K rotundě. On your left is the Devil's Column ⑮, said to be left by the devil after losing a wager with a priest. At the end is St Martin's Rotunda (see p44) ⑯, a small Romanesque church built in the late 11th century and restored in 1878. Turn left, walk downhill to Cihelná (Brick) Gate ⑰, built in 1741 and home to a small museum that houses six of the original statues from Charles Bridge. Go down Vratislavova Street to Výtoň tram stop on the Vltava Embankment.

The Neo-Gothic Church of St Peter and St Paul ⑬

TIPS FOR WALKERS

Starting point: Vyšehrad metro station, line C.
Length: 1.5 km (1 mile).
Getting there: The walk starts at Vyšehrad metro station and ends at Výtoň tram stop. Trams 3, 17 and 19 go back to the city centre.
Stopping-off points: Relax in the park next to the church of St Peter and St Paul. There is a café in front of the Basilica of St Lawrence and more outdoor cafés in the summer.

TRAVELLERS' NEEDS

WHERE TO STAY

Since the "Velvet Revolution" of 1989, Prague has become one of the most visited cities in Europe. Thanks to investment in new hotels, helped by huge injections of foreign capital, Prague has developed enough accommodation to meet every tourist need. Many old hotels have been rebuilt, while others have been fully re-vamped. Most of the renovated hotels are as smart as any in Europe – and they are often just as expensive. Unfortunately there is little scope for the budget traveller.

Doorman at the exclusive Palace hotel (see p193)

The few cheap hotels tend to be old-fashioned places in the centre of the city, or smaller, pension-type hotels located in the suburbs. We have inspected over 100 hotels in every price bracket in Prague, and on pages 188–95 we recommend 30 of those that offer especially good value. A cheap alternative is to stay in a flat or a room in a private home, which is usually booked by an agency (see p186). Hostels and campsites offer other budget options (see p187).

The Ungelt hotel (see p189)

WHERE TO LOOK

As Prague is such a small city, it is best to stay near the centre close to all the main sights, restaurants and shops. Most hotels are found around Wenceslas Square. Here you are at the hub of everything, and the prices of some (but not all) of the hotels reflect this. Another popular area is the nearby Náměstí Republiky, but the best area is around Old Town Square, a few minutes' walk from Charles Bridge. Hotels here include large, international establishments, old-fashioned Czech places, and some small, much more exclusive hotels.

To the south, in the New Town, there are a few cheaper hotels only a few metro stops from Old Town Square. But the area is less picturesque and some of the streets suffer from heavy volumes of traffic.

For a view of the river Vltava, stay in the Jewish Quarter, although most hotels here are new and expensive. There are also a few botels (floating hotels) moored along the embankments away from the city centre. They are a bit cheaper, but the small cabins are very cramped and uncomfortable, and most of the boats would benefit from some renovation.

Over Charles Bridge, in the Little Quarter, you will find a handful of interesting hotels in delightful surroundings, but there are far fewer by Prague Castle in Hradčany. Further north of this area, there are some large and particularly unappealing hotels. The city's suburbs too, have a number of rather nondescript places a few of these being new. These have some good facilities, but are often as expensive as their equivalents in the centre with the added inconvenience of travelling time and cost – the metro stops at midnight and taxis can become expensive.

HOW TO BOOK

To reserve a room you can book online or send a letter by fax (the best deals are often done online; a popular website is www.HRS.com). It is important to receive written confirmation of your booking by letter or fax in advance, something that will save you time and trouble when you arrive. Most hotel receptionists speak English, so you can always ring them for advice, otherwise ask your tour operator for help;

Pool-side bar at the luxury Praha Renaissance (see p193)

◁ **Rear view of the equestrian statue of St Wenceslas on Wenceslas Square** a number of UK operators specialize in Prague *(see p186)*. When arriving by car, park in the hotel garage or ask at reception about secure parking in the area.

FACILITIES

Following the large investment in many of Prague's hotels, most rooms now have en suite WC and shower or bath, telephone and TV, which may also offer video and satellite channels. Many hotels offer a reasonably-priced laundry service, and the larger hotels usually have 24-hour room service and mini bars. Guests are expected to vacate rooms by midday, but most hotels are happy to keep luggage safe if you are leaving later.

Foreign-owned hotels sometimes import managers, but the Czech staff generally speak good English so you should encounter few communication problems.

DISCOUNT RATES

The price structure for hotels in Prague is fairly flexible. One way to get a cheap rate is to turn up at the hotel and negotiate, although this practice is being phased out. The popular seasons are Christmas, New Year and Easter, when rooms are often hard to find. For cheap rooms in summer it is worth looking at student houses. Most of these have two bedrooms and a kitchen on the same floor, plus a small shop selling hot and cold drinks.

HIDDEN EXTRAS

All hotels include tax (currently at 19%) and service charges in their tariff, but do check these details when you book. Telephone charges can be a shock when you receive your bill so be aware of the mark-up rate. All telephone boxes in the city take phone cards and many take credit cards; phone cards are much cheaper than using cash *(see p232)*. Some expensive hotels charge an extra fee for breakfast, others include a

The Pařiž is a protected monument *(see p189)*

continental breakfast, but hot dishes cost extra. Buffet-style continental breakfasts are popular, and usually offer fresh fruit, cereals, yogurt, muesli, cold meat and cheese, and juice, jugs of coffee and tea.

Tipping is now common and is expected in many hotels. As in most countries, single travellers receive no favours. There are few single rooms, particularly in newer

The modern Praha Hilton hotel dominates the area *(see p195)*

hotels, and a supplement is charged for single occupancy of a double room; expect to pay about 70–80% of the standard rate.

DISABLED TRAVELLERS

Most of the newer hotels in Prague have wheelchair access. For information on accomodation suitable for the disabled, contact the **Czech Association of Persons with Disabilities**, the **Prague Association of Wheelchair-Users** *(see p234)* or the Embassy of the Czech Republic in your country.

TRAVELLING WITH CHILDREN

Children are accommodated by most hotels, either in family rooms or with extra beds, but Prague is not geared to their needs. Hotel breakfasts offer plenty of choice, and although all the fresh milk is pasteurized, hotels also provide long life milk. Few places offer high-chairs or baby-sitters. It is worth asking if there are discounts, or if children can stay free in parents' rooms.

DIRECTORY

UK AGENCIES

British Airways Holidays
London Road,
Crawley, West Sussex
RH10 2XA.
Tel 0870 850 9850.
www.baholidays.com

Čedok Travel
www.cedok.com

Cresta Holidays
Tabley Court,
32 Victoria St, Altrincham,
Cheshire WA14 1E2.
Tel 0870 161 0900.
www.cresta
holidays.co.uk

Crystal Holidays
Kings Place,
Wood Street,
Kingston-upon-Thames,
Surrey KT1 1JY.
Tel 0870 166 4971.
www.crystal
holidays.co.uk

Czech Tourist Centre
13 Harley Street,
London W1G 9QG.
Tel 020 7631 0427.
www.czechtourism.com

Osprey Holidays
Broughton Market,
Edinburgh EH3 6NU.
Tel 0845 310 3031.
www.osprey-
holidays.co.uk

Page & Moy Ltd.
Compass House,
Rockingham Rd,
Market Harborough,
Leicestershire LE16 7QD.
Tel 08708 334 012.
Fax 01858 461 956.
www.pageandmoy.com

Prospect Music and Art Tours
94–104 John Wilson Park,
Whitstable, Kent CT5 3QZ.
Tel 01227 743 307.
Fax 01227 273 263.
www.prospecttours.com

Thomson
Kingsplace, 12–42 Wood
St, Kingston-upon-Thames
KT1 1SH.
Tel 0870 888 0225.
www.thomsoncities.co.uk

US AGENCIES

Friends of Czech Greenways
Suite 1B, 515 Avenue I
Brooklyn, NY 11230.
Tel 718 258 54 68.
Fax 718 258 56 32.
www.pragueviennagreen
ways.org

FLATS AND ROOMS IN PRIVATE HOMES

IN UK
The Czechbook
Jopes Mill,
Trebrownbridge,
Nr. Liskard,
Cornwall PL14 3PX.
Tel & *Fax* 01503 240 629.
@ agnes.michael@
czechbook.com
www.czechbook.com

Regent Holidays
15 John Street,
Bristol BS1 2HR.
Tel 0845 277 3317.
Fax 01179 254 866.
www.regent-
holidays.co.uk

IN PRAGUE
Akasi
28 Října/Jungmannovo
náměstí 9.
Map 3 C5.
Tel 22 22 43 067.
Fax 22 42 37 235.

American Express Travel Service
Václavské náměstí 56.
Map 3 C5.
Tel 22 22 10 106.
www.american
express.cz

Autoturist Travel Agency
Londýnská 62.
Map 6 F4.
Tel 22 25 12 053.
Fax 22 25 20 242.
www.autoturist.cz

AVE Ltd
Hlavní nádraží (main
station). **Map** 4 E5.
Tel 25 10 91 111.
Fax 25 15 56 005.
www.avetravel.cz

Čedok
Na Příkopě 18.
Map 4 D4.
Tel 22 41 97 616.
www.cedok.com

Estec
Vaníčkova 5, Prague 6.
Tel 25 72 10 410.
Fax 25 72 15 263.
www.estec.cz

Pragotur
Arbesovo náměstí 4.
Tel 22 17 14 130.
Fax 22 17 14 127.
www.prague–info.cz

Prague Information Service (PIS)
Staroměstské náměstí 1.
Map 3 B3.
Tel 22 17 14 130.
www.pis.cz
Hlavní nádraží (main
station).
Map 4 E5.
Tel 22 17 14 130.
Fax 22 17 14 127.
www.pis.cz

e.travel.cz
Ostrovní 7.
Map 3 B5.
Tel 22 49 90 990, 0808
238 1322 (UK), 1 877 214
1286 (US).
www.e.travel.cz

Top Tour
Revoluční 24.
Map 4 D2.
Tel 22 48 13 172.
Fax 22 48 12 386.
www.toptour.cz

Travel Agency of Czech Railways
V Celnici 6.
Map 3 C4.
Tel 97 22 33 930.
Fax 97 22 33 809.
www.cdtravel.cz

HOSTELS

Dlouhá
Dlouhá 33.
Map 3 C3.
Tel 22 48 26 662.
Fax 22 48 26 665.
www.travellers.cz

Koleje a Menzy
Opletalova 38.
Map 4 D5.
Tel 22 49 30 010.

Petros
Hilbertova 69,
Louny.
Tel 41 56 58 580.
Fax 41 56 58 497.
www.hostel.cz

Petros Agency
www.ckm.cz

CAMPING

Aritma Džbán
Nad Lavkou 5.
Tel 23 53 58 554.
Fax 23 53 51 365.
www.campdzban.eu

Kotva Braník
U ledáren 55,
Braník.
Tel 24 44 61 712.
Fax 24 44 66 110.
www.kotvacamp.cz

Troja
Trojská 129, Troja.
Tel 28 38 50 482.
Fax 28 38 50 482.
www.volny.cz/campdana

DISABLED TRAVELLERS

Czech Association of Persons with Disabilities
Karlínské náměstí 12,
Prague 8.
Map 5 B2.
Tel 22 48 15 915.
www.svaztp.cz

Embassy of the Czech Republic
26 Kensington Palace
Gardens,
London W8 4QY.
Tel 020 7243 1115.
www.mzv.cz/london

Hotel in a quiet street of a
historic neighbourhood

PRIVATE ROOMS AND SELF-CATERING APARTMENTS

Over the past few years,
the number of private rooms
to rent in Prague has grown
enormously. Although cheap
and popular, they may be
some distance from the
centre. Private rooms in
homes start at about Kč600
per person per night, usually
with breakfast. There are also
self-contained apartments –
a fairly central one-bedroom
apartment costs about
Kč1,600 per night. Most
agencies that offer private
rooms also rent out apartments
(see Directory opposite).

To book a room or apart-
ment, tell the agency exactly
what you want, for how many,
when and in which area. The
agency will suggest places.
Find out the exact location

and the nearest metro before
accepting; if you are in Prague,
see it yourself. Make sure
you receive written, faxed
or emailed confirmation of
a booking to take with you.
On arrival in Prague, pay the
agency in cash; they give you
a voucher to take to the room
or apartment (sometimes you
can pay the owner directly).
If the agency requires
advance payment by banker's
draft go direct to the
accommodation with your
receipt. Agencies may ask for
a deposit on bookings from
abroad, or charge a registration fee payable in Prague.

HOSTELS

There are also many hostels
in Prague, and the **Petros
Agency** provides up-to-date
information on availability.
Useful websites include
www.hoteldiscount.cz,
www.bed.cz, and www.
travellers.cz.

Whilst some hostels are
open all year round, many
only open during the high
season. A few hostels operate
curfews, so it's worth
checking this before you
book. Also, it's often a good
idea to bring your own
sleeping bag, despite linen
usually being available for
hire. Sometimes it can be
better value to choose a hostel
further away from the city
centre, as some of the more
central establishments can cost
just as much as a cheap hotel.

If you are visiting between
June and mid-September, it's

worth investigating the
thousand or so very basic
student rooms available to
the public in the summer
holidays at Prague's
university, the Karolinum
(Tel: 224 913 692). These,
whilst unluxurious, offer
an excellent option for the
budget traveller. Some other
Czech colleges also offer a
similar service.

CAMPING

Most campsites in or near
Prague are closed from
November to the start of April.
They are very cheap with
basic facilities, but are well
served by transport. The
largest site is at **Troja**, 3 km
(1.5 miles) north of the centre.
Aritma Džbán, 4 km (2.5
miles) west, is open all year
for tents, and **Kotva Braník** is
6 km (4 miles) south of the
city on the banks of the
Vltava. For details contact the
PIS *(see Directory opposite)*.

PENSIONS

In the Czech Republic, pensions, or guesthouses, are a
cosy, inexpensive type of
accommodation. They offer
guests reasonably priced
standard rooms with ensuite
bathrooms, and most include
breakfast in the price. Look
out for their signs along the
roads approaching Prague –
the word *pension* is usually
in green. Pensions tend to be
located outside the city centre
and are therefore convenient
for visitors arriving by car.

CONCIERGES

Many hotels have a concierge
who can help guests with
theatre tickets and dinner
reservations. A concierge with
connections may be able to
find you good seats for a
show or secure a reservation
at one of the best restaurants
in Prague. You can also turn
to your hotel concierge for
help when making travel
arrangements and sightseeing
plans, and if you need to
make use of local services or
deal with an emergency. It is
polite to tip a concierge who
has helped during your stay.

Entrance of the Domus Henrici hotel *(see p190)*

Choosing a Hotel

The hotels in this guide have been selected across a wide range of price categories for the excellence of their facilities, location or character. The chart below lists the hotels in price categories within each particular area, starting with the Old Town and moving on to hotels further outside the city centre.

PRICE CATEGORIES
The following price ranges are for a standard double room and taxes per night during the high season. Breakfast is included.
Ⓚ up to Kč3000
ⓀⓀ Kč3000–4500
ⓀⓀⓀ Kč4500–6000
ⓀⓀⓀⓀ Kč6000–8000
ⓀⓀⓀⓀⓀ Over Kč8000.

OLD TOWN

Central
Rybná 8, Praha 1 **Tel** *22 48 12 041* **Fax** *22 32 84 04* **Rooms** *69* 🅿 🍴   ⓀⓀ
Map *3 C2*

An old-style hotel, the lobby and reception have had a cursory facelift, but this fades as you climb the stairs. The bedrooms, though old-fashioned, are clean and the bathrooms immaculate. The location, on the border of the Jewish Quarter and Old Town, is great and explains the high prices. **www.orfea.cz**

Cloister Inn
Konviktská 14, Praha 1 **Tel** *22 42 11 020* **Fax** *22 42 10 800* **Rooms** *75* 📶 🅿 🍴 🖥   ⓀⒾ
Map *3 B5*

Just a few minutes' walk from Charles Bridge, the Cloister Inn is, despite the name, a modern hotel offering large, well-furnished rooms with en suite bathrooms. A good buffet breakfast is served in a high-ceilinged dining room, while tea and coffee is on offer all day in the lobby. **www.cloister-inn.com**

Best Western Meteor
Hybernská 6, 110 00 Praha 1 **Tel** *22 41 92 559* **Fax** *22 42 20 681* **Rooms** *82* 📶 🅿 🍴 🖥   ⓀⓀⓀ
Map *4 D3*

Though part of the international Best Western group, the Meteor still has a cosy, old-fashioned feel so rare in chain hotels. Some parts of the hotel are slightly scruffy, but most of it has been modernised while retaining character. Most bedrooms are small, and the celler has a nice restaurant. **www.hotel-meteor.cz**

Betlem Club
Betlémské náměstí 9, Praha 1 **Tel** *22 22 21 574* **Fax** *22 22 20 580* **Rooms** *21* 🅿 🚹   ⓀⓀⓀ
Map *3 B4*

Beautiful, pastel-green medieval house on a quiet square, a short distance from the Old Town Square. Rooms are rather small and blandly decorated, but all have a private bath and WC. There is much character in the building, especially the original vaulted cellar where the excellent buffet breakfast is served. **www.betlemclub.cz**

U Zlatého Stromu
Karlova 6, Praha 1 **Tel** *22 22 20 441* **Fax** *22 22 20 441* **Rooms** *22* 🅿 🍴   ⓀⓀⓀ
Map *3 B4*

Set in a 13th-century house, this charming hotel has smallish rooms with real character. Furniture and fittings are all tasteful and classic, including wooden, beamed ceilings. While the garden out back is a haven of peace and quiet, some of the rooms facing the busy street are not. **www.zlatystrom.cz**

Clementin
Seminářská 4, 110 00 Praha 1 **Tel** *22 22 21 798* **Fax** *22 22 21 768* **Rooms** *9* 🍴 🖥   ⓀⓀⓀⓀ
Map *3 B4*

Located at the crossroads of ancient and modern Prague, this hotel is an ideal starting point for discovering and enjoying the city. It is housed in the narrowest and greenest building and dates to 1360, though it has only been recently converted to hotel use. Rooms are small but all have en suite bathrooms. **www.clementin.cz**

Élite
Ostrovní 32, 110 00 Praha 1 **Tel** *22 49 32 250* **Fax** *22 49 30 787* **Rooms** *79* 📶 🅿 🍴 🖥   ⓀⓀⓀⓀ
Map *3 B5*

The Élite is housed in a building which dates from the late-14th century. Its cosy atmosphere is aptly augmented by a stylish grill club on the ground floor, offering excellent Mediterranean and Argentinian cuisine, as well as a cocktail bar providing jazz and Latino music. An open atrium contains a day-bar with a small garden. **www.hotelelite.cz**

Grand Hotel Praha
Staroměstské náměstí 25, Praha 1 **Tel** *22 16 32 222* **Fax** *22 16 32 558* **Rooms** *31* 📶 🍴 🖥   ⓀⓀⓀⓀ
Map *3 C3*

With marvellous views of the Old Town Square it is no wonder that the large rooms and apartments are often fully-booked. Rooms are furnished classically and simply, but all have the necessary amenities the modern world demands. Breakfast is served in the historical U Orloje restaurant and beerhouse. **www.grandhotelpraha.cz**

Metamorphis
Malá Štupartská 5, Praha 1 **Tel** *22 17 71 011* **Fax** *22 17 71 099* **Rooms** *24* 📶 🅿 🍴 🚹 🖥   ⓀⓀⓀⓀ
Map *3 C3*

In the centre of Old Town, in the wonderful Tyn Courtyard, the Metamorphis offers rather strangely-styled but large rooms, with en suite bathrooms. Many rooms retain original features from the 14th century, when the building was built. The hotel's restaurant makes great pizzas. **www.metamorphis.cz**

Key to Symbols *see back cover flap*

U Prince

Staroměstské náměstí 29, Praha 1 **Tel** *22 42 13 807* **Fax** *22 42 13 807* **Rooms** *24*   **Map** *3 C3*

Great views of the Old Town Square from every room make this a popular choice for visitors. While the building itself is centuries old, the decoration and facilities inside are thoroughly modern, the hotel having only opened in 2001. The terrace (served by a glass lift) is a favourite feature of this little jewel. **www.hoteluprince.cz**

Ungelt

Štupartská 7, 110 00 Praha 1 **Tel** *22 48 28 686* **Fax** *22 48 28 181* **Rooms** *10*   **Map** *3 C3*

Tucked away in a quiet street behind the Old Town Square, this elegant hotel has more than just an air of exclusivity. The accommodation is in suites, simple yet stylish, and some rooms feature magnificent wooden ceilings. The restaurant is simple and there is a shady terrace. **www.ungelt.cz**

Four Seasons

Veleslavínova 2a, 110 00 Praha 1 **Tel** *22 14 27 000* **Fax** *22 14 26 000* **Rooms** *79*   **Map** *3 A3*

This luxury hotel, located close to the Charles Bridge needs no introduction. There are a variety of rooms and suites to choose from, and all have stunning views over the Vltava. The hotel's Allegro restaurant is often rated the best in the Czech Republic. **www.fourseasons.com**

Paříž

U Obecního domu 1, 110 00 Praha 1 **Tel** *22 21 95 195* **Fax** *22 42 25 475* **Rooms** *86*   **Map** *4 D3*

This Neo-Gothic building with a number of Art Nouveau elements was built by the celebrated architect Jan Vejrych, and was declared a historic monument in 1984. The rooms have been modernised in international style and everything is in pristine condition. **www.hotel-paris.cz**

Ventana

Celetná 7, Praha 1 **Tel** *22 17 76 600* **Fax** *22 17 76 603* **Rooms** *29*   **Map** *3 C3*

Classic Prague hotel in the heart of Old Town. A narrow building that makes great use of the space available, such as the modern lift inside the old staircase. The rooms are imaginatively designed, some on two levels, and all have rather grand four-poster beds. The reception area is an Art Deco treat. **www.ventana-hotel.net**

JEWISH QUARTER

Bellagio

U Milosrdných 2, Praha 1 **Tel** *22 17 78 999* **Fax** *22 17 78 900* **Rooms** *46*   **Map** *3 B2*

Wonderful, pastel-hued hotel on a quiet street minutes from the river. The tastefully decorated bedrooms are large and all have well-sized bathrooms. While the lobby bar is one of the city's trendiest drinking locations, the Isabella restaurant downstairs is also becoming a popular attraction in its own right. **www.bellagiohotel.cz**

Casa Marcello

Řásnovka 783, Praha 1 **Tel** *22 23 11 230* **Fax** *22 23 13 323* **Rooms** *32*   **Map** *3 C2*

Beautiful, rather exclusive hotel alongside St Agnes's Convent. The rooms, in two buildings surrounding lovely gardens, are not so much large as grand, with enormous bathrooms and luxurious furnishings. Sauna and small fitness room onsite. The vaulted lobby bar is a great place for an evening drink. **www.casa-marcello.cz**

Josef

Rybná 20, Praha 1 **Tel** *22 17 00 111* **Fax** *22 17 00 999* **Rooms** *110*   **Map** *3 C3*

This ultra-modern hotel is a wonderful contrast to the historic Jewish Quarter. Well furnished rooms, with probably the best showers in Prague, are situated in two bulidings: the Orange House and the Pink House, separated by a lovely courtyard with manicured lawn. Breakfast is served all morning. **www.hoteljosef.com**

Maximilian

Haštalská 14, 110 00 Praha 1 **Tel** *22 53 03 111* **Fax** *22 53 03 110* **Rooms** *71*   **Map** *3 C2*

Total renovation and redecoration in early 2005 makes this one of the most up-to-date and fashionable places to stay in the city. Exquisitely furnished rooms with over-sized beds are the order of the day at the Maximilian. Each room has classical drapes from Venice, a large en suite bathroom and internet access. **www.maximilianhotel.com**

President

Curieových náměstí 100, Praha 1 **Tel** *23 46 14 111* **Fax** *23 46 14 110* **Rooms** *130*   **Map** *3 B2*

Totally refurbished after the 2002 floods, the President now boasts an executive floor, a casino and health spa, and fabulously furnished rooms and suites. Unique amongst Prague's hotels you can select from one of four great views: the Castle, river, Old Town or St Agnes's Convent. **www.hotelpresident.cz**

Rott

Malé náměstí 4/138, Praha 1 **Tel** *22 41 90 901* **Fax** *22 42 16 761* **Rooms** *84*   **Map** *3 B3*

This central, but nevertheless quiet, hotel near the Old Town Square delights all with its charm, evocative architecture and original wooden furniture. Rooms are large and all have super-sized beds. The glass-roofed reception area and atrium is a joy, as is the adjacent restaurant specialising in game. **www.hotelrott.cz**

Grand Hotel Bohemia
Králodvorská 4, Praha 1 **Tel** *23 46 08 111* **Fax** *22 23 29 545* **Rooms** *78*   **Map** *4 D3*

A mustard-coloured Art Nouveau hotel, as grand and as imperial as the name would suggest. Rooms are enormous, staff are friendly and the hotel's café is one of the city's most popular meeting points. The buffet breakfast is equally famous amongst regular visitors to Prague. **www.grandhotelbohemia.cz**

Inter-Continental
Náměstí Curieových 43–45, Praha 1 **Tel** *29 66 31 111* **Fax** *22 48 11 296* **Rooms** *372*   **Map** *3 B2*

An imposing 1970s building set on the banks of the Vltava, this hotel has health and fitness facilities and a swimming pool. There is nothing Czech about the place, but it is a good example of a five-star international hotel. WiFi in all public areas, high-speed broadband in all rooms. **www.intercontinental.com/prague**

PRAGUE CASTLE AND HRADČANY

U Zlaté Studně
U Zlaté studně 166, Praha 1 **Tel** *25 70 11 213* **Fax** *25 75 33 320* **Rooms** *20*   **Map** *2 E2*

Luxury rooms in a former house which is almost as old as Prague itself, just minutes from the castle. Views of Prague from the rooftop restaurant and terrace are stunning, and the rooms are well furnished with original touches. Bathrooms, too, are comfortable, which is something of a rarity in these parts. **www.zlatastudna.cz**

Hoffmeister
Pod Bruskou 7, Praha 1 **Tel** *251 01 71 11* **Fax** *251 01 71 20* **Rooms** *37*   **Map** *2 F2*

The closest, quality hotel to Prague Castle, the imposing Hoffmeister offers a spa and fitness centre alongside its individually furnished rooms. Views from the rooms of the river towards the old town are terrific. The location, half-way up Chotkova, is not a great choice for the elderly or disabled, however. **www.hoffmeister.cz**

Savoy
Keplerova 6, Praha 1 **Tel** *22 43 02 430* **Fax** *22 43 02 128* **Rooms** *61*   **Map** *1 B3*

Splendid period building inside which a luxury, modern hotel plays host to the great and good. The list of famous people who have stayed here is as endless as the services that the hotel offers. Rooms are large and plush, all with what are probably the largest bathrooms in Prague. **www.hotel-savoy.cz**

LITTLE QUARTER

Residence Malá Strana
Mělnická 9, Praha 1 **Tel** *25 15 10 372* **Fax** *25 15 10 406* **Rooms** *35*   **Map** *2 F5*

Smart hotel in a lovely Neo-Classical building in the Little Quarter. Rooms are large, more like suites, and have small kitchens and a separate dining area. A filling breakfast is included in the price. There is a nice lounge with garden view on the ground floor, perfect for relaxing after a day's sightseeing. **www.hotelresidence-mala-strana.com**

Sax
Jánský vršek 3, Praha 1 **Tel** *25 75 31 268* **Fax** *25 75 34 101* **Rooms** *22*   **Map** *2 D3*

With a great location close to Prague Castle, the Sax and its classical white façade, is ideal for serious sightseers who want to be among the first up Hradčany hill in the morning. The rooms are simple but immaculate, overlooking a courtyard, and the common areas are well kept. **www.sax.cz**

U Žluté boty
Jánský vršek 11, Praha 1 **Tel** *25 75 32 269* **Fax** *257 53 41 34* **Rooms** *9*   **Map** *2 D3*

The sparsely furnished but tasteful and elegant rooms at U Žluté boty are all individually decorated, some with lots of wood, others with a more modern feel. The rooms are large and have well-sized bathrooms. The courtyard at the back is very pleasant during the summer. **www.zlutabota.cz**

Best Western Kampa
Všehrdova 16, Praha 1 **Tel** *25 74 04 444* **Fax** *25 74 04 333* **Rooms** *84*   **Map** *2 E5*

A 17th-century armoury, the Kampa is minutes from Charles Bridge, tucked away on a peaceful side street surrounded by lovely gardens. In the large reception hall, a bar and restaurant are combined under a huge Baroque-vaulted ceiling. The furnishings are simple and bedrooms are clean. **www.euroagentur.cz**

Domus Henrici
Loretánská 11, Praha 1 **Tel** *22 05 11 369* **Fax** *22 05 11 502* **Rooms** *8*   **Map** *1 C3*

Part of the Hidden Places hotel group, you may have trouble finding this establishment. It's difficult to get much closer to the castle than this, so sightseers will love the location. Rooms are enormous and tastefully decorated. An excellent buffet breakfast is served on the terrace during the summer **www.hidden-places.com**

Key to Price Guide *see p188* **Key to Symbols** *see back cover flap*

U Brány

Nerudova 21, Praha 1 **Tel** *25 75 34 050* **Fax** *25 75 32 767* **Rooms** *17*   **Map** *2 D3*

With one of the best addresses in Prague, U Brány is a popular spot, often full at busy times. Reserving your room well ahead is essential. The rooms, all of which are in fact two-, three- or four-roomed suites, are large and luxuriously decorated. The bathrooms are splendid. **www.ubrany.cz**

Biskupský Dům

Dražického náměstí 6, Praha 1 **Tel** *25 75 32 320* **Fax** *25 75 31 840* **Rooms** *45*   **Map** *2 F3*

Completely refurbished in the 1990s, this upmarket hotel is located in an old house overlooking the Royal Route. Rooms are classically furnished, evoking a bygone age. Those on the upper floor have stunning high ceilings with wooden beams and all sorts of awkward but enchanting nooks and crannies. **www.starshotelsprague.com**

Constans

Břetislavova 309, Praha 1 **Tel** *23 40 91 818* **Fax** *23 40 91 860* **Rooms** *32*   **Map** *2 D3*

Located on a quiet, medieval street below the castle, this recently-renovated hotel combines old-world class and taste with modern amenities. Rooms are large, with big beds and classic but simple furniture. The charming restaurant is a fine place to spend long evenings with friends. **www.hotelconstans.cz**

Dům U Červeného lva

Nerudova 41, Praha 1 **Tel** *25 75 33 833* **Fax** *25 75 35 131* **Rooms** *21*   **Map** *2 F3*

With views of the Royal Route, Prague Castle or the serene Petrin Hill Orchards, the Red Lion is absolutely ideal for sightseers. Add in the hand-painted Renaissance ceilings, original period furniture and parquet floors and you have a real historical treat. There is a traditional Czech beer hall too. **www.hotelredlion.com**

Pod Věží

Mostecká 2, Praha 1 **Tel** *25 75 32 041* **Fax** *25 75 32 069* **Rooms** *12*   **Map** *2 F3*

In the heart of the historical centre, this is a delightful, family-run hotel. Pod Věží offers a peaceful ambience, highlighted by the charming roof garden and the sidewalk café, which is open – and usually full – all day. Rooms are well appointed if not huge, and breakfast is included in the price. **www.podvezi.com**

U Páva

U Lužického semináře 32, Praha 1 **Tel** *25 75 33 573* **Fax** *25 75 30 919* **Rooms** *27*   **Map** *2 F3*

Located in a quiet part of the Little Quarter, U Páva provides visitors with stylish surroundings during their stay. Historical features are enhanced by traditional, wooden furniture, crystal chandeliers and attractive rugs. Personal touches give the hotel an individual feel, and the bedrooms are spacious. **www.romantichotels.cz**

U Tří Pštrosů

Dražického náměstí 12, Praha 1 **Tel** *25 72 88 888* **Fax** *25 75 33 217* **Rooms** *18*   **Map** *2 F3*

Just beside Charles Bridge, the hotel "At The Three Ostriches" began life as the home of Jan Fux, an ostrich-feather dealer. It is one of the best-known hotel/restaurants in Prague. Family run, it has an intimate atmosphere, and children are especially welcome. The bedrooms have recently been refurbished. **www.utripstrosu.cz**

Aria

Tržiště 9, Praha 1 **Tel** *22 53 34 111* **Fax** *22 53 34 666* **Rooms** *52*   **Map** *2 E3*

A charming, unusual little hotel where each of the fantastic, though not large, rooms are modelled to honour a particular musical legend, be it Dizzy Gillespie, Puccini or Mozart. The hotel even has a musical director who will recommend music to suit your mood, while also advising on concerts that you may attend. **www.ariahotel.net**

Waldstein

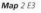

Valdštejnské náměstí 6, Praha 1 **Tel** *25 75 33 938* **Fax** *25 75 31 143* **Rooms** *15*   **Map** *2 E3*

The rooms in this historical hotel are furnished with superb antique furniture, yet all come with modern amenities, including internet connections and satellite TV. Some rooms even have mosaics on the ceilings. The breakfast, served in an original vaulted cellar, is excellent. **www.avehotels.cz**

NEW TOWN

Evropa

Václavské náměstí 25, 110 00 Praha 1 **Tel** *22 42 28 215* **Fax** *22 42 24 544* **Rooms** *90*   **Map** *4 D5*

The Evropa is Prague's most beautiful – and possibly most famous – hotel, with superb Art Nouveau decor, and a ground-floor terrace-café that is in itself a major attraction, boasting stunning glasswork. The rooms are not as fancy or impressive, but are large and all have private bathrooms. **www.evropahotel.cz**

Pension Březina

Legerova 41, Praha 2 **Tel** *22 42 66 779* **Fax** *22 42 66 777* **Rooms** *35*   **Map** *6 D2*

Located on a busy street, the somewhat faded exterior belies a super bed-and-breakfast hidden within. Rooms are modern if somewhat simple, and many have views of the small garden at the rear of the building. Two apartments ideal for families are available. Breakfast is served in the small dining room. **www.brezina.cz**

Pension Museum

Mezibranská 15, Praha 1 **Tel** *29 63 25 186* **Fax** *29 63 25 188* **Rooms** *12* **Map** *6 D1*

Large rooms, most with separate bedrooms and a small living area, are what distinguish the Pension Museum. Great service, an excellent breakfast and a super location at the top of Wenceslas Square, make this converted school just about the best value bed-and-breakfast in central Prague. **www.pension-museum.cz**

Junior

Senovážné náměstí 21, Praha 1 **Tel** *22 42 31 754* **Fax** *22 42 21 579* **Rooms** *15* **Map** *4 E4*

Expect excellent value-for-money if you stay at this cheap hotel, just a few minutes' walk from the top of Wenceslas Square. Rooms are not luxurious but are well equipped with private bathrooms. A good pizzeria downstairs does a roaring trade, and there is a bowling alley onsite too. **www.euroagentur.cz**

Luník

Londýnská 50, 120 00 Praha 2 **Tel** *22 42 53 974* **Fax** *22 42 53 986* **Rooms** *35* **Map** *6 E2*

Located in a quiet street lined with trees, this good value, historic hotel is in immaculate condition. The decor is simple, with whitewashed walls and good-quality wooden furnishings. Rooms are small but have en suite bathrooms with bath, shower and WC. A buffet breakfast is included in the price. **www.hotel-lunik.cz**

Na Zlatém Kříži

Jungmannovo náměstí 2, Praha 1 **Tel** *22 42 19 501* **Fax** *22 22 45 418* **Rooms** *8* **Map** *3 C5*

A challenger for the narrowest hotel in Prague award, the charming Golden Cross offers deceptively large, and rather luxurious double rooms and apartments, all with private bathrooms. A good buffet breakfast is served in the hotel's Gothic-style cellar. Transfers to and from the airport are possible. **www.goldencross.cz**

Opera

Těšnov 13, Praha 1 **Tel** *22 23 15 609* **Fax** *22 23 11 477* **Rooms** *67* **Map** *4 F2*

Although nowhere near the opera, this hotel is a classy Neo-Renaissance affair built in the late-19th century. Rooms are classically furnished and all have enormous windows with views of the small park opposite. The hotel bar is pure kitsch, with its 1950s-style booths, and shouldn't be missed. **www.hotel-opera.cz**

Tchaikovsky

Ke Karlovu 19, Praha 1 **Tel** *22 49 12 121* **Fax** *22 49 12 123* **Rooms** *19* **Map** *5 C2*

Ten-minutes' walk from Wenceslas Square on a quiet side street, the smart, Neo-Classical Tchaikovsky hits all the right notes with its simple charm and elegance. Rooms are well sized if low on frills, and bathrooms are huge and wonderfully decorated. A buffet breakfast is included in the price. **www.hoteltchaikovsky.com**

U Klenotníka

Rytířská 3, Praha 1 **Tel** *22 42 11 699* **Fax** *22 42 21 025* **Rooms** *11* **Map** *3 B4*

A small, but lovely hotel and restaurant in a converted house halfway between the Old Town Square and Wenceslas Square. Rooms are reasonably sized and offer great value for money. There is a small paternoster elevator for luggage. Excellent buffet breakfast is served in the downstairs restaurant. **www.uklenotnika.cz**

U Medvídků

Na Perštýně 7, Praha 1 **Tel** *22 42 11 916* **Fax** *22 42 20 930* **Rooms** *33* **Map** *3 B5*

Classic Czech restaurant, beerhouse and pension. The more expensive rooms have wooden beams and a definite medieval flavour, but all are large and full of character, and have private facilities. U Medvídků is one of the few hotels, which have a brewing museum in the basement. **www.umedvidku.cz**

Axa

Na poříčí 40, Praha 1 **Tel** *22 48 12 580* **Fax** *22 42 14 489* **Rooms** *132* **Map** *4 E3*

This block-style hotel is slightly dispiriting in appearance, yet reasonably priced and centrally located. Inside, things are much better, and all the recently-renovated rooms have a private bath and WC. There is also a large fitness complex in the hotel, including an indoor swimming pool, sauna and solarium. **www.hotelaxa.com**

Elysee

Václavské náměstí 43, Praha 1 **Tel** *22 14 55 111* **Fax** *22 42 25 773* **Rooms** *70* **Map** *4 D5*

If you are looking for a good value, but not luxury hotel on Wenceslas Square, then this place could be your best choice. The large, tastefully decorated rooms are fine for all but the fussiest visitors, and the location is perfect. Good insulation keeps noise from the busy street below to a minimum. **www.europehotels.cz**

Harmony

Na poříčí 31, Praha 1 **Tel** *22 23 19 807* **Fax** *22 23 10 009* **Rooms** *60* **Map** *4 E3*

The rather bleak looking Harmony is, in fact, in pristine condition after reconstruction. A compact place, it is run by young, friendly staff. Two small restaurants, one with tables on the pavement, give a choice of cuisine. Ask for a room away from the busy central street, which can be noisy at night. **www.euroagentur.cz**

Adria

Václavské náměstí 26, Praha 1 **Tel** *22 10 81 111* **Fax** *22 10 81 300* **Rooms** *87* **Map** *4 D5*

The Adria is bright and chic with an entrance on Wenceslas Square. Clever use of glass and mirrors makes the reception seem bigger than it is, and with plenty of gleaming brass the impression is light and up-beat. The bedrooms are bright, cheerful and smartly furnished. **www.adria.cz**

Key to Price Guide *see p188* **Key to Symbols** *see back cover flap*

Carlo IV
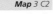

Senovážné náměstí 13, Praha 1 **Tel** *22 45 93 111* **Fax** *22 42 23 960* **Rooms** *152* **Map** *4 E4*

This magnificently decorated hotel with shimmering marble floors, intricate hand-painted frescos in a Neo-Classical building, is in the heart of the city. Part of the Boscolo Group, it is all startlingly wonderful, from the Box Block restaurant to the cigar bar, while the spa features Europe's best hotel swimming pool. **www.boscolohotels.com**

Hotel Maximilian

Haštalská 14, 110 00 Praha 1 **Tel** *22 53 03 111* **Fax** *22 53 03 110* **Rooms** *70* **Map** *3 C2*

A short walk from the Old Town Square and Charles Bridge, this four-star hotel boasts a stylish contemporary interior. All rooms are equipped with DVD players and internet access and most look out over a courtyard. Communal areas include a drawing room with a fireplace, a library and a garden terrace where breakfast is served. **www.maximilianhotel.com**

Liberty

28. října 11, Praha 1 **Tel** *22 42 39 598* **Fax** *22 42 37 694* **Rooms** *32* **Map** *3 C4*

Simple elegance meets modern efficiency in this fine boutique hotel in the centre of Prague. Spacious rooms and bathrooms, wonderful halls and luxurious services make this a popular choice with the well-heeled. The hotel's Relax Club offers fitness equipment, sauna, whirlpool, massage and solarium. **www.hotelliberty.cz**

Praha Renaissance

V celnici 7, Praha 1 **Tel** *22 18 22 100* **Fax** *22 18 22 200* **Rooms** *310* **Map** *4 E3*

The gleaming glass front of this relatively new hotel has taken over one entire corner of Náměstí Republiky. The opulent bedrooms include soft furnishings, plump bedcovers, plush carpets and fluffy bathrobes. There is a choice of fantastic restaurants, a beer hall and health club with a swimming pool. **www.renaissancehotels.com**

Seven Days

Žitná 46, Praha 2 **Tel** *22 29 23 142* **Fax** *22 29 23 222* **Rooms** *50* **Map** *6 D2*

Fabulous Neo-Classical hotel in the centre of Prague's New Town. Rooms are all large and superbly furnished with good taste, while the stylish common areas are impressively opulent. A sauna and whirlpool are available to guests for a small fee. Internet TV in all rooms. **www.hotelsevendays.cz**

Esplanade

Washingtonova 19, Praha 1 **Tel** *22 45 01 111* **Fax** *22 42 29 306* **Rooms** *74* **Map** *4 E5*

This imposing six-storey hotel opposite the opera house is known for its long history of luxury. The Art Nouveau façade hides an elegant interior, and all the rooms are well furnished. The hotel's café has a summer terrace, while the onsite French restaurant is world class. Service is exceptional. **www.esplanade.cz**

Marriott

V celnici 8, Praha 1 **Tel** *22 28 88 888* **Fax** *22 28 88 889* **Rooms** *293* **Map** *4 E3*

The Prague Marriott is one of the best hotels in the Marriott chain, and has a great location close to the Old Town gate. Every amenity and luxury imaginable is on offer in all the rooms. There is a great health club with a swimming pool, free to guests. The restaurants here are considered to be among the best in the city. **www.marriott.com**

Palace

Panská 12, 110 00 Praha 1 **Tel** *22 40 93 111* **Fax** *22 42 21 240* **Rooms** *124* **Map** *4 D4*

Located on a quiet side street close to Wenceslas Square, the mixture of styles – modern, Art Nouveau and traditional – with lashings of brass, glass, mirrors and fake flowers, may not be to everyone's taste, but the hotel succeeds in providing any luxury guests may require. Rooms are enormous. **www.palacehotel.cz**

Radisson SAS Alcron

Štěpánská 40, Praha 1 **Tel** *22 28 20 000* **Fax** *22 28 20 100* **Rooms** *211* **Map** *6 D1*

The views from the upper floors of this exquisite hotel could be an attraction in themselves. But that would be to forget the other joys of staying at this Radisson hotel, including enormous bathrooms, divine chocolates at bedtime and plush carpets. Expensive but worth every penny. **www.radissonsas.com**

FURTHER AFIELD

Apollo

Kubišova 23, Praha 8 **Tel** *28 46 80 628* **Fax** *28 46 84 570* **Rooms** *42*

Modern, non-descript hotel offering small, simple rooms with en suite facilities and satellite TV at reasonable prices. Situated in a quiet residential area in the north of the city, it is a tram or a metro ride away from the centre. A buffet breakfast is included in the price. **www.avehotels.cz**

Best Western Alta

Ortenovo náměstí 22, Praha 7 **Tel** *22 04 07 082* **Fax** *22 28 22 833* **Rooms** *87*

It may be some distance from the city centre, but the Alta is close to the metro and offers large, very good value, if plain and somewhat formulaic rooms. As part of Best Western, however, you can be assured that service is very good and always comes with a smile. Excellent breakfast included in the price. **www.hotelalta.com**

Carol
Kurta Konráda 12, Praha 9 **Tel** *28 40 19 911* **Fax** *28 40 19 977* **Rooms** *52*

This hotel is Dutch-owned, and the atmosphere is relatively relaxed for Prague. Bedrooms feature minimalist decor, but are immaculate and comfortable. The indoor swimming pool and sauna are a real treat. The only disadvantage is the distance from the city centre. **www.carol.cz**

Kafka
Cimburkova 24, Praha 3 **Tel** *22 42 25 769* **Fax** *22 42 25 769* **Rooms** *59*

A simple, clean but somewhat Spartan and soulless hotel a short walk away from Old Town. The building is a classic though, and a large number of triple and quad rooms make it a good choice for families on a budget. If you want to park in the hotel's carpark you need to pre-book a space. **www.ckvesta.cz**

Kavalír
Plzeňská 177, Praha 5 **Tel** *25 72 16 565* **Fax** *25 72 10 085* **Rooms** *50*

Cheapest hotel in the good value H&Hotels chain, this place is not without charm. Rooms are impressively large – some have two large double beds – and all the common areas are well kept, bright and breezy. Staff are friendly and communicate in a number of languages. It is some way from the city centre though. **www.europehotels.cz**

Abri
Jana Masaryka 36, Praha 2 **Tel** *22 25 11 568* **Fax** *22 42 54 240* **Rooms** *26*

Comfortable hotel in a quiet residential area of Prague, Vinohrady. Smallish rooms are well furnished and decorated, and all have private bathrooms. A small garden terrace is a pleasant place to unwind with a drink after a long day of sightseeing. Guarded parking and onsite restaurant. **www.abri.cz**

Anna
Budečská 17, Praha 2 **Tel** *22 25 13 111* **Fax** *22 25 15 158* **Rooms** *22*

Housed in an elegant Neo-Classical building with Art Nouveau interiors, this excellent value hotel is only a 10-minute walk from Wenceslas Square. Rooms are spacious and have large, comfortable beds, but some of the bathroms can be small. Staff are helpful, multilingual and very friendly. **www.hotelanna.cz**

Arcotel Teatrino
Bořivojova 53, Praha 3 **Tel** *22 14 22 111* **Fax** *22 14 22 222* **Rooms** *73*

Once a theatre, this design hotel is a well-priced, high-quality alternative to more expensive retreats. Located in residential Žižkov, its finest feature, besides the large, well-furnished rooms, is the spendid restaurant – situated in what was once the stalls – overlooked by the theatre's original balconies and boxes. **www.arcotel.at**

Ariston
Seifertova 65, Praha 3 **Tel** *22 27 82 517* **Fax** *22 27 80 347* **Rooms** *61*

Great value three-star hotel not too far from the city centre in a quiet residential area. Rooms are simple but clean and well-sized, with high ceilings and sturdy wooden desks. All have private bathrooms, and some larger rooms take a third bed. Non-smoking and disabled-friendly rooms are also available. **www.europehotels.cz**

Barceló
Na Strži 32, Praha 4 **Tel** *24 14 40 022* **Fax** *24 14 41 023* **Rooms** *213*

Situated some distance from the city centre, the Barceló – part of the Spanish hotel chain of the same name – is a fine, high-rise hotel catering mainly to large tour groups and business travellers. There is much to enjoy however, as rooms are large and those on higher floors have stunning views of the city. **www.barcelopraha.com**

Duo
Teplická 492, Praha 9 **Tel** *26 61 31 111* **Fax** *28 38 80 141* **Rooms** *553*

Massive hotel cum mini-resort on the northern edge of town, the Duo offers large rooms and super services at great prices. It also has the best sports centre in Prague, with a swimming pool, fitness centre, whirlpool, sauna and bowling alley. There are also three restaurants, a beer garden and an internet café. **www.hotelduo.cz**

Green Garden
Fügnerovo náměstí 4, Praha 2 **Tel** *22 42 61 181* **Fax** *22 42 62 182* **Rooms** *55*   **Map** *6 D3*

Comfortable if not luxurious hotel situated somewhat uncomfortably between the main Prague-Brno highway. It does overlook a small, green garden, however, and pricewise it is competitive. The large, airy and bright terrace is its best asset, where lazy afternoons maybe spent while drinking coffee. **www.hotelgreengarden.cz**

Julián
Elišky Peškové 11, Praha 5 **Tel** *25 73 11 150* **Fax** *25 73 11 149* **Rooms** *32*

Good value hotel where, though the rooms are on the small side, everything is done to make up for that one drawback. Service is fantastic, there is a sauna, solarium and a small fitness room, and children are especially welcome. All rooms are accesible by wheelchairs, and one room has a specially adapted bathroom. **www.julian.cz**

U Blaženky
U Blaženky 1, Praha 5 **Tel** *25 15 64 532* **Fax** *25 15 63 529* **Rooms** *13*

You are guaranteed to feel special just arriving at this villa conversion in one of Prague's best residential districts. The excellent value – though by no means cheap – rooms are modern and spacious, full of extras and nice touches, while the dining room is home to fine local cuisine and an excellent winelist. **www.ublazenky.cz**

Key to Price Guide *see p188* **Key to Symbols** *see back cover flap*

U Tří Korunek (Three Crowns)

Cimburkova 28, Praha 3 **Tel** *22 27 81 112* **Fax** *22 27 80 189* **Rooms** *58*

It may today cost rather more than three crowns to stay here, but the value for money is good, even if the location – out in the less than salubrious suburb of Žižkov – isn't. Rooms are simple and without any fuss but well appointed with everything you'll need. Service from the friendly staff is always good. **www.3korunky.cz**

Art Hotel Praha

Nad Královskou oborou 53, Praha 7 **Tel** *23 31 01 331* **Fax** *23 31 01 311* **Rooms** *24*

With its permanent display of Czech modern art, the Art Hotel is a cool, quiet place to escape the capital's tourist trail. Rooms are individually decorated, all with panache and taste. The lighting is a big feature: subtle and designed to catch your mood. Excellent buffet breakfast included in the price. **www.arthotel.cz**

Carlton

Táboritská 18, Praha 3 **Tel** *22 27 11 177* **Fax** *22 27 11 199* **Rooms** *49*

Not perfectly located, the Carlton is nevertheless a stylish, good-value hotel, offering large rooms at reasonable prices. The lofty celings and wooden beams make the top-floor rooms a preferred choice. Buffet breakfast served in a small cellar restaurant. One room is specially adapted for disabled visitors. **www.europehotels.cz**

Mövenpick

Mozartova 1, Praha 5 **Tel** *25 71 51 111* **Fax** *25 71 53 131* **Rooms** *502*

Though not centrally located, this luxurious hotel situated in two buildings linked by a funicular is wonderful. All of the rooms – some of which are split over two levels – are large, comfortable and cater to all needs. The hotel's restaurants are well regarded, and it's also famous for ice cream. **www.movenpick-prague.com**

Praha Hilton

Pobřeží 1, 186 00 Praha 8 **Tel** *22 48 41 111* **Fax** *22 48 42 378* **Rooms** *788* **Map** *4 F2*

French-owned and designed, this is the biggest hotel in the country, and despite the huge size, it does have a certain style. The bedrooms are tastefully decorated with all the comforts you would expect to find in a large international hotel, while the cost of staying in one is far lower than you may have thought. **www.prague.hilton.com**

Ametyst

Jana Masaryka 11, Praha 2 **Tel** *22 29 21 921* **Fax** *22 22 91 999* **Rooms** *84* **Map** *6 F3*

Fine, modern townhouse-style hotel with air-conditioned rooms, all with private bath or shower and internet access. The attic rooms with sloping, beamed ceilings are especially attractive. Sauna and massage also available. Ametyst has a small restaurant with some fine decor. **www.hotelametyst.cz**

Corinthia Towers

Kongresová 1, Praha 4 **Tel** *26 11 91 111* **Fax** *26 12 25 011* **Rooms** *544*

Situated beside the Vyšehrad metro stop, the Corinthia Towers is only a few minutes from the city centre. Built in 1988 as a modern high-rise filled with glass, brass and marble, it has an impressive health centre and a beautiful indoor swimming pool. The good-sized bedrooms are well decorated and comfortable. **www.corinthia.cz**

Diplomat Praha

Evropská 15, Praha 6 **Tel** *29 65 59 213* **Fax** *29 65 59 207* **Rooms** *398*

This hotel is located right at the end of metro line A, but is only 12 minutes from the city centre. It opened in 1990 and still feels very new. Efficiently run by Austrians, it offers excellent facilities including a nightclub, numerous restaurants, shops and even a whirlpool in the health club. **www.diplomatpraha.cz**

Mucha

Sokolovská 26, Praha 8 **Tel** *22 23 19 047* **Fax** *22 48 16 641* **Rooms** *39* **Map** *4 F2*

Perhaps a little overpriced, the Mucha is nevertheless a good hotel, in a great location, minutes from the city centre. The legacy of Czech painter Alphonse Mucha for whom the hotel is named is not forgotten, with reproductions of his work all over the building, which is also something of an Art Deco masterpiece. **www.avehotels.cz**

Praha Hotel

Sušická 20, Praha 6 **Tel** *22 43 41 111* **Fax** *22 43 11 218* **Rooms** *124*

When the Praha opened in 1981, it was regarded by its architects as the height of modernity, with its unique design, all curves and waves. Built to accommodate visiting heads of state and dignitaries, it is today open to all, though its secluded location still makes it a favourite of VIPs. **www.htlpraha.cz**

Andel's

Stroupežnického 21, Praha 5 **Tel** *29 68 89 688* **Fax** *29 68 89 999* **Rooms** *239*

Designed by the same team who came up with the multi-award winning One Aldwych in London, this is a modernist fusion of elegance and practicality. Rooms are spacious, bathrooms have separate shower and bath, and the onsite Delight restaurant is one of the city's best. The hotel is a metro ride from the city centre. **www.andelshotel.com**

Riverside

Janáčkovo nábřeží 15, Praha 5 **Tel** *23 47 05 155* **Fax** *23 47 05 158* **Rooms** *45*

Classy, and – as the name suggests – handy for the river, this hotel is not cheap but is certainly impressive, with small touches of elegance and fine living at every turn. From the basket of complimentary high-end toiletries in the bathrooms to the original, contemporary Czech art on the wall, your stay here will be enjoyable. **www.riversideprague.com**

RESTAURANTS, CAFÉS AND PUBS

Restaurants in Prague, just like the economy, seem to be getting better. For 40 years state-licensed eating and drinking establishments had little incentive to experiment or improve. But attitudes are rapidly changing. Fuelled by the booming tourist industry, new restaurants are opening constantly, many of them foreign-owned, offering the discerning eater an ever-increasing choice. The restaurants described in this

The Good Soldier Švejk at U Kalicha *(see p207)*

section reflect the change, though many only serve a limited range of standard Western dishes as well as staple Czech meals. *Choosing a Restaurant* on pages 202–3 summarizes the key features of the restaurants and cafés, listed by area. Full listings can be found on pages 202–7 and information on pubs, beer halls and bars appears on pages 208–9. Compared to Western prices, eating out in Prague is still cheap.

TIPS ON EATING OUT

Because of the huge influx of tourists, eating out has changed in character. The lunch hour is still early – between 11am and 1pm, and for most Czechs the normal time for the evening meal is around 7pm. However, many of the restaurants stay open late and it is possible to get a meal at any time from 10am until 11pm. Kitchens close 30 minutes to one hour earlier than stated closing times.

During spring and summer, the large numbers of visitors tend to put a strain on many of Prague's more popular restaurants. To be certain of a table, especially in the very well-known restaurants, it is advisable to book in

advance. The city centre is full of restaurants, and there are several off the normal tourist track. Prices also tend to be lower the further you go from the centre.

PLACES TO EAT

The importance of a stylish yet comfortable setting, and food which is inspired rather than just prepared, is slowly beginning to trickle down to Prague's better and more innovative restaurants. The places which follow this maxim are generally the best.

One of the simplest places to eat is the sausage stand, a utilitarian establishment which is very common in Central Europe. It offers Czech sausages, which can either be eaten standing at

Modern Czech restaurant

the counter or taken away cold. For a late-night meal your best bet is often a snack bar *(bufet)*.

For greater comfort, head for a café *(kavárna)*. Cafés range from loud, busy main street locations to quieter bookstore establishments. All have fully stocked bars and serve a variety of food from simple pastries and sandwiches to full-blown meals. Opening hours differ widely, but many open early in the morning and are good for a quick, if not quite a Western-style, breakfast.

A restaurant may be called a *restaurace* or a *vinárna* (one that sells wine). The best are those geared to non-Czech clientele. While usually cheap by Western standards, they are pricier than Czech places, but in return offer better service and higher quality food.

Plain Czech food is normally available at the local beer hall or pub *(pivnice)*, though the emphasis there is normally on drinking rather than eating.

Diners enjoying their meal at U Kalicha *(see p207)*

Tourists eating at the outdoor cafés in the Old Town Square

READING THE MENU

Never judge a restaurant by the standard of its menu translations – mistakes are common in every class of restaurant. Many menus still list the weight of meat served (a relic of communist rationing). Bear in mind that most main courses come with potatoes, rice or dumplings. Salads and other side dishes must be ordered separately *(see pp198–9 for The Flavours of Prague.)*

Restaurant sign

THINGS TO BEWARE OF

In some restaurants or bars the waiter may bring nuts to your table. Yes, they are for you to eat, but at a price equal to, or higher than, an appetizer. You will not insult

Fine dining amid stained-glass Art Deco splendour

anybody by telling the waiter to take them away. The same applies to appetizers brought round by the waiter.

Check your bill carefully, because extra charges are often added – this is quite a common practice in Prague. However, legitimate extra costs do exist. Cover charges range from Kč10–25 and such basic items as milk, ketchup, bread and butter might be charged for. Finally, a 19% tax, normally included in the menu.

Severe cases of food poisoning are rare in Prague, but mild cases are more common. Avoid stands selling food in the street, as the ingredients are exposed to bacteria and may not be cooked thoroughly. In general, restaurants in Prague have a high standard of hygiene, equal to the rest of Europe.

ETIQUETTE

You don't have to wait to be seated in snack bars and smaller eateries. It is also quite normal for others to join your table if there is any room. No restaurant has an official dress code, but people tend to dress up when dining in up-market restaurants.

PAYMENT AND TIPPING

The average price for a full meal in the centre of Prague is about Kč360. In some restaurants the waiter may write your order on a piece of paper and then leave it on your table for the person who comes around when you are ready to pay. Levels of service vary, but generally a 10% tip is appropriate. Add the tip to the bill, do not leave the money on the table. More and more restaurants now accept major credit cards, but always ask before the meal to make sure. Traveller's cheques are not accepted.

VEGETARIANS

Even vegetarians are well catered for in Prague. Fresh vegetables are available throughout the year, including winter, and numerous restaurants offer vegetarian and vegan options. Nevertheless, even when a dish is described as meatless, it's always worth double-checking. Vegetarians should particularly beware of menu sections called *bezmasa* as, whilst the literal translation of this word is "without meat", its actual meaning is that meat is not the main ingredient in the dishes listed.

DISABLED

Restaurants do not cater specifically for the disabled. The staff will almost always try and help, but Prague's ubiquitous stairs and basements will defeat all but the most determined.

RESERVATIONS

There is generally no need to reserve a table at lunchtime or on weekday evenings in Prague. If you are planning to eat dinner on a Friday or Saturday evening, however, particularly in Prague's better known eating places, it is advisable to book in advance. Tables can be reserved in person or by telephone. Some restaurants also take bookings on the internet, through their website. Alternatively, online booking companies will make a free reservation for you at many of the city's restaurants. Your booking is confirmed by email and you pay as usual at the restaurant.

The Flavours of Prague

While no visitor comes to Prague for the food, there is far more to contemporary Czech cuisine than the Central European norm of meat, potatoes and rice. Czech food remains based on seasonally available ingredients, while a simple, no-fuss approach allows natural flavours to dominate most dishes. The staples of Czech cooking are pork, beef, game and carp, which tend to be served grilled or roasted, accompanied by a light sauce and vegetables. They are also used in sour soups, known as *polévky*. It is also unlikely that you will leave Prague without tasting *knedlíky* (dumplings), either savoury or sweet.

Blueberries

Atmospheric U Pinkasů cellar bar and restaurant *(see p206)*

MEAT

The Czech favourite is pork *(vepřové)*. It appears in countless dishes, including soups, goulash and sausages, or can be served on its own, either grilled or (more commonly) roasted. It is invariably served on the bone, just slightly the burnt side of well-done. It also appears in other forms,

notably as Prague ham *(Pražska šunka)*, a succulent, lightly smoked meat usually eaten with bread at breakfast or with horseradish as a starter at suppertime.

Veal, usually served in the form of breadcrumbed, fried Wiener schnitzel *(smažený řízek)*, is popular and good.

Beef in the region has never been up to international standards, and needs to be prepared well to be edible.

The Prague favourite is *Pražská hovězí pečeně*, roast beef stuffed with bacon, ham, cheese, onion, and eggs. If cooked well it can be tender and delicious. Beef is also used in goulash and stews. Most of the beef served in top restaurants is likely to be imported. Czech lamb *(jehněčí)* is not the best in the world, either, though for a short period from mid-March to mid-May

Apple strudel   *Trdelník* (eclair)

Honzova buchta (fruit buns)

Čokoládový řez (chocolate cake)

Český koláč (plum jam bun)

Bublanina (apple crumble tart)

Selection of typical Czech cakes and pastries

LOCAL DISHES AND SPECIALITIES

Knedlíky (dumplings), either savoury (špekové) in soups or sweet (ovocné) with fruits and berries, are perhaps Bohemia's best-known delicacy. Once a mere side dish they have now become a central feature of Czech cuisine, as Postmodern chefs rediscover their charms and experiment with new and different ways of cooking and serving them. Other specialities of the region include *Dršťková polévka*, a remarkably good tripe soup, which – although an acquired taste – has also seen something of a revival in recent years as better restaurants add it to their menus. Duck and pheasant remain popular in Prague and, with the city surrounded by fine hunting grounds, such game is always of top quality. Pork, though, is the city's (and the nation's) most popular food, served roasted on the bone, with red cabbage.

Stuffed eggs

Polévka s játrovými knedlíčky
Soup with liver dumplings is the most common dish in the Czech Republic.

Wild chanterelle mushrooms from the forests around the city

there is good lamb available in Prague's markets, where it is usually sold whole, complete with the head which is used to make soup.

GAME

There is a wide variety of game to be found in the forests around Prague. Depending on the season (the best time is autumn) you will find duck, pheasant, goose, boar, venison, rabbit and hare on many menus. Duck is probably the most popular game dish, usually roasted with fruits, berries or sometimes with chestnuts, and served with red cabbage. Small pheasants, roasted whole with juniper and blueberries or cranberries, are also popular, while venison is often served grilled with mushrooms. Rabbit and hare are usually presented in spicy, goulash-style sauces.

VEGETABLES

Czech vegetables can be fabulous, if strictly seasonal. Note, however, that Czechs tend to boil their vegetables into oblivion before serving them. While more and more imported, out-of-season produce is finding its way

Fresh vegetables on a Prague market stall

into supermarkets, many Czechs are unwilling to pay the higher prices these goods demand. As a result, the hardy cabbage remains the country's top vegetable, used in numerous different ways, such as raw as a salad, or boiled as an accompaniment to roast meats. The Czech version of *sauerkraut, kyselé zelí*, is ubiquitous. Mushrooms, too, are well liked, and find their way in to many sauces, especially those served with game.

BEST LOCAL SNACKS

Sausages Street stalls and snack bars all over the city sell traditional sausages (*klobásy* and *utopence*), frankfurters (*párky*) or bratwurst, served in a soft roll with mustard.

Chlebíčky Open sandwiches on sliced baguette are found in any delicatessen or snack bar in Prague. Toppings are usually ham, salami or cheese, always accompanied by a gherkin (*nakládaná okurka*).

Pivní sýr Beer cheese is soaked in ale until it becomes soft. It is served spread on bread and eaten with pickles or onions.

Syrečky These tasty cheese rounds have a pungent aroma and are served with beer and onions.

Palačinky Pancakes are filled with ice cream and/or fruits and jam, and are topped with lashings of sugar.

Pečený kapr s kyselou omáčkou *Carp with sour cream and lemon is popular, especially at Christmas.*

Vepřové s křenem *Pork is served roasted, on the bone, with red cabbage and either sauerkraut or horseradish.*

Ovocné knedlíky *Sweet dumplings are filled with fruits or berries, usually blueberries or plums.*

What to Drink in Prague

'Golden Tiger'
beer mat

Czech beers are famous around the world, but nowhere are they drunk with such appreciation as in Prague. The Czechs take their beer *(pivo)* seriously and are very proud of it. Pilsner and its various relations originate in Bohemia. It is generally agreed that the best Pilsners are produced close to Pilsen – and all the top producers are not far from Prague. Beers can be bought in cans, in bottles, and best of all, on draught. Canned beer is made mostly for export, and no connoisseur would ever drink it. The Czech Republic also produces considerable quantities of wine, both red and white, mainly in Southern Moravia. Little of it is bottled for export. Mineral water can be found in most restaurants; Mattoni and Dobrá voda (meaning good water) are the two most widely available brands.

Gambrinus, legendary King of Beer, and trademark of a popular brand of Pilsner

Traditional copper brew-kettles in Plzeň

PILSNER AND BUDWEISER

The best-known Czech beer is Pilsner Urquell. Clear and golden, with a strong flavour of hops, Pilsner is made by the lager method: bottom-fermented and slowly matured at low temperatures. The word "Pilsner" (now a generic term for similar lagers brewed all over the world) is derived from Plzeň (in German, Pilsen), a town 80 km (50 miles) southwest of Prague, where this type of beer was first made in 1842. The brewery that developed the beer still makes Plzeňské pivo as well as the slightly stronger Plzeňský prazdroj (original source), better known as Pilsner Urquell. A slightly sweeter beer, Budweiser Budvar is brewed 150 km (100 miles) south of Prague in the town of České Budějovice (in German, Budweis). The American Budweiser's first brewer adopted the name after a visit to Bohemia in the 19th century.

Budweiser logo

This higher percentage refers to the original gravity, not the alcohol content

Světlé means light   Alcohol content

Pilsner Urquell logo

Reading a Beer Label
The most prominent figure on the label (usually 10% or 12%) does not refer to the alcohol content. It is a Czech measure of original gravity, indicating the density of malt and other sugars used in the brew. The percentage of alcohol by volume is usually given in smaller type. The label also states whether it is a dark or a light beer.

BEER AND BEER HALLS

Staropramen   **Gambrinus**   **Velkopopovický kozel**   **Budweiser Budvar**   **Plzeňský prazdroj (Pilsner Urquell)**

The real place to enjoy Czech beer is a pub or beer hall (*pivnice*). Each pub is supplied by a single brewery (*pivovar*), so only one brand of beer is available, but several different types are on offer. The major brands include Plzeňské and Gambrinus from Plzeň, Staropramen from Prague, and Velkopopovické from Velké Popovice, south of Prague. The usual drink is draught light beer (*světlé*), but a number of beer halls, including U Fleků (*see p155*) and U Kalicha (*see p154*) also serve special strong dark lagers (ask for *tmavé*). Another type you may encounter is *kozel*, a strong light beer like a German *bock*.

A half litre of beer (just under a pint) is called a *velké* (large), and a third of a litre (larger than a half pint) is called a *malé* (small). The waiters bring beers and snacks to your table and mark everything you eat and drink on a tab. In some pubs there is a tacit assumption that all the customers want to go on drinking until closing time, so don't be surprised if more beers arrive without your ordering them. If you don't want them, just say no. The bill is totted up when you leave.

People enjoying a drink in one of Prague's beer gardens

WINES

Czech wine producers have not yet emulated the success of other East European wine-makers. The main wine-growing region is in Moravia, where most of the best wine is produced for local consumption. Some wine is also made in Bohemia, around Mělník, just north of Prague. The whites are made mostly from Riesling, Müller-Thurgau or Veltliner grapes (*polosuché* is demi-sec and *suché* is sec). Rulandské (Pinot) is an acceptable dry white. The reds are slightly better, the main choices being Frankovka and Vavřinecké. In the autumn, a semi-fermented young, sweet white wine called *burčák* is sold and drunk across the capital.

Rulandské, white and red

CZECH SPIRITS AND LIQUEURS

In every restaurant and pub you'll find Becherovka, a bitter-sweet, amber herbal drink served both as an aperitif and a liqueur. It can also be diluted with tonic. Other local drinks include Borovička, a juniper-flavoured spirit, and plum brandy or Slivovice. The latter is clear and strong and rather an acquired taste. Imported spirits and cocktails are more expensive.

Becherovka

Choosing a Restaurant

These restaurants have been selected across a wide price range for their good value or exceptional cuisine; they are listed area by area, starting with Old Town and moving on to restaurants further outside the city. The entries appear alphabetically within each price category, and any special features are indicated by the symbols.

PRICE CATEGORIES
These have been calculated to represent the cost of an average three-course meal for one, including half a bottle of wine, and all unavoidable charges.
Ⓚ Under Kč250
ⓀⓀ Kč250–450
ⓀⓀⓀ Kč450–650
ⓀⓀⓀⓀ Over Kč650.

OLD TOWN

Bohemia Bagel
Ⓚ

Masná 2, Praha 1 **Tel** *22 48 12 603*   **Map** *3 C3*

The best breakfast deal in Prague is available from 7am until midnight at this always-busy bagel shop and café. High-speed Internet is also provided at reasonable rates throughout the day. It's become so popular, that four other branches have opened around central Prague.

Beas
ⓀⓀ

Týnská 19, Praha 1 **Tel** *60 80 35 727*   **Map** *3 C3*

Spartan, cheap and tremendously popular vegetarian curry house. Food is served on rather utilitarian trays, yet it is good, hotter than the Prague norm, and comes with free water to alleviate the effect of the spices. As cheap as they come, this place attracts rich, poor and anyone who likes real Indian food.

Country Life
ⓀⓀ

Melantrichova 15, Praha 1 **Tel** *22 42 13 366*   **Map** *3 B4*

This is part of the international group of vegetarian restaurants, but few others anywhere in the world can compete with its sublimely picturesque setting. It gets crowded at lunchtimes with vegetarians and non-vegetarians alike, all hungry to try their excellent pizzas, salads, soups and desserts.

Dahab
ⓀⓀ

Dlouhá 33, Praha 1 **Tel** *22 48 27 375*   **Map** *3 C3*

Right in the heart of the Old Town, Dahab is perhaps the only place in Prague where you can puff on a genuine *hookah* pipe after your meal. The combination of tearoom, patisserie, café and restaurant works well, and it has a nice selection of Middle Eastern dishes, including several vegetarian options.

Klub Architektů
ⓀⓀ

Betlémské náměstí 5A, Praha 1 **Tel** *22 44 01 214*   **Map** *3 B4*

This hidden jewel is tucked away in a warren of tunnels and arches, reached through a discreet courtyard close to the Bethlehem Chapel. The servings are hearty, and, unusual for an inexpensive Prague dining room. The menu includes a good, varied vegetarian selection.

Patriot X
ⓀⓀ

V Celnici 3, Praha 1 **Tel** *22 42 35 158*   **Map** *4 D3*

This is a Czech restaurant, café and bar which, quite distinctively, takes a Scandinavian "less is more" approach to decor, yet keeps the portions traditionally ample. The café is upstairs, while the restaurant and bar are downstairs. It has a terrace with great views of the Old Town.

Restaurace Století
ⓀⓀ

Karolíny Světlé 21, Praha 1 **Tel** *22 22 20 008*   **Map** *3 A4*

Arched ceilings, sepia prints and old china all evoke a gentler era in this quiet, intimate restaurant. The menu is inspired by the famous of yesteryear; for example, you can order a Marlene Dietrich (stuffed avocado with whipped Roquefort and marzipan) or an Al Capone (roast chicken leg with hot salsa and papaya).

Chez Marcel
ⓀⓀⓀ

Haštalská 12, Praha 1 **Tel** *22 23 15 676*   **Map** *3 C2*

Chez Marcel is a touch of real France in the centre of Prague. This is where business people and students alike come for regional *plats du jour*, as well as steak *au poivre*, fresh mussels and probably the best French fries in the city. Surprisingly for such a good establishment, the food is reasonably priced.

Don Giovanni
ⓀⓀⓀ

Karolíny Světlé 34, Praha 1 **Tel** *22 22 22 060*   **Map** *3 A4*

This, the first upscale Italian restaurant in Prague to open after 1989, was named after the opera which Mozart debuted a few blocks away in the National Opera House. Besides excellent contemporary Italian dishes, the seafood selection includes lobster and crab, fresh from the in-house aquarium.

Key to Symbols *see back cover flap*

James Joyce

Liliová 10, Praha 1 **Tel** *22 42 48 793*　　　　　　　　　**Map** *3 B4*

The James Joyce was the first Irish pub in Prague, and it's still just about the best, catering mainly to expats, not stag parties. Home to hearty meals, including enormous Irish breakfasts, "door-stopper" sandwiches and the best Irish stew in Prague. The staff are friendlier than at most other Irish pubs in town.

La Provence

Štupartská 9, Praha 1 **Tel** *800 15 26 72*　　　　　　　**Map** *3 C3*

It's well worth taking the trip down the winding staircase from the lively Banana Bar to this reasonably priced French provincial restaurant. The menu includes the usual countryside game favourites such as rabbit, pheasant and duck (in season), while the cluttered, original, rustic decor has a charm of its own.

Red, Hot and Blues

Jakubská 12, Praha 1 **Tel** *22 23 23 364*　　　　　　　**Map** *3 C3*

Located in what were the royal stables some 500 years ago, this place is renowned for good, hometown New Orleans and Creole cooking; chilli, chowder, burgers with all the trimmings, and *étouffé*. There's live jazz or blues on most nights, and it's popular with a trendy crowd. A real Bohemian hangout.

Reykjavik

Karlova 20, Praha 1 **Tel** *22 22 21 218*　　　　　　　**Map** *3 A4*

This is an Icelandic restaurant serving dependably good seafood favourites such as *frutti di mare*, shrimp cocktails and Icelandic salmon – in this case grilled *á la Norvegienne*. Vegetarian dishes are also available. The service is unobtrusively efficient and it's a pleasantly cosy nook on a cold winter's day. During the summer there is alfresco dining.

Bellevue

Smetanovo nábřeží 2, Praha 1 **Tel** *22 22 14 43*　　　　　**Map** *3 A5*

Situated by the river, Bellevue has a stunning view of the castle. The interior is an Art Deco triumph, all inlaid wood walls and marble floors. The menu includes Antipodean delicacies such as *carpaccio* with New Zealand lamb, which is yet to be seen on any other menu in Prague.

Kamenný Most

Smetanovo nábřeží 195, Praha 1 **Tel** *22 40 97 100*　　　**Map** *3 A4*

The menu here, at what is probably Prague's most adventurous Czech restaurant, will have even the most seasoned and jaded foodie in rapture. To complement the excellent cuisine there is an equally adventurous winelist, and the terrace – with its superb view of the Charles Bridge – is a jewel.

Le Saint-Jacques

Jakubská 4, Praha 1 **Tel** *22 23 22 685*　　　　　　　**Map** *3 C3*

Le Saint-Jacques is managed by a French proprietor who is as attentive as his cuisine is sumptuous. Try any fish dish from the constantly evolving menu. A pianist and violinist gently serenade patrons every night, making this one of the city's top romantic locations.

Mlýnec

Novotného lávka 9, Praha 1 **Tel** *22 10 82 208*　　　　　**Map** *3 A4*

Chef Marek Purkart was the first man in the Czech Republic to receive the Michelin Bibendum twice, so expect only the best food and the highest prices here. Crispy roasted duck with red and white cabbage and Karlovy Vary dumplings are recommended. Traditional Czech food – but with a twist.

Opera Grill

Karolíny Světlé 35, Praha 1 **Tel** *22 22 20 518*　　　　　**Map** *3 A4*

There are only seven tables here, which gives it the feel of a private dining room. It also means it's a good idea to book ahead. The menu features excellent international dishes, such as lamb, pasta and steak, as they are all superbly cooked and presented. The desserts are to die for.

Seven Angels

Jilská 20, Praha 1 **Tel** *22 42 34 381*　　　　　　　　**Map** *3 B4*

There has been a restaurant on this spot since the 13th century, but whatever the changes of management have been since then, Seven Angels remains one of the most charming, small dining rooms in Central Europe. The house specialty is traditional Bohemian cuisine, with a particular focus on game. A lively folk band plays Wed–Sun evenings.

Staroměstská

Staroměstské náměstí 19, Praha 1 **Tel** *22 42 13 015*　　　**Map** *3 C3*

Housed in a medieval building in the heart of the Old Town Square, this popular restaurant has been an inn for over fifty years. Its classic Czech cuisine can be paired with the famous Pilsner beers. A selection of Czech and other wines is also available. In warmer weather, the outside tables offer a great view of the busy square (prices are higher though).

U Modré Růže (The Blue Rose)

Rytířská 16, Praha 1 **Tel** *22 42 25 873*　　　　　　　**Map** *3 B4*

There's something for everyone on the Czech and international menu of this upscale but very much underground restaurant, with beef, lamb, game, seafood and vegetarian dishes all vying for space. The setting is certainly unique, in beautifully restored 15th-century catacombs.

JEWISH QUARTER

Orange Moon
Rámová 5, Praha 3 **Tel** *22 23 25 119*   Ⓚ Ⓚ
                                                                                      Map *3 C2*

Immensely popular since its opening, Orange Moon bucks the local propensity for toning down traditionally spicy food by having its dishes listed with a one-, two- or three-red pepper rating – that's spicy, very spicy or burning. Rest assured some of the Thai and Burmese dishes have a "no pepper" rating.

U Sádlů
Klimentská 2, Praha 1 **Tel** *22 48 13 874*   Ⓚ Ⓚ
                                                                                      Map *4 D2*

The rather kitsch aspects of this medieval-themed restaurant are achieved with much aplomb. Every dish has a thematic name, including several under the heading "Meat from an Apocalyptic Piglet!" Cheerful staff, and a lively crowd most evenings make this a good choice for small groups of friends.

Barock
Pařížská 24, Praha 1 **Tel** *22 23 29 221*   Ⓚ Ⓚ Ⓚ
                                                                                      Map *3 B2*

An eclectic and excellent range of modern European and Japanese cuisine is served by efficient staff in this perennially fashionable restaurant. But it's not merely a trendy venue; the food really is authentic, and more than up to international standards. Popularity means you should reserve a table to be sure of getting in.

La Degustation (Boheme Bourgeoise)
Haštalská 18, Praha 1 **Tel** *22 23 11 234*   Ⓚ Ⓚ Ⓚ
                                                                                      Map *3 C2*

Using ingredients from around Europe and combining it with traditional Czech dishes, this restaurant offers one of the most intriguing dining experiences in Prague with a choice of three, seven-course taster menus. Dishes range from ravioli filled with lobster and prawn in vanilla sauce to Argentinean organic entrecôte with foie gras parfait.

Les Moules
Pařížská 19, Praha 1 **Tel** *22 23 15 022*   Ⓚ Ⓚ Ⓚ
                                                                                      Map *3 B2*

Czechs claim otherwise, but the best beer in Prague is served here, and it's Belgian, not Bohemian. What really brings in the crowds though are the pots of tasty, steaming fresh mussels, flown in daily from Belgium. Other treats on the menu include young tender racks of lamb cooked in beer.

King Solomon
Široká 8, Praha 1 **Tel** *22 48 18 782*   Ⓚ Ⓚ Ⓚ Ⓚ
                                                                                      Map *3 B3*

The light, pleasant interior of the King Solomon, in the heart of the Jewish Quarter, extends to its winter garden. The food is impeccably prepared and presented, complemented by kosher wines from the Czech Republic and beyond. They also deliver special Shabbat meals to hotels throughout Prague.

Pravda
Pařížská 17, Praha 1 **Tel** *22 23 26 203*   Ⓚ Ⓚ Ⓚ Ⓚ
                                                                                      Map *3 B2*

A wonderful blend of old and new encompassing elegant gilt-and-white dining rooms and waiters in chic uniforms, Pravda will tempt the diner with its Asian- and Scandinavian-inspired fare. This includes relatively expensive seafood dishes such as Cajun crawfish and poached cod. The desserts are excellent.

La Bodeguita del Medio
Kaprova 5, Praha 1 **Tel** *22 48 13 922*   Ⓚ Ⓚ Ⓚ Ⓚ
                                                                                      Map *3 B3*

Papa Hemingway stares down at diners enjoying seafood and Creole delights at this eclectic place. Once dinner is over in the downstairs restaurant, you can then head upstairs to enjoy original and classic cocktails and a great selection of Havana cigars until the early hours.

PRAGUE CASTLE AND HRADČANY

Palffy Palace Restaurant
Valdštejnská 14, Praha 1 **Tel** *25 75 30 522*   Ⓚ Ⓚ Ⓚ
                                                                                      Map *2 E2*

Enter at Valdštejnská 14, then climb the stone staircase to this wonderfully alternative restaurant, in what feels like an aristocrat's private rooms. Soft melodies seep through the walls from a musical academy on the premises, providing the perfect accompaniment to a regularly changing menu.

Peklo (Hell)
Strahovské nádvoří 1, Praha 1 **Tel** *22 05 16 652*   Ⓚ Ⓚ Ⓚ Ⓚ
                                                                                      Map *1 B4*

Peklo is near the Strahov Monastery, which belongs to the order of the Premonstratensians. They've been keeping wine in the cellars here since the 14th century. The restaurant offers fine Czech and international cuisine and, as you may expect, a fabulous array of wines.

Key to Price Guide *see p202* **Key to Symbols** *see back cover flap*

LITTLE QUARTER

Cantina 🎵🍴 ⓌⓌⓌ
Újezd 38, Praha 1 **Tel** *25 73 17 173* **Map** 2 E5

Everything is super-sized here, from the enormous margaritas to the massive portions of good value Tex-Mex food. All the usual favourites are on the menu, including super *burritos* and authentic tacos. The usual Czech problem of "not spicy enough" persists, ask for extra spices if you like hot food.

Dinitz 📋 ⓌⓌⓌ
Na Poříčí 12, Praha 1 **Tel** *22 23 14 071* **Map** 4 D3

Café, bar and casual bistro-influenced restaurant owned by Israelis yet not serving kosher food. Instead you'll find a good mix of light meals, desserts and snacks in an easy going atmosphere. Very popular with trendy shoppers taking a break from pounding the streets of nearby Náměstí Republiky.

Hungarian Grotto 🚶📋🎵🍴 ⓌⓌⓌ
Tomášská 12, Praha 1 **Tel** *25 72 20 370* **Map** 2 E3

The land of Tokay, Bull's Blood, goulash and paprika has inspired this reasonably priced, romantically rustic cellar restaurant with a pleasant outdoor courtyard. To add to the atmosphere, the premises are supposedly haunted by a cuckolded baker from the 17th century.

Mount Steak 📋♿ ⓌⓌⓌ
Josefská 1, Praha 1 **Tel** *25 75 32 652* **Map** 2 E3

Very much a place for meat-lovers only, this restaurant offers over 60 different steaks, including boar, venison, kangaroo, shark and ostrich. All are cooked as you wish, either roasted on the bone or grilled, and served with hearty portions of potatoes and vegetables. Good side salads too.

Nebozízek (Little Auger) 📋🚶♿🍴 ⓌⓌⓌ
Petřínské sady 411, Praha 1 **Tel** *25 73 15 329* **Map** 2 D5

During spring and summer, the outdoor patio at this renowned restaurant half-way up the Petřín funicular is very popular, offering wonderful views of Old and New Town. Inside, it is cosy and elegant. The menu is diverse, with seafood, Chinese and Czech dishes, steaks and more.

Cowboys 📋🎵🍴 ⓌⓌⓌⓌ
Nerudova 40, Praha 1 **Tel** *800 15 26 72* **Map** 2 D3

This is a sprawling complex of bars and dining rooms, serving slightly overpriced but always enjoyable steaks and seafood against a lavishly eccentric decor. The upper terrace, however, affords diners one of the best views of central Prague and fills up quickly in spring and summer. Reservations needed.

David 📋♿ ⓌⓌⓌⓌ
Tržiště 21, Praha 1 **Tel** *25 75 33 109* **Map** 2 E3

It's a steep incline up a cobblestone lane to David, but gourmets will find it worth the exertion. The set lunch is a serious two to three hour affair, with an interesting selection of Czech, European and New World wines on offer with which to wash down the supreme and intense flavours.

Kampa Park 🚶📋🍴 ⓌⓌⓌⓌ
Na Kampě 8b, Praha 1 **Tel** *25 75 32 685* **Map** 2 F4

The most famous contemporary restaurant in Prague, Kampa Park has been playing host to the great and good. If you want to impress someone, then this is the place to come, if you can get a reservation. The fusion cuisine is mildly adventurous and always good.

Square 📋🍴🕐 ⓌⓌⓌ
Malostranské nám. 5/28, Praha 1 **Tel** *25 75 32 109* **Map** 2 E3

There has been a hostelry on this site since 1874, though today Square is as contemporary as restaurants come. It serves inventive Italian and Mediterranean cuisine to Prague's jetset. Check out the daily specials – always good value – on the chalkboard as you make your way inside.

U Malířů (At the Painter's) 🚶📋🕐 ⓌⓌⓌⓌ
Maltézské náměstí 11, Praha 1 **Tel** *25 75 30 318* **Map** 2 E4

There has been a restaurant on this spot since 1543. Even back then, U Malířů received high praise: King Rudolf II's foodtasters gave it three Royal stars. Today you can expect equally high quality, traditional and contemporary French cuisine in superb, sumptious surroundings still fit for a king.

U Tří Pštrosů (At the Three Ostriches) 📋📋 ⓌⓌⓌⓌ
Dražického náměstí 12, Praha 1 **Tel** *25 75 32 410* **Map** 2 E3

The dining room of At The Three Ostriches is somewhat reminiscent of a Bavarian hunting lodge, but the cuisine is 100 per cent bona-fide Czech. Adventurous diners may wish to try their ostrich specialities of goulash and *roulade* "Prague style", while there are simpler but equally good dishes for the less brave.

Valdštejnská Hospoda (Waldstein Inn)   ⓀⓀⓀⓀ
*Valdštejnské náměstí 7, Praha 1 **Tel** 25 75 31 759*   **Map** 2 E3

The Waldstein Inn, as it sounds, was once a typical local pub, but renovations and redecorations have exposed the original features of this 15th-century building, such as painted ceilings and stonework. The menu of Czech favourites has an emphasis on game. There is a good hotel above *(see p191)*.

NEW TOWN

Fish & Chips   Ⓚ
*Rytířská 19, Praha 1 **Tel** 22 42 26 105*   **Map** 3 C4

Reasonably authentic though not brilliant, British Fish & Chips comes to Prague to cater primarily for the marauding English stag parties who eschew sophisticated cuisine. Locals appear to have taken to it too, judging by the long queues at weekends. Cod, plaice and rock salmon available.

Buffalo Bill's   ⓀⓀ
*Vodičkova 9, Praha 1 **Tel** 22 49 48 624*   **Map** 5 C1

Quite the sensation when it opened in 1993, Buffalo Bill's Wild West-memorabilia covered cellar still draws locals, expat and tourists alike with its great mixture of Tex-Mex dishes and its wide range of ribs and wings from the American grill. Definitely child-friendly, with some of the best waiting staff in town.

Café Imperial   ⓀⓀ
*Na Poříčí 15, Praha 1 **Tel** 24 60 11 440*   **Map** 4 D3

This high-ceilinged café is laden with original Art Deco tilework. This is affordable elegance, however, with light breakfasts, lunches, suppers and snacks all served in the atmosphere of a traditional Continental coffeehouse. Staff are polite and formal, though the place can get a little smoky.

Hotel Evropa Café   ⓀⓀ
*Václavské náměstí 25, Praha 1 **Tel** 22 42 28 117*   **Map** 3 C5

The café that remains perenially popular is an Art Nouveau classic, even if it is now slightly shabby around the edges. Still a favourite with the Prague literati, it simply oozes character, and the small terrace is one of the city's most popular. The food is distinctly average, but that is not why people come here.

Jáma   ⓀⓀ
*V jámě 7, Praha 1 **Tel** 22 42 22 383*   **Map** 5 C1

Popular lunchtime spot serving great burgers – probably the city's best – and *burritos* to office workers and tourists alike. The evenings are very lively, when this becomes one of the city's top drinking spots, and getting a table can be difficult without a reservation. There's a small terrace at the rear.

Radost FX Café   ⓀⓀ
*Bělehradská 120, Praha 1 **Tel** 22 42 54 776*   **Map** 6 E2

Good vegetarian food is a rarity in Prague, but the food is so good that many non-vegetarians come here for business and working lunches. Beyond the restaurant is a bar serving lethal absinthe cocktails and an art gallery. Downstairs is Prague's most upmarket disco, home to extravagant theme parties.

U Fleků   ⓀⓀ
*Křemencova 11, Praha 1 **Tel** 22 49 34 019*   **Map** 5 B1

This cavernous and often raucous brewery and restaurant with its many rooms and lounges is thought to have been founded in 1499, though nobody seems to know for sure. What's certain is that there's been an onsite brewery since the early 1900s, and the food is good, reliable upmarket Czech pub fare.

U Pinkasů   ⓀⓀ
*Jungmannovo nám. 16, Praha 1 **Tel** 22 11 11 150*   **Map** 3 C5

This has been a cheap and great value Czech beer hall since 1843. The food is simple but hearty, making this a very popular lunchtime destination. There are three levels: a traditional beerhouse in the basement, a bar area for light meals and snacks on the ground floor, and a more formal dining room upstairs.

Beograd   ⓀⓀⓀ
*Vodičkova 5, Praha 1 **Tel** 72 49 03 734*   **Map** 5 C1

For years there was a Serb restaurant on this patch, and though the latest incarnation is pure Czech, the owners have kept the old name out of respect for the past. Somewhat more upmarket than the average Czech hostelry, prices are somewhat higher than the norm. The food is good, however, with game featured on the menu.

Café Restaurant Louvre   ⓀⓀⓀ
*Národní třída 20, Praha 1 **Tel** 22 49 30 912*   **Map** 3 B5

An excellent place for a late and lazy breakfast on the terrace, Louvre has been in business since the early 1900s. A full restaurant menu of Czech and European cuisine, they also have an excellent selection of cakes, pastries and coffees. There's a smart billiards room on the premises.

Key to Price Guide *see p202* **Key to Symbols** *see back cover flap*

Marie Teresie

Na Příkopě 23, Praha 1 **Tel** *22 42 29 869*   **Map** *3 C4*

A fluorescently lit shopping arcade is left behind on entering this spacious cellar restaurant, named after an Austrian Habsburg princess, who spent a great deal of time in these parts. The fare is traditional Czech, served with a silver service flourish. You can feel like royalty for very little money.

U Kalicha (At the Chalice)

Na bojišti 12–14, Praha 1 **Tel** *29 61 89 600*   **Map** *6 D2*

The look of this restaurant, including its cartooned walls, is based on the famous Czech novel *The Good Soldier Švejk*. Author Jaroslav Hašek was a frequent visitor and set some of his novel's pivotal scenes here. Traditional Czech cuisine is available at prices aimed more at Western tourist budgets.

U Korbele

V celnici 7 (Renaissance Prague Hotel), Praha 1 **Tel** *22 18 22 433*   **Map** *4 E3*

Heaps of traditional wood panelling, decorative Moravian plates and surprisingly affordable prices make this restaurant in the Renaissance hotel a great choice for genuine Czech food. Seasonal specialities come and go, refreshing the menu every couple of months. Every Czech beer imaginable is also on the menu.

El Gaucho

Václavské náměstí 11 – Kenvelo Centre, Praha 1 **Tel** *22 16 29 410*   **Map** *3 C5*

Step downstairs from a mini mall (devoted to just one fashion house and its offspring) and into a surprisingly genuine Argentine restaurant. Huge, juicy steaks are cooked on an authentic "asado" grill, waiters are dressed as gauchos, and there is a good selection of South American wines.

La Perle de Prague

Rašín Building, Rašínovo nábřeži 80, Praha 1 **Tel** *22 19 84 160*   **Map** *5 A2*

Situated on the seventh floor of the Rašín Building (also known as the Dancing House), with views of the Vltava and Prague Castle, this is a reasonably priced, upscale French restaurant. The wine menu is quite extensive and the knowledgeable staff can help you choose. There's a well-stocked cocktail bar too.

FURTHER AFIELD

Ambiente

Mánesova 59, Praha 3 **Tel** *22 27 27 851*   **Map** *6 E1*

This eclectic restaurant, which features everything from American Southwestern to Italian cuisine, is renowned for its salads, and probably serves the best Caesar salad in Prague. A second Ambiente, at Na Příkopě 22 (inside the Slovanský Dům shopping centre) serves the same mix of dishes.

Koliba Praha

Gregorova 8, Praha 11 **Tel** *27 29 41 340*

The open-plan cooking and dining area of this panoramic restaurant, up in the hills above Prague, fills up most evenings during the summer as genuine gypsy musicians lead the locals and tourists alike in a sing-song. Simple, but very good steak and fish dishes bolster what is otherwise standard Czech cuisine.

Krásná Řeka

Anglická 6, Praha 3 **Tel** *22 42 18 154*   **Map** *6 E2*

Open for what seems an eternity, this is still the best Chinese restaurant in Prague, although with small portions, you may decide to order an additional main course. Everything is good and authentic, with dishes ranging from tofu to duck. There is a refreshingly large variety of vegetarian options as well.

Taj Mahal

Škrétova 10, Praha 3 **Tel** *22 42 25 566*   **Map** *6 E1*

On a small street behind the National Museum, this Indian restaurant is popular with Prague's expat community. The menu is quite extensive, and its Oriental decor and sitar player add to the exotic atmosphere. Food is authentic though it may not be as hot as you are used to. Ask for extra spices if you feel the need.

U Marčanů

Veleslavínská 14, Praha 6 **Tel** *23 53 60 623*

Folk music, dancing and singing every night make this a favourite of visitors to Prague. A taxi-ride from the city centre, it is a pleasant villa in a residential area serving real Czech food to diners seated at long tables, enjoying huge portions and even bigger glasses of beer. Good times guaranteed. You will need to make a reservation.

Aromi

Mánesova 78, Praha 1 **Tel** *22 27 13 222*   **Map** *6 E1*

One of Prague's finest Italian restaurants, Aromi offers an authentic taste of Italy in simple surroundings. The cream and brown decor is restrained and the atmosphere relaxed. Specialities here are seafood and pasta and there are also excellent wines from around the world. Good value.

Pubs, Beer Halls and Bars

Prague suits practically everyone's taste, from sophisticated cocktail bars to traditional Czech cellar pubs. A new breed of pub, the themed Irish, English or sports bar caters to the large number of young English men who travel to Prague on so-called stag weekends. The real charm of drinking in Prague is that it's possible to stroll around the Old Town and find places to drink and fraternize with Czechs and expatriates alike, regardless of the time. If you sit at an empty table, don't be surprised if others join you. In traditional Czech pubs a waiter will automatically bring more beer as soon as you appear close to finishing, unless you indicate otherwise. It pays to expect the unexpected in Prague – in some supposedly upmarket places, the waiters' attitude can be surly and unhelpful, while in the humblest pub you may find service to be efficient and courteous.

TRADITIONAL PUBS AND BEER HALLS

Traditionally, Czech pubs either serve food or are large beer halls dedicated to the mass consumption of beer. The words *hostinec* and *hospoda* used to indicate a pub with food, whereas a *pivnice* served only beer, but over time the distinctions have faded.

Recommended for the brave, **U Zlatého tygra** (The Golden Tiger) is a loud Czech literati pub, wall-to-wall with, mostly male, regulars. (This is where the Czech president, Vaclav Havel took Bill Clinton to show him local beer culture.) **U Fleků** has brewed its unique beer, Flekovské, since 1499. For authenticity, and Budvar, try **U Medvídků** which is not far away from the National Theatre *(see pp156–7)* and the Old Town Square. **Olympia** serves traditional Czech cuisine in a stylish setting. The top-rated dish here is roasted boar leg served with Pilsner Urquell beer. The traditional *hospoda* scarcely comes more so than **U Pinkasů**, hidden behind Wenceslas Square in a quaint courtyard. **Pivovarský dům** brews its own beer, and is a slightly more up-market take on the usual Czech pub.

COCKTAIL BARS

Prague now has almost more cocktail bars than you could shake a swizzle stick at,

but there are some that stand out. On Pařížská, Prague's Fifth Avenue, you'll find **Bugsy's**. This bar has even printed their own cocktail bible, though towards the end of the week it does become somewhat overtaken by burly men in long coats. That fate has yet to befall the neighbouring **Barock**, a cocktail bar and restaurant with a noticeably chic clientele. Nearby **Tretters** combines smart looks with a slightly more down-to-earth attitude.

IRISH PUBS AND THEME BARS

Prague now has theme bars in all shapes and sizes, with still the most common being the ubiquitous Irish pub. **Caffreys** is one of Prague's most popular – and pricier – Irish bars, located off the Old Town Square. **Rocky O'Reilly's** is the biggest Irish pub in town, and a rowdy place, packed to the rafters if there is a big football match on the television. The **James Joyce** is but a stone's throw away from Charles Bridge, and is probably Prague's most upmarket Irish pub. Its neighbour is possibly the only Irish-Cuban hybrid pub anywhere, the noisy and fun **O'Che's**.

There is karaoke at **Molotow Cocktail Bar**, while **La Casa Blu** is a South American bar where the Chilean, Peruvian, Mexican and Czech staff create a carnival-type atmosphere.

BOHEMIAN HANGOUTS

Not only in the geographical heart of Bohemia, these bars also represent the unconventional side of Prague city-life. **Al Capone's** is one of the most famous, not to say notorious, drinking dens in the Old Town, host to a parade of visitors and locals. The large, red velvet drinking emporium that is the **Marquis de Sade** also epitomizes that spirit, built as it is in a 19th-century brothel. Over the Vltava in the Castle district you'll find **U Malého Glena** which translates roughly to Glen's house, and is one of the longest surviving expatriate bars in the city. Not far away is **Jo's Bar & Garáž**, which has also stood the test of time as an expat hangout. It's a small, cavernous pub, Mexican eatery and disco, and becomes quickly packed. Over in Žižkov is the large converted cinema and cultural centre **Akroplis**, home to an ever-changing programme of live music and DJs.

SPORTS BARS

Sports bars have taken off in Prague, with places like **Legends**, a long, polished cellar bar with a deck of TV screens. **Jágr's Sports Bar** is also for sports enthusiasts, owned as it is by Czech ice hockey hero Jaromír Jágr.

CAFÉ SOCIETY

The city is embedded in café society, ranging from old-fashioned smoky joints to cafés within bookstores, boutiques and billiard halls. Some are restaurants, others focus on drinking, but all serve alcohol. **Lávka** has the finest setting in the city. Situated at the foot of the Charles Bridge, it offers a great view of the castle. Other places to see and be seen are **Ebel** in the Old Town and **Slavia**, by the river opposite the National Theatre. For a perfect meeting place, try the **Grand Café Praha** opposite the clock tower in Old Town Square. **Globe** café and bookstore is a legend amongst Prague's expat community and serves the best cappuccino.

DIRECTORY

TRADITIONAL PUBS AND BEER HALLS

Lávka
Novotného lávka 1.
Map 3 A4.
Tel 22 22 22 156.
www.lavka.cz

The Beer House
PIVOVARSKÝ DŮM
Lípová 15.
Map 5 C2.
Tel 29 62 16 666. www.
gastroinfo.cz/pivodum

Trilobit
Palackého 15.
Map 3 C5.
Tel 22 49 46 065.

The Black Bull
U ČERNÉHO VOLA
Loretánské nám 1.
Map 1 B3.
Tel 22 05 13 481.

The Golden Tiger
U ZLATÉHO TYGRA
Husova 17.
Map 3 B4.
Tel 22 22 21 111.
www.uzlatehotygra.cz

The Shot Out Eye
U VYSTŘELENÉHO OKA
U Božích bojovníků 3.
Tel 22 25 40 465.

U Fleků
Křemencova 11.
Map 5 B1.
Tel 22 49 34 019.
www.ufleku.cz

U Kalicha
Na Bojišti 12–14.
Map 6 D3.
Tel 29 61 89 600.
www.ukalicha.cz

U Medvídků
Na Perštýně 7.
Map 3 B5.
Tel 22 42 11 916.
www.umedvidku.cz

Olympia
Vítězná 7.
Map 2 E5.
Tel 25 15 11 080.
www.olympia-
restaurant.cz

U Pinkasů
Jungmannovo náměstí
15/16.
Map 3 C5.
Tel 22 11 11 150.
www.upinkasu.cz

COCKTAIL BARS

Alcohol Bar
Dušní 6.
Map 3 B2.
Tel 22 48 11 744.
www.alcoholbar.cz

Bar Bar
Všehrdova 17.
Map 2 E5.
Tel 25 73 12 246.
www.bar-bar.cz

Barock
Pařížská 24.
Map 3 B2.
Tel 22 32 92 21
www.barockrestaurant.cz

Bugsy's
Pařížská 10. **Map** 3 B2.
Tel 22 48 10 287.
www.bugsybar.cz

Cheers
Belgická 42. **Map** 6 F3.
Tel 22 25 13 108.
www.cheers-restaurant.cz

Tretters
Kolkovně 3.
Map 3 C5.
Tel 24 81 11 65.
www.tretters.cz

Ultramarin
Ostrovní 32. **Map** 3 B5.
Tel 22 49 32 249.
www.ultramarin.cz

Zanzibar
Lázeňská 6. **Map** 2 E4.
Tel 60 27 80 076.
www.monin.cz

IRISH PUBS AND THEME BARS

Caffreys
Staroměstské nám. 10.
Map 3 B3.
Tel 24 82 80 31.
www.caffreys.cz

George & Dragon
Staroměstské nám. 11.
Map 3 B3.
Tel 22 23 26 137.
www.georgeanddragon
prague.com

James Joyce
Liliová 10. **Map** 3 B4.
Tel 22 42 48 793.

J.J. Murphy's
Tržiště 4. **Map** 2 E3.
Tel 25 75 35 575.
www.jjmurphys.cz

La Casa Blu
Kozí 15.
Map 3 C2.
Tel 24 81 82 70.
www.lacasablu.cz

Molly Malone's
U Obecního dvora 4.
Map 4 D3.
Tel 22 4 8 18 851.
www.mollymalones.cz

Molotow Cocktail Bar
Karlovo náměstí 31.
Map 5 B2.
Tel 22 22 30 226.
www.molotow.cz

O'Che's
Liliová 14. **Map** 3 C3.
Tel 22 22 21 178.
www.oches.com

Rocky O'Reilly's
Štěpánská 32. **Map** 3 A5.
Tel 22 22 31 060.
www.rockyoreillys.cz

BOHEMIAN HANGOUTS

Al Capone's
Bartolomějská 3.
Map 3 B5
Tel 22 4 2 12 192.
www.alcapone.cz

Confessions
U Milosrdných 4.
Map 3 B2.

Duende
Karolíny Světlé 30.
Map 3 A4.
Tel 77 51 86 077.
www.barduende.cz

Jet Set
Radlická 1, Prague 5.
Tel 25 73 27 251.
www.jetset.cz

Jo's Bar & Garáž
Malostranské nám 7.
Map 2 E3.
Tel 25 75 31 422.
www.josbar.cz

Marquis de Sade
Templová 8.
Map 3 C3.
Tel 22 23 27 790.

Merlin
Bělehradská 68A.
Map 6 E2.
Tel 22 25 22 054.

www.merlin-pub.cz

Mu Kafé
Mánesova 87.
Map 6 F1.
Tel 60 89 59 883.
www.mukafe.cz

U Malého Glena
Karmelitská 23.
Map 2 E4.
Tel 25 75 31 717.
www.malyglen.cz

SPORTS BARS

Jágr's
Václavské nám. 56 - Palác
Blaník. **Map** 3 C5.
Tel 22 40 32 481.

Legends
Týn 1. **Map** 3 C3.
Tel 22 48 95 404.
www.legends.cz

Sportbar Sparta ve Slavii
Smetanovo nábř. 1012/2.
Map 3 A5.
Tel 22 42 18 493.

Zlatá Hvězda
Ve smečkách 12.
Map 6 D1.
Tel 29 62 22 292.
www.sportbar.cz

CAFÉ SOCIETY

Café Imperial
Na Poříčí 15.
Map 4 D3.
Tel 22 23 16 012.

Ebel
Řetézova 9. **Map** 3 B4. *Tel
22 22 22 018.*
www.ebelcoffee.cz

Globe
Pštrossova 6. **Map** 5 A1.
Tel 22 49 34 203.
www.globebookstore.cz

Grand Café Praha
Staroměstské nám. 22.
Map 3 B3.
Tel 22 16 32 522.
www.grandcafe.cz

Hotel Evropa Café
Václavské náměstí 25.
Map 3 C5.
Tel 22 42 28 117.

Slavia
Smetanovo nábř. 2.
Map 3 A5.
Tel 22 42 18 493.

Nightlife

Nightlife in Prague is now as lively as in other European cities. A constant stream of visitors and a spirited local crowd has seen to that. Cheap drink, cutting-edge performers, liberal gambling and prostitution laws all help pull in the crowds. Prague is also now firmly established as a tour-stop for major American and UK pop and rock acts, with arenas such as the T-Mobile and Sazka playing host to big names at least once a month.

On a more local level, Prague's club scene is a proven testing ground for up-and-coming bands, and the dance/music events, heavily influenced by that of nearby Berlin, is renowned for being experimental. Prague's gay and lesbian scene is buzzing, and the local population, despite its deep catholic roots, is among the most tolerant in mainland Europe. For similar reasons, Prague is also now well known for its adult venues.

DISCOS AND NIGHTCLUBS

The biggest club in the city is the **Lucerna Bar**, which offers a varied programme – either live local bands or a DJ playing classic hits – in an unusual basement ballroom in the beautiful, but run down, Lucerna building. It fills up quickly however, so make sure you get there early. **Karlovy Lázně** is another large club, which sometimes has live bands. **Zlatý Strom** offers techno/house together with 1970s, 80s and 90s dance tunes until 5am in a spectacular medieval cellar setting.

The trendier clubs, more likely to be playing cutting-edge music, include **Celnice** and **Radost FX**, where the city's most affluent are attracted by a constant diet of house music and plush decor, together with **XT3** and **Kulturní dům Vltavská**. The **Double Trouble** is popular with visiting stag parties, which means it can get quite rowdy. For genuinely experimental and original hardcore house and techno music, the best place to go is **Roxy**, where sets are often accompanied by art house video projections. Roxy regularly hosts live rock bands, including a number of big named bands.

If it is cabaret you are after, try **Tingl Tangl**, a club well known for its lively transvestite shows.

ROCK AND POP CLUBS

Lovers of live rock music are well served in Prague. One school of thought feels that the anarchic influence of Prague's pioneering 1980s rock bands helped – however inadvertently – bring down the communist regime. There are today a large number of popular rock venues – generally small clubs and cafés – which host a variety of different groups. The indigenous scene continues to thrive – Prague's own rock bands play both their own compositions as well as cover versions of more famous numbers, many singing in English. Higher-profile, more internationally renowned Western bands play in Prague regularly, usually at the **T-Mobile Arena** or the new **Sazka Arena** *(see p223)*.

The **Rock Café** and the **UZI Rock Bar**, both very popular venues, offer regular concerts followed by discos. Other venues include the **Futurum Rock Club**, open till the early hours. The Lucerna Bar and Roxy also hosts regular bands.

JAZZ

The roots of jazz in Prague can be traced not only to the American tradition but also to the pre-war heyday of Prague's famous jazz players, such as Jaroslav Ježek. Even during the communist period, Prague was an internationally renowned centre of jazz, never failing to attract the biggest names. Dizzy Gillespie, Stan Getz, Duke Ellington and Buddy Rich all played in Prague during the 1960s and 1970s.

Today, Prague's many jazz clubs play all forms, from Dixieland to swing. One of the leading and most popular jazz venues in the city is the **Jazz Club Reduta**, which has daily jazz concerts at around 9pm. When former US President Bill Clinton asked his Czech counterpart Vaclav Havel if he could play some jazz during a state visit to Prague in January 1994, the Czech president took him to the Jazz Club Reduta. The popular **Metropolitan Jazz Club** holds late-night concerts until 3 or 4am. At the **AghaRTA Jazz Centrum**, you can hear a high standard of playing while eating in its café. **U Malého Glena** has regular live blues, jazz and funk, while **Dinitz Café** serves delicious international cuisine with jazz, swing or blues every night from 9pm. For serious enthusiasts, the International Jazz Festival *(see p52)* during October attracts talent from all over the world. For a more bluesy experience, head to **Ungelt Jazz & Blues Club** or **Red Hot & Blues**.

GAY AND LESBIAN VENUES

With even mainstream clubs such as **Radost FX** and **Mecca** holding regular gay nights, it is no wonder that Prague is considered Europe's hottest gay destination. The scene is liberal and diverse. Clubs are split into various categories, with **Alcatraz** a popular, hardcore leather and rubber venue, specialising in special events and theme parties. **Drake's Club** is a less in-your-face venue, and popular with visitors, while the city's most famous gay venue, **Friends**, has recently re-opened in a new venue after the previous location was ruined in the 2002 floods. As Prague's best gay cocktail bar, Friends has a steady following among expat and local men who are less interested in cruising than in just having a drink with like-minded folks. Temple, a gay centre, features a bar, disco, sex shop and hotel on the same premises.

The website www.prague. gayguide.net is a valuable resource for all things gay in Prague, including gay-friendly hotels, guesthouses and groups and associations.

ADULT PRAGUE

Like it or not, Prague has seen itself become the sex tourism capital of Europe since 1989, a result of cheap beer and the mistaken assumption that prostitution in the Czech Republic is legal. The law is, in fact, deliberately opaque, though the country's liberal ministers

are keen to remove all doubt from the law and fully legalise the practice. For the time being, the emphasis remains on tolerance, and visitors are free to indulge themselves at any number of what are known as "Relax Clubs". Some are more respectable than others, and many are tourist traps which should be avoided.

DIRECTORY

DISCOS AND NIGHTCLUBS

Celnice
V Celnici 4. **Map** 4 D3.
Tel 77 75 02 505.
www.clubcelnice.com

Double Trouble
Melantrichova 17.
Map 3 B4.
Tel 221 632 414.
www.doubletrouble.cz

Karlovy Lázně
Novotného lávka.
Map 3 A4.
Tel 222 220 502.
www.karlovylazne.cz

Kulturní dům Vltavská
Bubenská 1.
Tel 220 879 683.
www.vltavska.cz

La Fabrique
Uhelný trh 2. **Map** 3 B4.
Tel 224 233 137.
www.lafabrique.cz

Lucerna Bar
Vodičkova 36.
Map 3 C5
Tel 224 217 108.
www.musicbar.cz

Misch Masch
Veletržní 61, Praha 7.
Tel 603 272 227.
www.mischmasch.cz

Radost FX
Bělehradská 120.
Map 6 E2.
Tel 22 42 54 776.
www.radostfx.cz

Tingl Tangl
Karolíny Světlé 12.
Map 3 A5.
Tel 224 238 278.
www.tingltangl.cz

Újezd
Újezd 18. **Map** 2 E5.
Tel 257 316 537.

XT3
Rokycanova 29,
Praha 3.
Tel 222 783 463.
www.xt3.cz

Zlatý Strom
Karlova 6.
Map 3 A4.
Tel 222 220 441.
www.zlatystrom.cz

ROCK AND POP CLUBS

Futurum Music Bar
Zborovská 7, Praha 5.
Map 2 F5.
Tel 257 328 571.
www.musicbar.cz

Klub Lávka
Novotného lávka 1.
Map 3 A4.
Tel 22 10 82 299.
www.lavka.cz

Meloun
Michalská 12.
Map 3 B4.
Tel 774 000 313.
www.meloun.cz

Rock Café
Národní 20.
Map 3 B5.
Tel 224 933 947.
www.rockcafe.cz

Roxy
Dlouhá 33. **Map** 3 C3.
Tel 224 826 296.
www.roxy.cz

T-Mobile Arena
See p223.

UZI Rock Bar
Legerova 44.
Map 6 D3.
Tel 777 637 989.
www.demon.barr.cz/uzi

JAZZ CLUBS

AghaRTA Jazz Club
Železná 16.
Map 3 C4.
Tel 222 211 275.
www.agharta.cz

Dinitz Café
Na Poříčí 12.
Map 4 D3.
Tel 222 314 071.
www.dinitz.cz

Jazz Club Reduta
Národní 20.
Map 3 B5
Tel 224 933 487.
www.redutajazzclub.cz

Metropolitan Jazz Club
Jungmannova 14.
Map 3 C5.
Tel 224 947 777.

Red Hot & Blues
Jakubská 12.
Map 3 C3.
Tel 222 323 364.

U Malého Glena
Karmelitská 23.
Map 2 E4.
Tel 257 531 717.
www.malyglen.cz

U Staré Paní
Michalská 9.
Map 3 B4.
Tel 603 551 680.
www.jazzlounge.cz

Ungelt Jazz & Blues Club
Týnská 2.
Map 3 C3.
Tel 224 895 748.
www.jazzblues.cz

GAY AND LESBIAN VENUES

Alcatraz
Bořivojova 58,
Praha 3.
Tel 222 711 458.

Drake's Club
Zborovská 50,
Praha 5.
Map 2 F5
Tel 257 326 828.
www.drakes.cz

Friends
Bartolméjska 11.
Map 3 B5.
Tel 739 352 174.
www.friends-prague.cz

Jampadampa
V tůních 10.
Map 6 D2.
Tel 73 95 92 099.

Temple
Seifertova 3, Praha 3.
Tel 222 710 773.

Termix
Třebízského 4a
Tel 222 710 462.
www.club-termix.cz

Valentino
Vinohradská 40.
Map 6 F1.
Tel 22 25 13 491.
www.club-valentino.cz

SHOPPING IN PRAGUE

With its wide, pedestrianised streets, classy shopping malls, souvenir shops and antiques *bazars*, Prague is now established as one of Europe's leading shopping destinations. Almost all of the major US and West European retailers have estalished outlets in the city, and since 1989's Velvet Revolution, the quality of goods manufactured in the Czech Republic – always good – has improved considerably. Most of Prague's best shopping areas

Bohemian crystal

are in the centre of the city, and you can spend a whole day just diving in and out of small speciality shops and large department stores. For a different shopping experience, the few traditional markets in the city offer everything from vegetables to fresh fruit and to imported Russian caviar, toys, clothes, furniture, Czech crafts, electrical spare parts and even second-hand cars. Larger out-of-town malls are now also springing up, and are proving to be very popular.

OPENING HOURS

Most of Prague's shops open from 9am to 6pm Monday to Saturday, although supermarkets are open till late. However, shops are often more flexible than that, as many rely almost entirely on tourists for their trade. The more expensive gift shops have adapted their opening hours to the needs of their Western customers and tourists, often opening at 10am and closing much later in the evening. Many also open on Sundays as well.

Food stores open earlier, most of them at 7am – reflecting the early working day of many locals – and close at around 7pm. A few shops also take a break for lunch, which can vary from any time between noon and 2pm. Department stores and the big shopping centres and malls also open early but tend to close later, often around 10pm. Some open on Sundays.

All the shops are at their most crowded on Saturdays and for stress-free shopping it's often better to wander around them during the week. Prague's markets are

A set of Russian dolls available from one of the many street shops

generally open early every weekday morning but have varied closing times.

HOW TO PAY

Most staple goods, such as food, are cheaper than comparable items in the West, as long as they do not need to be imported. However, with more and more multinationals, such as Boss and Pierre Cardin, moving into the city, prices are slowly starting to rise.

The total price of goods should always include Value Added Tax (this is 19 per cent of the total price, depending on what is being sold), although all food is exempt from

One of the many antique shops in Bridge Street in the Little Quarter

this. Cash payments can usually only be made in Czech crowns, though some shops now take Euros, albeit at extortionate exchange rates. Smaller shops appreciate it if you pay the exact amount and at times may refuse to accept banknotes above Kč1,000. All major credit and charge cards are widely accepted, except American Express *(see p230)*.

Global Refund is a programme for non-EU residents that allows tax-free shopping for purchases exceeding Kč2,000. When you make a purchase at a shop displaying the Global Refund sign, ask at the cash till for a tax-free cheque. On leaving the country, show your items, receipts and cheques to customs officials, who will stamp the cheques, and you will get your VAT back. For more details, go to the Global Refund website (www.globalrefund.com).

SALES AND BARGAINS

Following the examples of the Western stores, sales are becoming more popular. As a result, it is now quite normal for clothes to be sold off cheaper at the end of each season. There is also an increasing number of post-Christmas sales in the shops found around Old Town Square, Wenceslas Square, Na Příkopě and 28. října.

If you want vegetables, fruit, meat or other perishable produce, buy them at the beginning of the day, when the best quality goods are still on sale. There is no point in waiting till the end of the day in the hope of getting bargains, as is the case in Western shops that reduce prices to get rid of perishable items.

WHERE TO SHOP

Most of Prague's best shops are conveniently located in the city centre, especially in and around Wenceslas Square, though the souvenir shops lining Nerudova on the way up to the castle are also well worth your time. Many of these shopping areas have been pedestrianized, making for leisurely window-shopping, although they can get rather crowded. There are a number of department stores which sell an eclectic range of Czech and Western items, with more opening all the time. The best-known department store, **Kotva** (The Anchor), lies in the centre of the city. It was built in 1975

and its four storeys offer a wide range of Western goods, particularly fashion and electronics, with the bonus of an underground car park. But compared to Western department stores, Kotva has a smaller selection of goods than you may be accustomed to – with the exception of food such as smoked meats, for example. Prices for some of the more luxurious items on sale, such as perfumes, can often be equivalent to the Western ones. **Dům módy**, another department store, stocks more upmarket clothing for men and women.

Another popular store is **Tesco**. This has a good selection of Czech and Western products in a bland 1970s building in the centre of town. The city's oldest department store is **Bílá Labut'** (The White Swan) in Na Poříčí. It was opened shortly before the occupation of Czechoslovakia in 1939 and was the first building in Prague to have an escalator. It has since been refurbished, and now specializes in furniture and interior accessories. **Debenhams**, another famous name from Western Europe, recently opened an enormous store on Wenceslas Square, and its home furnishings department on the third floor is very popular with locals.

The outskirts of Prague are now home to massive shopping parks, with large hypermarkets. Tesco has a huge branch at Zličín (at the end of metro line B), next to the equally enormous **IKEA**.

DIRECTORY

DEPARTMENT STORES

Bílá Labut'
Na Poříčí 23.
Map 4 E3.
Tel 224 811 364.

Debenhams
Václavské nám. 21.
Map 4 D5.
Tel 221 015 022.

Dům módy
Václavské nám. 58.
Map 6 D1.
Tel 224 217 005.

Kotva
Nám. Republiky 8.
Map 4 D3.
Tel 224 801 111.

Marks & Spencer
Na Příkopě 19/21.
Map 3 C4.
Tel 224 235 735.

Tesco
Národní 26.
Map 3 B5.
Tel 224 227 971.

MARKETS AND MALLS

Prague city centre is not blessed with a great market for most of the year, though the Christmas Gift Market in Old Town Square is well worth visiting. The city's major central market, **Havel**, sells mainly fresh produce. A better option for something surprising is **Holešvice** in the north of the city (take the metro to Vltavská). The best of Prague's flea markets, however, is **Buštěhrad Collectors Market**, a glorified car-boot sale close to Lidice.

Western-style shopping malls are now a common sight in Prague. The centre of the city is home to **Slovanský dům** *(see p217)* and **Černá růže**, while further afield **Flora Palace** *(see p217)* and the **Vinohradský Pavilion** *(see p217)* provide a genuinely Western European retail-therapy experience. Flora Palace is probably the better of the two, offering three levels of stores and direct access from Flora metro station. There is also a large mall at Zličín, the **Metropole Mall.**

A second-hand bookshop in Karlova Street

What to Buy in Prague

The massive selection of goods available in Prague's shops means that everyday items, such as food, books, camera film and toiletries are ubiquitous. Prague's more traditional products, such as Bohemian crystal, china, wooden toys and antiques, make great souvenirs, and there are still some real bargains to be picked up, though you will need to shop around. Increasingly popular are the more unusual goods which are sold by many of Prague's street shops. These include Soviet army medals, Red Army uniforms, Russian dolls, wooden puppets, ceramics and a wide selection of jewellery.

GLASS AND CHINA

Bohemian glass and china have always been ranked among the finest in the world. From huge, decorative vases to delicate glass figurines, the vast selection of glass and china items for sale is daunting. Crystal, glass and china can be quite different depending on where they are made. Lead crystal ranges in lead content from 14 to 24 per cent, for example. Always make sure you are fully aware of what you are buying.

Some of the best glass and china in Bohemia is produced at the Moser glassworks at Karlovy Vary and sold at **Moser**. The large Crystalex glassworks at Nový Bor and Poděbrady produce some of the most highly-decorated glass, sold at **Crystal**.

Other shops which sell a good selection of glass and china include **Bohemia Art Crystal, Dana-Bohemia** and two outlets called **Glass**. **Artěl** is a store selling mouth-blown glassware – designed by Karen Feldman – while **Arzenal** is another popular shop, with glass from the Czech's leading designer, Borek Šipek, whose collections are found in institutions ranging from MOMO in New York to the Design Museum in London. Billing itself as a cross-culture junction, there is a Thai restaurant on-site too.

However, prices for certain goods, especially classically designed vases, decanters and bowls are starting to reflect the increasing popularity of Bohemian crystal. The days when such goods could be purchased in Prague for half

the Western European price are over. Yet, value for money remains high, and you can still pick up bargains if you shop around carefully. Remember that many of the modern pieces are just as lovely and much cheaper.

Bohemian porcelain, while not as celebrated as Bohemian crystal, also makes an excellent gift or souvenir. **Český Porcelán**, the country's most famous factory, is in the town of Teplice, an hour's drive towards the German border from Prague, and its factory shop offers wonderful bargains. Other names worth looking out for include **Royal Dux Bohemia, Haas & Czjzek, A. Ruckl & Sons** and **Toner**.

Because of the fragile nature of the goods, many shops will pack anything you buy there. But if you go for a more expensive piece, it is worth looking into insurance before you leave Prague.

ANTIQUE SHOPS

Given its history as a major city in the Hapsburg empire, Prague is a great place to hunt for antiques. Hidden treasures seemingly lurk around every corner, and prices are still generally lower than in the West. Most of the city's shopping districts have a large number of antique shops: Old Town is full of them, as is the Royal Route from the castle. Look out for Bohemian furniture, glass and porcelain, as well as military and Soviet memorabilia.

Antique shops that are well worth exploring include **Dorotheum** and **Starožitnosti**. **Antique Clocks** sells exactly

what it says and **Military Antiques** is a haven for all army fanatics. For goods over Kč1,000, check with the shop whether you will need a licence to export them. You should watch out for an increasing number of fakes which are now appearing in the market.

Prague also has several *bazar* shops which stock a range of items at cheaper prices. Items are often unusual and good bargains can be found. **Bazar B & P** is a small, popular shop full of second-hand goods. For furniture bargains **Bazar nábytku** is well worth a visit.

TRADITIONAL CRAFTS

The traditional manufacture of high-quality, hand-crafted goods still survives. The variety of the merchandise available in the shops – hand-woven carpets, wooden toys, table mats, beautifully-painted Easter eggs, baskets, figurines in folk costumes and ceramics – are all based on Czech and Moravian folk crafts and then enriched with modern elements. You can buy them from many market stalls as well as a fair number of shops.

Czech Traditional Handicrafts offers a huge choice of hand-carved decorative items. Other arts and crafts shops include **Pottery Keramika Tupesy**. You should also look out for a new chain of shops called **Manufaktura** (Handmade), which sells goods made only in the Czech Republic. A number of street vendors around Old Town Square also sell handmade items including jewellery and puppets. Czech wooden items are also of the highest quality (*see* Speciality Shops, *pp216–17*).

BOOKS

There are numerous bookshops in Prague, reflecting its literary heritage, and many sell English-language books. Indeed, Prague is now a popular centre for young American novelists. One of the main bookshops is **U Černé Matky Boží**. Here, you'll find a range of English-language books (including Czech works which have been translated into English) as well as a fair number of German and French editions. Another well-stocked outlet is the **Big Ben Bookshop**. Maps and guides to Prague in English can be bought at **Academia**. Other specialist bookshops include **Palác knih**, **Kanzelberger** and **Fišer's Bookshop**.

Prague also has second-hand bookshops – look in Golden Lane and Karlova Street – which stock some English-language books, and they all offer the visiting bibliophile hours of enjoyable browsing. **Antikvariát Dlážděná** is one of the best and has a vast selection. **Antikvariát Ztichlá Klika** deals in antiquarian books as well as 20th-century avant-garde works. The legendary **Globe** café and bookstore is a good place to find second-hand English books

and enjoy the city's best cappuccino since 1993, when the shop opened in a poorer part of the capital by five entrepreneurial Americans. Now relocated to the city centre, the Globe hosts regular literary events, and art exhibitions, as does the newer **Shakespeare & Sons**, out in Žižkov, which is attempting to repeat the success of the Globe. The owner of **Anagram**, in Týn, claims to be able to order any book you want.

DIRECTORY

GLASS AND CHINA

Artěl
Vinohradská 164.
Map 6 F1.
Tel 27 17 32 161.
www.artelglass.com

Arzenal
Valentinská 11.
Map 3 B3.
Tel 22 48 14 099.
www.arzenal.cz

Bohemia Art Crystal
ČESKÝ KŘIŠŤÁL
Železná 14. **Map** 3 C4.
Tel 22 42 27 118.
One of several branches.

Bohemia Crystal
ČESKE SKLO
Kozí 9. **Map** 3 C2.
Tel 22 48 11 671.

Český Porcelán
Perlová 1.
Map 3 B4.
Tel 22 42 10 955.
www.cesky.porcelan.cz

Crystal
Karlova 5. **Map** 3 A4.
Tel 22 22 20 064.
One of several branches.

Dana-Bohemia
GLASS, CHINA, CRYSTAL
Národní 43. **Map** 3 A5.
Tel 22 42 14 655.
One of several branches.

Dům Porcelánu
Jugoslavska 16.
Tel 22 15 05 320.
www.cibulak.cz

Glass
SKLO
Malé náměstí 6.
Map 3 B4.
Tel 22 42 29 221.

Also at: Staroměstské náměstí 26–27.
Map 3 C3.
Tel 22 42 29 755.

Moser
Na příkopě 12.
Map 3 C4.
Tel 22 42 11 293.
www.moser-glass.com

ANTIQUE SHOPS

Antique Clocks
STAROŽITNOSTI UHLÍŘ
Mikulandská 8.
Map 3 B5.
Tel 22 49 30 572.

Antique Kaprova
Kaprova 12.
Map 3 B3.

A.D. Starožitnosti
Skořepka 8, Prague 1.
Map 3 B4.
Tel 224 238 599.

Bazar B & P
Nekázanka 17.
Map 4 D4.
Tel 22 42 10 550.
www.nekazanka.cz

Bazar nábytku
Libeňský ostrov.
Tel 266 310 726.
www.antik-bazar.cz

Dorotheum
Ovocný trh 2.
Map 3 C4.
Tel 22 42 22 001.
www.dorotheum.cz

Military Antiques
Charvátova 11.
Map 3 C5.
Tel 29 62 40 088.
One of several branches.

Starožitnosti
Náměstí Kinských 7.
Tel 25 73 11 245.
www.antique-shop.cz

GIFTS AND SOUVENIRS

Czech Traditional Handicrafts
Karlova 26.
Map 3 A4.
Tel 221 111 064.
Melantrichova 17.
Map 3 B4.
Tel 22 22 20 433.

Handmade
MANUFAKTURA
Melantrichova 17.
Map 3 B4.
Tel 22 16 32 480.
www.manufaktura.biz
One of several branches.

Pottery Keramika Tupesy
Truhlářská 9.
Map 4 D3.
Tel 22 23 11 156.

BOOKS

Anagram
Týn 4.
Map 3 C3.
Tel 22 48 95 737.
www.anagram.cz

Antikvariát Dlážděná
Růžová 5.
Map 4 D4.
Tel 22 22 43 911.
www.adplus.cz

Antikvariát Ztichlá Klika
Betlémská 10–14.
Map 3 A5.
Tel 22 22 21 561.

Big Ben Bookshop
Malá Štupartská 5.
Map 3 C3.
Tel 22 48 26 565.

Fišer's Bookshop
FIŠEROVO KNIHKUPECTVÍ
Kaprova 10.
Map 3 B3.
Tel 22 23 20 733.

Franz Kafka Bookshop
Staroměstské nám. 11-12.
Map 3 B3.
Tel 22 23 21 454.

Globe
Pštrossova 6.
Map 5 A1.
Tel 22 49 34 203.
www.globebookstore.cz

Kanzelberger
Václavské náměstí 4.
Map 4 D5.
Tel 22 42 19 214.

Knihkupectoí Academia
Václavské náměstí 34.
Map 4 D5.
Tel 22 42 23 511.

Palác knih
Václavské náměstí 41.
Map 4 D5.
Tel 22 42 16 201.

Shakespeare & Sons
Krymska 10, Prague 2.
Tel 27 17 40 839.
www.shakes.cz

U Černé Matky Boží
Celetná 34.
Map 4 D5.
Tel 22 42 11 155.

Markets, Malls and Speciality Shops

Take your pick – super-modern mall or traditional market. Prague has them both, although do remember that Prague's main market is at some distance from the city centre at Holešovice. Malls are springing up everywhere in the city, and Prague has made a name for itself as a leading place to find all sorts of odd bits and pieces in any number of speciality stores. From Faberge eggs to Jewish *yarmulkas*, you'll find it in Prague.

MARKETS

Prague's markets offer a vast range of goods in a very friendly atmosphere where bargaining is all part of the fun. The largest market in the city, **Prague Market**, is in Holešovice. It was converted from a former slaughter-house. The market now sells fresh fruit and vegetables, all kinds of poultry as well as fish, textiles, flowers, electronics and even second-hand cars and vehicle parts. These are all sold in several large halls and in outdoor stalls. The market is generally open from Monday to Friday, 6am to 5pm.

In Havelská, right in the centre of the city, is the small **Havel Market**, which mainly sells fruit and vegetables. Other well-known markets in Prague include the **Smíchov Market** and a small one on the street V kotcích. Remember that some of the goods sold at all these markets, especially clothes and shoes, can be of very poor quality. Nevertheless, they are an excellent place to hunt for a bargain.

You will also enjoy foraging through the junk, antiques, furniture and military memorabilia (none of which comes with a promise of a refund or guarantee) at the out-of-town **Buštěhrad Collectors Market**, allegedly the third-largest market of its kind in Europe. You can get there by public transport, taking a bus from Dejvická metro station. The market is only open on the second and fourth Saturday of the month, from 8am to noon.

Old Town Square plays host to an excellent and very popular Christmas Gift Market from the end of November to the middle of January. Besides the stalls selling gifts and toys, there are others selling hot wine and sausages, and there is also a small children's play area. The Square also hosts the city's Christmas tree (which fell down in 2003 causing great damage) and a number of open-air winter concerts.

MALLS

There is an increasing number of Western-style shopping malls in Prague, which are more popular and often much better than the old depart-ment stores, offering better value and a greater range of high-quality goods. **Vinohrad-ský Pavilion** has been re-opened as a shopping mall, following extensive moderni-sation, as has **Koruna Palace**. In the very centre of the town, on Na příkopě, the upmarket **Slovanský dům** is home to a great number of chic boutiques, jewellery stores, the fabulous Kogo restaurant and a multiplex cinema, while **Myslbek**, across the road, is a deceptively large shopping centre with a better range of shops that are more accessible to the aver-age pocket. Other shopping arcades include the enormous **Flora Palace** (Palác Flora: take the metro to Flora), which is home to hundreds of shops, and the slightly smaller **Nový Smíchov** (metro Anděl) home to Carrefour and more.

Just outside Prague, at the Zličín terminus of the metro line B, is **Metropole**, Prague's biggest mall. It offers hun-dreds of stores, including a huge C&A, the biggest Kenvelo in Prague and a special children's area. There is also a ten-screen cinema, **Cinema City** (see p221).

STREET STALLS

Street stalls and wandering vendors are not officially allowed to operate in most areas of Prague, though a number of vendors are permitted to sell souvenirs around Charles Bridge. Street stalls are allowed near the entrance to the Old Jewish Cemetery in the Jewish Quarter, and they also line the Old Castle Steps from Malostranská metro station up to the castle's eastern gate.

As most of these sellers are well vetted, the goods on sale tend to be reasonably good quality, though you are unlikely to find any real bargains, and much of what is on sale can be bought cheaper in souvenir stores. At the Old Town's largest outdoor market, **Havelská tržnice**, stalls are crowded with produce as well as handicrafts and textiles, on sale Monday through Friday.

SPECIALITY SHOPS

Bohemia and Moravia have long been known for their fine wooden toys. You will find a number of shops selling them throughout the city, especially in Old Town, but beware cheap imports. You can be sure of the genuine article at **Hračky** near the castle, Beruška in New Town and **Sparky's House of Toys**, just off Na Příkopě, a veritable treasure trove for children of all ages. Older children might also like **Games & Puzzles** on Jungman-nova, which specializes in all sorts of mind teasers, including exquisite hand-made wooden labyrinths.

If you are looking for some-thing a little quirky, but very Czech, try **Dr. Stuart's Botanicus** on Old Town Square, which sells all-natural and all-Czech health and beauty products, from soap to massage oil. Another popular store is **Qubus**, which sells anything and everything, as long as it is the height of modern design.

Most of the weird and wonderful things on sale

were designed by young Czechs. There are a number of other weird and wonderful stores in Prague. The **Spanish Synagogue Gift Shop** sells torah pointers, *yarmulkas*, watches and other Jewish gifts. **Le Patio** on Národní is a shop specializing in original illuminations and candelabra, as well as top-quality restored furniture imported from India, and tables and chairs made by some outstanding Czech blacksmiths. Another favourite for design fans is **de.fakto**, an upmarket version of IKEA, in the centre of the city. More practical perhaps

for souvenir hunters is **Philharmonia**, a music store on Pařížská stocking every great work in the Czech musical lexicon. Yet, the prize for most bizarre shop in Prague must go to **American Heating**, a store specializing in the restoration of historic stoves.

FOOD AND DELICATESSENS

Prague's supermarkets are well stocked with the basic foodstuffs. **Delicacies-lahůdky** is a small shop with meat and fish counters. A specialist food shop, selling smoked

sausage, cheeses and other local delicacies, is **Jan Paukert**. For freshly baked bread visit the bakers around Wenceslas Square and Karmelitská Street. **Paneria Pekařství** shops sell a good selection of patisseries and sandwiches.

For the best selection of local and international delicacies, however, try the **Fruit de France** store on Jindřišská, just off Wenceslas Square. Fine French and Czech foods and ingredients make it popular with the city's better chefs. You can meet them here if you arrive early enough in the day.

DIRECTORY

MARKETS AND MALLS

Buštěhrad Collectors Market
Buštěhrad.

Flora Palace
PALÁC FLORA
Vinohradska 151.
Map 6 F1.

Havel Market
Havelské náměsti.
Map 3 C4.

Havelská tržnice
Havelský trh.
Map 3 C3.

Koruna Palace
Václavské náměsti 1.
Map 3 C5.
Tel 22 42 19 526.

Metropole Mall
Zličín.
Tel 80 08 76 076.
www.metropole.cz

Myslbek
Na příkopě.
Map 3 C4
Tel 22 42 39 550.

Nový Smíchov
Plzenská 8.
Tel 25 72 84 111.

Prague Market
Bubenské nábřeži 306.
Praha 7.
Tel 22 08 00 945.

Slovanský dům
Na příkopě 22. **Map** 3 C4.
Tel 22 14 51 400.
www.slovansky-dum.cz

Smíchov Market
Náměsti 14. října 15.
Map 3 C4.
Tel 25 73 21 101.

Vinohradský Pavilion
Vinohradská 50.
Map 6 F1.
Tel 22 20 97 111.
www.pavilon.cz

SPECIALITY SHOPS

American Heating
Karmelitska 21.
Map 2 E4.
Tel 25 75 34 203.
www.starakamna.cz

Beruška
Vodičkova 30.
Map 3 C5.
Tel 22 41 62 129.

de.fakto
Vejvodova 3. **Map** 3 B4.
Tel 22 42 33 815.
www.defakto.cz

Dr. Stuart's Botanicus
Týnská 3.
Map 3 C3.
Tel 22 48 95 446.
One of several outlets around the city.

Games & Puzzles
Jungmannova 8.
Map 3 C5.
Tel 22 49 46 506.
www.hras.cz

Hračky Traditional Toys
Loretánské náměsti 3.
Map 1 B3.
Tel 60 35 15 745.

Le Patio
Národní 22.
Map 3 A5.
Tel 22 49 34 402.
www.patium.com

Philharmonia
Pařížská 13.
Map 3 B3.

Qubus
Rámová 3.
Map 3 C2.
Tel 22 23 13 151.
www.qubus.cz

Spanish Synagogue Gift Shop
Věžeňská 1.
Map 3 B2.

Sparky's House of Toys
Havířská 2.
Map 3 C4.
Tel 22 49 30 257.
www.sparkys.cz

FOOD AND DELICATESSENS

Bakeshop
Kozi 1.
Map 3 C2.
Tel 22 23 20 195.

Delicacies-lahůdky
ZLATÝ KŘÍŽ
Jungmannova 34.
Map 3 C5.
Tel 22 11 91 801.

Fruit de France
Jindřišská 9.
Map 4 D4.
Tel 22 42 20 304.
www.fdf.cz

Jan Paukert
Národní 17.
Map 3 B5.
Tel 22 42 14 968.

Paneria Pekařství
Valentinská 10/20.
Map 3 B3.
Tel 22 48 27 912.
www.paneria.cz
Also at: 28. října 10.
Map 3 C5; Nekázanka 19.
Map 4 D4; Vinohradská 23. **Map** 6 E1; Vodičkova 33. **Map** 3 C5.

PHARMACIES

*It is not usual for pharmacies to have individual names, so look out for **Léky** (drugs) or **Lékárna** (pharmacy).*

Belgická 37.
Map 6 E2.
Tel 22 45 93 396.

Národní 35.
Map 3 B5.
Tel 22 42 30 086.

Václavské náměsti 28.
Map 3 C5.
Tel 22 42 27 532.

Lékárna u Anděla
Stefanikova 6,
Prague 5.
Tel 25 73 20 918.
Open 24 hours.

ENTERTAINMENT IN PRAGUE

Since the Velvet Revolution in 1989, Prague's range of entertainment has become increasingly varied. Whether you prefer opera to jazz or mini-golf to a football match, the city has plenty to offer. Movie buffs can choose from many of the latest Hollywood blockbusters, a lot of them in English with subtitles. For the adventurous, mime and fringe theatre are both thriving. Prague has a superb musical tradition, which includes symphony orchestras, opera, musicals, jazz and folk music. Concerts are performed throughout the year, in venues which range from Baroque palaces to public parks and gardens. Even if you don't speak Czech, you can still enjoy the city's cultural offerings. Some plays can be seen in English, and for many types of entertainment, music, dance and sport, a knowledge of the language isn't necessary at all.

Street musicians entertaining the crowds

PRACTICAL INFORMATION

The best place to look for information about what's on and where in Prague, is in the English-language newspaper *The Prague Post (see p235)*. This provides details of the best entertainment and cultural events which will be of interest to an English-speaking audience. Those events that are in English or have translation facilities are marked. Other sources of information are the leaflets and City Guides given out at the ticket agencies in the city, such as **Ticketpro** or **PIS** *(see p226)*, as well as the many weekly alternative newspapers. These are generally printed in Czech, English and German. You can also use the free booklet *Přehled*, printed in English

A performance of *Cosi Fan Tutte* at the Mozart Festival

and available from any PIS office. For a comprehensive rundown of events, buy *Culture in Prague*, a detailed monthly publication listing information on a variety of local exhibitions, concerts and theatre.

BOOKING TICKETS

Tickets can be bought in advance from the box office at most venues. You can also book tickets in advance by writing to, or ringing, the venue. Remember that many of the city's box offices may not have any English speakers available. Tickets for the opera or for the National Theatre can also be booked online; visit www. opera.cz or www. narodni-divadlo.cz respectively. The more popular events tend to become heavily booked up in advance by tour groups – particularly during the summer – and by season-ticket holders. However, standby tickets are usually available about an hour before the show. If this isn't practical and you want to

PUPPET THEATRE

Puppetry has a long tradition in Prague and is still strongly represented. The most famous puppet show in the city is held at the **Spejbl and Hurvínek Theatre** *(see p221)*. The show revolves around Daddy Spejbl and his reprobate son Hurvínek. Other puppet theatres include the **National Marionette Theatre** *(see p221)*, which uses all-string marionettes featured in regular performances for children at weekends. The Theatre in the Old Town *(see p221)* and the **Puppet Empire** *(see p221)* also put on puppet shows occasionally. Check listings *(see p226)*.

Theatre puppets

be sure of a ticket on a particular day, it is better to buy them at a booking agency. The drawback to using agencies, however, is that commission on these tickets can be high, sometimes doubling the original price. Your hotel receptionist may also be able to get you tickets.

TICKET PRICES

Ticket prices are very cheap compared to Western prices, except for certain performances, most notably during the Prague Spring Music Festival (see p50). Prices range from around Kč100 for a small fringe production to up to Kč3,000 for a performance by an internationally famous orchestra. Paying by credit card is usually only acceptable at ticket agencies.

TICKET TOUTS

There has been a recent spate of counterfeit tickets on sale, especially for the larger rock concerts. To be safe, always buy your tickets at reputable agencies or at the venue itself.

LATE-NIGHT TRANSPORT

Prague's metro (see p242) stops running shortly after midnight, while the normal bus and tram service ends around 11:30pm. Then the city's extensive night bus and tram service takes over. Time-tables are displayed at each stop. Night trams and buses

A view of the Rudolfinum auditorium (see p223)

The Neo-Classical Estates Theatre (Stavovské divadlo)

are regular and efficient and it is likely that there will be a tram or bus stop near your hotel. Taxis provide the most certain form of late-night transportation, but beware of unscrupulous drivers trying to overcharge you (see p245).

Sparta Stadium (see p223)

Try to walk a little way from the theatre before you hail a cab; the fare will probably be a lot cheaper. Ask your hotel before you go out what the best transport options are.

MUSIC FESTIVALS

The most famous music festival of all is the Prague Spring Music Festival, held between May and June. Hundreds of international musicians come to Prague to take part in the celebrations. Other music festivals include the Mozart Festival (see p51), held in the summer, the Prague Autumn Music Festival (see p52) and the International Jazz Festival (see p52), that takes place in the autumn.

BOOKING AGENTS

Bohemia Ticket International
Malé Nàmèsti 13. **Map** 3 B4.
Tel 22 42 27 832.
www.bohemiaticket.cz

Na Příkopĕ 16. **Map** 4 D4.
Tel & *Fax* 22 42 15 031.
www.ticketsbti.cz

Lucerna
Štĕpánská 61. **Map** 5 C1.
Tel 22 42 12 003.

Pragotur
Staroměstské nám.1. **Map** 3 B3.
Tel 22 17 14 128/130.
Fax 22 17 14 127.
www.prague-info.cz

Prague Information Service (PIS)
Staroměstské náměstí 1. **Map** 3 B3.
Tel 12 444.

Ticketpro
Klimentská 22. **Map** 4 D2.
Tel 296 329 999.
Fax 234 704 204.
www.ticketpro.cz
Also at: Rytířská 12. **Map** 3 B4;
Václavské náměstí 38. **Map** 3 C5.

Týnská Galerie
Staroměstké náměstí 14.
Map 3 B3.
Tel 22 48 26 440.
www.viamusica.cz

Via Praga
Žatecká 1. **Map** 3 B3.
Tel 22 48 19 322.
Fax 22 48 19 324.
www.mozart.cz

The Performing Arts

Prague has always been known for its artistic heritage. Theatre has played an important role in the city's cultural development, and recently the range of entertainment has expanded considerably. Even during the communist period Prague remained a centre of experimental theatre, not least the emergence of Black Light Theatre in the 1960s. Today, this tradition continues, with new theatre groups emerging all the time, ever more experimental. In general, the theatre season runs from September to June. During the summer, open-air performances are given in Prague's gardens and parks. For those who prefer to dance till dawn, relax to the sound of jazz or take in a movie – you will find plenty to entertain you in this city.

ENGLISH-LANGUAGE PERFORMANCES

Many theatres in Prague have started to stage a number of English-language productions, especially in the summer months. Even if the play is not performed in English, many venues have installed simultaneous translation facilities. For details, check the listings (see p227).

MAJOR THEATRES

Prague's first permanent theatre was built in 1738, but the city's theatrical tradition dates from the Baroque and Renaissance periods.

The National Theatre (see pp156–7) is Prague's main venue for opera, ballet and plays. The neighbouring New Stage is another important venue. It is also the main stage for the multimedia **Laterna Magika** company, which is one of Prague's best-known theatre groups as well as being at the forefront of European improvisational theatre.

Other major theatres in the city include the "stone theatres." These gained importance during the 19th century and include the **Vinohrady Theatre**, the **Estates Theatre** (see p65) – one of the most respected in Prague – and the **Prague Municipal Theatre**, an acting company whose plays appear in turn at the **ABC Theatre**, the **Comedy Theatre** and the **Rokoko Studio of Drama**. The **Kolowrat Theatre** is based in the Kolowrat Palace.

FRINGE THEATRES

These originated during the 1960s and won renown for their fight against the status quo. The groups are still very innovative and largely experimental. They perform in small theatres, and many of Prague's best actors and actresses have developed their skills while working for some of these companies.

Fringe theatres include the **Dramatic Club**, well known for its supporting ensemble; the **Ypsilon Studio**, with one of the finest acting companies in the city; **Theatre Na Fidlovačce**, which stages a mix of musicals and straight drama; the large **Theatre Below Palmovka**, renowned for its mix of classical and modern plays; and the **Theatre in Celetná**. One of Prague's most spectacular theatrical and music venues is **Křižík's Fountain**, at the Exhibition Ground, where classical concerts are held and full orchestras perform to stunning lightshows. The **Semafor Theatre** is the home of the tremendously popular comedian, Jiří Suchý.

PANTOMIME, MIME AND BLACK LIGHT THEATRE

Some of the most popular theatre entertainment in Prague is Black Light Theatre, where black-clad actors move objects against a dark stage without being seen – a stunning visual spectacle, pantomime and mime. None of the three requires any understanding of Czech and all are strongly represented.

Jiří Srnec's Black Light Theatre is one of the major venues for Black Light Theatre performance. **Ta Fantastika** is another. These and others are listed in the directory (see p221).

DANCE

In Prague, opera and ballet companies traditionally share the National Theatre, where the Czech Republic's best permanent ballet company is based. The **Prague State Opera** also has a resident ballet ensemble, and has in recent years, been keen to usurp the reputation of the **National Theatre** company as the city's best, something it came close to achieveing in 2003, when it incorporated the now defunct Prague Chamber Ballet. This new company has since set high standards of innovative dance. The tickets for the ballet at both major venues are even lower than for opera performances. You can also watch ballet performances at the **Estates Theatre**. The **Duncan Centre** concentrates on contemporary modern dance and organises the Festival of Dance Theatre.

CINEMAS

Although Prague doesn't show all the latest Hollywood blockbusters, more than 80 per cent of the films shown are recent US productions and a third of them have Czech subtitles. Out-of-town multiplex cinemas are now big business. The largest of these – the **Cinema Cities** at Flora and Zličin – boasts 10 screens.

The listings magazines (see p227) show which films are on and in what language. There are still some major cinemas situated around Wenceslas Square, including **Lucerna** and **Slovanský Dům**; others are listed in the directory. The **Bio Konvikt Ponrepo** cinema shows old films.

DIRECTORY

THEATRES

Animato Black Light Theatre
ČERNE DIVADLO ANIMATO
Na příkopě 10.
Map 3 C4.
Tel 28 19 32 665. www.
animato.webpark.cz

Broadway
Na příkopě 31. **Map** 3 C4.
Tel 22 51 13 311. www.
divadlo-broadway.cz.

Dramatic Club
ČINOHERNÍ KLUB
Ve Smečkách 26.
Map 6 D1.
Tel 29 62 22 123.
www.cinoherniklub.cz

Estates Theatre
STAVOVSKÉ DIVADLO
Ovocný trh. **Map** 3 C3.
Tel 22 42 15 001.
www.narodni-divadlo.cz

Jiří Srnec's Black Theatre
ČERNÉ DIVADLO JIŘÍHO SRNCE
U Lékárny 597, 15600
Praha 5.
Tel 25 79 21 835.
www.blacktheatresrnec.cz

Kolowrat Theatre
DIVADLO KOLOWRAT
(IN ESTATES THEATRE)
Ovocný trh.
Map 3 C3.
Tel 22 49 01 448.
www.narodni-divadlo.cz

Křižík's Fountain
KŘIŽÍKOVA FONTÁNA
Výstaviště, Praha 7.
Tel 22 01 03 280/295.
www.krizikovafontana.cz

Laterna Magika
Národní 4.
Map 3 A5.
Tel 224 931 482.
www.laterna.cz

National Theatre
NÁRODNÍ DIVADLO
Národní 2.
Map 3 A5.
Tel 22 49 01 448.
www.narodni-divadlo.cz

National Marionette Theatre
NÁRODNÍ DIVADLO MARIONET
Žatecká 1. **Map** 3 B3.
Tel 22 48 19 322.
www.mozart.cz

Prague Municipal Theatre, ABC Theatre
MĚSTSKÁ DIVADLA PRAŽSKÁ, DIVADLO ABC
Vodičkova 28.
Map 3 C5.
Tel 22 42 15 943.
www.ecn.cz/abc

Prague Municipal Theatre, Comedy Theatre
MĚSTSKÁ DIVADLA PRAŽSKÁ, DIVADLO KOMEDIE
Jungmannova 1.
Map 5 B1.
Tel 22 42 22 734.
www.divadlokomedie.cz

Prague Municipal Theatre, Rokoko Studio of Drama
MĚSTSKÁ DIVADLA PRAŽSKÁ, DIVADLO ROKOKO
Václavské náměstí 38.
Map 4 D5.
Tel 22 42 12 837.
www.rokoko.cz

Puppet Empire
ŘÍŠE LOUTEK
Žatecká 1.
Map 3 B3.
Tel 22 23 24 562.
www.riseloutek.cz

Reduta Theatre
DIVADLO REDUTA
Národní 20. **Map** 3 B5.
Tel 22 49 12 246.
www.redutajazzclub.cz

Semafor Theatre
Divadlo Semafor,
Dejvická 27.
Tel 23 39 01 383.
www.semafor.cz

Spejbl and Hurvínek Theatre
DIVADLO SPEJBLA A HURVÍNKA
Dejvická 38.
Tel 22 43 16 784.
www.spejbl-hurvinek.cz

Ta Fantastika
Karlova 8. **Map** 3 A4.
Tel 22 22 21 366.
www.tafantastika.cz.

Theatre Below Palmovka
DIVADLO POD PALMOVKOU
Zenklova 34, Praha 8.
Tel 283 011 172.
www.divadlopodpalmovk
ou.cz.

Theatre in Celetná
DIVADLO V CELETNE
Celetná 17.
Map 3 C3.
Tel 22 23 26 843.
www.divadlovceletne.cz

Theatre in the Old Town
DIVADLO V DLOUHÉ
Dlouhá 39.
Map 3 C3.
Tel 22 48 26 807.
www.divadlovdlouhe.cz

Theatre Na Fidlovačce
DIVADLO NA FIDLOVAČCE
Křesomyslova 625.
Map 6 E5.
Tel 26 12 15 722.
www.fidlovacka.cz

Vinohrady Theatre
DIVADLO NA VINOHRADECH
Náměstí Míru 7.
Map 6 F2.
Tel 296 550 111.
www.dnv-praha.cz

Ypsilon Studio
STUDIO YPSILON
Spálená 16.
Map 3 B5.
Tel 22 49 47 119.
www.ypsilonka.cz

DANCE

Duncan Centre
Branická 41.
Tel 24 44 61 342.
www.duncanct.cz

National Theatre
NÁRODNÍ DIVADLO BALET
Národní 2.
Map 3 A5.
Tel 22 49 01 448.
www.narodni-divadlo.cz

Prague State Opera
STÁTNÍ OPERA PRAHA
Wilsonova 4.
Map 6 E1.
Tel 22 42 27 266.
www.opera.cz

CINEMAS

Bio Konvikt Ponrepo
Bartolomějská 11.
Map 3 B5.
Tel 22 42 37 233.
www.nfa.cz

Cinema City Flóra
Vinohradská 149.
Praha 3.
Tel 25 57 42 021.
www.cinemacity.cz

Cinema City Zličín
Řevnická 1.
Praha 5.
Tel 25 79 50 966.
www.cinemacity.cz

Evald
Národní 28.
Map 3 B5.
Tel 22 11 05 225.
www.evald.cinemart.cz

Lucerna
Vodičkova 36.
Map 3 C5.
Tel 22 42 16 972.
www.lucerna.cz

Mat
Karlovo náměstí 19.
Map 5 B2.
Tel 22 49 15 765.
www.mat.cz

Multiplex Cinema Nový Smíchov
Plzeňská 8.
Tel 25 71 81 212.
www.palacecinemas.cz

Perštýn
Na Perštýně 6.
Map 3 B3.
Tel 22 16 68 432.

Slovanský Dům
Na Příkopě 22.
Map 3 C4.
Tel 22 14 51 214.
www.palacecinemas.cz

Světozor
Vodičkova 39.
Map 3 C5.
Tel 22 49 46 824.
www.kinosvetozor.cz

Village Cinemas Anděl
Radlická 1.Praha 5.
Tel 25 11 15 111.
www.villagecinemas.cz

Music and Sport

Prague may not match the vibrancy of Vienna or Budapest, but it certainly can hold its own among Europe's leading cultural destinations. Opera and ballet are well represented, while music is provided by some excellent orchestras. Prices offer good value.

Sports fans are well served too, with top-class ice hockey and Champions League football, both attracting crowds during the season, from September to May.

OPERA

Since Richard Wagner's *The Mastersingers of Nurnburg* officially opened Prague's State Opera House on 5 January 1888, Prague has been a centre of operatic excellence. Today, two highly competitive world-class opera companies give opera top billing on Prague's cultural calendar. And while the low Soviet-era prices of yore are now long gone, top-price seats range from Kč1,000 to 1,200, which makes opera in Prague more accessible than most cities in Europe.

The two major companies, the National and the State, both perform exclusively in their own theatres – the National Opera Company in the **National Theatre** *(see pp156–7)*; the State Opera Company at the **State Opera**. The latter presents a predominantly classical Italian repertoire, always in the orginal language, and performances are always popular. Tickets should be bought in advance. The National Opera Company has a more experimental repertoire, and most of its operas are performed in Czech.

To view a Czech opera, by Czech composers Smetana or Dvořák, the National Theatre is your best opportunity to do so. A lesser known opera company based at the **Estates Theatre** *(see p221)* performs mainly classical, Italian operas in the original language.

CLASSICAL MUSIC

The Czech Philharmonic Orchestra (CPO) has been based at the magnificent **Rudolfinum** *(see p84)* since giving its first concert there in January 1896, when it was conducted by no less a personality than Anton Dvořák, whose name the Rudolfinum's grand hall now carries. Finding immediate success with the public in Prague and abroad (the Philharmonic travelled to London on tour as early as 1902), the orchestra is today recognised by music lovers as one of the finest in the world.

The post of chief conductor of the CPO is one of the most competed for appointments in classical music; the post is currently held by Zdeněk Mácal, appointed in 2003. Almost all contemporary Czech music, including the celebrated recent work *Requiem* by Milan Slavický, premiered at the Rudolfinum, though the programme is varied, and the works of Czech composers share the limelight with those of their foreign counterparts.

Besides the Rudolfinum, the main concert venue for classical music is the Smetana Hall, found in the **Municipal House** *(see p64)*. Other permanent concert halls include the **Atrium in Žižkov**, a converted chapel, the **Clementinum** and the imposing **Congress Centre Prague**. **Bertramka** is another venue with the added attraction of being the place where Mozart stayed when he was in Prague.

MUSIC IN CHURCHES AND PALACES

Concerts performed in the numerous churches and palaces around Prague are extremely popular. Many of these buildings are normally closed to the public, so this is the only chance to see them from inside. Major churches include the **Church of St James** *(see p65)*; the **Church of St Nicholas** *(see pp128–9)* in the Little Quarter; the **Church of St Nicholas** *(see p70)* in the Old Town; the **Church of St Francis** in Knights of the Cross Square *(see p79)*; St Vitus's Cathedral *(see p100)* and **St George's Basilica** *(see p98)*. Other important venues are the **National Museum** *(see p147)*; the **Lobkowicz Palace** *(see p99)* and the **Sternberg Palace** *(see pp112–13)*. It's worth checking the listings magazines *(p226)* for the specific dates and timings of concerts.

ETHNIC MUSIC

A small number of clubs and bars in Prague offer ethnic music. The **Palác Akropolis** hosts diverse performances daily in an atmospheric, converted 1920s-theatre building. The Akropolis hosts the likes of Ani Difranco, Apollo 440 and Transglobal Underground. A variety of bands can be seen from around the world in an unusual setting, at the **House of Culture**. Some of the better jazz clubs *(see pp210–11)* also feature ethnic musicians and bands on a regular basis. Another place worth checking out is **La Bodequita del Medio**, a Cuban restaurant that features Cuban performers most weekend evenings.

SPORTS

Czechs are crazy about most sports, and given their habit of winning international competitions in any number of events on a regular basis, it is not surprising. The biggest spectator sports are ice hockey and football, in that order of importance.

Czech ice hockey has long been rated second only to the US NHL, and the 2004–2005 season saw a large number of NHL players in action in the Czech league, a result of a season-long strike in the NHL. Prague has two teams in the top division, Sparta and Slavia. Sparta plays its home games at the **T-Mobile Arena**, where tickets cost from Kč50 onwards. Slavia play at the new **Sazka Arena**, built for the 2004 Ice Hockey World Championship, held in, but surprisingly not won by, the Czech Republic. Tickets here cost Kč140 and up. There are three games a week throughout the season, from September to May, so you should be able to catch a game.

Czech football has long been admired throughout the world, and the national team has often been among the world's best. It should have won the 2004 European Championship in Portugal, but was beaten in the semifinal by the eventual surprise

winners, Greece. The domestic league is less admired, as almost all of the country's top stars play in richer leagues elsewhere in Europe. The country's leading team, Sparta Prague, though is a perennial qualifier for the European Champions League, guarantees a procession of big-name opponents. Tickets for Champions League games (played September to December, depending on Sparta's progress) sell out quickly. Home matches of the Czech Republic are also played at **Sparta Stadium**, also known as the Toyota Arena.

If you want to get active yourself, you may have to

travel a little further out of town, as sports facilities are not extensive in central Prague. Squash, however, is currently all the rage, and there are number of courts in the city centre, including **ASB** on Wenceslas Square. Golf, mini-golf or tennis are on offer at the **Motol**, the **Exhibition Ground** *(see p162)* and **Štvanice Island**. Swimming pools are also out of the city centre, including two at **Divoká Šárka** and **Kobylisy**. There are beautiful natural lakes at **Lhotka** and **Šeberák** and a whole range of watersports is now on offer at **Hostivař Reservoir** and **Imperial Meadow**.

DIRECTORY

MUSIC VENUES

Academy of Music
HUDEBNÍ FAKULTA AMU
Malostranské náměstí 13.
Map 2 E3.
Tel 257 534 206.

Atrium in Žižkov
ATRIUM NA ŽIŽKOVĚ
Čajkovského 12, Praha 3.
Tel 222 721 838.
www.atriumzizkov.cz

Bertramka
BERTRAMKA MUZEUM
W A MOZARTA
Mozartova 169, Praha 5.
Tel 257 318 461.
www.bertramka.com

La Bodeguita del Medio
Kaprova 5. **Map** 3 B3.
Tel 224 813 922.
www.bodeguita.cz

Church of St James
KOSTEL SV. JAKUBA
Malá Štupartská.
Map 3 C3.

Church of St Nicholas (Old Town)
KOSTEL SV. MIKULÁŠE
Staroměstské náměstí.
Map 3 B3.

Church of St Nicholas
KOSTEL SV. MIKULÁŠE
Malostranské náměstí.
Map 2 E3.

Church of St Francis
KOSTEL SV. FRANTIŠKA
Křižovnické náměstí.
Map 3 A4.

Church of Sts Simon and Jude
KOSTEL SV. ŠIMONA A JUDY
Dušní ulice.
Map 3 B2.
www.fok.cz

Clementinum
ZRCADLOVÁ SÍŇ KLEMENTINA
Mariánské náměstí 10.
Map 3 B3.

Congress Centre Prague
KONGRESOVÉ CENTRUM PRAHA
5. května 65, Prague 4.
Tel 261 171 111.
www.kcp.cz

Lobkowicz Palace
LOBKOVICKÝ PALÁC
Jiřská 1, Pražský hrad.
Map 2 E2.
Tel 257 534 578.

Music Theatre in Karlín
HUDEBNÍ DIVADLO KARLÍN
Křižíkova 10.
Map 4 F3.
Tel 22 18 68 666.
www.hdk.cz

National Museum
NÁRODNÍ MUZEUM
Václavské náměstí 68.
Map 6 D1.
Tel 224 497 111.

Prague State Opera
STÁTNÍ OPERA PRAHA
Wilsonova 4.
Map 6 E1.
Tel 224 227 266.
www.opera.cz

Rudolfinum – Dvořák Hall
RUDOLFINUM – DVOŘÁKOVA SÍŇ
Alšovo nábřeží 12.
Map 3 A3.
Tel 224 893 111.
www.czech philharmonic.cz

St George's Basilica
BAZILIKA SV. JIŘÍ
Jiřské náměstí,
Pražský hrad.
Map 2 E2.

St Vitus's Cathedral
KATEDRÁLA VÍTA
Pražský hrad.
Map 2 D2.

Sternberg Palace
ŠTERNBERSKÝ PALÁC
Hradčanské náměstí 15.
Map 1 C3.
Tel 233 250 068.

ETHNIC MUSIC

House of Culture
KULTURNÍ DŮM VLTAVSKÁ
Bubenská 1.
Tel 220 879 683.
www.vltavska.cz

Palác Akropolis
Kubelíkova 27.
Tel 296 330 913.
www.palacakropolis.cz

SPORTING VENUES

Divoká Šárka
Praha 6.

Exhibition Ground
VÝSTAVIŠTĚ
Sports stadium, U Elektrárny 419, Praha 7.

Hostivař Reservoir
K Jezeru, Praha 10.

Imperial Meadow
CÍSAŘSKÁ LOUKA
Prague 5.

Kobylisy
Praha 8.

Lhotka
Praha 4.

Motol
V Úvalu 84,
Praha 5.

Sazka Arena
Ocelářská 460/2, Praha 9.
Tel 266 121 122.
www.sazkaarena.cz

Šeberák
K Šeberáku, Praha 4.

Sparta Stadium
TOYOTA ARENA
Milady Horákové, Praha 7.
www.sparta.cz

Štvanice Island
Ostrov Štvanice 1125,
Praha 7.

T-Mobile Arena
Za Elektrárnou 419,
Praha 7.
Tel 266 727 475
www.hcsparta.cz

SURVIVAL
GUIDE

PRACTICAL INFORMATION

Over the last ten years, Prague has become more and more open to visitors. The city has responded well to the enormous influx of tourists, and facilities such as hotels, banks, restaurants and information centres have improved considerably. Even so, a little forward planning is always worthwhile.

A Martin Tour sightseeing bus

Reading up about a sight, checking it is open and how best to get there, can save a lot of time and inconvenience. Prague's transport system is straightforward and most of the city's sights are within walking distance. In general, prices are still considerably lower than in the West, but a few of the more up-market restaurants and hotels are priced according to Western rather than Czech wallets. Despite a small increase in petty crime, especially pickpocketing, Prague is still safer than the majority of Western cities.

TOURIST INFORMATION

There are a number of tourist information offices and specialized agencies. These can provide advice on anything from accommodation and travel to restaurants and guided tours. Many employ English speakers and print English language publications. The efficient **Prague Information Service (PIS)** is the city's best tourist information point. It has three offices in the city centre and it provides visitors with maps, advice, listings (see pp218–9) and other types of information in English, German and Czech. To help you find your way around the city, **Kiwi** has a large selection of maps and guides in English.

Čedok street sign

TIPS FOR TOURISTS

In Prague, there are enough English speakers to make booking a room, buying a ticket or ordering a meal relatively simple. A smattering of German may also help, as many Czechs have a working knowledge of the language.

One of the best times to visit Prague is during the summer, although it can be rather crowded. Other busy times of the year are Easter and major Catholic festivals (see pp50–53). The main sights, such as the Old Town Square, are always packed during these periods, but the crowds give Prague a carnival atmosphere. Street entertainers, buskers and small street stalls spring up around the most popular attractions. If the crowds do get too much, just turn off into one of the smaller streets and you are almost guaranteed peace and quiet. Bring a light raincoat for the summer and some warm, woolly clothes for the rest of the year.

OPENING HOURS

This guide lists the opening hours for the individual museums, galleries and churches. Most of the city's major sights can be seen throughout the year, but many of Prague's gardens and the castles outside the city are only

A branch of the Prague Information Service in Staroměstské Náměstí

Entry tickets for some of Prague's major tourist sights

open from 1 April to 31 October. Visiting hours are normally from 9am to 5pm, daily, but during the summer months opening times are extended to 6pm. Note that final admission times can often be as much as an hour earlier. Gardens stay open until 8pm in July and August. All museums and several castles are closed every Monday. The National Museum is closed on the first Tuesday of the month and the Jewish Museum is closed on Friday afternoons and on Saturdays. Museum Night in June is an opportunity to visit collections between 7pm and 1am for free. A free transport service between the museums also operates.

Opening hours of Prague's shops vary widely. Some businesses are open between 7am and 6pm, Monday to Friday, and 8am to noon on Saturdays. Some department stores are open until 7pm on Saturdays and Sundays. Prague does not have any standard late-night shopping, although many of the more expensive tourist shops stay

A horse-drawn carriage in the Old Town Square

open until around 10pm. Banks open from 8am to 4pm, Monday to Friday. Restaurants, cafés and bars all have varied opening hours *(see pp196–7)*. Most of the city's bars open from 10am and as there are no licensing laws, often stay open until everyone leaves.

LISTINGS AND TICKETS

There are some 160 galleries and 40 museums scattered throughout the city, and to find out what's on it is best to look in a listings paper. The English-language newspaper *The Prague Post* gives detailed listings of most events and exhibitions. Available from newsstands in the city centre, it also give tips for the visitor and informative articles on Prague, its politics and its people. The **PIS** has a free monthly English-language listings book.

The price of entry tickets for museums varies widely, from Kč60 to around Kč300. Most churches are free, with a collection box at the door. Tickets for entertainment events can be bought from the booking agencies in the city, or at the venue itself. Some of Prague's hotels can get you tickets, or try a large travel agent in the centre.

SIGHTSEEING TIPS

A good way to see Prague is to take a sightseeing tour. Many firms offer trips around Prague's major sights as well as outings to castles such as Karlstein and Konopiště *(see pp168–9)*. Tours usually start from Náměstí Republiky (Republic Square) and from

the upper part of Václavské náměstí (Wenceslas Square). These trips can be expensive but prices vary, so it is worth checking what's on offer before you make a booking. The Jewish Museum *(see p87)* organizes trips around the Jewish Quarter. For those on a tight budget, **PIS** offers some of the cheapest tours.

A trip on tram No. 91, run by the Museum of Municipal Mass Transport, is one of the cheapest and best city centre tours. It starts off at the Exhibition Ground *(see pp178–9)* and travels around the Old Town, the New Town and the Jewish Quarter. It runs from Easter to the middle of November every weekend and public holiday. Tickets can be bought on board. Trams 22 and 23 will take you from the city up to the castle. Sightseeing trips in horse-drawn carriages (fiacres) are run from the Old Town Square, and in summer, a "fun train" from Mostecká Street runs through some of the loveliest parts of Hradčany and the Little Quarter.

A Czech signpost located in the Old Town Square

DIRECTORY

INFORMATION CENTRES AND TOUR OPERATORS

Akasi
28.října. **Map** 3 C5.
Tel 22 22 43 067.
Fax 22 42 37 235.

Na Příkopě 3–5. **Map** 3 C4.
Tel 22 42 36 118.
Fax 22 42 37 235.

American Express
Václavské náměstí 56. **Map** 6 D1.
Tel 22 28 00 111.
Fax 22 22 11 131.
www.americanexpress.com

Best Tour
Václavské náměstí 27. **Map** 6 D1.
Tel 28 48 14 141.
Fax 28 48 14 144.
www.besttour.cz

Čedok
Na Příkopě 18. **Map** 3 C4.
Tel 22 41 87 777.
Fax 22 42 24 421.

Rytířská 16. **Map** 3 C4.
Tel 24 22 77 23.
www.cedok.cz

Cityrama
Štěpánská 21. **Map** 5 C1.
Tel 22 22 30 208.
Fax 22 22 32 429.
www.cityrama.cz

Kiwi
Jungmannova 23. **Map** 3 C5.
Tel 22 22 30 107.
Fax 29 62 45 555.
www.kiwick.cz

Martin Tour Praha
Štěpánská 61. **Map** 5 C1.
Tel 22 42 12 473.
Fax 22 42 39 752.

Corner of Staroměstské náměstí/ Pařížská 1. **Map** 3 B5.
www.martintour.cz

Pragotur
Staroměstské náměstí 1.
Map 3 B3. *Tel 22 44 82 562.*
Fax 22 44 82 380.

Arbesovo náměstí 4.
Tel 23 60 02 562.
Fax 23 60 02 380.
www.prague-info.cz

Prague Information Service – PIS
Staroměstské náměstí 1.
Map 3 B3.
Tel 22 17 14 130.

Main station, Hlavní Nádraží.
Map 4 E5. **www**.pis.cz

Personal Security and Health

Compared to many Western cities, Prague is relatively safe. Though you may not need emergency help from the police, you should feel free to approach them at any time for advice of any kind; they are generally very helpful to the tourist population. If you should need emergency medical care during you stay in Prague, it will be given free. There is also a number of English-speaking services available, including health centres, pharmacies and dentists, as well as US and British information centres.

A Prague police sign

ADVICE FOR VISITORS

Prague is a safe and un-threatening city to walk around. Violent crimes against tourists in the city centre are rare. The main crime problems that affect tourists are petty pilfering from cars, hotels and pockets; violence with robbery is very unusual. Using your common sense should help you to avoid Prague's only real plague – its pick-pockets. The crowded summer months are a favourite time for these thieves. Always remember to keep your bag in sight and avoid carrying your passport, wallet and valuables in your back pocket or an open bag. Thieves do tend to operate around the popular sights, such as Charles Bridge, and

Municipal police badge

State police badge

many use diversionary tactics, one knocking into you while the other steals your belong-ings. It is very unlikely that anything stolen will ever be recovered. Never leave anything of value in your car. Car alarms have proved not to be a deterrent. Try and park your car in an underground car park, especially if you are driving a foreign make. Always take out adequate insurance before visiting Prague, as it is difficult to arrange once there. Report any thefts to the police for future insurance claims. Avoid getting drawn into a street card game known as shells. It is a classic con game.

Women may encounter a few stares and comments, but this is about as far as sexual harassment will go.

However, one place to try and avoid at night if you are a woman alone is Wenceslas Square. Most men will assume you are one of the city's prostitutes. Unfortunately, Prague has too few reputable bars and cafés that stay open into the early hours. The words "non-stop" and "herna" are synonymous with shady characters; the latter are filled with slot-machines and gam-bling addicts. See our bars and cafés listings for recom-mended places *(see pp208–9)*.

It is an unwritten law that you should carry your passport at all times and although you are unlikely to be asked to produce it, having it could save a lot of problems. Before you travel take photocopies of all essen-tial documents as replacing them can be difficult and time-consuming.

THE POLICE AND SECURITY SERVICES

In Prague you will come across several kinds of policemen and women and members of various security services. Report any problems to a uniformed state police officer at a police station. The main stations are marked on the Street Finder maps *(see pp246–57)*. The state police carry guns and can arrest a suspect. They patrol the streets on foot or drive green and white patrol cars. The municipal police are the other main security force, have greater powers, and are di-vided into different sections. Traffic police ensure the smooth running of traffic and regulate parking, speeding and drink driving. Fines for illegal parking and speeding are huge. It is illegal to drive with any alcohol in your

A male state police officer   **A municipal police officer**   **A female state police officer**   **A "black sheriff"**

State police patrol car

Prague ambulance

DIRECTORY

EMERGENCY NUMBERS

Ambulance
Rychlá lékařská pomoc
Tel 155.

Police
Tísňové volání policie
Tel 158.

Fire
Tísňové volání hasičů
Tel 150.

Emergency Operator
Tel 112 (in English).

MEDICAL CENTRES

Diplomatic Health Centre
Nemocnice Na Homolce
Roentgenova 2.
Tel 25 72 72 146.
www.homolka.cz

First Aid/Emergency Dental Care
První pomoc zubní
Palackého 5. **Map** 3 C5. *(7pm–6:30am Mon–Thu, 4pm–6:30am Fri, 6:30am–6:30pm & 7pm–6:30am Sat, Sun.)*
Tel 22 49 46 981.

General Health Care Corporation
Krakovská 8. **Map** 6 D1.
🚇 Muzeum. *Tel* 22 22 11 206.
www.ghc.cz

24-hour Pharmacy
Štefánikova 6. 🚇 Anděl.
Tel 22 49 46 982.
Palackého 5. **Map** 3 C5.

Vojenská Nemocnice
U Vojenské Nemocnice 01/1200.
Tel 97 32 03 203. **www**.uvn.cz

GENERAL HELP

American Centre
Americké středisko
US Embassy, Tržistě 15. **Map** 2 E3.
Tel 25 75 30 663.
www.usembassy.cz

British Council
Britské kulturní středisko
Politických Vězňů13. **Map** 4 D5.
Tel 22 19 91 160.
www.britishcouncil.cz

Car Breakdown Service/Road Accidents
Tel 1230, 1240.

Lost and Found
Ztráty a nálezy
Karoliny Světlé 5. **Map** 3 A5.
Tel 22 42 35 085.

bloodstream. Occasionally the police have a clamp down on drink driving and if you are caught, the penalties are severe. The traffic police are also responsible for car clamping and collecting the fines *(see pp240–1)*. Finally, if you have a traffic accident, you must immediately ring **Road Accidents**. It is against the law to move anything before the police get there.

There are also a number of private security guards. These are often called "black sheriffs" (many of them actually wear black uniforms) and tend to guard banks and be used as security at football matches and so on. They are not armed.

HEALTH CARE

Any EU national who falls ill in the Czech Republic is entitled to free health care. To claim medical treatment, visitors must have a European Health Insurance Card (formerly form E111) which should be presented to the physician along with a valid form of identification. However, not all treatments are covered by the card so additional medical insurance is a good idea.

Pharmacy sign

Your hotel should be able to put you in touch with a local doctor, but if you need more prompt service, Prague's emergency services are on call 24hours a day and you can call an ambulance if necessary. Hospitals with casualty units are marked on the Street Finder maps at the back of this book *(see pp246–57)*.

There are also 24-hour pharmacies (lékárna) *(see p217)* and a **First Aid/Emergency Dental Care Centre** giving advice and simple remedies. If you want an English-speaking doctor, visit **Vojenská Nemocnice**, (Army Hospital), or else go to the **Diplomatic Health Centre** for foreigners at Na Homolce. You will need to take a passport and a means of payment if you use either of these.

Those with respiratory problems should be aware that between October and March, sulphur dioxide levels in Prague regularly exceed the World Health Organization's accepted levels – often by up to three times. With increasing car ownership and a lack of money for alternative fuels, this seems unlikely to decrease in the near future.

Money, Banks and Currency Exchange Offices

A bureau de change sign in Prague

Compared to many European cities, Prague is a relatively cheap city to visit. Hundreds of banks and bureaux de change have been established, some staying open all night. For the lowest charges and, unfortunately, the longest queues, it is best to change money in a bank. Credit cards are becoming more and more accepted. Traveller's cheques can only be changed in banks.

BANKING

Hundreds of private banks and bureaux de change have been opened in Prague since 1989. The large, modern banks – generally found in the city centre – all open between 8am and 5pm Monday to Friday. The banks may not close at lunch. There are always long queues at the exchange tills so make sure you get there well before closing time. Hundreds of Bureaux de change are found in tiny shops throughout the city. However, despite offering much better exchange rates than the banks, their commission charges are huge, often as high as 12% compared to the bank's 1–5%. But there is a minimum bank commission of Kč20–50. The main advantage of these exchange offices is their convenience. Many are open late every day, some offer a 24-hour service, and queues are rare.

Most of the larger hotels will also change foreign currency for you, but again commission rates may be very high. If you find you have some Czech currency left over from your stay, you can reconvert your money. All banks will reconvert your extra crowns for a small commission. Finally, never change your money on the

black market. As well as being illegal the rate is not any higher than banks or exchanges and it is likely you'll be given notes that are not legal tender.

There are also may ATM machines in the centre of Prague. Some of these are in the entrance to banks and are open even when the branch

An automatic teller machine for dispensing cash

is closed. They accept Mastercard, Visa and Eurocard, and information is in English, German, French or Czech.

CREDIT CARDS

Paying by credit card is becoming more popular. Even if a shop or restaurant window sports a credit card sign, do not assume they will take them as payment; always ask before you eat your meal. The cards most often accepted are: American Express, VISA, MasterCard and Access. Most banks will allow cash advances (up to your limit) on your card. Only a few restaurants, shops and hotels accept American Express.

Façade of the Československá Obchodní bank

DIRECTORY

BANKS

Česká Národní Banka
Na příkopě 28. **Map** 3 C4.
Tel 22 44 11 111.
Fax 22 44 13 708.
www.cnb.cz

Česká Spořitelna
Rytířská 29. **Map** 3 C4.
Tel 22 41 01 111.
www.csas.cz

Commercial Bank
KOMERČNI BANKA
Spálená 51. **Map** 3 B5.
Tel 22 24 11 111.
www.kb.cz
One of several branches.

Czechoslovak Commercial Bank
ČESKOSLOVENSKÁ OBCHODNÍ BANKA
Na příkopě 14. **Map** 3 C4.
Tel 26 13 51 111.
www.csob.cz

GE Money Bank
Opletalova 4. **Map** 4 D5.
Tel 22 44 90 631.
www.gemoney.cz

Unicredit Bank
Revoluční 7. **Map** 4 D2.
Tel 22 11 19 779.
Fax 22 11 19 762.
www.unicreditbank.cz

BUREAUX DE CHANGE

American Express
Václavské náměstí 56.
Map 3 C5.
Tel 22 28 00 237.
Fax 22 22 11 131.
www.aexp.com
One of several branches.

Exact Change
Na Poříčí 13.
Map 4 D3.
Tel 22 48 19 744.
One of several branches.

Interchange
Železná 1. **Map** 3 C4.
Tel 22 42 21 839.
One of several branches.

CASH AND TRAVELLER'S CHEQUES

Currency comes in Czech-crowns and hellers. There are 100 hellers to the crown. It is legal to bring Czech currency into and out of the Czech Republic. Traveller's cheques are by far the safest alternative to carrying cash. It is recommended that you take well-known brands – American Express, Thomas Cook, for example – although it is unlikely that the major banks will refuse any. However, traveller's cheques are not accepted as currency by any shops or restaurants and must be changed at exchanges or banks. The American Express office sells and cashes traveller's cheques. They don't charge commission for cashing their own cheques.

Banknotes

Czech banknotes are now in circulation in the denominations Kč20, Kč50, Kč100, Kč200, Kč500, Kč1,000, Kč2,000 and Kč5,000.

Kč5,000 note

Kč2,000 note

Kč1,000 note

Kč500 note

Kč200 note

Kč100 note

Kč50 note

Kč20 note

Coins

Coins come in the following denominations: 50 hellers; Kč1, Kč2, Kč5, Kč10, Kč20 and Kč50. All the coins have the Czech emblem, a lion rampant, on one side.

50 hellers

1 crown (Kč1)

2 crowns (Kč2)

5 crowns (Kč5)

10 crowns (Kč10)

20 crowns (Kč20)

50 crowns (Kč50)

Communications

The Czech telephone and postal service, Telecom, has undergone a major modernization programme. Digital phones have replaced the older coin-operated ones, and the postal service has become much more efficient. There were some problems in the transition, but the upgrading and improvements have been completed and few problems should be experienced.

telephone calls and internet services. On all phones in the country the dialling tone is a short note followed by a long one; the ringing tone consists of long regular notes, and the engaged signal has short and rapid notes.

USING PUBLIC TELEPHONES

Although there are plenty of public phones on street corners, you can also find them in post offices, where you have to leave a deposit, make the call, and then pay what you owe to the attendant. In hotels, you can usually get a direct line but commission charges on the calls are often exorbitant. Remember also that international calls are extremely expensive, no matter what time of day you phone. But they are at least somewhat cheaper after 7pm, and also

on Saturdays and Sundays. The cheapest way to call abroad is after 5pm and on weekends via Telecom's Xcall service (ring 970 00).

There is an increasing number of modern phonecard telephones in Prague. You can buy the cards *(Telefonní karta)* for these phones from most tabáks and newsstands, and from post offices, supermarkets and petrol stations. Two very popular cards are Karta X, a pre-paid calling card which allows you to make national and international calls from any phone, and TRICK, a multifunctional card which can be used to pay for

PROBLEM NUMBERS

If you have problems getting through to a number in Prague, it is very likely that the number has changed due to the modernization of the phone system. To check, ring the directory enquiries number and ask for an English speaker.

INTERNET CAFES

There are several internet cafés in Prague. On the whole, prices are modest, and the lines are reasonably fast for email access. One of the best is **Káva**, in the New Town. There is also one at the Trades Fair Palace *(see pp164–65).*

USING A COIN-OPERATED TELEPHONE

1 Lift the receiver and wait for the dialling tone.

2 Insert a 1, 2 or 5 crown coin in the slot.

3 The digital display shows how much credit is left. If you need to insert more money, the message *Vložte mince* appears.

4 When the words *Volte číslo* come up, dial the number then wait to be connected.

5 When you have finished speaking replace the receiver. Any coins that were unused are returned here. These phones do not give change.

Coins (also Kč10 & Kč20) that can be inserted into coin-operated phones

Kč1   Kč2   Kč5

USING A PHONECARD TELEPHONE

1 Lift the receiver and wait for the dialling tone.

2 The message *Vložte telefonní kartu*, asks you to insert your card. The display also shows you how much credit you have left on your phonecard.

3 When the words *Volte číslo* appear, dial the number and wait to be connected.

4 The card is ejected automatically when it runs out of credit.

By pressing this small button on the phone at any time during your call, you can have an English translation of the instructions.

Emergency numbers

The multi-purpose TRICK phonecard

POST OFFICES

There is a number of post offices in Prague *(see Street Finder on pp246–57).* The best and largest one is the **Main Post Office** in Jindřišská, just off Wenceslas Square. It has a huge variety of services, including a large phone room where you can make international calls. This service operates from 7am to 11pm.

This post office has recently undergone a complete refurbishment, and is now astonishingly modern and straightforward to use, with easy-access information in English. Take a ticket when you enter the building and then follow the number on it to the correct booth, which will be indicated by an electronic display. Much to the delight of locals, the former long queues have at

Post Office sign

last been replaced by swift and efficient service.

The main post office on Jindřišská is open from 2am to midnight.

SENDING A LETTER

The postal service is now fast, but prices for all the post office services are expected to increase slightly in the future.

REACHING THE RIGHT NUMBER

	Dial
• Internal (Czech) directory enquiries	1180
• Prague directory enquiries and the operator	1180
• International exchange and to make a collect call *(ask for an English-speaker)*	1181
• International call followed by the country code	00
• International directory enquiries	1181
• **In case of emergencies (Police)**	**158**
• **Emergency operator (English)**	**112**

Tobacconist's, where you can also buy stamps and phonecards

There is no first or second class mail in the Czech Republic, but the majority of letters usually arrive at their destination within a few days.

If you want to send something more valuable through the post, use the registered mail service, which is reliable and efficient. Aerogrammes abroad do not exist.

Postcards or letters can be posted in the many orange post boxes scattered around Prague. Both take around five working days to arrive in England and about a week to get to America.

Stamps can be bought from post offices, newsagents or tabáks – who will also tell you what stamps you need. All parcels and registered letters need to be handed in at a post office.

For emergency parcels and packages, you can use an international courier service, such as **DHL**.

POSTE RESTANTE

Post restante letters are delivered to the Main Post Office in Jindřišská Street. Go to window 28 (open Monday to Friday 6:30am to 8pm and Saturday 6:30am to 1pm) with your passport or other official identification. The **American Express** office will also hold mail and parcels for up to a month for anyone who is a registered card holder.

USEFUL ADDRESSES

Main Post Office
Jindřišská 14. **Map** 4 D5.
Tel 22 11 32 113. **Tel** 800 10 44 10 (general information).
Open 2am–midnight daily.
www.cpost.cz

American Express
Václavské náměstí 56.
Map 4 D5.
Tel 22 28 00 237.
Fax 22 22 11 131.
www.aexp.com

DHL
Václavské náměstí 47.
Map 4 D5. *Tel 800 103 000.*
Fax 22 15 12 424.
www.dhl.cz

Káva
Národní 37. **Map** 3 B5.
Tel 22 42 28 862.
Open 7am–10pm daily
(from 9am Sat & Sun).
www.kava-coffee.cz

Post to all destinations

Collection times of the mail

One of the new-style post boxes

Additional Information

Visitors enjoying tax-free shopping on Na Příkopě

DISABLED TRAVELLERS

Facilities for the disabled are few and far between. Occasionally you will come across a ramp at the entrance to a building to allow the disabled easier access, but this is the exception rather than the rule. There are few organizations that campaign for the disabled and, unfortunately, those that do are currently hampered by both public inertia and a lack of funding.

Despite, this, these attitudes are slowly changing and, although transport around the city is a major problem, groups do now exist who can help you with advice, sightseeing tours, accommodation and getting around the city. Two of the best organizations to contact in advance of your trip are: the **Czech Association of Persons with Disabilities** and the **Prague Wheelchair Association**.

Czech Association of Persons with Disabilities
Karlínské náměstí 12.
Map 5 B2. **Tel** 22 48 15 914.
www.svaztp.cz

Prague Wheelchair Association
Benediktská 6.
Map 4 D3.
Tel 22 48 27 210/22 48 26 078.
Fax 22 48 26 079.

CUSTOMS REGULATIONS AND IMMIGRATION

A valid passport or, where applicable, an ID card is needed when entering the Czech Republic from countries outside the Schengen Zone of 24 European nations. Visitors are advised to contact the Czech embassy or consulate, or check details with their travel agent to confirm visa requirements before travelling. British nationals must have a valid passport or identity card, but visas are not required (www.czechembassy.org.uk/consular.htm). Visitors from the United States, Canada, Australia and New Zealand need a valid passport with a minimum of 90 days remaining on it, and can stay for up to three months without a visa. Anyone wishing to stay longer than 30 days will need to register with the border police. Your hotel can usually arrange this for you. If you require a visa you can obtain one from your nearest Czech embassy or consulate.

For non-EU visitors, customs allowances per person are 2 litres (3.6 pints) of wine, 1 litre (1.8 pints) of spirits, 200 cigarettes or equivalent tobacco products. Goods under 175 euros in value can be imported duty-free.

You can take in as much foreign currency as you like, however, it is illegal to take more than Kč350,000 out of the Czech Republic. To export authentic antiques you need to obtain a special licence *(see Shopping p214)*. VAT (value added tax) can be claimed back on items totalling Kč1,000 or more which are carried out of the country within 30 days of purchase.

STUDENT INFORMATION

If you are entitled to an International Student Identity Card (ISIC), it is worth getting one before travelling to Prague. Admission charges into most of Prague's major tourist sights are cheaper on production of a valid ISIC card. Students can also get cheaper coach and train travel. There are a couple of youth hostels in the centre of the city *(see Where to Stay, pp186–7)*. For further information about what is available contact the tour operator **Koleje a Menzy**.

Koleje a Menzy
Jednota Youth Hostel, Opletalova 38. **Map** 4 D5. **Tel** 22 49 30 010. **Fax** 22 49 30 361.

EMBASSIES AND CONSULATES

Australian Consulate
Klimentská 10. **Map** 4 D2.
Tel 29 65 78 350. **Open** 9am–1pm, 2–5pm Mon–Fri.

Canadian Embassy
Muchova 6.
Tel 27 21 01 800. **Open** 8.30am–12.30pm Mon–Fri.
www.canada.cz

New Zealand Consulate
Tel 22 25 14 672. **Fax** 22 42 54 640. (Can be unattended. Lost passport: contact UK Embassy; in emergency: call Consulate in Berlin: 00 49 30 20 62 10 or 00 49 17 27 20 69 92 out of hours).

United Kingdom Embassy
Thunovská 14. **Map** 2 E3.
Tel 25 74 02 111.
Open 9–11:30am Mon–Fri.
www.britain.cz

United States Embassy
Tržiště 15. **Map** 2 E3. **Tel** 25 75 30 663. **Open** 9am–4:30pm Mon–Fri. **www**.usembassy.cz

NEWSPAPERS, TV, RADIO

Prague has a number of newspapers including two weekly English-language ones, *The Prague Post and Prague Business Post*. They are both well produced and provide useful tips for visitors

The two English-language news-papers published in Prague

to the city as well as up-to-date and informative pieces on Prague, its people and politics. The former includes a good leisure supplement, *Night and Day*.

Most of the newsstands that are around Wenceslas Square and other popular tourist spots sell the main European papers and the *International Herald Tribune*. A wide selection of international papers is also available at the news-agent's in Jungmannova 5.

These days there is a larger choice of television in Prague than ever before. Western films are interspersed with well-made nature

A two-prong and a three-prong plug adaptor for use in Prague

programmes and classic Czech films. The stations also show many soap operas, like *Dallas*. Various satellite channels are also available, plus numerous programmes in English, including the daily news. Foreign films are often shown with optional Czech dubbing.

You can listen to the BBC World Service on 101.1FM, but one of the most popular radio stations is Europe II on 88.2MHz playing a blend of mainstream pop. Other stations include Radio I on 91.9MHz, Radio Golem on 90.3MHz and Radio Bonton on 99.7MHz. Reception can be very bad outside the city. You can also listen to the BBC on the Internet (www.bbc.co.uk/).

CONVERSION CHART

Imperial to Metric
1 inch = 2.54 centimetres
1 foot = 30 centimetres
1 mile = 1.6 kilometres
1 ounce = 28 grams
1 pound = 454 grams
1 pint = 0.6 litre
1 gallon = 4.6 litres

Metric to Imperial
1 millimetre = 0.04 inch
1 centimetre = 0.4 inch
1 metre = 3 feet 3 inches
1 kilometre = 0.6 mile
1 gram = 0.04 ounce
1 kilogram = 2.2 pounds
1 litre = 1.8 pints

ELECTRICAL ADAPTORS

The electricity supply in Prague is 230V AC and two-pin plugs are used. For British or US plugs, an adaptor is needed. Adaptors may not be easily found in Prague and it is wise to buy one before leaving home.

PRAGUE TIME

Prague is on Central European time, which is Greenwich Mean Time (GMT) plus 1 hour. Summer time runs effectively from the end of March up until the end of October – this is GMT plus 2 hours.

RELIGIOUS SERVICES

Anglican
St. Clement's; Klimentská 5.
Map 4 D2. ✝ *11am Sun.*

Baptist
Baptist Church of Prague;
Vinohradská 68. **Map** 6 F1.
Tel 22 27 11 047. ✝ *11am Sun.*

Hussite Church
Church of St. Nicholas;
Staroměstské náměstí. **Map** 3 C3.
Tel 22 42 15 402. ✝ *10:30am Sun.* **www**.husiti.cz

Interdenominational
International Church;
Peroutkova 57. **Tel** 29 63 92 231.
www.internationalchurchof
prague.cz
✝ *(in English) 10:30am Sun.*

Jewish
Old-New Synagogue *(see pp88–9).*
Jerusalem Synagogue;
Jeruzalémská 7. **Map** 4 E4.
www.kehilaprag.cz ✡ *(in Hebrew) Sundown Fri; 9am Sat.*

Methodist-Evangelical
Ječná 19. **Map** 5 C2.
Tel 22 43 15 613, 25 75 30 020.
www.praguefellowship.cz
✝ *4:30pm Sun.*

Roman Catholic
Services are held in many churches. Some are:
Church of the Infant Jesus of Prague, Karmelitská 9.
Map 2 E4. **Tel** 25 75 33 646.
www.apha.cz ✝ *(in English) noon Sun.* Church of St. Thomas,
Josefská 8. **Map** 2 E3. **Tel** 25 75 32 675. 5 *(in English) 11am Sun.*

A Roman Catholic service

GETTING TO PRAGUE

Prague is located at the heart of Europe and – apart from the Czech Republic's lack of motorways – has good transport connections with the rest of the continent. There are direct flights every day from most of Europe's major cities and, via ČSA, from Newark, in the USA. However, there are no direct flights from Australia. International coach transport is efficient and cheap. But the journey is about 20 hours from London compared to an hour and a half by air. International rail transport is a popular method of travelling to Prague, but trains tend to get booked up early, especially in the summer. The main train station (Hlavní nádraží) is close to Wenceslas Square and the city centre and, except for the airport, other major points of arrival are also fairly central.

ČSA aircraft

AIR TRAVEL

There are 50 international airlines which now fly to Prague airport. If you are flying from the United States, **Delta Air** operate scheduled flights from the east coast of America. But these are not direct flights – there is a stopover in Frankfurt. There are no Australian or New Zealand carriers flying to Prague, although you can fly **British Airways** with a stop in London. Other airlines include **Air France**, **KLM**, **Air Canada** and **Czech Airlines (ČSA)**. It takes about one and a half hours to fly from London to Prague and about nine hours from the east coast of America – not including the stopover.

DISCOUNT FARES

Because of the increasing popularity of Prague as a tourist destination, many new airlines are starting to fly to the city. Increased competition

has led to a significant drop in the price of flights.

Charter flights have been introduced by a few agents. They are set to become more popular and it is well worth investigating their availability. Remember that these can be subject to last-minute changes and cancellations. Check the ads in the travel sections of major papers for special fares.

APEX (advanced purchase) tickets can be good buys, but they have stringent conditions attached to them. These include having to book your ticket at least a month in advance and severe penalties if you cancel your flight.

If you ring well in advance, airlines will quote you the standard fare, but the price may be lowered nearer the time if seats remain unsold – this is rarely the case in the summer months. Students, senior citizens and regular business travellers may all be able to get discounts. Children under two (who do not occupy a separate seat) pay 10% of

Porters at Ruzyně

the adult fare. Remember fares are more expensive in July and August. If you do manage to get a cheaper deal, ensure that you will get a refund if your agent goes out of business.

AIRLINE OFFICES

Air Canada
Ruzyně Airport. **Tel** 22 48 10 181.
www.aircanada.ca

Air France
Jungmannova 34. **Map** 3 C5.
Tel 23 30 90 933. **www**.airfrance.com

British Airways
Ruzyně Airport. **Tel** 23 90 00 299
www.britishairways.com

Czech Airlines (ČSA)
V Celnici 5. **Map** 4 D3.
Tel 23 90 07 007. **www**.csa.cz

Delta Air Lines
Národní 32. **Map** 3 B5.
Tel 22 49 46 733. **www**.delta-air.cz

KLM
Jungmannova 34 **Map** 3 C5.
Tel 23 30 90 933. **www**.klm.com

Lufthansa
Ruzyně Airport. **Tel** 23 40 08 234
www.lufthansa.com

The recently modernized interior of Ruzyně Airport

RUZYNĚ AIRPORT

Prague's only international airport, Ruzyně, is 15 km (9 miles) northwest of the city centre. The 1936 airport is small, but modern, clean, efficient and functional. It was modernized during the 1960s and now offers all that you would expect from an international airport: 24-hour exchange facilities; car rental offices; a duty-free shop; post office and a left-luggage office.

Sign for passport control

The airport was bought by Air France in 1992 and has undergone further modernization, including the addition of a new terminal, opened in 2005. The North 1 terminal is used for inter-continental flights, including those to the UK, North America, the Middle East, Africa and Asia. Flights within the EU and other European destinations are served by the new North 2 terminal. Other changes include a new business class lounge and catering facility.

TRANSPORT FROM THE AIRPORT TO THE CITY

The airport is linked to the city centre by a regular mini-bus service run by **CEDAZ**. For the return trip to the airport, these can be picked up at Náměstí Republiky and Dejvická metro stations. For a group of one to four people, the trip into town costs Kč480; for five to eight people it is Kč960. The buses can also take you to addresses outside the city, and can even be used to tour the Czech Republic. Whatever your desti-

The airport forecourt, from which buses and taxis can be taken into town

Sign for the CEDAZ airport bus at Náměstí Republiky metro station

nation, make sure to book the bus a couple of hours in advance. The buses can be ordered from 8am to 10pm daily. There is also a regular service to the airport from Dejvická metro (bus 119) and from Zličín metro (bus 100).

Alternatively, there is always a rank of taxis waiting in front of the terminal. Ask at the information booth about the price you should expect to pay for a taxi into town; it is likely to be about Kč600–1,000.

CEDAZ
Tel 22 01 14 296 or 22 42 81 005.
Fax 22 01 14 286.
www.cedaz.cz

PRAGUE'S EUROPEAN AIR CONNECTIONS

Prague, situated at the centre of Europe, has good flight connections to most major European cities. It can be reached in less than two and a half hours on direct flights from all the airports marked on the map.

The spacious interior of the railway station, Masarykovo Nádraži

TRAVELLING BY TRAIN

Prague is connected by rail to all the major capitals of Europe. Rail travel can be an enjoyable, if rather slow, way to travel to and from Prague. International trains have dining cars and couchettes, and tickets are cheaper than air fares. The railways in the Czech Republic are run by the State (České Dráhy – ČD).

The façade of Hlavní nádraží

There are information offices at stations, and these usually have English speakers, so you shouldn't have any trouble booking a ticket. PIS and Čedok (see p227) will help you with timetables and prices. There are four types of train run by ČD. These are the *rychlík* (express) trains; the *osobní* (passenger) trains, which form a local service and stop at all stations, often travelling as slowly as 30 km/h (20 mph); the EX, or national express; and the EC (Eurocity) or international express. International trains are

the fastest, but get delayed at borders. Tickets can be bought in advance or on the day at stations or at the **Travel Agency of České Dráhy** (see p186), however, trains tend to get booked up quickly. If you do want to buy a ticket just before your train leaves, be warned that queues at ticket booths can be long. When you buy your ticket, specify exactly where and when you want to go, whether you want a single or return and what class of ticket you want. First class carriages exist on most trains and guarantee you a seat. In the timetable, an 'R' in a box by a train number means you must have a seat reserved on that train. An 'R' without a box means a reservation is recommended. If you are caught in the wrong carriage, you have to pay an on-the-spot fine.

TRAIN STATIONS

The biggest and busiest railway station in Prague is Hlavní nádraží which is only a five-minute walk from the city centre. In the 1970s, the original Art Nouveau structure was enlarged and a modern departure hall now dominates

the whole terminal. The station is large, efficient and clean with a good-sized, inexpensive, 24-hr left-luggage office in the basement. The nearby luggage lockers are convenient and very cheap. There are also food stalls, bureaux de change and a number of booking and information services in the departure hall.

The other rail stations in the city are Masarykovo nádraží – Prague's oldest terminal, the Holešovice Station and the smallest, Smíchov Station.

TRAVELLING BY COACH

A uniformed ČD railway porter

Coach connections from Prague to many of the major European cities can be infrequent and are often very booked up. However, many of these coach routes are much cheaper, and often faster, than the slower trains. The city's main bus terminal is Florenc, situated on the eastern edge of the New Town. During the summer months there are hundreds of coach trips to all the major coastal resorts in southern Europe. These get booked up quickly by Czechs, so buy your ticket in advance and be sure to reserve yourself a seat. International bus timetables are confusing; check with PIS (see p227) for more detailed information. Coach travel is cheap, but long-haul journeys can be uncomfortable and are slower than air.

Passengers boarding a long-haul coach

PRAGUE'S MAJOR RAIL AND COACH STATIONS

The major points of arrival by train and coach are all fairly central and easily accessible by metro – the nearest metro to each terminal is shown in the boxes along with more detailed travel information.

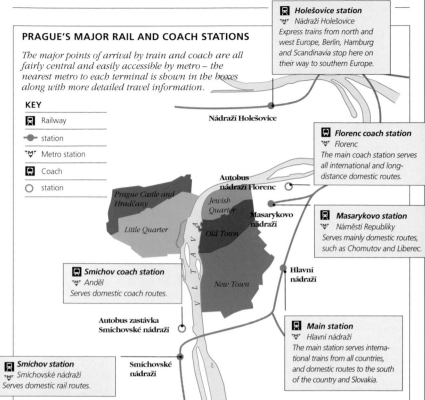

KEY

🚊 Railway

🔴 station

Ⓜ️ Metro station

🚌 Coach

⭕ station

Holešovice station
Ⓜ️ Nádraží Holešovice
Express trains from north and west Europe, Berlin, Hamburg and Scandinavia stop here on their way to southern Europe.

Nádraží Holešovice

Florenc coach station
Ⓜ️ Florenc
The main coach station serves all international and long-distance domestic routes.

Autobus nádraží Florenc

Prague Castle and Hradčany

Jewish Quarter

Little Quarter

Old Town

Masarykovo station
Ⓜ️ Náměstí Republiky
Serves mainly domestic routes, such as Chomutov and Liberec.

Masarykovo nádraží

Smíchov coach station
Ⓜ️ Anděl
Serves domestic coach routes.

New Town

Hlavní nádraží

Autobus zastávka Smíchovské nádraží

Main station
Ⓜ️ Hlavní nádraží
The main station serves international trains from all countries, and domestic routes to the south of the country and Slovakia.

Smíchov station
Ⓜ️ Smíchovské nádraží
Serves domestic rail routes.

Smíchovské nádraží

A Czech motorway sign

TRAVELLING BY CAR

To drive a car in the Czech Republic you must be at least 18. Most foreign driving licences, including Canadian, US and EC ones, are honoured – New Zealand and Australian drivers should get an International Driving Licence. If you bring your own car to Prague, by law you must carry the following with you at all times: a valid driver's licence, vehicle registration card, a hire certificate or, if you are borrowing the car, a letter signed by the owner and authorized by a recognized body, such as the AA or RAC, giving you permission to drive it and a Green Card (an international motoring certificate for insurance). If you drive on the motorway, you will also need to display a special card available at the border, petrol stations and post offices. Other items you have to carry at all times are a set of replacement bulbs, red warning triangles and a first-aid kit. You also have to display a national identification sticker. Headlights must be used even during daylight hours between November and April, and whenever visibility is poor. It is compulsory to wear seatbelts if fitted, and children under 12 are not allowed in the front seat. When you are driving it is strictly forbidden to have any alcohol in your blood and to use a mobile phone.

There are now good connections to all the major cities in the Czech Republic, including Bratislava and Brno, and many more are currently under construction.

Road signs are clear and easy to follow. The speed limit on motorways is 130 km/h (81 mph); on dual and single carriageways 90 km/h (56 mph) and in urban areas 50 km/h (31 mph). The traffic police patrolling the roads are very vigilant, and any infringements are dealt with harshly. There are also occasional road blocks to catch drunken drivers.

The popular, Czech-made Škoda car

GETTING AROUND PRAGUE

The centre of Prague is conveniently small and most of the sights can be reached comfortably on foot. But to cross the city quickly or visit a more remote sight, the public transport is efficient, clean and cheap. It is based on trams, buses and the underground (metro) system, all of which are run by the Prague Transport Corporation (Dopravní podnik). Throughout this guide, the best method of transport

Walking around the city

is given for each sight. The metro and trams serve the city centre, while buses are used to reach the suburbs. The entire system is simple to use – only one ticket is needed for all three forms of transport. Bus, tram and metro routes are found on city maps, available at most city centre tabáks, bookshops and newsagents; or refer to the map on the inside back cover of this guide.

DRIVING A CAR

Most visitors are better off not driving around the centre of Prague. The city's complex web of one-way streets, the large number of pedestrianized areas around the historic core of the city and a very severe shortage of parking spaces make driving very difficult. Prague's public transport system is a much more efficient way of travelling around the city centre.

If you do decide to use a car, remember that on-the-spot fines for traffic violations are common, especially if you are caught driving in one of the city's restricted areas, such as Wenceslas Square. Prague's motorists have become less disciplined and caution is often needed, You must drive on the right and the law states that both driver and front- and back-seat passengers should wear seat belts, if they are fitted. The speed limit in the city is 50 km/h (31 mph) unless a sign indicates otherwise. Traffic signs are similar

One-way traffic and No stopping except for supply lorries

to those in Western Europe. Cars can be useful for seeing sights outside the city. Car rental is inexpensive, but public transport is almost as efficient getting out of the city as in it (see pp236–9).

PARKING

Car parking spaces in the city centre are scarce and the penalties for illegal parking, harsh. Many parking areas are restricted and the oniy places to park legally on the street

Pedestrian zone

Pedestrian crossing

Street or square name and Prague district

Street number

City registration number

PRAGUE ON FOOT

Walking around Prague is the most enjoyable way to see the city. Some pedestrian crossings are controlled by traffic lights, but be sure to cross only when the green man is flashing, and even then, check the road carefully. It is now illegal for drivers to ignore pedestrian crossings, but for years they were allowed to do so, and old habits die hard. Those crossings without lights are still ignored by drivers. Remember that trams run in the centre of the road and go in both directions, which can be confusing. They also travel at high speeds, occasionally coming upon you with little warning. With the uneven cobbled streets, steep hills and a mass of tram lines, flat comfortable shoes are strongly recommended.

Brown street signs with tourist information

are in front of the New Town Hall in Karlovo náměstí, in Na Florenci and at Hlavní station. Unfortunately, car theft is rife, and expensive Western cars are a favourite target. It is safer to park in an official – preferably underground – car park *(see the Street Finder pp246–57)*. But these are expensive and tend to get full early on in the morning. Many parking spaces are reserved for office workers and disabled drivers. Parking at central hotels is limited, with only a few spaces allocated. It is better to park at one of the guarded car parks at the edge of the city and use public transport. Parking meters are rare in Prague but traffic wardens are not.

Parking sign

TOWING AND CLAMPING

Many Prague locals park on the pavement. But ignoring *No Parking* signs may well mean that you find your car has been towed away or clamped. Both the municipal and the private firms that patrol the city are vigilant and ruthless with illegally parked cars, especially with foreign cars. If your car has disappeared, ring 158 to find out if it has been towed away or stolen. To reclaim your towed-away car, you have to go to one of the parking lots (the police will tell you which one) and pay a hefty fine before the car is released. Wheel clamping is becoming

Prague's colourful clamp, also known as the Denver Boot

very popular. You must pay a fine of 1,300 crowns at a police station (the ticket on your windscreen will tell you the address) and return to your car to wait for the clamp to be removed.

THE TRANSPORT SYSTEM

The best way to get around the city centre is by metro or tram. Prague's rush hours are between 6am and 8am and 3pm and 5pm, Monday to Friday. But more trains, trams and buses run at these times, so crowding is not a problem. Some bus routes to the suburbs only run during peak hours. From 1 July to 31 August a summer timetable operates and the entire transport system is reduced. There are information offices at Muzeum and Můstek metro stations (7am–9pm daily), at Ruzyně Airport (7am– 10pm daily) and at Nádraží Holesovice; English is spoken.

One of the many newsstands in Wenceslas Square

TICKETS

Paying on the transport system relies on the honour system, with periodic checks by plain-clothes ticket inspectors who levy an on-the-spot and large fine if you don't have a valid ticket. A transfer ticket covers the entire system – bus, tram and metro – and allows 75 minutes of travel after validation on weekdays and 90 minutes at the weekend. Buy the ticket before you travel and validate it in the machines provided, or you will be travelling illegally. You can buy single ride tickets, from tabák stores and metro stations, or from the driver on buses, with exact change. There are automatic ticket machines in the metros *(see p242)*. Charges vary according to type of journey: up to 20 minutes with no changes (or 30 minutes and four stops on the metro), or up to 60 minutes with the possibility of changing your route. You can

also buy network tickets *(sít'ová jízdenka)*. These offer unlimited rides on buses, trams and metro for periods ranging from 24 hours to 30 days.

Three-day pass   **Transfer ticket**

Travelling by Metro

The underground railway, known as the metro, is the quickest and most comfortable form of transport in Prague. Managed by the Prague Transport Corporation *(see p240)*, its construction began in 1967. It has three lines, A, B and C, and 55 stations. The straightforward layout and clear signs make finding your way around the system very easy. Trains run between 5am and midnight.

Můstek

The metro sign for
Můstek metro station

FINDING YOUR WAY AROUND THE METRO

Metro entrances are not always easy to spot. Look for a sign displaying the 'M' within an upside-down triangle *(see right)*. The street entrance will normally lead you down a flight of steps. A high-pitched bleep (for the blind) at some entrances can also help to guide you.

Once you have purchased your ticket and passed through the unmanned ticket barriers, continue down the fast-moving escalators to the trains. At the bottom of each escalator is a long central corridor with a platform on either side for trains travelling in either direction. Signs suspended from the ceiling indicate the direction of the trains *(see opposite page)*. The edges

of the platforms are marked with a white, broken line which should not be crossed until the train stops. Most of the metro doors open and close automatically (you may have to push a button on some trains), giving a recorded message when they are about to close. During the journey the name of the next station is announced in Czech.

Maps of the underground system can be found above each metro door.

Line A is the most useful for tourists, because it covers all the main areas of the city centre – Prague Castle, the Little Quarter, the Old Town and the New Town – as well as the main shopping area around Wenceslas Square.

Displayed above some seats are disabled signs. These seats should be given up for the elderly, disabled, and those with small children.

The spacious interior of Můstek metro station

AUTOMATIC TICKET MACHINES

You can buy transport tickets at designated ticket sellers *(see p241)* or at the automatic ticket machines in the metro station. The ticket machines, and tickets themselves, may vary in design and colour, but they are still applicable to all forms of transport. The machine offers a choice of tickets at varying prices, for adults, children, bicycles and other bulky items. Once it has been validated, a single-journey ticket is valid for an hour.

1 Check which price band is the right one to meet your requirements, then press the appropriately labelled button.

3 If you are happy that you have selected the right type of ticket, then press the *výdej* button to confirm your choice. (If you are unsure, press the button labelled *storno* and start the process again.)

JÍZDENKY, FAHRKARTEN, TICKETS

851

2 The visual display unit confirms which type of ticket you are in the process of selecting.

4 When you have confirmed your choice of ticket, insert coins into this slot. Most machines give change.

5 Collect your ticket, and any change that may be due to you, from the large slot at the base of the machine.

MAKING A JOURNEY BY METRO

1 The letters, each in a different colour, indicate the three metro lines. The number above the letter is the time it takes to get from one end of the line to the other.

This metro map can be bought from most metro stations, tabáks and news-agents. A metro map has also been included at the end of this book.

2 To decide which line to take, find your destination on the *Street Finder (see pp252–7)*, its nearest metro station and then plot your route on a metro map.

3 You can use single-journey tickets *(left)*. Alternatively, transfer tickets *(below)* and network tickets give you unlimited travel for a set period of time, and are also valid for buses and trams *(see p241)*. Generally, a child's ticket costs half that of an adult's.

The central corridor with platforms either side and signs indicating the direction of trains

4 Before going down the escalators, you must stamp a single-journey ticket in one of these machines. If the ticket has not been stamped, it is not valid and you will have to pay a fine if caught. Do not stamp tourist tickets.

5 This sign, hanging from the ceiling, is visible when you come down the escalator. It shows the direction of the trains on each platform. This one says that the train's final station *(Stanice)* on the left is Háje, so from the metro map you know the train is travelling south.

"Stanice" means station

"Směr" means direction

Name of station

The white circle indicates which station you are in

6 This sign along the central platform indicates the station on line C where you are (white circle) and those stations where you can transfer to the other lines (A and B). For stations to the left of the white circle follow the arrow to the left, and vice-versa for stations to the right.

7 Once you are at your stop, follow the exit signs *(Výstup)* leading out of the metro system.

Travelling by Tram

Trams are Prague's oldest method of public transport. Horse-drawn trams appeared on the streets in 1879, but by 1891 the first electric tram was in operation. After the metro, the tram system is the fastest and most efficient way of getting around the city. Some lines only operate in the rush hour and there are a number of night trams, all of which pass by Lazarská in the New Town.

Tram Signs

These are found at every tram stop and tell you which trams stop there, and in what direction each tram is going.

Name of the tram stop

Tram logo

The direction each tram is heading in

Numbers indicate which trams stop here

TRAM TICKETS

The tram system is run by the Prague Transport Corporation *(see p240)*. Tram tickets are also valid for the metro and buses *(see p242)*.

You have to buy your ticket before you board a tram. Once you have entered, you will see two or three small punching machines on metal poles just inside the door. Insert your ticket and it will be stamped automatically.

If you do not punch your ticket it is not valid and, if you are caught by a ticket inspector, you will have to pay an on-the-spot fine *(see*

p241). A single-journey ticket is valid for one journey only *(see p241)*, however long.

Each tram stop has a timetable – the stop underlined is where you are standing. The stops below that line indicate where that tram is heading.

Trams run every 10 to 20 minutes. Doors either open and close automatically or by pushing a button and each stop is announced in Czech. After the metro closes, a small number of night trams run every 30 minutes or so. These trams (numbers 51 to 58) are marked by blue numbers at the tram stop. For more information see www.dp-praha.cz.

One of the new trams on the streets of Prague

USEFUL TRAM ROUTES

These three tram routes are the most useful for getting around the centre of Prague. They pass many of the major sights on both sides of the Vltava, so are also a cheap, pleasant way of sightseeing.

Hanavský Pavilion

Letná Park

Hradčany

Belvedere

Jewish Quarter

Náměstí Republiky

Little Quarter

Rudolfinum

Powder Gate

Old Town

Charles Bridge

Strahov

Church of St Nicholas

New Town

Wenceslas Square

Hotel Europa

Strahov Monastery

Petřín Park

Charles Square

National Theatre

Church of St Peter and St Paul

Vyšehrad

KEY

——— Route 14

——— Route 17

——— Route 22, 23

Travelling by Bus

You are unlikely to use a bus unless you want to visit the outer suburbs. By law, buses are not allowed in the city centre (they produce noxious fumes and the streets are too narrow), so they transport people from the suburbs to tram and metro stops outside the centre.

Bus stop logo

BUS TICKETS

A typical public bus in Prague

Unless you have small change, you must buy a ticket before you board a bus. Tickets are available from all the usual agents *(see p241)*.

Again, you must validate your ticket in the punching machine on the bus. If you buy a single-journey ticket, it is only valid for one journey. Each time you change bus, you will have to buy a new ticket, unless you have a tourist ticket *(see p241)*. The doors open and close automatically and the end of the boarding period is signalled by a high-pitched signal. You are expected to give up your seat for the elderly and disabled.

Bus timetables are located at every stop. They have the numbers of all the buses that stop there and the timetable for each route. The frequency of buses varies considerably. In the rush hour there may be 12 to 15 buses an hour, at other times as few as three.

Throughout the night there are 12 buses which go to the outer areas not served by the tram and metro system. For more information see www.dpp.cz.

Travelling by Taxi

For visitors to Prague taxis are a useful but often frustrating form of transport. After decades of public ownership, all taxis are now privately owned, but there are many unscrupulous drivers who are out to charge as much as they can get away with. For this reason it's worth taking a few simple precautions. For a start, find out how much a fare should cost.

An illuminated taxi sign

TAXI FARES

One of the many taxi ranks in the centre of the town

As soon as you enter a taxi there is a minimum charge. After that, by law the fare should increase at a set rate per kilometre. However, this set charge is rarely, if ever, adhered to and taxis can be a very expensive way of getting around the city. Taxi meters can be set at four different rates but for journeys in the city it should be set at one (the cheapest). However, rather than depend on the meters –

they are often rigged – it is a wise move to negotiate a fare you think is reasonable before you enter the cab. Vigorous bargaining can often bring the price down. Few taxi drivers speak more than the most rudimentary English, so communication can be difficult. Unless your Czech pronunciation is good, write down your destination for them in Czech. At night, charges will increase, sometimes by 200 or even 300 per

Taxi receipts, if requested, are required to be given by law.

The distance travelled   Amount charged

eb european business solutions

cent. Be sure surcharges are included in the figure you negotiate beforehand. If problems do arise at the end of the journey, ask for a receipt before you pay. This will normally deter drivers from trying to overcharge you. Avoid taxis around the main tourist sights, these can often be the worst offenders. Despite occasional problems, taxis are a safe form of transport and women should feel comfortable alone in them.

The meter displays your fare and surcharges.

Fare   Surcharges   Rate

STREET FINDER

The map references given for all the sights, hotels, restaurants, bars, shops and entertainment venues described in this book refer to the maps in this section. A complete index of street names and all the places of interest marked, can be found on the following pages. The key map (right) shows the area of Prague covered by the *Street Finder*. This map includes sightseeing areas, as well as districts for hotels, restaurants, pubs and entertainment venues.

In keeping with Czech maps, none of the street names in the index or on the Street Finder have the Czech word for street, *ulice*, included (though you may see it on the city's street signs). For instance, Celetná ulice appears as Celetná in both the index and the Street Finder. The numbers preceding some street names are dates. In our index we ignore the numbers, so that 17. listopadu (17 November), is listed under 'L'.

KEY TO STREET FINDER

■	Major sight
■	Places of interest
□	Other building
Ⓜ	Metro station
▤	Train station
▣	Coach station
▤	Tram stop
▤	Funicular railway
▬	River boat boarding point
▤	Taxi rank
P	Car park
ⓘ	Tourist information office
✚	Hospital with casualty unit
▤	Police station
✝	Church
✡	Synagogue
⊠	Post office
==	Railway line
—	City wall
==	Pedestrian street

SCALE OF MAP PAGES

```
0 metres          200
                        1:8,400
0 yards           200
```

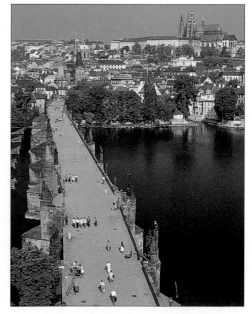

View of the Little Quarter, Hradčany and Prague Castle from the Old Town Bridge Tower

Aerial view of the Baroque Church of St Nicholas in the Old Town Square, from the tower at the top of the Old Town Hall

MILADY HORÁKOVÉ

2 **3** **4**

NÁBŘEŽÍ EDVARDA BENEŠE

V L T A V A

NA FRANTIŠKU

REVOLUČNÍ

Jewish Quarter

NERUDOVA

Karlův most

Little Quarter

Old Town

WILSONOVA

SMETANOVO NÁBŘEŽÍ

ÚJEZD

NÁRODNÍ

0 metres 500

0 yards 500

5 **6**

ŽITNÁ

ANGLICKÁ

SLEZSKÁ

New Town

JEČNÁ

KORUNNÍ

RAŠÍNOVO N. BŘEŽÍ

SOKOLSKÁ

LEGEROVA

V L T A V A

SVOBODOVA

SVORNOSTI

RADLICKÁ

VNISLAVOVA

SEKANINOVA

KŘESOMYSLOVA

JAROMÍROVA

The imposing twin towers of the Church of St Peter and St Paul on top of Vyšehrad rock

Street Finder Index

The order of the names in the index is affected by the *háček*, the accent like an inverted circumflex (*háček* means "little hook"). In the Czech alphabet, **č**, **ř**, **š** and **ž** are treated as separate letters. Street names beginning with **ř**, for example, are listed after those beginning with **r** without an accent.

Churches, buildings, museums and monuments are marked on the Street Finder maps with their English and Czech names. In the index, both forms are listed. However, English names for streets and squares, such as Wenceslas Square, do not appear on the maps. Where they are listed in the index, the Czech name is given in brackets in the form that appears on the map.

<table>
<tr><td colspan="2">USEFUL WORDS</td></tr>
<tr><td>dům</td><td>house</td></tr>
<tr><td>hrad</td><td>castle</td></tr>
<tr><td>kostel</td><td>church</td></tr>
<tr><td>klášter</td><td>convent, monastery</td></tr>
<tr><td>most</td><td>bridge</td></tr>
<tr><td>nábřeží</td><td>embankment</td></tr>
<tr><td>nádraží</td><td>station</td></tr>
<tr><td>náměstí</td><td>square</td></tr>
<tr><td>sady</td><td>park</td></tr>
<tr><td>schody</td><td>steps</td></tr>
<tr><td>třída</td><td>avenue</td></tr>
<tr><td>ulice</td><td>street</td></tr>
<tr><td>ulička</td><td>lane</td></tr>
<tr><td>zahrada</td><td>garden</td></tr>
</table>

General Index

Acknowledgments

Dorling Kindersley wishes to thank the following people who contributed to the preparation of this book.

Main Contributor

Vladimír Soukup was born in Prague in 1949. He worked for the daily newpaper, *Evening Prague*, for 20 years, eventually becoming Deputy Chief Editor. He has written a wide range of popular guides to Prague.

Additional Contributors

Ben Sullivan, Lynn Reich.

Editorial and Design

Managing Editor Carolyn Ryden; *Managing Art Editor* Steve Knowlden; *Senior Editor* Georgina Matthews; *Senior Art Editor* Vanessa Courtier; *Editorial Director* David Lamb; *Art Director* Anne-Marie Bulat; *Production Controller* Hilary Stephens; *Picture Research* Ellen Root; *DTP Editorial* Emma Anacootee, Claire Baranowski *Designer* Nicola Erdpresser, Sangita Patel; *Consultant* Helena Svojsikova; *Maps* Caroline Bowie, Simon Farbrother, James Mills-Hicks, David Pugh (DKCartography).Russell Davies, Stephanie Driver, Fay Franklin, Alistair Gunn, Elaine Harries, Charlie Hawkings, Jan Kaplan, Dr Tomáš Kleisner, Jude Ledger, Susannah Marriott, Marianne Petrou, Robert Purnell, Marian Sucha, Daphne Trotter, Christopher Vinz.

Additional Photography

DK Studio/Steve Gorton, Ian O'Leary, Otto Palan, M Soskova, Clive Streeter, Alan Williams, Peter Wilson.

t = top; tl = top left; tc = top centre; tr = top right; cla = centre left above; ca = centre above; cra = centre right above; cl = centre left; c = centre; cr = centre right; clb = centre left below; cb = centre below; crb = centre right below; bl = bottom left; b = bottom; bc = bottom centre; br = bottom right; d = detail.

Works of art on the pages detailed have been reproduced with the permission of the following copyright holders: Aristide Maillol *Pomona* 1910 © ADAG, Paris, and DACS, London, 2006: 164cr. Gustav Makarius Tauc (An der Aulenkaut 31, Wiesbaden, Germany) under commission of the Minorite Order in Rome: 35br. The publishers are grateful to the following individuals, companies and picture libraries for permission to reproduce photographs or to photograph at their establishments: ALAMY IMAGES: Chris Fredriksson 199c; PjrFoto.com/Phil Robinson 227bc; Robert Harding Picture Library 10bl; ARCHEOLOGICKÝ ÚSTAV ČESKÉ AKADEMIE VĚD: 20t; ARCHIV FÜR KUNST UND GESCHICHTE, BERLIN: 17b, 18tl (d), 18tr, 18bc(d), 18br(d), 19tl(d), 19tc(d), 19tr(d), 19c(d), 19bc(d), 20clr, 20bl, 23cb(d), 29cla(d), 32t(d), 32bl, 34ca(d), 35ca(d), 35bl, 43tl, 50b(d), 105cr, 118t, Erich Lessing 28ca(d), 31bl(d), 88c, 89cb; ARCHIV HLAVNIHO MĚSTA. PRAHY (CLAM-GALLASŮV PALÁC): 23cl, 24bl, 28bl, 28br, 30b, 33clb, 33bc, 72t, 136br, 137br(d), 138ca, 168c. BILDARCHIV PREUSSISCHER KULTURBESITZ: 4t(d), 19bl(d), 29br, 34bc, 68tr, 104bl(d); BRIDGEMAN ART LIBRARY, London: Prado,

Madrid 29t; Rosegarten Museum, Constance 26ca. ČESKÁ TISKOVÁ KANCELÁŘ: 19br, 35cbr, 203cr; COMSTOCK: George Gerster 12cla; ČSA: 244t; JEAN-LOUP CHARMET: 18bl(d), 21c, 31br, 33t, 33bl, 33br(d), 34tr(d), 34bl, 62c, 69tc; ZDENEK CHRAPPEK: 50c; CORBIS: Gail Mooney 199tl; JOE CORNISH: 58–9, 60, 148br; CZECH NATIONAL BANK: 239. MARY EVANS PICTURE LIBRARY: 9, 59, 138cb, 183, 225. GRAFOPRINT NEUBERT: 31clb, 38clb, 116c. ROBERT HARDING PICTURE LIBRARY: Michael Jenner 128tl; Christopher Rennie 24ca, 103tr; Peter Scholey 30t, 129tl; HIDDEN PLACES RESIDENCES & BOUTIQUE HOTELS: 187bl; HUTCHISON LIBRARY: Libuše Taylor 51b, 52t, 177tl, 205c. THE IMAGE BANK: Andrea Pistolesi 14b; Courtesy of ISIC, UK: 242c. KANCELÁŘ PREZIDENTA REPUBLIKY: 20–1, 21tr, 21bl, 21br, 22c; KAPLAN PRODUCTIONS: 117t; OLDRICH KARASEK: 11tr 56cb, 62tr, 101bl; 101crb, 134t, 135b; 176t, 201c, 219t, 233cl, 246c; KARLŠTEJN: 25tl; Vladimír Hyhlík 24–5, KAREL KESTNER: 35cbl; KLEMENTINUM: 23tl; Prokop Paul 22t; THE KOBAL COLLECTION: 35tl; DALIBOR KUSÁK: 164bl, 168–9 all, 170-1 all. IVAN MALÝ: 218t, 218c; MUZEUM HLAVNÍHO MĚSTA PRAHY 32–3; MUZEUM POŠTOVNÍ ZNÁMKY: 149cl. NÁRODNÍ FILMOVÝ ARCHIV: 34br; NÁRODNÍ GALERIE V PRAZE: 24br, 40b; Grafická sbírka 26t, 27bl, 31t, 67b, 69c, 100t, 102b, 121t, 125cb, 129br, 138b, 157cb, 175b, 180b; Klášter sv. Anežky 39tr, 83t, 92–3 all, 133b; Klášter sv. Jiří 16, 37br, 38t, 39tr, 97clb, 106–7 all, 108–9 all, Šternberský palác 38ca, 112–3 all, 114–5 all, Veletržní Palac 164–5 all; Zbraslav 40b; NÁRODNÍ MUZEUM, PRAHA: 147b; NÁRODNÍ MUZEUM V PRAZE: Vlasta Dvořáková 20clb, 26–7, 26bl, 26bc, 26br, 27t, 27cl, 27cr, 27br, 29bl, 39cb, 75b, 72b, Jarmila Kutová 20c, 22bl, Dagmar Landová 28bc, 126c, Muzeum Antonína Dvořáka 39b, Muzeum Bedřicha Smetany 32ca, Prokop Paul 75b, Tyršovo Muzeum; 34cb, 149bl; NÁRODNÍ TECHNICKÉ MUZEUM: Gabriel Urbánek 41t. OBRAZÁRNA PRAŽSKÉHO HRADU: 98b; ÖSTERREICHISCHE NATIONALBIBLIOTHEK, WIEN: 25clb, 26cb. PHOTO- GRAPHERS DIRECT: Chris Barton 10cra, Eddie Gerald 11bl; PIVOVARSKÉ MUZEUM: 200tr, 200c; PRAGUE INFORMATION SERVICE: www.prague-info.cz 226bc; BOHUMÍR PROKŮPEK: 25bl, 30t, 120c, 121c, 121bl, 163b. REX FEATURES LTD: Alfred 35tr, Richard Gardener 240t. SCIENCE PHOTO LIBRARY: Geospace 13, 38crb; SOTHEBY'S/ THAMES AND HUDSON: 104c; STÁTNÍ ÚSTŘEDNÍ ARCHIV: 23b; STÁTNÍ ÚSTAV PAMÁTKOVÉ PÉČE: 23tc; STÁTNÍ ŽIDOVSKÉ MUZEUM: 39ca, 85t, 85c, 90t; LUBOMÍR STIBUREK, www.czfoto.cz: 55b, 145ca, 163t, 176c, 243cl, 244cr, 251bca, 252cr; MARIAN SUCHA: front endpaper Lbl, 55t, 56cb, 94, 127b, 174t, 205bl, 205t, 233bl, 237tr, 245c; SVATOVÍTSKÝ POKLAD, PRAŽSKÝ HRAD: 14t, 21tl, 24t, 24cb, 28t, 40tr. MARTIN TOUR, PRAHA: 226tr; UMĚLECKOPRŮMYSLOVÉ MUZEUM V PRAZE: 39tl, 40tl, 149c, 149br, Gabriel Urbánek 28clb, 41b; UNIVERZITA KARLOVA: 25tr. U PINKASU RESTAURANT: 198cla; PETER WILSON: 4b; 197tl, 224-5, 246. ZEFA: 33cra. Front endpaper: all special or additional photography except (centre) JOE CORNISH. JACKET: Front - CORBIS: Dallas and John Heaton main image; DK IMAGES: Jiri Kopriva bl. Back – JOE CORNISH: bl, tl; DK IMAGES: Jiri Dolezal cla; Jiri Kopriva clb. Spine – CORBIS: Dallas and John Heaton t; DK IMAGES: Peter Wilson b. All other images © Dorling Kindersley. For further information, see: www.dkimages

Patricia Cornwell recognized as one of the world's top
bestselling crime authors with novels translated into thirty-
six languages in more than 120 countries. Her novels have
won numerous prestigious awards including the Edgar,
the Creasey, the Anthony, the Macavity, and the Prix du
Roman d'Aventure. Beyond the Scarpetta series, Cornwell
has written a definitive book about Jack the Ripper, a
biography, and two more fiction series among others.
Cornwell, a licensed helicopter pilot and scuba diver,
actively researches the cutting-edge forensic technologies
that inform her work. She was born in Miami, grew up in
Montreat, NC, and now lives and works in Boston.

www.PatriciaCornwell.com

@1pcornwell

Facebook.com/Patricia.Cornwell

1pcornwell

ALSO BY PATRICIA CORNWELL

Patricia
Cornwell
CHAOS

HarperCollinsPublishers

HarperCollins*Publishers* Ltd
1 London Bridge Street
London SE1 9GF

www.harpercollins.co.uk

This paperback edition 2017
2

First published in Great Britain by HarperCollins*Publishers* 2016

First published in the United States by William Morrow,
an imprint of HarperCollins*Publishers* 2016

Printed and bound by CPI Group (UK) Ltd, Croydon, CR0 4YY

Typeset in Meridien by Palimpsest Book Production Ltd,
Falkirk, Stirlingshire

MIX
Paper from
responsible sources
FSC™ C007454

FSC™ is a non-profit international organisation established to promote the
responsible management of the world's forests. Products carrying the FSC label
are independently certified to assure consumers that they come from forests that
are managed to meet the social, economic and ecological needs of present and
future generations, and other controlled sources.

Find out more about HarperCollins and the environment at
www.harpercollins.co.uk/green

To Staci
—In Memory of Tram—

THERE IS LOVE IN ME THE LIKES OF WHICH
YOU'VE NEVER SEEN. THERE IS RAGE IN ME
THE LIKES OF WHICH SHOULD NEVER ESCAPE.

—Mary Shelley, *Frankenstein*

CHAOS

From the Ancient Greek (χάος or kháos)
A vast chasm or void
Anarchy
The science of unpredictability

PROLOGUE

TWILIGHT
WEDNESDAY, SEPTEMBER 7

Beyond the brick wall bordering Harvard Yard, four tall chimneys and a gray slate roof with white-painted dormers peek through the branches of hardwood trees.

The Georgian building is a welcome sight no more than fifteen minutes ahead as the crow flies. But walking wasn't smart. I was foolish to refuse a ride. Even in the shade it feels like an oven. The atmosphere is stagnant, nothing stirring in the hot humid air.

Were it not for the distant sounds of traffic, the infrequent pedestrian, the vapor trails overhead, I might believe I'm the only human left on a post-apocalyptic earth. I've never seen the Harvard campus this deserted except maybe during a bomb scare. But then I've also not been witness to such extreme weather in this part of the world, and blizzards and arctic blasts don't count.

New Englanders are used to that but not temperatures

1

edging past a hundred degrees Fahrenheit. The sun is molten in a bone-scrubbed sky that the heat has bleached the blue out of as I've heard it described. *The greenhouse effect. Global warming. God's punishment. The Devil's in his workshop. Mercury in retrograde. El Niño. The end times.*

These are some of the explanations for one of the worst heat waves in Massachusetts's history. Business at my headquarters, the Cambridge Forensic Center, has gone through the roof, and that's the paradox of what I do. When things are bad they're normal. When they're worse they're good. It's a gift and a curse that I have job security in this imperfect world, and as I take a shortcut through the center of the campus in the stifling heat, I tweak the talk I'm going to give at the Kennedy School of Government tomorrow night.

Cleverness, a play on words, provocative stories that are real, and maybe my sister Dorothy isn't the hopeless tool I've always believed. She says that I have to be entertaining if I'm to get an auditorium full of jaded Ivy League intellectuals and policy makers to listen. Maybe they'll even walk around in my shoes for once if I share the dark side, the underbelly, the scary basement no one wants to enter or acknowledge.

As long as I'm not expected to repeat insensitive jokes, certainly not the ones I constantly hear from the cops, rather dreadful slogans that end up on T-shirts and coffee cups. I'm not going to say *our day begins when yours ends* even if it's true. Although I suppose it's all right to quip that the more dire the straits the more necessary I am. Catastrophes are my calling. Dreadful news gets me out of bed. Tragedy is my bread and butter, and the cycle of life and death remains unbroken no matter our IQ.

This is how my sister thinks I should explain myself to hundreds of influential students, faculty, politicos and global leaders tomorrow night. In my opinion I shouldn't need to explain myself at all. But apparently I do, Dorothy said over the phone last night while our elderly mother was ranting loudly in the background to her thieving South American housekeeper, whose name—no kidding—is Honesty. Apparently Honesty is stealing vast amounts of jewelry and cash again, hiding Mom's pills, eating her food and rearranging her furniture in the hope she'll trip and break a hip.

Honesty the housekeeper isn't doing any such thing and never did or would, and sometimes having a nearly photographic memory isn't to my advantage. I recall last night's telephonic drama, including the parts in Spanish, hearing every word of it in my head. I can replay Dorothy's rapid-fire self-assured voice advising me all the while about how not to lose an audience since clearly I will if left to my own devices. She told me:

Walk right up to the podium and scan the crowd with a deadpan face, and say: "Welcome. I'm Doctor Kay Scarpetta. I take patients without appointments and still make house calls. Wouldn't you just die to have my hands all over you? Because it can be arranged." And then you wink.

Who could resist? That's what you should tell them, Kay! Something funny, sexy and non-PC. And they're eating out of your hand. For once in your life you need to listen to your little sis very carefully. I didn't get where I am by not knowing a thing or two about publicity and marketing.

And one of the biggest problems with deadbeat jobs, no pun intended, like working in funeral homes and morgues, is nobody knows the first thing about how to promote or sell anything because

3

why bother? Well to be fair, funeral homes are better at it than where you work. It's not like it's part of your job description to make a dead person look presentable or care if the casket is pretty. So you have all of the disadvantages of the funeral business but nothing to sell and nobody to say thank you.

Throughout my career as a forensic pathologist my younger only sibling has managed to equate what I do with being a mortuary scientist or simply someone who deals with messes no one else wants to touch.

Somehow it's the logical conclusion to my taking care of our dying father when I was a child. I became the go-to person when something was painful or disgusting and needed tending to or cleaning up. If an animal got run over or a bird flew into a window or our father had another nosebleed, my sister would run screaming to me. She still does if she needs something, and she never takes into account convenience or timing.

But at this juncture in life my attitude is the two of us aren't getting any younger. I've decided to make a real effort to keep an open mind even if my sister might be the most selfish human being I've ever known. But she's bright and talented, and I'm no saint either. I admit I've been stubborn about acknowledging her value, and that's not fair.

Because it's possible she really might know what she's doing when she mandates that I should speak less like a legal brief or a lab report and more like a pundit or a poet. I need to turn up the volume, the brightness and the color, and I've been keeping that in mind as I polish my opening remarks, including cues such as underlines for emphasis and pauses for laughter.

I take a sip from a bottle of water that's hot enough to

brew tea. I nudge my dark glasses up as they continue to slip down my sweaty nose. The sun is a relentless blacksmith hammering in twilight's fiery forge. Even my hair is hot as my low-heeled tan leather pumps *click-click* on bricks, my destination now about ten minutes out. Mentally I go through my talk:

Good evening Harvard faculty, students, fellow physicians, scientists and other distinguished guests.

As I scan the crowd tonight I see Pulitzer and Nobel Prize winners, mathematicians and astrophysicists who are also writers, painters and musicians.

Such a remarkable collection of the best and the brightest, and we are extremely honored to have the governor here, and the attorney general, and several senators and congressmen in addition to members of the media, and business leaders. I see my good friend and former mentor General John Briggs hiding in the back, slinking low in his seat, cringing over the thought of my being up here. [Pause for laughter]

For those of you who don't know, he's the chief of the Armed Forces Medical Examiner System, the AFMES. In other words, General Briggs would be the forensic surgeon general of the United States were there such a position. And in a little while he's going to join me during the Q&A part of the program to discuss the Columbia *space shuttle disaster of 2003.*

We're going to share what we've learned from materials science and aeromedicine, and also from the recoveries and examinations of the seven astronauts' remains that were scattered over a fifty-some-mile scene in Texas . . .

I have to give Dorothy credit.

She's dramatic and colorful, and I'm somewhat touched that she's flying in for the lecture even if I have no idea why. She says she wouldn't miss tomorrow night but I don't believe her. My sister's not been to Cambridge in the eight years I've headed the CFC. My mother hasn't either, but she doesn't like to travel and won't anymore. I don't know Dorothy's excuse.

Only that she's never been interested until now, and it's a shame she had to choose tonight of all nights to fly to Boston. The first Wednesday of the month, barring an emergency, my husband Benton and I meet for dinner at the Harvard Faculty Club, where I'm not a member. He is and not because of his FBI status. That won't get you any special favors at Harvard, the Massachusetts Institute of Technology (MIT) and other Ivy League institutions in the area.

But as a consulting forensic psychologist at the Harvard-affiliated McLean Hospital in nearby Belmont, my FBI criminal-intelligence-analyst husband can avail himself of the most marvelous libraries, museums, and scholars in the world anytime he wants. He can help himself to the Faculty Club to his heart's content.

We can even reserve a guest room upstairs, and we have on more than one occasion been given enough whiskey or wine during dinner. But that's not going to happen with Dorothy flying in, and I really shouldn't have said yes when she asked me to pick her up later tonight and drop her off at her daughter Lucy's house, which will get Benton and me home after midnight.

I don't know why Dorothy asked me specifically unless it's her way of making sure we get to spend a little alone time together. When I said yes I'd come and Benton would be with me, her response was "I'm sure. Well it doesn't matter." But when she said that I realized it does matter.

She has something she wants to discuss with me privately, and even if we don't get the chance tonight, we have time.

My sister left her return flight open-ended, and I can't help but think how wonderful it would be if it turned out I'd always been wrong about her. Maybe her real reason for venturing north to New England is she feels the same way I do. Maybe she at long last wants to be friends.

How amazing if we become a united front when coping with our aging mother, with Lucy and her partner Janet, and with their adopted nine-year-old son Desi. And also their newest addition Tesla, a rescue bulldog puppy who's staying with Benton and me in Cambridge for a while. Someone has to train her, and our greyhound Sock is getting old and likes the company.

1

My shoes swish through the hot dry grass, and sweat trickles beneath my clothes, down my chest, my back. I'm moving again, seeking shade as the sun settles lower and the slanted light shifts.

Every time I escape the glare it finds me again, the walled-in center of the Harvard campus a maze with its greens and lawns, its quadrangles and courtyards connected by paths and walkways. The stately brick-and-stone buildings draped in ivy live up to the stereotype, and I remember what I felt when I was given a tour at the age of fifteen. It's as if I'm back in time with every step I take, sweetly, sadly.

It was on one of my few trips outside of Florida during my senior year in high school when I began exploring colleges and what I might amount to in life. I'll never forget walking exactly where I am now and experiencing a limbic rush at the same time I was self-conscious and out of place. The memory is interrupted when I'm startled by a vibration, what feels and sounds like a large insect buzzing.

I stop walking on the piping-hot sidewalk, looking around, noticing a drone flying high over the Yard. Then I realize the buzzing is my own phone muffled by my suit jacket pocket, where it's tucked away from the heat and sun. I check to see who's calling. It's Cambridge Police Investigator Pete Marino, and I answer.

"Is there something going on that I don't know about?" he says right off, and the connection is pretty bad.

"I don't think so," I puzzle as I bake on the bricks.

"Why are you walking? Nobody should be out walking in this shit." He's curt and sounds irritated, and I'm instantly alerted this isn't a friendly call. "So what the hell got into you?"

"Errands." I feel on guard, and his tone is annoying. "And I'm walking to meet Benton."

"Meeting him for what reason?" Marino asks as our cellular connection continues to deteriorate from good to spotty, back to okay and then fractured before it's better again.

"The reason I'm meeting my husband is to eat dinner," I reply with a trace of irony, and I don't want a tense time with yet another person today. "Is everything all right?"

"Maybe you should be the one telling me that." His big voice suddenly booms painfully in my right ear. "How come you're not with Bryce?"

My chatterbox chief of staff must have informed Marino about my refusing to get back into the car at Harvard Square, about my *violation of protocol and reckless disregard for safety*.

Before I can answer, Marino begins confronting me as if I'm a suspect in a crime. "You got out of the car about an hour and a half ago, were inside The Coop for maybe twenty minutes," he's saying. "And when you finally exited the store on Mass Ave? Where'd you go?"

"I had an errand on Arrow Street." The sidewalks in the Yard form a brick spiderweb, and I find myself constantly making adjustments, taking the most efficient path, the quickest and coolest.

"What errand?" he asks as if it's any of his business.

"At the Loeb Center, picking up tickets for *Waitress*, the Sara Bareilles musical," I reply with forced civility that's beginning to waver. "I thought Dorothy might like to go."

"From what I hear you were acting as squirrelly as a shithouse rat."

"Excuse me?" I stop walking.

"That's the way it's been described."

"By whom? Bryce?"

"Nope. We got a nine-one-one call about you," Marino says, and I'm stunned.

He informs me that his police department was contacted about "a young guy and his older lady friend" arguing in Harvard Square about 4:45 P.M.

This young guy was described as in his late twenties with sandy-brown hair, blue capri pants, a white T-shirt, sneakers, designer sunglasses, and a tattoo of a marijuana leaf. The tattoo isn't right but the rest of it is.

Supposedly the concerned citizen who called the police recognized me from the news, and it's disturbing that my clothing description is accurate. I do in fact have on a khaki skirt suit, a white blouse, and tan leather pumps. Unfortunately it's also correct I have a run in my panty hose, and I'll strip them off and toss them when I get where I'm going.

"Was I mentioned by name?" I can't believe this.

"The person said words to the effect that Doctor Kay Scarpetta was arguing with her pothead boyfriend and stormed out of the car." Marino passes along another outrage.

"I didn't storm. I got out like a normal person while he stayed behind the wheel and continued to talk."

"You sure he didn't get out and open the door for you?"

"He never does and I don't encourage it. Maybe that's what someone saw and misinterpreted it as him being angry. Bryce opened his window so we could talk and that was it."

Marino lets me know that next I became abusive and physically violent, slapping Bryce through the open window I just described while repeatedly jabbing him in the chest with my index finger. He was yelling as if I was causing him injury and terror, and to put it succinctly, what a crock of shit. But I don't say anything because of the uneasiness in my gut, a hollow tight feeling that's my equivalent of a red warning flag.

Marino's a cop. I may have known him forever but Cambridge is his turf. Technically he could give me a hard time if he wants, and that's a new and insane thought. He's never arrested me, not that there's ever been a good reason. But he's never so much as given me a parking ticket or warned me not to jaywalk. Professional courtesy is a two-way street. But it can quickly become a dead end if you're not careful.

"I admit I might have been a little out of sorts but it's not true that I slapped anyone—" I start to say.

"Let's start with the first part of your statement," Marino the detective interrupts me. "How little's a little?"

12

"Are you interviewing me now? Should you read me my rights? Do I need a lawyer?"

"You're a lawyer."

"I'm not being funny, Marino."

"I'm not either. A *little* out of sorts? I'm asking because he said you started yelling."

"Before or after I slapped him?"

"Getting pissy doesn't help anything, Doc."

"I'm not pissy, and let's be clear about who you're even referencing. Let's start with that. Because you know how Bryce exaggerates."

"What I know is supposedly the two of you were fighting and disturbing the peace."

"He actually said that?"

"The witness did."

"What witness?"

"The one who called in the complaint."

"Did you talk to this witness yourself?"

"I couldn't find anybody who saw anything."

"Then you must have looked," I point out.

"After we got the call, I cruised the Square and asked around. Same thing I usually get. Nobody saw a damn thing."

"Exactly. This is ridiculous."

"I'm concerned someone might be out to get you," he says, and we've been through this so many times over the years.

Marino lives and breathes his phobic conviction that something horrible is going to happen to me. But what he's really worried about is his own self. It's the same way he was with his former wife Doris before she finally ran off with a car salesman. Marino doesn't understand

13

the difference between neediness and love. They feel the same to him.

"If you want to waste taxpayer dollars you can check the CCTV cameras around the Square, especially in front of The Coop," I suggest. "You'll see I didn't slap Bryce or anyone else."

"I'm wondering if this has to do with your talk at the Kennedy School tomorrow night," Marino says. "It's been all over the news because it's controversial. When you and General Briggs decided to make a presentation about the space shuttle blowing up maybe you should have expected a bunch of fruit loops to come out of the woodwork. Some of them think a UFO shot down the *Columbia*. And that's why the space shuttle program was canceled."

"I'm still waiting for a name of this alleged witness who lied to one of your nine-one-one operators." I'm not interested in hearing him obsess about conspiracists and the pandemonium they might create at the Kennedy School event.

"He wouldn't identify himself to the operator who took the call," Marino says. "He was probably using one of those track phones you can buy right there at the CVS. It's one of those numbers you can't trace to anyone. Not that we're done trying, but that's how it's looking, and it's pretty much what we're up against these days."

I pass through the shade of a huge old oak with low-spreading branches that are too lush and green for September. The early evening heat presses down like a flaming hand, flattening and scorching the life out of everything, and I switch my shopping bag to my other arm. My messenger-style briefcase also has gotten very heavy, packed with a laptop, paperwork and other personal effects, the wide strap biting into my shoulder.

"Where are you exactly?" Marino's voice is cutting in and out.

"Taking a shortcut." I'm not interested in giving him my precise whereabouts. "And you? You're muffled every other minute or talking in a barrel. Are you in your car?"

"What'd you do, take the Johnston Gate so you can cut through the Yard to Quincy Street?"

"How else would I go?" I'm evasive now in addition to being slightly breathless as I trudge along.

"So you're near the church," he says.

"Why are you asking? Are you coming to arrest me?"

"As soon as I find my handcuffs. Maybe you've seen them?"

"Maybe ask whoever you're dating these days?"

"You're gonna exit the Yard through the gate across from the museums. You know, at the light that will be on your left on the other side of the wall." It seems like a directive rather than an assumption or a question.

"Where are you?" as my suspicions grow.

"What I just suggested would be most direct," he says. "Past the church, past the Quad."

15

2

I walk through a black wrought-iron gate in the brick wall bordering the Yard, and I look up and down Quincy Street.

On the other side of it the entire block is taken up by the recently renovated brick-and-concrete Harvard Art Museum that includes six levels of galleries under a glass pyramid roof. I wait near a line of parked cars glaring in angled sunlight that is slowly waning, and I check the time and weather on my phone.

It's still an oppressive ninety-three degrees at 6:40 P.M., and I don't know what I was thinking a little while ago. But I simply couldn't take it anymore as Bryce prattled nonstop while he drove along the river toward the Anderson Memorial Bridge, turning right at the red-roofed Weld Boathouse, following John F. Kennedy Street to Massachusetts Avenue.

I didn't think I could listen to one more word, and I instructed him not to wait for me as I climbed out of the SUV in front of the college bookstore, The Coop. Harvard Square with its shops and Red Line subway stop is always populated even in the most miserable weather. There's going to be foot traffic and a fairly steady panhandling population 24/7.

It wasn't an appropriate place for Bryce to roll down his window and argue like a boy-toy lover with a lady boss mature enough to be a cougar. He wouldn't listen or leave me, and started sounding slightly hysterical, which unfortunately is his personality. He wanted me to state "for the record" why I no longer desired his assistance and to inform him "chapter and verse" if he'd "done something." He kept repeating that he just knew he'd "done something" and wouldn't listen each time I denied it.

The curious were watching like hawks. A homeless man sitting on the sidewalk in front of CVS, shading himself with his cardboard sign, stared at us with the beady eyes of a magpie. It wasn't exactly an ideal spot to park a vehicle that has OFFICE OF THE CHIEF MEDICAL EXAMINER and the CFC's crest, the scales of justice and caduceus painted in blue on the doors. The SUV's back windows are blacked out, and I understand the impact when one of our marked vehicles pulls up.

After I managed to shoo Bryce off, I shopped inside The Coop for gifts for my mother and sister. I made sure my clingy chief of staff really was gone when I finally emerged from the air-conditioning into the brutal heat, heading out on Brattle Street.

I swung by the American Repertory Theater, the ART in the Loeb Center, to pick up six tickets for *Waitress*, having reserved the best orchestra seats in the house. After that I backtracked on Massachusetts Avenue, cutting through the Yard and ending up where I am now on Quincy Street.

I pass the Carpenter Center for the Visual Arts on my

17

left, and I must look like a holy mess. After all the trouble I went to before my ill-advised ride, showering in my office, changing into a suit that's now wrinkled and sweat-stained. I dabbed on Benton's favorite Amorvero perfume that he finds in Italy. It's the signature fragrance of the Hotel Hassler in Rome, where he proposed to me. But I can't smell the exotic scent anymore as I sniff my wrist, waiting at an intersection. Heat rises in shimmering waves from the tar-smelling pavement, and I hear Marino's big voice before I see him.

"You know what they say about mad Englishmen and dogs going out in this shit?"

I turn around at the garbled cliché and he's stopped at a light, the driver's window open of his unmarked midnight-blue SUV. Now I know why the reception was so bad when we talked a moment ago. It's what I suspected. He's been cruising the area looking for me, talking to people in the Square. He turns on his emergency flashers and whelps his siren, cutting between cars in the opposite lane, heading toward me.

Marino double-parks, climbs out, and I don't think I'll ever get used to seeing him in a suit and tie. Smart attire wasn't designed with the likes of him in mind. Nothing really fits him except his own skin.

Almost six-foot-five, he weighs two hundred and fifty pounds give or take thirty. His tan shaved head is smooth like polished stone, his hands and feet the size of boats. Marino's shoulders are the width of a door, and he could bench-press five of me he likes to brag.

He's handsome in a primitive way with a big ruddy face, heavy brow and prominent nose. He has a caveman jaw and strong white teeth, and he tends to explode out of business clothes like the Incredible Hulk. Nothing dressy and off the rack looks quite right on him, and part of the problem is he shouldn't be left to his own devices when he shops, which isn't often or planned. It would be helpful if he would clean out his closets and garage occasionally but I'm pretty sure he never has.

As he steps up on the sidewalk I notice the sleeves of his navy-blue suit jacket are above the wrist. His trouser cuffs are high-waters that show his gray tube socks, and he has on black leather trainers that aren't laced all the way up. His tie is almost color coordinated and just as unfashionable, black-and-red-striped and much too wide, possibly from the 1980s when people wore polyester bell-bottoms, Earth Shoes and leisure suits.

He has his reasons for what he wears, and the tie no doubt is woven of special memories, maybe a bullet he dodged, a perfect game he bowled, the biggest fish he ever caught or an especially good first date. Marino makes a point of never throwing out something that matters to him. He'll wander into thrift shops and junk stores looking for a past he liked better than the here and now, and it's ironic that a badass would be so sentimental.

"Come on. I'll drop you off." His eyes are blacked out by vintage Ray-Ban aviator glasses I gave to him a few birthdays ago.

"Why would I need a ride?" The entrance to the brick path leading from the concrete sidewalk to the Faculty Club is just up ahead, a minute's walk from here at most.

But he isn't going to take no for an answer. He steers me off the sidewalk, raising a big mitt of a hand to stop traffic as we cross the street. He's not holding me but I'm not exactly free as he guides me into the front seat of his police vehicle, where I struggle awkwardly with my bags while the run in my panty hose races from my knee down to the back of my shoe as if trying to escape Marino's madness.

I can't help but think, *Here we go again.* Another spectacle. To some it might look like I'm being picked up and questioned by the police, and I wonder if I'll be hearing that next.

"Why are you riding around looking for me, since it seems that's what you're doing?" I ask as he shuts the door. "Seriously, Marino." But he can't hear me.

He walks around and climbs into the driver's seat, and the interior is spotless and tricked out with every siren, light, toolbox, storage chest and piece of crime-scene equipment known to man. The dark vinyl is slick and I smell Armor All. The cloth seats hardly look sat on, the console as clean as new and the glass sparkles as if the SUV was just detailed. Marino is meticulous about his vehicles. His house, office and attire are another story.

"Did I tell you how much I hate the damn phone?" he starts complaining as he shuts his door with a thud. "Some things we don't need to be talking about on a wireless device that has access to every damn thing about your life."

"Why are you dressed up?"

"I had a wake. Nobody you know."

"I see." I don't really.

Marino isn't the type to put on a suit and tie for a wake. He'll barely do that for a funeral or a wedding, and he's certainly not dressing up in weather like this unless he has a special reason he's not saying.

"Well you look nice, and you smell good. Let me see. Cinnamon, sandalwood, a hint of citrus and musk. British Sterling always reminds me of high school."

"Don't change the subject."

"I didn't know we had a subject."

"I'm talking about spying. Remember when the biggest worry was someone riding around with a scanner," he says. "Trying to hack into your house phone that way? Remember when there weren't cameras in your face everywhere? I stopped by the Square a while ago to see who might be hanging around, and some snotty asshole college kid started filming me with his phone."

"How do you know it was a college kid?"

"Because he looked like a spoiled little brat in his flip-flops, baggy shorts and Rolex watch."

"What were you doing?"

"Just asking a few questions about what they might have seen earlier. You know, there's always the usual suspects hanging out in front of The Coop, the CVS. Not as many in this heat but they'd rather be free and footloose in the great unwashed outdoors than in a nice shelter out of the elements. Then the kid was pointing his phone at me like I'm going to shoot someone for no reason and maybe he'll get lucky and catch it on film. Meanwhile some damn drone was buzzing around. I hate technology," he adds grumpily.

"Please tell me why I'm sitting here because clearly I don't need a ride since I've already arrived at my destination."

"Yeah you don't need a ride, all right. I'd say the damage is already done." He looks me up and down, his sunglasses lingering too long on the run in my hose.

21

"And I'm sure you didn't pick me up just to tell me that."

"Nope. I want to know what's really going on with Bryce." Marino's Ray-Bans seem to pin me in my seat.

"I didn't know anything was—beyond his being more frazzled and annoying than usual."

"Exactly. And why might that be? Think about it."

"Okay, I'm thinking about it. Possibly because of the heat and how busy work has been. As you well know we've had an overload of weather-related cases, and he and Ethan are having trouble with that same abusive neighbor, and let's see . . . I believe Bryce's grandmother had her gallbladder removed the other week. In other words there's been a lot of stress. But who the hell knows what's going on with him or anyone, Marino?"

"If there's a reason we shouldn't trust Bryce, now's the time to spill it, Doc."

"It seems to me we've discussed this enough," I say over the blasting air-conditioning, which is going to chill me to my marrow because my clothes are so damp. "I don't have time to ride around with you right now, and I need to make some effort to clean up before dinner."

I start to get out, and he reaches for my arm again.

3

"Stay." He says it as if he's addressing his German shepherd Quincy, who's currently not in the cage in back. As it turns out, in addition to being a failed cadaver dog, he's also a fair-weather man's best friend.

Named after the legendary medical examiner on TV, this Quincy doesn't venture out to any crime scene when the conditions are inclement. I suspect Marino's furry sidekick is safely at home right now on his Tempur-Pedic bed in the den with the air-conditioning and DOGTV on.

"I'm going to drop you off the last damn fifty feet. Sit and enjoy the cool," Marino says.

I move my arm because I don't like being grabbed even gently.

"You need to hear me out." He shoves the gearshifter in drive. "Like I said, I didn't want to go into it over the phone. We sure as hell can't know who's spying anymore, right? And if Bryce is compromising the CFC's security or yours I want us to find out before it's too late."

I remind Marino that we use personal proprietary

23

smartphones and have the benefit of encryption, firewalls and all sorts of special and highly secure apps. It's unlikely that our conversations or e-mails can be hacked. My computer-genius-niece Lucy, the CFC cyber-crimes expert, makes very sure of that.

"Are you talking with her at all about any of this?" I ask. "If you're so worried we're being spied on don't you think you could take it up with her? Since that's her job?"

Just as I'm saying this my phone rings and it's Lucy requesting her own version of FaceTime, meaning she'd like us to see each other as we talk.

"What timing," I say right off as her keenly pretty face fills the display on my phone. "We were just talking about you."

"I've only got a minute." Her eyes are green lasers. "Three things. First, my mom just called and her plane is going to be delayed a little bit. Well, I shouldn't say *a little bit* even if that's how she described it. We don't know for how long at this point. And I'm not a hundred percent sure what's going on with air traffic control. But there's a hold on all outbound traffic at the moment."

"What's she being told?" I ask as my heart sinks.

"They're changing gates or something. Mom and I didn't talk long but she said it may be closer to ten thirty or eleven by the time she gets here."

It's nice of my sister to let me know, it flashes in my mind. As busy as Benton and I are, and she wouldn't think twice about making us wait at the airport half the night.

"Second, the latest just landed from Tailend Charlie." Lucy's eyes are moving as she talks, and I try to figure out where she is. "I haven't listened to it yet. As soon as I'm freed up from the nine-one-one bullshit call I will."

"I assume what was sent was another audio clip in Italian," I point out because Lucy isn't fluent and wouldn't be able to translate all or possibly any of it.

She says yes, that at a glance the latest communication from Tailend Charlie is like the other eight I've received since the first day of September. The anonymous threat was sent at the same time of day, is the same type of file and the recording is the same length. But she hasn't listened, and I tell her we'll deal with it later.

Then she asks, "Where are you? In whose car?" She's vivid against a backdrop of complete darkness, as if she's in a cave.

Yet her rose-gold hair is shiny in ambient light that wavers like a movie is playing in the background. Shadows flicker on her face, and it occurs to me she might be inside the Personal Immersion Theater, what at the CFC we call the PIT.

I tell her I'm with Marino, and that brings her to the third and most important point; she says, "Have you seen what's on Twitter?"

"If you're asking then I'm sure it's not good," I reply.

"I'm sending it to you now. Gotta go." And then Lucy is gone from the small rectangular screen just like that.

"What?" Marino is scowling. "What's on Twitter?"

"Hold on." I open the e-mail Lucy just sent, and click on the tweet she cut-and-pasted. "Well as you suspected, there appears to be a video of you talking to some of the usual suspects in Harvard Square."

I show it to him and can feel his wounded pride as he watches the distant figure of himself lumbering about, barking questions at homeless people loitering in front of various businesses. Marino herds one man in and out of the shade as this person tries to duck questions in a most animated fashion. The indistinguishable noise of Marino raising his voice while the man shuffles from pillar to post is embarrassing. And the caption is worse. *OccupyScarpetta* with a hashtag.

"What the hell?" Marino says.

"I guess the gist is that you're territorial about me and were asking a lot of questions because of it. I presume that's how my name ended up in the tweet." His lack of a response answers my question. "But I doubt it will do any real damage except to your ego," I add. "It's silly, that's all. Just ignore it."

He isn't listening, and I really do need to go.

"I'd like a minute to clean up." It's my way of telling Marino I've had enough of being held hostage in his truck full of gloom and doom. "So if you'll unlock the doors and release me please? Maybe we can talk tomorrow or some other time."

Marino pulls away from his illegal double-parking spot. He eases to the curb in front of the Faculty Club, set back on acres of grassy lawn behind a split-rail paling.

"You're not taking this seriously enough." He looks at me.

"Which part?"

"We're under surveillance, and the question is who and why. For sure someone's got Bryce tagged. How else can you explain the marijuana tattoo?"

"There's nothing to explain. He doesn't have a tattoo of any description."

"He does. Specifically, a marijuana leaf, as it was referred to in the call," Marino says.

26

"No way. He's so afraid of needles he won't even get a flu shot."

"Obviously you don't know the story. The tattoo is right here." Marino leans over and jabs a thick finger at his outer left ankle, which I can't see very well from where I'm sitting even if I knew to look. "It's fake," he says. "I guess you didn't know that part."

"It would seem I don't know much."

"The marijuana leaf is a temporary tattoo. It's a joke from last night when he and Ethan were with friends. And typical of Bryce? He figured he could wash it off before he went to bed, but a lot of these temporary tattoos can last for the better part of a week."

"Obviously you've talked to him." I look at Marino's flushed shiny face. "Did he reach out to you?"

"I got hold of him when I heard about the nine-one-one call. When I asked him about the tattoo he sent me a selfie of it."

I turn away to look in the sideview mirror at cars moving past. It occurs to me that I don't know what Benton is driving tonight. It could be his Porsche Cayenne Turbo S or his Audi RS 7. It could be a bureau car. I was busy with the dogs, with Sock and Tesla, when my husband left this morning at dawn, and I didn't see or hear him drive away.

"The tattoo's a problem, Doc," Marino says. "It gives credibility to the phone call. It pretty much proves that whoever complained about you and Bryce disturbing the peace saw you—unless there's some other reason this person knows about the tattoo and what the two of you were wearing."

I recognize the sound of a turbocharged engine changing pitch, and I listen as it gets closer, louder.

"You're still picking her up tonight?" Marino asks.

"Who?" I watch Benton's blacked-out RS 7 coupe glide past slowly, downshifting, sliding into the space in front of us.

"Dorothy."

"That's the plan."

"Well if you need any help I'm happy to get her," Marino says. "I've been meaning to tell you that anything I can do, just say the word. Especially now since it's sounding like she's going to be so late."

I don't recall telling him that my sister was coming—much less who was picking her up at the airport. He also didn't just hear this for the first time when Lucy called a moment ago. It's obvious he already knew.

"That's nice of you," I say to him, and his dark glasses are riveted to the back of the Audi as Benton maneuvers it so close against the curb that a knife blade barely would fit between it and the titanium rims.

The matte-black sedan rumbles in a growly purr like a panther about to lunge. Through the tinted back windshield I can make out the shape of my husband's beautiful head, and his thick hair that's been white for as long as I've known him. He sits straight and wide-shouldered, as still as a jungle cat, his gray-tinted glasses watching us in the rearview mirror. I open my door, and the heat slams me like a wall when I step back out into it, and I thank Marino for the ride even though I didn't want it.

I watch Benton climb out of his car. He unfolds his long lank self, and my husband always looks newly minted. His pearl-gray suit is as fresh as when he put it on this morning, his blue-and-gray silk tie perfectly knotted, his engraved antique white-gold cuff links glinting in the early evening light.

28

He could grace the pages of *Vanity Fair* with his strong fine features, his platinum hair and horn-rim glasses. He's slender and ropy strong, and his quiet calm belies the iron in his bones and the fire in his belly. You'd never know what Benton Wesley is truly like to look at him right now in his perfectly tailored suit, hand-stitched because he comes from old New England money.

"Hi," he says, taking the shopping bag from me but I hold on to my briefcase.

He watches Marino's dark blue SUV pull back out into traffic, and the heat rising off the pavement makes the air look thick and dirty.

"I hope your afternoon's been better than mine." I'm conscious of how wilted I am compared to my perfectly put-together husband. "I'm sorry I'm such a train wreck."

"What possessed you to walk?"

"Not you too. Did Bryce send out a *be on the lookout* for a deranged woman with a run in her stockings prowling the Harvard campus?"

"But you really shouldn't have, Kay. For lots of reasons."

"You must know about the nine-one-one call. It would seem to be the headline of the day."

He doesn't answer but he doesn't need to. He knows. Bryce probably called him because I doubt Marino would.

4

A bicycle bell jingles cheerily on the sidewalk behind us, and we step out of the way as a young woman rides past.

She brakes in front of us as if she might be going to the same place we are, and I offer a commiserating smile when she dismounts, wearing sporty dark glasses, hot and red-faced. Unclipping the chin strap of her robin's-egg-blue bike helmet, she takes it off, and I notice her pulled-back long brown hair, her blue shorts and beige tank top. Instantly I get a weird feeling.

I take in her blue paisley printed neckerchief, her off-white Converse sneakers and gray-and-white-striped bike socks as she stares at her phone, then at the Georgian brick Faculty Club as if expecting someone. She types with her thumbs, lifts her phone to her ear.

"Hey," she says to whoever she's calling. "I'm here," and I realize the reason she's familiar is I met her about a half hour ago.

She was at the Loeb Center when I was buying the theater tickets. I remember seeing her as I wandered into the lobby to use the ladies' room. At most she's in her early twenties, and she has a British accent, what strikes me as a slightly affected or theatrical one. I was aware of it when she was talking with other staff and several actors at the American Repertory Theater.

She was across the room taping index cards of recipes on walls already covered with hundreds of them. In this particular production of *Waitress* members of the audience are invited to share their own favorite treats and tasty family secrets, and before I left I wandered over to take a look. I love to cook, and my sister loves sweets. The least I could do is make something special for her while she's here. I was jotting down a recipe for peanut butter pie when the young woman paused as she was taping up another card.

"I warn you. It's lethal," she said to me, and she had on a whimsical gold skull necklace that made me think of pirates.

"Excuse me?" I glanced around, not sure at first that she was talking to me.

"The peanut butter pie. But it's better if you add chocolate, dribble it over the top. The real stuff. And don't swap out the graham-cracker crust for anything you think might be better. Because it won't be, I promise. And use *real* butter—as you can tell I'm not into low-fat anything."

"You don't need to be," I replied because she's wiry and strong.

This same young woman is in front of Benton and me on the sidewalk along Quincy Street, holding her iPhone in its ice-blue case, clamping it back into its black plastic holder, and she accidently fumbles her water bottle, sending it tumbling. It thuds to the sidewalk, rolling in our direction, and Benton bends down to pick it up.

"Sorry. Thanks very much." She looks hot, her face flushed and dripping.

"You definitely don't want to be without this today." He returns the bottle to her, and she secures it in its holder as I notice a young man trotting through the grass of the Faculty Club.

Her rimless sunglasses are directed at him as she remounts the bike, steadying herself, the toes of her sneakers touching the sidewalk. He's dark and thin, in slacks and a button-up shirt as if he works in an office. Then he's in front of her, hot and grinning, handing her a FedEx envelope that's labeled but not sealed.

"Thanks," he says. "Just put the tickets in and it's ready to go."

"I'll drop it off on my way home. See you later." She kisses him on the lips.

Then he trots away, back toward the Faculty Club, where I gather he must work. She puts on her helmet, not bothering with the strap that's supposed to be snug under her chin. Turning to me, she flashes a smile.

"You're the peanut-butter-pie lady," she says.

"What a nice way to be characterized. Hello again." I smile back at her, and I almost remind her to lock her chin strap.

But I don't know her. I don't want to be overbearing, especially after being accused of yelling at Bryce and disturbing the peace.

"Please be careful out here," I say instead. "The heat index is hazardous."

"What doesn't kill you makes you stronger." She grips the flat riser handlebars, pushing down the pedals with long strong strokes.

"Not always," Benton says.

I feel the hot air stir sluggishly as she rides past.

"Enjoy the pie and the play!" she tosses back at us, and she reminds me of my niece, sharp-featured, bold and extremely fit.

I watch her bare legs pumping, her calf muscles bunching as she picks up speed, cutting across the street, threading through the same gate I used earlier. I remember being that age when the best and worst was before me, and I wanted to know everything up front as if my fate could be negotiated. Who would I be with and what would I become? Where would I live and would I make a difference to anyone? I speculated, and at times tried to force my life in the direction I thought it should go. I wouldn't do that now.

I watch the young woman's retreating figure getting smaller, more distant and remote as she pedals through the Yard, between the sprawling brick Pusey and Lamont libraries. I don't understand why anyone would want to know the future. I wonder if she does, and the conservative answer is probably. But the more likely one is absolutely. Whereas I don't anymore.

"What did Marino want?" Benton lightly, affectionately touches my back as we follow the sidewalk.

Up ahead on our left is the split-rail paling, and set far back is the brick-and-white-trimmed neo-Georgian building, two stories with a glass-domed conservatory. The four tall chimneys rise proudly and symmetrically from different corners, and ten dormers stand sentry along the slate hipped roof.

The long walkway of dark red pavers winds through rockery and ornamental shrubs. The sun has dipped behind

33

buildings, and the oppressive air is like a steam room that's slowly cooling.

Benton has taken off his suit jacket, and it's neatly folded over his arm as we walk past the bright pink bottlebrushes of summer sweet, purple mountain laurel, and white and blue hydrangeas. None of it stirs in the breathless air, and only a scattering of dark green leaves shows the slightest blush of red. The longer it's hot and parched, the more unlikely it is that there will be much in the way of fall colors this year.

As Benton and I talk, I do the best I can to answer his questions about Marino's intentions, explaining he was emphatic that he didn't want me out walking by myself. But I don't think it's his only agenda. I have the distinct impression that Benton doesn't either.

"At any rate," I continue telling the story, "he was out and about all the while he was on the phone, basically bird-dogging me while he pretended he wasn't. Then he drove me the last fifty feet, and that's where you found me a few minutes ago."

"The last fifty feet?" Benton repeats.

"It's what he mandated. I was to get into his car and he would drive me the last fifty feet. Specifically the last *damn* fifty feet."

"Obviously what he wanted was to have a private face-to-face conversation with you. Maybe it's true he didn't want to talk over the phone. Or he used that as an excuse. Or it could be both," Benton says as if he knows, and he probably does because it's not hard for him to profile Pete Marino.

"So tell me why you decided to go for a stroll all by yourself, dressed in a suit and carrying heavy bags?" Benton

34

gets around to that. "Aren't you the one who warns everybody about the heat index—the way you just did with the woman on the bicycle a minute ago?"

"I suppose that's why there's the cliché about practicing what you preach."

"This isn't about practicing what you preach. It's about something else."

"I thought a walk might do me good," I reply, and he's silent. "And besides I had the theater tickets to pick up."

I explain that I also had gifts to find at the college bookstore, The Coop. The T-shirt, nightgown and handsome coffee-table book may not be the most original presents I've ever bought but they were the best I could muster after wandering the aisles. As Benton knows all too well, my sister is difficult to shop for.

"But that doesn't mean I don't know what she likes," I'm saying, and he isn't answering.

A popular musical and a peanut butter pie, for example, and Dorothy also will be very pleased with the skimpy Harvard tee that she can wear with her skimpier leggings or jeans. Her Ivy League shirt will be amply filled by her surgically enhanced bosom, and no doubt she'll inspire many scintillating conversations in the bars of South Beach and Margaritaville.

"And the Cambridge photography book is something she can carry back to Miami as if it was her idea," I explain as Benton listens without a word, the way he does when he has his own opinion and it's different from mine. "And that's exactly how my sister will play it when she shares pictures of Harvard, MIT, the Charles River with Mom. It will be all about Dorothy, which is fine if it means Mom enjoys her gift and feels remembered."

"It's not fine," Benton says as we pass through the deepening shadows of tall boxwood hedges.

"Some things won't change. It has to be fine."

"You can't let Dorothy get to you this way." His tinted glasses look at me.

"I assume you've heard the nine-one-one call." I change the subject because my sister has wasted quite enough of my time. "Apparently Marino has a copy but he wouldn't play it for me."

Benton doesn't respond, and if he's listened to the recording he's not going to tell me. Had he been made aware of it, he might have requested a copy from the Cambridge Police Department, citing that the FBI wants to make sure a government official wasn't misbehaving or being threatened.

My husband could come up with anything he wants to gain access to the 911 recording, and he's quite friendly with the commissioner, the mayor, pretty much everybody who's powerful around here. He didn't need Marino's help.

"As you may or may not know, someone complained about me supposedly disturbing the peace." It sounds even more bizarre as I hear myself describe such a thing to someone whose typical day involves terrorists and serial killers.

I glance at him as we near the proud brick building in the gathering dusk, and his face doesn't register whatever reaction he might be having.

"I assume Bryce told you about it after Marino confronted him, wanting to know exactly what happened in Harvard Square when he dropped me off," I add.

"Marino's feeling insecure about you," Benton says, and I can't tell if he's making a statement or asking a question.

36

"He's always insecure," I reply. "But he's also acting oddly. He was pushy about wanting to drive to the airport. He was overly interested in helping pick up Dorothy."

"I wonder how he knows she's coming here. Did you tell him? Because I didn't."

"Since we had almost no warning, I really haven't had a chance to tell hardly anyone," I reply. "Maybe Lucy mentioned it to him."

"Or Desi might have. He and Marino have gotten to be real pals," Benton says, and he can mask his emotions better than anyone I know but he can't fool me.

I can tell when something hurts him, and the blossoming relationship between Marino and Desi obviously does. I've worried it would as Marino spends increasing amounts of time with a mercurial and insatiably inquisitive boy whose genetics are largely unknown to us. We don't know what to expect. We can't predict who he might take after.

It should be Janet's late sister Natalie since it was her egg she'd had frozen when she was only in her twenties. Long before she did anything about it she was researching surrogate mothers and sperm donors. I remember her talking about being a single parent, and in retrospect it seems she had a premonition that her days on earth would be few. And they were. Seven years after Desi was born she would die of pancreatic cancer. It's such a shame she's not here to watch him change rapidly like a butterfly breaking out of its cocoon.

"Look, I get it," Benton is saying. "I'm not nearly as much fun as Marino. He's already taken Desi fishing, started teaching him about guns, given him his first sip of beer."

"Fishing is one thing but I'm not happy if Lucy and Janet think the rest of it is okay."

"The point is—"

"The point is that you don't need to be fun the same way Marino is," I reply. "In fact I'm hoping you might be a good example."

"Of what? A boring adult?"

"I was thinking more along the lines of a sexy brilliant federal agent who drives fast cars and wears designer clothes. Desi just doesn't know you yet."

"Apparently Desi does know me. Marino told him I'm a retired school principal, and Desi asked me about it. I told him it was a hundred years ago when I was just out of college and working on my master's degree," Benton says.

"Did you explain that when you were getting started, a lot of FBI agents came from educational and legal backgrounds? That in other words yours was simply a sensible career path?" Even as I say it I'm aware that it's too much explanation, and the well has been poisoned.

"There was no reason for Marino to bring that up except to make Desi afraid of me. Which is harmful and ill-advised because he's headstrong enough already. I've noticed that increasingly he doesn't like being told what to do."

"I agree he doesn't like to be controlled. But then most of us don't."

"Marino's goal is to be Good Time Uncle Pete while I'm the school principal," Benton says, and I watch the darkness settle heavily, hotly.

We've reached the wide brick patio arranged with wooden tables, red umbrellas, and potted shrubs and flower beds. On this last Wednesday of September, there shouldn't be an empty chair out here. But there's no one sitting outside the Faculty Club, no one in the world but us.

38

5

The entrance could belong to a private home, and that's what the Faculty Club has become to my FBI-profiler husband, who didn't graduate from Harvard. Benton went to Amherst just like his father and grandfather did.

A home away from home. A portal to another place where pain, fear and tragedy aren't allowed. Benton can spirit himself away to his immaculate neo-Georgian escape in the heart of the campus and pretend for a brief spell that there's no such thing as ignorance, bigotry, politics, and small-minded bureaucrats.

He can enjoy a cloistered retreat where everyone celebrates enlightened ideas and our differences, and there's no such thing as violence or aggression. Benton feels safe here. It's one of the few places where he does. But not so safe that he's not carrying a gun. I can't see a pistol but I have no doubt he has one in his briefcase, and his backup somewhere on his person. His Glock 27 or concealed-carry Smith & Wesson Model 19 that he won't leave home without.

We've stopped in front of flanking pilasters that are painted white, and there's a transom over the dark red door. I gaze up at the perfect symmetry of the brick facade, and my attention lingers on the multipaned bay windows of the upstairs guest rooms.

"Maybe another time." Benton looks up too and knows what I'm thinking.

"Yes, I guess there will be no sleepover tonight, thanks to my sister. But if I had anything to change into I'd rent a room anyway right now and take a shower." I can almost hear the creaking carpeted old wooden stairs leading up to the second floor.

I remember the sound and feel of the fabric-covered walls, the cozy elegance and most of all the narrow beds where Benton and I don't get much sleep. Ours is a well-practiced ritual that we engage in regularly and don't talk about with anyone but each other. It belongs exclusively to the two of us, and I wouldn't call it a date but consider it more like therapy when we come here once a month, assuming the stars are properly aligned.

So often they're not, but when they are we get a welcome reminder that decency and humanity still exist in the world. Not everybody lies, steals, rapes, abuses, neglects, tortures, kidnaps and kills. Not everybody wants to ruin us or take what's ours, and we're so lucky to have found each other.

We walk into the chilled quiet of formal antiques, fine paintings and Persian rugs. Benton closes the door behind us, and we're surrounded by sconces and mahogany paneling, dark tufted leather furniture, and wide-board flooring. Fresh flowers are arranged on the entryway table, and tonight's menu is displayed on a Victorian oak podium.

I detect the layers of familiar scents, the cut lilies and

roses, and beeswax with a patina of musty staleness, that are reassuring and part of an old-world charm that makes me think of poetry, cigars and rare leather-bound tomes. I could close my eyes and know where I am. The energy is different in here. There's a gravitas, a formality that should be expected in a place that's hosted heads of state and some of the most accomplished people in the world.

I pause in the entryway, in front of an antique oval mirror, running my fingers through my limp blond hair. I stare into the pitted glass at the tall handsome man behind me in pale gray, hovering over me like a breathtaking apparition.

"Do I know you?" I ask Benton without turning around.

"I don't think so. Are you waiting for someone?"

"Yes."

"What a coincidence. I am too. I've always been waiting for someone."

"So have I."

"Well not just someone. The right person." His reflection looks at me.

"Do you think there's only one right person for each of us?" I ask the mirror on the wall.

"I can only speak for myself."

We don't have a name for our little game, and nobody is wise to our delightful choreography of meeting as if we're strangers. It's refreshing, sobering but also good psychology if one can handle the truth. What would happen if we really were meeting for the first time right now in the entryway of the Harvard Faculty Club?

Would we notice each other? Would he still find me as attractive as he did the first time we met? It's not always the same for men when their wives get older, and some

41

mates may say they're just as in love when they're not. It's brave to ask such questions and face the truth unflinchingly. What might we feel were we to meet now instead of decades ago when Benton was married and I was divorced and we worked our first case together?

There's no scientific method for answering such a question, and I don't need one. I have no doubt we'd fall in love with each other all over again. I'm certain I would have an affair with him that would result in my being called a home wrecker. And I wouldn't care because it's worth it.

Benton places his warm graceful hands on my shoulders, and rests his chin on top of my head. I smell his earthy cologne as we look at our reflections in the convex mirror, our faces Picasso-like abstractions where the silvered glass is eroded.

"How about some dinner?" he says into my hair.

"Will you excuse me for a moment?"

I check my shopping bag in the coat closet, and step inside the ladies' room with its formal wallpaper and vintage Victorian theater posters. I set my leather messenger-bag briefcase on the black granite countertop and dig out a cosmetic kit. I face the mirror over the sink, and the woman in khaki staring back at me is slightly shopworn and disheveled.

Actually there's nothing slight about it, I decide. I look like hell, and I take off my damp suit jacket and drape it over a chair. My bra has soaked through my white blouse, and I turn on the hand dryer and blast hot air inside my collar, doing what I can so I don't sit around in wet underwear. Then I dig out powder, lipstick, a toothbrush. I contemplate my appearance and what else I intend to do about it. Not much.

42

I can't reverse the effects of lousy sleep, of running myself ragged and walking in the extreme heat. I feel a touch light-headed, and I'm weary and hopelessly clammy. I need food and drink badly. I need a shower most of all, and I take off my ruined panty hose and toss them in the trash. I douse a hand towel with cold water, cleaning up, but there's no quick remedy for rumpled sweatiness.

It's as if I were soaked and agitated in a washing machine, and I notice I've gotten a bit thinner in recent weeks. That usually happens when I neglect to exercise, and I haven't been jogging for a while, certainly not during the heat wave. I haven't touched my TRX bands, and Lucy's been after me to go with her to the gym.

I powder my face, and shadows in the low light of a crystal chandelier accentuate my prominent cheekbones and nose, and the angle of my strong jaw. I'm reminded of what journalists say, almost none of it relevant or kind. I'm *masculine* and *off-putting*. Or my favorite unflattering line that's been recycled excessively in stories: *Dr. Kay Scarpetta is compelling in appearance with an inaccessible, secretive and domineering face.*

I wet my fingers and muss my hair. I give it a once-over with a volumizing spray. I brush my teeth, and dust my forehead and cheeks with a mineral powder that blocks ultraviolet light and doesn't cause cancer. I don't care that it's about to be pitch dark out. I do it anyway. Then I dab on an olive oil lip balm and find the Visine and a small tube of shea butter.

I feel much improved but as I survey my wilted suit and blouse, I can hear Dorothy's voice in my head as clearly as if she's inside the ladies' room with me. She'd say the same thing she'll probably say when Benton and I pick

43

her up in a few hours. I have a terrible sense of style. I'm boring and sloppy. I get dirty and dress in stuffy suits like a frump or a man. She can't understand why I don't wear stilt-like heels, heavy makeup or acrylic nails and gaudy polish.

It's lost on her why I wouldn't emphasize my body parts, as she puts it, "especially since both of us were endowed with big knockers," she likes to boast about what's most important. I don't dress or conduct myself anything like my sister. I never have and couldn't possibly.

Ever since I can remember I've been incompatible with fragile female accoutrements and empty-headed attitudes. We simply don't get along.

Benton is waiting for me, chatting with the hostess Mrs. P at her station.

He grips his black leather briefcase with one hand, and in the other he holds his phone, typing on it with his thumb. He slips it back in a pocket as he notices my return from the ladies' room, and I understand what's meant by one's heart leaping. Mine is happily jolted by the sight of him. It always is.

"A big improvement? Hmm?" He takes his glasses off, making a big production of appraising me, his eyes glinting with a playful light. "Do you agree, Mrs. P?" he asks her as he winks at me.

In her early eighties, she has a nimbus of wispy grayish-white hair, and round wire-rim glasses like a caricature of a prim and proper New England matron. Her face is doughy and wrinkled like dehydrated fruit, and her dress and matching jacquard jacket are a rose-trellis design in greens and reds that reminds me of a William Morris pattern.

44

Mrs. P tends to eye me curiously even when I don't look overcooked and disheveled, as if there's much she wonders about but isn't going to verbalize. Several times now her eyes have dropped down to my bare legs, and then she looks up quickly as if she's seen something she shouldn't.

"What do you think?" Benton asks her.

"Well I'm not sure." Her glasses wink as she turns her head back and forth like a tennis match, from him to me, looking at one, then the other, and the two of them have their shtick. "You know not to put me on the spot that way," she affectionately reprimands him.

Mrs. P's surname is Peabody, pronounced with an emphasis on the first syllable, a drawn-out PEE-b'dy, like the city near Salem. I've never addressed her by her first name, Maureen, and have no clue if those close to her call her that or Mo or something else. In the years we've been coming here she's simply been Mrs. P, and Benton is Mr. Wesley. If she refers to me by name it's Mrs. Wesley, although she's well aware of my other life where most everyone else calls me Dr. Scarpetta or Chief.

It's a sad secret that Mrs. P knows what I do and who I am even as she politely pretends otherwise. Not long after Benton and I moved to Cambridge, her husband was killed in a car accident literally in front of their house, and I took care of him. Now it's as if that never happened, and what I remember most about her husband's case is his widow Mrs. P's refusal to talk to me. She insisted on going over her late husband's autopsy report with one of my assistant chiefs, a man.

But then Mrs. P started at the Faculty Club in a day when things were very different for women. You could be

45

on the faculty here and find yourself relegated to the ladies' dining room or discover there's no place in the dorm and you're not welcome in the same libraries or housing as your male classmates. When one of the greatest legal minds of our time, Ruth Bader Ginsburg, arrived for her first year at Harvard Law School she was asked to justify her taking up a seat that could be occupied by a man.

"I think you need your head examined if you go outside in this," Mrs. P is saying to Benton, and he widens his eyes, staring at her with mock disappointment. "You'll melt like a candle," meaning that's what she thinks I look like.

Benton says to me with a shrug, "I guess that's a no. Sorry, Kay. It would seem Mrs. P thinks you still look like something the cat dragged in."

"I would never say such a thing!" Mrs. P laughs her soft self-conscious laugh, placing three fingers over her pink lips, shaking her head as if my husband is the naughtiest human being on the planet.

She's quite fond of Benton, who of course is teasing both of us. If you don't know him it would be difficult to recognize because his humor is as subtle as a cobweb you can't find but keep brushing from your face. He knows damn well my appearance isn't greatly improved. I don't have hose on, and the leather insoles of my unstylish scuffed shoes feel as slimy as a raw oyster that's been sitting out for hours.

"Let's not rub it in," I say to him as Mrs. P gathers two menus and the thick black notebook, the extensive *carte des vins*. "I realize it wasn't your intention to have dinner tonight with something the cat dragged in."

"Depends on the cat." Benton opens his briefcase with bright springy snaps of the clasps.

He trades his sunglasses for bifocals, the kind you get in the drugstore. I shoulder my messenger bag again, and we follow Mrs. P into the north dining room with its tall arched windows and exposure to the front lawn, which is cloaked in darkness.

Our feet are quiet on deep red carpet as we pass beneath exposed dark beams in the white plaster ceiling, through a sea of white-cloth-covered tables beneath brass chandeliers with small red shades over their candlelike lights. We're the only guests so far, and Benton and Mrs. P chat amicably as she shows us to our usual corner.

"Not until closer to eight tonight," she's telling Benton that the Faculty Club is going to be quite slow until then. "We have two private dinners upstairs but not much down here. It's too hot, you know."

"What about power outages?" Benton asks. "Have they affected you?"

"Now that's trouble when it happens. The power goes out and stays out, and you can't stay inside but can't go outside either. Let's hope that doesn't happen again, especially not while you're in here trying to enjoy a nice quiet dinner."

Mrs. P then begins to update us on Felix the Cat. That's his real name but she just calls him Felix for short, and apparently Felix hasn't fared well during the heat wave.

"He did very poorly the last time the power went out, which was just yesterday at noon, at least that's what I found out later because I was here at the time. Where I live is one of the worst areas on the grid map or something like that," she explains to both of us. "And you know Felix is old with all the problems that go along with it. I don't always know if the power's out in the house, you see. I

47

might be fine here and have no idea poor Felix is suffering with no air-conditioning."

"Maybe there's a neighbor or someone who can check on him?" I suggest.

"My neighbors are in the same boat if the power goes out," she says. "And my children don't live nearby. Now my grandson's working part-time here while he tries to make it as a musician, and he helps out when he can. But he's twenty-three and allergic to cats."

"Could you bring Felix to work?" Benton asks, and Mrs. P just laughs.

"Why couldn't you?" Benton is serious.

"Well I couldn't." She looks across the dining room, making sure no one else has come in.

6

Our corner table is to the right of a big fireplace framed by a burled-wood mantel that reaches from the carpet to the ceiling. Perpendicular to it the gold-damask-covered wall has been arranged with fine British, Dutch and Italian art that wasn't here when we were last month.

The new exhibit includes a seascape, a religious allegory, and a still life that has a skull in it. There are oil portraits of stern men in colonial dress, and powdered women with corseted waists too cinched to be anatomically possible without bruised ribs and crowded organs. I never know what I'm going to see from one visit to the next because most of the art is on loan from the surrounding Harvard museums, which hold one of the finest collections anywhere.

The paintings constantly rotate, and this appeals to Benton in particular because it's not dissimilar to how he grew up. His wealthy father invested in art and constantly moved priceless paintings in and out of the Wesley home, a brownstone mansion not so different from the Faculty Club.

How amazing it must be to pick a Pieter Claesz this week and a J. M. W. Turner or Jan Both the next. And maybe a Johannes Vermeer or a Frans Hals while we're at it, I think as I scan our private gallery, each painting illuminated by a museum light and framed in gold.

It's difficult to imagine growing up the way Benton did when I compare it to the minimalist and decidedly nonglamorous conditions of my Miami upbringing. He comes from Ivy League New England stock while I'm the only one in my second-generation Italian family who went to college. As hard as it was to have so little in every sense of the word, I'm grateful that when I was growing up I didn't get what I thought I wanted.

Benton was deprived in a different way. He got everything his parents wanted. He lived their dreams, and in many ways it only made him more impoverished and lonely. I imagine I was sad and isolated at times when I was a child. But what I remember most is feeling driven, having no choice but to learn to make do, whether it was the way I dressed, what shampoo I could afford or how long I could make something last.

I became adept at experiencing the world through books, photographs and movies because there was no such thing as a vacation or traveling anywhere for any reason until I finally began visiting colleges in my midteens. Benton on the other hand lacked for nothing except attention and a normal boyhood. He says he never felt rich until we met, and it's the nicest thing anyone's ever said to me.

He moves the table a little, angling it as he pleases, as if the dining room belongs to him. "I'm worried you're going to be cold."

"So far I'm all right. Other than the way I look."

"Which is beautiful. Always the most beautiful person I've ever known." Benton smiles at me as he pulls out my chair.

"I think you're made delusional by the heat." I sit down.

Scooting in closer to the table, I tuck my messenger bag under my chair, and we never position ourselves so that our backs are to doors or any other egress. We don't place ourselves in front of windows that might make us as conspicuous as fish in a bowl.

In fact we really aren't shown to a table as much as we're deployed to one. Benton and I locate ourselves where we can keep up our scan of what's around us, making sure nothing could surprise us from behind or through glass. In other words, in my husband's safe home away from home, we sit at dinner like two cops.

We couldn't relax if we didn't, and it's the little habits that are sobering. It's impossible not to be reminded that we belong to a small and special tribe. The tribe of the public servants who are traumatized.

"Are you sure you're going to be all right in the air-conditioning?" Benton asks as a waiter heads our way, an older man who must be new. "Would you like my jacket?" Benton starts to take it off, and I shake my head.

"I'm fine for now. I'll manage. Again I apologize for ruining what was left of our night."

"I don't know what you're talking about. You haven't ruined anything." He opens his white napkin and drapes it in his lap. "Well, maybe your panty hose. How did that happen by the way?"

"Oh my God. Is there anything I've not been asked today?" Then I feel irrepressible bubbles of laughter rising up my throat as Benton watches me quizzically.

"Is there something I'm missing?" he finally asks, but the waiter is waiting.

He stands by our table in his white jacket, starched and buttoned up, and he has the gaunt face and loose skin of someone once handsome who lost a lot of weight. He looks at Benton, the pen resting on the order pad. We'd like water before anything else, my husband says, and suddenly I remember my panty hose in the ladies' room trash and I'm amused again.

"I'm sorry." I dab my eyes with my napkin. "But sometimes I'm struck by the absurdity. To answer your question, I ran my hose just like any other woman, I'm sure."

"I doubt it." He's watching the waiter talking with the young man we saw out front a few minutes earlier, both of them checking on a big table set for a large party, fussing with silverware, repositioning the flower arrangements. "Usually your mishaps involve sharp weapons, body fluids, and blowflies," Benton adds.

"I ran my panty hose on a gurney, one of those cadaver carriers with a crank for raising and lowering. As I was helping lift a body off I got snagged, possibly on one of the casters."

"And then what?" and it begins to penetrate that he really is asking for a reason. "You didn't change into a new pair of panty hose," he says. "Why not?"

It's not a frivolous question after all. Of course nothing he asks really is even when he's being funny.

At my headquarters, Bryce is in charge of keeping certain necessities in stock including coffee, snacks, standard toiletries—and extra pairs of panty hose.

If he doesn't oversee the supply of such things there's a

52

good chance they won't enter my mind because skirts and stockings aren't my friends even if I pretend otherwise. Given the choice, I wear my usual field clothes of flame- and insect-resistant cargo pants, the more pockets the better, and tactical shirts embroidered with the CFC crest.

And of course sturdy cotton socks and low-profile boots. I'm also partial to parkas, packable jackets, baseball caps, and I suppose it all goes back to those impressionable years in medical school and the Air Force. When I was getting started I lived in scrubs and BDUs, and if I had my way I still would.

But since I'm often summoned to testify in depositions, in court and before lawmakers, I have to keep other accoutrements on hand that are appropriate for a director and chief who can influence the type of body armor our soldiers wear or whether someone should land in prison.

"I go through several pairs of hose a week at work," I'm explaining all this to Benton. "And I suppose Bryce hasn't been shopping much in this heat. Or maybe he's been too busy with his own dramas to bother ordering things online. So yes, I wasn't happy when I discovered I had nothing to change into after I ruined my hose. But I don't know why it didn't enter my mind to stop in the CVS myself at Harvard Square and pick up another pair so I'm not sitting here bare-legged. I suppose that's yet another miscalculation on my part."

"Then what you're saying is Bryce has been letting you down, and you were upset with him even before he drove you to the Square. When you realized you had nothing to change into, that was the catalyst." Benton slides his reading glasses out of their case. "But the fuel load was already laid."

"And what fuel load might you mean?" I smooth my napkin over my skirt and am reminded of how badly I want to get out of these clothes.

"I think you know."

What he's leading up to is my family—specifically my reaction to my sister's uninvited and unexpected visit, and I glance at the time. I'd planned on heading to Logan by nine thirty but now I'm not sure what to do. Lucy says Dorothy might be late. Well it would be nice of my sister to let me know so Benton and I don't race away from here and end up sitting outside the baggage area for hours.

"Bryce stopped by my office around four thirty to give me a ride to The Coop, to take me on any errands and then drop me off here," I begin recounting what happened this afternoon. "And that was fine except he wouldn't stop talking. I honestly couldn't take it."

"Talking about what?"

"That's very difficult to reconstruct when it's Bryce. It seems he's convinced I don't feel the same about him, that I don't like him or want him around, and this predates today's incident with the panty hose. Lately I've gotten the impression he has some strange notion that I've distanced myself and am thinking of firing him or who knows what."

"Based on?" Benton slips on the reading glasses, parking them low on his straight narrow nose, his hazel eyes finding me over the top of the frames.

"Based on his repeated questions about what else he'd done wrong. He kept asking that when he was arguing with me in front of The Coop."

"Were you arguing or was he?"

"I've always heard it takes two."

Benton laughs. "It doesn't when it's him. Bryce is pretty good at playing both sides of the net."

"I didn't argue. I just resisted and denied, telling him I needed to go. He was so worried about the broiling heat, and here I was standing out in the middle of it because he wouldn't leave me alone."

"So in other words, he's reacting to you." Benton picks up the thickly bound wine list that was on top of his menu.

"As usual but it's more extreme, it seems."

"This may shape up to being one of those unfortunate situations that's all about bad timing." Benton turns several thick creamy pages, glancing at wines. "I hope not. But it was bad timing for you to get out of sorts with him while a detractor, possibly a stalker, was watching. Normally we could let it go, dismiss it as a deranged rambling. But the marijuana-leaf tattoo is a problem. If it wasn't for that detail I wouldn't give any credence to someone calling in what sounds like a completely frivolous complaint. I wouldn't even bother listening."

"What are you saying?" I reply. "And how did you know about the tattoo?"

But Benton turns another page in the wine list. He doesn't answer.

"Are you suggesting that you've listened to the nine-one-one recording? Is that what you're telling me?" I ask him next.

7

The waiter has returned with a bottle of still water, and we're quiet as he fills our glasses.

We say nothing unless it's related to appetizers and how lovely it is to have the dining room all to ourselves for as long as it lasts. Benton always gets the crab cakes with grilled scallions and pickled banana peppers, and I usually indulge in the lobster bisque with lemon brown butter.

But it's too hot for either, we decide, and instead we pick the Mediterranean salad with heirloom tomatoes and crumbled feta. I ask if we can substitute purple onions for sweet ones and have extra dressing on the side with crushed red pepper to add a kick. I order another bottle of water, this one sparkling with lots of lime. The instant the waiter has moved on I return to what Benton was saying.

"What do you mean you wouldn't bother?" I ask. "Your wife is the subject of a police complaint and you wouldn't bother to pay attention? Even if it's chickenshit?"

"This wouldn't be the first time unstable people have spotted you in public and called the police and the media."

Benton turns another page in the wine list, and the light catches his gold signet ring engraved with his family coat of arms. "You're recognizable, Kay, and people associate you with sensational crimes and disasters. I could tell you otherwise but it wouldn't be the truth. So yes." He glances up at me. "I might not have paid attention or as close attention as I should have."

"You've listened to the recording." I won't let him evade the question. "I'm going to keep asking."

He silently reads the wine list, and I can see his eyes moving up and down a page of white Burgundies. I'm not sure why. The most he can have is a glass. In a while he has to drive, and I think of Dorothy and get only more adamant with Benton. I can't seem to help it.

"I want to hear the recording," I tell him. "Do you have a copy? And I'm not interested in the transcript. I want to hear the bastard lie about me."

"Marino should play it for you," Benton says as he turns pages back and forth between different types of wines. "I assume he's investigating your egregious disturbance of the peace just like any lead detective worth his salt would spend his time doing."

"I told you he wouldn't tell me scarcely anything the person said. He wouldn't discuss it in detail, and legally I can push this, Benton. I have a right to face my accuser, and in this case the accuser is the person who's lying about me on that recording. I want to hear it for myself—with my own ears. There are no legal grounds for withholding that recording from me unless you think I'm implicated in a federal crime. And last I checked, disturbing the peace wasn't."

This is exactly what Benton wants me to do—to threaten him in a confrontational offended way that doesn't really reflect my true feelings. What I mustn't do is treat him like my husband when it comes to this particular matter, which ironically he wouldn't know about in the first place if we weren't a couple. He needs to be Special Agent Benton Wesley this moment and I need to be the Chief, and we've been down this road many times.

He turns another page in the *carte des vins*. "I think we should have white wine," he says. "But it depends on what you want to eat. We'll have just enough to taste and cork the rest for later, after we finally get home."

"It would take nothing more than a Freedom of Information Act request. But it's stupid to make me go through that. I was thinking about fish. Something light." I open my menu without picking it up as he reaches down next to his chair and finds his briefcase.

He places it in his lap, and I hear the bright snap of the locks again.

"Remember what my eighth-grade teacher said to me?" He pulls out his wireless headset in its zip-up case. "Good ol' Mr. Broadmoor . . ."

"Who declared that one day you're going to get what you ask for and be sorry," I finish the anecdote for Benton, one he repeats often when he's sure it applies to me.

"It won't be pleasant and I'd rather spare you." He unzips the small black case. "But as you know, the laws about nine-one-one recordings are rather murky in Massachusetts. There's no statute that tells me you can't listen. You're right about that."

He hands the headset to me and I put it on. He places his phone in the middle of the table, and touches several prompts on the display. I hear static and clicking in stereo. Then:

"Nine-one-one, what is your emergency?" The dispatcher is a woman, and I recognize her voice from the chronic radio chatter in my life.

"Hello. It's not exactly an emergency but I think the police should know that one of our esteemed public servants is disturbing the peace in front of God and everyone in Harvard Square."

The caller's voice is mellow and flows at a rhythmic slow pace, bringing to mind someone pulling taffy. It's as if the person is stoned or putting on an act, and I remember what Marino said about not being able to tell if the caller is male or female. I'm not sure either.

"What's the address of your emergency?" the dispatcher asks.

"I don't know precisely but I should think a good way to describe the Square is it's the area around the T station."

"Is there an address of a business you can give me?"

"No." The caller coughs several times.

"What number are you calling from?"

"It's my cell phone so it's not going to tell you my location. You won't be able to confirm anything about me like that . . ."

At this point the caller becomes abusive and argumentative in his slow, languid way, and I think of him as a *him*. But I honestly can't say because the voice is low and husky in a pleasant range somewhere between a baritone and a tenor.

As I listen to him describe what he allegedly witnessed it enters my mind that my so-called shit fest with my "boyfriend" isn't something that was happening while this witness who's a liar was on the phone with the dispatcher. What he says seems too rehearsed to be happening in real

59

time, and instantly I'm suspicious he's reporting his made-up story after the fact.

"Do you know where the female subject is now?" The dispatcher is asking about me in the recording as I stare down at the white tablecloth and listen carefully through the headphones.

"No, but she's a C-U-Next-Tuesday if I ever saw one, and I sure as hell wouldn't want her showing up at my damn house if somebody died. Jabbing her damn finger, slapping the fool out of some poor sissy kid who looks like a real loser. I can't imagine what sort of bedside manner a nasty bitch like that would have . . ."

"Where are you?" the dispatcher asks as the caller coughs and clears his throat again. "Are you outside?"

"With the birds and the bees. Of course I'm outside! How the hell else could I be reporting something that's going on outside in the elements right before my very eyes?"

This goes on until she lets him know the police are on their way, and she asks the caller's name.

"You don't need my name, lady, what you need is to pay attention to their names. You hear me?"

"I need a name so the police can find you—"

"Don't try that shit with me. I know what you're doing. You're going to cover this up just like you do everything about the damn government, and it's time for the intolerance and fascism to end . . ."

The vileness goes on for almost a minute total, and it's difficult to hear such awful things about me. My anger spikes. I take off the headset, returning it to Benton.

"It would seem this individual has a personal problem

60

with me for some reason." I'm shaken and incensed, and it's the only thing I can think to say.

"Is the voice familiar?" Benton's eyes don't leave mine.

"No it's not. What time was the call made?"

"Twelve minutes past six." His stare doesn't waver as the meaning hits me.

June twelfth or six-twelve is my date of birth. Usually I would assume this is nothing more than a coincidental overlap with my personal life except for a not-so-minor problem. Six-twelve p.m. is also the exact time Tailend Charlie has been e-mailing his recorded threats to me since September 1.

"So it was almost an hour and a half after the fact." I reach for my water glass. "Bryce and I were talking in front of The Coop at closer to four forty-five. Are we sure there's no way the time could be faked?"

"I don't see how, Kay. The time stamp is on the nine-one-one recording."

"Then the call was definitely made after I'd left the Square. At six-twelve I'm certain I was walking through the Yard. That's also in the ballpark of when Marino reached me on my cell phone."

"Can you check?" Benton indicates my phone on the table.

I pick it up and look at the incoming calls. "He tried me first at six-eighteen," I reply. "I remember what building I was walking past when my phone vibrated, and it was him."

"What this suggests is he must have been contacted the instant the police got the complaint about you," Benton says, and I don't know if he's asking or telling.

"Don't forget Rosie's always been a little sweet on him. They dated a few times. She probably didn't waste a minute getting hold of him."

"Rosie?"

"The dispatcher," I remind him. "I recognized her voice. Her name is actually Rosemary but Marino calls her Rosie."

"Which brings me back to the same question. Was there anything familiar, anything you noticed about the voice you just listened to in the nine-one-one call? Anything that struck you?" Benton looks down at his phone, but the screen has gone to sleep and there's nothing to see but a glassy black rectangle.

He unlocks it and the displayed video file reappears with its frozen PLAY arrow.

"Beyond how arrogant and hateful the person sounded?" I'm thinking hard. "Nothing struck me, not really."

"It sounds like you're not sure."

I look up at the plaster ceiling and replay the 911 audio clip in my head. "No," I decide. "It's unfamiliar, just a normal pleasant voice. I'm not sure what else to say about it."

"And you're equivocal again." Benton's not going to tell me why he thinks that.

It's not his style to lead the witness even if the witness is his wife, and I take another drink of water as I think for a moment. He's right. I'm uncertain, and then it occurs to me why.

"It's too uniform, too homogenous," I explain what I've been picking up on but couldn't identify. "There aren't the variations I might expect. There's something stilted and unnatural about it."

"In other words it sounds artificial or canned. Fake, in other words," he says, and I wonder if this came from Lucy. "We can't tell if it's synthetized." He answers my unspoken question about my niece. "But Lucy agrees that it's strangely consistent from one comment to the next. She says that if it's been enhanced or altered—"

"Wait a minute. If you got the audio file from the police, then how could it have been altered?"

"Lucy introduced the idea of a voice changer similar to what gamers are into. There are a lot of these apps on the market, although not the quality of whatever this person used. The typical voice disguised by software tends to sound obviously fake like a poor animation. It's within the realm of possibility the caller has proprietary highly sophisticated software that changes your voice as you speak into the phone—"

"And it sounds different from your usual voice but normal to whoever's on the other end." I finish his thought because I already know what's next.

Benton asks if I think it's possible that my cyber-stalker Tailend Charlie is the one who called 911 and lied about me.

"Indicating this individual is stepping things up," my husband adds. "Escalating whatever his game is, and we know without question that Tailend Charlie is technically sophisticated."

"Let's hope that's not who placed the nine-one-one call because it would suggest he was in close proximity to me today," I reply. "And I've been hoping whoever the cyber-bully is he's not in Cambridge. Preferably he's on the other side of the planet."

"It strikes me as a little too coincidental that you began getting the e-mailed threats only a week ago, all of them altered audio clips. And now this," Benton says.

"So tell me, Mr. Profiler." I press my leg against his, and the fabric of his suit is smooth and cool against my bare skin. "What do you have to say about someone who calls nine-one-one to report your wife for being a C-U-Next-Tuesday?"

8

"Male. And not old. But not young," Benton says. "I doubt it's a student unless we're talking about a mature one."

"As in a graduate student?"

"Don't know, forties at least," he replies. "Older but not so old as to preclude this person from moving about freely in all sorts of weather. More like someone from the homeless population around the Square but that doesn't mean it's what we're dealing with. He's educated but could be self-educated.

"He probably lives alone, probably has a psychiatric history. And he's intelligent, way above the norm. He's antigovernment, which means anti-authority, and yes, I'd say there's genuine hostility toward you. He's the sort to overidealize relationships and even assume ones that don't exist." Benton ticks all of this off like a grocery list.

He doesn't even have to think about it.

"Could it be someone I know?"

"Yes. But it's more likely you don't. Possibly you've never met."

"Marino thinks this person was using a prepaid phone, a TracFone, something that isn't traceable," I reply. "And that makes sense if you don't live the sort of life that involves monthly phone bills, et cetera. But how does that fit with using some sort of voice-changing software that has to be installed?"

"It would seem to me that you could install software on just about any type of smartphone and still use it with prepaid cards."

"Yes. And we associate such things with homeless people but there's something else I'm sure you've considered . . ." I start to say, but the waiter is back with our sparkling water and lime.

Benton raises his hand to signal we'll fill our glasses ourselves. When the waiter drifts away I mention the Obama Phone, a rather irreverent reference to a government program for low-income people that provides a free cell phone with unlimited minutes, texting and all the rest.

"That's typically the sort of device we're talking about in the homeless population we find in area shelters and out on the streets with their cardboard signs," I explain as Benton listens. "But you have to apply and register for an Obama Phone, for lack of a better word. And I would think that if the person who called in the bogus complaint about me was using such a thing, then the number would trace back to the carrier."

"SafeLink," Benton says, and I can tell he's already thought about it. "It's one of the biggest and most popular noncontract cellular services."

"But if the phone is part of a government program?"

"That would be the difference. You have to be registered. You have to enroll to qualify, and you have your own account." He picks up the bottle of water and refills our glasses.

"That's exactly what I'm getting at," I reply with a nod. "So Lucy possibly could have traced the phone that made the nine-one-one call if the person were part of this program."

"Yes she could," Benton agrees.

"Then the witness who's such a fan of mine wasn't using an Obama Phone," I summarize, and Benton just stares at me.

He knows that I'd rather the crank caller was using an Obama Phone, and that's the bigger point. I'd prefer to take my chances with someone who truly might be a regular at the Square, perhaps some disenfranchised person who's unpleasant and unstable but not harmful. What I don't want is to be on the radar of an experienced criminal. Especially one sophisticated enough to create software that sends all of us down the wrong path.

If we can't recognize evil, then we can't say for sure it's not in our midst. Whoever made the call, whoever Tailend Charlie is, even if they're one and the same? The miscreant could be right in front of us. And there's no thought much scarier than that. It would be devastating to learn that the person who lied about me to the police is someone I know. It would be worse if whoever is sending me death threats in Italian is someone I care about and trust.

"Who called you about the nine-one-one recording?" I ask Benton. "How did you get involved by the way?"

"Well I'm married to you. Start with that. But Bryce called me as I was finishing up a meeting and about to head out of the office. The lamb or the halibut? You decide. I'll have what you're having."

"I'm going to try the halibut with brussels sprouts. How did you get a copy of the recording? I can't imagine the Cambridge police gave that to Bryce."

"They didn't. I think we should go for a Burgundy. A Chablis *premier cru.*"

"The 2009 Montée de Tonnerre." We've had it before, and the wine is refreshingly clean and pure with a chiseled finish.

"Very good," Benton says, and he's not going to tell me if he got the 911 audio clip from his friend the police superintendent, and I'm not going to ask further because I'm not sure I want to know.

The waiter is back with our salads, and both of us order the pan-seared halibut with brussels sprouts for our main course.

I ask for sides of spaghettini vegetables and wild mushrooms, and we order the Chablis. Then we wait in silence until he walks away again and can't overhear our conversation, and I'm beginning to get the sense that he's lingering. But only a few people have started to trickle in, and he's probably bored.

"By the way, in case you didn't know, we issued a new terror bulletin a few hours ago," Benton says to me, and he means the FBI has.

"It's hard to keep up with them. I just make it a habit to assume we're on high alert all of the time. Anything specific?"

"Just that it's something major, and there's reason to suspect we're talking the East Coast. Hopefully not Boston again but there's a lot of chatter out there about it and also D.C."

"Thanks for passing it along." I look at him because I feel him watching me closely. "Is there something else? Because you look like you have a question. I can practically see it in a bubble over your head."

"Maybe I shouldn't say it."

"And now you have to after a loaded comment like that."

"All right. I'm wondering if it's possible that Bryce is acting a little loosely wrapped because you are."

"I'm loosely wrapped? I don't believe I've heard that before. I've heard a lot of things including very vulgar things, but never that."

"Let me ask you an important question. If Dorothy wasn't suddenly coming to town, do you think the incident at Harvard Square would have happened?"

"No. Because I wouldn't have had to bother with gifts or theater tickets."

"That's not the only reason, Kay. She's coming here. She didn't ask, she told, and as usual you accommodated. You paid for her ticket and even offered her a room in our house."

"Which fortunately she declined because she'd rather stay with Lucy." I feel anger rising like heat from a lower level of my psyche, a region of my inner self that I don't approve of and might just hate.

"I have a feeling the person she'd rather stay with is Marino," Benton says. "But only if he lived in a penthouse."

I set down my glass too hard, and water slops over the rim. I watch the white tablecloth turn gray where the water soaks in. Then Benton uses his napkin to pat dry the mess I've made while I stare at him in disbelief.

"What are you talking about?" Noticing Mrs. P lighting

a candle with an electric match several tables away, I try not to look upset.

I don't want it to appear that I'm fighting with someone else. I realize how thin my skin is right now.

"I mentioned it when all of us were in Miami last," Benton says as our waiter reappears with two glasses and the wine.

I think back to our most recent trip this past June, and remember that Marino and Dorothy started driving together to pick up takeout food. He rented a Harley and took her for a ride, and I recall Benton making a comment. When I'm with my family in Miami and also dealing with Lucy, Janet and Desi, I can be very distracted. But it's also true that what Benton is alluding to is something I wouldn't want to notice. I wouldn't want it to be true. I can't think of much that's more frightening than the idea of Marino and my sister together.

The waiter slides out the cork with a soft pop, and hands it to Benton. He lifts it to his nose and watches as a small amount of the pale cold Chablis is poured.

"You do the honors." He hands me the glass, and the wine is sharply clean, waking up my tongue.

Benton nods for the waiter to pour us each a taste.

"Happy Wednesday." Benton touches his glass to mine in a toast, and this is the second time in the past hour that I've felt that an insect is in my clothing.

My phone vibrates in my jacket pocket.

"Now what?" I set down my glass as I check who's calling. "Speaking of . . . It's Marino again."

After all that's gone on, even he wouldn't interrupt dinner unless there was a good reason. Now Benton's phone is buzzing.

I catch a glimpse of a 202 area code before he says, "I've got to take this," and he answers, "Wesley here."

"Hold on," I tell Marino without saying hello, and Benton and I are both getting up from our chairs. "You know where I am so it must be important. I assume I need to get somewhere I can talk."

"Do it now." Marino's voice is hard.

"I'm walking out. Hold on," I say to him as Benton and I collect our briefcases.

We drop our napkins next to our barely touched salads and glasses of wine. We leave as if we're not coming back.

9

We're calm and reserved as we walk with purpose through the dining room, avoiding the curious glances of other couples being seated.

Benton and I are together but separate, each of us on the phone. To look at us, you'd never know anything out of the ordinary was going on. We could be talking to our Realtors, our bankers, our brokers, our pet sitters.

We could be a well-heeled couple getting calls from our adoring children, and Benton would be the rich handsome breadwinner. While in comparison I'd be the hardworking rather peculiar and difficult wife who always looks shopworn and halfway blown together. Our eyes are slightly downcast as we weave between tables, and I recognize the fixed stare, the flexing of his jaw, the tenseness of his hands.

I know the way he gets when something is serious. He's probably listening to his employer, the U.S. Department of Justice. Not his divisional office but Washington, D.C., possibly someone high up in the FBI or the director himself, and it could be the White House. It's not Quantico, where Benton got his start and used to work. That's not the area code I just saw on his phone when it vibrated.

My husband's special power is his ability to get into the mind of the offender, to discover the why and the what for, and unearth whatever traumas and bad wiring unleashed the latest monster into our midst. Benton's quarry could be one individual. It could be several or a group of them, and when he goes after them, he must become an empathic Method actor. He has to think, anticipate and even feel what evildoers feel if he's to catch them. But it's not without a price.

"Yes, speaking," Benton says, and he listens. Then, "I understand. No, I'm not aware of it." He glances at me. "It's the first I've heard." He looks down at the red carpet. "Please explain. I'm listening."

"I'm walking out," I quietly tell Marino.

Something has happened, and my imagination is getting the better of me. I sense a presence that's suffocating, heavy and dark. It's palpable like ozone in the air, like the eerie vacuum right before a massive storm breaks. I feel it at a visceral level.

"What is it exactly that you'd like me to do?" Benton turns his head away from people looking at us.

"Should be there . . . in three." Marino's voice is fractured in my earpiece, another bad connection, and everything that's weirdly unfolded in the past few hours suddenly is crashing around me. "No one saw anything . . . that we know of. But two girls, these two twins found her . . ." he says, and I do my best to decipher.

But it's as if I've walked into a tornado. There's so much

72

flying around I can't tell what's up, down, inside out or backward.

"Hold on," I again say to him because I won't discuss a case until no one can overhear me.

"Turning off Kennedy . . . On Harvard Street now," his voice is choppy.

"Give me two more seconds. I'm finding someplace quiet," I reply, and I can hear the sound of his engine as sirens wail in the background.

Past Mrs. P's empty station, Benton takes a right at the entryway's round table with its sumptuous fragrant arrangement of cut lilies and roses. I keep going back to what he said just moments ago about an anticipated terrorist attack on the East Coast, possibly in the Boston area again. Now something has happened here in Cambridge, and he's on the phone with Washington, D.C., as the terror alert is off the charts. I don't like what I'm feeling.

I don't like the way Benton glanced at me as he said over the phone that he wasn't aware of something, that he hadn't been informed of whatever it is. As if there's something happening in the here and now that he should know about, that both of us should. Whatever's going on isn't simply a local problem, and as I think this I also know I'm ahead of myself. The two of us getting important if not urgent calls simultaneously doesn't mean they're related. It could be a coincidence.

But I can't shake the ominous signals I'm picking up. I have a feeling I'm going to discover soon enough that Benton and I are about to have the same problem but won't be able to discuss it much if at all. In our different positions we won't handle it the same way, and we could even end up at odds with each other. It wouldn't be the first time and certainly won't be the last.

"Doc . . .? Did you get the part about . . .? Interpol calling . . .?" Marino says, and I must have misheard him.

"I can hardly understand you," I reply in a loud whisper. "And I can't talk. One second please."

Benton heads into the drawing room, and I wish the drapes had been pulled across the tall expansive windows. It's completely dark out with only vague smudges of distant lamps pushing back the inkiness, and I'm conscious of the night and what might be in it, possibly close by, possibly watching. Maybe right under our very noses. I detect something sinister has been tampering with us all day and probably for longer than that.

I return to the entrance, where I avoid the old corroded mirror on the wall, and I stand with my head bent, facing the front door but not really seeing anything as I listen to Marino over the phone.

It's difficult to hear everything he's saying. We have at best a spotty connection, and I'm beginning to get jumpy. I don't know who's doing what or spying on whom, and in light of everything else it's hard not to feel hunted and disoriented.

"Okay, stop. You need to say that again only much more slowly." I huddle near an ornate cast-iron umbrella stand, and I don't want to believe this is happening. "What do you mean she's already stiff?"

"The first guy there checked her vitals said she's already stiff," Marino replies, and the connection is almost perfect suddenly.

"And have you seen this yourself or is it what you've

been told?" I reply because what he's saying sounds completely wrong.

"I was told."

"Were there any attempts at resuscitation?"

"She was obviously dead," Marino says clear as a bell.

"That's what you were told."

"Yeah."

"What was obvious about it?" I ask.

"For one thing she was stiff. The squad didn't touch her."

"Then how did they determine she's stiff?"

"I don't know but apparently she is." Marino again reminds me he hasn't been to the scene.

"As far as we know, the first responding officer is the only one who's touched her?" I want to know.

"That's what I've been told."

"And what about her temp? Warm? Cool?"

"Warm supposedly. But what do you expect when it's still ninety degrees out? She could be out there all day and not cool off."

"I'll have to see when I get there. But the rigor doesn't make sense," I tell Marino. "Unless she's been out there much longer than one might initially assume. And that wouldn't make sense either. Even in this weather there are still some people out and about, especially near the water. She would have been found long before now, I would think."

For rigor mortis to be obvious, the victim would have had to be dead for several hours at least, depending on what muscles are noticeably affected and how advanced the postmortem process has gotten. The high temperatures we've been having would escalate decomposition, meaning rigor would set in sooner. But it's extremely unlikely that what Marino's been told is correct. That's also not surprising. Patrol officers are often the first responders, and they can't always know what they're looking at.

". . . Got him waiting with the twins . . . uh, who found the body . . ." Marino is saying, and then I lose the rest.

"Okay. You must be in a bad space again." I'm getting exasperated, but at least it sounds like he has the scene secured.

But I can't imagine what he meant when he said that Interpol was trying to call him.

"Looks like someone was hiding in the trees, waiting," he then says, and the connection is much better again. "That's what I'm guessing. No eyes or ears."

"Not if it were the middle of the day," I point out as I continue glancing around me, making sure no one can hear. "And if she's been dead for hours as her alleged rigor would suggest? There would have been eyes and ears because it would have been broad daylight, possibly early or midafternoon."

"I agree with you. That part can't be right."

"It doesn't sound it. But I'll see when I get there," I repeat. "What else can you tell me?"

Marino begins to describe what he knows about a violent death that may have happened within the past hour not even a mile from here. The woman's body is on the fitness path along the river. Some of her clothing has been ripped off, her helmet more than twenty feet away, and there's visible blood. It appears she died from a blow to the head, or that's what the first responding officer told Marino.

"He says you can see where she was struggling, moving

around as her head was banged against the path," Marino adds, but what I alert on is his mention of a helmet. "Like someone was waiting until she was passing through a thick clump of trees where nobody could see, then grabbed her and she fought like hell."

"What helmet?" I ask. "The victim was on a bicycle?"

"It appears she was attacked while she was riding," Marino answers, and I can hear his excitement in his tense tone while I feel a chill along my spine.

I can't help but think of my encounter earlier today, first at the repertory theater and then on the sidewalk along Quincy Street. Suddenly the young woman with the British accent is in my mind, and I wish she weren't.

"She was on the path that cuts through the middle of the park," Marino is explaining, "and it happened in the spot where there's a small clearing in a stand of trees. I'm thinking it was planned like that to ambush her."

"And her helmet was off and some twenty feet from the body?" It's another detail that like her rigor defies logic, and I wonder what color the helmet is.

I hope it's not a robin's-egg blue.

"That's the story," Marino says, and I know exactly what he sounds like when something big goes down.

Not just big. But explosively bad. The blitz attack he's describing will create a public panic if it's not handled properly. I feel slightly sick inside. I remember the young woman on her bicycle looking at me quizzically as Benton handed her the bottle of water she dropped. She put her helmet back on before she rode off, and she didn't bother fastening the chin strap. I remember seeing it dangling as she rode off across the street, through the Yard, heading in the direction of the Square and the river.

This would have been close to seven P.M., barely an hour ago as the sun was setting. I tell myself if it turns out the victim is the woman I saw, it would be a bizarre twist of fate, an almost unbelievable one. I almost hope the detail about rigor turns out to be accurate. If it is, the victim couldn't be the young cyclist in Converse sneakers.

But even as I reassure myself, I also know that what Marino said about the rigor can't be true. Or the reporting officer is confused. Because I don't think it's possible—even in this weather—for a dead body on the fitness path inside John F. Kennedy Park not to be discovered for hours. I suspect the death happened recently, and then I envision the young woman's flushed face and smile again.

What doesn't kill you makes you stronger. I hear her voice in my head.

"I've already talked to your office," Marino says in my earpiece. "Rusty and Harold are bringing a truck."

"I need a big one."

"The MCC," he says, and the tri-axle thirty-five-foot mobile command center is a fine idea if there's a place to park it.

"We're going to need a barricade," I remind Marino, and I can't get the woman's face, her sporty sunglasses and self-assured smile, out of my thoughts.

"That's what I ordered. Remember who you're talking to."

When he headed investigations at the CFC, he was in charge of our fleet. In some ways he knows more about the nuts and bolts of our operations than I do.

"I want a place to duck out of the heat and away from the curious," I reply. "And we'll need plenty of water."

"Yeah, there's not exactly a 7-Eleven handy, and the park is dark as shit. We're setting up lights."

"Please don't turn them on yet. The scene will blaze like Fenway."

"Don't worry. We're keeping everything dark until we're ready. Doing what we can to keep the gawkers away, especially any assholes trying to film with their phones. There's student housing everywhere. Eliot House is right there on the other side of Memorial Drive and it's as big as the Pentagon, plus you got the Kennedy School, and traffic on Memorial Drive. Not to mention the bridge is right there, and across the water is Boston. So we got no plans of lighting up the scene right this minute."

"Do we have a name?" I ask.

"An ID was found on the path near her bike. Elisa Vandersteel, twenty-three years old from the UK. Of course that's if it's the dead lady's. I'm guessing it probably is," Marino says, and my mood sinks lower. "I'm told the picture looks sort of like her, for what it's worth. And I just pulled up in front of the Faculty Club. You coming out?"

"Where in the UK?" I almost don't want to ask.

"London, I think."

"Do you know what kind of shoes she had on?" I envision the cyclist's off-white Converse sneakers, and I'm pretty sure I caught a peek of bike socks, the kind that are below the ankle.

"Her shoes?" Marino asks as if he didn't hear me right.

"Yes."

"Got no idea," he says. "Why?"

"I'll see you in a minute," I reply.

10

I step away from the front door, pausing by the antique entryway table with its big flower arrangement.

Inside the drawing room Benton is discreetly tucked to one side of a window near the baby grand piano. He's on the phone, his face hard and somber. There's nobody else inside with him, and I wish I could tell him about the woman on the bicycle. He saw her too, and now the worst may have happened.

But I don't get any closer. I know when not to disturb him, and I notice that Mrs. P is back at her station, her round old-fashioned glasses staring at me. As I glance at her she quickly looks down and begins to open menus, checking the printed pages inside. I can tell she senses something is wrong.

I can't hear what Benton is saying to whoever he's on the phone with, but I get the impression based on his tone that he's not talking to the same person he was a moment earlier. I catch his eye and indicate I have to go, and he nods. Then he turns away. He doesn't place his hand over his phone to ask what's happening or offer what might be going on with him. And that makes me wonder if we really are being contacted about the same case.

But I don't see how that would be feasible. At this stage there's no reason I can think of for the FBI to be interested in a local death, possibly of a young woman from London named Elisa Vandersteel. But it's disturbing that Marino mentioned the International Criminal Police Organization, Interpol. I don't know why he did or if I might have misheard. But I can't stop thinking of the cyclist with the blue helmet and Converse sneakers who called me the *peanut-butter-pie lady*.

I realize the ID found near her body might not be hers, but when I met her she sounded British, possibly from London, and my stomach clenches harder. I feel a sense of urgency that's personal. As if I knew the woman who's been killed. As if I might be one of the last people she ever spoke to or saw. And I will myself to control my thoughts.

I can't say for a fact whose dead body is in the park or how the death occurred or why, I remind myself. I open the door and step out into the dark oven of the patio, where no one is sitting in the stifling night air. I follow the walkway, looking all around me with every step I take. I listen for the quiet nocturnal sounds of insects, of birds lifting off branches in a startled burst, their wings whistling.

I listen for the creaking of old trees, the rustle of leafy canopies or chirp of a katydid. But it's dead quiet except for traffic that gusts like the wind, rushing, then lagging before it picks up again. I'm aware of the solid roughness of the bricks beneath my softly tapping shoes, mindful of the thick static air and the bright bug eyes of vehicles on Quincy Street.

I pass the same foliage and rockery I did earlier when I was with Benton, but it seems I'm on another planet now, surrounded by unfamiliar voids of lawn, and hulking dark shapes and shadows. Nothing moves except traffic beyond the split-rail paling silhouetted ahead. I can see the libraries sleepily lit up across the street in the Yard, where I was walking not even an hour and a half ago. I reach the sidewalk, and Marino's SUV is parked at the curb behind Benton's Audi.

It seems like déjà vu as I climb in and stare at the rear of my husband's blacked-out Batmobile illuminated in the glare of headlights. Only he's not in it now, and I feel a pang of loneliness as I see the empty dark space where he was sitting behind the wheel, watching us in the rearview mirror but a very short time ago.

Benton is still inside the Faculty Club, and I continue watching for him to emerge from the red front door, to see him illuminated in the entrance light as he steps outside and follows the walkway. But there's no sign of him. He must still be on the phone, and it enters my mind that in the midst of all this chaos he has to take care of banal matters such as paying for a dinner we didn't get to eat. I didn't think of asking for the check. I simply walked out.

As I pull my door shut and set my briefcase by my feet, I ask Marino what else he instructed my two autopsy technicians Rusty and Harold to bring to the scene.

"And have they already left?" I pull my shoulder harness across me and the steel tongue snaps into the buckle that as usual I had to dig out of the crack in the seat. "Because I need protective clothing and a scene case. I don't have anything with me, not even a pair of gloves. And there's no time for me to stop by my office."

82

"You need to relax," Marino says. "I've got it covered."

He looks the way he did when I saw him last, except he's taken off his tie. I see it on the backseat, sloppily coiled like a polyester snake.

"Please assure me we're keeping the lights off." It's not possible I'm going to relax. "We turn on portable flood-lights and we may as well send out invitations and a press release."

"Remember where I used to work? Remember who used to take care of all that and still knows how?" He checks his mirrors. "I know the drill." His eyes are darting and he's sweating. "I guess Benton's staying?" Marino stares at the Faculty Club, boxy and dignified in the distant dark.

A pale gold light fills the tall twelve-paned windows, and I can see inside the drawing room, the masculine leather furniture, the sparkling chandelier, the gleaming baby grand, and I look for Benton. But there's no way he's lingering in front of windows for all the world to see.

"I'm not sure what he's doing," I reply. "He was on the phone with Washington when I was leaving."

"Let me guess," Marino says, and right off he's assuming Benton's call is related to what's just happened in John F. Kennedy Park.

"I don't have any idea," I reply as we pull away from the curb. "I don't know what's going on but he did mention earlier that the terror alert is elevated."

Marino turns on his emergency lights but not his siren. "Something's going on, Doc. I'm just telling you. And he's not passing along the info because that's what the FBI does, doesn't matter that you're married to them."

"I'm not married to the FBI. I'm married to Benton." I've said it before and I'll say it again.

"If the reason he's on the phone with Washington is the Vandersteel case, there's no way he's going to tell you," Marino says as if he knows my husband better than I do. "He could be talking to Interpol, which might explain the call I got—that's assuming news of the case here has shot up the chain already, and if so I'd like to know how the hell that's possible. But Benton won't tell you shit unless it suits his purposes because right now he's the Feds. And yeah, you're married to them. Or maybe worse? He is."

"This is several times now that you've mentioned Interpol." I'm not interested in hearing his disparagements of Benton, the FBI or anything else at the moment. "Why?" I ask.

"They didn't call you too, did they?" Marino glances at me, his brown eyes glaring and bloodshot.

"No." I'm mystified. "Why would they and about what?"

Marino guns a right on Harvard Street, and the route he takes basically will retrace my steps from my earlier ill-fated walk.

Only now it's completely dark, and the stars and quarter moon are blotted by a hot haze that for days has been filmy over the horizon, intensifying the colors at twilight from pastel tints to wide brushstrokes of gaudy orange, magenta and deep rose.

"Let me start at the beginning and spell it out," Marino says. "I was actually on my way to the CFC."

"What for?" I look at his wide-eyed flushed face as he streaks past apartment buildings, a bookshop, a bank, a café and other businesses that form blurred chains of light on either side of the two-lane road.

"Because Lucy and I were trying to see if there's anything

else we could figure out about the bogus nine-one-one call made by someone using voice-changing software," he says, and that addresses at least some of what I've been wondering.

Unsurprisingly, Lucy picked up on the subtle but odd uniformity of what we suspect is an altered voice on the audio clip. She must have said something to Marino and also to Benton.

"She's in her lab," Marino says. "Or she was right before I called you."

"Then what?" I ask him as we speed through the middle of the Harvard campus. "You're with her at the CFC, and what happened next?"

There are more people out now, on the sidewalks, walking through the Yard. But certainly it's nothing close to the usual crowds, the typical hustle and bustle of Cambridge, which I've always said is a concentrated version of any huge metropolis in the world and all the problems and advantages that go with it.

"Then I get the call from Clay," Marino says.

"Do I know him?"

"Tom Barclay."

"The investigator?"

"Yeah."

"I see," I reply, and this changes things.

I look out the windows, and the park and the river are just minutes ahead. I can see the brick Widener Library with its teal cupola, and the stone slate-roofed department of linguistics. I'm surprised and unsettled by what Marino just told me. If Tom Barclay was the source of the information, that's unfortunate.

"I see," I again say. "So it wasn't a patrol officer who was the first responder."

"Nope. It was Clay," Marino answers, and Clay, or Investigator Barclay as I know him, recently was transferred from property crimes to the major case unit.

I haven't really worked with him directly but one of my medical examiners had a case with him earlier in the week and complained about him. Barclay is much too sure of himself and doesn't know when to shut up. He may have attended the crime-scene academy but that doesn't give him the expertise to identify and interpret artifacts such as rigor and livor mortis, and other changes that occur after death. A little knowledge can be a dangerous thing when you're cocky.

"The detail about rigor is perplexing and troublesome," I tell Marino over the thunder of his driving like a rocket. "He's been around dead bodies before."

"Not many."

"But some. And he should recognize certain obvious postmortem changes," I add, "and hopefully not confuse or misrepresent them. But it would seem like a strange mistake to make if he's stated for the record that she's already going into rigor when in fact she's not. And he shouldn't be stating anything to you that you in turn pass on to me. All of it constitutes a paper trail, a record that we might wish we didn't have."

I emphasize *for the record* because Marino's relaying to me what Investigator Barclay reported could become problematic if it's documented or circulated. The dead woman and any associated biological evidence are my legal jurisdiction, meaning I'm present in an official capacity.

I'm not here as Marino's mother, wife, friend, partner, mentor or pal, and very little is private anymore. Unfortunately, any information we exchange doesn't constitute some sort of legally protected small talk. We can get asked anything when we're under oath.

"Clay's new. He's never worked a homicide, and he thinks he's a genius. Beyond that what can I tell you?" Marino replies. "I guess we'll see for ourselves, but he said she was stiff. He touched her and she felt as stiff as a mannequin. That's what he told me."

"If he wasn't sure or didn't know, I wish he hadn't said it." This is disappointing and may come back to bite us. "It's worse because it's a detective saying it."

"I know," Marino says. "That's why I'm always telling him and everyone else to think before you open your damn pie hole and be careful what you write, e-mail and post on freakin' Facebook."

At Harvard Square, the SUV's strobing red and blue lights bounce off street signs and are reflected in the windows of buildings and cars we pass. I remind him of Interpol, steering him there.

"Why were you called?" I want to know.

"The million-dollar question."

"And when was this?"

"Let me roll back the tape so you can appreciate the timing," Marino says. "First I get the call from Clay. I tell Lucy I gotta go and am heading downstairs—"

"You were actually with her in her lab when Investigator Barclay called you?" I ask, and Marino nods, explaining he'd just gotten there and they were getting started going over the 911 recording.

"Then my phone rings and it's Barclay. He says he's at a homicide scene in JFK Park on the riverbank."

"Did he actually use the word *homicide*?" I ask. "Because I wish he hadn't said that either."

"He said it looked like an attempted sexual assault, and that she was beaten to death."

"I don't know why you bothered to pick me up." Cops like Barclay can create dangerous problems. "It appears he's happy to do my job." I'm going to have to have a word with him before the night is over. "Why did I bother interrupting my dinner?"

"Yeah he pisses me off too," Marino says. "You got no idea. Talk about someone who doesn't look before he leaps. It never occurs to him that maybe he's not a damn expert at whatever it is."

"I hope he's not freely offering these same opinions to everyone he talks to," I add, "because this is how misinformation ends up all over the place. Let's get back to Interpol. Tell me about the phone call."

"Like I was saying, Clay asked me to meet him at the scene. Then he wanted to know if he should contact your office, and I said I would take care of it. By the time I'd walked out of Lucy's lab, taken the elevator down to the lower level and was getting in my car in the parking lot, my phone was ringing again," Marino tells the story loudly, over the noise of the engine.

"This time the call's from an unknown number. You know, when a call comes up with a row of zeros? Like when caller ID is blocked and it's not somebody in your contacts list?" he says. "So I answered, and it was Washington, D.C."

11

"It was Interpol," Marino states as if there can be no doubt about it.

I ask him how he could be so sure. "You said the number was blocked. So I'm not clear on how you knew who was calling," I add, and other drivers are moving out of our way.

"The person identified himself as an investigator from their Washington bureau, the NCB, and said he was trying to reach Investigator Peter Rocco Marino of the Cambridge Police Department."

Interpol's United States headquarters, the National Central Bureau (NCB), reports directly to the attorney general. And neither the NCB nor Interpol's global head-quarters in France would be interested in any U.S. case unless there's reason to suspect criminal activity that extends beyond our national borders. That thought brings me back to the cyclist with the British accent, and I hope she's not dead.

I envision her blue helmet with the unbuckled chin

strap, and I should have said something. I should have told her to fasten it.

"I asked the NCB guy what he was calling in reference to, and he said he was aware of the developing situation in the park on the waterfront," Marino explains.

"Those were his exact words? *The developing situation*?" Now I'm really baffled.

"I swear to God. And I'm thinking, What the hell? What situation could he know about? How could he know there's a body in the park by the water here in Cambridge?"

"I don't understand . . ." I start to say.

"I asked how he could be aware of any situation period around here," Marino talks over me. "What was his source? And he said that was classified."

"I don't understand," I repeat myself. "How is it possible that Interpol's call to you was in reference to Elisa Vandersteel, assuming that's who's dead?" It's completely illogical. "Was her name mentioned?"

"No, but he was talking about a sudden death. That was how he phrased it, *a sudden death that had international consequences,* which is why Interpol is involved," Marino says.

"Elisa Vandersteel would have international consequences," I reply, "since she's not American. Once again, that's assuming the driver's license is the dead woman's."

"It felt like that was the situation he was referencing. That he somehow knew about it."

"Tell me how it's possible? I've never heard of something like this happening," I reply. "The local media hasn't even caught wind of it yet. Is there something on the Internet I've not been told about? How could Interpol know about a death before you've been to the scene or called the medical examiner?"

"I asked Lucy if anything had been tweeted or whatever," he says. "I called her right after I hung up from talking to the Interpol investigator. Nothing's out there about the Vandersteel case that we know of. Assuming that's who she is. But you're right. It seems Interpol knew before either of us did, and I don't understand that either."

Marino's portable radio is charging upright in the console, and it hasn't escaped my notice that there's very little chatter. In fact it's so quiet I forget the radio is in the car until I notice it. I've heard nothing go over the air that might alert anyone about the dead body awaiting us at the park.

"But how would Interpol investigators or analysts know about a body found in a Cambridge park near the water in the past thirty-some-odd minutes?" I ask. "I'm sorry, something's off about this, Marino. And it's not the way the process works. Local law enforcement requests assistance because there might be an international interest—"

He interrupts, "I know how it's supposed to work. You think this is my first friggin' rodeo?"

"I don't believe I've ever heard of Interpol initiating contact about a homicide scarcely anyone knows about yet," I emphasize. "We don't know she's a homicide for that matter. We also haven't verified the victim's identity. We don't know a damn thing."

"All I can tell you is the investigator who called said he was from their counterterrorism division. He said he understood we have a situation," Marino uses that word again. "A death with international consequences, and I got the feeling he was thinking about terrorism, based on the words he used. I sure as hell wish I had a recording of what he said."

91

"And where did the information come from?" I'm going to keep pounding that drum. "Just because a British driver's license was found on a bike path? And how would he even know about that unless Barclay told him? This is absurd."

"When I asked him how the hell he could know about anything going on in Cambridge, and why he was calling me directly, he said they'd received e-mailed information that listed my name and number as the contact." Marino stares straight ahead, and he must be thinking the same thing I am, but he won't want to admit it.

"Interpol doesn't work that way." I'm not going to back down because this is something I know about, and Marino has been duped. "And they don't hire psychics with crystal balls who can predict cases before the rest of us know about them, last I heard." I instantly regret saying this because he'll take it as a slight directed at him, when it's not. "It's implausible if not impossible that they could know about a scene and a dead body we've not so much as looked at yet."

"Well I'm not the one who's pals with the secretary-general," Marino replies with a sarcastic snap. "Maybe you should call him up and ask him how the hell they found out so damn fast."

I've been to Interpol's headquarters in Lyon, France, numerous times, and am on friendly terms with the secretary-general Tom Perry, who's actually American, a Rhodes scholar, a former head of the National Institute of Justice, and a bona fide Renaissance man.

"If need be I will," I reply reasonably, ignoring Marino's sting, careful of my tone because I don't want to argue with him. "How was it left?" I ask.

"The investigator said the Washington headquarters, the

92

NCB, was contacted but didn't say by who. He said it was protected information, the same shit I use as an excuse all the time. So I didn't think much about it," Marino explains, but I can tell he's thinking about it now.

"This is sounding too much like the nine-one-one complaint," I reply, in hopes he'll make the same connections I am.

I'd rather he draw his own conclusion so he doesn't kill the messenger.

"Yeah, and the guy coughed."

"Who did?"

"The Interpol guy coughed several times and I remember wondering if he had a cold. And now that I'm thinking about it, the person who left the bogus nine-one-one coughed too."

Marino has a hard edge to his glumness, and his face is deep red.

"I'm beginning to think that whoever murdered Elisa Vandersteel has anonymously reported his own damn case to Interpol because he wants the entire damn planet to know about it," he then says above the noise of his car, and I can see his pulse pounding in his neck. "And God only knows who else has been contacted."

That may be Marino's biggest worry. But it's not mine.

The angrier he is the calmer I get.

"There had to be a source," I persist anyway, because I deal with international cases far more often than Marino does, and I know the routines and the protocols. "Did a police officer contact Interpol? In other words did another cop contact the NCB in Washington about the Cambridge case? Because that shouldn't be classified."

"Got no idea who the source was but somebody sure as hell told somebody something," he almost yells over the roar of his engine. "Hell no, Barclay didn't, though. He wouldn't without clearing it with me. He wouldn't even think of it."

"Interpol's very careful who it talks to. You have to be authenticated and verified." I gently lead him closer to what will most assuredly be an unpalatable truth.

"I don't think it was a phone call. It sounds like they got an e-mail," Marino says, and the ugliness he's about to face is going to enrage him.

I look at his profile inside the dark SUV, at the big dome of his bald head, his strong nose, and the hard set of his heavy mandible.

"I do know that e-mail is the quickest and simplest way to report something to them," he's saying. "The forms and everything are right there on the Internet. They've got it all on a website. It's easy but it's also going to be monitored and traceable."

"So we certainly would expect that the Washington office of Interpol, the NCB, would know if an e-mailed tip was bogus," I say pointedly. "In other words, the NCB should know if it weren't from a real member of the law enforcement community or someone else in an authorized position to report an incident or a threat." I know what I'm suspicious of, and Marino doesn't like the tack I'm taking.

"You sure as hell would think so," he says with a hint of defensiveness, which is what I expect because he should know what's coming.

He should have figured it out before I did, but it's an unpleasant truth. And those take longer. They're harder to swallow.

"And it also could be that Interpol hasn't been contacted by anyone legitimately," I suggest. "And that you weren't either," I add, and he acts as if he didn't hear me.

"You would think the investigator who called me could have helped out a little by saying they weren't sure the tip was credible, that maybe some whack-a-do is jerking everybody around." Now Marino sounds personally offended, and he continues to ignore what I just said. "But I took what I was told at face value."

"Are you absolutely certain it was an Interpol investigator who called you?" I begin to confront Marino with what I suspect, and he's silent.

To borrow his colorful and bewildering vernacular, this is the real piece of cake, the poison in the ink, the snake under the tent, and the elephant in the woodpile. I'm asking him who he was really talking to, because all the signs point at his having been played for a fool. Or at least that's exactly how it's going to feel to him.

"I'm wondering what made you believe it was Interpol on the phone besides what the person claimed?" I try that approach next, and I can feel Marino getting stubborn like concrete setting.

Then he says, "I guess the only way I'm going to know is if I try to call the asshole back."

He picks up his cell phone from his lap. He unlocks it and reluctantly hands it to me as if he's turning over evidence that will get him into a world of trouble.

"Open it to my notepad," Marino says with his unblinking eyes fixed on the road, "and you'll see the number. Just click on the app and you can see where I typed what he gave me."

"Why? So you could call him back and report what we're about to find?"

"Hell if I know. He just gave me a number and said to update him, that we'd touch base tomorrow," Marino says, and this is sounding only more like a taunt, a hoax, with every second that passes.

Throughout my career I've worked closely with Interpol. We've always enjoyed a close relationship because when it comes to death and violence the world is a small place. It gets smaller all the time, and it's increasingly common for me to deal with color-coded international notices about fugitives and people who have vanished or turn up dead and nameless in the United States.

I also deal with Americans who die abroad, and now and then a decedent turns out to be undercover law enforcement or a spy. I know how to dance the dance with the Department of Justice, the Pentagon, the CIA, the United Nations Security Council and various international police agencies and criminal tribunals. I can honestly say that what Marino is describing to me isn't at all the way the process works.

"Then you want me to call this?" I look at what he typed in an electronic note, a phone number with a Washington, D.C., area code.

"Why not?" he says, and he's like a pressure cooker about to blow.

"I don't want to talk to whoever it is since it's your phone and not mine." I look at the phone in my hand, at the number displayed on an electronic message pad.

"Quit thinking like a damn lawyer. Just call it. May as well go ahead, and both of us can listen to it on speaker-phone. Let's see if the investigator answers."

"You never did tell me his name. Who will you ask for?"

"John Dow. Dow as in Dow Jones." Marino's jaw muscles clench.

"Or as in John Doe?"

"I'm pretty sure he pronounced it Dow." The redness in his face is spreading down his neck.

I click on the number and am given the option to CALL, which I select, and I wait for it to connect. And it does, ringing loudly, wirelessly through intercom speakers in the SUV.

"Thank you for calling the Hay-Adams. This is Crystal, how may I assist you?" a female voice answers.

"Hello?" Marino says with a blank expression that turns into a murderous scowl. "This is the Hay-Adams? The hotel?" He turns his baffled furious face to me and silently mouths, *What the fuck?*

"This is the Hay-Adams in Washington, D.C. How may I assist you, sir?"

"Would you mind reading back your number to make sure it's what I was given?" Marino says, his glaring eyes on the road.

"Were you trying to contact the Hay-Adams Hotel, sir?"

"It would be helpful if you'd tell me your number. I think I might have dialed the wrong place," Marino says, and after a pause the woman recites the same number that's in the electronic note I looked at.

"Thanks. My mistake." Marino ends the call. "Goddamn son of a bitch!" He slams his meaty fist on the steering wheel.

What he wrote down is the general number for the hotel. It's what was given to him by someone who identified himself as a counterterrorism investigator for Interpol. This is worse than a typo or even a deliberate and mocking misdirect. It's personal, and not just directed at Marino. It may not be directed at him, period, but now's not the moment to tell him that. The Hay-Adams means nothing to him and I doubt he's ever stayed there.

But the hotel is close to the Capitol, the White House, and convenient to FBI headquarters, and also its academy and behavioral analysis unit in northern Virginia. The Hay-Adams is our first choice when Benton and I are in Washington, D.C., together, and we were there several weeks ago for business and pleasure. We visited museums, and Benton had meetings in Quantico while I conferred with General Briggs about our space shuttle presentation at the Kennedy School.

I think back to anything else that stands out about the trip. But nothing extraordinary occurred. I had work and so did Benton. We were in and out of offices and around a number of different people. Then the last night we were there we had dinner with Briggs and his wife at the Palm with its cartoon-covered walls.

We sat in a booth near a host of iconic characters. Nixon, Spider-Man, Kissinger, and Dennis the Menace, I recall.

12

Sirens scream as a Cambridge patrol car squeals a tight left off Winthrop and falls in behind us. We're a light show flashing along John F. Kennedy Street, and other drivers are slowing down and moving out of the way.

"Shit, shit, shit. Damn son of a bitch," Marino continues cussing a blue storm, to borrow another of his uniquely crafted clichés.

He's glancing in his mirrors as I sit back in my seat, hoping we don't crash. We're not going as fast as it seems but it's nerve-racking, and Marino's in a treacherous mood because of the phone call to the Hay-Adams Hotel. He rarely treats a death scene as an emergency. Usually lights and sirens aren't needed. Usually it's too late for us to prevent or save much, but he's impatient, aggressive, in a blind fury.

"Jesus Christ! Who the hell was that? Who the hell was I just on the phone with?"

He's been going on and on since he ended the call. There's nothing I can say, and I know when it's best to mostly listen. Marino needs to vent, then he'll be okay. But he won't forgive and forget. He never does. Whoever makes a fool of Pete Marino will have hell to pay. It may take years. In some instances it's taken decades.

"I can't believe it. I freakin' can't believe it! And what the crap does Roberts think he's doing?" Marino glares into the rearview mirror at the marked unit flashing and wailing behind us. "Did you hear me ask for his assistance? Did you hear me request a backup or yell *Mayday*?"

He glances angrily at me, and he's almost shouting. I'm silent as I sit snugly strapped in my seat, watching the lights pulsing in my side mirror, waiting for him to calm down.

"No, I didn't think so," he loudly answers his own questions. "This is what's called playing cops and robbers. The idiot Roberts is all dressed up with no place to go because I don't need his damn help."

Marino glares in the mirror every other second, his jaw muscle doing its rapid-fire flexing again. He snatches his portable radio out of the charger.

"Unit thirty-three," he holds the radio close to his lips, practically spitting he's so pissed.

"Thirty-three."

"Ask one-sixty-four to call me." He's instantly polite with a touch of sweetness as he talks to the dispatcher he refers to as Rosie.

"Roger, thirty-three," she says, and her tone is different with him too, and it needles me a little.

Marino loves women but he's never known what to do with them besides the obvious courting, badgering, acting out, being led by the nose and in general being controlled by his *lesser member*, as Lucy not so delicately puts it. No relationship he's had has ever lasted, not with his former wife Doris, who in my opinion he's never gotten over. He's also fallen out with me more than once, badly, almost irreparably.

I think of him flirting with my sister in Miami. Benton swore the two of them started something when we were there earlier in the summer, and I wonder how I could have missed the cues. I watch him return the radio to the charger as Rosie calls unit 164 and passes on the message.

I check my phone for any further updates about when my sister is set to land at Logan. I'm about to send Lucy a message about my inability to show up at the airport in light of what's just happened, but I'm distracted again when Marino's cell phone rings through the SUV's intercom.

"What can I do you for? What's up?" A male voice fills the car, and Officer Roberts sounds hyper and too cheerful.

"What's up is you." Marino isn't nice about it. "I see you bird-dogging me and need you to peel off and get the hell away." He sounds vicious.

"You're one to talk, all lit up like the Fourth of July. You know what they say. Monkey see, monkey do—" Unit 164 fires back as if he's having a grand time, and Marino interrupts because now he's really angry.

"Turn your fucking lights and fucking siren off, Roberts. If I need a meat puppet you'll be my first damn call," Marino snaps.

If he had a handset and could hang up with a slam, I'm sure he would. But he can't. He presses a button on the steering wheel to end his tirade.

"I'm not sure what he was responding to," I puzzle. "I've not heard anything on the radio that might hint we have a possible homicide in the park."

"He knows something big is going on there. He may

101

not know what but everybody out here knows something's up. The radio silence is deliberate, and then he sees us go by, and that's his excuse to fall in behind me," Marino growls.

I remind him that it might not have been the best idea to turn on his own lights and siren. Certainly it's attracting attention.

"Well that doesn't mean you follow me like a damn parade. It's not a damn party or a spectator sport," Marino talks at the top of his voice. "Everybody wants to be a damn detective until they have to do paperwork, deal with lawyers, get sued, get called out at all hours and all the other bullshit we put up with."

I can see the patrol car in the side mirror, dropping back, receding into the distance. The red and blue strobes have gone dark, the siren ended in a whimper. Unit 164 slows and turns left on South Street as we flash, pulse, yelp and wail through a well-lighted stretch of restaurants, coffee shops, taverns and breweries.

"Maybe it really was Interpol," Marino says, and it's a good thing I'm accustomed to his non sequiturs. "Maybe I wrote down the number wrong." He picks up where he left off about the bogus phone call from a bogus investigator. "Maybe that's all it is."

"I seriously doubt it. I'm sorry to say but I think the call you got is exactly what it appears to be, Marino, and I'm sure it's upsetting." I don't add that it might be somewhat the way I felt when Benton played the 911 recording for me that Marino refused to share.

I know all too well what it's like to be falsely accused, excluded, belittled, treated suspiciously or simply tormented and harassed. But when Marino is upset, he doesn't

102

necessarily compare notes with others, including me. There are no other notes. Only his.

"Wait till I get my hands on whoever it is," and he's enraged all over again. "How the hell did this person come up with my name and get my cell number? Where did he get the information? How did he know to call me about anything?"

"I don't know." I'm saying that a lot.

"Well it's the biggest and most important thing we need to find out. Who gave the info to this asswipe joker?"

"It's probably not the biggest or most important thing we need to find out at the moment." I stare at him, and I hate that someone has targeted him like this.

I know how Marino gets. He can't endure being boondoggled. He can't tolerate being made to feel as unimportant and powerless as he did while he was growing up on the wrong side of the tracks in New Jersey.

"I recommend you put this on a shelf for now," I tell him. "We'll worry about Interpol later. At your earliest convenience I suggest you have Lucy take a look at your phone to see if she can trace the unknown call that supposedly was from the NCB's counterterrorism division."

"Right," he says tersely, and he's furious with himself.

Marino was tricked, and it will be unfortunate if other cops find out about it.

I think of Roberts, for example, who Marino just emasculated. The way he goes after his comrades will come back to him a hundredfold if they discover he fell prey to a hoax of the worst order. They'll be merciless, but it's not a joke. It's no laughing matter. Marino might have been talking to the same anonymous person who, it would seem, used voice-altering software to complain about me in a 911 call today.

Marino could have been talking to Tailend Charlie, for all we know. Or if Elisa Vandersteel is the dead woman and she's a homicide, then Marino might have been talking to her killer. There's no telling who Marino was on the phone with but I'm convinced it wasn't Interpol. I'm no-nonsense as I tell him he really must let it go. With what we have ahead of us there's no room to spare for personal outrage or embarrassment.

"Let's just do this." I raise my voice above the noise of our roaring through Cambridge in a juggernaut of brilliant strobes and urgent tones. "It's been a hell of a day but we've been through much worse. How many years has it been? And here we are. We're still here, and we'll figure it out. We always do."

"That's the damn truth," he says, and I feel him glumly settle down a little, getting steadier. "I just can't believe it happened."

"I know. But it could happen to anyone."

"Even you?" He glances at me, and I nod. "Bullshit," he says.

"Anyone at all," I reassure him, but it's not entirely honest.

I seriously doubt I would have fallen for the same ruse the same way Marino did or at all. I would have asked more questions. I would have been suspicious instantly if I'd gotten such a call on my personal cell phone from a so-called NCB investigator. I would have recognized the corruption of a process I know better than Marino does.

"Well I feel stupid as shit," he confesses, and suddenly I feel stupid too but for a very different reason.

I suddenly remember Dorothy again. I'm startled and dismayed as I envision the disapproval, the *I told you so* look in her eyes and the gleam of satisfaction. She loves it when I screw up, and by the time I'd gotten into Marino's SUV at the Faculty Club my attention had been diverted from my sister and her last-minute plan of an unscheduled visit.

She's on her way here even as Marino and I are headed to a death scene, and I think of his flirting with the dispatcher Rosie. His annoying womanizing enters my mind. I resist looking at him as I'm unhappily reminded of what Benton accused, and it's more disturbing when I think of Marino's repeated offers to pick up Dorothy at Logan tonight.

Last I heard she's supposed to arrive from Fort Lauderdale around nine thirty but she's going to be late, according to Lucy. It's already almost eight thirty, and I have no doubt my sister is expecting Benton and me to be waiting for her with bells on no matter when she lands.

That's not going to happen, and Marino can't be there either, not that I'd encourage it. Next it occurs to me as an additional blow that I left my shopping bag in the cloakroom at the Faculty Club. I won't have gifts for the chronically dissatisfied Dorothy. Dammit. That figures, and the fact is I can't possibly do anything for her right now. I can't pay attention to her or make the slightest gesture of welcome. I've failed, and that's exactly how she'll look at it.

She'll view it negatively and as an unfairness directed at her personally. It won't occur to her that she wasn't quite as inconvenienced as the person who's dead. Dorothy's not even as inconvenienced as I am, but that won't enter her head. Once again I'm the busy and inaccessible Big Sis, and if she reaches out and makes herself vulnerable, this is what happens. I can hear her now. I could script it.

I send a text to Lucy and Janet: *Unable to make it to airport.*

Possibly you could get Dorothy? Or she could Uber? Very sorry.

Almost instantly Janet answers: *No problem. We'll take care of Lucy's mom. Maybe stop by later? We'd love to see you.*

It always jolts me when Dorothy is referred to as Lucy's "mom." It never sounds right, and it's at moments like this when I'm reminded of how bonded I am to a niece I've raised like a daughter. I admit I might be a little possessive, just the tiniest bit territorial and jealous.

13

The bulky shapes of centuries-old trees and tall dense hedges are etched against the night as we enter the John F. Kennedy Park.

Marino has slowed the SUV to a crawl. He's turned the emergency lights and siren off. I count four patrol cars and one unmarked SUV parked bumper-to-bumper barely off the pavement. Deeper in it's too dark to make out much, little more than impressions of something there. Maybe a distant mountain range. Maybe thick woods in murky shades of dark muddy colors.

If I didn't already know what was around me, I couldn't tell from what I can see. The darkness transforms benches, paths, trash cans, the bend in the river into a scene that could be almost anywhere. But I would know Boston across the water. Instantly I would recognize the Hancock skyscraper topped by its lance-like antenna, and the Prudential Tower. I couldn't miss the lit-up Citgo sign, also known as the *C-it-Go* sign because so many Red Sox home runs have sailed over it.

We can drive but only so far, as there are no roads through the park, which is wide where we are but in other parts very narrow. Motorized traffic is prohibited inside the acres of well-kept grass, shrubs and hardwood trees that stretch between the Charles River and Memorial Drive. I've been here many times. It's a favorite hike from our house near the northeastern edge of the Harvard campus.

If Benton and I keep up a good pace we can make the round trip on foot in roughly an hour. That's if we take the most direct route, and we don't always. Now and then we wander from one newsstand and outdoor café or market to another, making our leisurely way to the water, especially when the weather is as sublime as it can be in the spring and fall. On Sundays when it's warm and not raining we love to drink Peet's coffee and read armloads of newspapers on a bench by the Charles.

In the winter we might hike or snowshoe here and sit bundled up and close to each other, sharing a thermos of steaming-hot cider. All of this is going on in my mind as an emotional subroutine that I don't focus on but can't block. I feel the distant echo of nostalgia, of loss, as I'm reminded of how rare it is that Benton and I have had much time to ourselves for leisure—for doing nothing, whatever that means.

We treasure conversations and activities that are unencumbered by broken laws and tragedies. We treat it as a special occasion if no one is committing violent acts or has died during the hours or a weekend when Benton and I are paying attention to each other. This is why our regular outings at the Faculty Club are important and cherished. It's why having favorite secret places like hotels, the ocean, the river, and scenic areas where we hike is necessary to good relationships and our good health.

The park is a popular place to get away, to have a picnic, to sunbathe, read, study or play a pickup Frisbee game. Only cyclists and people on foot are allowed but that doesn't stop Marino from sacrilegiously bumping his big police vehicle over grass and a narrow unpaved path. He halts between a big maple tree and a tall iron lamp that glows wanly in the near pitch-blackness, the SUV nose-in toward the Charles River. The headlights illuminate the red-roofed brick boathouse, and to the left of it the bridge I drove past during my fateful ride with Bryce what now seems days ago.

I watch a lighted necklace of cars moving to and fro overhead, their lights diamond white and blood red. And below, the water is sluggish, greenish black and rippled. I don't see any boaters out. Most of them will have gone in at sunset. On the opposite shore, Boston's Back Bay is softly illuminated by the glowing windows of old brownstones and row houses. In the distance, the downtown skyline sparkles, and the night sky is a lighter shade of black, a deep charcoal over the harbor and the ocean, which I can't see from here.

Marino turns off the engine, and we open our doors. No interior lights blink on because he's always kept those switches off for as long as I've known him. It makes no difference what he's driving. He doesn't want to be an easy target, a deer in the headlights as he puts it, and we never have been in all of the miles I've ridden with him. Most vehicle-related mishaps when we're together occur because I can't see where I'm stepping, what I'm sitting on or exposed to when I'm in and out of anything he pilots.

But to give him credit, he's much more meticulous about his cars, trucks and motorcycles than he ever was when we first started working together. I'll never forget his tricked-out Crown Vics with their monster engines, and their long looping antennas bobbing like fishing poles. The ashtrays overflowed, the windows and mirrors at times were opaque from smoke. There were fast-food bags and chicken boxes everywhere, and usually I was sitting on salt that looked like sand everywhere. If you didn't know what it was you might think Marino lived near a beach.

Overall he's become more highly evolved. He still smokes but nowhere near as much, and when he does the great outdoors is his ashtray. He wouldn't think of dirtying or stinking up his car, not that this is anything to brag about. When he eats while on the road he doesn't rip into the packets of salt and ketchup the way he used to, and he's much better about cleaning up. Nonetheless I prefer to see what I'm climbing into when he rides me around after dark.

I've earned my share of purple hearts from grease and various condiment stains on pants and skirts. I've banged my lower extremities against riot guns stored between or under seats, and slipped on running boards that are slick with Armor All. I've snagged my hose on a deer antler and hooked my thumb on a fishing lure in the glove box, which also is never lighted. Once we bumped over a bad pothole, and a *Playboy* centerfold fell out of the visor and into my lap. It was several editions old. Marino had forgotten it was there, I guess.

I lower my pumps to the dirt path, standing up, and the heat slams into me like a wall. It's not as bad as it was when I walked out of the Faculty Club but that doesn't mean it's much better than tolerable. It doesn't mean it's safe for long exposures without risking hyperthermia, and I'm assuming we'll be working the scene for hours.

When the truck is here it can serve as a staging area where we can duck into the air-conditioning at intervals. We'll have plenty of water, snacks, and urine-collection devices, UCDs—more popularly known as *piddle packs*.

"We've got to figure out exactly how we're going to do this," Marino says, and we shut our doors.

The quiet heat is broken by the rumble of traffic on the street behind us and on the bridge. I hear little else. Maybe a plane passing overhead. Nothing is stirring, the heated air inescapable.

"A high recon," I reply simply as I shoulder my messenger bag. "Then a low one where we move in and collect evidence."

"You going to leave the body out here even longer than it's already been?"

"Longer than what? We don't know how long it's been. We know when the police got the call, which I'd estimate was what? Thirty or forty minutes ago? I'll factor all of this in, and the numbers and data will be as exact as anything can be. It's business as usual in other words, and will be fine."

"So we just leave her as is." He pushes a button on his key fob and pops the tailgate.

"Why are you worrying so much?"

"Because I wish we could get the body out of here. That would solve most of our problems, Doc."

"And at the same time create bigger ones. I don't want to wait any longer than necessary but I don't have much choice if I want to see what I'm doing."

"It's just too bad this had to happen with Dorothy flying

in," he says, and that may be the very last thing I want to talk about right now.

"Plus I have nothing with me, no protective clothing, nothing," I pick up on what I was saying before he rudely brought up my sister. "I came straight from a dinner where I didn't have my car or anything else. Under normal circumstances, I wouldn't have left for the scene yet."

We've walked around to the back of the SUV, and I don't rub it in that Marino continues to enjoy a special status and special treatment. Had he taken the required steps that other detectives don't typically deviate from, he would have called the CFC investigative unit he used to head.

He would have discussed the case with whoever answered. After routine questions were asked and an electronic report was created, one of my medical examiners on call would have been contacted. Most likely that doctor would have responded but only after a truck and all needed supplies and personnel were deployed first.

If I ended up at the scene at all, it wouldn't be now. It might not be for another hour at least. I probably could have finished my dinner with Benton first, and if I'd had enough wine I wouldn't have shown up at all. I wasn't supposed to be working tonight. I was to be with my husband and go pick up my sister. But Marino bypassed all of the usual protocols and checks and balances just as he always does.

I won't tell him that I don't really mind. When he calls I know it's serious. We have a routine that's familiar and comfortably rutted like an old wagon trail. I watch him lift open the tailgate, and of course no light goes on. I may as well be staring into a cave.

*   *   *

"I've got gloves, coveralls," he says halfheartedly because he knows I can't wear anything that might fit him. "And the usual stuff, except no thermometer. I should just toss one in so you have it if you need it. I keep meaning to get around to it."

"We're going to have to wait," I say it again, and I have no doubt he won't be the only one who's about to get impatient.

Everyone will be champing at the bit to collect whatever forensic treasures might be out here. Every cop—and Marino most of all—will want to know what happened to the victim. I can't begin to answer that until I examine her, and I can't do that until I deem it safe. Right now it's not.

Turning on the lights at this exposed location would be the same as doing it inside a glass house. Anyone around us will have a ringside seat, and as I spell this out, Marino agrees reluctantly.

"We'll start with photographs. We'll get the lay of the land," I say as we continue to discuss what makes the most sense. "I'm sure the truck will be here any minute."

"But it will be another good twenty or thirty minutes after that with all the setting up to be done." Marino is halfway inside the back of his SUV, using his phone flashlight to illuminate the precisely arranged and packed crime-scene accoutrements and equipment. "And it's going to be hard as hell to see in the meantime." His voice is muffled inside as he roots around. "And my damn night vision's not what it used to be either. It's like everything turns to shit the minute you hit forty."

I stare through the velvety darkness at the river flowing sluggishly like liquid dark glass. Marino hasn't seen forty in a while, and when he gets like this there's not much I can say. But I don't blame him. I would be licking my wounds too if I'd just been duped the way he was.

"Getting old sucks," he gripes, and I know when he's feeling belittled and obsessive. "I hate it. I freakin' hate it," he adds, and the Interpol impostor has done a number on him.

"You're not old, Marino." I've heard enough, and we have a lot to take care of. "You're in great shape and weren't born yesterday. You're experienced. So am I, and we know exactly what to do out here. We've worked far more difficult scenes than this. Forget about the phone call for now. Put it out of your mind. I promise we'll get to the bottom of it. But that's not what should be preoccupying you at the moment."

He continues digging around inside his truck, and I begin my scan as if I'm a lighthouse sweeping everything around me, looking for what needs to be protected or ignored. Since we don't know what happened and exactly where, we'll start well outside the perimeter the police will have secured.

I can't see any yellow tape from where we're parked, but I have a pretty good idea it begins at the clearing where a dead body and a bicycle await us. But if this is a case of violence involving the perpetrator and victim physically encountering each other, then the clearing isn't where the scene begins. It can't be. And Marino is thinking the same thing.

"Whoever did it had to get in and out of here somehow," he says. "Unless it's a damn elf that lives in a tree."

"Assuming Investigator Barclay's description of the body has even a semblance of truth?" I reply. "If she really were

114

assaulted and beaten? Then yes, her assailant or someone involved had to access the park. Whether she was killed here or dumped, the person was in and out, and we can't assume he didn't take the same route we're about to. I'm not saying it's a *he*."

"Yeah I know." Marino hands me a box of extra-large nitrile gloves that he'll use and I won't. "But if it was a sexual assault or an attempt, we're probably talking about a male. I'm already looking for tire tracks, especially gouges and flattened areas of grass. So far I'm not seeing it, but he could have entered the park a number of different ways."

"A lot of streets dead-end here and along the river," I point out. "And there's no wall obviously, so he could have been parked in a variety of nearby locations. But from there how did he get the body in here?"

"Carried it." Marino is shoving heavy cases of equipment around in the back.

"I doubt it."

"I didn't say that's what I think. I'm just saying it's possible."

"How would that explain her bicycle being near her body?" I ask.

"Exactly, because I think we already know she wasn't dumped." He tears open a cardboard box. "She was murdered right where she was found." He hands me one folded pair of disposable coveralls, still in the cellophane package, size double-XL.

"Let's be reminded that we don't know that she was murdered." I watch him and I constantly look around. "We have no idea why she's dead."

Lights reflected in the water's slow current flicker like

a vast school of silvery fish, and on the other side, Boston is a glittering empire of centuries-old stone and brick, and modern high-rises. But almost no ambient light dispels the darkness immediately around us, and I dig into my messenger bag for the small tactical flashlight I always carry. I force the box of gloves, the coveralls to fit inside so my hands are free.

"We have to establish the perimeter," Marino says. "We've got to start somewhere but as dark as it is? We're pretty much guessing."

"That's why we start here. We'll look where we're going and get an overview," I reply, and I deeply regret what I'm wearing.

I might have to burn this suit when I finally scrape it off me. I don't enjoy disposable clothing that swathes me in bright white Tyvek rather much like a building under construction. But right about now I find myself coveting, almost lusting for, a loose-fitting pair of coveralls and light-weight ankle boots.

"We can mark anything we see with cones or flags and then come back a second time once we have the luxury of time, privacy, and appropriate visibility," I continue the discussion with Marino. "I'm assuming you talked about barriers with Rusty or Harold? I know we have the basics in our big trucks, but there's nothing basic about this situation. The scene is wide open from virtually every angle and perspective once we turn on the lights."

"I told Harold we're going to need more than the usual walls that we prop up with a few sandbags to make sure people can't see shit from street level." Marino slides a big scene case to the lip of the open tailgate. "But for something like this, you got that right. We're going to need a tent because you got all kinds of people looking down at us from buildings and the bridge."

I glance up at the long string of headlights moving above us, crossing the river in both directions. I watch aircraft lit up like small planets, clustered around Logan Airport, and I think of Dorothy again. Marino digs in a box of evidence-marking cones in bright primary colors, each of them numbered. He stacks a dozen of them, and it always reminds me of the Cap the Hat board game that my father found at a yard sale in our Miami neighborhood when I was a little kid.

"I said we want a roof," Marino tells me what he told Harold. "I said we're going to need the full monty out here."

14

We follow the same dirt footpath we just drove over, gradually veering off it and into the grass. Dry and several inches deep, it whispers against my shoes and tickles my bare ankles as we watch where we step, moving deeper into the wooded park, toward the hard-packed sandy fitness path that winds through the middle of it.

The tall iron lamps are few and far between. They would offer little more than vague yellowish smudges as you sit on a bench or take a stroll at night. It's very dark in here, and I have my small tactical light while Marino has his phone flashlight pointed out and slightly down.

In his other hand he tugs the heavy-duty black plastic scene case that's big enough for a small body. Its wheels make a quiet gritty crunch as he rolls it along, leading the way, both of us careful not to trample evidence or stumble. So far we haven't seen anything that might make us stop and plant a small colorful cone.

The parched grass is a carpet of brownish-green sharp little blades in the glare of our lights, and my scuffed tan leather shoes are vivid. I can hear fragments of conversation up ahead, what sounds like children talking in excited quiet voices. It's not a happy excitement but a different brand of cortisol-fueled enthusiasm that I associate with fear, with shock. But there's something else I'm picking up. The childish sounds don't strike me as normal.

They bring to mind haunted places with otherworldly conversations that drift on the air in creepy tales. Here, then gone, the laughter of dead children frolicking in the woods, of dead children picking berries and playing hide-and-seek or tag.

The peculiar disembodied voices in the distance ahead remind me of horror movies, and I feel a chill touch the back of my neck as the park spreads out darkly, peacefully, on either side of the fitness path where someone has died. Someone I may have met twice earlier today, and I continue to hope I'm mistaken.

We approach a clump of trees with full canopies that offers a perfect place for a predator to lie in wait. Marino points this out to me as we walk deeper inside shadows where the dead and the living are gathered, waiting for us. It feels uncanny and weird as if we're headed to a surprise party where everyone crouches in the dark until the guest of honor appears and the lights switch on.

I remember the early years when we really didn't have to worry about cameras everywhere and huge indiscretions trending on the Internet before I can finish an autopsy or get lab results. In the old days every Tom, Dick and Harry weren't filming with cell phones. By the time photo journalists showed up with telescopic lenses, the body was either gone, safely zipped up in a pouch, or detectives would be gathered around holding up sheets or their coats to protect a victim's privacy. Life and death are much more complicated now.

"I don't think this was random," Marino is saying. "Someone knew her patterns."

"Do we know if she had patterns?" It's my way of cautioning him again about jumping to conclusions, but it's a waste of breath.

"Everybody has patterns," he says, and I listen as I wait for Rusty and Harold to rumble up in our diesel mobile command center.

I'm wondering where they're going to park it and what commotion it's going to generate in the very lap of Eliot House. Looming over the park is one of the biggest housing complexes on the campus with its seven brick buildings and numerous courtyards that remind me of Oxford and Cambridge or the palace of Versailles. I imagine students peering out their windows and venturing outside.

The truck will be spotted immediately, and if people zoom in or get closer they'll see OFFICE OF THE CHIEF MEDICAL EXAMINER and the CFC crest and Massachusetts state seal on the doors. I expect that any minute the Harvard campus will begin waking up to the stunningly sad realization that someone has been killed virtually under its proverbial nose. The second we turn on the lights we're going to need more uniforms for crowd control.

"Because there's nothing to stop people from ducking under the tape," I say to Marino as we inch our way through the woods. "There's nothing to stop traffic on the bridge from detouring so people can drive through the park to rubberneck. This could become a major fiasco pretty fast."

"I'll bring in more units when we're ready," he says, and I begin to make out the scene materializing several hundred feet ahead. "If I make the request now? A squadron of cars roll in and only draw more attention. The minute the tent's up, I'll request backups, as many as it takes."

I count the silhouettes of the six battery-powered LED spotlights that have been set up on tripods. They're perched about like tall praying mantises, quiet and dark as if sleeping.

I see the shapes of uniformed cops milling around, talking in the hushed way people do when it's dark. The sound of childish voices is an indistinct and perplexing staccato in the impenetrable background. I can't determine the source but it's eerie, as if the dark wooded area is haunted by agitated sprites.

Marino and I duck under the yellow perimeter tape, which is where I thought it would be. We enter a clearing in the trees where the body is half on the path, and half on the grass. I can make out the paleness of her bare arms and legs, and the whiteness of her sports bra and light color of her shorts. She's on her back with her legs straight but splayed, her arms up and spread as if she's been positioned in an X.

What I see sends a mixed message of mockery, of sexual degradation—and also nothing like that. At first glance it seems she's been displayed to shock whoever discovers her, but it's unusual that her shorts and bra are still on. Typically when a body is lewdly, hatefully displayed it's nude. Often other contemptuous touches are inserted and added to further disgrace and disfigure, and I'm not seeing anything like that yet.

But I've also learned the hard way to be overly conservative about making assumptions based on previous cases I've worked. A detail in one death may mean something else entirely in another. As we get closer I make out that the bicycle is on its side in the middle of the unpaved gritty path. I recognize the tall broad-shouldered Cambridge investigator Tom Barclay off to one side, near the trees, about fifty feet from the body. The spritelike voices I've been hearing belong to the two girls he's with, and they look too young to be out alone at this hour. But it's hard to tell.

They could be ten or twelve or maybe slightly older, and they're identical twins, one in pink, the other in yellow. Restless like two plump little birds, they turn their heads in synchrony, their eyes darting about, and it's obvious there's something not quite right about them. As we approach I can see that Barclay is shining a light on whatever he's holding. He's asking a question I can't quite hear.

"I might have," the girl dressed in pink drawls loudly in the voice of one who doesn't hear very well as she peers at what Barclay is showing the two of them on his phone, and Marino and I get closer.

"I don't know. Usually there's lots of people and I stay out of the way of bikes," the girl in yellow says slowly in the same blunted tone, and no matter what I was told, I can't quite believe what I'm seeing in the uneven illumination, the chiaroscuro created by our flashlights.

During one of our badly connected phone conversations as Marino was on his way to pick me up, he mentioned twins. I didn't give it much thought but to stand before them especially under the circumstances is extremely disconcerting. I find myself literally doing a double take as I look from one to the other, both of them dark-haired with identical unflattering helmetlike cuts.

The matching unstylish glasses they have on remind me

of yearbook pranks, of inking nerdy black frames on the face of a rival's photograph. The girls are built the same, under five feet tall and heavy. They wear striped T-shirts, shorts and sandals that fortunately for me don't match. If the twins weren't wearing different colored clothing I'm not sure I could tell them apart.

"Wait here, okay? You know what to do, don't you? You stay right here and don't go anywhere. Stay. And I'll be back." Barclay talks to the girls as if they're a lower order of a pet such as a rabbit or a lizard.

He strides toward us, and I check my phone to see if there's any word from Rusty and Harold.

I hear the truck as I'm about to call, and I press END.

The rumble of the diesel engine is unmistakable, and I look back in the direction of John F. Kennedy Street. I can see headlights cutting through the park as a white CFC truck that's bigger than an ambulance bumps off the pavement and creeps under trees. The low-hanging branches scrape the boxy metal roof, making a terrible screeching sound that has the effect of nails on a chalkboard.

"Good. Maybe we can get going here so we can figure out who we need to be notifying and talking to," Barclay says too authoritatively as he reaches Marino and me. "The sooner we can process the scene and get the body to the morgue, the better," he adds as Marino ignores him.

My eyes have adjusted to the contrasting shades of light and shadow, and I can better make out the twins some distance from us where Barclay was a moment ago. A female uniformed officer is with them now, asking if they need water or food. She wants to know if they'd like to wait in an air-conditioned patrol car. She says it as if they've been asked this before, and they shake their heads no. I have a pretty good idea what will happen next.

In a while she's going to transport them to the department and place them in a daisy room, as police call a comfortable nonthreatening setting they use for interviews with children. A counselor will be in to talk to and evaluate the girls, but the female officer isn't going to mention that out here in the middle of the park.

She's not going to explain that the twins will be treated the same way abused children are, and I can't help but feel judgmental. It's not appropriate for me to have personal opinions about cases I work, but it's inevitable some things are going to hit me harder than others. I'm not good with bad parents, bad caretakers and bad pet owners.

The twin sisters are young and impaired, and what sort of person would allow them to be out and about unchaperoned, especially after dark? Is anybody wondering why they aren't home and where they are?

"We can turn on the lights whenever you're ready," Barclay tells us rather than asks.

"The problem, Clay, is the minute we do it's like we've lit up a baseball field," Marino answers in an artificial avuncular tone, as if the young investigator is dim-witted and useless but a nice enough boy. "And if you build it, they'll sure as hell come. So nope, Clay." Marino says the name every chance he gets. "Not yet, right Doc?" He looks at me.

"Flashlights only for now," I agree, and the diesel sound gets louder, then stops as the engine is cut. "It's going to be difficult enough when people start noticing our mobile command center parked out here in addition to all the police cars." I look at the twins watching us with owl eyes.

124

"It's pretty obvious there's something going on, and I don't want to draw attention until we can set up a barrier."

I explain that right now the body is exposed to anyone who happens by or trains a telescopic lens on it. I can't turn the lights on, and I can't work without them, and it's a familiar catch-22. I wouldn't think of examining the body in situ without lighting if I'm given the choice, and I can't cover her with a sheet before I examine her or I run the risk of disturbing or displacing evidence. So for the moment we're stuck in the dark with only flashlights, and my attention wanders back to the twins again. I can't stop looking at them.

I'm keenly aware of their disproportionately small heads, their thin upper lips and flat midfaces. They probably won't get much taller, will have an ongoing struggle with their weight, and their small eyes are spaced far apart like a nonpredatory animal, a horse or a giraffe. The thick glasses, hearing aids, the silver braces on their teeth and everything else indicate a catastrophic failure that likely happened in utero.

Possibly it was due to what the unborn twins were exposed to, and if what I suspect is correct, it's unspeakably tragic. It's careless and cruel. Fetal alcohol syndrome is preventable. Just don't drink during pregnancy, and I wonder if the two girls are in special classes in school. I worry how functional they are, and what obstacles we face in using them as witnesses in this case.

I wonder how much I can rely on what they tell me now about how they happened upon the body and what they might have tampered with. Are they cogent? Are they truthful? And what kind of parents or guardians would allow them to wander about at night or at all?

I feel anger stir like an ember glowing hotly when it's fanned. Then Barclay is next to Marino and me, showing us the photograph on his phone of Elisa Vandersteel's driver's license.

"That's what I found on the path," Barclay says proudly, as if he discovered the smoking gun. "Obviously, I didn't pick it up. I thought I'd wait until you got here." He directs this to Marino as I look at the photograph on the phone display.

Elisa Ann Vandersteel. DOB: 12–04–1998. London, and the post code is the exclusive area of Mayfair, on South Audley Street near the Dorchester Hotel and the American embassy. The photograph could be the woman I encountered twice earlier today, but I'm not certain.

I'm not going to say anything to Marino or anybody else until I have more information. Any sightings of the victim are important in determining when she died, and I'm mindful of being cautious about what I pass along without verification. Not that driver's-license portraits are very good in general, but in this one Elisa Vandersteel is heavier than the cyclist I met. The face in the picture is broader, and the brown hair is short, whereas the young woman in Converse sneakers was lean and had a ponytail. But we don't know how old the photograph is. She might look very different now.

"Anything else?" I ask. "Any other personal effects? A lot of cyclists have bike packs or saddlebags for their wallets, keys and other belongings."

I don't add that I don't remember seeing something like that when I encountered the cyclist on Quincy Street. But Barclay says he didn't see a bag of any sort attached to the bicycle or nearby.

126

"That doesn't mean there wasn't one," he adds. "It might have been stolen by whoever did this."

"And we don't know if this is a homicide." I'm just going to keep saying it. "We don't know anything yet." I return his phone to him.

"How many people have you had to chase off since you got here?" Marino asks him what's gone on since the call was broadcast over radio.

"A handful have wandered in or tried to."

"How close did they get?" Marino has yet to really look at him while they talk.

"They didn't get anywhere near."

"At least not the ones we know about." Marino abruptly walks off in the direction of the twins.

"A couple of students, three to be exact," Barclay tells his retreating back. "I turned them away before they could see anything. They couldn't see there's a dead body," he directs this at me, and I wonder what he was doing before he showed up here.

15

He's sleek and quite an eyeful in parachute pants, a polo shirt, and leather high-tops, everything black.

His pistol is holstered on his right hip, his detective's badge displayed on his belt, and Investigator Barclay looks like the star of his own TV show with his lean muscular build, Ken-doll face and buzz-cut blond hair. I can smell his cologne from several feet away, and I know his type, what we used to call a hotshot.

Marino has cruder terms for vain young bucks like Clay, as he hails him. I can't imagine the two of them are friendly with each other or would be under any circumstances imaginable. As this is going through my mind I have second thoughts about Barclay's nickname. Or better put, something comes to me as a warning.

"Does everybody call you Clay?" I ask, but what I'm really wondering is if anybody does besides Marino.

"I don't know why he suddenly started doing that unless it's to tick me off as usual." He watches Marino talking to the twins. "My first name's Tom, my middle name's David.

People call me Tom. It's just another one of his stupid jokes that he thinks are so brilliant. I guess his point is to encourage other corny bullshit. First it's *Clay*. Then it's *Dirt*. Or *Play-Doh*. Or if I do something wrong my name will be *Mud*. But it goes with the turf when you get promoted to working major cases." He shrugs. "You get picked on."

Barclay continues to nail Marino with a stare, and Marino continues talking to the twins as if he's oblivious. But he's not. The sophomoric jokes, the juvenile behavior are a special skill set of his, and he has the acumen of a hawk. He doesn't miss Barclay's slightest twitch, and it's a good thing I didn't call him Clay. Marino would have thought that was hilarious, and it may very well be that he's the only one who's ever called him that.

But chances are good that Marino won't be the last. Unfortunately when he comes up with a nickname or new "handle" for someone, there's no undoing it. I wouldn't be surprised if soon enough everyone in the Cambridge Police Department was talking to and about Clay Barclay, as if the lame redundancy really is his name.

"How you doing, Doctor Scarpetta?" He's boisterous and too friendly as if we've just run into each other at a reception or in a crowded bar.

"Thanks for doing a good job keeping things quiet out here . . ." I start to say.

"If this was in daylight can you imagine a more exposed spot?" He watches me dig in my bag for a notepad and a pen. "Not to mention working a scene when it's over a hundred degrees. At least it's a cool eighty-eight now."

I'm methodical and not in a hurry as I pull out Marino's package of coveralls and the box of gloves. I set them on top of his nearby scene case. Then I walk back to

Barclay, my tactical light pointed down at the grass with each step.

"I'll take the ambient temperature as soon as the truck is here," I let him know, and the real point I'm making is he needs to be careful about throwing around information the way he's been doing.

I'm mindful that he's already gone out on a limb by deciding the victim is Elisa Vandersteel when identity hasn't been confirmed by DNA, dental records or any other legitimate means. And an ID found on the fitness path in a public park isn't a confirmation. Not even close.

He's also said she's an assault, a murder, and I can't know any such thing when I've not so much as looked at her yet. Possibly most dangerous is what he's also passed along to at least one person—Marino—that the body is as stiff as a mannequin. In other words, it's in an advanced stage of rigor mortis. That directly impacts the estimated time of death, and I wish Barclay had kept his opinion to himself.

These are the sorts of seemingly benign mistakes that can haunt you in court, and time of death is especially tricky. It's not an exact science but is crucial to any alibi. It's a favorite bone for defense attorneys to chew on, and how quickly strangers can lose faith in what an expert witness like me testifies. I have no intention of causing jurors to doubt my credibility because an inexperienced detective thought he could do my job for me at a death scene.

While it was appropriate for Barclay to check that the victim was actually deceased, he shouldn't have begun playing the role of a medical examiner by making determinations about rigor mortis and how advanced it is or

130

isn't. He needs to be careful about information he finds on the Internet. He shouldn't accept as gospel what the temperature in Cambridge is based on a weather app.

What part of Cambridge? There could be quite a difference between a shady spot near the water and the hot bricks of Harvard Square, for example.

"I'm assuming you got the temperature from some sort of app on your phone," I say to Barclay after a silence I can tell he's eager to fill. "So the detail about it being eighty-eight degrees Fahrenheit or thirty-one degrees Celsius? We'll keep that out of any reports since we don't know what the temperature is in the exact location where the body was found."

"If you got a thermometer I can put it over there next to her," he says, and I realize how aggressive he is.

"No thanks. That's not what I was suggesting. I don't have my scene case yet, but when I do I'll handle any temperatures that need to be taken of the body, the ambient air, and all the rest." I speak slowly and in a measured tone, resorting to what I think of as my neutral voice. "It might be cooler here because of the river," I suggest as if it's no big deal.

But he knows it is. He feels disrespected and criticized, and I'm witness to his mood's rapid shift. It's something I suddenly remember observing about him on the few occasions I've been in his presence. He's volatile. He goes from hot to cold with not much in between.

"If only there was a breeze." He looks away from me, toward the river, and it's obvious when his narcissism is winged. "It's hard to breathe. Damn suffocating."

He's practically turned his back to me.

*　　*　　*

"What time was the body found?" I ask him that next, and he can keep his back to me the rest of the night if it makes him happy.

After a sulky silence Barclay says, "We got the call about forty-five minutes ago. But oh! Wait a minute!"

He turns around and feigns a eureka moment, flashing his white teeth in the dark.

"The time came from my phone." He throws a snarky dart, and it won't find its mark with me.

"Is that okay? Or should I trust my watch instead?" he asks, and I won't engage.

"The time I have written down for when I got the call is nineteen-oh-six-hundred hours." He says it as if I won't know what that is.

I jot it down. "Twenty-three-twenty Zulu time. Twenty minutes past seven EDST." Then I ask, "How was the call classified when it was broadcast? What was said exactly? Because it would seem the media isn't aware of anything yet."

"It came in as a ten-seventeen." He waits for me to ask him what that is, but I know the police ten-codes probably as well as he does.

I've been hearing them my entire career, and a 10-17 is common. It literally means "meet complainant."

"I'm assuming it was about the twin sisters," I interpolate, and Barclay stares at me as I think, *What a dick.*

He says nothing went out over the air that might alert reporters monitoring Boston-area law enforcement radio frequencies. This continues to argue against Marino's suspicious phone call being from anyone legitimately involved in the case. It would seem Barclay absolutely didn't contact Interpol's National Central Bureau in Washington, D.C. I have a feeling that Marino's right. The inexperienced investigator probably wouldn't think of it and might not even know what the NCB is. Not every cop does.

Marino certainly didn't initiate the contact, and of course I didn't. It couldn't have been anyone at my office. We didn't know about the death at the time the alleged NCB investigator called Marino's cell phone. What's becoming more apparent is that the person responsible is someone up to no good, to understate the problem.

"I happened to be on Memorial Drive and got here in maybe three minutes max," Barclay then answers what I didn't ask about why he was the first responder or paid attention to a low-priority call.

Meeting a complainant suggests someone wants to talk to a police officer, usually to report a concern or upset of one sort or another. A general request like that could be about anything. Much of the time it's about nothing, and it surprises me that a detective would pay much attention to such a call unless it was specifically directed at him. But Barclay is new to the Major Case Squad. Maybe he's overly eager. Maybe he was bored.

"And the two girls who found her?" I ask, and I'm watching Marino talk to them out of earshot. "Are they students? Because they look too young for college."

From where I'm standing they're barely pubescent, and I'd hazard a guess neither is old enough to have a driver's permit.

"No, ma'am, they're not in college," Barclay says, and he flips through pages in his notebook. "They go to the school near Donnelly Field, in the eighth grade. Or that's what they told me and I got no reason to think they're making something up or hiding anything. Or that they knew the victim. They said they didn't."

These strike me as callous remarks to make about two girls

who have been traumatized by a discovery that will stay with them the rest of their days. I wonder if he's implying that he briefly considered them suspects—if it crossed his thoughts that the twins might think it was a fun idea to ambush someone on a bicycle. I suppose anything is possible, and I notice his small flashlight is turned off. It's as if he's forgotten he has it, and he checks through his notes. He finds the page he wants as if he can see in the dark like a cat.

The girls live near the Highland Laundromat off Mount Auburn Street, he tells me as he loudly flips through pages. It makes sense that their route would have taken them from Harvard Square, along John F. Kennedy Street toward the river. The plan was to walk along the water through the park, then cut up Ash Street, which would take them home. All told the outing was just under a mile round trip.

"Usually they would cut over to Mount Auburn, which is more direct," Barclay explains what he gleaned from questioning the sisters. "But it's so hot they've been detouring through the shaded park and sticking near the water as much as possible."

"Why were they out at all?" I'm making notes.

"They said they were heading home from the Square, from Uno's, and I'm thinking who can eat pizza in this weather? I heard on the news this morning that in another day the heat will break. Then it's rain and we'll go straight to winter. You grew up in Miami, right? So I guess this weather's a piece of cake for you. Not me. This is way too hot for my thick blood."

I don't ask where he's from but it's probably not here, not originally. He has a trace of a midwestern accent.

"I've only been to Miami a couple times," he says, and I don't follow up on that either.

16

He waits to see if I'll engage in small talk and banter, but I'm not interested. My attention keeps going back to Marino talking to the twins some distance away, angling his phone flashlight in a way that won't illuminate much to anyone who might be watching with binoculars or a telescopic lens.

But I recognize what he's doing. He wants to see the expression on the sisters' faces as he questions them, and I can tell that the girls find him reassuring. I intuit it by the way they gaze up at him. I sense it by how they cluster close to him beneath the dark canopy of a spreading oak tree as if they're passing through an evil forest and Marino is their guide.

"Anyway," Barclay says, pointing toward rhododendron bushes about twenty feet ahead of where we are, and to the left of the body. "You might want to be careful where you're walking around here and I don't mean because of any evidence we've not collected yet. But one of the girls got sick over there."

"When was that?"

"When I first got here, right as I was walking up. She was coming out of the bushes, wiping her mouth on the back of her hand and kind of glassy-eyed. I don't know which one or if she threw up or what. Trust me, that's one thing I decided not to investigate too closely."

"Do you know if either of them touched the body?" I get to the most important question. "What exactly did they tell you they did?" I glance at the time on my phone, and the glow from its display is bright like a TV screen in the dark.

It's 8:22 P.M., and I make a note of it.

"When I got here there was no one else around, and they weren't close, were at least twenty feet from her," Barclay says. "They were real shook up, and they said they didn't touch it. I must have asked them half a dozen times, and they said no. The closest they got to it was maybe a yard," he adds, holding his hands about three feet apart as if I can't envision what he's describing.

"It?" I ask.

"The dead lady."

He continues to regard the victim as an object while he treats me like a lesser mortal who has no right to be here. I'll take it a little longer. Then I'm going to share a few of my thoughts with him. I'm going to give him some free advice.

"They wandered close to check it out, and then retreated, were probably scared shitless," Barclay says. "They stayed back and called the police."

The girls have matching backpacks, and I have no idea what might be inside them. But at a glance I don't see that either of them has a phone.

"How did they call for help?" I ask.

"I don't know. Nine-one-one." It's his way of flipping me off.

"I'm aware that nine-one-one was called. My point is at least one of them must have a phone."

"I don't know. I didn't search them," he says. "But tell you what. When I get them in the daisy room and can distract them, I'll go through their backpacks. I guarantee their phones and who knows what else is in there."

I return him to the subject of the body being found, and he tosses out the same details I've already heard. The girls were walking home and noticed something ahead on the path.

"They got closer," Barclay says, "and at first they thought it was someone who'd been in a bad bike accident. Like it was getting dark and she ran into a lamppost or something, hitting her head so hard it knocked her helmet off. They could see blood and that she wasn't moving."

"What do you mean *at first*?" Before I talk to the twins I want an idea of how much he may have tainted them. "At first they thought she'd had a bike accident? That's what they said?"

"Well I doubt they think that now. They think somebody did something bad to her."

"How did they get a good enough look to notice blood and decide she was dead?" I ask, and if the girls suspect foul play it's probably because Barclay has his mind made up about what type of case this is.

He hasn't hesitated saying it's a homicide—a sexual one at that.

"It's extremely dark, and the shadows are especially thick where she is," I point out. "Do they have a flashlight?

Because I don't know how they could have seen very much otherwise."

"Maybe in one of the backpacks. I don't know. They told me they were pretty sure she was dead. They said she smelled dead."

"That's interesting. Meaning what?"

"And they also said she smelled like a hair dryer." He smirks.

"I'm wondering what they meant by that," I reply, and he laughs.

"Who the hell knows? They're retarded, right?"

"It's not my job to test their IQs and I doubt it's yours either, and that's not a good word to use." I look on as Marino takes photographs and sets down a numbered cone, and it's all I can do not to blast Barclay but good. "The girls meant something by what they said," I add in my most reasonable tone. "It would be smart to figure out what it was instead of assuming they're talking nonsense."

"Probably what they were noticing was the blood. Blood plus heat equals an odor. Kind of a metallic smell? Like a hair dryer maybe? And her blood's going to be decomposing for sure in no time at all because of how hot it is."

"Unless you want to swap jobs with me, Investigator Barclay, that's another detail you really shouldn't be discussing." I glance back at the sound of footsteps and wheels rolling slowly along the gritty path.

"Another detail? As in more than one?" He might be flirting now. "But hell yeah. I'll swap jobs anytime. I've always thought I'd be a good doctor."

I detect low voices, and Rusty and Harold with all their gear and equipment are two floating lights and a shadowy caravan. I can just make them out as they enter the woods that lead to the clearing.

They wear hands-free headlamps like miners to light their way as they steer two trolleys. I don't have to see them to know they're loaded with a mountain of scene cases, boxes, sandbags, and the privacy barrier, which is disassembled and packed inside what looks like a stack of long black body bags. Tied down with bungee cords, the bulky dark shapes of the advancing cargo bring to mind a morbid Santa's sleigh as it lumbers closer. I send Harold a text:

Once inside the tape, begin to unload. Will check with you in a few.

"It should take no more than twenty minutes to get all this set up," I say to Barclay. "While this is going on Marino and I will do a walk-through, taking photos, getting an idea what we need to identify, protect and preserve before we assemble the barrier in place over the body. Once that's done we'll turn on the lights and I'll examine her inside an enclosure that affords us privacy."

"How big an area can it cover?" Barclay stares back at my transport team.

"Big enough to enclose the bike and the body," I explain. "What we're putting together is basically a tent. And if you've never been through this before, we have to take steps in a well-thought-out logical order so one procedure doesn't mess up another."

I watch the twins talking to Marino, and I look at the bicycle some twenty feet ahead of where I'm standing, and then the body a good ten feet beyond that. Usually when I conduct a high recon or preliminary walk-through I get the lay of the land and a good idea of what I'm dealing with. But what I'm seeing out here is a contradiction. It's haphazard, almost quirky, as if someone staged the scene but didn't have a clue what it should look like.

Had the victim fallen from her bicycle, her body wouldn't be ten feet from it. A bicycle can't throw you like a horse, and even if it could, what I'm seeing doesn't add up. Why is her helmet so far from where the bicycle went down? Even if her chin strap wasn't fastened, that still wouldn't explain it. How did she hit her head so hard as to be killed almost instantly, it seems? I also can't imagine that she died in the position she's in with her arms up, her legs wide, her knees and elbows barely bent as if she's in the middle of a jumping jack.

"You ready to take a look at her?" Barclay asks, and what I'd really like is for the overbearing new investigator to leave me alone with my thoughts for a moment.

"And it goes without saying that you didn't disturb the body. You didn't move it." I click my pen closed and ask in the way of a coda.

"I said I didn't. I checked her vitals, and it sure seems like she's been dead for a while."

"Her vitals? Where?"

"Her wrist. I'm pretty sure it was her right one. I picked it up to check for a pulse, and her arm was stiff. That was it. That was all I did. Like I keep telling everybody I didn't move her," he says, and I wonder who *everybody* is.

I suppose Marino could constitute a crowd all by himself when he's after someone.

"When the squad got here did you tell them you were sure she'd been dead for a while?"

"I gave them my opinion. I said she was already stiff, and yeah she was warm because you could fry a freakin' egg out here."

140

"One thing you really should keep in mind, Investigator Barclay, is it's important not to be the origin of unsubstantiated opinions." As a parting gesture I offer him a piece of my mind, a free moment of mentoring that he's certain not to appreciate.

"No matter how well intended your opinions may be," I add in a quiet voice that means business, "be very careful before you speak. I don't care what you're told or what you see. I don't care what you're absolutely certain you believe. Think twice. Think three or four times."

"I have a right to my opinion—" he starts in, and I cut him off.

"Not if it has to do with science, medicine or some other area that's not your expertise. I advise that you report your observations but don't interpret or make decisions based on them." I don't take my eyes off him. "Because loose talk and misinformation are fodder for lawyers."

"I'm just telling you she's stiff and therefore been dead awhile . . ."

"Paralysis can make someone stiff. That doesn't mean the person's dead. Again, please don't interpret or offer your opinions—especially not medical or forensic ones."

"Since I'm the one who witnessed it, that makes what I'm saying a fact, not an opinion," he fires like a loaded bowstring. "And maybe there's an odor. I might have smelled rotting blood." After a hostile pause he takes the next shot. "And now I'm getting what all the chatter was about. All the shit that was on the radio earlier."

I don't ask him what he means. I have a feeling I know as I'm unpleasantly reminded of the 911 complaint about my supposedly fighting with Bryce and disturbing the peace. Maybe Barclay knows all about it. Maybe everyone in his department does. I conclude my business with him by asking that he wait over there, and by that I mean a healthy distance from me.

He stalks off toward Marino and the twins, and the dashing investigator whose name isn't Clay doesn't like me. It couldn't be more apparent. Not that I particularly care. Marino walks in my direction. He crouches by the big black plastic Pelican case he rolled from his SUV.

"You need to keep your eye on him." I say it under my breath. "Because he's brand-new and already he doesn't think he answers to anyone. An attitude like that will get only worse."

"I got his number more than you know." Marino moves around the case unsnapping clasps. "He's got a weird thing with older women, some fucked-up mother complex. I'm just giving you fair warning."

"I remind him of his mother?"

"An aunt, a mother. Because you're older than him."

"That doesn't mean I remind him of his mother or aunt or anyone else for that matter."

"I'm just telling you he thinks he's a gift to women but unlike yours truly here he doesn't like them. Not really." He opens the lid of the case.

Inside is a supply closet of forensic necessities perfectly organized and neatly packed. He finds a camera and a large flashlight with a detachable shoulder strap. Then he pulls disposable booties over his shoes, and he works a pair of gloves over his huge hands.

"I know these will swallow you, Doc." He hands me a pair of booties and gloves.

I ask him for two rubber bands to adjust the booties, making them half the size so I don't walk out of them or step on my own feet. I pull on the extra-large gloves and have inches of room to spare in the floppy purple nitrile fingers.

"Let's go," he says, and we move on to the second stage, the inner perimeter, not bothering with other protective clothing, not yet.

There's no risk of contamination if we're careful not to step on or disturb anything. With rare exceptions we won't collect evidence until the inner scene is protected and the lights are on. We start in the clearing, using our flashlights to sweep the gritty swath in front of us, and the trees and grass on either side.

With each step Marino stops as if he sees something. He leans closer, grunts softly, indicating it's nothing, and he takes photographs. I hear the constant whir of the shutter. The blinding bursts of the flashgun are disorienting as we continue our well-practiced synchronized approach. It's a deeply ingrained procedure, like the proper way to hit a tennis stroke, and we rarely need to coach each other anymore.

"Stop," I say to him as the silhouette of an unlit lamppost materializes in the dark up ahead, close to the overturned bicycle at the outer rim of the clearing, just before the woods begin again.

The lantern on top of the black iron pole is out, and we shine our lights at it, discovering a glass pane is wide open, the bulbs inside shattered. Bits of broken glass flash and flare as we probe the grass, and splinters sparkle all around the bike.

"From this perspective, it almost seems it might have crashed into the lamppost," I comment. "Maybe what Barclay suggested is right."

"He's never right," Marino snipes.

Perhaps the person riding couldn't see and had an accident. But that wouldn't explain the destroyed lightbulbs inside a lantern some ten feet off the ground. It wouldn't explain why the body isn't nearby.

"Got no idea." Marino stares up at the dark metal frame of the lantern at the top of the lamppost. "Maybe somebody opened the access pane and smashed the bulbs."

"It's weird that the glass is blown all over the place. How would that happen if you opened the pane and smashed the bulbs? And unless you're a giant I don't think you could reach the lantern to unlatch it."

"I'm thinking the same thing. How come the glass is blown everywhere? The bulbs couldn't have been shot out or the outer glass panes would be broken, and I don't see how a rock could do it unless you were up on a ladder and used it to smash the bulbs." He shines his light around, looking for one anyway. "But to be honest, we don't know for sure when the damage happened."

"I wouldn't expect the park to leave a broken light out here for very long," I reply.

"Well it sure as hell makes it darker in this immediate area where she went down on her bike when she got attacked," he says as we probe nonstop with our lights. "So maybe some psycho smashed out the lamp. Maybe he shimmied up the lamppost, who the hell knows, and then waited for her or some other victim. That's exactly what it's looking like, meaning this was premeditated."

"Or maybe the light was already out and she had an accident." Not that I think this at all, but I'm reminding him to be cautious about locking one idea or another into his mind. "We don't know for a fact that she was assaulted," and I've said this multiple times but nobody seems to be listening.

Another step, and another, then one more until we're about four feet from the bicycle on its side. The body is some ten feet from it, and already I can see the drag marks.

"Dammit!" I mutter, and regardless of what Barclay claimed, I had a feeling this was what I'd find. "She's been moved."

17

They're easy to discern when you're accustomed to looking for disturbances in soil or foliage. It's second nature for me to scan for anything that might suggest an area was trampled on and disturbed either accidentally or deliberately.

The drag marks indicate the body was moved but not much, and that's another oddity to add to a list of them. Her upper body is in the grass. Her hips and legs are on the path, and I can see the displacement of the gritty surface that begins inches from the backs of her low-cut socks. What immediately comes to mind is at least one person began pulling her and either was interrupted or stopped for some other reason. And I wonder what happened to her shoes.

Her shoes like her shirt seem to be missing, assuming she was wearing them prior to her death. Maybe they're out here somewhere, I decide. There may be quite a lot of things we find once we have proper lighting, and I envision the cyclist in the blue helmet again.

I remember her sneakers. I've been hoping the dead

woman isn't wearing Converse. I can't be sure since something has happened to her shoes. She's not wearing a blue paisley bandanna or gold necklace like the cyclist was. But something could have happened to those too, and it's an act of will not to take a close look right now, to stride right up and satisfy an unbearable curiosity mixed with dread.

I could get inches from her. I could shine my flashlight on her face to see if it's the woman with the British accent. And if both of them are Elisa Vandersteel. But I know better. I need to work my way to the body one little piece at a time, patiently, carefully. Pretending I don't know what might be up ahead in the dark. Pretending not to care. I'm not supposed to have feelings or reactions about anyone I take care of or investigate but of course I do.

I glance back at the distant racket of Harold and Rusty unloading the trolleys and unzipping the big black vinyl bags. I hear the low murmur of the two of them talking.

"Do you mind?" I trade my small tactical light for Marino's big one.

I crouch down in the middle of the path, looking all around, making sure I don't compromise or interfere with whatever might be out here. The turbo six-thousand-lumen light is made of metal and weighs several pounds. It has a wide lens with six LEDs, and the brilliant beam paints over the path, igniting hard-packed sandy minerals like quartz and silica.

They sparkle like something alive wherever the light touches, and bits and slivers of broken glass flicker and flare when I illuminate the area around and under the bicycle. I do this slowly, thoughtfully, and I pay attention. Once a scene has been entered and intruded upon, there's no going back. There's no undoing it, and when possible

I take all the time I need no matter how much it might irritate everyone else. I point the light past the bike, another ten feet to the body.

I can see more clearly where her heels dragged through the loose surface as she was pulled a short distance; at most eight inches, it looks like from here. I can only suppose this must be what Investigator Barclay misinterpreted as evidence of a struggle. She has on grayish-looking footie-type socks similar to what the cyclist had on but I won't be able to tell until I get closer.

"I'm not sure what's happened out here but I'm not liking it," I say to Marino. "Something's very off about this. It's as if her bike went down right here where the lamp's access pane is open, the bulbs shattered and glass every-where. Yet her body's over there? And I doubt she rode a bike in her socks. I need to get closer. If you don't mind hanging back for a minute, and keep taking pictures." I get up from my crouched position.

I make scraping sounds as I move about in my ill-fitting jerry-rigged shoe covers. I direct the beam along the path, following it to the body, and from several feet away I see the long brown hair is in disarray. I see her attractive young face with its turned-up nose and delicate chin, her pale skin, the dirt on her parted lips, and her eyes staring dully through barely open lids. The sunglasses she had on earlier are missing, assuming the dead woman and the cyclist I met are one and the same.

I'm increasingly convinced they could be, and that's thinking of it conservatively. That's not including what my gut is telling me. In the intense light I can see that the shorts are light blue, and there are pinstripes in the socks. Soaked into the grass under her neck is blood. From where

148

I am I don't see a lot of it, and I don't notice bruises, lacerations or other injuries to her face. Only dirt and vegetable debris, as if she took a tumble.

But the position of her arms is telling. They're over her head, wide-spread and palm up, and that corroborates my growing conviction that she was pulled by her wrists. It never ceases to amaze me what people don't think about in the uproar of the moment. It would have been simple to brush away the drag marks and position the body, making it not quite so obvious what was done after the fact. I glance at the twins again, and their faces are riveted to me. I have a bad feeling they're lying.

They claim they didn't get near the body, no closer than three feet, according to Barclay. But somebody did. It may have been more than one person. There may have been two people of similar strength and each one of them pulled the dead woman by an arm, then stopped. I wonder again about the helmet some twenty feet away, upside down in the grass like a beached turtle. Did someone toss it there? What happened to her shoes and shirt? What about sunglasses, a necklace, a bandanna? If she had them, where are they?

I paint the light over the bicycle as I slowly make my way around it. I look for damage to the tires, the white frame with blue accents and a racing stripe, and the gel seat. I don't notice dents or scrapes. But the black plastic phone holder clamped to the flat handlebars is empty. The clamp that would have held a phone in place has been released. There's no phone in sight, and I get that feeling again, only more strongly. It comes back as a pang in my stomach accompanied by a sinking sensation, and I take a deep, slow breath.

I try to control my thoughts about the woman I encountered twice today as I brace myself for an inevitability that's crashing over me like a tidal wave. The bike's definitely familiar. I didn't have a reason to study in detail what she was riding but I'm certain there were blue markings on a light-colored or white frame. I remember noticing the blue was the same shade of robin's-egg blue as the helmet she had on, and my light picks it up again in the grass near a Japanese maple tree.

"That's just weird," I say to Marino, and I envision the face of Elisa Vandersteel in the ID I just looked at. "The helmet's some twenty feet from the body. Why?" I ask.

"It could have happened when she resisted, maybe tried to run from whoever grabbed her," he proposes, but so far I'm not seeing evidence that she fought anyone or ran anywhere.

"Or did the sisters toss it there, and if so why?" I reply. "And it would seem unlikely that they would remove the victim's shirt, but where is it? Where are her shoes?"

I don't mention the phone, bandanna, the necklace or the sunglasses, because I wouldn't know about them if I'd never seen the woman before. I'm not ready to introduce the subject to Marino. If it's even remotely possible I'm mistaken about having met the victim earlier, it could launch him in the wrong direction. It could hurt the case in court. I shine the light and comment that the area around the bicycle and the body aren't very disturbed except for the drag marks.

"I see nothing so far including blood that might indicate there was a pursuit or a struggle," I'm explaining. "But what I do see isn't making sense as I continue to point out. It's chaotic."

Then my light flicks past what looks like two shiny threads curled on the path inches from each other.

The segments are six or seven inches long, and I realize what we've found is a delicate gold chain that's been forcibly broken into pieces.

"Possibly part of a necklace," I say to Marino as I look back at the overturned bicycle.

It's close by, several yards behind us, and I scan the path around the broken chain, looking for any sign of a confrontation, a struggle. But the tan unpaved surface is smooth and undisturbed as if nothing dramatic happened here.

"A necklace someone ripped off, and it doesn't look like it's been out here long." Marino sets down another tiny evidence marker, a blue cone with the number 7. "I wonder if something was on it, a locket, a cross or whatever that might have looked valuable. Or maybe it was taken as a souvenir."

"Possibly," I reply, and I sweep the area around the pieces of the chain, looking for a pendant, ring, lucky charm, anything at all that might have been part of a necklace.

A skull, for example, like the cyclist had on. It was hard to miss when we met at the box office and then again on the sidewalk. I noticed a necklace with a gold skull, a cartoonish whimsical one. I remember she flipped it around to her back as she pedaled off, making sure the dangling chunk of metal was out of her way and didn't hit her in the teeth as she rode, I can only suppose.

As I walk through the grass I don't see her shirt, and I remember it was a beige tank top, a Sara Bareilles tour souvenir from several years earlier, I'm pretty sure. I see nothing like that. But I finally find her sneakers scattered, one here, the other way over there, off-white Converse, the laces still tied in bows as if she literally were scared out of her shoes.

I may not be sure of her name but I have little doubt that she's the cyclist I saw earlier at the theater and then in front of the Faculty Club, and I keep myself in check. I can't react to it. I can't give any indication I have a personal reaction to anything I'm doing out here. And I make a decision as we set down cones, making notes and taking photographs. It's time to give Marino a heads-up.

"I can't prove this," I say to him, "and I'm not sure it matters. But I may have seen her earlier tonight."

"You're shitting me." He stops walking and stares at me as if I have five heads.

I briefly explain it to him, starting with my encounter at the American Repertory Theater, and then later in front of the Faculty Club.

"Benton and I both met her on the sidewalk," I add. "And this would have been about six forty-five as the sun was setting. But it wasn't dark yet."

"If that's who it is then she couldn't have been dead very long when the girls found her," he says. "We got the nine-one-one call at about seven thirty."

"Which is why what Barclay said is illogical," I answer. "If she'd been dead less than an hour when he checked for a pulse, she shouldn't have been in full rigor or even an easily discernible stage of it."

I glance back at the twin sisters, and their attention is all over the place as Barclay talks to them. I'm reminded that they aren't as comfortable with him as they were with Marino, and it's obvious. Since he was with them they've turned into a matching pair of frightened bookends, weary and wild-eyed.

I catch Barclay saying something to them about their mother. He's asking about her in a way that makes me suspect he was asking earlier. They shake their heads, and if there's a father in the family mix, I've yet to hear a mention.

"She usually asleep this early . . . at eight thirty?" Barclay says.

"It depends."

"Sometimes."

"When she doesn't feel good."

"Maybe that's why she's not answering the phone . . .?" he asks, and I can't tell which girl is responding to him.

"No," one of them says. "Don't wake her up if she's asleep. She won't like that."

"When she doesn't feel good she doesn't like it," the other echoes, and I sense they're accustomed to taking care of their mother.

I can catch only snippets of the conversation but it's enough to indicate trouble. I wouldn't be surprised to learn that Mom is divorced, and the reason she's not answering the phone is because she's drunk. She probably hasn't a clue that her daughters haven't returned home, and I hope I'm wrong. I unlock my phone and I send a text to Harold:

Heading your way.

I say to Marino, "I think we've seen enough for now. Let me make sure Rusty and Harold are on the same page with us about how to set up. I'll be right back. Then we can suit up and hopefully get the lights turned on in a few minutes."

Marino stares in the direction of crime-scene tape in the

woods, about the length of a football field from where Rusty and Harold are waiting. Then he looks at the twins some fifty feet ahead to the left, at the outer edge of the grassy clearing, close to trees. Their eyes dart around restlessly as Barclay continues saying things I can't hear.

"I'm going to wander over and talk to them," Marino lets me know.

"I'll meet you there." I look at the twins looking at us. "It would be very helpful if they told me in their own words what they might have done out here. That's what I'd like to find out before anything else if you have no objections."

"Yeah," Marino says. "I think we already know there's something they're hiding. Like why the dead lady was dragged, and why her shit's everywhere or missing."

18

Rusty and Harold are the CFC's *Odd Couple*. My two top autopsy technicians are so different from each other they shouldn't get along.

Rusty in his surf pants and hoodies looks like a hippy leftover from the golden era of tie-dye and Woodstock while Harold is a former Army man who eventually became a funeral-home director. He has thinning gray hair, a neat mustache, and lives in suits, single-button conservative ones in solid subdued shades of black and gray.

"How long are we talking about?" I look at what they have to assemble with nothing to guide them but flashlights. "Can we be up and running in twenty minutes max?"

"I think so." Harold crouches, and then Rusty does, their headlamps flicking over the roller storage bags unzipped and spread open all around us.

Inside are folded aluminum frames, polyurethane-coated black sidewalls and an awning fabricated of heavy-duty black polyester. Still tied down on the trolleys are the requisite sandbags, ground stakes, the scene cases, the boxes of gloves, and the plastic-wrapped packages of disposable protective clothing.

Any additional supplies we might need including water and nonperishable food such as protein bars will be inside the big truck. And I plan to head that way soon. I need something to drink and to get out of the heat for even a few minutes. More importantly, I want to call Lucy, and I don't intend for anyone to hear our conversation. I'm going to ask her about a twenty-three-year-old woman named Elisa Vandersteel whose driver's license lists a London address. I want to see what Lucy can find out about her, and we need to start now.

It doesn't matter that the identity isn't certain. At the moment and after what I've seen so far, a confirmation will be little more than a formality. The rest of the story is a baffling mystery, as are other disturbing events that continue to unfold, and we should get started on any line of inquiry that might be helpful.

Who was Elisa Vandersteel? Why was she in the United States? What was she doing in Cambridge, and was riding her bicycle along the river at sunset a habit? If she did it routinely, then a stalker or some other dangerous person could know.

"I'm sorry to make this so inconvenient," I explain. "But the thing we really have to worry about is up there, and I don't mean God." I point up, indicating the bridge, the surrounding buildings, and also news helicopters that will show up the minute the word is out. "We have exposure from every direction including overhead."

"That's what we get paid the big bucks for," Rusty says, and he says it a lot.

"Do you know what killed her?" Harold asks.

156

"I've not examined her because I don't want to get that close until we have privacy and adequate light. But from a distance I can see signs of trauma. It appears her body was repositioned and moved."

"Well that's bad," Harold says. "You're sure she's been tampered with?"

"There are drag marks."

"Crap," Rusty replies. "A couple kids found her?"

"And who knows what all they did before the police got here," Harold adds somberly.

"Some of her belongings also appear to be unaccounted for. Others are scattered, and possibly a necklace was broken and whatever might have been on it is missing at the moment." I don't mention the gold skull.

I don't want to tell anybody what to look for. I continue to remind myself to be careful about influencing the investigation because of a personal theory I might have based on an experience that may be nothing more than a fluke. So what if I met Elisa Vandersteel—if that's what turns out to be the undisputed truth? What does that have to do with her death or anything we may or may not find here?

Even as I try to dismiss the encounter as irrelevant I know it's not. If nothing else, it won't be helpful if it comes out in court that I met her not long before she was murdered. It won't make the case stronger. Quite the opposite. The defense will use it against me. I'll be accused of not being objective, of being influenced and distracted by crossing the path of the victim not once but twice just hours before her death.

"Forcibly removed," Harold assumes about the broken chain I mentioned.

"Assuming the jewelry is hers, that's what it looks like," I reply.

"Sounds like there was a violent struggle and the perpetrator tried to stage something after the fact," he suggests, and their headlamps are blinding when they turn toward me.

"There was violence," I reply. "But I can't say if there was a struggle because I don't know enough yet. As soon as we have the enclosure up, I'll know a lot more."

"We had a discussion about what would be best. We thought you'd want the canopied tent, and we recommended that to Marino." Harold always sounds a little unctuous, as if he's greeting people at the chapel door or giving a tour of a casket showroom or a slumber parlor. "We know the area of course. But we also pulled up a map."

I glance up at Eliot House's upper-story student apartments, and I can see several people looking out the lighted windows. I look at the bridge, and there's a steady stream of cars on it in both directions. Aluminum clinks and clacks, and I hear the sound of bags shoved around on the ground.

"Will you post her tonight?" Rusty asks.

"Usually I would wait until the morning. But this isn't usual," I reply.

"Because I'm wondering if Anne should come in." He lifts out another folded frame that's cumbersome but lightweight, and his headlamp is a blazing Cyclops eye. "If so, she should be heading back to the CFC now, in other words."

The scaffolding of tent sections going up around us brings to mind a crazed Stonehenge fashioned of silver tubes.

"I'll get a van for transporting her when it's time." Rusty is talking about the body now.

"How do you plan on handling that?" I ask. "Without driving right through the middle of the scene."

"I think we pull in as close as we can without messing up anything," Rusty says. "Then by the time you're ready for us to carry her out, she'll be pouched with an evidence seal. And that's all anybody's going to catch on camera, just the usual pouched body on a stretcher. I'm thinking we'll have her in the receiving area by nine P.M. if all goes well." The two of them look at each other, and nod.

"I can notify Anne," Harold says.

She's the CFC's chief forensic radiologist, and I'm going to want the victim in the CT scanner as soon as possible. I reply that yes, Anne needs to come back in if she can. It would be wise to mobilize now, I couldn't agree more.

"You're thinking she was murdered," Rusty says.

"I don't know what I think yet."

"To play devil's advocate," he adds, "I'm wondering if she could be a heat-exposure death. Like she's riding her bike, faints, wrecks and hits her head. We sure have had our share of heat-related fatalities of late, a lot of them weird-ass stuff."

"A bike accident wouldn't explain her belongings strewn everywhere," Harold says thoughtfully.

"It depends on who touched her stuff and when it happened," Rusty disagrees. "You know, like if somebody was looting? Like in small-plane crashes? If you don't get there fast, people steal everything."

"But not out here. That's not going to happen here," Harold says somberly.

"Stealing happens everywhere." Rusty unrolls another section of black polyurethane siding.

I tell them more about the twins who found the body, and that we can't be certain who did what. Kids don't always understand consequences, Rusty drawls in his slow

159

amicable way, the headlamp cushioned by the do-rag over his long shaggy hair.

"They move something, take something. They don't know any better at first." He interlocks the frame of a large panel. "Then maybe they freak out and lie because they're afraid of getting in trouble."

"We'll build the components here out of the way," Harold says to me as I survey the trolleys and what I want from them now. "Then we'll finish the final assembly in the target area when you're ready and feel it's safe for us to work over there."

"We'll mark off a perimeter, and you can set up the tent right over the bicycle and the body." I add that Marino will use spray paint to clearly designate the footprint for the tent, a safe zone for laying something down.

I take off the ill-fitting gloves he gave to me, and the huge shoe covers fitted with rubber bands. I drop them into a bright red biohazard trash bag.

I collect my gear, grabbing a scene case, what's essentially a large tough plastic tool chest. I pick a box of purple nitrile gloves size small, several pairs of shoe covers with traction soles, and packaged hooded coveralls. I leave Rusty and Harold to their construction project, and follow the path, reentering the clearing.

I direct the flashlight downward and slightly ahead of me, careful I don't step on any possible evidence even though Marino and I already have been over this area. I never stop looking down and around because it's quite possible to walk past something several times without noticing it. So far I've seen nothing except the victim's scattered personal effects that we've already marked with

160

cones. The park is clean. Any scrap of litter I notice appears to have been out here for a while.

I'm aware of my breathing, of the sound of my feet on the gritty path, then the swishing as I walk through grass. I hear the steady rush of traffic on the bridge, the rumble of trucks and cars, and the whine of a motorcycle on John F. Kennedy Street. The air is hot and heavy. It doesn't move. I slow down as a figure materializes in the darkness up ahead, striding toward me. The female officer I saw earlier approaches me with purpose.

"Doctor Scarpetta?" She's keyed up, almost breathless, stopping several feet from me, directing her flashlight at the ground. "You ever notice how you find something when you're not looking for it?" The shiny steel nameplate on her short-sleeved dark blue uniform shirt reads N. E. FLANDERS.

"It happens all the time," I reply. "What did you find?"

"I was walking over to check on your guys, see if they needed anything." She stares off in the direction of Rusty and Harold. "And I noticed something. It's probably nothing but it's a little strange. I think someone was sick in the bushes over there. I'm pretty sure it's recent." She turns and points behind her. "In the woods just off the path and not very far from the bike and the body."

"Investigator Barclay mentioned that one of the girls might have been sick," I reply, and I get the feeling Officer Flanders knows nothing about this because he didn't bother sharing information. "He told me that when he first got here he saw one of them coming out of the bushes, and that it appeared she might have thrown up."

"Someone did for sure."

"I'm happy to look if that's what you're asking. I was headed that way."

"What time frame are we talking about for getting some lights on out here?"

I tell her it shouldn't be long for the tent. After that, I'll get the body to my office as quickly as I can.

"If you don't mind me saying so, it doesn't seem right to just leave her lying there out in the middle of everything."

"I'd do her a far greater disservice if I compromised evidence in any way," I reply.

"We can't put anything over her? A sheet or something?"

"I'm afraid not. I can't risk dislodging or losing evidence, especially trace evidence. If I cover her before going over her carefully with a lens, I won't have any idea what I might be messing up."

"Well if she's been out here for a while anyway, I guess waiting an extra half hour isn't going to change anything," Officer Flanders decides.

"What makes you think she's been out here for a while?"

"Well that's what Barclay thinks."

"It would be best if we don't circulate rumors," I reply, and she shines her flashlight on what I'm carrying.

"Can I help with something? It's too hot to be hauling anything heavy."

"I'm fine. And if any of you need water or to step out of the heat, we have our truck."

"As long as there's nothing dead in there," she jokes.

"You'll be happy to know that we don't transport bodies in the same truck where we rest, drink, eat, and work. We'll have a van here for the body," I explain, and Officer Flanders has a broad face that's neither pretty nor unattractive.

She's what my mother used to call "plain," by which she meant an unremarkable-looking girl who was worse off than "the ugly ones." That's how she would say it, and her explanation for such a vile statement couldn't have been more logical. At least in her limited way of thinking, and also in Dorothy's because she shares the same point of view. Pretty girls don't try at all because they don't have to. Ugly girls try harder for obvious reasons.

That leaves plain girls, which usually is synonymous with smart girls, and they need to try but don't know any better or can't be bothered. So plain girls have the distinction of finishing first and last in the categories of accomplishment and attractiveness respectively. It's my mother's own weird version of "The Tortoise and the Hare," I suppose, only there's no moral and no one really wins.

N. E. Flanders is the brand of plain that Dorothy wouldn't have a single kind word to say about. I estimate the officer's age is mid- to late forties, her chunky short-waisted figure not helped by her creaking black leather duty belt and low-riding trousers. Her dark hair is tucked behind her ears in a pageboy, and a white T-shirt peeks out of the open neck of her uniform shirt.

"I'll show you." She motions me to follow her. "It's a rag, a cloth, a towel, I don't know. But someone threw up on it as best I can tell. I mean I didn't get more than a few feet from it, and I didn't touch it of course."

We light our way as we walk, looping around the bicycle, and stopping at the edge of the woods between the path and the river. I recognize the clump of rhododendron bushes Barclay pointed out earlier, and as Officer Flanders probes the dark dense shadows with her light, I smell the evidence before I see it.

"There." She points the beam of light at what looks like a wadded-up cloth caught in branches near the ground as if shoved there.

I set down the scene case, and as I bend closer and shine my light I decide what the officer has discovered isn't a rag or a towel. It's a shirt, off-white, possibly beige, and I can make out a portion of a date, a partial image of a silkscreened face. I remember the woman on the bicycle was wearing a beige Sara Bareilles concert tank top.

"I assume this hasn't been photographed." I unfasten the clasps of my scene case.

"No. All I did is notice it with my light. And then I saw you coming."

"We need to get Marino here." I balance on one leg at a time, pulling the shoe covers with traction soles over pumps that are still damp and sticky against the bare skin of my feet.

I work my hands into a pair of gloves, small ones that fit this time. I open a transparent plastic evidence bag, and next retrieve a pair of sterile disposable forceps. I explain that typically I wouldn't store anything in plastic unless the item is completely dry. Blood and other body fluids including vomit will degrade and rot as bacteria and fungus proliferate, and any evidence such as DNA will be lost.

I'm explaining this to Officer Flanders when I hear Marino before I see him. His big bootie-covered feet are getting closer on the path.

"What's up?" his voice booms in the dark, and I show him what we've found. "What makes you think it's hers?" He directs this at me, and I'm relieved he makes no allusion to what I told him a little while ago.

He doesn't ask me if the shirt looks familiar. He doesn't come right out and confront me with what I remember about how the cyclist looked or was dressed when I encountered her twice earlier.

"It's a T-shirt, and it's wet, apparently covered with vomit," is what I say. "It would appear to be recent since nothing would stay wet out here for very long."

As he takes photographs I explain that the shirt is too messy for a paper bag. I'm going to package it in plastic but only temporarily. I'll have the CFC truck deliver the evidence directly to my headquarters. I'll make sure everything is properly preserved. We'll recover any evidence from the shirt and hang it in a drying cabinet—I spell out exactly what we'll do. Then I cover my nose and mouth with a surgical mask.

"How 'bout you go over and hang out with the two girls," Marino says to Officer Flanders. "Keep everybody away from them, and don't ask them nothing. Just stay with them, and the Doc and me will be right there."

She walks off, and I hand Marino a mask. He puts it on and starts taking photographs.

"Shit," he complains, and underbrush crackles and snaps beneath his feet as he moves around. "Some things you never get used to. Goddamn it!"

"Are you all right?"

"It's like when some kid throws up on the bus. Then everybody does."

"Well don't unless you're going to do it in a bag. Would you like one?"

"Hell no. I've been around worse shit than this."

I hand him the pair of disposable forceps and he grips the shirt with them, extracting it from the rhododendron bush. He guides it over the transparent plastic bag I hold open, and I can see at a glance that the T-shirt is from a Sara Bareilles concert and it's damaged. There are tears in the cotton fabric but I don't notice blood. If the victim was wearing the shirt when she was attacked or injured, there should be blood on it.

Marino and I discuss this briefly because it doesn't make sense.

"I'm not getting how her shirt came off." He continues to poke around in the bushes. "And there's no blood on it?"

"I need to examine it carefully, which I'm not going to do out here."

"Unless the girls did it. Maybe they took it off the body because they wanted it."

"Then why does it have tears in it? Why is it damaged?" I pinch the bag's seal closed with my fingertips.

"How do we know it wasn't already torn?" Marino says.

I don't recall that the cyclist's T-shirt was torn. But I wasn't looking carefully. At the time I had no reason to make a mental note of her every detail as if I were filling out an investigative report in advance.

"We'll figure that out when we get it to the labs," I reply. "But what I can tell you with certainty right now is there are multiple tears in the shirt and it's covered with vomit."

"Then what? How did it end up in the bushes? The answer is: It didn't walk here by itself. And there's a lot of disturbed dead leaves and soil back here."

He looks in the direction of the twin sisters. I can see Officer Flanders's back, and the moving beam of her flashlight as she's about to reach them.

"Come on." Marino steps out of the bushes, onto the grass. "Let's go find out what the hell they did."

19

I introduce myself as Kay Scarpetta, which means nothing to them.

I don't say I'm a doctor, a Ms. or a Mrs. Maybe I'm a cop. Maybe I work with social services. I suppose I could pass for Marino's girlfriend. I can't tell what the twins think of me or what assumptions they might make about my reason for showing up to chat with them about a dead body they stumbled upon.

"How are you both holding up?" I set down my scene case and smile.

"Fine."

They look flushed and tired but from what I understand they've refused every opportunity to sit in an air-conditioned car. They're content to stand outside in the hot dark night, and it occurs to me they might crave attention. I have a feeling they spend much of their time picked on or ignored, and I wouldn't be surprised if they put up with more than their share of being ostracized and bullied.

"She'd like to ask you a few things," Marino says to them about me. "Then we'll get you someplace where you can get cool, have a nice drink, a snack. How would you like to see what a real police department looks like?"

"Okay," one of them says.

"Where are the TV cameras?" the other asks. "How come this isn't on the news? It should be on the news!"

"We don't want any TV cameras or reporters here right now," Marino replies.

"But why aren't they?"

"Because I'm in charge," Marino says flatly. "That nice lady officer you were with a few minutes ago? Officer Flanders is going to give you a ride to my headquarters in her police car."

"Are we in trouble?"

"Why would you be in trouble?" Marino asks.

"Because somebody's dead."

"Because somebody did something bad."

As Marino and I were walking here, he informed me that the girls are fourteen years old. Their names are Anya and Enya Rummage—as in the ROOMage and not the RUMmage sisters, God help them, I can't help but think. What unfortunate names for identical twins. As if they don't get ridiculed enough, I'm guessing. I give them another reassuring, sympathetic look as if all of us are out in the miserable heat and in this mess together, which of course couldn't be further from the truth.

"I'm wondering exactly where you were when you noticed the body," I say to them as if I'm perplexed and need their help.

"There." Anya in pink points toward the distant trees

168

behind us where Rusty and Harold are assembling the tent scaffolding.

"So you were walking through the woods, following the path toward the clearing," I reply.

"Yes, and we saw the bike on the ground."

"Then we saw her."

"When you were entering the park from John F. Kennedy Street, did you see anyone? Hear anything at all? I'm wondering how long she might have been here when you found her."

They say they didn't hear or see anything unusual as they cut through the park. They didn't hear anyone talking and certainly they didn't hear shrieks or someone yelling for help. As both of them continue to recount what happened, I get a picture of them walking along the fitness path the same way Marino and I did a while ago.

When they reached the clearing they saw what they at first assumed was a bicycle accident. It was almost completely dark by then, and there was no one else around. The park was empty as far as they could tell except for "animals," they continue to say. A squirrel, possibly a deer, they tell me. I ask what time it was when they discovered the bicycle and the woman's body, and the girls shake their heads. They don't know.

"Then what did you do? Do you think you can describe for me exactly what happened next?" I ask, and both of them look at Marino for approval, and he nods. "How close did you get to her?" I inquire.

"Tell her. It's okay," he reassures them. "She's a doctor and is trying to help."

But it's not quite the right thing to say. The twins stare

in the direction of the body as if it's not too late for a doctor's intervention.

"I'm a doctor who works with the police," I explain to them without using any of the buzzwords like *medical examiner, coroner* or *forensic pathologist*. "We need to find out what might have happened to the person you discovered. It's my job to figure out now she got hurt and died."

"She must've wrecked," Enya in yellow says. "Or someone jumped out at her maybe because she couldn't see very well. You ride slow because you can't see? And then a bad person is waiting to get you."

"It was too dark," the other sister says.

"Too dark to be riding a bicycle through the park?" I go with their train of thought, and they nod.

"So what made you decide to walk through here?" Marino asks. "Did you worry about how dark it is?"

"No because we do it all the time."

"Not all the time," Anya in pink disagrees. "Not usually after dark but our pizza was slow."

"Because you added sausage. Even though I didn't want it."

"So what if I did?"

"You got here and it was dark. And you weren't scared walking through here alone?" Marino asks, and they shake their heads.

"We watch out for cars. And there's no cars through the park. Mom doesn't like us walking around cars."

"We don't come here in the rain, though."

"We only walk through here sometimes. Not in the winter or when it's too cold near the water."

"Mostly when it's hot."

"Mom gives us money for food when she doesn't feel good."

"She doesn't feel good today."

"She's very tired."

"She's asleep and doesn't want to get up."

I look from one face to the other, from Anya to Enya. Or maybe it's Enya to Anya. Both of them have on stretch shorts with drawstrings, and tees with tulip hems. As I continue to ask questions, they tell me the same story I heard from Barclay. They got close to the body but didn't touch it, and their eyes jump around as they describe this. When I ask them how long they waited before they called the Cambridge police, neither of them replies, and they won't look at me.

I ask Enya, the sister in yellow, if she made the call, and she shakes her head, no.

"What about you?" I ask Anya in pink.

"No." She shakes her head vigorously, and now both of them stare at me.

"Maybe you'll let me see your phone," Marino says. "I'm betting one or both of you have a phone, right?" And the girls indicate they don't. "So neither of you called the police?" Marino asks. "Now come on. Somebody had to, right? How'd we know about it if you didn't call us?"

"I didn't call the police," Enya says slowly in her blunted tone.

As both of them continue to assert what seems a blatant lie, I get a sneaking suspicion it isn't. I have an idea what might have happened.

We know the Cambridge police received a 911 call about a person down in the park, and that would indicate the girls had access to a phone. But if they literally don't own the phone in question, then that might suggest they used one that belongs to someone else.

To this equation I add my earlier observation when I briefly looked at the bicycle on the path. The phone holder on the handlebars is empty. If the woman I met earlier was Elisa Vandersteel, as I suspect, then I saw her clamp her iPhone into the holder before she rode off across Quincy Street and into the Yard. So what happened to her phone after that? I might know, and if I'm right it could explain why Anya and Enya are swearing they don't have a phone.

Maybe they don't—not one of their own. They claim they didn't call the police, and very possibly they couldn't have. Not literally if the phone didn't belong to them—not if it was locked and they didn't have the password. They absolutely couldn't dial the Cambridge Police Department. They couldn't even call 911 without getting past the locked screen, and I doubt they'd know how to do that in emergencies unless someone had shown them.

I propose this to Enya in yellow. I ask her if she knows what an iPhone is, and she does. It would seem her mother has one, and yes she understands about swiping the locked screen to the right, to the password keypad. At the bottom on the left side is the word *emergency*. All you have to do is touch it and you're given a dial pad that allows you to enter your country's emergency three-digit number, which is 911 in this case.

So neither Enya nor Anya dialed the Cambridge Police Department's general number. One of the sisters pressed EMERGENCY, and then entered 911, afterward pressing SEND. Literally, that's what Anya in pink—not Enya in yellow— admits to having done.

"How'd you know to do something like that?" Marino acts impressed.

"Mom showed us," they say in unison.

"She showed you how to use her phone in case there's ever an emergency?" I suggest, and they nod.

"If we need to call an ambulance," Anya adds.

"Is that what you thought you were calling? You thought you were asking for an ambulance?" I ask, and they verify that was their intention.

"Then you didn't think about the police," Marino picks up where I leave off. "You didn't know the police would come if you called for help. That's not who you were asking for."

They confirm that they didn't want the police and never intended for them to come. They tell us they wanted to help her, and the police don't help anybody. The police are who you call when you want to get someone into trouble.

"When someone's mean," Anya says, "and you have to lock them up in jail."

Marino and I realize without having to say it that the girls weren't deliberately misleading us about the phone and who they did or didn't call. It's clear there are limitations in what they comprehend, and an emergency isn't the same thing as a crime. One requires medics. The other the police. What this might suggest is that at first the sisters weren't sure the victim was dead, and they weren't assuming she'd been attacked. Their immediate thought was she'd had an accident, and their response was to get medical help, which is exactly as their mother has taught them, it seems.

"You weren't asking for the police to come." Marino makes sure. "You wanted an ambulance."

173

"Yes."

"Did you think she was alive?" He's going to keep asking until he gets a satisfactory answer.

"She didn't move."

"And the bad smell." Anya in pink wrinkles her nose.

"Can you describe it?" I ask.

"It smelled like mom's blow dryer when it won't work."

"You noticed an odor that reminded you of your mother's blow dryer?" I try to decipher what she means, pretending it's the first I've heard of a strange smell.

I'm not going to let on that Barclay told me something similar.

"It gets too hot," Enya says.

"An electrical smell?" I suggest as I think of the broken lamp.

"If you thought somebody had done something bad to her would you have called the police?" Marino then asks, and after a pause the girls shake their heads in unison.

They shrug and say they don't know. Then he points toward the clearing, asking them to remember their initial impression when they saw the bike and the woman on the ground. They continue to assert that they thought she was in an accident at first.

"You wanted to help her," he says, and they nod. "You saw she was hurt," and they nod again.

"We didn't want her getting more hurt."

"Like if another bike might run over her," Anya in pink says, and her handoff couldn't be smoother.

"That's the danger when someone's down in the middle of the path, right?" Marino doesn't miss a beat. "Maybe you moved her out of the way a little? So no one would run over her?" he asks, and they nod.

It's as simple as that.

"What happened to make you sick?" Marino asks either one of them since we don't know who did what.

"My stomach," Enya says.

"And the shirt you cleaned up with?" Marino boldly powers forward. "Did she have it on when you first saw her?" He assumes the girls removed the shirt from the body, but they shake their heads, no, and they don't look unnerved.

They don't look the least bit frightened or unhappy anymore.

"It was in the bushes where the thing was. It scared me and made me sick." Anya points.

"Hmm," Marino frowns. "I'm wondering if it's the same bushes where we just found it."

"All I did was see what it was. And then something was in there." Her eyes suddenly widen behind her glasses. "It tried to kick me and I screamed."

"Who do you think it was?" Marino asks as if her comment was normal.

"It might have been a deer."

"And maybe she heard it too as she was riding past, and it scared her. So she wrecked."

"Did you actually see a deer?" I ask.

"I heard it," Anya says excitedly. "I heard it running away."

"What about you?" Marino asks Enya.

"I heard it too!" she exclaims the way kids do when they realize everyone is eager to hear a story they're telling. "I heard it run away in the dark, and then the policeman got here."

"So let me make sure I get this straight," Marino says.

175

"You heard something run out of the bushes, and then Investigator Barclay showed up. You got any idea how many minutes passed between when you heard the commotion in the bushes and when Barclay got here?"

"One minute," Enya says.

"I don't know," Anya chimes in.

"One minute and I don't know?" Marino looks at both of them. "Which is it?"

"Maybe more than one minute. I don't know."

"I was scared and then he was walking toward us. Are we in trouble?" Enya looks uncertain again.

"Now why would you be in trouble?" Marino asks.

"I don't know."

"Hmm." He pauses, puts on the big act of entertaining an unhappy thought. "Wait a minute. Hold the phone. Have you done something I don't know about? Something that you're worried might get you in trouble?"

Technically, the answer is yes. It appears they've tampered with a crime scene and perhaps tried to abscond with an expensive phone taken from a dead person. Even if they borrowed it initially, it would appear they intend to keep it unless there's a better explanation for what happened to it. But I think it's safe to say they won't be held accountable—nor should they be. I'm not sure they know better.

Then as if Enya can read my mind she picks up her knapsack, which is in the grass by her feet. It's pink with small hearts, and her sister's is just like it. Enya digs into a front pocket and slides out an iPhone in an ice-blue case—like the one I saw the cyclist clamp into the holder on her handlebars.

Marino doesn't touch the phone. He doesn't act surprised

176

and certainly not suspicious or judgmental. He opens a brown paper evidence bag and holds it in front of Enya. He instructs her to drop the phone inside it.

"Well now that's really helpful," he says to both girls, and I can imagine Barclay's smoldering resentment when he finds out what Marino's just done. "You know what I can't figure out?" He looks at both of them.

"What?"

"How you got hold of this. How did you manage that?"

Anya in pink admits with a hint of pride that she saw the phone "on the handlebars" and "borrowed" it.

"That was a pretty smart idea to borrow the phone to call for help," Marino says, and they look pleased.

He wants to know if they'd mind him taking a peek at what's inside their knapsacks. Maybe there's something else they have that might be helpful.

"Okay," Enya says, and she takes his hand.

She presses it to her face as if she might love him.

20

Twice now in the past forty minutes I've trekked alone through the clearing, following the path to the edge of the park where an auxiliary diesel generator hums in the dark.

I'm getting more frustrated with each minute that passes. I was hoping to be back at my headquarters before now, and yet I've scarcely started. The body should be in the CT scanner. I should be setting up my autopsy station.

Already I should have a good idea what happened to her, and I don't. Not to mention hypervigilance is fatiguing. When you have to think about everything you do and say, and watch every place you touch or step, it wears you down. Especially in this weather.

It's already 9:30 P.M. and the tent isn't close to ready. I could put on the big show of hanging around outside instead of retreating to the quiet comfort of an air-conditioned monster truck. But there's not much I can help with at the moment, and one thing I've learned over the years is to pace myself. If I don't keep hydrated, if I'm not careful about overheating, if I don't plan and strategize I won't be much good to anyone.

The CFC's mobile command center is the size of a small yacht hitched to a super-duty crew cab, white with the CFC crest and the state seal on the doors. There are no windows in the trailer. But inside it's lit up and cool, a combination lounge and war room where first responders and other essential personnel can rest, work, teleconference, use computers, and safely store evidence destined for the labs. When I stopped in here the first time it was to drink water, change my clothes, and safeguard the packaged soiled T-shirt by locking it inside an evidence mini-refrigerator.

Now I'm back again, fortifying myself with more water and a protein bar while trying not to fantasize about the dinner I missed at the Faculty Club. I'm hungry and restless as I wait to hear from Lucy. She was pushy about having a discussion with me a while ago when I couldn't talk. Now that I'm alone with a few minutes to spare, of course I can't get hold of her. I'll have to see what I can find out on my own about Elisa Vandersteel, and I sit down at a workstation.

Logging onto the computer, I spend a few minutes searching the name, and it gives me an uneasy feeling when nothing comes up, not a single file returned. I try the surname Vandersteel and Mayfair, London, and have no better luck, which is odd. It's pretty difficult to avoid any mention on the Internet these days but if my searches can be trusted, it would seem that Elisa Vandersteel doesn't exist.

She also isn't on social media, it seems. I can't find her on Instagram, Facebook or Twitter, and that's extremely unusual for someone young. The woman I noticed taping up recipes at the ART certainly didn't seem shy or introverted. I also realize that doesn't mean much. One can be confident and friendly but private, and maybe she's had issues in the past that cause her to stay below the radar. But the more key words I enter without success, the more wary I get.

I think of the photograph of the UK driver's license that Investigator Barclay showed me. I remember that the street listed in the Mayfair address was South Audley, not far from the American embassy. But I didn't pay close attention to the house number. I search what I recall and nothing comes up, and I'm grateful that my routine searches aren't the final word on Elisa Vandersteel.

I'm not Lucy. I can't begin to approach her level of technical sophistication, and as soon as we have a private moment I'll get her to search. I check my phone again, and can tell by the digits displayed in the icons of certain proprietary apps whether anything new has landed. Nothing has that I consider a priority at the moment, and I hope Lucy's all right. When I think about what's happened so far today I can easily imagine her state of mind. I have a very good idea what she's thinking.

Or better put, who's shadowing her thoughts, gaining on her in leaps and bounds right about now, and it's depressing. It's a falling off the wagon of sorts because an enemy, a nemesis will become an addiction if one's not careful. Lucy isn't and never has been. She can't be. It's too personal for her. She's going to get worked up and paranoid in a way that Marino, Benton and I never have and won't when it comes to a certain human virus who infected her decades ago.

I decide I may as well head back out into the elements

to see how we're coming along with the canopied barrier, which has been trickier than we anticipated. Spray-painting the footprint has been a frustration and a headache because we can't turn on the auxiliary lights without exposing the entire scene to anyone who might be watching and ready with cameras. It's very dark despite the multiple flashlights poking and prodding. The terrain is uneven, and there are tall hedges, benches and lampposts in the way.

The first attempt wasn't working so we had to stop, and trying again has proven a worse mess than imagined. First Marino's bright orange outline had to be painted over in black, then the area was measured again and reconfigured as we made sure we weren't going to be setting the tent on top of evidence. The second attempt wasn't much better, and as I'm thinking this I'm well aware that Marino, Rusty and Harold are still at it and will be for a while longer.

It's become quite the engineering challenge to enclose the bicycle, the body, and as many personal effects as possible while avoiding bushes and trees, and causing any potential damage to the scene. But if they don't manage to get the tent pitched fairly soon, I'm going to have to improvise. This has gone on too long already. It's not according to plan, and someone's going to say something. Probably Tom Barclay.

Marino wouldn't allow him to accompany the twins to the police station, and the cocky and annoying investigator is still here, trying to watch everything I do while pretending he's not. Maybe he's hoping to learn something that might make him better at his job. Maybe he's waiting for me to screw up.

But most likely he's simply behaving in character—a magpie carrying every glittery bit of gossip back to his nest.

Information is his currency, and while he may not mean any harm, people like him are dangerous.

I get up from a chair bolted to the stainless-steel diamond-plate floor, and the mirror-polished metal is cold beneath my bare feet.

I was able to ditch my silk blouse, my skirt and suit jacket for a pair of teal-green scrubs but sadly I'm stuck with my scuffed clammy pumps. Storage bins in here include scene gear for all conditions except the Sahara Desert, which is what it feels like in Cambridge of late. But in general the CFC isn't prepared for unrelenting extreme heat because it almost never happens in New England.

I can't exactly trade my uncomfortable shoes for what's available, which are rubber hip waders and waterproof fire boots, one size fits all. Opening a cabinet, I find a fresh pair of shoe covers with grip soles. I step back into my damp pumps, and the thin leather linings have become unglued and feel slimy against the bare soles of my feet. I pull on the booties but I won't bother with coveralls or gloves yet. I check my phone again, and still nothing.

I've let Lucy know that I need her help, but I haven't said why. I'm not about to immortalize my suspicions in writing or voice mails no matter how safe I'm told my communications are. Especially when my phone has been acting up the way it has, and Lucy is even more careful about leaving an electronic trail than I am. I wonder what she's doing. I wonder if she's working in her lab or the Personal Immersion Theater, the PIT.

Or maybe she's with Janet and Desi, and as I envision the three of them I think what an extraordinary family they've become. Janet is an environmental attorney. She's former FBI, and her history with Lucy includes college and Quantico. They practically grew up together, and I couldn't ask for a better partner for my niece. I would choose Janet time and time again were it up to me. She's humane, smart and gentle—as was her sister Natalie, who died a year ago this past summer.

Janet and Lucy have created an ideal home for Desi, all of us an extended family, a supportive and protective matrix. He would be an orphan otherwise, and what a loss that would be. Such an irresistible lovely boy, the incarnate Christopher Robin, my sister says, his blue eyes mesmerizing, his mop of light brown hair streaked blond by the sun.

Nine now, Desi is growing up fast, all legs and arms, and his face has become more angular. He's nimble, fearless and scary smart, and I've begun to tease Lucy that at last she's met her match. Who wouldn't want to be part of a family unit like that? And I'm unpleasantly reminded of what Benton said before our dinner was interrupted.

He suggested that Dorothy and Marino might have more than a playful flirtation going on. Now she's on her way here when she's never bothered once the entire time I've lived and worked in the northeast. Marino has bonded with Desi, taking him fishing, teaching him how to play baseball, giving him his first taste of beer, and the track my thoughts are running along is too unpleasant to dwell on.

It's distasteful if not enraging to imagine Dorothy with Desi. My selfish sister who couldn't be bothered with Lucy. My male-addicted only sibling who always forgot about her daughter the instant the newest suitor was at the door.

And now all I hear from Dorothy is Desi this and Desi that, as if there's nothing she adores more than to nurture and attend to a child, especially a male child. It's obscene. It's the height of hypocrisy, and then I can't bear to think about it anymore. I blank it out.

Dorothy should be landing at Logan fairly soon, assuming her plane hasn't been further delayed. Lucy, Janet and Desi are probably picking her up, and that's why Lucy isn't getting back to me, I tell myself. She's busy driving one of her demanding supercars or tricked-out armor-clad SUVs. But who knows what anybody is doing, including my husband. I have no idea what Benton's phone call from Washington, D.C., was about. I haven't a clue where he is.

It's surreal that our dinner date has come to this, and then I click on the phone app for the security cameras we use to monitor the dogs. Sock and Tesla were in the living room a while ago. Now they're sleeping in their memory-foam bed in the kitchen, and I back up the recording to when Page the dog sitter is walking in. Obviously Benton has let her know something has come up and we're not certain when we'll be home.

Clearly she's staying over, in pajama bottoms and a T-shirt, barefoot, no bra, and I don't like it when she's in the downstairs guest room. I don't want to say such a thing out loud but it's true and probably means I'm a selfish person. I sincerely dislike having anyone in our house but there's no choice now that Tesla is in the mix. She needs training, socializing, and she shouldn't be left without human companionship for long periods of time.

I watch Page filling the dog bowls with filtered water she pours from a pitcher. A friend of Lucy and Janet's, she's imposing, her upper-body strength from competitive swimming impressive, almost unbelievable for a female. It's entered my mind that she might take steroids because I can't quite believe her bulk is solely from long hours in the gym or some earlier stint in the Navy when she was accepted into the Basic Underwater Demolition or BUD training program for SEALs.

Tall with curly dark hair, all brawn, Page is the gentle giant with dogs, kind but in control. She couldn't be more thoughtful or attentive toward an aging greyhound rescued from the racetrack or an English-bulldog puppy once abused by children and abandoned.

"Who's gonna potty and then get a beddy-bye treat?" Page asks Tesla and Sock.

I hear their nails click furiously as they run to the back door.

Walking through an air-conditioned cloud of LED light, I pause in the galley with its coffeemaker, small refrigerator, microwave and laminated white countertops.

Tossing empty water bottles into the recyclable trash, I look around at the workstations, equipment cases, forensic instruments, and multidrawer cabinets of tools and other supplies. I make sure there's nothing else I need for what I'm about to do. I don't think there is. And Harold and Rusty know the drill. On my way here I gave them my scene case and other necessities. They will have everything set up under the tent by the time I get there, and everything will be as it should.

But I'm restless and my mood is tense, my thoughts burdened. When I think of the second time I encountered the woman who I now believe is dead and about to become

185

my patient, she literally rode off into the sunset. I don't know where she went after that or when she finally entered the park, but it was completely dark by seven thirty.

Supposing she was killed around that time, it means that for the better part of two hours her body has been left out in the middle of a public park surrounded by Harvard student housing and other populated buildings. In an ideal situation I would have gotten her out of here a good hour ago.

This is taking too long but it's not surprising. Things rarely go as quickly as we'd like, and in a difficult death investigation it's the rule rather than the exception that very little goes as planned. But the world is less forgiving than it used to be, and already I'm preparing for criticism.

Someone will decide I didn't show proper respect, that I carelessly left a dead body exposed for all to see. I'm callous and uncaring. Or I'm negligent. I'll read about it in a blog or hear about it on YouTube. I always do.

21

I scroll through the latest news feeds, and so far so good.

There's no mention of the police or personnel from my office working a bicycle accident, an assault or anything else at the edge of the Harvard campus. I see nothing about a dead body in a Cambridge park or even the most vague allusion to the *developing situation* on the waterfront that the alleged Interpol investigator mentioned to Marino.

I come across nothing I consider a cause for concern except what Benton told me earlier about the elevated terror advisory. I skim an online article in the *Washington Post* about the bulletin published earlier today:

. . . The Secretary of Homeland Security has issued a National Terrorism Threat Advisory alert due to an imminent threat against transportation hubs, tourist hot spots, and the sites of major public events such as sporting competitions and concerts. Of specific concern are possible planned attacks in Washington, D.C., Boston and their neighboring communities. This is based on detailed chatter U.S. intelligence has intercepted on the Internet suggesting these potential targets, and that self-radicalized homegrown actor(s) could strike with little or no notice . . .

When the status has gone from *elevated* to *imminent* the threat is considered credible and impending, and that makes me wonder about airport security. It will have been beefed up—especially in Boston. That may be why my sister's plane was delayed. It could explain why the TSA was overwhelmed in Fort Lauderdale, the line of passengers out the terminal and on the sidewalk "unless you're first class like me," as my sister informed Lucy, who then passed it along to the rest of us.

I don't have any updates directly from Dorothy. She can't be bothered to tell me she's running late or that she's on the plane. I had to get the information secondhand, and even so I don't know what to expect. I guess it really doesn't matter since I'm not the one picking her up anyway, and I feel a twinge I recognize as disappointment with a sprinkle of hurt for good measure.

A part of me expects more of my only sister. I always have, and for me to feel that way after all I've been through with her is not only baseless it's irrational. It's time to get over it. Dorothy has always been exactly who she is, and for me to hope for anything better reminds me of a quote attributed to Einstein: *Insanity is doing the same thing over and over again and expecting a different result.*

Dorothy is predictable. She does the same thing repeatedly and expects not a different result but the same one she got the last time she did whatever she wants with little regard for anyone else. So maybe she's the sane one, I think ruefully, and as I go through my messages and alerts I'm surprised that General John Briggs just tried to get hold of me. For some reason I missed a call from his home phone minutes ago.

I have a special ring tone for all of his numbers, and I make sure my ringer is turned on. It is. But it was silent, and I don't know why because our electronic communications are excellent in here. They have to be. Lucy makes sure of it in all of our vehicles, utilizing range extenders, boosters, repeaters or whatever it takes. And I'm seriously beginning to wonder if there's something wrong with my smartphone. It isn't one you can buy in a store or online, is virtually *hack-proof* according to Lucy. But maybe she's wrong. It depends on who's doing the hacking.

She's constantly developing special apps and encryption software that aren't available on the open market, doing everything possible to make sure our computers, radios, phones and other devices are as secure as anything can be in this day and age. But nothing is infallible. I touch the PLAY arrow, expecting to hear the voice of the chief of the Armed Forces Medical Examiners, the head of U.S. medical intelligence, my friend and former mentor Briggs.

But it's his wife who tried to reach me, and I know instantly that her news won't be good. A classic military spouse from an earlier more traditional era, Ruthie has devoted her life to her formidable husband, moving with him whenever his newest orders have come in, running interference and enabling him while she prays he doesn't get hurt, kidnapped or killed in the destabilized war-ravaged hellholes he frequents.

Iraq, Afghanistan, Syria, Turkey, Cameroon, Yemen, and she's never really sure. Often she's not told but lives the anguish of knowing that whenever he boards a military transport jet or lands on an aircraft carrier she may never see him again. Her life has been Briggs and nothing but Briggs, and if she doesn't want someone to access him, that person won't, including me. Depending on what's at stake, if he doesn't want to deal with me directly, it's Ruthie I hear from.

So I'm accustomed to her mediation, her triangulation, and now and then it tests my patience. But she sounds unusually raw and emotional in the message she's just left, and I can't tell if she's been crying, drinking, is sick or maybe all of the above. I play the voice mail again. Then again, pausing at intervals, listening carefully, trying to determine if something is wrong with her or if she's simply feeling bad about the reason she's calling. I'm pretty sure I know what it is. I've been expecting it.

"Kay? It's Ruthie Briggs," she begins in her slow Virginia drawl, and she sounds tired and congested. "I'm hoping you'll pick up. Are you there?" she says stuffily. "Hello, Kay?" She clears her throat. "Are you there? I know how busy you are but *please* pick up. Well when you get this please call me. I want to make sure you've been told . . ."

But her voice is muffled, and then it's as if she's swallowed her words and I can scarcely hear her. It occurs to me that she might be holding something, perhaps tissues in front of her face, and that she's turning away from the phone as she speaks.

"For the next little while I'm at this number, then . . . Well as you can imagine there's a lot to do, and I just can't believe . . ." Her voice quavers. ". . . Well please call me as soon as you can." In her befuddlement she leaves her phone number as if I don't have it.

And the voice mail abruptly ends.

If what I suspect has come to pass, there's no reason for Ruthie to be upset. It couldn't be helped, and at least the cancellation isn't as last minute as it could have been.

All along I've been primed for getting a call literally right before Briggs and I are supposed to be onstage at the Kennedy School. At least I've been given almost twenty-four hours' notice, and it's not like I haven't been warned repeatedly. He's told me from day one that he might not be able to appear with me tomorrow night. It all depends on the mood at the Pentagon and NASA, he's said, and he's apologized in advance for what's probably just happened.

Most likely Ruthie tried to reach me to tell me I'm on my own tomorrow night. Briggs won't be on the panel with me. So it's not really a panel anymore because that leaves me alone onstage. But I'll manage, and it occurs to me that were I to step outside the mobile command center I could see the imposing red-brick complex from here, tucked behind trees.

The Kennedy School backs up to the park, and I can't help but think about how everything seems weirdly linked and familiar. It's as if I'm traversing a landscape that's turned out to be an intricate maze, and I don't know how big it is, what it connects or how to get out.

I'm not going to learn anything further about why Briggs has had to cancel until I talk to him, assuming I can reach him. He also could have been deployed somewhere, and

I know how much he hates to let anyone down, especially me. Big Army man that he is, he'll duck a confrontation if it includes being the bearer of bad news. I redial his and Ruthie's home number. No one answers, and I hear a peculiar clicking on the line.

"Ruthie, it's Kay. I'm sorry I missed you," I leave her a voice mail, and now I'm hearing an echo as if two of me are talking on top of each other. "For some reason my phone didn't ring. I'm working an outdoor scene and may be in spots where the signal is bad or I can't answer. But please keep trying me."

Then I send a text to Harold and Rusty, making sure that one of our transport vans is on the way. It may have to wait awhile but let's go ahead and get it here, I tell them.

10-4, Boss. Moving slow. Unavoidable. Stay cool ALAP, which is Rusty speak for *as long as possible*, and he includes a frowning, red-faced emoji.

On the right side of the trailer, beyond the galley, is a deep stairwell that leads outside. My Tyvek-covered shoes thud down the metal steps, and at the bottom I open the door. I emerge outside in the hot night and am blinded by blazing HID headlights. I hear the guttural rumble of a powerful engine. I smell high-octane gasoline exhaust that can't be coming from the mobile command center's auxiliary diesel generator. Then everything goes silent and black.

"Hello?" A thrill of fear touches the roots of my hair as I hear the swish of grass, of someone walking fast. "Who is it? Who's there?"

A lean figure materializes in the night like a ghost rushing toward me.

*   *   *

"Aunt Kay, it's me. Don't be startled," Lucy says, but it's too late.

My adrenaline is out the gate. Flustered, I click on my tactical light then point it down so I don't blind her. Just as quickly I turn off the bloody thing, feeling foolish, then angry.

"Dammit, Lucy!" My heart is flying, my thoughts scattered like a flock of crazed birds. "Don't sneak up on me like that." My pulse pounds. "Jesus. It's a good thing I don't have a gun."

"I don't know if it's a good thing. Especially now."

"I could have shot you. I'm not joking."

"There's nothing to joke about, and I wasn't sneaking." She's scanning all around us as if we're not alone. "I just this second pulled up and saw you walking out. I was coming to find you."

"Why?" I take a deep slow breath, and the hot air seems to barely fill my lungs.

"I'm glad you're okay." She looks at me, then back at the street, and up and around as if we're about to be attacked.

"What do you mean *especially now*? What's going on?" Something is, and she's in high gear. "Why wouldn't I be okay?"

"You've been leaving me messages," she says, and I detect the brittleness in her voice, the flinty aggression. "So here I am. Let's go inside."

I recognize her mood and probably know what it means. "I didn't demand we talk in person. I have a simple question, and a phone call would have been fine. I was going to ask you to search a name for me—"

"It's too hot out here," she cuts me off, not seeming to listen.

193

"What's the matter?"

"I don't like what's going on." Her staring eyes are deep-set shadows, her mouth grim.

"Someone's dead, and there's nothing to like about that or a lot of things at the moment." But I know that's not what she means.

"I don't like it," she repeats, and her attention is everywhere again. "I've been trying to tell you. There are things you don't know, and it's fucked up." Her low voice is fierce in the dark, and I get a feeling deep down, a mixture of emotions that I can't easily describe.

Disappointment. Frustration. The numbness of homicidal rage turned stony and cold like something ancient that's petrified. I've become increasingly desensitized, especially in recent years, and it's true about crying wolf. Lucy may not do it audibly but I know when a certain subject is constantly on her mind.

She rarely comes across as excitable. She's not the sort to go off the rails, to be impetuous, to act nervous or scared or raise her voice. But she can't fool me. I can always sense when she's about to fly apart the way she is right now. It won't be pretty. It never is. When she gets like this I usually know why. Or better stated, I have a good idea who it's about.

"What is it that's fucked up, Lucy?" I brace myself for what's next as my eyes adjust to the dark again.

I'm pretty sure I know what she's going to say. I could have predicted her reaction after the 911 complaint that we now think was made with voice-altering software. If she knew about another bogus call a little while ago, this one supposedly from Interpol, she'd be only more convinced of her curdled worldview. Lucy accepts as unimpeachable her own version of original sin, which is that all horrors and humiliations come from the same malignant source.

As if there's only one devil. Only one mortal enemy. Only one cancer. And if only that were true.

"Let's go inside and get something to drink." Her face is so close to mine I can smell cinnamon on her breath and the subtle spiciness of her Escada men's cologne.

She's acting as if we're being watched. Maybe she worries she was followed here, and I stare past her at what's parked behind the CFC truck. She jokingly considers her Ferrari FF a family car because it has a backseat and a boot for luggage.

I can't make out the color in the dark. I know it's a vivid shade of blue called Tour de France, and the interior is quilted *cuoio* or a racing-yellow Italian leather. But she could have thundered up in anything, an Aston Martin, a Maserati, a McLaren, a different Ferrari.

Lucy is a genius. I don't use the word lightly or as a term of endearment. It's not an adoring aunt's hyperbole but an accurate description of someone who by the age of ten was programming software, building computers and acquiring patents for all sorts of inventions. Before Lucy was old enough to buy liquor or vote she'd earned an incomprehensible fortune from creating search engines and other technologies.

While still in her teens she landed on the *young and filthy-rich list*, she likes to quip, and began to indulge her passion for helicopters, motorcycles, speedboats, jets and other fast machines. She can pilot pretty much anything, and I focus my attention on her all-wheel-drive FF with its long sloping nose parked silently, darkly on the grass. She drove it to work this morning, and the reason I'm certain of this is because the Ferrari was picked up by the CFC security cameras while I was upstairs in my office, sitting at my desk with its multiple computer displays.

On one of them I watched Lucy drive her four-hundred-thousand-dollar so-called family car inside the bay where ambulances and other transport vehicles pick up and deliver bodies. Not even the cops can park in there, and I was unhappily reminded that often she tucks her expensive modes of transportation out of the dirt and grime, out of the weather. It's rather selfish, and now and then some members of the staff make comments. But that's not what has me thinking about this now. It's the flight suit she has on.

When the cameras picked up Lucy this morning as she climbed out of her electric-blue 650 horsepower V-12 coupe, she was wearing ripped-up jeans, a baggy T-shirt and sneakers. I remember she was holding a large coffee, and slung over a shoulder was her tactical black backpack, roomy with lots of compartments, basically a portable office and armory.

Now that I'm thinking about it, the backpack is what she typically carries when she's flying somewhere. Then at some point today she changed into one of her flame-resistant flight suits in lightweight khaki Nomex, the CFC crest embroidered in red and blue on the left chest pocket. It's not uncommon for her to fly her twin-engine bird whenever and wherever she pleases.

But it's late. It's pitch dark. We're in the middle of an extreme weather alert and a difficult death scene. Her mother is on a plane headed to Boston. I don't understand.

"I'm wondering why you changed your clothes." I bring it up tactfully, and she looks down at her flight suit as if she's forgotten what she has on. "Are you flying somewhere? Or maybe you were earlier?"

But it wouldn't make sense. At its most miserable today the temperature crept past a hundred degrees with more than 70 percent humidity. The hotter and more humid it is, the less efficient the helicopter, and Lucy is meticulous about weather conditions. She has to factor in payload, torque, engine temperatures, and I think back to how many times I was around her today.

At a staff meeting, on the elevator, and I ran into her in the break room when I was looking for Bryce. The last time I saw her probably was around four P.M. after I left the autopsy room with my assistant chief, Dr. Zenner, and we walked past the PIT.

Lucy was inside replacing several projectors, and we chatted with her for a while. She wasn't in a flight suit then.

197

22

She's blasé about it, claiming she spilled coffee and had to change her clothes.

I know when my niece is evasive. It's as obvious as her rose-gold hair and as plain as the narrow nose on her intensely pretty face. I check my phone, mindful of the minutes creeping by, and still nothing from Harold or Rusty about how the tent is coming along.

Usually Lucy would volunteer right about now, asking if she could go check on them. Technical engineer that she is, maybe there's something she could do to help. But she doesn't offer and isn't going anywhere. It's obvious she has an agenda, has shown up unannounced for a reason, and I may as well see what it is as I wait, tamping down my impatience, glancing at my phone every other second.

I don't want to hound Rusty and Harold. It's not helpful if I continue interrupting them while *they struggle with their erection*, as Marino put it rather horribly the last time I checked. But probably I shouldn't stand out here in the dark talking to my niece either. A better idea is to head back to the clearing and find out for myself how things are going. I want to make sure no one is overheating or needs anything, and I'm mindful of rumors.

I don't want an ugly one starting about my sitting in the air-conditioning, relaxing with my feet propped up while everybody else toils in what feels like Death Valley after dark. I don't want it said that I was taking my sweet time fraternizing with my niece, who thundered up to the scene in a Ferrari that costs more than a lot of houses. My mother still preaches that appearance is everything. These days she has no idea how right she is.

It doesn't take much for people—especially cops—to question your competence and credibility. It takes less for them to wonder about your honesty, and even less than that to doubt your human decency. Any suggestion that I'm entitled or lazy could influence a jury in a negative way. The truth is almost anything can.

"Lucy, I need to head out and check on things . . ." I start to say, and she moves closer to me, touching my arm in a way that's arresting.

"Let's cool off and get something to drink," she replies, and it's not a suggestion.

I glance around at flashlights probing the distant night. I look back at the jeweled vehicle lights flowing along John F. Kennedy Street, and up at the steady traffic on the bridge. I survey the growing number of police cars parked everywhere. No one is inside them. I don't notice a single person near enough to eavesdrop.

But I don't doubt that Lucy feels the breath of the enemy on the back of her neck, and nothing I say is going to change that appreciably. It's like people who suffer from post-traumatic stress disorder. You'll never convince them there's nothing to feel anxious about. You won't talk them out of their nightmares and phobias. It won't help to wish them happy thoughts and sweet dreams.

Lucy's early passions, triumphs, disasters and flirtations are part of her programming. Most indelibly etched are her Quantico experiences, what truly were the very best and worst times of her young adult life. With my blessing and under my direction she took a road less traveled and slammed head-on into a monster. Their collision was cataclysmic and I never saw it coming. Lucy's not the same, and neither am I. No one would be.

Psychic injuries can become faults that like disk errors and other glitches aren't always fixable. It's disturbing to contemplate how often my niece's hair-trigger responses aren't warranted by what she's convinced she perceives. Most of the time I don't say much. I wait for her to have clarity, and she doesn't seem to have that as often anymore. It's gotten increasingly difficult to be sure what to trust. What's real? What isn't? Even Lucy doesn't always seem to know, and if I could wipe the monstrous psychopath Carrie Grethen off the face of the earth it would be for that alone.

She's managed to rob my de facto daughter of any peace of mind she might have had in this life, and I can't seem to do much about it. God knows I've tried. God knows how much I regret the damage that's been done. Were I really Lucy's mother, I'd be a failed one. She's the most important thing I should have gotten right.

I won't forgive Carrie Grethen for that either, and it's moments like this when I recognize how much I want her eradicated. Completely and forever. Like a plague. Like a scourge.

"All right." I go along with Lucy's request in a noncommittal way, revealing nothing important on the off chance we're not alone. "We'll duck out of the heat and grab a drink but we need to make it quick. As you've probably gathered, setting up is taking longer than I'd hoped."

"Murphy's Law."

"Once we're ready to go, I can't stall."

"He who waits." Lucy chats away in slangy clichés, and it's obvious she's doing it for the benefit of whoever she thinks is watching us.

Lately it seems all I hear about is spying, tailing, peeping, trolling, spoofing, stalking, hacking, sniping, snooping. And maybe Carrie really is out here in the dark somewhere having a grand time monitoring our every word, our every move.

The more I think about her, the more I seethe, and I say nothing else to Lucy. I'm silent as I enter my personal access code in the digital keypad on the trailer's side door.

"Be careful." My niece's cinnamon breath is in my ear, and I'm aware there are telescopic lenses that could capture the numbers and symbols I entered.

I know there are all kinds of skimmers that can grab data from a considerable distance. I couldn't be more mindful that Carrie is adept in such things and so much more, and I'm worn out from the warnings. In addition to Lucy's deadly projections I have to contend with Marino's endless fear-biting hypotheticals about all the different ways I might be followed or stalked and for all sorts of far-flung reasons.

"I'm always careful." I open the aluminum door. "Not

infallible but certainly not cavalier," I add as I step inside, and the cold air is biting.

Lucy follows me in, shutting the door after her. "I still think we should switch our vehicles to fingerprint locks."

"I know you do, and maybe someday it won't be so impractical." The air-conditioning is a relief but I'm going to freeze.

"I just wish these suckers were armored. They should be."

"That would be even more impractical. Are Janet and Desi okay?" I bring them up now that we're inside the trailer's metal stairwell, which isn't bulletproof but at least no one can overhear our conversation.

"They're at Logan driving around in circles because there's no place to wait longer than a nanosecond." She tugs on the door handle again, double-checking that it's secure. "I told Janet not to head out so early but she did anyway, don't ask me why. Mom isn't close to landing yet."

"Do we have an idea why?" I start climbing the steps.

Lucy is right behind me. "First there was a delay in Fort Lauderdale because of an unattended bag at the same gate Mom was using. So her flight took off more than an hour late because of that, and then she was sitting on the tarmac for a while."

"And you know this how? I wouldn't think a left bag at my sister's gate would be trending on the Internet."

"Mom's been e-mailing updates to Janet," Lucy says, reminding me that my sister can't extend the same courtesy to me.

"And I guess it's one of those situations where there's not time to go home." The hurt I feel is as old as time, but I won't let it show. "She'd much rather have to turn around and go back," I add.

"Also traffic is backed up in New York airspace like it has been all week because of the heat wave. Sea fog, thermals are a problem because the air is so much hotter than the water right now, and a lot of flights are on ground holds or are being rerouted. Depending on fuel, Mom won't be landing until at least ten thirty."

I check the time and it's almost ten.

"And she's got luggage," Lucy says. "A lot of it."

"Sounds like she's planning to stay with you awhile."

"I just hope her damn phone battery doesn't die, and I'm worried about Janet connecting with her. Apparently Logan's a real shit show, and you know Mom," Lucy says as our feet thud dully to the top step. "Usually the last one on the plane. Good luck with her bags being there, and Janet can't possibly go inside to help."

"It's going to be a very late night for Desi."

"He's been texting me that the traffic is terrible. State troopers are herding everyone, barely letting you stop your car when you drop off or pick up."

"Well I'm sure he must be excited about Dorothy's visit," I comment halfheartedly as we enter the bright white Formica and stainless-steel galley.

"Yes, since she spoils him rotten. Have you talked to Benton?"

"Not since the Faculty Club," I answer, and Lucy's green eyes have that distant look I know so well and have come to dread.

She may be here in the flesh but in spirit she's somewhere else, some remote emotional space she doesn't share. Beautiful, brilliant, in her midthirties but much younger than that in many ways, and compared to most of the population, Lucy has every advantage. How sad that

203

an obsession would become the path of least resistance for an overachieving highflier like her. Not that there's anybody like Lucy, and her uniqueness is part of the tragedy.

What a waste that she naturally gravitates to Carrie's isolated hateful place like water seeking its own level. Lucy believes she's the captain of her own ship, the master of her own fate. That she has free will. But I'm not so sure anymore.

"Why? Have you talked to him?" I ask.

"Yes," she says, and I would remove this curse from her if I could.

I would take it upon myself if it meant freeing Lucy. I would do almost anything. And strangely I think of the woman on the bicycle and what she said to me before she rode across the blistering hot street:

What doesn't kill you makes you stronger.

But what if it *does* kill you? That's what we should be asking because Carrie isn't making us stronger. It's too late. We crossed that divide two years ago when she let us know in the worst way imaginable that she's still alive. Since then we're on the side of diminishing returns as she's chipped away, bled and maimed us while we flail in a state of perpetual sensory deprivation.

We don't see or hear Carrie. We don't experience her unless it's on her terms, and her greatest gift is her implied nonexistence. Saying she did something heinous has become rather much like saying the Devil did. Except I have provable scars from her, and a lot of people have died.

"I've been curious about what Benton's doing." I sound calm, which isn't at all how I feel. "He got a call from Washington about the same time Marino called me about this case. How did he seem to you?"

"Hard to tell. I'm pretty sure he was in a car when I reached him," Lucy says.

"A car? Or his car?" I lean against the countertop across from her. "I'm wondering if he's with other FBI agents, if something's happened. He mentioned the terror alert's been elevated and includes Washington, D.C. And also here, the Boston area."

"He didn't offer what he was doing or who he was with," she says, and in the bright light I can make out the subtle bulge of the pistol beneath the cuff of her right pant leg.

23

The holster is strapped above her boot.

I can't tell what she's carrying but it's probably her Korth PRS 9mm. There's no telling what she has in her car, a high-capacity pistol for sure and possibly a lot more firepower than that.

"I don't know if he was driving or being driven somewhere but his tone made me think he wasn't alone." Lucy plants the palms of her hands behind her on the edge of the counter.

Hoisting herself up, she sits, resting her back against a cabinet, her booted feet dangling, the pistol's black holster peeking out. She folds her strong graceful hands in her lap, and I'm aware of the plain platinum Tiffany wedding band on her left ring finger.

None of us were invited when she and Janet were married in a civil ceremony on the Cape last year after Natalie died. But as Lucy and Janet both explained, they didn't do it to prove their love and commitment. They didn't need to prove it to each other or anyone else, they said. They did it because they intend to adopt Desi.

"You called Benton for what reason?" I ask. "And when was this?"

"A little while ago. After I listened to the latest from Tailend Charlie," she says to my dismay.

"Why on earth would you bother him about that with everything else going on?" I can't believe it.

"There are new developments you're unaware of. Some old developments have resurfaced too. It's important or I wouldn't bother you." Yet as she says this I have my doubts.

There's something Lucy isn't telling me. I can see it in her face. I can feel it. Benton is involved, and I ask her again if he's okay. She says he's really busy, and I reply that all of us are. Then she proceeds to explain that Tailend Charlie's latest audio clip was sent at the usual time, twelve minutes past six P.M. More than three hours ago, and my frustration boils over. I don't see why this merits our undivided attention in the middle of a death investigation.

"I don't mean to be rude," I say to her. "But that's not new information, Lucy. Every one of his crank communications is sent at six-twelve P.M. As you continue to point out, it's intentional, and let me guess? The new recording is cookie-cutter identical to the others except for the content of the message. In other words the recording is canned and precisely twenty-two-point-four seconds long."

"And two-twenty-four was the street address of your house when you and Mom were growing up in Miami." Lucy isn't going to back down from what she's decided without the benefit of real evidence.

"Two-twenty-four and twenty-two-point-four aren't the same thing at all."

"Symbolically they are."

"I'm not sure we should be so quick to assume intentional symbolism." I pick my words carefully so she doesn't get defensive. "The time stamp of six-twelve, the length of two minutes and twenty-four seconds, could be nothing more than meaningless remnants of programming code."

"And six-twelve also is the exact time the bullshit nine-one-one call was made to the Cambridge police," Lucy reminds me as if she didn't hear what I just said.

"That's true. But all of it could be coincidental . . ." I don't finish because I know it probably isn't.

I check my phone again. Nothing from Rusty and Harold, and I send Marino a text:

How are we doing?

"Listen, Aunt Kay," Lucy says to me as I look down at my phone, waiting for an answer from Marino. "I don't like to admit that I was at a disadvantage because of multiple things happening at once."

She pats down the pockets of her flight suit, sliding out a small tin of her favorite cinnamon mints. They rattle softly as she opens the lid, offering them to me, and I think about her choice of words. *Multiple*, as in many. There's something she's not going to tell me, and I take a mint. The fiery-sweet flavor rushes up my nostrils, making my eyes water.

"When we talked a couple hours ago I was preoccupied with the nine-one-one call." Lucy tucks the tin back in a cargo pocket, buttoning the flap. "I was tied up with trying to figure out what the hell happened, who was behind it and why. I can't do everything at once."

"Not even you can." I move the mint to the other side of my mouth and take a sip of water.

She goes on making her case, claiming that early this evening we were attacked simultaneously on multiple fronts—and she uses that word again.

Multiple.

"The timing is deliberate. I believe we're talking about connected attacks that involve the same person or persons. And that suggests to me there are more on the way," she adds.

But the real problem isn't what's been done or might be next. Or how. Or why. It's the *who* in the equation, and all along I've maintained it's obsessive and dangerous to assume that behind every aberrant act is the same diabolical puppeteer.

I'm not naïve about Carrie Grethen. I'm intimately familiar with her nefarious proclivities and treacherous capabilities. I know what it is to be physically mauled by her, almost die at her hands, and work her crime scenes and autopsy her victims.

So it's not as if she's an abstraction to me. But unfortunately she's not the only horror show, and I open the text that just landed. Marino writes:

A clusterf**k. Stay put for now. Nothing U can do.

I wish he hadn't called the scene out here a clusterfuck. I hope that doesn't come home to roost at some point.

"Suffice it to say that what little I could decipher in the audio file was worse than usual." Lucy continues telling me about the latest harassment from Tailend Charlie. "It's too close for comfort, and no telling about the rest of it."

"What does Benton say?" I ask.

"I wasn't going to get into it with him on the phone, not with other people around, especially a bunch of suits," she answers, and I puzzle over how she can know who he's with if he didn't say. "And I sure as hell wasn't going to bring up the stuff about Natalie," she adds to my astonishment.

"You mean Janet, not Natalie." I assume Lucy has misspoken.

"I mean Natalie," Lucy says. "You'll get it when you start thinking about her last few months, when Janet and I were frequently in and out of Virginia. Then you and Benton were with Natalie a number of times late in the game when she was in hospice in particular, and if you think back to some of the things she was saying? They take on a very different meaning now, a disgusting one."

"I can't fathom why you and Benton would be talking about her in the context of everything else." I feel a flutter of uneasiness as I wait for the rest of the story.

"Remember the fights you and Mom used to have when you were kids?" Lucy adds to my confusion. "Remember what you nicknamed her after you got really pissed off?"

"Sister Twister. Because of her wicked pinching in addition to her other ambushes. Twisting and yanking your hair or cutting it off in your sleep or who the hell knows. Although to hear her tell the story it was you who was the nasty fighter." Lucy reminds me of what I've not thought about in years.

"Dorothy's always been quite the fiction writer." That's as much as I'm going to say.

I've spent most of my adult life being extraordinarily circumspect about what I tell Lucy about her mother.

"We've got to figure out who might know what went on in your house when the two of you were growing up in Miami." Lucy plugs her phone into the charger on the countertop she's perched on.

"Who besides my mother and Dorothy? And me obviously? No one comes to mind but I'll give it some thought." I open a closet and find a dark blue CFC windbreaker to put over my scrubs because I'm getting chilled.

"I suspect that certain things are connected and have been for a lot longer than we've realized," Lucy says. "Going back to summer before last when Natalie was dying, and longer ago than that."

"Such as?" I zip up the windbreaker, and it's so big it hangs midthigh. "What things?" I open the stainless-steel refrigerator reserved for beverages and edibles, no evidence allowed. "Water or Gatorade?"

"Starting with I no longer believe her death was the private family matter we thought it was. Gatorade would be good. In a bottle, not a can."

"Cool blue or lemon-lime?"

"There should be orange."

"Natalie's death wasn't private?" I question as I root around for orange Gatorade. "As in someone was spying on her? I've not heard you mention this before as if it's a certainty. I know only that Natalie was very paranoid. She worried she was being monitored."

"She should have been worried. That's what I'm getting at. I think someone was attempting to spy during her most intimate final weeks, days, hours, moments with all of us." Lucy's green eyes blaze. "I can't say for sure how far it went because none of us were expecting surveillance or looking for it. So things could have been missed."

"Because we didn't take Natalie's fears seriously enough," I say.

"No we didn't. And what I can't swear to now is whether

211

there were any other devices in her house or later in hospice. I wasn't looking for them."

"Any others?"

"Besides Natalie's computers, specifically her laptop." Lucy opens the bottle I handed to her. "But we can't be sure what else might have gone on. I wasn't conducting counterspy sweeps every time I went to Virginia. Janet wasn't either. We didn't think we had a reason."

"And now you're sure there was spying going on?" I ask, and Lucy nods. "As Natalie was dying?"

"During some of it, I'm guessing. We may never know how much."

"It would take a very special type of degenerate to do something like that."

"And we know exactly who fits the bill. I have a very strong feeling she's up to something really special this time."

She means that Carrie is, and I'm back to the same suspicion, only more strongly. Something else has happened. But she's not sharing that information with me for some reason, and I keep thinking about Benton. She was talking to him earlier. I don't really know about what. Lucy isn't going to say a word if he's told her not to, and I herd her back to what started this conversation.

I ask her if Natalie might have been aware of the nickname I coined for Dorothy when we were kids. Might she ever have heard someone mention Sister Twister?

"If so, I don't know about it." Lucy tilts back her head and takes a swallow of Gatorade.

"I'm wondering if the subject may have come up in Carrie's presence years ago when she, Janet, Natalie and you were still friendly with each other."

"I don't think so."

"I can't see any other explanation for how some anonymous cyber-menace would know unpublished personal details about my family. Unless it came directly from the source," I add.

"You mean unless it came from Sister Twister herself. My mother the mad pincher," Lucy says, and I don't correct her.

It's not true that pinching and pulling hair were Dorothy's real crimes but I'm not going to tell Lucy that. I've never elaborated on just how sneaky, untruthful and violent my sister could be, grabbing an arm, an ankle, and twisting the skin quick and hard in opposite directions. What was called a snakebite or Indian sunburn back then was her specialty.

When executed with sufficient skill and force, it's quite painful and leaves little evidence beyond a redness that early on I learned not to complain about. If I did, Dorothy simply would say that I had a sunburn. Or I was suffering from an allergic reaction. As usual I was wrongly accusing her. I was trying to get her into trouble, and when questioned, she would concoct the most elaborately imaginative falsehoods to explain my inflamed sore flesh.

If I was sitting near the windowsill reading, and my arm or ankle got burned, she'd tell our mother. Or the sun hit me at a certain angle while I was sleeping. Or I must be coming down with a fever, a rash. Possibly I got a spider bite or was developing an allergy to gardenias, to mangoes. Or I was "coming down" with cancer like our father.

Dorothy got exponentially bolder and out of bounds as he got sicker. She decided he wasn't able to stick up for *Daddy's pet* anymore, rendering me defenseless, she assumed. I wasn't. But I didn't tattle or retaliate with corporal punishment.

There are better ways to deal with bullies, and in some respects I'm actually grateful to my sister. Thanks to her I learned the art of silence, the power of listening and the added potency that comes with waiting. As our father used to say:

A volte la vendetta é meglio mangiata fredda.

Sometimes revenge really is better served cold.

"What I'm wondering is if my sister might have mentioned the silly nickname to Natalie, to Janet." I suggest this to Lucy because I'm seriously beginning to wonder who Dorothy has been talking to—not just recently but over the years.

"I don't know," Lucy says, "but there's no way Mom ever passed on that story or anything else to Carrie."

"Not unless we're mistaken in what we've always assumed about the two of them not knowing each other. Are we absolutely certain of that?"

"They've never met and Mom knows nothing about her." Lucy's adamant, and I'm going to push harder.

24

"What about in the very beginning?" I ask Lucy. "Are you sure you didn't mention Carrie when you started your internship at Quantico? It would make sense when you went home to Miami or talked on the phone if you might have said something to Dorothy about your FBI supervisor, your mentor—especially one who gave you so much special attention."

Carrie couldn't have been more generous or charming, and Lucy was flattered out of her mind. She didn't have a chance.

"I know you don't like to think about it," and I don't want to be provocative, "but you were bowled over by her in the beginning. You couldn't talk enough about her. At least to me."

"I think you know why I didn't mention her to Mom." Lucy's stare has turned hard and edgy. "I didn't talk about Carrie or anybody else I so much as had a beer with."

Dorothy is bitterly disappointed by her only child's "lifestyle," as my sister continues to refer to being gay. It doesn't matter how many times I tell her that who any of us falls in love and partners with isn't a lifestyle like belonging to the country club or living in the suburbs. My sister doesn't get it. In my opinion she doesn't want to get it because it's easier for her to define Lucy as a bohemian or a tomboy, which is Dorothy's euphemism for being gay. It's easier if Lucy and I both suffer from penis envy, and that's my sister's euphemism for not being male-dependent the way she is.

Penis envy really is a thing, she loves to declare, preferably in front of our mother. Or more recently, in front of Marino when we were in Miami this past June and he was giving Dorothy motorcycle rides and who knows what else.

"There's quite a lot Benton and I don't discuss with Dorothy," I reassure Lucy. "She wouldn't have any idea who Carrie Grethen is unless you've shared that part of your life. Or someone else has." Marino enters my thoughts, and I hope Benton is mistaken.

It gives me a sick feeling to think of Marino being sweet on Dorothy, of him talking to her about us or anything else that's none of her business and is possibly dangerous. The idea is too galling, and I dismiss it.

"You're saying that Tailend Charlie mentioned Sister Twister." I get back to that because I want to make sure I'm clear on where it came from. "As you know, Lucy, I've not listened to the audio clip yet. So I'm assuming it's not been transcribed or translated unless you got someone else to do it."

"I haven't and won't," she answers. "It's important you do it since you're the intended target. The recording was made for your benefit."

"It hasn't been translated and yet you know what it says?"

"Bits and pieces. Easy ones." Lucy takes another swig of Gatorade. "My Italian may be clunky but I know *sorella* means sister, and I recognized *Sorella Twisted* or *Sister Twister* when I played the clip. I've heard the nickname from Mom when she's regaled me with stories of how terrible you were to her."

I feel another rush of resentment that's as fresh as it's old.

"I recognized your name, your initials, and the word *chaos*," Lucy continues to describe what she could make out in the most recent audible harassment. "Apparently *chaos* in Italian is pretty much the same thing in English."

"In Italian there's no *h*. It's spelled *c-a-o-s*." I pronounce it for her.

"Yes." Lucy nods. "That's exactly what I heard. *Chaos is coming*, or something like that."

She goes on to explain that the audio file is consistent with the others I've received since the first day of fall.

"Cheesy rhymes, insulting, and promising your death," Lucy says.

In each of them the Italian-speaking voice has been synthesized. The lyrical baritone sounds like my father, who died when I was twelve.

She finds the audio file on her phone and turns up the volume as high as it will go, touching PLAY. The familiar computer-manufactured voice begins loudly:

Torna di nuovo, K.S. A grande richiesta!

The rhyming cyber-threats greet me with the same opening line every time. Translated: *Back again, K.S. By popular request, no less!* And as I listen, I feel blood vessels dilate in my face. My pulse picks up.

217

I don't want to hear a voice that sounds like his because then he's in my mind again. As if my father's still here. As if he's still alive. But he's not. What I'm hearing isn't him, and he would never talk to me unkindly. He would never wish me dead, and pain flares. I go hollow inside.

"I don't have time to deal with this now." I tell Lucy to stop the recording, and she does. "You think Tailend Charlie is Carrie Grethen. That's what you've come to tell me," I address the elephant in the room.

"I think she's behind it, that it's part of something else she's up to. Yes. That's where I am in this." Lucy's face is defiant.

"You've decided it."

"Because I know."

"And I needed to be told immediately because if Carrie is Tailend Charlie?" I fill in the blanks. "Then maybe she's also the one who disguised her voice and called nine-one-one about me. Maybe she's doing everything that's going on right now including magically interfering with the damn tent so I can't work the damn scene."

"Try not to get so irate. Especially not in this heat. It's not good for you."

"You're right, it's not."

"I believe she's in league with whoever Tailend Charlie is." Lucy's green eyes are unblinking. "Carrie's found someone to help her. It's her MO. It's what she does when she's mounting her next major offensive. She builds her army of two."

"Her latest Temple Gault, Newton Joyce, Troy Rosado." My mouth is as dry as paper, and I take another swallow of water, careful to keep my sips small so I'm not constantly looking for a piddle pack.

"She's taken about a year to regroup after her last blood-bath when she killed Troy's father. Then when she'd used up Troy she almost killed him. Carrie's easily bored." Lucy says these things as if there can be no debate. "You don't really think she's been sitting around doing nothing since then, do you?"

I keep my eyes on her and don't say a word. There's not much to say. She's either right or she isn't, and I have nothing to add.

"Hell no," she answers her own question. "We know Carrie better than that by now. She's been industrious while she's been away." Lucy's tone lacerates. "And her newest minion is some techy-geek anonymous worm who calls himself Tailend Charlie," she adds, and for an instant I'm stunned by her jealousy.

Lucy is threatened by my latest cyber-stalker because so far she's failed at tracking him, and Lucy doesn't fail. Yet she's rather much failed at everything she's attempted since Tailend Charlie's mocking communications began. Failure is Lucy's Kryptonite. She can't endure it.

"I don't know who he is but Carrie isn't working alone," Lucy says as I'm distracted by my phone on the countertop.

The display suddenly has illuminated for no apparent reason.

I pick it up, unlocking it, taking a look. The ringer is turned on, the ring tone on vibrate, exactly as I set them. Apparently I haven't missed any more calls due to some sort of glitch, and nothing looks out of the ordinary.

I place the phone back on the counter I'm leaning against, and it unsettles me that Ruthie Briggs hasn't tried me again. Nor has she texted or e-mailed.

"After a while certain things can suddenly make more

sense." Lucy is talking about Natalie's death a year ago almost to the week, on September 18, and I'm becoming obsessed with the damn tent.

It's now past ten and nothing from Rusty and Harold. Not a peep from anyone. What the hell could be taking so long? I start to send Marino another message but I hold my horses. I don't need to drive everyone crazy. When they're ready for me, they'll let me know.

"Janet had been careful about getting the necessary passwords," Lucy is talking about Natalie's electronic devices now. "I just figured she was so overwhelmed she forgot or wrote down something wrong."

After Natalie died it turned out Janet and Lucy couldn't access the most important device of all: the personal laptop that had been in Natalie's bedroom and later in the hospice facility. The password she'd given Janet didn't work.

"And getting into it wasn't a piece of cake." Lucy avoids the word *hack*. "Natalie worked in digital accounts management. She was computer savvy."

I look at Lucy as she talks, and her eyes are windows to the carnage inside her. It wouldn't show up on a CT scan. It wouldn't be visible in an autopsy. But evidence of the massacre is beneath the surface like the footprint of a fort rotted away centuries ago and buried by layers of sediment and soil. Lucy has rebuilt her big powerful life on top of what Carrie ruined, and were the two of them face-to-face in mortal combat, I no longer wonder who would emerge liberated and whole.

I'm confident that neither of them would.

"I honestly thought Natalie was going overboard in her worries about spying," Lucy continues to explain, and

I can tell she feels guilty. "I worried she was getting demented, that the cancer had spread to her brain."

"Understandably," I reply, but what I'm thinking is there are some things that can't be restored anymore.

There are some battles that can't be won. And if I imagine Lucy and Carrie in a duel, who would kill whom anyway? I hope I'm wrong. I hope it won't prove to be the case that they can't go on without each other. What would motivate either of them in their endless bloody tennis match if the other wasn't across the net? I don't know the answer but as Benton likes to say about dysfunction, *It's hard to give up your iron lung.*

"I remember you telling me that Natalie had covered her computer cameras with tape," I bring that up. "A lot of people do it but apparently she didn't until she knew she was dying."

"She put black tape over the webcams on her desktop, a tablet and also the laptop," Lucy replies. "It's an easy low-tech way to prevent someone from using your own computer to spy on you. Natalie routinely disabled built-in cameras on any personal electronic device she owned because she knew they can be activated remotely. And if the hacker is really skilled he can remotely alter the camera chip, disabling the indicator light so it no longer turns on when you're being secretly recorded."

"So taping over the camera lens was added for good measure," I reply.

"At the time it just seemed wacky."

"But what if it wasn't?"

"That's why we're talking about this," Lucy says. "I should have taken her seriously. If she hadn't been so sick and saying such weird shit, I would have."

"Did she ever mention concerns about Carrie?"

"No reason. All of us thought she was out of the picture for good."

"Because she was locked up in a forensic facility for the criminally insane," I presume. "And then after she escaped she got killed. Or that's what we believed."

"Like the rest of us, Natalie was convinced Carrie went up in flames with Newton Joyce when his helicopter crashed off the coast of North Carolina," Lucy says.

"Who did she think was spying on her?"

"The Feds. Or maybe a foreign government, other lawyers, lobbyists, reporters. You name it. The law firm she was with dealt with a lot of heavy-hitting politicos."

"And when she was moved to the hospice facility, this personal laptop went with her." I envision it on the bedside table where Lucy had set it up.

25

I don't recall seeing black tape over the camera lens on the silver frame of Natalie's personal computer. But I'm remembering other things that were going on at the time.

Almost concurrently, Lucy was finding oddities in the CFC computer system. Then as more weeks passed she confirmed that someone had hacked into our e-mail and possibly the database. Months later after Natalie died, Lucy began to find other reasons for concern, she says.

"I was going through her computer logs, checking all processes that were running and at what times of day and night," she explains, and it's the first I've heard her go into detail about what she did back then. "And I found possible indicators of Trojan horses, of malware parading as legitimate programs, of a number of things."

"I assume you discussed this with Janet?" I ask because Lucy's never discussed it with me.

"I told her I wasn't sure. For example, there can be lots of explanations for a corrupt registry file. There can be more than one reason for a number of things. And if there's no cause for suspicion because you're far more worried about losing somebody you love and dealing with her seven-year-old kid? Then maybe you're not really looking either."

"But now you're suspicious."

"It's gone way beyond that."

"You've decided it was Carrie who was hacking. It was Carrie who was spying on Natalie, and basically on all of us." I don't ask because it's not a question.

"She was probably using a RAT, a Remote Administrator Tool to control Natalie's computer or computers." Lucy moves around the small galley as she talks, opening cabinets and cupboards like a fidgety kid. "And who knows how long it had gone on."

"How old was Natalie's laptop?"

"She'd refurbish and upgrade her personal computers, keeping them for a while. The one in question was six years old at the time, and some of the questionable files went back that far. So it's possible she was being hacked even earlier but those computers or devices are long gone. I can't check."

"If Carrie had been monitoring Natalie for at least six years," I reply, "then it wasn't triggered by her diagnosis or even by you and Janet getting back together. None of that had happened yet."

It's not adding up that the spying went on for an extended period of time. If it continued even after Janet and Lucy broke up well over a decade ago, why would Carrie still be watching Natalie? As I remember it, Carrie found her boring and referred to her as *The Old Shoe*. But clearly there's a lot I don't know, and I don't want to interrogate my niece.

I've never been given a satisfactory explanation for why she and Janet reconnected several years ago after more than a decade of being apart. I don't know if they were in contact all along or whose idea it was to get back together. But one day Janet reappeared, and next I knew Natalie was in hospice care and Desi was living here.

"Carrie's an addict, you know," Lucy then says as she walks into the main area of the trailer, her booted feet loud on the shiny steel floor. "She's addicted to us. In a sick way we're all she's got."

"She doesn't have us. She's never had us." I feel myself harden with anger.

Lucy sits down at a workstation and wakes up the computer mounted on the built-in desk.

"Somewhere mixed in with her mutated alchemy is this raging insatiable need to be important to someone." Lucy types a password. "And when she's in control of her victim—because everyone she partners with is a victim— she couldn't be more important to that person. For a while she's God. But then it always ends the same way. And she's alone again. The irony is, she needs us."

"She's not God and I don't give a damn what she needs." I return to the same bolted-down chair I was sitting in earlier.

"Benton says if you can't see her as a human, you'll never figure her out." Lucy's eyes meet mine. "And if you never figure her out, you'll never stop her."

I take a look at my phone again. Nothing. What the hell is going on? And I halfway expect that we're going to open the trailer door and find the entire park has vanished. As if we're in some hideous twilight zone and are being controlled remotely the same way Natalie's laptop may have been.

"Even if Carrie's behind all this, please explain how she would know the first thing about my father." I'm thinking of the canned recordings that sound like him, and I type a text to Marino as I talk. "If she's partnered with some other deranged person, how would he or she know?" I say to Lucy. "My father wasn't recorded, as far as I know, and Carrie never met him. She hadn't even been born by the time he died."

"I have to think there must be something of him out there somewhere," Lucy says, and it's not the first time she's said it.

"I'm not aware of it."

"You've never heard a recording of him but you can still hear him in your head."

"Like it was yesterday."

"What about Mom?"

"I don't know what Dorothy remembers."

"And there's no way she has a recording or knows about one?"

"She wasn't helpful. I asked her that a few days ago when we were discussing her trip." I didn't tell her why I was curious.

"There must be some kind of recording somewhere," Lucy says. "There has to be, and if there is? All someone had to do was get hold of it and pull out phonetic blocks and fabricate sentences. You could do the same thing to synthesize a voice speaking in Italian."

"Why can't we find this person?" I ask her point-blank. "What's so different this time that you haven't been able to trace a single communication from Tailend Charlie?"

"I think we're dealing with someone who's setting up virtual machines. If it were me, that's what I'd do."

"Please explain what you mean."

"It means we're sort of screwed," she says.

"What you do is hack into some open machine or network. University campuses are prime targets for this, and we've got more than our share around here," Lucy explains what she believes Tailend Charlie is doing.

"Once you create your own virtual machine, you use it to create a virtual mail server," she adds. "After every e-mail you eradicate the server and create a new one, and this goes on and on into perpetuity."

"And there's no trail, no IP or anything?" I assume.

"Maybe there will be an IP in the packet logs of routers along the way. But it's the worst kind of wild-goose chase. Every time you track down an e-mail it's gone and a new one pops up from a totally different location."

"It sounds like something Carrie would do," I admit. "It's technology I can imagine her knowing about."

"You can pretty much take it to the bank that she knows the same things I do," Lucy says reluctantly, and it's hard for her to give Carrie that much credit.

It's even harder for me to hear it. Then Lucy brings up Bryce and I've been waiting for her to get around to him. She says he has no concept of who he leaks intel to in the course of what he considers normal conversations.

"Including the detail about a fake tattoo, which couldn't have been visible to anyone who might have been watching." Lucy picks up her phone. "He would have had to pull down his sock, and even so, the tattoo is small and faded after he scrubbed the hell out of it."

She explains that when she heard about the 911 call she asked Bryce to take a photograph of the tattoo and e-mail it to her right away. She hands me the phone, and the marijuana leaf above Bryce's right ankle is Crayola green but dull. It's about the size of a quail egg.

Now that I'm looking at the image I'm not surprised that none of us at work today were aware of the inconspicuous temporary tattoo. I don't see how anyone could notice it without being in close proximity to Bryce as he has his sock pulled down or off. Or maybe the wrong person somehow heard about Bryce's botched party trick, and from there the detail somehow found its way into the false 911 complaint made to the Cambridge Police Department earlier this evening.

"The pool of suspects should be small," Lucy concludes. "It had to be someone who knew what Bryce was doing last night."

"What did he tell you?" I ask.

"That he got a fake tattoo at dinner with friends. Nothing was posted on social media, and he hasn't a clue how anybody would have known beyond the buddies he was with. That's the extent of his note to me. I've not actually talked to him."

"Maybe we should." I take another sip of water and try not to think about how empty my stomach is or how late it's getting.

I block out the *grand cru* Chablis Benton and I didn't drink, and the clammy shoes that feel glued to my bare feet. I keep checking my phone. According to Marino's latest update a few minutes ago, the tent's not completely set up yet because there was a problem arranging the panels around several large trees. A section of scaffolding collapsed. Then the canopied roof didn't fit quite right. Or something like that.

"Have you ever told Bryce that when you were growing up in Miami, some of the kids in school called you a Florida cracker?" Lucy asks that next, and I'm feeling pelted by rotten eggs from my past.

"You've got to be kidding," I reply.

"Tailend Charlie again, and he had to get it from somewhere. That's why I'm asking."

"Sister Twister and Florida cracker are mentioned in the latest rhyming tripe?"

"Yes," Lucy says, and indignation stirs in its secret place. I feel shame that was dormant but the anger is very much alive as my privacy, my past, continues to be invaded, distorted and vandalized by some anonymous bastard bard.

"Let's get to the bottom of this," I say from my metal chair as I dig my hands into the pockets of my windbreaker. "Bryce knows something even if he doesn't think he does. Let's ask him."

Several clicks of the mouse, and Lucy opens a file. Then in no time she has my chief of staff Bryce Clark on live video, the app her own enhanced rendition of Skype or FaceTime. She goes straight to the point, asking him if he knows much about my childhood in South Florida. Might he have been discussing it with anyone? Especially recently?

"Well we all know they were as poor as church mice," he replies. "But I can't say exactly what she might have mentioned when we've just been sitting around shooting the breeze. Is she with you?"

"Yes," I speak for myself.

"Not that it's very often we have nothing better to do than sit around the office shooting the breeze, right, Doctor Scarpetta?" He waves, his attractive boyish face staring blearily from the computer display. "Full disclosure?" He holds up a brown bottle of Angry Orchard hard cider with its whimsical scowling-apple-tree label. "My second one but I'm not drinking on the job since I'm home? Even if I'm talking to you?" He's saying this to me, I think, and I'm not sure if it's a question or a comment, if he's being funny or not, and that's not unusual with him.

"The friends you were telling me about earlier." Lucy rests her chin on her hand, addressing him on the computer display as if he's sitting across the desk from her. "Do you talk to them about work?"

"Never inappropriately," he says, and I can tell from the background that he's sitting in his living room and has paused the TV.

"What about her?" Lucy says to him as she looks at me.

"Are you suggesting I'm disloyal?" Bryce protests. "Are you saying I'm talking about Doctor Scarpetta behind her back?"

"I'm not saying anything. I'm asking questions. Are you sure there's no possibility one of these friends you had dinner with last night might have posted something about your tattoo online? Not that I've seen anything anywhere yet . . ."

"You won't because there's nothing," he retorts. "Why would it be on the Internet?"

"That's exactly what we're trying to figure out. How someone might have known about it," Lucy says.

"Perhaps someone who had no idea it could cause a problem?" I offer him a chance to save face.

"Hell no. Anyone who matters knows that stuff like that can get me into trouble because of who I work for," he says as if suddenly I'm not present anymore. "That anything can be used against anyone in court."

He rambles on for a long moment, suggesting in his convoluted way that it's routine for him to be called to testify in trials and have his credibility attacked. It's not. He's never summoned for anything except jury duty, and he's always excluded.

"Where did you go last night?" Lucy asks him.

"We had two other couples over for Mexican home cooking, our specialty, as you know." Bryce smiles on the monitor, warmed by the memory. "Firecrackers with fresh jalapeños, a seven-layer dip with my famous guacamole, plus tacos, and the most amazing margaritas made with a really nice *añejo* tequila that we've been saving since Christmas? The one from your mom?"

My mind blanks out for a moment. Then I realize he's referring to Dorothy. It dawns on me what he's talking about.

26

In Miami over the holidays last year, I got my fill of hearing about my sister's wonderful generosity and what *a simply scrumptious doll she is*, to quote Bryce.

It seemed that every time he and I had business to discuss over the phone, the topic of conversation managed to bounce back to Dorothy. If he thought she was in earshot, he'd tell me to pass along how much they were enjoying the tequila. Or he'd yell hello as if she could hear him. Or he'd ask me to convey a comment or a question. It was rather awful.

"Oh, what's the name?" Bryce snaps his fingers several times on the computer display. "This really fancy Patrón and it came in a leather box? And she has this fantastic recipe with agave nectar and fresh lime juice, straight up like a cosmo in a chilled glass, no salt. I told her I would practice so we can have her over while she's in town. And as you can imagine, the six of us had *way* too much fun." He rolls his eyes. "Just ask our cranky neighbor."

"Which friends are you talking about? Who were you

drinking tequila with?" Lucy wants to know. "And when did you tell my mother this?"

Bryce recites four names I've heard him mention often over the years as Lucy begins typing information into search fields. My slightly tipsy chief of staff continues to defend what he perceives as the tarnished honor of his best pals, who he's known "since forever?" He says it like a question.

"And you know what? I can promise you they have nothing to do with the lying piece of shit who made the nine-one-one call about Doctor Scarpetta abusing me in public," he adds with feeling.

"I didn't abuse you." I remind him to pay attention to his choice of words. "Please be careful what you say, Bryce."

"I'm just repeating what was reported to the police by some jerk-off concerned citizen." His face is sincere with his fixed blue stare and spiky blond hair.

"When did you tell my mother you would make her margaritas?" Lucy steers him back to that.

"Well today's Wednesday. So I guess it was Monday night when we were going over her flight info and other things."

"And the fake tattoo? Where were you when you were messing around with that last night?" Lucy asks. "And who saw?"

"Wow! Get out the rubber hoses! Or these days, the waterboard? In our living room. There was nobody else there. We were safe and sound in our own home. It's too hot to go out and I'm not one for making scenes. Not that a fake tattoo and margaritas are a felony, last I heard."

"What time was it?" Lucy asks.

"Let's see. It was after dark obviously, and we'd eaten. I'm thinking around the same time it is now. Nine forty-five, ten o'clock. Maybe as late as ten thirty, which is about when I realized to my shock that the tattoo wasn't *temporary* as advertised? It wasn't going to come off easily, and I'm thinking of contacting the company about it and complaining."

"So let's talk about nicknames for a minute," Lucy says.

"Well I'm sure I have a lot of them. And maybe I don't want to hear what some of them are?"

"I'm actually talking about your chief," Lucy says to him as she looks at me.

When she quizzes him about nicknames from my child-hood that he might have overheard, he asks, "Like what?"

"You tell me." Lucy isn't going to give him certain unseemly details if he doesn't already have them.

"She might have been called a know-it-all." Bryce frowns the way he does when he's thinking hard. "But that's to be expected, I guess. No insult intended," he adds for my benefit, I assume.

"Let me know if you think of anything else," Lucy says to him. "Any comment, no matter how innocent. Any person you know who might have passed along something without realizing it."

He promises he will, and with a click of the mouse he vanishes from the monitor.

"That narrows it down but doesn't make me feel any better." Lucy swivels her chair around, facing me as I recheck my phone for updates. "If this business with the fake tattoo had gone on in a bar, a restaurant or somewhere else in public?" she says as I read a text from Harold:

Tent up and ready for you.

"It might make more sense that someone could have been watching. But in the living room of his own home?" Lucy is saying.

234

The scene is waiting. I tell her I've got to go, and then I ask her to see what she can find out about Elisa Vandersteel. I tell her briefly about running into the woman who I fear is now dead, and if Lucy is surprised, she doesn't show it. But I catch a flare in her green eyes like light touching an emerald.

"How did you get the name?" She goes into interrogation mode, and I tell her about the British driver's license.

"Where was it and why are we thinking that's who she really is?" she then asks.

"On the fitness path between the body and the bicycle. Marino can e-mail you a picture of it."

"Most cases aren't complicated, Aunt Kay. Most end up being pretty much what they appear to be. But this one isn't going to be simple." She sounds reasonable but beneath her calm words is a threatening undercurrent, and I get up from my chair.

"There's something you're not telling me." It sounds so trite.

I sound naïve, almost laughable, because there's always something Lucy isn't telling me. There's plenty I don't tell her either, especially about Dorothy.

"I have a hunch about something. That's as much as I'll say right now." Lucy stares at me the way she does when she doesn't want me asking her anything more about a particular subject. "I'll be back with you when I have info I can confirm."

I remember what she said earlier. She referenced *multiple things happening at once*, and I inform her about the phone call Marino got allegedly from Interpol. All Lucy has to say about it is *more of the same*.

235

"Lucy, don't be so quick to decide everything is Carrie."
I come right out and say it.

"I haven't decided anything," she replies, and I feel her stubbornness like a slab of concrete beneath thin carpet.

"Well you know where I'll be. And I'm sure it comes as no surprise that it's not looking like I'll see my sister tonight." I stubbornly avoid referring to her as Lucy's mom or mother whenever I possibly can. "Please tell her I'm sorry Benton and I couldn't pick her up—that both of us apologize."

I almost say that we're looking forward to spending time with Dorothy, that we can't wait to have her over to the house, to cook for her and take her to the theater. But it wouldn't be true, and Lucy knows it's not. I can't tolerate the idea of lying, especially to someone who's been hoodwinked and mistreated by a parent who isn't a nice person unless it suits. Maybe I'm not a nice person either because there are some things I simply can't forgive. And I can't forgive my sister. I won't.

"Tell her I hope she isn't too exhausted after what's sounding like a not-so-pleasant flight," is the best I can muster as I open the door at the bottom of a metal stairwell that brings back memories of riding the school bus.

I remember missing it because Dorothy thought it was amusing to change every clock in the house. She thought it great fun to hide my homework, and I would miss the bus because of that too.

"I'm going to work in here for a while." Lucy's voice follows me out into the hot darkness where the greedy night crouches, waiting for me like some insatiable entity cloaked in suffocating black.

*   *   *

The humming vibration of the truck's generator, the sounds of traffic begin to recede into the inky distance behind me.

As I head back to a clearing I can't see it anymore, just a dark void because of the black tent up ahead, acres away, I'm haunted by what I just heard. It's been a while since I've thought about what happened ten months ago when Dorothy gave Bryce and Ethan a very expensive bottle of tequila.

I remember thinking it odd that she was suddenly extravagant with people she'd never shown any interest in, although typically my sister is quite the hit with gay men. She adores South Beach, and it adores her back. She finds it gratifying and entertaining to *dress to kill*, as she puts it, to hold court in gay bars, to march in gay pride parades or better yet ride on a float, preferably in a formfitting low-cut dress, showing off her eye-popping curves, waving to all her fans as if she's Sofía Vergara, whom Dorothy idolizes.

Whatever Italian my sister learned as a child, she's managed to forget so completely she can barely say *ciao* or order pasta, although she doesn't bother with either. I'm not sure when it happened, but somewhere along the way Dorothy decided she's South American.

She's fluent in Spanish and all things Latino. The Miami Sound Machine. The hip-hop scene. She loves Cuban and Mexican cuisine, and suddenly Bryce does too. I didn't give her handmade aged tequila much importance until a few minutes ago.

I didn't realize what it might signify and why would I? It's not out of the ordinary for my sister to make grand gestures when the mood strikes. It's not unusual for her generous acts to be at my expense. Not so coincidentally I was in Miami with Dorothy and my mother when Bryce

237

and Ethan received the Gran Patrón, specifically the Burdeos, which of course is Spanish for "Bordeaux," and that's the type of barrels it's aged in.

In other words, I heard all about it ad nauseam, and as I think back I recall assuming Dorothy's motive was to outdo or annoy me, and so what? I wasn't going to give her the satisfaction. But I find myself facing the ugly possibility that her Christmas splurge wasn't random or whimsical.

It wasn't simply her showing off and rubbing my nose in it. Not during the holidays or later at Easter, on Bryce's birthday or Ethan's and most recently and significantly Desi's. She's sent a deli basket, scented candles, potpourri, and treats for their pets. Desi got a Miami Heat jacket and a check, and I remember that Dorothy also called him.

All this when she didn't used to give any of us the time of day, really. Certainly she never paid attention to my chief of staff on the rare occasion she would call me at work. Until not so long ago she was condescending and dismissive to Bryce on the phone. She had no interest in Desi until his mother died. Dorothy never wanted to come north for a visit until now, and I wonder how often she and Bryce talk.

I will myself not to think about this now. Each gritty step I take along the unpaved path draws me closer to a young woman who shouldn't be dead no matter the cause. Still nameless and a mystery, she patiently awaits me inside a tent beyond the woods on the far side of the clearing.

Now that I'm seeing what Rusty and Harold have been struggling with for the better part of two hours, I understand what a job it was—or to quote Rusty's favorite shopworn pun, what an *undertaking*. Several acres away, the rectangular enclosure could accommodate a small wedding or a funeral.

The pitch-dark boxy shape blocks out tall old trees and shrubs, and the vague stars and quarter moon. I no longer can see the smudged lamps, the lights reflected in the river or the spreading empire of Boston neighborhoods and skyscrapers on the other side.

As I walk closer it's as if I'm reaching the end of the earth or diving in a shallow reef that abruptly drops off thousands of feet to the lightless bottom of the sea. I have the eerie sensation of floating in outer space, of being jettisoned to some awful remembered place where I don't want to be. And what continues to enter my mind is something Benton began to say at the beginning of our time together what now seems a different life ago.

I remember his exact words long before we had any concept of how trite and understated they one day would prove to be:

Carrie Grethen hasn't finished ruining people.

That was the simple prediction Benton Wesley, the FBI's legendary profiler, made long before we knew who she was, long before she was apprehended. He continued to predict her malevolence after she was indicted and convicted, and he didn't stop voicing his warnings when she was locked up on the women's ward of Kirby Forensic Psychiatric Center in New York City.

27

Criminally insane, deemed mentally unfit to stand trial, Carrie was warehoused on Wards Island in the middle of the East River, and it was a catastrophic mistake.

I don't know why it surprised anyone when she escaped. Benton had predicted as much, and he said that the miscreant who airlifted her to freedom, Newton Joyce, wasn't the first or last Clyde to her Bonnie. As a child, Joyce was horrifically disfigured in a fire. After his death, police searched his house and found a freezer full of his victims' faces. Carrie had encouraged him to keep the souvenirs. They probably were her idea.

I'm sure there were other partners after him, who knows how many before she exploited and had her fill of Troy Rosado. Carrie has a pattern of partnering with people she's convinced she can control, usually fatally flawed males like Troy, like Joyce, and before them Temple Gault, who Carrie worshipped and couldn't dominate.

A rare breed of glorious monster, Gault was a self-indulgent flamboyant Caligula, only he also was disciplined and supremely competent. Slight and limber, he was lithe and as lethal as a razor-tipped whip. He could strike as fast as a cobra, slicing open a throat or kickboxing the person to death, and he had a fetish for biting. As I walk through the heavy hot air I see his light blond hair, his blue eyes wide and staring like Andy Warhol's.

I've hardly thought about Temple Gault in years, and it's as if he's suddenly all around me. For an uncanny instant I feel his evil presence in the stagnant night, and I'm grateful he and Newton Joyce are gone for good. Dead. Unfortunately Carrie isn't, and I envision her dyed black hair and baseball cap, her unnaturally pale skin that she obsessively protects from ultraviolet light and toxins. This was what she looked like about a year ago, at any rate, and we have no idea about her appearance now. It could be anything.

But I would know those eyes, eerily blue like cobalt radiation, as if the decay of her very core emits a sapphire glow that darkens with her worsening moods, deepening to an angry purple like a damselfish when it turns aggressive. Carrie once was physically exquisite, born with exceptionally beautiful attributes and a stellar intellect. Her splendor was part of her curse.

The rest of it was her deranged religious freak of a mother who was pathologically jealous with a plethora of personality disorders and delusional ideations. Carrie had no siblings that would survive. After her birth, her mother miscarried twice. The brother born on the third try died soon after the father went to prison, and I remember looking up the autopsy records and lab reports when I was the chief in Virginia.

I remember thinking that a lot of mysterious deaths like

241

eleven-month-old Tailor Grethen's were signed out as sudden infant death syndrome or SIDS when maybe they shouldn't be. I remember wondering how he really died as I imagined little angelic-looking Carrie doing something undetectable to her precious baby brother. Wedging his head between the mattress and the side of the crib. Positioning him in a way that ensured he couldn't breathe. Smothering him. To quote Benton quoting Gilbert O'Sullivan:

Alone again, naturally.

Carrie would remain an only child in a blighted universe all by herself. Homeschooled, she had no classmates, friends or ordinary activities. She didn't go to the movies, take music lessons, play sports or read for pleasure. The only television programs she was allowed to watch were fundamentalist religious ones about Jesus and judgment, about who's saved and who isn't. *The Jim and Tammy Show. The 700 Club.* Jerry Falwell. She listened to TV preachers threaten eternal damnation and other hellfire scares, and by the time she was six, Carrie knew all about sin.

Her mother made sure of it. Benton believes she not only didn't stop her daughter from being sexually abused, it was the mother's idea. She egged it on, enticing a host of men with her pretty child as a party favor. Carrie was lagniappe, a little something extra that her mother freely offered and would severely punish her for afterward. Carrie was forced to beg for forgiveness, to forsake her evil ways and perform degrading acts of penance after every battery and rape.

Her superior mental discipline and ability to dissociate have made her a supremely successful psychopath, possibly the most successful one he's ever encountered, says Benton, who has studied and pursued her much of his career. She can transport herself mentally, detaching herself so completely that she doesn't feel stress or pain, and she knows how to wait. Carrie will delay gratification for decades if the reward is worth it, and lying and truth are different sides of the same reality to her. She could say the world is flat, the moon made of cheese, and she'd pass a polygraph.

Emotions such as fear, remorse and sorrow are colors missing from her palette, and it was Lucy's bad luck that this perfect storm of a malicious human being would be her supervisor at the FBI's Engineering Research Facility. My innocent and immature niece literally was assigned to Carrie during the college internship I personally arranged, using my influence and connections. Lucy wasn't much more than a child at the time.

She never really had a chance to fall in love with the right person, and maybe she would have if I'd not had the bright idea of sending her to the FBI Academy. If only she'd never stepped foot in Quantico, Virginia. Maybe her first significant relationship wouldn't have been with someone who seduced her, stole her heart and in some ways her very identity and soul. Maybe Lucy would have felt differently about Janet long ago and also now. I wouldn't want to be Janet.

I wouldn't want to be the one who comforted Lucy after Carrie came close to destroying all of us. It's not a level playing field. It never has been, and Janet's smart enough to realize there are but a few degrees of separation between murderous hate and erotic love. They are different extremes of the same raging passion, and she evokes neither in Lucy.

Janet is somewhere between the best and the worst of everything when it comes to life with my niece, and I constantly feel bad about it even as I say nothing. It's not my business. But I worry I'm to blame. Maybe Lucy would have been better off had I not tried to do so much for her, had I not insisted on rescuing her from powerlessness, from loss and every other perceived bogeyman that plagued my childhood.

Maybe Dorothy is right when she says that I'm the one who's done the real damage to a niece I couldn't love more were she my own daughter. The irony is that Dorothy doesn't know about the worst mistake I made. She doesn't know about Carrie Grethen. My sister could be sitting next to her on the plane and not know who she is or why it matters.

Heading toward the big boxy tent silhouetted against the night, I realized how unsettled I am by Lucy showing up and giving shape and form to her worst fears. I resent walking around in the dark with Carrie on my mind, and I feel myself begin to resist her as I've done countless times.

"How are we holding up?" I say to one of the uniformed cops as my sweat-soaked Tyvek-covered feet quietly crunch past on the unpaved path that stretches ahead of me.

"Hanging in."

"Stay cool," I say to another officer.

"You too, Chief."

"If anybody needs any water, let us know," I offer the next one I encounter.

"Hey, Doc? We got any idea yet what happened to her?"

"That's where I'm headed," I reply, and I have a similar exchange with all of them.

There are at least twice as many uniformed officers stationed about, and I have no doubt that Marino's made sure the park is surrounded and buttoned up. No one uninvited can come in and out, and I find myself constantly listening for news helicopters, grateful I'm not hearing them yet. I don't need them hovering low and churning up the scene with their rotor wash.

I reach the tent and for the second time tonight am startled by a figure stepping out of the shadows.

"Marino's inside waiting for you," Investigator Barclay says officiously as if I've just shown up late for an appointment.

Velcro rips as I push my way through the side flap of the canopied enclosure. For an instant I'm dazzled by auxiliary lights, the scene as bright as an operating room. I stop just inside, setting down my shoulder bag, placing my phone on top of it.

I survey some forty-by-thirty feet of the John F. Kennedy Park that includes the iron lamp with its shattered bulbs, the bicycle and the body, all of it lit up like high noon. Marino and I are alone, no one else allowed inside until we say so. He moves about in white protective clothing that starkly contrasts with the black-paneled walls and twelve-foot-high black roof supported by a scaffolding of gunpowder-gray aluminum poles.

As I watch him make notes and take photographs I feel as if we're immersed in a black-and-white postmodern photograph. The only noticeable colors are the margins of green grass, the tawny fitness path, red biohazard warnings, and the dead woman's light blue shorts. From where I'm standing I can't see the blood but it will be coagulated, tacky and a dark reddish brown on the way to dry black.

That's based on what I noticed earlier when I got close,

and also on the weather conditions, which remain extreme. Already I can feel the trapped humidity from the river. The hot air is sticky and low pressure like a tennis bubble. There's a plastic smell, and it won't be long until the stuffy environment bristles with a foul stench as bacteria teem and dead flesh and fluids putrefy.

"I went through the knapsacks," Marino calls out to me, and I assume he's talking about Enya and Anya.

"Are the girls safe and cool in a daisy room, I hope?" I find an equipment case to sit on so I can suit up.

"Eating snacks, drinking sodas. Flanders is babysitting, and I've got a couple uniforms making a wellness check on the mom." Marino's booming voice is amplified by the enclosure.

"She's still not answering the phone?"

"Or the door. Poor kids. I feel bad for them."

"And they're still saying she's supposed to be home?"

"Asleep in bed when they left the house, and I have a feeling I know what that means. Dead drunk, how much you want to bet?" Marino says. "I'm going to have to get DCF involved because it's obvious there's a problem."

The Department of Children and Families is the agency in Massachusetts responsible for neglected and abused kids. I tell Marino that no matter what happens in this case, he should make certain the twins are safe. It would seem they don't have adequate adult supervision. The way they're headed they're going to end up hurt or worse, and I don't think they understand the different kinds of trouble they can get into.

"Like stealing. Like tampering with evidence and obstruction of justice," Marino agrees. "Call it what you want? That's what it is when you pick up something that's not yours at a scene and decide to keep it. And guess what?" He hunches his shoulder to wipe sweat off his chin. "It turns out they were in possession of the dead lady's sunglasses. Which is too freakin' bad because I would have liked to see where they found them. How close to the bike or the helmet, that sort of thing?"

He lowers the camera and heads toward me as I begin pulling off the shoe covers I wore walking here.

"Do I dare ask what else was in their knapsacks?" When children stumble upon a violent scene it's bad for every reason imaginable.

"Leftovers from dinner," Marino says as he reaches me. "Bread wrapped in napkins, little packets of stuff like Parmesan cheese, red pepper flakes, salt, salad dressing." His big face is framed in white Tyvek like a nun in a habit, his cheeks bulging and a sweaty deep red.

"Sounds like they're not being properly fed." I look up at him from where I sit. "But you're not really going to know until you get inside their house. Are you okay, Marino? I'm worried you're very hot."

"Well they don't exactly look like they're starving. Yeah I'm hot. This sucks."

"One can be overweight and malnourished," I remind him. "In fact that's often the case, especially if the diet is mostly sugar and fast food. And left to their own devices, that's what kids will eat morning, noon and night."

"It appears they were telling the truth about having pizza for dinner and why they were out wandering around," he says. "I get the feeling they do this sort of thing a lot in all kinds of weather, probably because you're exactly right. Their mother's not taking care of them."

"It may be that she's never taken care of them, including

247

when she was pregnant." I suggest that the twins may be suffering from fetal alcohol syndrome.

"That would explain why between the two of them they couldn't light up a ten-watt bulb," Marino says. "They're street-smart but that's about it. And it's shitty. Little kids shouldn't have to be street-smart."

"The sunglasses they picked up," I go back to that. "What do they look like?"

"Maui Jims, sporty ones."

"Rimless with amber lenses?" I inquire as I get a sinking feeling again.

"Yeah," he says. "They were near the body, according to Enya. The lenses are dusty and scratched real bad, and I'm thinking the victim may have been wearing them when she was attacked. Assuming they weren't already damaged."

"We need to be careful about saying she was attacked." I don't like it when he makes me feel like a scold.

"When you saw the lady riding her bike earlier did you notice if her sunglasses were damaged?"

"I didn't notice, assuming that's for sure who this is."

"I think we know." He pulls off his gloves and tosses them into the nearby biohazard trash bag hanging on a metal stand. "It's hard to imagine we're talking about two different women who look similar, are about the same age, and both had on Converse sneakers and a Sara Bareilles concert T-shirt. And maybe the same type of sunglasses. And they appeared in the same part of Cambridge at the same time."

"Even if they're the same person that doesn't mean we know who she is." I'll continue reminding him to be conservative even if he doesn't listen.

"And the other thing the girls had squirreled away?"

He picks up a roll of paper towels, tearing off several squares to wipe his face. "A pendant. A gold skull about the size of a quarter, like from a necklace. I'm thinking it came from the broken gold chain."

"Where was it found?"

"They said on the path near the bike. Based on where they showed me, I'm thinking it was in the general area where the pieces of chain were." He tosses the wadded paper towels into the bright red trash bag next, and I follow them with my used shoe covers.

"The woman I encountered earlier was wearing an unusual necklace shaped like a skull. It was gold and looked fairly substantial, not flat like a medallion but rounded with contours," I inform him. "I noticed her flip it around to her back, tucking it into the back of her shirt when she rode across Quincy Street, heading into the Yard."

"It's gotta be her, and I'm not liking that you saw her twice right before she got whacked. I keep worrying that she's got some connection to you, Doc."

"I can't imagine what it would be," I reply. "I don't believe I'd ever seen her before today."

Then I tell him about my Internet searches for Elisa Vandersteel. I couldn't find her in London or anywhere.

28

"The driver's license could be fake," he says. "These days technology makes it a piece of cake to counterfeit IDs that look like the genuine article."

"It's odd that whoever Elisa Vandersteel is she doesn't seem to be on social media either," I inform him. "What young person isn't these days? And I came across nothing in the news about anyone with that name that might be her. But I only looked for a few minutes."

"I agree it's strange. Unless she had reason to stay below the radar." Marino pulls down his white hood, patting dry his shiny head with paper towels. "Jesus, I'm sweating like a whore in church. Or she had a fake ID card, and there's no such thing as an Elisa Vandersteel with that DOB and address. And maybe that's why there's no one with that name on social media."

"Lucy's working on it. Let's see what she comes up with." I tear open a packet of coveralls.

"More than she's been coming up with, I sure as hell

hope." It's an unfortunate dig at her failed efforts with Tailend Charlie, and I won't get into it with him.

I scan the lighted area of the park inside the flat-topped block-shaped enclosure, my attention wandering over the grass, the hard-packed path, the laid-down bike and the body. The scene looks eerily undisturbed as if it's not possible someone died violently here.

"How are we doing?" I ask Marino to fill me in on what might have developed since we last communicated. "Have you found anything interesting that we missed the first time? We're going to want to wrap this up as quickly as we safely can. It's awful in here, and I don't want either of us or anyone else getting overheated."

"Mostly I've been collecting what we already know about. The pieces of gold chain, the driver's license. And her helmet, which didn't look damaged to me."

"Do you think Enya and Anya might have picked up other evidence?"

"Where would they hide it? I searched their knapsacks, and we've got the glasses, the skull pendant, the phone. Plus we found the shirt one of them threw up on in the bushes."

"Unless they hid something somewhere," I propose. "Money, for example. Credit cards, cash? The victim was riding her bike out here alone with no money and no keys?"

"All I can tell you is they swear they didn't *borrow* anything else." Marino takes off his gloves and unzips a small black Harley-Davidson cooler bag that belongs to him personally. "They turned their pockets inside out for me. Nothing."

"I suppose it depends on whether they trust you enough

251

to be truthful," I reply as he lifts out a dripping bottle of water and offers it to me. "No thanks. I'm all set at the moment. It depends on whether you trust them in return," I add about the twins. "Do you?"

"Hell, by now I've got them thinking they're going to be sworn in as junior detectives any minute. So I'm pretty sure if they had anything else they would have handed it over."

"I'm also curious about why they didn't bother picking up the driver's license." I begin working the synthetic white pant legs over my horrible shoes. "It was still on the path when Investigator Barclay arrived. I'm wondering how it got where it was and why the girls took other things but left that for some reason."

"Probably because, the way they figure," Marino says, "a dead person's ID would get them caught red-handed. It's not like they thought it was fine and dandy to take the belongings of someone who's been injured or in this case killed. Point being, at some level they know right from wrong. They were thinking finders, keepers. And they assumed the dead lady wasn't going to need sunglasses, a phone or a gold skull pendant anymore."

"They said that?"

"Pretty much."

"Well she wouldn't be needing money anymore either."

"I know. But unless they've got it hidden in their under-wear?" He gulps the water, and the bottle is almost empty when he returns it to the cooler bag. "But I'll have Flanders check into that because there was no way in hell I was going to and be accused of manhandling them."

"Let's hope there's nothing else they've squirreled away that the victim wasn't going to need anymore." I replay my encounters with the cyclist when we were in front of the Faculty Club.

I didn't notice much in the way of jewelry.

"I didn't see a watch, for example," I pass on to Marino. "But the phone, the sunglasses and any other items Anya and Enya picked up and tucked inside their knapsacks will be a problem if this goes to court."

"I hope they didn't mess up anything that matters." He splays his fingers, working his hands into new gloves. "Not that there's anything much to mess up. So far I'm not seeing discernible footprints, no fresh cigarette butts. No blood drips or anything that might make you think there was a struggle. It's like she was already dead when she hit the ground."

"It certainly appears that she didn't move." I stand up and work my arms into the slippery white sleeves. "Based on what I'm seeing, I suspect once she was on the ground she was unconscious and dying," I add as my phone rings.

It's Lucy, and I put on my earpiece. I tell her I hope she's found something.

"South Audley Street, Mayfair. Off Grosvenor Square," she says.

"Elisa Vandersteel's address?" I sit back down on top of the equipment box, and I look up at Marino.

"A six-thousand-square-foot house valued at around thirty million pounds," Lucy tells me. "That's the address on the driver's license, and one of the reasons her name's not coming up in ordinary searches is it's not her or her family who lives there."

"The address is fake then."

"It's not. The owner is the CEO of a tech company, William Portison. British, went to MIT, wife's name is

Diana." Lucy's voice sounds in my earpiece. "Does that mean anything to you?"

"I don't think so."

"That's who owns the house where Elisa Vandersteel was living as an au pair for the past two years," Lucy says with no lack of confidence. "It could explain why the Portisons' ritzy Mayfair address is on her British driver's license. And being an au pair might be why she's not on social media. Not every employer wants that if they're private and careful with their kids."

"You might be right but it's odd," I reply.

"A lot of au pairs work in exchange for room and board," Lucy says next. "They basically become part of the family."

"Yes but usually not literally," I reply. "I wouldn't think living with a family entitles you to hijack their address and use it as your own. If the South Audley Street house isn't Elisa Vandersteel's legal residence, then it really shouldn't be on her driver's license or other forms of identification. If nothing else it presents a liability to the Portisons."

"Well it seems they didn't stop her from using it when she moved to London two years ago and got the license," Lucy says. "She lists it on a number of things and got mail there. So I assume they knew what she was doing."

"Moved from where?" I ask.

"Canada," Lucy says in my earpiece. "She exchanged her driver's license for a British one. And the obvious reason to do that would be if she planned to drive in the UK for more than twelve months."

She goes on about it with a certainty that perplexes me, and I'm not going to ask how she's managed to find out all this. When I searched the Internet for Elisa Vandersteel

I came up empty. But I don't know where Lucy looked. Possibly the Deep Web, the Undernet, and I don't venture into the Bermuda Triangle of cyberspace, where terrorists and deviants prowl, and unsuspecting people and their property are wrecked and forever lost.

Lucy reminds me rather constantly that nothing is private anymore. Maybe what I'm seeing with the Tailend Charlies of the world is simply the price of doing business these days. But I admit I hate it. At times I feel like Rip Van Winkle waking up to discover decades have passed. Only it feels more like a century. Life used to be more civilized than it's become, that's for sure.

"And it's likely her work visa was up or a problem of one sort or another," Lucy adds as if she's had access to a dossier, "which explains why she's no longer in London."

"The woman I met earlier today definitely sounded British, not Canadian," I reply. "In fact, my first thought was that she might be from London."

"Elisa Vandersteel was in London for the past two years but not from there."

"And before that?"

"A student at Leicester University, and before that it was Toronto, where she was born."

"And do we have any idea why she was in Cambridge?" I ask. "It would seem she has something to do with the repertory theater or the musical *Waitress* since that's where I ran into her the first time."

"She's not a student here," Lucy says as if it's common knowledge. "Her name also doesn't come up with the ART, the Loeb Center, *Waitress*, or anything related or even similar. Maybe she was a volunteer or something. It will be easy enough to find out."

"I'm wondering if she might have been living with someone here the same way she was in London." I tell her about the young man she kissed in front of the Faculty Club.

"That's my guess. She's staying with someone, explaining why I'm not finding anything to indicate she has an address in the greater Boston area. There's nothing listed in her name. No rentals. Nothing owned. Not even a hotel room or sublet that I'm seeing so far," Lucy says, and I feel Marino's curious stare.

"We got an ID?" he asks, and I indicate it's looking that way.

The UK driver's license found on the fitness path is genuine. The dead woman is twenty-three-year-old Elisa Vandersteel, a college graduate, a former au pair. But we won't release her name publicly until we've gotten a confirmation with DNA or dental charts and have notified her next of kin. For now Marino and I will assume this is who we're dealing with, and I feel stunned all over again.

I feel horrible. Actually I'm not even sure how I feel, how I should feel, how anybody should feel. It's as if I had a chance to change Elisa Vandersteel's destiny, and I didn't. She was in front of me twice today mere hours before her death. But it made no difference. If only I could have stopped her. If only I'd suggested she fasten the chin strap of her helmet or that she get out of the heat. Maybe I could have gotten her to think twice.

Maybe she would have changed the ultimate route she took or changed something, anything at all. If only I could have delayed or diverted her, maybe told her not to ride alone after dark through a deserted park. Of course I didn't know she was going to do that. I didn't know enough to tell Elisa Vandersteel a damn thing that might have prevented her from dying. And I need to stop this or I'll drive myself crazy.

"Her father was Alexander Vandersteel, and he committed suicide in 2009 at the age of forty-one," Lucy tells me what she's finding so far, and I hear keys click in the background as she continues her searches. "I got his obituary right here, and it looks like he ran a charity that got decimated by some Madoff-like investment scam. He hanged himself from a rafter in the garage," she says, and I can't imagine a detail like that was in his obituary.

"What about Elisa's mother?" I stand up and zip the coveralls to my chin but save the dreaded hood for later.

"Not sure yet," Lucy says. "But her parents were divorced."

"So let me see if I have this straight. The father's dead, who knows about the mother, and they were divorced," I repeat. "I guess we go to plan B because it would seem that Elisa Vandersteel's familial relationships may not help us with her identity."

I sit back down and start pulling on a new pair of shoe covers.

"We're probably not going to be able to confirm who she is," I add, "until we recover certain personal items such as her toothbrush, her hairbrush."

"I'm guessing she was staying with someone around here," Lucy says. "And I can promise that somebody at the theater is going to have at least some of the answers we need. I thought I'd wander over there before everyone's gone for the night, just do a little snooping, maybe find out where the boyfriend lives and where she's been staying. I'll find something."

257

I glance at the time on my phone. The evening performance at the repertory theater will have ended more than an hour ago.

"How will you explain your interest?" I inquire. "We want to be careful about word getting out."

"Oh I forgot. I'm new at this," says my former FBI, ATF agent niece who spent years undercover and doesn't need my coaching.

I tell her to be careful, and she says she'll see me later.

"Probably back at the office at some point," she adds, and I don't ask if Dorothy and her mountain of luggage are in the car with Janet and Desi yet.

I end the call, not inclined to bring up my sister in front of Marino, who watched me the entire time I was on the phone. I have a feeling he's thinking about her but I'm not going to give him an entrée to talk about it. If what Benton said is true and Marino and Dorothy have started something unbeknownst to me, I don't want to hear it now. I have enough to deal with.

"Ready?" I say to him.

29

"The ambient temp's eighty-seven degrees," Marino says, and I spot the thermometer he placed on top of my scene case near the body.

I pull on purple nitrile gloves, and already I'm sweating through my scrubs.

"Thanks." I find my notepad.

"What are you going to do about taking her temp?" he asks. "I'm worried we should have just gone ahead and done it when we first got here."

"With flashlights in the dark when we don't know what evidence we might be disturbing or contaminating?"

"I know. And I'm with you, Doc. But just saying I've heard some comments, you know, cops talking about you sitting in the cool truck and not bothering."

"And we've heard such comments before, and we'll hear them again."

"Should we turn her over or something? Because I don't see how you're going to put a thermometer in her armpit when both arms are straight up." He lifts his arms above his head, and when he's swathed in white protective clothing I'm reminded why Bryce sometimes calls him The Yeti.

"We're fine at the moment. I won't need to turn her to take her temp."

"Okay. But it seems like the longer she's out here . . .?"

"I know how it seems," I reply. "But as you've pointed out, her arms are straight up over her head. Even if I reposition her, it wouldn't be ideal for getting a core temperature."

That leaves the option of using the rectum. But there's no way I'm inserting a thermometer and possibly introducing injury or have some pugilistic defense attorney accuse me of it. I'll opt for the less convenient technique of making a small incision in the right upper abdomen to get the temperature of the liver.

I'll do this before anything else, and I return to the body. Kneeling close with a sterile disposable scalpel, I get a whiff of decomposition and another odor that's most noticeable near her head. The stench from blood breaking down is mixed with something else, and I try to isolate what it is.

"I'm smelling something acrid," I say to Marino as dark red blood oozes from the tiny buttonhole incision I make.

"I don't smell anything." He looks away as I push in the long thermometer.

Marino's not squeamish until he is. Then some things really bother him. I reposition myself closer to Elisa Vandersteel's head to find the source, getting down on my knees, leaning close to look carefully.

"Not me," Marino says. "All I smell is rotting blood."

"This." I show him singed hair near her neck and right jaw.

"Shit. I swear you're part bloodhound."

I also notice tiny fragments of glass. They shine like grains of sand in her disarranged ponytail, but I see nothing like that on her clothing, skin or adhering to the dried reddish-brown blood in her right ear.

"So maybe she has a head injury," Marino says as he follows where I'm touching and looking. "That can make you bleed out of your ears."

"It depends on what type of head injury."

"How about one caused by a gun?" he proposes, and he's not being funny. "We don't know that she wasn't shot." His eyes are hidden by his camera again as he takes more photographs. "We've sure as hell seen our share of cases where you don't know they've been shot until you get them to the morgue."

"At the moment we don't know much," I agree, and I have little doubt that at this early stage of things Marino wishes the victim had been blasted with a shotgun, had a knife in her back or an ax buried in her head.

Then he'd know exactly what he's dealing with, and most of all he wants to work the case because he's already working it. It's natural to want to fit facts with a gut feeling, and that's the problem I routinely face because it's hard for cops to back off. There's no conquest, commendation or adrenaline rush if Elisa Vandersteel died from natural causes or an accident.

"She could have been shot." Marino doesn't stop but he will eventually. "And if you were shot in the ear at close range you could get burned hair from the muzzle flash."

"I'm fairly certain that's not what we're seeing." I study wisps and stubble that remind me of melted nylon as I think about what Anya and Enya said they noticed when they were close to the body.

They mentioned an odor that reminded them of their mother's overheated blow dryer, and possibly what they were detecting was burned hair. If so they were telling the truth about that, and the more I observe at close range, the more reality shifts right in front of me.

What began as the scene of an attempted mugging, robbery or sexual assault turned deadly is quickly becoming something else entirely. Marino won't want to hear it. Not at first. But after spending most of my professional life with him, I'm used to talking him down from the ledge, and he returns the favor. Now and then I'm guilty of bias too. I don't know anybody who isn't.

Marino probably is the most relentless cop I've ever worked with, and his kneejerk reaction will be to resist the track my thoughts are taking. When a detective worth his salt sinks his teeth into a theory, he doesn't want to let go. If one isn't careful, an investigation becomes a competition, a contest when it shouldn't be about winning. It should be about truth.

"Maybe she burned her hair when she was drying it after the shower this morning," he suggests. "It's important to remember we don't know when it happened. Maybe it's got nothing to do with what killed her."

"She dried her hair after the shower this morning?" I call attention to what he just said. "Do we know that's what she did?"

"Negatory since we barely know who the hell she is. But what I'm trying to say is we have no idea when it happened. I've seen people burn their hair from grills, the stove, cigarette lighters," he reminds me.

But what he's really referring to is that he's experienced each of the above more than once. Marino hasn't changed much. He still makes me crazy when he starts squirting lighter fluid during backyard barbecues. I can't count the times I've said to him: *What is it you don't understand about more not always being better?*

"Back in the days when I had hair to worry about, I scorched it when I was lighting a flare one time," he says, and I remember that too. "Took a long damn time to live that down." This was in Richmond, and he didn't live it down. "Point being, we don't know when she singed her hair and it might have nothing to do with anything."

Her eyes stare dully at me from slitted lids.

If only you could speak, I always think. She will in her own way and in her own time. The language of the dead is silent and difficult, and the message I keep getting is Elisa Vandersteel looks remarkably clean and uninjured. I haven't turned her over yet, and I'll know more when I can examine her internally. But already I feel confident that her singed hair is directly related to her death.

That doesn't mean she's a homicide. I believe she was killed by a predator but that doesn't mean it was human. She may be an electrocution, and I'm scanning for any possible source of current. I'm looking around for something damaged, a shorted circuit that she could have come in contact with.

My attention continues going back to the obvious suspect, the iron lamp with its broken bulbs. I keep looking up at the sky only to be reminded that I can't see it because of the canopy. I'm thinking about power lines and lightning, and I tell Marino that whatever singed her hair likely occurred at or around the time of her death. If she'd burned her hair at an earlier time I don't believe we'd smell it now.

"Except I don't smell it." He bends close to the body, shrugging his broad shoulders.

"And I do," I insist. "And if it's this noticeable it probably was even stronger when Enya and Anya showed up a couple hours ago and found her."

Marino looks at the body, and he looks all around the lighted area of the park boxed in by the tent.

"The one thing that sticks out like a sore thumb is the blown-out lamp." He comes around to the idea begrudgingly, and now we're getting somewhere.

"That's exactly what I'm wondering. The damage to the lamp is telling us something important," I reply, and we start talking about power lines.

Most of them aren't underground in Cambridge, and Marino is quick to assert that if one were down we would have found it by now.

"Probably the hard way. Or the twins would have lit themselves up," he adds. "So tell me how it could be an electrocution, Doc? She would have had to come in contact with something electrically charged, and I'm not getting the mechanics of how it could have happened."

He points out there are no accessible electrical panels that might have live circuits, and no cords or tools to malfunction.

"And I'm not seeing transmission wires, cables, nothing like that exposed on the ground anywhere," he continues going down the list, and he should know.

Marino has his own machine shop. He has a monster garage, and thinks nothing of building an addition to his house or overhauling the engine of his truck. On more than one occasion in the past he's been the jack-of-all-trades I called in a pinch when I had a problem or electrical emergency. Especially in the earliest years when I lived alone, he was always over at my house for one reason or another, installing motion-sensor lights, repairing the garage door, changing the oil in my car, swapping out the garbage disposal.

"And it's a damn good thing, right?" he says. "Or maybe all of us would have been fried the minute we started walking around out here."

"That's an unpleasant thought." I step back on the path, looking at the lamp, at the pattern of broken glass.

The lightbulbs didn't merely crack or shatter. They were exploded with enough force to send pieces and shards many yards away. The lamppost is about ten feet tall, and I can't see the damage to the lantern. But clearly Marino has.

"The screws are still in the sockets, the three bulbs are totally destroyed." His face is red and sweaty as he circles the lamppost, looking up, his hands on his hips. "For the most part the filaments are gone."

"How can you see from here?" The lantern is too far above my head for me to look inside it.

"While they finished setting up, I used a stepladder and took photographs, which I can show you later," Marino says. "The metal latch is missing, maybe explaining why the glass door is open, and the question once again is when. Did the exploding bulbs cause the little latch, the hook, to break off? Or was it even there to begin with? We'll keep looking but it's not showed up so far."

I walk over to the bicycle on its side, and the rear tire is closest to the park entrance where Marino and I came in when we first got here. Apparently Elisa Vandersteel did the same thing, and I remember her pedaling through the Harvard Yard. I imagine her turning right off John F. Kennedy Street, entering the park from the east.

From there she would have followed the fitness path to the clearing, riding west as the sun slipped behind the trees and the shadows got darker and longer. Based on the position of the bike, something happened right here where I'm standing on the path, the iron lamp but several yards to my left. Her body ended up some ten feet away with glass in her hair, and her helmet is farther away than that.

As I think of lightning deaths I've worked I'm reminded that at first blush it almost always seems we're dealing with a violent assault. Clothing can be ripped, tattered or torn completely off, and I think of the T-shirt in the shrubbery. Shoes or boots will split wide open or come off like the Converse sneakers. Jewelry melts or breaks, and I envision the segments of gold chain we found. The broken ends looked shredded, and that's consistent with an electrical discharge. The current hits a metal object, dramatically heating it up, and it disintegrates.

Often victims are critically injured when the explosive force of an electrocution or a lightning strike hurls them to the ground. It's not unusual to die from blunt-force trauma, and it could be that's what killed Elisa Vandersteel. But I have my doubts.

30

My coveralls crinkle. The thin white material is slippery and whispery as I sit back on my heels to take a closer look at the unpaved path and the nearby grass.

It's past eleven, and the stench of decomposition has made the air deader and thicker. It's close to unbearable in here. But at least we're not dive-bombed by flies. The tent helps keep them out, and as a rule they're not active at night, not hunting for putrefying wounds and orifices in which to lay their eggs.

I study glass fragments as small as grains of salt that rained over the bicycle, sparkling like diamonds on the frame, the tires, and blades of grass.

"Not that I'm an expert in exploding lightbulbs," I say to Marino as I return to the bike's rear tire. "But right here where she went down there's a fair amount of glass that's been pulverized into dust."

"I've seen that before in electrical fires and arcing. Lightbulb glass is really fragile, and you give it enough juice it will blow to smithereens." He squats close to me, and I feel his heat and smell his sweat. "But some of what we're noticing probably is from the powder that coated the inside of the bulbs."

We look up at the empty lantern with its open access door, and below it a whitish residue is visible on the black iron frame. When the glass fragments blew out, they created a trail of what looks like fairy dust sparkling and twinkling across the fitness path, through the lawn, to the trees.

In my head I play it out like animation, envisioning the lamp violently exploding and the bicycle going down. The two events happen simultaneously as Elisa Vandersteel is jettisoned from the saddle. If that's what occurred, it could explain the tiny particles of glass on top of the downed bicycle. It might be the only explanation for the sandlike fragments caught in her hair.

"Well I think you're right about her burned hair being related to this." Marino cranes his neck looking up at the black iron lantern again. "But if the lamp malfunctioned as she was riding by? Wouldn't you also expect her to have cuts from flying glass?"

"That's a good point, and I can only say I've not yet seen any injuries like that." I think about how low Elisa Vandersteel might have been as she was riding by.

The lightweight hybrid has a small aluminum frame, low-rise handlebars, and a gel seat that I estimate would be approximately four feet off the ground were the bicycle upright. When she rode through the Yard she was bent over but not tucked into a racing position. I estimate the lantern would have been at least seven feet above her head when the lightbulbs exploded out the open door.

"The greater the mass, the greater the velocity," I'm explaining this to Marino. "And the bigger pieces, the shrapnel, would have flown over her head. But powder wouldn't travel far. It would drift down. That's assuming she was on her bicycle at the time, and I'm not seeing anything to make me think she wasn't," I add. "All of this is hypothetical. But it's significant that there's glass in her hair. It couldn't have landed on her where she is now."

"Nope. There's nothing over there because all the glass blew that way." He points in the general direction of the Kennedy School. "So we really don't think she was grabbed off her bike." He looks at me, and it's a good sign that he's started using the word *we*. "We're thinking there was no assailant—that she was just riding through the park and got zapped by a faulty lamp or heat lightning or something crazy like that."

"It's a possible scenario," I reply. "I don't see any sign of a physical confrontation."

"Then we're not calling this a homicide. Are we calling it anything when people ask?"

"It's undetermined for now. The less said the better."

"That's for damn sure. But to throw her ten feet like she was shot out of a cannon? All I can say is there must have been a hell of a lot of force. And I guess her helmet ended up even farther away than that because it's lightweight."

"And because possibly the chin strap wasn't fastened." I tell him when I saw Elisa Vandersteel ride across Quincy Street toward the Harvard Yard, the strap was dangling.

"Shit," he says. "Well that answers that."

"We'll know a lot more when it's determined exactly what happened to the lamp," I reply. "It won't be fun if you have to dig up the entire thing and haul it to the labs."

"Done it before. Will do it again."

269

I busy myself with my scene case, finding clear plastic and brown paper bags. I gather rolls of masking tape, Sharpies, and a gunshot-primer-residue collection kit I use when traces of debris are destined for the CFC's powerful electron microscopes. Changing my gloves, I return to the body. I kneel by her head, and in the intense illumination of the auxiliary lights, my flashspun polyethylene-covered knees are bright white against the green grass.

I remove the cap from a carbon-covered metal stub. I press the adhesive side against Elisa Vandersteel's scorched hair, collecting bits of glass, fibers, particles, anything I find. Sealing each stub inside a sterile vial, I label and initial it, prepping in the field, preparing specimens for the trace evidence lab.

This will make it easier for my chief microscopist Ernie Koppel to do the analysis when he gets to work first thing in the morning. The evidence will be waiting. It will save us time if all he has to do is sputter-coat the samples with gold. Then he'll mount them in a chamber and vacuum it down.

Palpating the scalp, I dig my fingers through Elisa Vandersteel's tied-back long chestnut hair. Gently, carefully I work my way around the curvature of her skull, and my gloves are smeared dark red.

"She's got a wound to the back of her head," I tell Marino, and I'm aware of the side of her face resting against my leg.

She's as warm as life, and I feel a flutter around my heart again. It's as if I've been touched by the breath of God, reminded of what I'm dealing with, and I steady myself. I can't have a personal reaction right now, and I move blood-crusted hair out of the way to measure the laceration with a small plastic ruler.

The injury is not quite two inches in length over the occipital bone. I tell Marino that the laceration was caused by skin splitting as a result of blunt-force trauma, and this likely is the source of most of the blood we're seeing.

"Possibly from striking her head on the hard-packed path," I add.

"And the reason there's blood under her back is because she was dragged and that's where it ended up." Marino is looking down at Elisa Vandersteel's feet with their light gray-and-white-striped bicycle socks. "And we can account for how that happened. We know who did that much at least."

He takes more photographs of marks in the dirt that are no more than six inches long, terminating at the back of the heels. The girls didn't pull her very far in their effort to get her out of harm's way. They didn't succeed if their goal was to make sure she didn't get run over, as they put it.

Her body isn't even close to being completely off the path, but I'm bothered that their impulse was to move it at all. I wonder if this is what they habitually handle at home, perhaps when their mother is in a drunken stupor or passed out cold on the floor.

I gently touch the wound to the back of the head, spreading the irregular ragged edges so I can see the slender threads of tissue bridging. They're a clear indication this isn't an incised wound caused by a weapon with a sharp edge. I tell Marino that the scalp and subcutaneous tissue were split by a crushing force over a bony prominence of her posterior skull.

"So she must have been alive when she got that or she wouldn't have bled out," he says.

"But she didn't bleed out very much, which suggests she didn't survive very long. The scalp is incredibly vascular," I explain. "There would be a lot of blood everywhere had she survived long enough to move, to walk around or try to run from someone."

I continue working my fingers through her hair, checking for boggy tissue or fractures. There are no other injuries to her scalp or skull, not that I can feel or see, and I ask Marino to bring a hand lens from my scene case. I hear him step away. Then he's opening drawers, and next he's back with the magnifying lens. I use it and a flashlight to get a better look at Elisa Vandersteel's right ear.

"No abrasion, charring, stippling or any other sign of injury," I inform him. "I'm seeing only dirt and dried blood, and I'm not likely to know what caused the bleeding until we get her into the CT scanner."

Placing my hands under the back of her head, I lift it a little. I turn it to the right, and there's dried blood in her left ear too.

"If she's an electrocution, why would she have blood in her ears?" Marino asks.

"Ruptured eardrums are the most common cause." I open her eyes wider.

I check them for burns, for hemorrhages, and the blue irises are becoming cloudy. Sliding the long thermometer out of the incision in the abdomen, I wipe off blood so I can read the calibrations. Elisa Vandersteel's core body temperature is thirty-four degrees Celsius or ninety-four degrees Fahrenheit, and that would be about right if she's been out here for several hours.

"And her rigor's beginning, which is also consistent with that. I can feel a little resistance as I move her neck." I show Marino. "But her right hand and wrist are completely stiff, as Investigator Barclay noted earlier, and it's beginning to make sense."

As I lift her arm I notice that on top of her wrist is a peculiar whitish linear burn about three inches long and so fine it's as if she were scorched by a fiery spiderweb. It wasn't noticeable when her arm was raised over her head, so I'm just now seeing it, and I wonder if her right hand was near her hair when it got singed. If so, what did she come in contact with? Marino takes photographs, and I show him that the right wrist and hand are as rigid as iron.

"Yet rigor's only moderately advanced in her right elbow and shoulder." I lift her arm again to demonstrate. "It's barely noticeable in other small muscles and not apparent anywhere else including her left arm." I move that too. "I assume when Investigator Barclay checked for a pulse, the wrist he touched was her right one."

"I'm going to ask him," Marino says. "But that's the only thing that adds up. And from that he decided she was in full rigor all over."

"She's not, and it would have been even less advanced a few hours ago. She would have been limber except for this." I indicate her right hand and wrist. "And I'm reminded of what we see in an electrocution when the victim touched something like a hot wire—and that's what the white mark looks like on her anterior wrist. It looks like a burn from touching something extremely hot, the kind of burn you get when you scorch yourself on the red-hot burner of a stove."

"But a burn wouldn't give you instant rigor," Marino

says. "And that's what this is even though I'm not sure I've ever seen it in person before."

A cadaveric spasm or "instant rigor" supposedly can occur when the death is preceded by a violent expenditure of energy that depletes muscles of oxygen and adenosine triphosphate (ATP). And the result is rigidity. The phenomenon is rare and believed by many experts to be apocryphal. But for sure something odd has happened here.

"So if her right hand was in contact with an electrical current," I tell Marino, "theoretically this could cause the muscles to continuously contract or clench, to go into what's known as tetany."

I pull the body partially on its side, just enough to check the back for livor mortis, or the settling of uncirculating blood due to gravity. I see only a slight pink blush. When I press down my thumb, the skin still blanches. Livor is in the early stages, and this also is consistent with her not having been dead very long.

There's also no question that when she landed on the ground she was either shirtless or her shirt was bunched up. Her back has the scratches and abrasions I'd expect in a bicycle accident, and there's dirt on her white sports bra.

When I turn the body a little more I'm surprised by what at first looks like a necrotic tattoo.

"What the hell?" Marino says.

"Her pendant," it dawns on me.

31

The burn is shaped like a skull.

"You can see the face. Well almost," I show Marino as we change our gloves, and we have a red biohazard trash bag full of soiled ones by now. "You can make out an eye and part of the grin, at any rate."

"Was she wearing the necklace backward when you ran into her?" He blots sweat on his chin with a paper towel, careful not to drip anywhere important, including the body.

"I wouldn't think so because I noticed the gold pendant was a skull with a whimsical face."

"Then it had to be turned over when it burned her, and it had to be inside her shirt so it was directly against her skin." He states what he wants to be true.

Marino doesn't want to think anything that might feed into his phobia of things that creak, groan and go clank in the night. He's getting spooked. I would expect as much after today, and it seems far from over.

"If you saw an injury like this and had no idea?" He goes on and on about it. "In the Salem days this would get you hung as a witch. They'd say it had to be a witch who zapped this person, and you'd better hope you never gave whoever it was the evil eye."

"Well fortunately we don't live in those days. But you're right. I probably would have been hanged as a witch." I pick up my hand lens, and he takes close-up photographs of the burn.

Dry and dark reddish brown, the partial impression of the skull's grinning face was caused by sparing when the metal pendant got extremely hot. The debossed or depressed mouth and an eye weren't in contact with skin, and those areas aren't burned. They've remained pale, explaining what looks somewhat like a grotesque emoji in the middle of Elisa Vandersteel's upper back. Even I would be the first to say that it's bizarre.

"It looks like a dead head." Marino's eyes race around. "Like something supernatural, like a stigma."

He means a death's-head and a stigmata, and the burn only looks like that if one knows what caused it.

"Can you help me hold her please?" Sweat runs down my chest, my belly, between my thighs, and the scrubs under my coveralls are soaking wet.

Squatting across from me, Marino steadies the body as I turn it completely on one side to give me a better look from head to toe, front and back.

"That's weird too," he says about the delicate whitish linear burns I find on the right shoulder and posterior base of the neck. "More of the same thing she's got on her stiff right wrist, and they're on the same side of her body. But if they're burns, they don't look anything like the one here." He indicates the angry red wound caused by the pendant.

I explain that when burns look leathery and white it usually indicates full thickness or third degree. I suspect that these whitish linear marks are from direct contact with whatever may have electrocuted her.

"Such as wires." I give him a hypothetical. "Except they would have to be very fine, almost hairlike."

"What wires?" Marino looks around nervously as if they might be close enough to get him.

"I have no idea—assuming that's what we're dealing with," as I notice she has something in the interior pocket of her blue running shorts. "The other burn is from the gold pendant making contact with this same electrical source. That's my guess."

Digging my fingers under the waistband, I find the small interior pocket and the hard flat shape inside it. I pull out a black plastic fob that appears to have a serial number on it.

"Bingo. Maybe it's the key to where she lives," Marino says as I drop the fob in an evidence bag I hand to him.

I get up and look around at the trees, the lamp, the trail of exploded glass. I try to come up with what could have been long and linear like fine wires that she might have come in contact with as she rode her bicycle out here. I think of her pedaling through the shadows, through the stifling heat, perhaps getting anxious and weary as it got later and darker.

Then suddenly something sears her bare right shoulder, the back of her neck, scorching her between her shoulder blades. It must have been excruciatingly painful and terrifying as she frantically grabbed at whatever it was, burning and shocking her right hand. It must have felt as if she were being attacked by an invisible swarm of hornets, and that might be the last thing she was conscious of as her bike went down and she was thrown clear.

Such a scenario could explain the linear burns, and it could account for her asymmetrical rigor. A powerful electrical current striking a gold pendant and passing through her body would have heated up moisture, turning it to steam, and that could have blown off and damaged her shoes and clothing. Heat could have broken the gold chain we recovered, and I check her neck again, looking for any sign the chain burned her before it broke free.

Using a magnifying lens and moving her hair, I find what look like several red hash marks, tiny red burns no bigger than dashes on the right and left sides of her neck. There's nothing in front, and then I envision Elisa Vandersteel again, hot and sweaty but alive and friendly on the sidewalk in front of the Faculty Club. She was wearing a neckerchief.

A blue paisley print, I'm fairly sure, and I recall having the impression it was somewhat faded, possible a little frayed as if it might be something old. I ask Marino if a neckerchief has shown up, and I describe it. Did the twins possibly have it in a knapsack, and he didn't realize where it came from?

"Nope," he says. "I didn't see anything like that but I'll have Flanders double-check while she still has them in the daisy room."

"If not, then it should be around here somewhere," I reply, "unless she took it off after I saw her on Quincy Street. The important point is if she were wearing something like that it might have protected the front of her neck if the fabric was under or partially under the chain

278

when it got heated up. If we find the neckerchief there may be burns that would verify this."

Then I tell him we also need to check on whether there might have been thunderstorm activity reported in the area early this evening. And I add that flipping the necklace around to her back may have been the worst thing she could have done.

"Even though she would have been sweaty and electricity loves sweat. But even so, skin isn't the best conductor," I explain. "But finding a chunk of gold is another story, and that may be why she's dead."

"Because the current would have hit her heart." Marino watches me work a small brown paper bag over one of the hands. "And there's a lot of resistance to pass through, which is why some victims have nothing more than burns after the fact. I know a guy who lost a finger but that was it."

"If the electrical charge didn't pass through her body, it's possible she would have survived," I agree. "And I'm betting we're going to discover her head injury isn't what killed her."

"That's why I'm careful about wearing jewelry when I'm around anything that can shock me. It used to piss off Doris because first I wouldn't wear the big clunky silver ID bracelet she gave me. Then I wouldn't wear my wedding ring, and she'd say it was so I could screw around on her." Marino confides this as if it's a new story, and at this stage of things very few of them are.

He hasn't stopped talking about his ex-wife in all the years they've been apart, which is at least twenty. Doris was his high school sweetheart, an uncomplicated woman, long-suffering until she wasn't anymore and ran off with another man. I know Marino hasn't gotten over her. I just hope he doesn't finally do it now because of my sister, and I try to block out what Benton said at the Faculty Club.

I secure the bags at the wrists and ankles with masking tape, making sure no evidence is added or lost during the trip to my headquarters.

"Now what?" Marino says at the sound of male voices outside the entrance of the tent.

I turn around as Velcro rips, and it's Investigator Barclay again, poking his head inside.

"You need anything?" he calls out.

"Yeah as a matter of fact, *Clay*?" Marino yells back. "I need you to stop coming in here and asking us that!" He rolls his eyes, and slowly shakes his head.

He waits until Barclay is gone to ask about the "freaky pattern" we sometimes see in lightning strikes, usually on a victim's chest or back. It reminds him of flying over the Low Country in Lucy's helicopter, he says. All those tidal creeks branching out everywhere through the salt marshes and mud flats, and what Marino refers to is arborization.

Also called *Lichtenberg figures*, it's the peculiar reddish pattern a lightning strike often leaves on the surface of the skin. If you don't know what you're looking at it's a freakish sight, and what causes it isn't completely understood. A good possibility is capillaries rupturing along the path the electric discharge takes through the body. And Elisa Vandersteel doesn't have a hint of this.

What bothers me more is if she were struck in her back and a thousand volts passed through the gold pendant, stopping her heart, then where's the exit? Lightning is predictable and it's not. It's as if it has a mind of its own, as if it's alive. It wants to race to the ground like some wild beast burrowing, and it's not uncommon to find an exit burn on the bottom of a victim's foot.

She doesn't have that either, nothing but dirt on her socks. There's not an exit anywhere I can find, and I tell Marino I'd like to see the pendant Anya and Enya picked up. He walks back to his big scene case.

Paper rattles as I open what looks like a plain brown grocery bag, and I work it over the hair, the entire head, all the way to the base of the neck, using more masking tape. I tear it with my gloved hands instead of using a blade.

I like something I can remove easily once the body is on the table in the autopsy room. A hair, a fleck of paint, a fiber, DNA—it could be anything. I'll move heaven and earth not to lose or contaminate it. But if one doesn't understand my reasoning, what I've just done looks like an appalling way to treat a dead body. It's what Marino calls a *whack and sack.* That's your reward for getting hit by a train, killed in a plane crash, for being murdered. *Dr. Death comes along and bags your pieces and parts like trash collected along the highway,* according to him.

At least I repositioned her arms from straight up over her head to down by her sides so we can fit her into a final bag, the biggest one, a body pouch, and I'm reminded that death and dignity don't belong in the same sentence. Opening drawers in my scene case, I find a sterile needle, and then Marino is back. I recognize the thickly contoured gold skull with its deep-set blackened eyes and gap-toothed grin.

I feel the weight of it inside its labeled bag, noting that the pendant doesn't look damaged, just dusty. I touch the needle to it through clear plastic and feel the faint magnetic tug.

"It must be gold-plated steel or there's some other alloy present. Gold is an excellent conductor of electricity but it wouldn't get magnetized unless it's not pure." I return the bag to Marino, and my fatigue is on its way to crushing.

I don't feel very good. I should take a break but there's not time.

"If it was lightning," Marino counters, "how come I didn't hear any thunder around here late this afternoon or early evening? You can't have lightning without thunder."

What he says is true because lightning causes thunder. One can't exist without the other. I propose that we might not detect so much as a rumble if the storm is twenty or thirty miles from here. We might not have a clue there's anything to worry about as we step outdoors for a walk, a swim, a game of golf. But a flash of lightning can travel a great distance from the storm generating it.

"That's where we get the expression *a bolt out of the blue*." My tongue is making sticky sounds as I talk. "And when you look at a chaotic scene like this you can understand people coming up with such ridiculous things as an *act of God* or *spontaneous human combustion*. When what they probably were dealing with was a damn lightning strike." I'm beginning to get irritable, to have sharp corners. "It would have been especially confusing if the nearest storm was many miles away, having already moved through."

"Except no storm has moved through," Marino says as Tailend Charlie violates my thoughts again, and I remember looking into the etymology after receiving the first mocking audio clip from him.

I say *him* but I don't know if the person is male. For the sake of convenience I refer to him as such, and Benton believes it to be true. My profiler husband says my cyber-stalker-poet is a man, an older intelligent and highly educated one, and the question from the start is why he gave himself a handle that's archaic British slang.

A *tail-end Charlie*, as it's more typically spelled with a hyphen, can mean the last batsman in cricket. But it also can also refer to a gunner in the rear of a fighter plane or the last thunderstorm in a squall line. As I pass this along to Chicken Little Marino, I realize all I'm probably doing is reinforcing his fear that the sky really might fall on our heads.

"In other words, just when you think something's over, the freakin' worst is yet to come," he complains as a whiff of rubbing alcohol fills my nostrils.

I watch him open packets of antimicrobial wipes, cleaning the six-inch plastic rulers we use as a scale when photographing evidence.

"One more curious coincidence in a day full of them." I'm aware that my stomach is somewhat unsettled.

"Yeah but is it really a coincidence?" Marino places each disinfected ruler into a sterile bag, returning all of them to a labeled drawer in his photography case. "You're saying it is, right? Because you only started getting those recordings a week ago. And now here we are." His eyes dart around as sweat trickles down his shiny red face framed in Tyvek.

I'm not saying anything one way or another, and I don't answer him as my patience rubs thinner. Everything is catching up with me. It's as if I feel the earth shift beneath my feet, a sinkhole about to open up.

"And if you think about it, Doc, a bolt out of the blue *is* a tail-end Charlie because it's the last part of a storm that's moved on, right? Kind of like a last flash for good measure."

I watch him drop wadded sanitizing wipes into the trash.

"What I'm saying is a rogue thunderbolt, in other words literally a tail-end Charlie, might be what killed this lady. Sure it could just be coincidental in a day full of shit like this—to quote you. It may have nothing to do with your rhyming troll." His bloodshot eyes look at me. "But what if it does?"

I don't reply because that's what I'm afraid of. I don't want to give my fear a name or form. I don't want to think or say it.

"What if it's all connected somehow?" Marino continues poking a stick at it. "What if it's all coming from the same source somehow? I mean we sure as hell have to consider it on top of everything else that's been going on."

It's overwhelming to contemplate a link between Tailend Charlie and Elisa Vandersteel since both are linked to me. It might imply that Carrie Grethen is behind all of it. Behind everything, and I'm too worn down to read tea leaves, to speculate anymore. Instead I suggest to Marino that we rely on science. Since nothing else seems very trustworthy, I advise that he check with the National Oceanic and Atmospheric Administration.

"NOAA should be able to tell us everything that's gone on weatherwise." I unlock my phone and my vision is bleary. "We'll find out if there was any thunderstorm activity within fifty miles of here." I feel whoozy and peckish as I text Rusty and Harold that we're ready to transport the body.

It's getting close to midnight and time to clear out. I've done as much as I can at the moment. The tent was a Rubik's Cube to set up, and we stopped taking breaks as the work dragged on stressfully, miserably. We're behind and overheated. I feel dehydrated, my mood deteriorating precipitously, and I have a headache that's getting worse.

When I hear familiar voices and Velcro ripping again, I'm dizzy and jumpy as I turn around. I almost lose my balance.

". . . They're just finishing up . . ." Investigator Barclay pushes through the tent's opening.

I can't see Benton but I hear him mention something about blocking in several police cars. He'll be out of their way in a few minutes, he says in a commanding serious voice, and I feel a nudge of dread.

32

"Like I said? Be ready because it stinks like holy hell in there . . ." Barclay announces in a stage whisper.

He's annoyingly present and officious as he holds open the tent flap for my important FBI husband, practically saluting him, showing him into our glaringly bright, baking-hot, airless, foul-smelling theater, where I'm about to pass out.

"Whatever you need, you know where I'll be."

"I've got it from here." Benton has had his fill.

"I almost went with the FBI, you know. I got no problem working with you guys," as if everybody else does. "Well you got my number if there are any other questions?"

"That's it for now." Benton's politeness hardens like epoxy as he tells the overbearing obtuse investigator he can leave—that nobody minds.

As I listen I'm finding it difficult to kneel in the grass, to concentrate. I'm packing up my scene case, feeling a little drunk, and I wonder what questions Benton was asking Barclay. What were they discussing as the presumptuous investigator escorted him here? I slam down the lid of what's nothing more than a big black toolbox.

"Bet you don't know many agents who started out as police investigators? Because I would think that would be a big draw . . ."

"You need to go," Benton snaps at Barclay.

And heavy plastic clasps snap. And my heart lurches. I feel strangely shaky and emotional.

Keep breathing. Keep moving.

Since I saw Benton last he's taken off his suit jacket and his tie. The sleeves of his white shirt are folded up to his elbows, and the pistol holstered on his hip is exposed.

He didn't drop by to say there's a lovely bottle of French Chablis waiting at home. He's here on official Bureau business, and I think of Lucy as my pulse hammers. I ask if she's okay and feel a stab of nausea.

"She's fine." Benton watches me from just inside the tent, near the equipment cases.

I'm getting increasingly agitated. Hostility smolders and sparks like an aggravated dragon while I act like everything is normal.

"We need to talk, Kay."

But I'm wondering how the hell he knows Lucy is fine unless he's been in communication with her recently. And if so, why? Don't gild the lily. Don't sugarcoat. Just tell me what I don't want to hear, tell the damn truth for once.

"Is she still working in the truck?" I hear myself ask even as I know the answer.

"No." Benton stares at me, and Lucy wouldn't still be here.

That was hours ago when we talked inside the

air-conditioning, and the stench is putrid and pervasive now. I'm insulated in it like a foul rotting gauze that I taste in the back of my throat as the dragon salivates, swallowing hard.

For God's sake, don't throw up.

I'd never live it down, and I watch Investigator Barclay vanish through the tent flap, what's become the wormhole to a parallel universe. He won't go far. No doubt he'll hover within earshot as he's done most of the time Marino and I have been working in isolation, conversing in private, speculating secretly, gossiping just between the two of us, not realizing some asshole wannabe was out there listening.

No telling what Barclay relayed to my husband, in other words to the FBI. After what Marino and I have been through with this scene, and the biggest damn threat is one of our own. The thought penetrates furiously as my heart pounds harder, and my eyes are watering. I take deep slow breaths, blinking several times, well aware that a common symptom of heat exhaustion is irritability. But knowing that doesn't do any good once you're caught in a vortex of uncontrolled fury.

"Hey Benton? Did Dorothy get in okay?" Of course Marino would ask sweetly, warmly about a woman who devours men like tartare.

Innamorato pazzo! as my father used to say.

Marino is crazy in love. Now that I'm looking for it, I can see it plain as day, and I pay attention while Benton tells him in a leaden voice that Dorothy is fine.

Other than one of her absurdly ostentatious oversize designer bags being lost, that is. I don't say it out loud.

She's landed safely with almost all her luggage, Benton

informs us about my vain self-important inconvenient sister who's always treated her own flesh and blood like shit.

"But she's finally in the car at least?" Marino has to make sure about his intended paramour. "Because I've not gotten a text from her in the last couple hours. She stopped answering."

Sotto l'incantesimo! my father would declare. Marino is under the spell. He and Dorothy have been in contact even as I've been by his damn side working this motherfucking scene, and he never let on. Then I'm horrified that I just said something so hideous as that out loud. Maybe I didn't. Maybe I thought it but didn't say it.

Marino's not behaving as if I did. I look closely and suddenly there are two of him all in white like Pillsbury Doughboys. Neither seems offended. But I can't tell and I close my eyes. Then I open them and Marino is by himself again and acting normal for him. I hope I didn't say *motherfucking*. Not that I'm a prude. But I rarely talk like that. I'm not thinking straight. I'm about to erupt like a volcano. My electrolytes are in the toilet, and it's bewildering.

"As long as she's okay," Marino is saying to Benton. "But the airport's a nightmare because of the elevated terror alert and who knows why else." He tries to be nonchalant about it and fails.

"She's with Janet and Desi." Benton's eyes don't leave me.

"Then she's in the car on the way to their house?" Marino probes but Benton isn't paying attention.

"We need to talk, Kay. I need you to come with me," and I detect sadness beneath my husband's iron will.

I push back my hood, my hair plastered to my scalp. I

289

pick up my scene case, and it seems incredibly heavy as I make my way to him.

"What's the matter, Benton?" Marino yells. "You getting bored hanging out with pencil necks? Couldn't stand missing out on all the excitement? Wanted to drop by and see what real investigators do?"

He's behind me, loud enough to break the sound barrier and not picking up on cues. Marino's too busy making cracks about the *FIBs*, as he calls the FBI when he's not calling them something worse. Then he falls silent mid-snark because Benton's grim expression is as rigid as a mask. He's oblivious to everything except me.

"Shit." Marino realizes something is seriously off. "Hey? What's going on?"

"You don't look good, Kay." Benton couldn't be more gentle or somber. "I need you to sit down."

He starts to touch me but I move away. I have blood on the cuffs of my sleeves. I need to decontaminate. I have to get out of this synthetic clothing before I suffocate. I feel claustrophobic wrapped up from stem to stern like a house under construction, and I'm breathing faster and shallower.

I will myself not to show that I'm on the brink of collapse. I'm keenly aware of the danger signs. One of them is not sweating enough. I'm not anymore.

"How about sitting down and drinking something?" Benton says because he's thoughtful.

He always has been, from the first time we found ourselves in the same room together, and I couldn't take my eyes off him. Benton was considerate and kind when he didn't have to be, when most people weren't. He didn't follow the lead of his male compatriots and think of me

290

as tits and ass in a lab coat. He never called me *ma'am* or *Mrs.* He'd say my name the way he still does. As if he meant it.

"Do we have Gatorade? Anything like that out here . . .?" He's asking because he would do anything for me.

"Not that I'm seeing so far but I'll keep digging." Marino is crouching by his Harley-Davidson cooler bag, and I blearily watch his thick fingers find the small metal tongue.

I hear the sound of a zipper as I sit down on top of my scene case. I begin taking off my coveralls, and everything's a struggle.

"We need to talk about Briggs," Benton says.

"Is this about him canceling?" It sounds pathetically lame when I ask, like wishful thinking on my part.

I know that's not why my husband, why Special Agent Benton Wesley has come for me. He didn't show up to pass along information about my event with Briggs but to haul me away because the U.S. government wants what only I can give. Or give up, and that's the more likely story. Whatever the FBI demands won't be in my best interest. It never is one hundred percent of the time.

"I'm sorry," Benton says as I reach down to pull off my dirty grass-stained shoe covers. "I didn't want you hearing this from somebody else."

"Ruthie tried to get hold of me and sounded upset." Blood pounds in my head. "That's what I thought she was calling about." But it wasn't, and I should have put more effort into finding out what she really wanted.

"He's gone," Benton says. "I'm sorry, Kay."

"Fuck!" Marino violently twists the cap off a bottle of water, handing it to me as his face turns a deeper shade of red.

"What the hell are you talking about?" He glares at Benton. "He's *gone*? General Briggs is dead?"

"I'm really sorry," Benton says to me, and how ironic that he would resort to a euphemism.

Gone. As in *passed away. No longer with us. Not here anymore.*

That can't be right. That's not what he means. But it is, and dread nudges harder. It throws an elbow into my solar plexus, knocking denial right out of me.

Dead.

Briggs went swimming at six P.M., and forty-five minutes later was found facedown in the pool, and I try to comprehend it.

Dead.

The stagnant foul air seems smoky as if I'm looking through a veil. I take another sip of water warm enough to bathe in. I pour it into my hands. I splash it on my face. I dribble it over my bare arms. I dig my fingertips into my temples as my head aches miserably, looking up and down, blinking several times.

I get back on my feet as Marino machine-guns questions, demanding to know if the FBI is thinking that what happened to Briggs *is connected to the dead lady here in the park*. It's unwise for Marino to ask that. He just made it easier for the rug to be pulled out from under him, and he does that a lot.

"Kay? You should sit." Benton's face is blurry. "Please take it easy. I want to make sure you can walk back. We probably should have you transported. What about a wheelchair?"

"Good God no. Just give me a few minutes." I'm a little queasy.

"Sit and drink water please."

"I'm fine." But I'm wobbly on the way to worse if I'm not careful.

I don't want to be sick, and I look away from him, from Marino. Don't stare. Fixating is a recipe for disaster, and I look here. I look there. Up and down. Moving around. I don't allow anything to hold my attention for more than a second or two, barely stopping my eyes from moving. Don't fixate because that's when it will happen.

That's when you lose it, and I can't count the people I've collected off the epoxy paint-sealed floor or presented with the ubiquitous plastic bucket. Mostly cops who gather around the stainless-steel autopsy table as if it's no big deal, and I always see it coming.

That fifty-yard stare as my scalpel slices through the chest, making the Y incision, running down the torso, detouring around the navel, reflecting back tissue with quick deft flicks of the blade.

Exposing gastric contents, the intestines, and it's not aromatherapy, to quote Marino. Only he pronounces, even writes it *Romatheraphy* with a capital *R*. As in the Eternal City. As in Romulus and Remus.

Two
Four
Six
Eight
Remember
Not
To
Fix-ate!

My little morgue ditty. Rhymes are an easy way to remember. Keep moving. Look here. Look there. Don't stare. I recite my little ditty in my mind because I'm the

293

one who needs it this time. And I keep my eyes moving. And my attention wanders . . .

Over the grass.

Across the tawny dirt path.

Back to the dead woman forlorn on her back.

In her white sports bra.

Her blue shorts.

And gray-striped socks.

Her head, each hand, each foot wrapped in brown paper like an uprooted tree in a burlap diaper.

Dead.

Packaged as evidence, disgraced and depersonalized, and that can't be the bold, proud, spirited woman I met earlier today. Not once. But twice. Attractive, quick-witted, fit, overflowing with confidence and life. Reminding me of Lucy. How could she be reduced to this? To detritus hauled away and carved up?

What doesn't kill you makes you stronger.

But it did kill her, and what a strange thing to say, as if a part of her knew and was trying to laugh it off. I should have stopped it somehow. She was in my presence twice and I didn't stop anything.

I look around the black cubical tent with its exposed gray aluminum frame. Then back at the body, and I remember her strong tan shoulders and bright smile as she taped recipes to the walls inside the Loeb Center. I remember her dropping her water bottle on the sidewalk in front of the Faculty Club.

You're the peanut-butter-pie lady.

She was hot, her tan skin covered in a sheen of sweat. The sun was going down. There were smudges of peach and pink along the horizon, and I watched her ride across Quincy Street.

Dead.

I look up at the trees. Their heavy green branches are motionless in stifling air that would be a clamorous symphony if odors were musical instruments in an orchestra of stench. I'd be hearing minor keys, sharps and flats, a crescendoing chaos swelling with percussion. Heavy with bass strings. Building to a suffocating coda.

Then the house would go dark after the encore of death, and the bloated teeming crowd would be too turgid and foul for me to force my way through anymore. Looking for an exit. Not finding one. There isn't one. Briggs would be the first to say it. I can't show up at the morgue in Baltimore for him.

It would only give the bad guys something to dig up that doesn't need to see the light of day, Kay.

I can hear him as if he's standing in front of me with his deep dimples and big smile. There's really only one rule in life, he preached. To do what's right. But he didn't always, and I wipe my eyes on the backs of my hands.

33

I rest quietly on top of my hard black boxy perch. I keep my back straight, breathing slowly, deeply, trying not to slouch.

I bought the heavy-duty plastic scene case on sale at Home Depot years ago, and it's an appropriate throne for the *Queen of Crime*, for *Her Travesty* and *Royal Hardship*. Bryce is quite the pun meister. He calls me a lot of things when he thinks I can't hear him.

I wait for my molecules to gather, for the dizziness to pass. My brain seems to slide around heavily, slowly, inside my skull like an egg yolk as I turn my throbbing head this way and that. I listen to Marino and Benton. Sipping water, I look closely at who's talking. Back and forth like a Ping-Pong match. Point and counterpoint like a Gregorian chant. The Pugilistic Crank versus the Unflappable Stoic.

I have a ringside seat as Marino questions, and Benton deflects and evades, not answering anything important about what's happened to our mutual friend John Briggs. But it's not lost on me that my husband doesn't hesitate to probe about the dead woman in our midst, a twenty-three-year-old Canadian who shouldn't be on the FBI's radar, certainly not yet.

I also don't trust Benton's imperviousness to the helicopter that's begun flying up and down the river. Or maybe it's more than one. But he acts as if he doesn't notice what at this hour isn't a sightseeing tour, and it sounds too big to be a local TV news crew. I have a feeling the Feds have started showing up or are about to, and I don't think Marino suspects what's going on. Probably because oblivion is better, and as I rest and hydrate I give him another second or two before he faces reality in a most unhappy way. I know a not-so-friendly takeover when I see one.

". . . The question's also going to be why she really left their employment," Benton is talking to Marino about the Portisons in London and their former au pair Elisa Vandersteel. "Because if the family was happy with her they would move heaven and earth to hang on to her. Why did she leave?"

"Maybe her visa."

"There are ways around that if the family wanted to keep her and she wanted to stay. The two boys are older though. Thirteen and fourteen, and it may be as simple as they don't need someone looking after them anymore."

"What two boys? How the hell do you know that? Did Lucy tell you?"

But Benton doesn't feel obligated to answer questions unless it suits him. He's asking and commenting about the case as if he's in charge, and Marino is beginning to fidget and get flustered. After carefully packing his Pelican case, he's suddenly kneeling back on the grass to reopen it as if he doesn't know what to do with himself.

"Yeah, I know what the questions are," he retorts, unsnapping clasps, and he's getting defensive and louder. "You must have talked to Lucy and I don't know why because last I checked this wasn't your damn case."

"Maybe she found out something from the people at the theater?" Benton doesn't answer that question either as he looks toward the body some fifty feet away. "For example, what or who brought her to Cambridge?"

Marino opens the big lid on his scene case.

"The question is whether Elisa Vandersteel was an intended target or simply random—in the wrong place at the wrong time."

"Whose question?" Marino begins rechecking the evidence he packaged, and I see his paranoia and anger grow by leaps and bounds. "I thought you were here to talk about Briggs." His hot flushed face stares warily at Benton as the truth sinks in.

Something has happened to the jurisdiction in the Vandersteel case. That would explain why Benton is here. If the FBI has taken over the investigation it would make sense that he's been prowling around the scene inside the tent, watching where he steps, scanning trees, the grass, the path, and the damaged lamp and exploded glass. When he's not looking at me, he's looking at everything else, and it's beyond his usual curiosity.

I can tell when he's making assessments. I know when he's in his profiler mode. I also know that the FBI shouldn't have been invited to assist in the Vandersteel case—not at this early stage. But Benton's demeanor, his heavy energy and quiet gravitas, are telling me he doesn't need an invitation.

What that suggests is a fait accompli, and it's a thought I find disturbing and unsettling. We don't know if she's a homicide, and since when is the FBI interested in electrocutions or lightning strikes?

I have no doubt Barclay divulged all sorts of things as he escorted Benton through the park. But by that point most of the damage had been done. A decision had been made or my husband wouldn't have shown up here to begin with, and Benton can't just walk in uninvited and help himself to a case. There's a process, and I wonder when Marino's going to catch on that Benton isn't treating him like an investigative colleague anymore.

I watch him pack up his coffin-size scene case, obsessively fussing with it the way he does with one of his monster tackle boxes or tool chests.

". . . A heart attack is my vote." He's like a moth batting against a window screen, determined he's going to extract more from Benton about Briggs, about anything.

But what I'm really witnessing is the agonal stages of Marino's lead role—or any role—in the Vandersteel investigation. He won't be involved with what's happening in Maryland either. But then, technically he never was.

". . . That's why I'm wondering if Ruthie said anything about him not feeling good," Marino says as Benton ignores him.

Marino hasn't been informed outright that his case has been co-opted by the Feds, and since they aren't collaborative that's the same as being fired. Something like that wouldn't come from Benton. That's not how it's done when a local investigator is removed from a case—or more accurately stated, when a case is removed from a local investigator. Benton won't be the one to say it and he doesn't have to for the ugly truth to be all around us like the stench and the heat.

"Like maybe he hadn't been feeling right, was having chest pains. Or maybe it had to do with the pacemaker he got eight or nine months ago?" Marino has begun to bluster, and Benton isn't answering. "But I can see you aren't going to tell me shit. In other words you're being a typical FBI dickwad."

Benton isn't really, and were Marino not so distracted by his discomfort and fatigue, by his usual power struggles and insecurities, he might realize what's glaring. Briggs had a top-level security clearance and regularly advised military leaders, the secretary of state and various directorates including the Departments of Defense and Justice.

He attended social events at the White House and was accustomed to briefing the president. For obvious reasons he's of keen interest to the U.S. intelligence community, which isn't going to insert itself directly into the domestic investigation of his death. The CIA is sneakier than that.

Typically it uses the FBI as a liaison or a front because global spymasters aren't supposed to deal directly with domestic medical examiners, cops and the likes. That's a sanitized way of saying that in the real world the CIA is the invisible witch rubbing the FBI's crystal ball, diverting and deploying its agents and experts like a squadron of flying monkeys.

What happens next suddenly and without warning is they descend upon your scenes, your witnesses, your offices, paper records, database, labs, morgues, your very homes and families. There's no regard for what damage might be done, and cops like Marino may never know what hit them or the reason. Having a major case overtaken by the Feds is every investigator's nightmare—especially if the agents involved are secretly doing the bidding of some cloak-and-dagger organization like the CIA.

I watch Marino watching Benton look around, assessing, contemplating, carrying himself as if he has the right to be here while I scarcely know the smallest thing about my mentor, my friend found dead in a pool. What pool? Was this at Dover Air Force Base in Delaware? I know he swam there religiously when he was overseeing the Charles C. Carson Center for Mortuary Affairs.

Or was Briggs traveling? He would use the hotel pool if there were one. But I have a feeling I know, and it would be tragically ironic. It would seem like an Old Testament judgment as I envision the quaint stone house in its charming Bethesda neighborhood off Old Georgetown Road. Briggs bought the property decades ago. One of the draws for him was its close proximity to Walter Reed National Military Medical Center, where we once worked together.

"Here." Marino looms over me, and I realize he and Benton have stopped talking.

Marino has dug up a sports drink that's as hot as the humid foul air. The bottle was hiding inside a rucksack for God knows how long but I don't care. I wipe lint and grime off it, twist the cap, releasing the seal with a pop. The fruity flavor is salty and cloying, and I feel it instantly like the hit of a cigarette or a shot of Scotch.

"I don't know if something like that can go bad after a while," Marino watches me sip, and his clothing is several shades darker from sweat. "Sorry it's not cold."

On the deck behind the house is the Endless Pool Briggs was constantly repairing.

I can see it in my mind as vividly as a photograph, and it pains me unbearably. Too frugal and stubborn to replace it, he held it together with spit and rubber bands, he liked to quip. To him it was a functional exercise machine no different from a treadmill or a stationary bike, and swimming in place was part of his daily routine when he was at his and Ruthie's Maryland home.

I was witness to it when I would stay with them, and the appointed time was six P.M., the witching hour between work and Johnnie Walker, as he liked to say. He'd step down into water heated to eighty degrees Fahrenheit, and turn on the current, selecting whatever resistance suited his mood and conditioning. Then he'd swim in place for thirty minutes. No more or less, and after all we've been through? After all my complaints about his jerry-rigged engineering? This is how it ends?

I ask Benton that. I need to know it for a fact. Where was Briggs? Was he at the house in Maryland? I want to know for sure and don't care if Benton doesn't want to talk in front of Marino or perhaps at all. I don't care whose case it is. I need to know a few things. I need to know them now.

"Yes, in Bethesda," Benton answers me while communicating with a look not to push him too far, that we can't be talking about this here.

"Where was Ruthie?" I push a little more. "Was she home?" He can tell me that much.

"She was making dinner."

The kitchen sink overlooks the redwood deck and fenced-in yard in back. But one can't see the pool because it's off to one side near the bird feeder and the toolshed. I told Briggs more than once it wasn't safe. If he had a

302

heart attack, if something happened, very likely no one would see him in time.

I badgered him about getting a defibrillator, about installing security cameras. When he got the pacemaker, I gave him a CCTV starter kit so Ruthie could monitor his exercise from different areas of the house.

Thanks but no thanks, he let me know. *I don't need to be spied on more than I already am.*

Approximately six hours ago, I'm told, he headed out the back door with his towel, his goggles, barefoot, and in swim trunks. I've been to the residence countless times. I can see the Endless Pool about the size of a home spa. I recall Briggs installing it on the deck maybe fifteen years ago when old football injuries started acting up and he began referring to himself as the *joints* chief of staff.

He gave up running for swimming, and at their Maryland home he'd wage war against the Endless Pool's artificial current. If he wanted to build endurance he didn't go longer but harder. He'd wear water mitts or scuba fins to increase resistance, and I ask if he had on either. Benton doesn't seem to know, and I watch Marino pick up a handle of his big Pelican case, rolling it closer to the tent entrance as I hear voices and the clatter of a stretcher.

Then Marino's cell phone startles the stifling quiet, the ring tone a World War II air-raid siren, an urgent alert I've heard before but not often. He steps away from his scene case and us as he answers someone high up in the Cambridge Police Department food chain.

"Yeah, I'm still here and about to wrap it up. What? You're kidding." His voice is exasperated but restrained. "Yeah, I'm hearing you. Not that I'm surprised." He glares at Benton. "When the hell was this?"

The tent flap opens again, and Harold walks in, weary but tranquil, smiling sympathetically at me. He asks if I need anything, and I would see it on his face if he'd heard the news about Briggs. The CFC exists because of General John Anderson Briggs. He helped shape the place and has spent considerable time with us over the years. Harold, Rusty and the rest of my staff will be crushed. But not as crushed as I'll always be.

". . . That figures. It's nice of him to tell me himself seeing as how I've been standing here talking to him for the past fifteen friggin' minutes." Marino gestures on the phone, stealing resentful sidelong glances at Benton.

"It's still hot as Hades out there." Harold solemnly nods, looking at me as if I'm a prospective project for an undertaker.

I can imagine him contemplating different glues and shades of makeup and whether I'm going to need putty.

"If you don't mind my saying so, Doctor Scarpetta . . .?"

"I do mind, Harold. I don't need to hear that I look worse than some of my patients right about now."

"Goddamn son of a bitch." Marino has ended his call.

"You just look like you could use a break someplace cool, Chief." Harold takes my empty sports-drink bottle from me, studies it with a frown before tossing it in the trash. "You did notice this was expired?"

"Well that makes two of us, Harold. Thanks and you know where I'll be." I look down at my damp dirty scrubs, at my loathsome pumps. "I'll see you back at the ranch."

"Well I don't know about you walking anywhere. You still look pretty hot to me . . . Oh dear." As he's pulling on a pair of gloves. "I didn't mean that kind of *hot*. Anyway

304

I'm not sure you should exert yourself in the least." His concerned face appraises me too carefully.

"Don't even think about it." I wag a finger at him.

"We do happen to have a stretcher handy and it's as clean as brand-new—"

"No. Thank. You." I emphasize each word like a gunshot.

"Fine. But we'll be bringing up the rear if you start feeling faint. It's a bit of a hike, and there seem to be a lot of people. Law enforcement of one sort or another," he adds, signaling that there are cops or agents in the park who weren't here earlier.

"What about the media?" I ask.

"Oh no. They can't get in. The park is completely sealed. They have the entrances blocked and have even closed off Bennett and Eliot Streets and University Road. Cruisers are all over the place, most of them with their emergency lights off, and there are a lot of unmarked cars lurking about. And I've been hearing a helicopter. Actually, it could be more than one."

Then he goes on to give me an update in the same earnest soothing tone. He says my troops are being mobilized, and that confirms what I suspect. He realizes it's not happenstance that Benton is here. Harold recognizes the signs of a coup on the way, and he's taken it upon himself to mount a defensive front while the new day is still young.

My radiologist Anne has agreed to come in to work right away, he confirms. So has Luke Zenner, and Bryce is already there. Rusty has driven the mobile command center back to the CFC and returned with a van to transport Elisa Vandersteel's body. Harold has saved me hours and possibly a lot more than that. This is one of many reasons why I couldn't possibly replace him, and I tell him thanks.

"I can use all the help I can get," I add. "I think the long night might have just gotten longer."

"I'm afraid you're right, Chief." His smile is somewhere between unctuous and pious.

Benton loops the strap of my briefcase over his shoulder, pretending he didn't hear anything we just said. He follows me as I duck through the black fabric flap, passing from glaring brightness to the pitch dark. For an instant I can't see. But the great hot outdoors is a pleasant relief, and I fill my lungs with air that's not as stifling and doesn't stink.

"How are you feeling? Are you okay to head out? Tell me the truth," Benton says, and maybe it's my muddled condition but I feel a vibration.

"As long as I don't jog." I detect the unmistakable *thud-thud*.

"Slow and easy please," he looks at me as my attention is pulled toward the river.

The *whomp-whomp-whomp* reverberates in my bones, percussing in my organs. I scan around us as mechanical turbulence bounces off buildings and bridges, making it difficult to pinpoint the location of what sounds big and scary.

I'm fairly certain it's the same helicopter we've been hearing or another one like it, and I notice a bright white light in the distant dark to the northeast, a searchlight probing, headed toward us. We stop walking to watch the blazing finger pick its way along the MIT and Harvard campuses.

It paints over the ruffled water, slashing through thick treetops and over the fitness path on this side of the river.

34

The Bell 429 thunders in low and slow, whirling and churning, lit up and strobing at an altitude of maybe four hundred feet and a speed of sixty knots. Rotor wash agitates the canopies of trees, shaking them violently, and it's a good thing we've collected the evidence. I wouldn't be happy if this thing had roared in before the tent was up.

"I hope it doesn't decide to hover here," I raise my voice to Benton as if he has something to do with the deafening spectacle, and maybe he does.

The twin-engine bird roars past in a fierce wind, and I recognize the gun platforms on the skids, the fifty-million-candlepower NightSun on the belly, the rescue hoist, the Forward-Looking Infrared (FLIR) camera.

The silhouette of the twin-engine warship brings to mind a monster tadpole, a carnivorous one, and I notice the doors haven't been removed or opened. Typically they would be if this were a tactical operation or a search-and-rescue mission, and that hints the objective is surveillance. But as far as I'm concerned, mostly what I'm seeing is for show.

"One of yours?" I ask Benton, our necks craned, looking up. "Because it's not Boston, the state police or Med Flight. It's not the Army, Marines, Navy or Coast Guard. And it's certainly not Lucy even though she changed into a flight suit a few hours ago. That's definitely not her helicopter," I add.

The searchlight is long and linear like a stick of neon-bright white chalk as the unmarked blacked-out bird banks sharply downriver, doing a one-eighty at the Harvard Bridge, near my headquarters.

"It wasn't my idea," Benton says as we stand outside the tent, looking up.

"And what idea are we talking about? Thundering up and down the river for what purpose?"

"Suffice it to say Carrie Grethen feeds off the attention but so do certain other people."

By *certain other people* he means his own, his fellow agents, and we watch the helicopter scream past again.

"I was against it, saying she'll only get off on it if she's goaded into overdrive. She'll just kick it up even higher, but I was outvoted," and that's all he's going to say about it.

The rest I can probably guess with a high degree of accuracy. The FBI is searching this area of Cambridge, and I'm betting they have choppers up in Maryland and possibly other places. If this is for Carrie Grethen's benefit it's truly stupid, and Benton is right about that. In fact the idea of intimidating her in such a fashion would be laughable if anything were funny at the moment.

The Bureau's big machines don't impress her, and more likely they've been deployed for appearance sake, to make sure the taxpayers know that Federal agents have stormed in to save the day. That's what Benton meant when he referenced that Carrie's isn't the only ego in the mix. There's nothing like being splashy. There's nothing like giving a false but dramatic impression, and this is why cops like Marino snipe about the Famous But Incompetent, another moniker tossed around about the FBI. It's why they're the FIBs.

It's why Marino resents and distrusts them, and as I think of Elisa Vandersteel's body being loaded on a stretcher right about now, I feel a rush of indignation. The FBI with its expensive equipment and slick agents hasn't mobilized for her sake. She's nothing more than a means to an end, and I ask myself the same thing I always do. What are the Feds really after?

The answer is almost always going to be mundane if not predictable. Add politics to power and season liberally with publicity. Then stir in the elevated terror alert for the Boston–Washington area that Benton mentioned earlier, and that's probably what I'm dealing with. In summary, it's why Marino has been marginalized and I'm about to be if I'm not clever.

"Remember this isn't a race," Benton says, and he's setting a very slow pace as we trek back to where he's parked near the entrance at John F. Kennedy Street. "If you start breathing hard or feeling unsteady, we're pausing and taking a break."

Overhead on the bridge, the traffic is much lighter between Cambridge and Boston's Back Bay. There aren't many cars or motorcycles, mostly trucks at this hour as the Charles River flows sluggishly like molten glass in the uneven glow of lamps along the shore. The helicopter is gone, at least for now, and our footsteps are quiet.

"What's really going on?" I ask. "I know what I think but would rather hear your side of things."

"Uh-oh. We're already talking about *sides*."

"Because you can't be on mine and I won't be on yours. Despite Marino's claims to the contrary, I'm not married to the FBI."

"I wanted to check on you for a lot of reasons, and it was important I tell you myself about Briggs. But that's not the only reason I'm here."

"Obviously not. You've been walking around and asking questions about a case that shouldn't be any of your business. You don't simply show up and insert yourself into a local investigation, and that tells me other things have gone on. Clearly they've gone on stunningly fast, in the blink of an eye."

"Yes, they have because so much has happened at once," and he tells me that before he got here he was on the phone with Gerry Everman, the commissioner of the Cambridge Police Department.

Benton doesn't say who initiated this conversation, but I can guess. The FBI did, and when they take over an investigation this is what it's like. It feels exactly the way it does right now as I walk with their senior profiler through the park toward densely shadowed trees beyond the clearing.

I listen to our shoes on the hard-packed path with its loose sandy surface that's a poor medium for footwear or tire tracks. Distant traffic sounds like a gusting wind. I catch fragments of conversation in the impenetrable dark, and am vaguely aware of people I can't quite make out talking in hushed voices.

I feel eyes on us as I catch the silhouettes in uniforms

and field clothes of cargo pants and polo shirts. Cops, possibly the Feds, and I think about Harold implying it was getting a little crowded out here.

"Electrical? I get the impression that's what you're deciding." Benton is almost too quiet to hear, and I walk very close to him. "It seems she was riding past a lamp and was electrocuted."

"And then logic begins to fail us because what I'm seeing is confusing if not contradictory." I take his hand and don't care who sees it. "Was the problem the lamp? Or was the lamp blown up by the same electrical current that killed her? And where did this current come from? If it came from the lamp then how does that explain her injuries? She has a linear pattern of burns that don't make sense. And I don't understand the FBI's interest this early on when there are more questions than answers."

"It's almost like she encountered exposed wires, from what I've gathered."

"Yes, I'm sure you've gathered quite a lot," I reply. "But there aren't any wires that we could see, and they would have to be some distance off the ground if they were going to make contact with her neck and shoulders. It's as if she was riding along and passed under something that's no longer present or visible."

"Or something passed over her," Benton suggests.

"Obviously you're assuming homicide when I don't know that for a fact yet."

"But why she would be targeted is a mystery," he says. "Elisa Vandersteel has no connection to us that I can fathom, and no connection to Briggs. I also don't see why she might be of interest to Carrie Grethen. The victimology perplexes me. Something's not right."

311

"Does it bother your colleagues? And yes, something's not right. That's quite an understatement."

"Elisa Vandersteel was a soft target. Random, in the wrong place at the wrong time. Briggs was a hard target. That's the theory."

"Is it your theory?"

"I'm not sure I have a theory but I know Carrie Grethen kills for a reason," Benton says. "She's not into random slaughter but rather prides herself on what she perceives as her own moral code and decency. It's not her MO to destroy people who don't deserve it, in other words. So why would she target a twenty-three-year-old Canadian au pair whose dream was to be an actress?"

"It sounds as if you might have learned more about her."

"Apparently the reason she was in Cambridge is she'd gotten an internship at the repertory theater, was helping in stage management in hopes of getting a chance to act. She'd started there about two months ago, at the beginning of August. Was bright, a hard worker, funny, but very private. This is according to several theater people Lucy's already talked to."

I think of the young man who handed Elisa Vandersteel a FedEx envelope in front of us, and I ask if anyone has tracked him down yet.

"There's a lot to dig into but she was seeing someone who works in the events-planning office at the Faculty Club. Apparently he's a vocalist who she met when he auditioned for *Waitress* but didn't get the part."

"Do they know his name?"

"They couldn't remember it."

"Do they have any idea why Lucy was asking about her?"

"I don't think so. She wandered backstage as if she was looking for her and started chatting. I definitely have the impression that Elisa Vandersteel was living with this guy we saw on the sidewalk."

"But we don't know where." I think of the key fob I found in her pocket.

"Not yet but it's close enough for her to get around on a bicycle, it would seem."

"Have you told Marino all this?" As I ask I remember that he has custody of Elisa Vandersteel's phone, and Benton saw her talking on it the same way I did.

But he doesn't bring it up.

"No, I've not told him," he says, and it occurs to me that he's not bringing up her phone for a reason.

Benton saw her talking on it the same as I did when we were on the sidewalk in front of the Faculty Club. He hasn't asked about it. If I don't mention it, he probably won't. Maybe someone else will but Benton will feign ignorance. Why would he know that Elisa Vandersteel had a phone? And I feel sure he hasn't told his compatriots that he encountered her not long before she died.

Already Benton is letting me know in his own subtle way that he's not going to interfere with me even as he does.

"Do you intend to tell Marino what you're telling me?" I ask. "And if not, when will he be informed that he's been fired from his case?"

"No one's been fired, Kay," Benton says slowly, gently, in rhythm with his steps.

"Technically, maybe not."

"I think we understand each other."

"Yes, and what I ask is you remember the most important thing."

"It doesn't need to be said."

"But I will say it anyway. She deserves the best we can give her." I mean that Elisa Vandersteel does.

"And I have no doubt you'll make sure she gets it, Kay. I can count on you to do what it takes."

He's letting me know that he personally won't get in my way. But the Bureau is another story. Then he asks my opinion about the cause of death, and this is when we step up the tempo and the subtle moves in our dance.

I'm required to pass along information even as the parties involved interfere with me. I won't withhold appropriate details from my FBI husband. I give him far more than I would most. But I don't tell him everything.

35

I explain what I can say with reasonable certainty, handing off to Benton what I would to other officials who have a right to know. But I'm nicer about it and we're holding hands as we walk through trees, rooftops peeking over them to our left, the glinting dark river to our right.

"An electrical charge passed through the pendant she had on, magnetizing it," I'm saying. "She was thrown off her bicycle, lacerating her scalp. Some of her belongings were scattered, and based on glass in her hair," I conclude, "I believe this happened at the same time the lamp exploded. But I can't tell you much more than that when she's not been examined at the office yet."

"It's sounds like you're talking about lightning."

"Similar, yes. But not quite, which is baffling. Lightning could account for the burn caused by the pendant but not the peculiar threadlike linear burns she has. I honestly have never seen anything like this before."

"Which brings me to the question we wouldn't want anyone to know we're asking," Benton says. "Is it possible we're dealing with some sort of DEW, a directed-energy weapon?"

"As opposed to what? Heatstroke? A heart attack?" I'm aware that the leather insoles of my ruined shoes make quiet squishy sounds as I walk.

"As opposed to sabotage," Benton says. "Such as doing something to booby-trap the lamp or an Endless Pool so that they malfunction catastrophically."

He turns to look behind us as if he can see the shattered lamp with its swath of exploded glass. But all of that is under the tent. It's like looking back at a black hole at the far end of the dark park with its smudges of illumination, and I detect people moving about almost invisibly. They keep their distance from us, watching in the velvety blackness, their tactical lights probing and flaring.

"This is what the Bureau is thinking?" I ask. "That someone targeted two different people in two different places with what's basically weaponized electricity?"

"Like a particle beam, a laser, a rail gun that uses energy instead of projectiles. The technology's out there. It's been only a matter of time before something terrible happened."

"And the delivery system in these two cases?"

"Something like a long-range laser gun. A manned aircraft. Or much more problematic would be a UAV, an unmanned aerial vehicle converted into a weapon of assassination or mass destruction."

"As in a drone you can buy off the Internet?"

"This is what we've been anticipating, and you've been hearing me say it for a while, Kay. A drone is going to take out a major passenger jet, a government building, a world leader. Sufficiently weaponized, a drone could take out a lot more than that. We're waiting and watching because it's a certainty when the capability is there."

"And unfortunately drones are everywhere. Not a day goes by when I don't see them somewhere," I reply, and it gives me an uneasy feeling that I spotted one earlier today. "Even when I was walking to meet you, even in this heat, there was one flying around," I add.

"Did it seem to be following you?"

"I didn't think that at the time. But as we're talking about it I remember being aware of one at the Square when Bryce was holding forth through the open car window before I went inside The Coop. And then there was the drone as I was walking through the Yard afterward. But I can't say it's the same one, and it didn't come close."

"Depending on how technically sophisticated the device is, it might not need to get close if it's being used to spy or stalk," he says. "Did you notice how many props it had? Was there anything about it that caught your attention?"

"It looked like a big black spider against the sun. That's the only impression I recall having because I didn't pay attention to it. I imagined some kid hanging out in his dorm room and having fun flying the thing. I honestly gave it almost no thought."

"Kids are high on our list for this very problem, only we've been expecting homemade weaponized UAVs— drones armed with explosives, with firearms, pipe bombs, poisonous chemicals, even acid. But there are worse things to fear. Especially if the objective is to terrorize," and as he talks I remember what Marino said a little while ago:

. . . *If you think about it, Doc, a bolt out of the blue is a tail-end Charlie* . . .

"You're right," I tell Benton. "You wouldn't want the

public to know you're asking questions like this. People would be afraid to leave their homes if they thought they might get attacked from the sky while they're swimming or riding a bicycle. What about burns? Do we know if Briggs has them?"

"There's a burn on the back of his neck. A round one about the size of a dime."

"Round?"

"Yes, and it's red and blistered," he says as I think of the skull pendant Elisa Vandersteel was wearing.

"Do we have any idea what caused this round burn?" I ask.

"No, but it must be something he came in contact with while he was in the pool."

"What about jewelry, anything metal he had on?"

"Nothing except the copper bracelet he always wore. The one that turned his wrist green."

"If it has alloys mixed in with the metal, it might have been magnetized."

"It was very weakly when the death investigator from the medical examiner's office thought to check. Apparently electrocution was top on the list because the pool clearly had malfunctioned for one reason or another," Benton continues telling me what the police have said.

When they checked they discovered the pump, the wiring to the lights, everything was fried, and I envision the gray 30-amp breaker subpanel on the back of the house, 50 amp, to the left of the door that led into the kitchen. I tell Benton I'm fairly certain the pool was the only thing on it, and he replies that the breaker was thrown.

Then I ask about the main breaker panel outside the house. Was anything thrown in there, and he says no. This suggests the possibility of a transient high-voltage electrical source that came in contact with Briggs or the pool while he was swimming. And this sounds much too similar to what we've been saying about the Vandersteel case.

"Something that was there but isn't now," I follow what Benton is considering. "Something like manufactured lightning—or a directed-energy weapon, a DEW in other words."

"Imagine if the water became electrified, and you have a pacemaker," Benton adds, and my thumb finds his wedding band, a simple platinum one, as I'm reminded of Marino's refusal to wear jewelry because it's dangerous.

I ask if Briggs had on anything else metal. Was there anything on his person or around him that could have completed the circuit if he'd come in contact with an electrical source?

"Just the bracelet," Benton says. "He wasn't wearing his wedding band or his dog tags."

"He wouldn't have been. He always took them off when he swam. The last time I stayed with them he'd place them in a dish on the kitchen table," I recall.

"That's where they are in photographs I've seen."

"Everything seems pretty normal." I stop again to shake another small rock out of my shoe. "He did what he usually does, and yet you instantly suspect foul play? I don't care that he's a three-star general with a top-level security clearance. Even spies can drown or have a heart attack. What did you say that got your employer sufficiently interested to mobilize this fast?"

"Literally all it took was one phone call," and Benton brings up the one he got from Washington, D.C., as we were leaving the Faculty Club.

*   *   *

319

It wasn't his director or the attorney general on the line.

My husband was being spoofed. He says he got the same type of call that Marino had gotten minutes earlier, and I don't know how Benton found out about that. Possibly Lucy told him. But as I replay what happened as we were leaving our untouched dinners, I realize that Marino was on the phone telling me about Interpol contacting him even as Benton answered his own bogus call.

"Someone supposedly from the National Crime Bureau, the NCB." Benton unlocks his phone, and the display is dimmed sufficiently so that it's hard to see from a distance. "And this person said he'd e-mailed me a photograph, and sure enough he did."

He holds his phone so I can see the picture, and I try to remember anyone acting oddly, perhaps loitering near us some ten days ago on Saturday night, August 27. I search my memory for someone who might have paid too much attention, staring or hovering, especially showing undue interest in General Briggs when we had dinner with his wife and him at the Palm in Washington, D.C., not even two weeks ago. The restaurant was packed with mostly a business crowd, and I remember it was loud.

"You weren't aware of anybody taking photographs, and haven't a clue who might have . . .?" I start to say as Benton shakes his head, no.

On the phone's display, Briggs is all smiles but the picture has been Photoshopped to include a heavy black *X* over his face. His arm is around Ruthie as they sit across from Benton and me. We're raising our glasses in a toast at our booth surrounded by cartoons of Dennis the Menace, Spider-Man, Nixon.

It was a festive evening with plenty of shoptalk mixed

with pleasure, and Briggs and I discussed our talk. We enjoyed several Scotches as we fine-tuned logistics about tomorrow night's event at the Kennedy School. As I look at the photograph I find it gut-wrenching and stunning that a happy moment captured in time would turn into something like this.

"Obviously someone was in the restaurant or near a window at some point while we were eating dinner," I say to Benton. "Do you think it was Carrie Grethen?"

"Frankly yes. I think she or someone directed by her were nearby or passing through, depending on what technology was used. But someone obviously and deliberately took the picture of us and I was none the wiser either."

"And the point?"

"Destabilizing us is certainly a big part of it," Benton says. "Keeping herself constantly at the center of our focus is important. She wants to remind us of her presence and that she's smarter than we are, always one step ahead. Never forget this is a competition."

But I do forget. I can't possibly spend my waking moments thinking about something like that. I've never understood people, including my own sister, who devote most of their resources to besting someone, to winning a match that's one-sided and imagined.

"She wants our attention and our fear," Benton continues to tell me what Carrie craves, and I've been hearing it forever. "Most of all she has to overpower us, to get in the last word. Control and more control."

"Who do you think you were actually talking to when you saw the 202 area code for D.C. and took the call?" I ask. "Did you assume it really was an NCB investigator?"

"I wasn't sure what was going on at first. The person

sounded male and reasonably credible until he launched in about the *developing Maryland investigation*. That was the language, and I had no idea what investigation he was talking about. So I listened, and I asked why he was calling me specifically and how he got my cell phone number. He said I was listed as the contact person on the case."

"What case specifically?" I look down at my shoes, and one of the heels is coming loose.

"In hindsight, obviously Briggs, who I wouldn't know about until a little bit later. But at the time this so-called NCB investigator was vague. When I pushed him on details he was in a hurry. He gave me a phone number that turns out to be the desk of the Hay-Adams Hotel."

"And since that's exactly what happened to Marino," I reply, "it can't be a coincidence."

"I agree. Two bogus phone calls within minutes of each other, both supposedly from NCB about two different cases that have barely happened yet, mysterious sudden electrical-type deaths occurring almost at the same time hundreds of miles apart," Benton says, and I remember him in the drawing room of the Faculty Club, on the phone near the grand piano.

"When this so-called investigator was talking to you, did you notice if he coughed?"

"It's interesting you would say that. Yes, he sounded like he might have asthma."

It's possible Carrie is utilizing voice-altering software, and I wonder if she's sick or maybe her accomplice is. Benton may have been talking to one of them and had no idea. It's even more bizarre to think Marino might have been. I touch the left arrow at the bottom of the phone's display to go back a screen to see who e-mailed the photograph.

Tailend Charlie sent it to Benton's FBI e-mail address some four hours ago, last night at eight P.M. This was an hour and fifteen minutes after Ruthie discovered her husband in the pool, and maybe forty-five minutes after the twins discovered Elisa Vandersteel's body here in the park and helped themselves to her phone, calling 911.

"We're supposed to know Briggs was a hit," Benton says. "That's why I got the photograph. It's a way of claiming responsibility. Calling Marino was a way of doing the same thing about the case here in Cambridge. It's what terrorists do, and never forget that's what Carrie Grethen is. She and whoever she's in league with are terrorists who won't stop until they're eliminated."

"I'm glad she's telling us what she thinks we need to know." I feel a prick of anger.

"If she took out Briggs herself, and I believe she did," he says, "then that could place her in Bethesda some six or seven hours ago."

"Depending on how she did it," I remind him. "If you're talking about something like a laser gun fired from an unmanned aircraft? I'm assuming that can be done from the desk of someone sitting thousands of miles away." Even as I say this I know where Benton is headed.

He and his colleagues will be going south to Maryland. But I won't be going with them. They'd be wise not to ask.

"I'm supposing she might be in the D.C. area because of the photograph taken of us in the Palm," Benton confirms what I suspect. "And if the ultimate goal of what we're seeing is some coordinated attack using UMVs on a

323

massive scale, then I can see her spending time in the Washington–Baltimore area," and there can be no doubt where this is going.

Or more precisely, where it's already gone. Over the next few hours, Benton will be on his way to D.C. or Baltimore. I'm supposed to be with him as FBI agents begin arriving at my headquarters, which conveniently will be missing its director and chief. Elisa Vandersteel's autopsy and virtually everything else will be witnessed and micromanaged.

We're about to be invaded. At least I'll be prepared, thanks to Harold, and I'm hoping Anne is already at the office.

36

She answers her cell phone on the first ring, and I can tell she's expecting my call.

"I'm pulling into the parking lot now," Anne's voice is in my earpiece, and she doesn't bother with hello.

"Any sign of visitors yet?" I ask.

"Not so far."

There may be a lot of people in and out, and it doesn't matter if we didn't invite some of them, I tell her. It's of no consequence if we don't like them or completely understand who they are. They must be taken care of properly. So we need beverages, especially coffee, and most of all we need food.

"Not much is going to be open at this hour if you're hoping for something decent to eat," Anne's easygoing voice says as I begin to make out John F. Kennedy Street through dense trees up ahead, and I don't see any traffic.

"That's why we have the locked freezer in the break room," I begin to explain confidentially as if I'm telling her how to access Fort Knox. "There should be pizza I keep for emergencies. Meat, vegetarian and vegan. Gluten-free and regular."

"Seriously?"

"What did you think was in there?"

"The last lawyer you didn't like. I don't know."

"I'm still at the scene but heading back. Benton is dropping me off." I keep my voice down.

I glance back at him, and the hulking shape of the tent looms in the dark distance behind us like a flattened thunderhead. He's politely walking some distance away because he doesn't want to overhear what I say. If he doesn't hear it he doesn't have to tell anyone, and it won't be Benton who pulls the evidence out from under me. But he won't stop it from happening either. That's assuming I don't beat his colleagues to the draw.

I'm suddenly alert and in overdrive as I explain to Anne that I need Ernie Koppel to come in right away. I'll also require someone from the histology lab to prepare specimens for him. We're about to be interfered with, overtaken, and if we don't begin testing evidence immediately there's a good chance it will all end up at Quantico, at the FBI crime labs.

We talk about this obliquely. Nothing is to be put in writing, and we're very careful what we say over the phone. Hopefully, by the time the government makes its official requests, I'll have done most of the analysis. I'll have done everything I possibly can to answer questions that I worry might languish otherwise or never be asked. Elisa Vandersteel needs me to finish what I've started.

She deserves the best I can give her, and the first order of business will be the CT scan. I suggest to Anne that whatever left the odd linear burns might have deposited microscopic evidence in the wounds.

"Lightning wouldn't do that."

"You're exactly right," I reply. "It wouldn't."

"But an electrocution might."

"And if so?" I ask her. "Electrocuted by what? What looks like lightning but isn't? We need to find out exactly what happened to her if for no other reason than to make sure that it doesn't happen to somebody else."

"And while we may care about that? No one else will," Anne says, and I know what she's really saying.

If the evidence ends up in Quantico, we have no control over who finds out what. The Feds have their own agenda, and it's not the same as mine.

"He'll be autopsied in Baltimore tomorrow. Well actually *today*." Benton has wandered back and slides his hand out of his pants pocket, glances at the luminescent dial glowing on his wrist. "Christ. It's already half-past midnight. How did that happen?"

"I assume you've talked to Doctor Ventor or someone has."

The chief medical examiner of Maryland, Henrik "Henry" Ventor is one of the finest forensic pathologists in the country, both of us affiliated with the Armed Forces Medical Examiner System, the AFMES. Briggs trained us, was our commander, our boss.

"Yes, and he's already been in touch with the police," Benton says.

"I assume that's where you're headed after you drop me off," I add.

"I took the liberty of getting Page to grab your bug-out bag from the hall closet at home, and we have it with us. Any other items hopefully you can pick up at the office. I realize you need to get out of your scrubs and clean up a bit. Then we'll head out."

"I'm not going with you, Benton."

"We'd like you there."

"Even if I didn't have responsibilities here, I wouldn't get involved. I don't need to tell you why that is."

"We could use your help, and the other doesn't matter anymore."

"It shouldn't matter but it could. Imagine what it would do to Ruthie if I got asked the wrong thing under oath."

"I promise you won't get asked."

"That's a promise you can't possibly keep, Benton. I can't be helpful in Maryland right now but I could do some harm. And I need to finish this case. I'm not about to walk off in the middle of it. So I'm staying put."

He goes on to remind me that the Army CID, the Pentagon, the FBI and various intelligence agencies want Briggs's autopsy witnessed by at least one other senior forensic pathologist, preferably a special reservist with the Air Force who's affiliated with the AFMES. In other words, ordinarily that senior person would be me, he says as if I didn't just tell him no several times.

"Page will take care of Sock and Tesla. I expect we'll be there for several days," he adds, and I can't possibly.

Benton wants to go after Carrie with guns blazing, and I have no doubt Lucy is more than happy to accommodate. Neither of them is comfortable with the idea of my staying here alone in the house with Page and the dogs, and I'm not about to move in with Janet and Desi, especially now that my sister is here.

"You'll work both cases with us, Kay. It will be like the old days."

"It wouldn't. The FBI doesn't work *with* anyone, and I won't work *for* you or them. I work for the victim.

Specifically, the dead woman I just spent several hours with in the tent."

"I don't want you staying here."

"I know you don't but that's the way it has to be," as we close in on headlights burning through the trees.

"Then stay at Lucy's new place in Boston. You'll be safe with Janet."

"I can't."

"Then they can move into our place while I'm gone, and all of you will be together."

I hear an engine idling, and Benton wouldn't leave his expensive Audi running with no one in it—not even for two minutes. He didn't come here alone, not that I'm surprised, and I wonder which agents are with him.

"I'm heading to Norwood, and from there to Baltimore," he says, and Lucy keeps her helicopter in Norwood, just outside of Boston, where she has her own hangar.

"I see. That's why she's in a flight suit. She's taking you," and I think about the timing of her showing up as I emerged from the trailer.

Benton must have let her know about Briggs's death hours ago.

"When I'm done here I'll come meet you," I promise as we approach a black Tahoe with dark-tinted windows and government plates.

The back door on the passenger's side opens, and I watch an unfamiliar man climb out.

"It will be at least a day or two," I say to Benton, "but I'll help Ruthie, do anything I can."

Off to our left the Kennedy School of Government hulks against the night, and for an instant it's hard to breathe.

37

Roger Mahant is the assistant special agent in charge, the ASAC of the FBI's Boston division.

He's driving the black Tahoe. Benton's riding shotgun, and I'm in the backseat sitting next to a man I've never met before. He could be FBI but acts more like the CIA, quiet, unreadable, self-contained. I don't trust him or anyone at the moment, not even my husband, not professionally. He has to take their side in here. He has to be one of them.

So Benton can't tell me everything that's going on—not in front of them. He can't act like my husband or much of a friend. It's nothing new but feels more lonely than usual as he sits in the front seat, his back to me, saying little or nothing, in his sponge mode. You forget he's there while he soaks in everything around him, and I can tell when he's doing it.

"Something else to drink?" Mahant's brooding dark eyes look at me in the rearview mirror.

"I'm fine for now." I have my messenger-bag briefcase

in my lap, and my arms are wrapped around it as if someone might try to take it.

Mahant saw me polish off a Fiji water and just now set the empty bottle on the floor like a litterbug. He looks at me constantly when he should keep his eyes on the road. I don't like it when he and Benton talk to each other in low quiet tones. It reminds me that my husband is part of a collective, a group, a tribe. I'm careful and observant as I sit quietly in back, out of my element and not in charge. The ride is a favor I didn't want but couldn't refuse, and any second they're going to pick my brain. They'll get every drop out of me before they finish what I've started— or they think they will.

In the few short minutes I've been inside the Tahoe I haven't asked questions. But I've gathered that the man in the backseat with me is from Washington, D.C., or that area. He might be from Quantico or Langley. I don't know what he does but it seems it was fortuitous that he was in Boston this week. I also don't know his name. He may have told it to me when I first climbed in but I don't think he did. I'm almost certain he didn't say a word as I buckled up.

The inside of the SUV smells like french fries, and the radio is on just loud enough for me to recognize Howard Stern bantering with his cohost Robin Quivers. I can't tell which taped segment it is. But I didn't realize Mahant is a fan of the show, and wouldn't have expected it. I almost like him better. But I don't. Even if I could it wouldn't be smart.

Don't let your guard down.

In his fifties, bald with thick-framed glasses, he has one hand on the wheel, and in the other he holds a Dunkin'

Donuts iced coffee he sips quietly, politely, through a straw. He's cordial enough whenever I've been around him, usually at professional receptions, holiday gatherings, that sort of thing. But we don't socialize. I try not to with the FBI.

Briggs warned me from day one not to trust the Feds. I always found that amusing since he is the Feds—or he was.

Work and play with them but never show your underbelly, he would say. *And for God's sake keep your knickers on, Kay, or you'll find out the hard way it's a man's world.*

It doesn't matter that it's unfair, he'd declare with a pointed finger. If life were fair, people like us would be unemployed, and in my head I hear his resonating voice. It demanded attention no matter what he was saying or to whom. But keeping my knickers on wasn't in the cards, and Briggs wasn't solely motivated by his strong moral sensibilities, no matter what he claimed.

He had feelings that went back to our very earliest days. We both did, and it took but one kiss, one protest that we should stop, and then we didn't. I remember the sounds of our breathing, the pattering rain. I'll never forget when he turned the headlights off as we sat in his ruby-red Karmann Ghia in front of the shabby stucco building where I lived with a toxicologist. Her name was Lola, which is Spanish for Dolores. It means sorrows, and that suited her to a T.

We were so young and inexperienced, recent hires at the Miami-Dade Medical Examiner's Office, where Briggs was my supervisor, and Lola was never happy, especially with me. I disappointed and annoyed her constantly and didn't understand it then. No doubt it was out of spite that she wouldn't always tell me when she was coming or going, as if she might make me jealous. But that rainy windy night I knew she wasn't home and probably wouldn't be for a while.

Ironically she'd made sure to rub it in as if to imply that she had quite the life and I didn't. Briggs asked me about her because he found her peculiar and abrasive. What was it like living together? Did I worry she might poison my cereal? When would she be coming home, and then the heavens opened. We laughed at the deafening drum roll overhead, at the flooded glass, and he turned the wipers off. Surrounded by a deluge, we fogged up the glass, wiping it off to steal glances up at the second floor, at the empty unlighted window of the cracker-box apartment I had to share because that was what I could afford.

It was obvious no one was home, obvious why Briggs wanted to walk me up with the umbrella and see me in safely. He wasn't being a gentleman, and I was no lady. It was a perfect storm of circumstances and had been from the start when my rattletrap car with its worn-out clutch happened to break down on Dixie Highway after dark.

Lola happened to be out with an ex, she made sure I knew. My sister Dorothy happened not to answer the phone, and neither did my mother. Briggs happened to be the only person I could reach after I'd hiked along the shoulder of the highway to a gas station pay phone. He happened to drive me home, and afterward he happened never to tell Ruthie the truth.

She'd already decided I was a home wrecker even before I was one. Why let her know she was a psychic or a prophet? Why tell her she was right?

Why give her one more reason to shun you, Kay? I can hear Briggs arguing with me.

Confessing to his wife would have been an apocalyptic ending to my relationship with him. We wouldn't have worked together again. My days with the AFMES would have ended before they began because she was overly sensitive, fragile and possessive, and at the time she had a powerful father at the Pentagon. This was according to Briggs, his rationale for why he needed to keep certain things from her. It was for her good and mine. It was for the best. Those are the sorts of things he'd say. I always knew he was kidding himself, and it might have been the only time I would have called him a coward.

"You doing all right?" Benton turns around and looks at me in the backseat, and truth be told, he's a bigger man than Briggs ever could be.

My husband doesn't run from what he wants or pick something because it's safe. He doesn't lie about what he loves. He may be deliberate and take his time. But he won't give up or settle for less, and we don't keep secrets from each other. Not the kind that would fray the bond between us.

I introduce myself to the man sitting next to me as the Tahoe turns onto Memorial Drive. Then I feel silly.

He must know who I am and why the FBI picked me up. In a few minutes they'll leave me at the CFC because I'm not as cooperative as they'd like me to be, and I begin watching for my titanium-skinned biotech building. I stare out at the dark early morning as we follow the river, and I realize how tired I am. I feel defeated and guilty. It's true what they say about your sins finding you out.

Only in my case it's more appropriate to say that my sins tend to find me, period. There are consequences to everything. But when Briggs and I had our moment it couldn't have occurred to me that this day would come. I couldn't have imagined I'd be called upon by the government to assist in his autopsy but would have to recuse myself for reasons I won't discuss. Even if I weren't up to my ears in the Vandersteel case, I wouldn't go to Baltimore tonight. It wouldn't be right.

". . . So I was just wondering what people call you."

I realize the man next to me is asking a question as he offers a packet of tissues, gently nudging it against my wrist. I take it from his strong smooth hand, opening the little cellophane tab.

"Thank you." I wipe my nose, my eyes. "You were saying?"

"I'm sorry about General Briggs. I've actually said it a couple of times. I understand he trained you."

"Yes. Thank you."

"Then I was asking how you're doing, since rumor has it you were in pretty bad shape out there, got heat exhaustion."

"I'm fine."

"And after that I was curious about what people call you. Kay or Doctor Scarpetta? And can we get you anything? Food? Something else to drink?"

"No thank you."

"To which question?" He's being flirty right in front of my husband.

Or literally behind his back.

"I don't need anything," I say to whoever the man is, and I don't want to look at him.

And I don't want him looking at me as I see myself the way he must. Wilted, my makeup gone and forgotten, my hair out of control. My deodorant stopped working hours ago, and the only scrubs I could find inside the trailer are too big. Not dressed but draped, I constantly find myself tugging at the V-neck of my salty sweat-stained shirt because if my bra strap doesn't show, cleavage does. And while I'm used to Marino staring, I'm not so forgiving to a perfect stranger.

"Tell me your name again." He hasn't told me at all, and when he answers I think he's kidding at first.

"Andrew Wyeth," he repeats, and then I wonder if he's making a nonsensical joke or a snide allusion to my husband's wealthy late father, an art investor.

There were Andrew Wyeth watercolors in the Wesley house when Benton was growing up. I stare at the back of his head as he looks down at his phone, and he has no reaction to what the man next to me is saying. Benton is ignoring him. He's ignoring all of us even as he follows our every word and intonation with the keenness of a hawk. I know it for a fact because that's what he does.

"Just think of the painter and it's not me," Special Agent Wyeth says as he shakes my hand a little too long, a little too tenderly, and his humor doesn't penetrate my smoldering mood.

I don't want to be in this car. I don't want to be with them, and it's not easy when Benton has to act this way. When we're forced to pretend we have something different with each other than we really do, it makes me feel cheated and dishonest. As if we're having an affair again. As if I'm a home wrecker again.

Sometimes our little games make me feel alone and unsupported, convinced nothing will be handled properly unless I do it myself. That's the way I feel now. I'm on my own.

"Were you named for the artist?" I'm blandly polite and barely listening as I think of all I've got to do quickly, stealthily, without showing my hand.

"No, ma'am. My father was," Wyeth reminds me how much I hate to be called "ma'am."

Thirty at most but more likely in his twenties, he must be a wunderkind to be keeping such important company. While I can't see him very well in the dark backseat I don't need to. He's very nice-looking and has a soothing voice that inspires trust I don't intend to offer. Muscles bulge from the short sleeves of his polo shirt and strain against the khaki fabric of his cargo pants.

Veins rope, and he has so little body fat it's as if he's been shrink-wrapped in his own skin. I can't imagine how much time he must spend in the gym or what he eats. Very little. Protein. Juices. Kale. Healthy things like that, I imagine, and he smells good. A subtle woodsy manly fragrance with a touch of citrus and musk.

Calvin Klein.

". . . You'll be in the very capable hands of Boston's finest, ASAC Roger Mahant, who you know." Andrew Wyeth is winding up his pitch about what I'm in for. "I believe you've seen him throw back a few at festive gatherings, so you know how entertaining he can be."

"Hey, I'm sitting right here. I can hear you," Mahant jokes in the mirror while Benton continues to ignore us as he does something with his phone.

"He'll be spending some time with you, Doctor Scarpetta, mostly for observational purposes so we can be up to speed on what's going on in the Vandersteel case," and Wyeth must be with the Bureau to go on like this as if he runs the place.

"We'll need accommodations for a few of us," and it's Mahant talking now. "A fairly large office with a couple of desks, a table and chairs," he says impertinently. "We also need private access to at least one restroom, and of course parking," he adds outrageously as I decide, *What a prick*.

38

The last thing I want is federal agents roaming around my headquarters, and Bryce will be even more out of control. He'll be a hot mess. Everyone will be.

But there's not much I can do, and it does no good to get incensed. I need to be clearheaded, and then Benton is reaching over the back of the seat, handing me his phone.

"Police photographs taken at the scene," he says, and I brace myself as I begin to go through them.

There's nothing of Briggs *in situ* as Ruthie discovered him because when the rescue squad arrived the first thing they did was pull him out of the water. That was about the extent of any heroic measures because it was quickly apparent that he was dead. In the pictures I'm looking at he's faceup on the deck near the wooden side of the Endless Pool.

I recognize the outdoor furniture, the back of his Bethesda house and the yard, and it pains me to be so familiar with what I'm looking at, to think of all the stories. He's wearing what he called his *dogaflage*, the baggy swim trunks his skilled-seamstress wife made for him a few years ago as a surprise. The green-and-brown camouflage pattern includes the cartoon dog from *Family Guy*, and Briggs had multiple pairs that traveled wherever he went.

It's awful to see his strong vibrant face slack and suffused a deep purplish red with barely open eyes, and I can make out the impression left in his skin by the goggles he was wearing when he died. There's foam protruding from his lips, and Mahant asks me about it.

"That's what you see in drownings, right?"

"Sometimes." I have to watch every word I say with bureaucrats like him.

I don't want to read my casual comments in a report or hear them on the news. Already I can tell he's not going to grasp much of what I talk about while he believes he knows more than I do about everything. Picturing him and his subordinates in certain areas of the CFC is worse than a bull in a china shop. They can do real damage that can't be fixed.

"But you don't just drown in a pool not much bigger than a hot tub," Mahant says. "It's what? Four feet deep? So obviously something happened."

"You can drown in a puddle or a bowl of soup. But yes, something happened," I agree with his banal assessment as his eyes glance at me in the mirror.

"And the sudsy stuff coming out of his mouth is from breathing, meaning he didn't die instantly."

"Almost nobody does," I reply. "Unless you're decapitated or blown to smithereens your brain takes a moment to shut everything down. That doesn't mean he was conscious as he took an agonal breath or two and aspirated water. If that's what happened, it could explain external foam in the mouth or nostrils."

340

"You're telling me if your heart stopped you could still breathe? Like for how long and how many breaths?"

"I don't know. It would be a little difficult to research something like that," I reply, and Wyeth smiles and stifles a laugh.

I click on other photographs, finding a close-up of the copper bracelet, then several others of his body turned on its side to show the odd round burn on the back of his neck. I hope Briggs was instantly incapacitated, that he never saw it coming, and for an instant I envision the drone I noticed earlier, silhouetted blackly against the sun. I think how simple it would be to do something hideous with one.

"I assume you won't be starting the autopsy right this minute," Mahant continues talking to me as my thoughts jump disturbingly to another recent case.

"There's a lot to do before that," I reply as I think about the Cambridge woman electrocuted this past Monday night.

Molly Hinders was watering her yard at sunset, and was found sometime later dead in the wet grass with a burn on her head.

"And I won't have much of a staff until everybody starts coming in to work." I'm not lying but I don't intend to be helpful—not the way he wants me to be.

"So I should get back here at what time, Kay?" Mahant asks.

"Whatever works for you. We'll be here."

"But what time do you plan to do her autopsy exactly? I'm assuming you have an electronic schedule I can access so I don't have to bother you? Anyway, set the time and I'll plan to meet you."

"We don't really schedule autopsies in the way you're describing. We're not like a hospital OR or a doctor's office."

I sound perfectly reasonable and not the least bit condescending even as I marvel over how uninformed he is.

"Yep. What's the hurry when your patients are dead?"
Wyeth quips.

"Why don't we just set a time." Mahant isn't asking, he's
telling, and he's about to be a real thorn in my side if I let him.

"That's a little tricky because first she has to go into the
CT scanner . . ." I start to say but it's too much to explain.

I'm not sure the Boston division's second in command
has ever been inside my building. I know I've never worked
with him, and that's no surprise. Officials like Mahant are
pencil necks and *suits*, as Marino calls them. They're not out
in the field investigating, and when they do show up at a
scene or the autopsy room you can be assured it's political.
There's an agenda that likely won't be shared, and no
matter how friendly and collegial the relationship begins,
it goes off the rails fast and rarely ends well.

I have no intention of honoring any sort of schedule
ASAC Roger Mahant might decide. But the writing's on
the wall. He's going to do everything he can to insert
himself into the business of the CFC, and I'll do everything
I can to make him wish he hadn't. For better or worse I
can be pretty good at that, and I remind him that when
he comes back later to be sure to bring shower supplies
and a change of clothing.

"Why?" His dark eyes are in the mirror.

"You'll want to clean up thoroughly afterward and stuff
what you've got on in trash bags. I remind you that the
odor gets into your hair, your clothing, way up into your
sinuses. In fact, I apologize because it's never a good idea
to be inside a closed car after you've been working a scene
for hours where the body is decomposing rapidly."

Benton lifts his arms and sniffs his folded-up shirtsleeves. "I think I'm all right but I wasn't there long or on top of everything like you were," he plays along with what I'm up to.

Mahant cracks his window an inch, turning the air-conditioning as far up as it will go.

"We have disposable gowns, hair covers, gloves and such that we'll supply," I say to him over the blasting air. "And we're also taking care of food. You're just not allowed to have anything to eat or drink in the autopsy rooms. But there's a break area upstairs."

"Eating in the autopsy rooms? Judas Priest. Do people really do that?"

"Not anymore. When's the last time you had a tetanus shot?"

"Hell if I know." Mahant's reflection in the rearview mirror looks impatient and unhappy.

"What about hepatitis A and B?" I ask that next.

Around a bend in the river, the Cambridge Forensic Center comes into view up ahead near the Harvard Bridge.

My seven-story metal-skinned cylindrical building has been compared to a lot of things. An unjacketed lead projectile, a dum-dum round, a snub-nosed missile, a pickle. It juts up like a tarnished metal silo across the road from a different section of the same fitness path where Elisa Vandersteel was riding her bicycle when she was killed. The scene I just worked is barely a mile from my office, although one would never know it because Mahant had to take a circuitous route as we left the park unless he wanted to bother flashing his creds and asking police to move barricades from streets closed off.

He turns left off Memorial Drive. Then another left, and

we stop in front of the CFC's ten-foot-high black PVC-coated privacy fence. I open my window and reach out to enter a code on a keypad mounted to the left of the black metal gate topped by triple-pointed spikes. With a loud beep it lurches to life and begins to slide open on its tracks.

The Tahoe drives inside the back parking lot, and I recognize the personal cars belonging to certain members of my staff. Bryce is here. So is Anne, and the Tahoe creeps past parked vans, SUVs and trucks, all of them ghostly white and silent at the quiet hour. We stop behind the unmarked white Ford Explorer in the first space to the left of a pedestrian door at the back of the building.

It's what I drove to work yesterday. But I left it here thinking I would be off the next day spending time with my sister, Janet, Lucy, Desi and everyone. I got a ride with Bryce, and then I would have ridden home with Benton from dinner. But nothing's turned out that way, and the next day is here. There will be no time off or family gathering in my immediate future, and I get out of the Tahoe.

"I'll be right there," Benton says to me, and he stays inside the SUV with the doors shut.

I can imagine at least some of what they're talking about. Mahant doesn't want me around when he and his cronies help themselves to my headquarters and everybody in it alive and dead. But that's too bad. No one is chasing me off, and I wait by the pedestrian door. I wait several minutes, then Benton steps out of the SUV. I scan my right thumb to unlock the biometric lock and we walk into a vehicle bay the size of a small hangar.

I smell fresh-scented disinfectant. The epoxy-sealed floor, the walls lined with storage cabinets, everything is spotless. Gleaming steel gurneys are neatly parked in a washing area, and in a far corner is La Morte Café, where Rusty and Harold drink coffee and smoke cigars at a table and chairs that can be hosed off.

"Lucy was able to hack into Elisa Vandersteel's phone," Benton starts in telling me what he thinks he can and probably more than he should.

As usual he's smarter than everybody else. He knew Lucy would get into the phone far more quickly than the labs in Quantico would.

"So we know who the boyfriend is, the kid we saw at the Faculty Club," Benton says. "Chris Peabody."

"As in Mrs. P?" I remember she mentioned her grandson was working part-time at the Faculty Club.

"Probably but we'll confirm. He lives in a one-bedroom apartment on Ash Street, west of here."

"Which was the direction Elisa Vandersteel was headed as she rode through the park," and I can tell by the look on Benton's face that he's very worried.

"The last phone call she made was to him at seven-oh-six P.M. as she was putting a FedEx in the drop box on JFK Street right next to the school of government," he says. "We know this because of the content of the voice mail when the boyfriend tried her back about ten minutes later, and based on everything else, I'm thinking she was dead by then. I'm thinking she did exactly what we thought, Kay. She entered the park off JFK Street, and as she rode near the lamp something got her."

"Does her boyfriend know?" I recall seeing him and other staff going in and out of rooms while we were at the Faculty Club.

No doubt there will be plenty of witnesses to vouch for his whereabouts at the time of Elisa Vandersteel's death, and it's unlikely he has anything to do with it. But Mrs. P's grandson is in for a god-awful time in every way imaginable.

"There are a lot of people to talk to. This is going to be a shit storm, and you've been up for twenty-something hours with no end in sight," Benton is saying. "Let Luke handle the autopsy, Kay. You've already done the hardest part. Why don't you come with us?"

"Us? Who else besides Lucy?"

"Wyeth." Benton walks me to the far end of the bay where a ramp leads up to another door. "As you may have gathered he's one of us, with our NCTC."

The National Counterterrorism Center monitors both domestic and international threats. It works hand in glove with U.S. intelligence agencies such as the CIA.

"If he's been in the Boston area for the past few days I assume he wasn't here because of Briggs unless you had intel about his death in advance," I reply, and our voices echo inside the vast hollow concrete space where we talk, just the two of us near a huge drain in the floor and a thick coiled hose. "And I hope that's not true. Because if you had even a glimmer—"

"We didn't. There was no forewarning that I'm aware of, just the photograph e-mailed, as I've said, and he was already gone by then." Benton uses that euphemism again.

Gone.

"Wyeth has been in the area on another matter." Benton pauses, his eyes on mine, and then he says, "I'm very concerned about the possibility of some major attack planned for the Washington area, and that what we're seeing right now is the tip of the iceberg."

He says he can't get into the details but Briggs was an important target in more ways than I know.

"It's been rumored on the Hill for a while that he's in line for an appointment to a cabinet-level position, something the new administration has in mind," Benton says. "I think Carrie is reminding us she can slay any dragon she likes and rob us of what we care about most. She can destroy our dreams. She can rob us of our family, and Briggs was exactly that, especially to you."

"I don't know if she's reminding us of that or anything." I take a deep breath as I feel angry and sad at the same time. "And rumors don't always have anything to do with fact. We should be careful what we infer and believe when there's so little we know," I add as the windowless bay door begins to retract.

The illuminated parking lot fills the opening as the massive rolling door lifts with metallic clanks, and headlights burn as the white van glides inside. Then the door begins to shudder down again loudly as Harold and Rusty climb out the front seat, walking around to the back, opening the tailgate, all of it amplified in here.

"I'll call you on a fuel stop." Benton hugs me, and the hard shape of the pistol on his hip reminds me that we never really know when we'll see each other again.

We don't live normal lives or have a normal relationship, and I'm not sure what it is to feel safe anymore. For a moment he holds me close, his nose and mouth buried in my hair as more headlights glare in the parking lot beyond. I swallow hard. This feels terrible.

"I'd appreciate it if you'd have Janet, Desi and Dorothy move into our place until I'm back. I know I've mentioned it but I mean it, Kay. Everybody's safer together," Benton faces me, his eyes unyielding. "I've already talked to Janet about it in case you decided to stay home, and I was pretty

347

sure you would. Page can help as needed with the dogs," he adds as I catch Luke Zenner out of the corner of my eye.

My blond Austrian assistant chief walks up to us, and I suspect he was sleeping when Anne summoned him. Possibly sleeping with her, it also occurs to me, as Luke is impossibly attractive and quite the ladies' man. I can see the wrinkles from his pillowcase imprinted on the right side of his face. He hasn't shaved, and it couldn't have taken long to throw on a Patriots T-shirt, baggy Bermuda shorts, and a pair of moccasins.

"I'll be upstairs for a while and will fill you in later," I say to him, and it's my way of signaling that we can't talk openly in front of Benton right now. "I'm thinking we should put her in the decomp room. She's getting into rough shape really fast."

"I can imagine and it sounds like a plan," Luke says with his German accent as his blue eyes meet mine. "We'll get going on that, then," and Harold and Rusty are wheeling the stretcher through the bay.

They push it up the ramp, and through the door leading inside as Benton and I say good-bye, although we don't really use that word. We try not to speak in terms of endings but to leave our separations light and airy with a *See you later* or *I'll call in a bit.* As if everything is fine when it's not.

I wait at the top of the ramp, my messenger bag slung over a shoulder of my sweat-stained scrubs. I watch my tall husband with his wide shoulders, his long stride and straight proud posture as he walks away. He reaches the huge square opening, and it frames him like a painting as he turns to smile at me.

39

The first stop when I enter my building from the bay is the brightly lit receiving area with its walls of stainless-steel coolers and freezers monitored by green digital readouts that turn yellow and red when they aren't happy.

The air is cool and pleasantly deodorized, and I'm greeted by bickering just inside the door, where Harold and Rusty have parked the stretcher on the platform floor scale. They've put on shoe covers, aprons, gloves and surgical caps, and I catch them in medias res, softly pecking at each other and oblivious to anyone who might be listening.

"Well what is it then?" Harold clicks open a pen and he has his notebook open.

"It's really annoying when you do this."

"Do what? I'm just asking for verification of what weight you said we should deduct."

"I didn't say because I don't need to." Rusty holds the long wooden measuring rod in one hand like a shepherd's crook as he unzips the pouch.

"Then what is it?"

"Why would it be different this time, Harold?"

"It's always smart to ask."

"And you always do. It's eighty-six pounds just like last time we weighed it."

"But you didn't check first when it was empty, did you. So we don't know that for a fact."

"No, I don't every single time because it's stupid," as Rusty measures the body from the top of the bag over Elisa Vandersteel's head to the bottom of the bags on her feet.

"What happens if we get asked in court whether we weighed the stretcher?"

"I've never heard anybody ask that or even bring it up except you."

"But they could and depending on the circumstances maybe they should. You never know when the tiniest detail can make all the difference. Let's see . . . if we subtract eighty-six from two-sixteen?" Harold does the math in his pocket-size notebook because he can't do it in his head. "We get a weight of one-thirty." He writes it down as I walk across the recycled-glass floor that's a shade of tan called truffle. "And the length?"

"Sixty-five inches."

I stop at the glass-enclosed security desk, what people here call the Fish Tank. On the outer ledge of the closed window is the big black leather-bound log, our Book of the Dead. It's anchored by a thin steel chain, and all case entries must be made in black ink with the ballpoint pen tethered by a length of the same white cotton twine we use for sutures.

I open the acid-free ledger pages, lightly rapping a knuckle on the glass to get my favorite security officer's attention. Georgia has her back to me as she collects a yellow RFID wristband from the 3-D printer. She returns to her desk and slides open her window.

"You look like you've lost more weight." I notice her dark blue uniform with its yellow trouser stripes seems a bit baggy as she sits back down at her computer, placing her hands on the keyboard, the mouse.

"Oh, now you're just being nice." She peers at me over her reading glasses as her peach acrylic nails begin clicking over keys. "Seriously, though?" Her brown eyes are pleased. "You can tell?"

"I certainly can."

"Almost ten pounds."

"I thought so."

"You've made my day and the sun's not even up yet."

"The most important question is what Weight Watchers has to say about pizza this morning. Is it legal?" I review entries about bodies delivered and picked up, catching up on what's happened since I was here last.

"That depends on what kind and whose it is. Now if it's your pizza, Doctor Scarpetta? I don't care if it's a thousand points because I'm eating it."

I watch her go through paperwork on her desk, accessioning the Elisa Vandersteel case, giving it a unique number.

16-MA2037

"But you might want to tell me what sort of party we're suddenly having," Georgia says, "and who I should be watching for in the cameras and worrying about. Am I right that we're battening down the hatches? Because you just say the word."

"It looks like we're having company, and we'll be as hospitable as we can muster." I'm careful what I say so nothing comes back to haunt me, and I turn another page in the log. "But no one's getting in the way of the work. We won't allow that."

"Well I sure knew something was going on with Anne showing up at this hour. And then Bryce wandering in, and after him Paula from histology? And now you and Doctor Zenner, and rumor has it Ernie Koppel's on his way. Damn." She glances up at me. "So who's the company we didn't invite?"

I tell her, and she blows out a loud breath and rolls her eyes.

"I could use some overtime help if you're interested," I add, scanning names, ages, addresses, suspected causes of death, and whether our patients are still with us or have been dispatched to a funeral home or cemetery.

"Starting when?" she asks.

"Starting when your shift ends six hours from now."

"O'Riley will be in then. At eight."

"Yes, and I'd like you to stay and help him, if you're willing. As long as you're not too tired." I want Georgia around because she's fearless and she's loyal. "Let's get as many backups here as we can."

"I'll get on the phone. It's better if I do it." She means instead of Bryce. "You know how he can get on people's last nerve."

"As many of our officers who are available. I want at least one on every floor if possible."

"To protect us from them." She means from the FBI, and I don't nod or answer.

I look her in the eye, and that's enough.

"You just let me know what you want me to do," Georgia folds her thick arms across her formidable chest, and I don't know how effective she'd be in a fight but I wouldn't want to challenge her.

"That will be largely decided by our guests," as I turn back several pages in the log, wondering if there's been a mistake.

"Well I can already tell you what they'll do," Georgia is getting worked up by the thought of her turf being overrun. "They're going to snoop into every damn thing they can while they have the chance."

"We won't give it to them," I reply as I continue to peruse the log, and I didn't expect Molly Hinders's body to still be here.

But it must be. Had it been released there would be a handwritten record of it, and as I read the entry made Monday, September 5, I'm reminded of the address.

Granite Street.

Bryce and Ethan live on Granite Street here in Cambridge very close to Magazine Park on the river. They moved there last spring, and I'm startled and not quite sure why.

"It appears Molly Hinders wasn't released after I left yesterday." I return the log to its spot on the ledge. "I thought she was being picked up by the funeral home. Did Doctor Wier run into some sort of problem?"

Lee Wier is one of my forensic pathologists, and she knows what she's doing because I trained her.

"Well that's turned into quite the cluster F."

I have a bad feeling Georgia's right about that. Molly Hinders is Investigator Barclay's case, and Marino needs to intervene.

"That poor lady couldn't have worse luck. Now everybody's drunk and fighting while she's all by her lonesome in a damn cooler," Georgia is telling me as I keep thinking about what Dr. Wier said as she was going over the case during staff meeting several mornings ago.

When Molly Hinders's body was found it was near a plugged-in stereo speaker that had fallen from its mount and was on the wet grass. It was the only explanation for how she could have been electrocuted in her backyard as she watered her plants with a hose. But it's really never made sense to me that a speaker circuit could kill anyone.

Her scalp and hair were burned from coming into contact with the electrical source that killed her.

This was the early evening of the Labor Day holiday, and she'd returned home from kayaking on the Charles River. She removed her kayak from her car's rooftop rack, dragged it into the backyard, then entered the house and poured herself a glass of wine. Still in her bathing suit, she went out to water the backyard, where there's a stereo system, a wrought-iron table and chairs, and a barbecue under a partially covered pergola overgrown with vines.

When the police arrived the stereo system had no power because the ground-fault circuit interrupter—similar to a breaker—had been tripped. That alone should have prevented her from being shocked, much less killed. For some reason it didn't, and I've found this puzzling from the start. But the case didn't grab my attention then the way it does now. Molly Hinders is reminding me too much of Elisa Vandersteel and General Briggs.

"Please explain why Molly Hinders is still here," I ask again.

"From what I gather," Georgia says, "her family has money, and she and her estranged husband weren't divorced yet. So he's fighting over who's claiming the body. They're fighting over everything because she was real young and there's no will, no nothing, and then the kicker?

They fired the first funeral home they picked, so we can't exactly be releasing her to anyone yet anyway."

"It's just as well, fortuitous in fact, because there may be other problems," I reply as I hear the sound of the elevator doors opening. "I don't want her released until I say. I want to check on a few things," I add as Bryce appears, and he's changed his clothes since we talked by phone in the trailer what seems an eternity ago.

"Who aren't we releasing?" my chief of staff says, and his blue eyes look a little bleary, maybe from hard cider.

He has on tight stovepipe jeans, a T-shirt and lots of Goth jewelry, spunking himself up for the Feds. Bryce loves to flirt, and the more it's not appreciated the better.

"Molly Hinders," I inform him. "Her manner of death will be undetermined pending further investigation. I need you to let Doctor Wier know." Then I ask Bryce if there's anything new on his marijuana-tattoo mystery. "I don't suppose we've figured out how that detail ended up in a nine-one-one call." I put it to him bluntly.

"Sure. Ethan and me got to the bottom of it," he says too flippantly as his boyish face turns red. "The weirdo next door? You know our jerk-off neighbor? It had to be him paying me back."

"How'd he know what's going on inside your own house?" Georgia pipes up, and obviously she's familiar with the tattoo story.

Bryce probably couldn't wait to tell her.

"Paying you back for what?" I ask him.

"Well . . ."

"Bryce? Your face is beet red. Obviously you know. Tell me how your neighbor found out about your fake tattoo."

"Well it seems I got a little drunker than I thought on

margaritas made with that to-die-for tequila your sister gave us? And apparently after our friends left I went to take the trash out, and I heard this same really weird noise and saw a strange light again. So of course I tripped on something and fell down, and then there he was trying to help me up. Only in that crazy moment it wasn't a *he*. It was this *thing*, and I really thought it had happened this time."

"What the hell?" Georgia has stopped typing, staring bug-eyed at him. "What are you talking about?"

"I really thought I was being abducted by aliens for some research project they must be doing."

"Jeeees-us." She starts shaking her head. "You sure do waste my time."

"I'm dead serious. I've been seeing weird lights in the sky at night."

"They're called stars and airplanes." Georgia just keeps shaking her head.

"Am I to assume it was your neighbor who showed up while you were out with the trash?" I ask.

"Donald the Nasty. I don't remember what happened but Ethan does because I guess he came out to look for me and heard the ugly things I apparently said. Ethan was upset, telling me to thank Donald for coming to my aid, can you imagine? And of course in my confusion I yelled, *How the frick do we know he's not the one who pushed me down?*"

"And he knew about your tattoo how?" I again ask.

"Because of his flashlight, and I had on shorts and was barefoot. So he saw it and made some crack about us being potheads, and that it figured. But I don't remember any of it."

"Marino needs to know every word," I reply. "Please call right away. Find him, and tell him we need to talk."

40

I reach through Georgia's window to remove the hand-held RFID reader from its charging cradle. Walking over to Cooler number two, I lift the big steel handle, and the huge polished door opens with a quiet suck and a puff of condensation that looks like fog but smells like death.

I move through the chilled foul air inside a huge frigid space filled with steel trays bearing body-shaped mounds, each pouch tagged with a chip embedded in a plastic sticker that should match the chip in the decedent's yellow wristband. Redundancy. Because one of the worst things you can do is lose someone, and I scan with the reader, holding it like a gun until I locate Molly Hinders.

My breath smokes out as I unzip her pouch, and the sound of blowing air is loud. I grab a pair of gloves from the box on a gurney, and momentarily I'm working my purple-sheathed fingers through her short curly black hair. Everywhere I touch is refrigerated cold as I feel around the sutured autopsy incision that follows her hairline, over her ears and around the back of her head, where I find the small gaping wound in her scalp.

Dr. Lee Wier did exactly what she was trained to do and what I recommended to her when we discussed this case. She made sure to surgically remove the burned tissue so we could have Ernie check it for microscopic particles of metals or other materials that might have been transferred to the wounds. She should have sent these samples to the histology lab days ago, and I walk back out of the cooler. Shutting the heavy door, I hope for a good signal on my phone as I try Paula in the histology lab.

"I finished up everything on that yesterday afternoon," she says in my earpiece after I ask how the case is coming. "Doctor Wier had asked me to get on it as soon as I could because of the prep time involved, so that's what I did."

"She specifically asked you to prepare wet samples for Ernie."

"Absolutely. I prepped four separate specimens from the burn on the victim's head."

"I'm very happy to hear it," I reply because the burned tissue would have to be dehydrated with acetone before it could be placed inside the vacuum chamber of an electron microscope, and this can take days.

Had Dr. Wier and Paula not been fast acting, there might not be anything to analyze until the weekend, and waiting couldn't be a worse idea. Depending on what we're dealing with, someone else might die, and up ahead I see the open door as I follow the empty corridor, passing labs and other work spaces that are dark at this early hour.

Inside the large-scale X-ray control room Anne's desk is empty, her pocketbook and keys on top of it. Through a leaded-glass window I can see her in the room on the other side, standing at the creamy-white large-bore CT scanner, a lab coat on over her jeans, talking to Luke Zenner, who's changed into scrubs. On the table in front of them is Elisa Vandersteel's pouched body, and I open the door connecting the control and scan rooms.

"You're just who I need to see," I say to Luke as I walk in.

I explain it's possible that Molly Hinders and Elisa Vandersteel aren't accidental deaths. They may be homicides that are connected, and I also let them know about Briggs. Luke and Anne begin asking questions I can't answer. They get increasingly upset.

"We can't get into it now," I finally tell them because we really can't. "We need to save our feelings for later. We have to focus and find out what's killing these people, and if it's electrical malfunctions, flukes or deliberate, such as some weapon we've not seen before."

"It's hard to imagine everything suddenly happening is coincidental," Luke says, and his eyes are hard and he's clenching his jaw.

"When you're done," I continue, "photograph the burns before excising them, and the tissue goes straight to Paula. Of primary interest are the very fine linear whitish leathery burns on her upper back and lower posterior neck, and also the top of her right hand and wrist."

"I'll need to take off the paper bags anyway," Luke says. "So I'll just do all of it in here, get everything ready for the labs. Then I'll have her moved into the decomp room."

"I'm going upstairs to clean up," I reply.

"Now that's an idea. Nothing like cleaning up before you do an autopsy in the decomp room," Anne says drolly, and she gives me an idea.

"I understand there have been some problems with the

ventilation in there," I point out, and Anne gets a blank look on her plain but pleasant face, then she frowns, and then she gets it.

"Oh *that*," she says as if she suddenly remembers. "You must be talking about the downdraft table in there," she recalls, but she's making it up. "The airflow wasn't pulling odors down and venting them away from people working, I believe that was the problem the other day, and I heard the stench was so bad it had legs," she improvs. "So I hope for the sake of our guests that we don't have a problem this morning."

"That would be too bad," I agree.

Thirty minutes later, upstairs inside my office suite, I emerge from the bathroom drying my hair with a towel.

Dressed in clean blue scrubs and black rubber surgical clogs, I walk through my sitting area of leather furniture in soothing earth tones, a conference table, and my personal collection of anatomical drawings by Max Brödel, Edwin Landseer, Frank Netter, in addition to eighteenth-century prints of William Hogarth's *Four Stages of Cruelty*.

Near my desk the data wall displays the time and other information in bright digits against glassy blackness. 3:08.45 AM EST . . . 3:09.50 . . . 3:10.00 . . . I watch the seconds silently advance as I select an app on my phone that offers a menu of CFC zones inside and out that are constantly monitored by security cameras. The data wall splits into screens that display live feeds, and my back parking lot has filled up considerably since I last checked.

There are several dark blue and black sedans and SUVs, and I pan and tilt, checking other zones and discovering the black Tahoe inside the bay where only Lucy is cheeky enough to leave her cars. Roger Mahant is already back, and he's come with quite a posse, it seems. I wonder why Georgia didn't let me know. Maybe she tried and I was in the shower.

I call her desk extension and it begins to ring as I watch digital seconds tick past. Ringing and ringing. 3:12.11 . . . 3:13.10 . . . 3:14.00 . . . Oddly there's no answer downstairs at her desk, and then my phone rings.

"What's going on?" I assume it's Georgia.

"Hello?" Ernie Koppel says. "Kay?"

"I'm sorry. I was trying to call downstairs . . ."

"Can you drop by?" he asks. "I don't usually say something's urgent but you need to see this before anybody else does. I'm waiting for a confirmation but if you've got a minute I think I've found something that's a first. At least for a crime lab."

He tells me where he is, which electron microscope, and I grab my lab coat off the back of my desk chair, hurrying out the door. I decide to avoid the elevator. Not only is it notoriously slow in my state-of-the-art biotech headquarters but I intend to duck and dodge the FBI every chance I get. A good way to start is by using the emergency stairs. While anyone can take them to exit the building, you can't access our floors without an ID badge or a code.

So I'm not likely to run into anyone, and my clogs echo on the metal-edged concrete steps as I descend to the lower level. It's as quiet as a bomb shelter in the stairwell as I go down and down, unlocking the door at the bottom. It opens into our evidence bay, where we process large items, typically cars and trucks, but we've also recovered evidence from supercars, motorcycles, Jet Skis, and even a homebuilt hang glider that obviously didn't work very well or it and its owner wouldn't have ended up here.

The lights are on a low, energy-saving setting, and I briskly walk through the gloom, passing exam spaces occupied by current cases. A boat under a tent will be fumed with superglue to develop possible latent prints, and two spaces down from that is the camper where a suspected murder-suicide occurred. Next to that, a stand-alone bay is covered in blood-spattered-and-streaked white paper from ceiling to floor to reconstruct a stabbing.

I head toward an illuminated red IN USE sign above the concrete bunker housing the transmission electron microscope, the TEM. Scanning my thumbprint on the biometric reader, I pass through the stainless-steel door as it slides open with a swoosh that always reminds me of *Star Trek*. I'm greeted by the familiar rush of positive-pressure air blowing my hair as I step inside, and the door whispers shut behind me.

"Howdy. Come on in and take a load off," Ernie says in the near dark from the console of the half-ton microscope. "Because you're going to want to sit down for this."

My top trace-evidence examiner always reminds me of a submarine pilot as he sits in front of a periscope-like thick metal tube that rises nearly to the ceiling and is topped by the assembly of the cathode, what most people call an electron gun but I tend to think of as more like a lightbulb. Its simple hairpin-shaped tungsten wire fires thermoionic emissions at whatever we decide to analyze, and I always find it cavelike in here, stuffy and claustrophobic.

The thick concrete walls are acoustically dead, and the dark fabric-covered fiberglass insulation seems to suck in all light. I have the sensation of being at the bottom of the sea, underground or lost in the cosmos. I always feel as if I'm passing into the unknown like Alice through the looking glass. And in a way I am because the world Ernie navigates can't be managed without instruments capable of detecting particles as small as one-billionth of a meter or seventy-five-thousandth the diameter of a human hair.

I could fit thousands of skin cells and specks of dust on such minuscule and ubiquitous evidence, what I think of as the universal detritus shed by negativity and bad karma. People leave all sorts of seemingly undetectable trash in their wake, and it's constantly recycled. It can end up in the damnedest places as we track the tiniest tattletales in and out, passing them from one person or object to another, from one continent to the next.

I think back to when I saw Ernie last, maybe a month ago, and since then his blond-streaked graying hair has gotten longer. I notice that peeking out under his lab coat are a black suit and a bolo tie with a silver-and-turquoise arrowhead slide. He has on a black lizard belt, matching black cowboy boots, and I'm betting his black Stetson with its gambler crease is in his office. He must have court later today, a deposition or some other reason to dress up, and I ask him that.

"Nope." His blue eyes sparkle in his weathered face. "Something much more important. I was planning on heading over to the Kennedy School after work to hear your talk. I doubt I'll have time to go home first. A bunch of us are going from here."

I'm touched and overwhelmed by sadness as I sit down. I tell him about Briggs.

"Goddamn," Ernie swears under his breath as I brief him on what I fear we might be dealing with.

363

"Energy or electricity that's been weaponized somehow," I tell him what Benton suggested.

"Well in a bizarre way that would make sense," Ernie says.

"You've found something that might hint at such a thing?"

"Not exactly and maybe. I actually got onto this yesterday before I left," he refers to the Molly Hinders case as I continue scanning the bank of monitors overhead, not making much sense of what I'm seeing.

Displayed are peculiar shapes illuminated in black and white, some in the nano range and magnified two hundred thousand times. I'm confronted by spectra that are puzzling as I recognize the atomic symbols for nickel and aluminum recovered from the burn on the scalp, and also the presence of silica and iron.

I'm not sure why titanium would show up, and I'm baffled by the presence of zirconium and scandium. They aren't everyday metals. One is commonly used in nuclear reactors, the other in the aerospace industry.

"I didn't want to tell you what I'd found," Ernie says, "until I'd verified it with a buddy of mine at ORNL."

Oak Ridge National Laboratory in Tennessee is one place we turn when we have extraordinarily unusual questions in the field of materials science. In other words, if we can't figure out what something is made of and why, then we reach out to ORNL, MIT, Caltech, even NASA. A good example is the very thing I'm supposed to talk about tonight—the *Columbia* space shuttle tragedy. A typical crime lab wasn't going to determine why a heat shield failed.

"And he literally just called me as you were on your way down to see me," Ernie is saying. "You've heard me mention Bill. He works in the superconductor lab they've

364

got down there and sleeps about as much as you do," he adds because it's not even four in the morning. Do you know what panguite is?"

"I don't think so," I reply. "In fact, I don't believe I know what you're talking about."

"This." He indicates a black-and-white image on a monitor that at 500X looks white and lumpy like misshapen molars.

41

"Panguite was discovered several years ago when geologists at Caltech were analyzing pieces of a meteorite that fell in northern Mexico in 1969." Ernie leans over to pull up a sock that's been eaten by his cowboy boot.

"I've never heard of a mineral called panguite," I reply.

"Named after Pangu, the god that split Ying from Yang or something," he says as my incredulity grows. "And what Bill says is just because panguite was recently discovered doesn't mean it's not present in other meteorites that have struck the earth. You'd have to go around testing space rocks in every museum in the world to know."

"How can you tell we're talking about a meteorite?" I indicate the monitors across the top of the room. "And you do realize how completely illogical this is? Molly Hinders certainly wasn't struck by a meteorite while she was watering her yard on Labor Day. Not that there's a case on record of anyone being struck by a meteorite but had she been? I would expect a lot more than a small burn on her scalp, and she certainly didn't die of blunt-force trauma. She's clearly an electrical death."

"The metals we're seeing are significant," Ernie points out. "Especially zirconium and scandium, but also iron, titanium et cetera."

"But there could be other explanations for finding them."

"But not for panguite. It doesn't naturally exist on earth." He points out peaks for Ti^{4+}, Sc, Al, Mg, Zr, Ca—the elemental components of what he goes on to explain is a new form of titania.

It occurs as fine crystals that at a magnification of 200,000X are reminiscent of pitted white bone or coral. I can see strange areas of red patina, and also irregular surface features including cracks, pits and crystal inclusions mixed with shiny fibers, what Ernie informs me are bundles of single-walled carbon nanotubes.

"Now you see our problem," he says.

"I certainly do."

"Mother Nature has been tampered with."

"You're thinking someone has built a weapon from a meteorite and carbon nanotubes?"

"Possibly."

Nanotubes are lightweight, incredibly strong, and structures made of these extremely fine fibers can be superfast and efficient at conducting electricity and heat. It's believed and feared that molecular nanotechnology is the future of everything, including war.

"Imagine making a small powerful bomb out of nano-thermite or super-thermite?" Ernie is saying. "Or how about mini-nukes? Or God forbid bioterrorism delivered in the nano range? Scary shit."

"Yes it is, and I understand the utility of building

something out of nanotubes, but what would anyone use panguite for?"

"That was my question too. And the possibility Bill came up with is if it's like titanium then maybe it's an under-coating, some sort of thermal protection."

"Then why not use titanium? And where might someone get hold of a meteorite, assuming the person doesn't work with them?"

"That's not hard," Ernie says. "You can buy all sorts of pieces and parts of meteorites off the Internet."

"But would they have panguite in them?"

"That's what I'm saying. We don't know. We can't know if they've not been analyzed. But I'm going to assume that this is rare." He means finding panguite is rare. "If the mineral was only recently discovered, it's hard for me to believe it's turned up often in the past or you might think it would have been discovered a long time ago."

"We're also talking about someone familiar with nano-technology," I reply. "And if this person is actually modifying materials at the atomic level? Then we're not talking about the average bear."

"What do I say if the FBI wanders in here and starts asking me what I'm doing?" Ernie asks.

"Keep your door locked and they won't be wandering in. If you're quiet they'll never find you down here."

"Because if something like this got out, Kay? It would create a panic if the public thinks meteorites are killing people or some new death-ray-like weapon is."

"Discretion is imperative right now." I get up from my chair.

*   *   *

After I leave Ernie, I return to the CT-scan room but it's empty now. I head back to the receiving area, where two FBI agents are drinking coffee near the door that leads out to the bay.

"I tried to call you," I say to Georgia as I pause by her desk.

"I bet you did right about the time I was out in the bay telling them they can't park in there. You see how much good it did. That big-ass SUV's still sitting in there, isn't it?"

"If it gets scraped by a stretcher they have no one to blame but themselves." I'm always warning Lucy about that.

She doesn't listen and nobody dings or sideswipes her cars. It hasn't happened once. But there's always a first time for everything, and I head in the direction of the autopsy room, which is dark and silent as I walk past its shut door. Beyond it is another autopsy room, what's really an isolation area for badly decomposed or possibly infected cases, and the two agents on either side of the steel door leading inside don't look happy to be here.

Using my elbow, I press a hands-free steel button on the wall and the door automatically swings open on a cloud of stench that sends both agents scurrying out of the way.

"How are we doing in here?" I ask cheerfully as I take my time holding the door open wide, and the foulness is thick and bristles like something alive.

Mahant, Anne, Harold and Luke are swathed in protective clothing and clustered around the only table in a room with a thirty-foot ceiling and banks of high-intensity lights, and I note that the observation window in the upper wall is empty and dark. Anne didn't think to tell our FBI visitors that they could sit behind glass in a teaching lab and avoid unnecessary unpleasantness if they preferred. They could drink coffee up there and monitor everything we're doing on a live audio-video feed. But Anne accidentally on purpose forgot to mention it, I guess.

Luke snaps a new blade into a scalpel. The paper bags have been removed from Elisa Vandersteel's hands, feet and head, and her sports bra, blue shorts, and socks are off and spread out on a white-paper-covered countertop. He begins to run the blade through her flesh, from clavicle to clavicle, then down her torso.

"It's looking like she has cardiac damage, possibly a torn posterior pericardium, and hemorrhage in the area of the left myocardium," he tells me what he observed on the CT scan. "Plus what looks like suffusion of blood in the interventricular septum."

"What about her head injury?" I reach for rib cutters on the nearby surgical cart, and situate myself across the table from Luke.

I'm shoulder to shoulder with Mahant.

"No skull fracture," Luke says as I cut through ribs, removing the breastplate, exposing the thoracic organs, and the putrid odor blooms up our nostrils like a dark deadly flower.

Mahant's face shield isn't going to save him, and I watch as he turns a tint of grayish green. Luke lifts the bloc of organs out of the chest cavity and sets it on a big cutting board with a wet heavy sound.

"Is something wrong with the air in here?" Mahant has inched back from the table, and he's staring at me without blinking.

"Too cold? Too hot?" Anne innocently inquires.

"I mean the ventilation." He swallows hard.

"It could be worse. We had a floater in here the other day." She looks at me as I snip open the stomach with surgical scissors. "In fact that's when the ventilation didn't seem to be working all that well."

"It's the heat wave," Luke says.

"How would that affect the ventilation?"

"It affects everything."

"You can imagine how hard our air-handling system has to work in this weather." I dribble the gastric contents into a plastic carton, and I'm surprised to find undigested peanuts and raisins.

"Obviously she had a snack not long before she died," I show Mahant the palm of my glove as he backs up another several inches.

"Maybe a trail mix or something like that?" Anne suggests as I snip through the connective tissue of the bowels, dropping sections into a plastic bucket on the floor while Luke removes a kidney from the scale.

"You might want to find out about that," I say to Mahant as Luke begins sectioning the kidney and Harold makes an incision around the top of the skull.

Then Bryce walks in, and he couldn't be more oblivious to what's normal for him and for all of us.

"Taking breakfast orders," he announces cheerily, and I resist looking at Anne, who clearly has gotten to him with her evil plan. "How many takers do we have for pizza?"

"Jesus," Mahant stares wide-eyed at him, and Harold pulls the body's face down like a collapsed rubber mask so he can access the top of the skull, gleaming white and round like an egg.

371

"Meat or veggie?" Bryce asks as Harold plugs the Stryker saw into an overhead cord reel. "And we have gluten-free." Bryce raises his voice over the loud whining of the oscillating blade cutting through bone. "But nothing *glutton-free*," he can't resist his favorite pun. "Because you can't stop eating it," he says.

Harold picks up a chisel to pop off the skullcap.

"The trick is to cut a little notch right here," he shows Mahant, who isn't blinking and hardly breathing anymore. "Then I insert the chisel and give it a little quick turn like a skate key." Harold does it as he talks, and then he's catching the ASAC as he topples like a tree to the tile floor.

"Oh dear. Let's get him some air." Harold holds him up and walks him to the door, and he's done this quite a lot in his career. "Here." He opens it and leads him out. "Let's find you a chair," he says in his best funeral-director voice. "Can one of you gentlemen please find a chair? He just needs a little air," he says to the agents in the corridor, and I must be a bad person.

I stay inside the decomp room and do nothing to help Mahant. As long as he doesn't throw up on the body or crack his head on the floor, I don't care if he's faint or queasy. I pretend I do but I know it's not true, and maybe he and his merry band of agents will leave and not come back.

"Take a look." Luke is slicing the heart on the cutting board.

He uses a towel to pat dry a section, and the fresh myocardial contusion is a tiny bluish-black spot on the pale heart muscle.

"Basically the electrical current walloped her heart and stopped it," he says.

"Do you think the injury to her head would have knocked her out?" Anne asks. "On CT she definitely has subarachnoid hemorrhage."

"It might have," I reply, "but it doesn't matter because the head injury didn't contribute to her death. Maybe it would have but there wasn't a chance. She was already dying when she hit the ground."

"Taking everything into account?" Luke adds as he takes photographs. "Death resulted from respiratory arrest due to electrocution. She probably didn't survive longer than several minutes, and I doubt she knew what hit her."

42

Across the river the rooftops of Boston are a gray dragon's back of slate tiles and chimney pots. I watch the darkness lifting on the horizon, the sun rising before my eyes.

From my office with a view I witness dawn touch the new day, the river turning variegated shades of blue with greenish hues. Iron lamps blink off along the pale gash of the fitness path where people are out riding bikes and jogging. The world is waking up as usual, as if nothing at all happened last night not even a mile downriver from here. The death in John F. Kennedy Park has hit the news but you'd never know it to look out my windows.

I walk across the carpet carrying a large very strong coffee I just made at the espresso bar. I sit down at my U-shaped desk with its bunker of large computer monitors, and I've been translating and transcribing for the better part of an hour.

I've decided spacing and line breaks based on cadence and pauses, doing my best to infer format from what I listened to in the Tailend Charlie audio clip e-mailed to me early last night:

> *Back again, K.S.—*
> *(By popular request, no less!)*
>
> *What's next*
> *will be worse*
> *than what was first.*
> *(Face it Florida cracker*
> *you were cursed at birth.)*
>
> *Chaos is coming*
> *in a stinging swarm,*
> *a death airborne.*
> *(Remember Sister Twister?*
> *Bet you won't miss her!)*

Interpreting meanings in cryptic messages and symbolism is like reading tea leaves, but what strikes me most about this last communication isn't the mentions of Florida cracker and Sister Twister. Lucy had told me about these when we talked in the trailer, and I don't care about insults right now. It's the threat that we need to pay attention to, and Lucy probably missed it because her Italian is inadequate.

What's next will be worse than what was first.

Was Molly Hinders first? Is this who Tailend Charlie is alluding to? And what's next? Would that have been Elisa Vandersteel? Or maybe he's talking about something or someone else entirely, and I wonder how much personal information about me came from years of Carrie spying on Janet's sister Natalie.

375

Carrie could have learned all sorts of things if she put her mind to it, and she could have passed on these details to an accomplice who's now using them to taunt and belittle. Someone brilliant but deranged, it enters my mind because that's the feeling I get when I'm subjected to his communications.

But why? There are so many things one might mock me about. Why pick silly names I was called as a child? Why not pick the much worse ones I'm called now? It's childish. In fact it reminds me of the way my sister used to fight with me when we were little kids. I decide it must be Carrie's new sidekick who's having such juvenile fun with verse recited in synthesized Italian that's supposed to be my father berating and disgracing me. I try Benton again. The call goes to voice mail again, and I leave another message:

Hey, it's me. I sent you my best effort with the latest troll-ish communication. Without being too specific, I think certain phrases in it might be of interest, and while I'm not the expert, it seems to promise something disastrous. The word aerotrasportato *or "airborne" was used, and I checked multiple times to make sure I heard the canned Italian word right. Call when you're able.*

It's almost seven A.M. here or about one P.M. in France, and I remember the last time I stayed at La Tour Rose in Lyon. It's hard to believe it's been six years since I last visited Interpol's headquarters, what looks like an intergalactic space station clandestinely situated out in the middle of nowhere along the River Rhône.

The secretary-general will be eating lunch because one thing I know about Tom Perry is he never turns down a civilized meal. So I'm not likely to get him but I try his office anyway, and his assistant Marie answers the phone.

"I'm sure he's at lunch," I say by way of an apology after we exchange pleasantries.

"He is," she replies in her heavy French accent. "But he happens to be eating at his desk as he finishes a long call."

"I want to pass on information and I could use his help with something."

"Hold on, please. And it's very nice to talk to you again, Madame Scarpetta. You must come back and visit soon."

I can hear her talking to the secretary-general in French but I have no idea what they're saying. Then he's on the line, and I know instantly by the tone of his voice that he's in the middle of something that is indeed serious. More serious than usual, at any rate.

"I wouldn't bother you, Tom," I say right off, "but I think it's time we talk about what's happening in Cambridge."

"And also in Bethesda, it seems," he says, and as I suspected he knows about Briggs.

Obviously Benton or one of his colleagues with the FBI has been in communication with Interpol, and I wonder who Perry was having the long phone conversation with right before I called. I wonder if it might have been Benton. His phone goes straight to voice mail every time I try him, and I would expect him to be informing the secretary-general of what's going on since some murderous miscreant is using Interpol's esteemed name in vain, basically spoofing the agency.

Possibly Carrie Grethen is. Possibly her accomplice is. Maybe both of them together are responsible for everything, but Interpol is more than a little familiar with her at least, I remind Perry as I explain why I'm reaching out to him. They got a bellyful of Carrie long years ago, and then like the rest of us believed she was dead until she decided to show us that she's not.

"I haven't had much sleep, so I hope I'm not rambling," I add. "But you know very well how dangerous she is, and I don't have an idea what the ultimate goal is but I know she has one."

"Why do you know that, Kay?"

"Because she always does, and I feel this is something really bad, that she's looking to make a statement."

"Certainly you know her better than I do," he says, and I don't like the way it feels when anybody points out that I know her at all.

"Based on information I've gotten from Lucy, it seems Carrie has been laying the groundwork for some sort of coup," I explain. "She's been planning something for years, and I'm concerned about more people being hurt or killed. I'm concerned about a lot of things."

"Well I'm glad you reached out to me, and I'm always grateful for your input, especially about a matter you've had so much personal experience with. What did you want my help with specifically?" The secretary-general has a Connecticut accent, and he doesn't sound surprised or impressed by anything I've said.

"Last time I visited you in Lyon we had a conversation over a very nice Bordeaux, and you made the comment that anything can be weaponized, and of course that includes fear."

"Which is the point of terror."

"If you can create a weapon that causes enough fear," I explain, "the fear itself can cause damage that's as paralyzing and destructive as any physical device like a bomb or a laser gun. Fear can make decent people behave irrationally and violently. And imagine suddenly worrying that something airborne might kill you as you ride your bike or swim in your pool."

"Yes, I agree," he says. "That would be extremely bad, especially if there really is a weapon involved. I understand your office is doing the autopsy this morning in the Vandersteel case."

"We're done," I reply. "By the time we got to it we already had a pretty good idea that she's an electrocution and most likely is a homicide. But what's new and somewhat of a surprise is there may have been an earlier victim."

"Where and how recently?"

"In Cambridge at the beginning of the week. In fact I'm fairly certain of it now, and that leads to my next question. Could there be others, including in places outside the United States? Cases of presumed lightning strikes or weird electrocutions, particularly if the person is around water and out in the open. It's also possible there are victims who survived. I'm not sure Elisa Vandersteel would have died had the electrical current not hit a metal necklace she was wearing."

"We're thinking the same way," Perry says. "You and I both know that things start small but the problem is, by the time we recognize these things, they're no longer small."

"If we're not careful."

"That's right. And we must be very careful because local terror in Massachusetts or the U.S. can be a proving ground for something international," he adds, and I tell him about Molly Hinders.

I describe her injuries, explaining that she was killed in Cambridge near the Charles River and so was Elisa Vandersteel.

379

Both of them were attacked as it was getting dark, meaning the visibility would have been poor, and moisture was a factor in each case. Molly was standing in wet grass as she sprayed a hose, and Elisa would have been sweaty. Moisture and electricity like each other.

"But it's curious. Why would Carrie Grethen be interested in either of the women?" Perry wonders over the phone.

"If you want my opinion? Carrie wouldn't be," and it's amazing how much I resist saying her name.

But I'm thinking of what Lucy said. If I make no effort to understand Carrie Grethen, I'll never have a hope of stopping her. And I do know her. I know her far better than I let on to anyone, including myself.

"Carrie would be interested in Briggs," I explain. "I can understand her targeting him, and mostly the choice is personal for her. Benton and I had worked with him for decades. You know how close I was to him. She's paying us back. Mostly she's paying me back."

"For what?"

I start to give him my stock flip answer of *who knows?* But I do know what Carrie will never forgive, and it's not really about Lucy or any of us. It's about Temple Gault. I killed him in a confrontation, stabbed a knife in his thigh and severed his femoral artery. I knew exactly what I was doing, and he gave me no choice. Carrie's never gotten over it, and according to Benton she's never gotten over him.

"But there's nothing personal about the victim selection with the other two," Perry says.

"There probably is but probably not for Carrie Grethen," I reply. "The more we're seeing, the less likely it is that she's working alone. So maybe her accomplice, her new Temple Gault, is killing the women while Carrie is on to bigger game like John Briggs or who knows who might be next."

"You know the problem with accomplices, don't you? They don't always do what they're told."

"Suggesting Carrie might not have anything to do with the Vandersteel and Hinders cases."

"If someone goes rogue."

"That would make her very angry."

"And her partners always go rogue. But let me ask you this first," Perry says over the phone. "From an evidence standpoint what justifies your deciding these cases are homicides? Has something turned up that I wouldn't know about?"

He wouldn't know about certain developments because the FBI doesn't yet, and I'm in no hurry to share the information. If the secretary-general of Interpol tells them, that's his business.

"Something has turned up, and you're about to be the only person I've told," I reply as I watch the sun peek above the horizon, painting streaks of orange across Prussian blue. "I've not told the FBI or anyone what I'm about to say to you. We need to be extremely strategic about how the information is shared because it appears we're dealing with a weapon that at least in part has been fashioned from a meteorite—"

"All right, hold on," he interrupts me. "Say that again."

I tell him about panguite as I keep thinking about what Ernie said.

You'd have to go around testing space rocks in every museum in the world . . .

Before he mentioned that, I wasn't thinking about museums. But now I am.

"Of course someone could have bought pieces of meteorites on the Internet but they wouldn't necessarily contain panguite. So we need to consider how someone acquired it and then had the ability to engineer it into something dangerous," I'm explaining to Tom Perry. "For example, was it stolen from a collection somewhere? Just as priceless art can be heisted from museums, so can rare rocks."

"Obviously you've not talked to Benton yet," Perry says, and I imagine the secretary-general's smiling eyes and easygoing manner.

No matter how busy he is, he never acts like he's in a hurry. Some of the nicest, longest business lunches I've ever had have been with him in Lyon, and he knows French wines dangerously well for an American.

"Obviously you've talked to Benton if you're asking me that. I've not talked to him since he left here with Lucy, headed to Maryland," I reply as light flares mirror bright on the surrounding Harvard and MIT apartment and academic buildings.

43

Shadows move over brick and granite. In the distance the skyline of downtown Boston is more sharply outlined and begins to glitter as the sun rises higher in the cloudless sky.

"Do you know who William Portison is?" Tom Perry says, and I'm betting Benton has talked to the man Elisa Vandersteel once worked for.

"Lucy says he's a tech CEO in London, clearly very wealthy," I reply. "The address for their Mayfair house is what Elisa had on her driver's license. We found it near her body."

"He's an alum of MIT, and so is his ne'er-do-well brother, both of them British. One is a mega-success worth billions and the other just as smart but missing a few wires or they're crossed or something. I'd call Theo in the spectrum, a whack-job genius."

"Theo?" I look out at pastel streaks changing in shape and intensity as sunlight flickers like shiny fish in the slow-moving current of the river across the street.

"Theodore Portison. He goes by Theo when he's not using an alias."

Rowers in colorful racing shells slice through the water, and rush-hour traffic sounds like a faraway train, a strong wind, a steady rain.

"Why would he use an alias?" I ask.

"He's paranoid people are out to get him. So he runs and hides, this is according to the brother," Perry says, and I feel sure the information actually came from Benton.

I seriously doubt the secretary-general of Interpol talked to William Portison himself, and my husband can get the most sensitive information from a stone.

"How old is the brother?" I ask.

"Theo Portison is forty-seven, single, never married. He taught quantum physics at MIT until he was fired about twenty years ago, and this has been checked out and verified."

He means that Benton has checked it out.

"Theo moved back to Cambridge about a year ago, and in fact I'm guessing that even as we speak he's either been visited by the FBI or is about to be," Perry lets me know, and I wonder where Marino is as all this is going on.

"Why was Theo fired?" I inquire, and I glance at new messages, and there's still nothing from Benton or Lucy.

"The short answer again is he's crazy," Perry says as I look out at the sunrise. "The long one is he was causing problems with female students. Apparently he would be overly attentive and then he'd start stalking them. Specifically what got him fired is he planted surveillance devices in one girl's dorm room. If you're going to spy? Maybe don't pick someone at MIT who's as smart as you are. He got caught."

"And what has he been doing for the past twenty years?" I ask.

"I don't think he has to do anything. His wealthy brother takes care of him, and in many ways always has. For a long time Theo lived with their mother in London but she died a few years back. As you're probably gathering, he has an adjustment disorder, to put it kindly."

"Would it be fair to say that the authorities have had their eye on Theo Portison for a while? I'm wondering if he has terrorist or radicalized leanings and it was brought to someone's attention?" After a long empty pause I ask, "Tom? Hello? Are you still there?"

"Yes."

"Yes what?"

"Yes it would be fair," and that's as far as he'll go in letting me know that the Portisons aren't a new problem. What they are is a different one. Especially Theo.

"Is there a reason Theo would be in possession of panguite or have access to it?" I ask the secretary-general, bringing us back to the traces of meteorite Ernie found.

"Well that's interesting because William Portison's business is aerospace technologies, and they build rockets among other things," Perry says. "He's into cars, space travel, timepieces, all sorts of things including rocks, and has his own museum, and guess who helped him with it? His limited brother. I think Theo is William's *Rain Man* aide-de-camp."

"Then it's likely Theo was acquainted with Elisa Vandersteel since she was living with his brother's family for the past two or so years. Is the rock collection in the house?" I ask, and there's much more to what Perry is saying than meets the eye.

"He keeps his collection in a safe room with a gun vault door."

"Someone needs to find out if anything is missing," I reply. "Specifically if any type of space rock is missing, and if so, what it is and most importantly what is the provenance. Where did he get it?" I explain what we need to be finding out. "The mineral fingerprint of the meteorite might be the only real evidence in this case. We can match it if it turns up again."

"But wouldn't Theo know that if he used to help with the museum?"

"It depends on whether his brother knows the details of what he bought or was given. William Portison might have acquired part of a meteorite and not known its precise elemental composition," as I hear the lock buzz free in my office door.

"Scotland Yard will be interested in all this, I'm sure," Perry says, adding to my suspicions that the authorities have more than one fish to fry.

I end the call as Marino walks in, and I'm reminded of his privileged character.

I haven't gotten around to deleting his fingerprint from certain biometric locks, including the one to the parking-lot gate, the pedestrian door that leads into the building and also the door to my office. It's been years since he headed investigations here. But I can't bring myself to eradicate all traces of him, and as I watch him walk in, I notice he's still in his same sweaty clothes he was working in earlier although he got rid of the navy jacket long ago.

He hasn't showered. That's apparent as he hovers by my desk like a predatory bird. On a scale of one to ten with ten the highest, I'd rate Marino's anger right now at a hundred. He's in what I think of as a white rage, his face livid, his eyes granite as he clenches his jaw muscles.

"You look about as pissed as I've ever seen you, and I hope it's not at me," I start to say.

"The fuckers," he growls, and I can see the pulse in his temple as a reddish-purple thrush creeps up his neck. "I'm sitting down with the guy and really getting somewhere, and the assholes showed up in fucking SWAT gear and had the mother-effing helicopter thundering over the damn house. When they realize it's just me and some local nutjob they call off the dogs, and then Mahant walks in like the new sheriff's come to town." Marino dusts off his hands. "The end."

"What do you mean *the end*? And who are you talking about?"

"Bryce's cranky next-door neighbor," Marino says to my shock. "I was just getting to the bottom of why he made the bogus nine-one-one call about you."

"Marino . . .?" as I think of what Tom Perry just told me about Theo Portison.

He's either been visited by the FBI or is about to be.

"It was exactly what Bryce said," Marino is talking fast and without pause. "To get him back for insulting him, and what better way to hurt him than to drag the big chief Doctor Scarpetta into the mix so maybe he gets fired—"

"What did you just call me?"

"Big chief?" Marino shrugs. "It's what he called you, not me."

"That's what Tailend Charlie calls me in some of the mocking audio clips."

"Well you can tell the FBI that but I'm not helping them a damn bit."

"Are you saying that they just showed up at Theo Portison's door while you were sitting in the living room with him?" I then ask.

"Who the hell's Theo Portison?" Marino scowls, looming over me. "Bryce's neighbor is John Smyth with a *y*, the English spelling. And I guess it's not enough for the Feds to take over the Vandersteel and Briggs cases but now they're looking into crank nine-one-one calls? I mean what the hell?"

"Did Mahant or someone tell you why they were there?"

"When do they ever tell us anything?"

"His name is Theodore Portison, and apparently he's known for having aliases because he gets paranoid." I push back my chair from my desk. "He was fired by MIT twenty years ago, and he knew Elisa Vandersteel. It's quite possible he's Tailend Charlie." I get up and take off my lab coat. "We'll see if I get any more audio files after this."

"Well they grabbed him," Marino says as we walk to my door, "They ended up arresting him."

"For what?"

"Hell if I know. But they've been digging through his landfill of a place. Shit. It's my case, Doc."

"The important thing is he was caught."

"But Carrie hasn't been."

"One down is better than nothing. Assuming he's Tailend Charlie, that he's the one who killed these two women."

"And has been harassing you, me, Benton. Using voice-altering software or whatever? Why?"

"Ask Benton," I reply. "But I'm betting it has to do with fantasies and power, and maybe the delusional thinking of a damaged brain mixed in. Does Theo Portison by chance have a drone?"

"He's got shit all over the place including what look like robot parts. The inside of his house looks like *Sanford and Son*. Think crazy-ass inventor meets homeless person, and it looks like his kitchen is also a lab, and part of it was under a plastic tent like he was making crystal meth or something."

"Does he have a cough?" I ask, and we're following my curved corridor to the elevator.

"He says he's got chronic lung disease, and I can't remember whose fault he said it was. He's one of those people who pretty much blames everyone for everything."

"I'm not surprised he has lung disease."

"Why?" Marino looks at me. "Just because of a cough?"

"If he works with nanotubes and doesn't do it in an appropriate clean room or under a HEPA-rated local capture hood—in other words a protected environment—he could have a serious respiratory problem from inhaling fibers and particles too small to see. And as you may remember, the phony Interpol investigator who called you had a cough. That's what you said. And maybe not so coincidentally, so did the phony Interpol investigator who called Benton."

"Nanotubes?"

I tell Marino about that next, and we're in the elevator now, the building restored to its usual sanctity and rhythm. People are coming in to work, and the FBI is no longer here. I'm sure Theodore Portison will keep them busy for a while, and Mahant may decide never to watch an autopsy again.

"I never did have any pizza," Marino says as the elevator slowly descends.

"That was a long time ago and you weren't here. How did you know about it?" I ask.

"Oh, I know your little tricks," he says. "I heard about the ventilation system and that you grossed out Mahant so bad he hit the deck."

"*Almost* hit it." I wave at Georgia as Marino and I pass through the receiving area, headed to the parking lot.

389

44

The limitations of human flesh, and I should know better than to think I can ignore them.

Driving home is an effort, and I find myself struggling to stay awake as I ease to a halt at a stop sign near the Harvard Divinity School in our Cambridge neighborhood. My blood sugar is low, and I'm feeling the crushing letdown that's a given after I've been fueled by nothing but high-octane adrenaline for hours.

Thankfully I live not even fifteen minutes away from the CFC, and I blast cold air on my face, listening to music, doing whatever I can to stay awake. It's a few minutes past nine, and the morning sun is bright overhead as I pull into the narrow brick driveway of our nineteenth-century timber-sided house, painted smoky blue with gray shutters and doors. There are tall chimneys at either end of the slate roof, and sunlight blanks out the upstairs windows as I park behind Janet's green Land Rover.

It has half of the detached garage blocked, and when Page returns from taking the dogs to the groomer, her pickup truck will block the other half. Good luck getting Benton's or my personal cars out should I need them for some reason.

Everybody's here, I think dismally, and then I feel selfish. As much as I love my family, what I'd like right now is privacy in my own home. And I need to give that up and get over myself. I need to be a good sport and remember not everything in life is about solving crime. Climbing out with my messenger-bag briefcase, I lock my CFC SUV that I wasn't going to leave at the office this time. Following pavers through the wooded front yard, I take the brick steps, aware of the early morning heating up. But by all accounts it's not supposed to reach ninety today. This weekend it's going to rain, and my garden and lawn could use it.

There's a lot of cooking I need to do, and I'm not prepared. Had I known this many people including Dorothy would be staying here I would have done major shopping, and maybe I'll find time this afternoon to get to the store before I have to get ready for the Kennedy School. Maybe I'll throw together something easy like lasagna that we can heat up after the event is over.

We'll open a few bottles of a nice Pinot Noir and drink a toast to Briggs, I decide as I stand on the front porch with keys in hand, looking around and listening. I hear a light breeze stir the old hardwood trees in the front yard, and I detect the earthy fragrances of loamy soil and mulch. A car drives by, one of our neighbors, and she waves.

Benton and I live on the northeastern border of the Harvard campus, across the street from the Academy of Arts and Sciences, and around us on all sides are lovely antique homes that are manifestations of enlightenment.

I love it here. I love fooling myself into believing I'm safe as long as I'm surrounded by smart people, and I look around some more, my hand on the door handle.

I don't hear anyone, and the dogs aren't here. But I detect a distant noise, a faint high-pitched whine like a table saw, and there's a house being renovated two doors down. Another car goes by, another neighbor, and I open the front door, noticing that the alarm isn't set. That doesn't make me happy. Stepping into the foyer of dark-paneled walls arranged with Victorian etchings I pause to listen, but I don't hear anyone, and it occurs to me that Janet, Desi and my sister might be in the backyard. In fact that sounds like a very nice plan. Maybe I'll drink coffee with them for a while. Then I'll try to sleep for a few hours.

At some point this afternoon I'll need to go over my talk for tonight because I've confirmed with my contact at the Kennedy School that I'm not going to cancel. I'm going to do this for Briggs. In spirit he'll be with me as I address policy makers about the dangerous planet we live on and why it's imperative to incorporate science and the highest level of training into everything we do if we're to expand our frontiers and protect ourselves.

Inside the kitchen I see used coffee pods on the counter near the Keurig, and someone had cheddar-cheese toast. Probably Desi, as he's become a big fan of Vermont cheddar since moving here and is quite particular about what color wrapper the block of cheese comes in. For him extra sharp is synonymous with purple, and in the mornings he asks for purple cheese toast, I'm told.

I set my briefcase on the breakfast table near a window, and I head to the back door, where Desi has parked the fishing pole, the baseball bat and glove Marino gave him for his birthday. The pole has a hard rubber casting sinker attached to a long sturdy leader line that's tied to the monofilament, and he's been teaching Desi how to cast the same way he once taught me. The nine-year-old is learning patience and precision, and not to muscle his way through life.

It's fine except for how it makes Benton feel, and as sorry as I might be about that, we have to do what's best for the child. Marino is good for Desi, and I don't mind them using the backyard as long as no one tramples my roses, and the rule is when the line gets tangled in trees, no one is climbing anything.

Safety first, and I begin to open the oak door leading outside. Then I stop because I don't understand what I'm seeing.

45

Lucy is in khaki cargo pants, a CFC polo shirt, a baseball cap and dark glasses. She's near the big magnolia tree with its circular bench, and Desi is standing woodenly next to her. He's holding what looks like an iPad, barefoot and in Miami Dolphins shorts and T-shirt, and he's wearing something blue around his neck.

I duck back into the quiet gloom of the hallway as I realize it can't be Lucy who's with Desi, and my heart lurches as if I almost stepped on a snake. She's in Maryland, and even if she magically were back this soon, the androgynous-looking person with short strawberry-blond hair is too thin to be my niece. I realize who I must be looking at as my heart pounds out of my chest, and I go to an app on my phone, turning the cameras on for the house and the property.

I duck into the pantry, where there's a flat-screen monitor on the butcher block. I zoom in on the backyard, tilting and panning, hoping Carrie Grethen doesn't know what I'm doing. She should have heard me drive up but maybe she didn't. Maybe she knows someone is inside the house watching but she might not, and I check every zone monitored by cameras, making sure I don't see anyone else on the property.

So far it seems Carrie is here alone, and I think of what I assumed was a white construction van parked on the side of the road just past our driveway. I saw it when I was pulling in, and I'm on edge, worried that any second Carrie's going to notice the cameras move. But she isn't looking. Her attention is all over the place. On Desi and also straight up at the sky and down at the tabletlike device he's holding, and across at my sister and Janet, who are out of frame but I know they must be sitting there. I just heard Dorothy's voice but I didn't catch what she said.

I turn up the audio on the HD cameras as high as it will go.

". . . I don't want to," Desi tells Carrie as he shakes his head no. "I don't want to sting anyone."

"Of course you do."

"It's bad to hurt people."

"Let me show you how much fun it is. Just click on that arrow key pointing at the word *enable*. It's in green on the display, and when you touch the key the color turns red because the TC is armed. A Tailend Charlie. Do you know what that is, son?"

"I don't want to play with you anymore. And I'm not your son," he says, and Carrie smiles radiantly.

"When you find out who you are it will be like discovering you're royalty. Prince Desi." She places a hand on his shoulder.

"You're scaring me," he says.

"But why are you doing this?" It's Dorothy talking again,

and I try to find her with the cameras. "I thought we were friends."

It would be like her to think she could persuade Carrie Grethen to cease and desist, to give up and go away or even more preposterous to believe that Carrie would like her and want to be friends. Of course my narcissistic sister would assume she's a match for someone who has caused misery and destruction for decades.

I lock in a camera on Dorothy and Janet sitting tensely in chairs some twenty feet from the magnolia tree. A small table with their coffees and bottles of water is between them. Both of them are in scrubs that they probably got from me, and neither of them moves. Their hands are in their laps, but I don't see any sign of restraints. Dorothy's eyes are wide, and the morning light isn't kind on her overfilled Botoxed face while Janet is quiet and steady.

I already know Janet doesn't have a gun. If she did she would have handled Carrie by now, and all of us have had to develop new habits with firearms now that a child is in the mix. I manipulate the cameras some more and I see the drone, what looks like a big black whirling spider with eight rotor blades hovering at the top of the magnolia tree. That's the high-pitched whining I was hearing. It's not construction at the neighbor's house.

I send Marino a text:

MAYDAY. She's at my house in backyard. Hostage sit & drone.

I don't call 911. I can't have regular patrol cars roar up. That's not how one deals with something like this, and it's sneaking up on me what Carrie is doing. She wants Desi to be inducted into her infernal family. She wants him to hurt someone, to kill someone with her weaponized drone.

Remember Sister Twister? Bet you won't miss her.

Carrie is going to kill Dorothy, and then she'll get rid of Janet. That leaves only Desi, and it's clear to me what she's planned to do as I think of her spying on Natalie. I wonder if Carrie was really spying on the boy.

"But why?" My sister never does know when to shut up, and Desi is a small statue holding the flight controller. "I don't understand. We had such a nice conversation on the plane," she foolishly says, and now I know.

Carrie must have orchestrated it so that she would be with my sister on the flight from Fort Lauderdale last night. No doubt she was sitting right next to her in first class, and that's probably why the alarm is off in the house and Carrie is in my backyard. Dorothy probably let her in just like she would some other new friend she's made, and my sister never meets a stranger.

She'll bring anybody home and did all the time when we were growing up. She never asked. It's always been her right to do whatever she wants, and this time it might cost her and all of us. My mind races crazily as I try to figure out what to do.

"I just can't understand why you're here being so awful, and after several drinks and our lovely conversation? I thought I had a new girlfriend, one who reminds me so much of my daughter, which is why we were so instantly taken with each other. And here I thought it was going to be such fun when I came north to see my grandson." My sister is crying. "Desi? Come over here right now and let's all go into the house like this never happened. And you just go on and leave us alone, do it now while you can," she warns Carrie, whose answer is to take the flight controller out of Desi's hands.

She moves the drone directly over my sister's head,

approximately six feet above her, and the flying blades stir her dyed blond hair, which is long and makes her look harsh.

"Just touch where it says *enable*," Carrie says to Desi, and she holds the flight controller close to show him.

"Don't do anything she says!" Dorothy cries.

"Shut up. Please," Janet says to her while not taking her eyes off Carrie.

But Janet has no weapon. If she did, she'd know exactly how to use it, and even as I'm thinking this I don't see a way out. Not in the usual sense of what one does in a dire emergency. It's very hard to shoot a drone. They're filled with empty spaces and even if you take out several rotor blades that doesn't mean you're going to stop it in time.

You'd need to take out the power source the same way you would an explosive device. But I don't have a water cannon handy, and taking the lock off the pistol I keep out of reach on a top shelf of a kitchen cabinet isn't going to help. Spraying bullets in a residential neighborhood is out of the question.

Page and the dogs are nowhere to be seen or heard. I hope they don't return from the groomer anytime soon, and my attention continues to land on the sports equipment rather sloppily tucked in the corner to the left of the door.

I see the fishing pole, and the baseball bat is wooden not metal. The baseball mitt is leather, and it, like wood and dry skin, is a good insulation against electricity. I also notice the empty hooks where Sock and Tesla's leashes hang, and it prompts me to send a text to Page:

DO NOT return home until U hear from me.

Carrie wouldn't hesitate to hurt anything we care about, including Page, including our pets.

"I'm going to show you," Carrie is saying to Desi as I continue to monitor the backyard with the cameras.

I watch the spinning drone hovering over my sister's head, and Carrie touches the display of the flight controller. The drone makes a vertical ascent, and at the same time I see the conductors lowering, four of them so fine they're barely visible, like thin gray pencil lines with something round and dark weighting each at the end.

Eerily the conductors vanish from view on and off. All I see are the round weights floating in space like tiny dark planets, and I think of the round burn on the back of Briggs's neck.

"I'm going to show you something cool," Carrie says to Desi, returning the flight controller to his unwilling hands. "But first you need to do something for me. An experiment. See the bottle of water on the table? Go pour it on Granny Dorothy's head."

"No."

"Do it."

"No."

I pick up the fishing pole.

"You need to learn how to be brave. What's wrong with you? It looks like I'm going to have to toughen you up." Carrie's face is transformed by anger. "See what happens when you're raised by inferiors? Well that's all about to change, Desi."

I've been fishing a few times in my life, mostly with Marino, who went to great lengths teaching me how to cast. I'm pretty good with my hands, and I flip back the bail on the spinning reel as I walk out the back door.

There's a chance the spinning blades will cut the leader and the line but I also know that even helicopters avoid monofilament. Lucy is careful flying low over beaches because of kites and helium balloons attached to hundreds of feet of fishing line.

Carrie stops me as her face turns murderous and at the same time pleased. I pull back the graceful long pole and snap it forward with just the right flick of my wrist, I hope, and the rubber sinker sails up in an arc toward the top of the magnolia tree. Sunlight catches the graceful monofilament line as it rises high and bends, falling over the whirling dervish, and I wait for the spinning blades to cut the line.

But they don't, and the drone jerks. At least one of the blades has stopped, and the sudden tugging cues me to start reeling as Carrie yells obscenities, the flight controller unable to override the lowest technology of modern time, a simple fishing pole.

"Run! Run!" Desi is yelling, and Janet is on her feet.

The drone careens like a wounded bird, and I reel and reel as Carrie's furious strides close in on me. Reeling furiously, and the drone is no more than ten feet away, loud like a whirling fan, the conductors dangling not far over her head.

I tug down hard on the fishing pole at the same moment Carrie pulls out a big stiletto and the long blade hisses out. Then blood is flying everywhere. I hear someone screaming and what sounds like a transformer blowing, and then I'm on the ground. I smell burned flesh.

46

For an instant I was Elisa Vandersteel sailing through empty space and landing on my back, remembering nothing. Except I came to in the emergency room. I'm not dead, not even close, and I sit up in bed to the sound of heavy rain.

It dully beats the slate roof and spatters the windows when the wind blasts, and Sock and Tesla are wedged warmly on either side of me. I hear their breathing, and then it's drowned out by howling gusts that just now whistled and moaned, and water thrashes and drums in different intensities and tempos. The early morning sounds moody and wounded. Or maybe it's me who feels like that.

The event at the Kennedy School night before last wasn't canceled but postponed, and that not only was wise but unavoidable. One speaker was dead, the other in the hospital. Whatever the drone's conductors came in contact with in addition to Carrie Grethen and her stiletto caused me to be thrown and knocked unconscious. I spent the

401

next day and a half being tested, prodded, probed and scanned, finally coming home last night.

So I didn't give my presentation to influential people, and here I am resting peacefully in bed with two dogs. I can't think of anything much better than that. Janet and Desi have been kind and thoughtful about looking after me, and Dorothy is around somewhere. Benton and Lucy should be home any minute, having left the helicopter behind in D.C. because of the weather. We'll have a wonderful brunch in a little while. I should get going, and I feel strangely lightweight as if someone turned down gravity.

It's as if the reign of terror has been lifted with the dry spell, the heat wave, as if the balance of life has been restored, and I feel happy in a way I've not been in a long while. Carrie Grethen was badly sliced up and burned, her skull fractured by the mechanical monster of her own design. When she's sufficiently recovered she'll be held in isolation at the local state psychiatric hospital, in a maximum security forensic unit for the criminally insane. She can't hurt anyone now, and her partner Theo Portison is in jail, neither going anywhere except to trial.

Meanwhile the police and FBI will continue their search for any other foot soldiers she may have recruited here or abroad. Lucy suspects Carrie can operate her drones remotely the same way military operators do. She could have had one docked in the Bethesda area and piloted it from South Florida to fly to Briggs's house and kill him. After that Carrie boarded the plane in Fort Lauderdale and enjoyed her friendly flight with my sister. I can't wait to hear what Dorothy has to say about that. Since I got shocked unconscious, I've not talked to her much.

I check my e-mail. My office is working overtime, and another note from Ernie confirms what we suspected, that the same panguite fingerprint we found in the Molly Hinders case was also present in the whitish linear burns on Elisa Vandersteel's body. Both women were electrocuted by carbon nanotube conductors that were retracted by spools into a monster drone powered by capacitors and coated in a thermal protective paint that includes panguite. The weights at the ends of the conductors, what resemble sinkers, also contain panguite.

Benton says making a weapon out of something stolen from his powerful brother was Theo's way of appropriating what he perceives as rightfully his. "Sort of like Jacob stealing Esau's birthright," my husband said, and he also believes that the murders in Cambridge were target practice, in a sense, except the selection of the women was emotionally driven by Theo's tendency toward erotomania and sexual violence.

Based on further information Benton has gotten from the brother William, it would seem that Elisa was friendly with Theo and likely had no idea that he was obsessed with her. Apparently after he returned to Cambridge a year ago he suggested that she should come here and try to get her foot in the door as an actress. She could stay with him while she interned, and she did for several weeks, living in a back room and helping with cooking and other chores.

Then she met Chris Peabody and soon after moved in with him, in part to get away from Theo, who by all accounts she was fond of but found increasingly annoying and overbearing. She thought him peculiar but likely never imagined that he was spying on her, stalking her, becoming increasingly enraged when he saw her with the young man she'd met and was falling for.

It's occurred to me that Theo may have been watching when Elisa rode her bicycle to the Faculty Club. I remember her kissing Chris Peabody on the sidewalk while Benton and I were there. It may very well be that Theo had been engaging in dry runs, practicing his drone maneuvers with her being none the wiser, and as she was riding through the park he may have decided to scare her. Maybe he didn't mean to kill her. But he did.

He wouldn't have shown up at the scene and taken the neckerchief or anything else from her body if he hadn't intended to kill her. The blue paisley-printed bit of cloth was a souvenir. Maybe Theo would have taken other items had Anya and Enya not appeared, and I wonder how long he might have hidden in the bushes watching them. It wasn't a deer that startled the twins. That's not what they heard running away in the dark.

There's much we'll never know unless Theo tells all. Or maybe his many recordings will offer an explanation. Benton believes the former MIT professor had been following Elisa and Molly remotely with his airborne camera. If so, there should be graphic proof of his voyeurism, dry runs, his kills. We'll get a peephole view into his violent sexual fantasies.

Benton and his colleagues will spend a lot of time going through boxes of carefully labeled audio-video storage devices. Apparently there are years and years of them inside Theo's landfill of a house, and it's a good thing he can't resist his compulsions. That may seem strange to say since people are dead, but many more would be had he been more disciplined.

The plan very well may have been to have these airborne directed-energy weapons stationed all over the place, and eventually Carrie would have an army of her own human drones operating mechanical ones. We may not know what she had in mind, and I suspect Benton won't find out no matter how much time he spends questioning her eventually.

Carrie isn't going to talk. If she does, nothing will be truthful. Or even if it is, it won't be helpful. Not to us.

I'm startled awake when Tesla suddenly sits up and barks, and I realize I must have drifted back to sleep. I fluff pillows behind me to prop myself up, and I pet her head as she barks again and Sock barely stirs.

"Yes, I know you've learned a big dog trick but please be quiet." I pet the small white bulldog with her brown-masked eyes as she barks and barks, her sides heaving in and out like bellows.

Woof—woof—woof—woof . . .!

"Okay, that's enough. What is it you think you hear?" I throw back the covers, and she won't stop.

I get up and pad barefoot to the curtained window across from the bed, and peeking out, I don't see anything except the rain lashing and flooding the driveway two stories down. The wind howls again, and Tesla barks more frantically as our brindle greyhound Sock continues to snooze.

"All right. Shhhh." I stroke Tesla gently, talking very soothingly, and it makes me feel better too. "It's just a storm." I rub her speckled ears, and the door to the bedroom opens.

"Rise and shine," Dorothy sings out as she enters, and now I know why Tesla was barking.

It was my sister she was hearing, and Dorothy is wearing a large T-shirt and nothing else as she carries two coffees.

"Mind if I come in?" as she hands me a steaming mug and sits on the bed. "Hush Tesla. I can't stand a yippy dog."

"I wouldn't exactly call her yippy. She sounds rather fierce."

"Well it's an irony, right? She's named for a car that's supposed to be quiet."

"Actually it's Lucy's joke. For someone with the biggest carbon footprint on the planet? Now she can tell people she has a Tesla."

"How do you feel? I've heard stories about people who get shocked almost to death or struck by lightning and suddenly they can play the piano or their IQ goes up ten points."

"I'll let you know. I've always wanted to play the piano."

"Did you have unusual dreams?"

"Not yet."

"Listen, Kay. I need to explain better what happened," my sister starts to say, and I stop her.

"How is Desi doing?" I ask because all of us should worry about how traumatized he might be.

"I'm telling you!" Dorothy brags as if she had something to do with it. "What a trouper that boy is! He seems fine."

"He's had plenty of practice putting on the brave front, Dorothy. That doesn't mean he's fine."

"You know? One of the things I've learned after writing how many children's books?" She smiles at her rhetorical question. "Plenty, right? The point is, I know kids. And I'm always amazed at how we're bothered by a lot of things that don't bother them in the least."

"Just because he's not showing something doesn't mean

he's not bothered. It will be good for Benton to talk to him when he and Lucy get home."

"Look." Dorothy sips her coffee. "That evil woman came up to me, and of course I did a double take because at first I thought she was Lucy."

"Stop."

"I was waiting at the gate, and she started talking to me, and what a coincidence our seats were next to each other—"

"Stop right there." I hold up a hand, and shake my head.

"But I need to explain what happened. You need to let me—"

"So far you've not explained it at all," I interrupt, "and we need to leave it that way, Dorothy."

"But I just said—"

"You've explained nothing. Period. We can't discuss what went on with you and Carrie at the airport, on the plane, or when she showed up here at the house after you invited her here and then let her in. Okay?"

"But I—"

"No."

"It's just that you must think I'm really stupid but it's not like anyone ever told me about her—"

"I'm a witness in the case the same way you are. Now not another word. Thanks for the coffee. It tastes sweet. Did you put sugar in it?"

"Agave nectar, just the way you like it."

"I don't take sweetener."

"Since when?"

"Since ever, Dorothy." And I have to laugh because the more things supposedly change the more they don't. "You were always the caretaker," I tease.

"I've never been one of those," she says sullenly, and she doesn't seem to be such a good one for herself either.

My sister's hair is too long and too blond, and whoever she's paying a fortune to for aesthetic work ought to be locked up. Her unnaturally round cheeks crowd her eyes when she smiles, her lower jaw is too heavy, and she couldn't frown if she tried, making it slightly more challenging to read her discontent and underlying chronic boredom.

"You have to understand this is the biggest thing I've ever done." Dorothy's over-enhanced breasts are on high alert, and it would suit me if her T-shirt were about ten inches longer.

"What's the biggest thing you've ever done?" I inquire. "I'm afraid I don't know what you're referring to."

"I helped catch someone. You've always been the crime buster, Kay. And I'm just this overblown pretty woman who's doing the best she can to keep her shit together while I just get damn older all the time. I mean look at me. No matter what I do."

I start to tell her to cut out the tanning booths. Her skin looks spray-painted tan, but I don't go there. She doesn't need my criticism, and maybe I'm not the only one who's pathologically insecure but doesn't show it most of the time.

"I'll tell you what's missing." I set down my coffee on the bedside table. "If you go into the closet and open the first cabinet on the left, you'll find something special I keep down here for rainy mornings just like this one."

"A joint would be nice," she says.

"A very nice Irish whiskey," I reply. "Go on in there and

408

pour us two shots. Then we'll talk as long as you don't ask me anything you shouldn't."

I watch my sister walk into the big cedar-lined closet, and I hear her going into the cabinet and pulling the cork out of the bottle.

"We should get Mom on the phone this morning. Both of us," I say as Dorothy returns.

"Not unless she puts her hearing aids in. I'm tired of yelling." She sets the shot of whiskey by my coffee. "You're never around. In fact you never have been ever since you left for college. So I've been on my own with her. And now I'm the one she picks on."

"I'm very sorry to hear that."

"The book business not being what it was? Kids don't want to read what I write, not this day and age."

"I don't believe that."

"I mean let's face it. I'm not going to be invited to Comic Con." My sister looks rather crushed.

"Never say never." I taste the whiskey and it's warm going down, warmer than the hot coffee but in a different way. "We spend our lives reinventing ourselves, Dorothy. I never knew that until I got a little older and wiser."

"Well our mother's decided I'm the failed one. It used to be you because of your divorce and no kids, and then you decided to be a doctor to dead people so you don't have to worry about losing patients, about them dying on you."

"I'm sure that's what mother says." I reach for my coffee.

"That and getting involved with a married man."

"Mom has to say we've failed because she feels she has," I reply. "She never had a chance to do any of the things we can, and maybe she questions what her purpose on this earth has been. If so, that's not a good way to feel when you're almost eighty years old."

"Well look." Dorothy throws back the whiskey as if she needs courage, which she doesn't. "We're the only sisters we've got, right? So we're in this together, and mainly I wanted to make sure you're okay with Pete and me."

"I don't really know much about Pete and you," I reply as I feel indignant inside when I have no right to feel that.

"It's the real thing, and one favor you could do me is make it sound like I did something helpful at least in catching that monster. What's her name? Carrie Gretchen."

"Grethen. And you were helpful," I reply, and it's true but not the way my sister would have intended.

She was helpful because she single-handedly brought Carrie to my door. It was Dorothy who began answering Facebook postings from someone who claimed to be a childhood friend from our early days in Miami. My sister bought into Carrie's traps hook, line and sinker, and began a correspondence that supplied more information to Carrie than she already had.

Dorothy happily volunteered nasty nicknames, and that my father had recorded a radio commercial for his small grocery store. Carrie must have gotten her hands on it or maybe Theo Portison did. There's nothing good to come of my rubbing it in that Dorothy engaged in a long conversation with a perfect stranger on a flight, and then invited this person to my house and almost got all of us killed and Desi abducted. Dorothy is no match for Carrie's machinations.

But then none of us really are or it wouldn't have taken this many years and destroyed lives to catch her.

47

"A minute please to wash my face and grab my robe." I walk away from the bed, heading to the bathroom. "Then we'll get Tesla and Sock downstairs and you can help me in the kitchen. What's Desi doing? Is he up yet?" I call out to Dorothy.

"He slept with Janet," I hear her say. "I think they're getting started on brunch. They wanted to surprise you by helping."

I smell sausage cooking. And Desi's quite the meat-eater in our midst, he and Marino.

"Why did she want him, Kay? Why would anyone go to such lengths to kidnap a nine-year-old child?"

I stop outside the bathroom door and look at her, wondering if she's serious, and sadly she is. "People have gone to much more extreme lengths than Carrie did," I reply, and my sister doesn't want to know some of the horrors I've seen.

"Well I honestly don't get it." Dorothy wouldn't get it because she couldn't be bothered with Lucy, and that's another thing I need to let go of.

We head downstairs, a rambunctious puppy bulldog and slow old greyhound at our heels, and in the kitchen Janet has the window open over the sink. The sound and smell of the rain is carried in on warm steamy air, and my thoughts are pulled away, outside into the storm. Desi is setting the table in the dining room while Dorothy makes more coffee but I'm not in here in my head.

I'm back in my Miami neighborhood, and I see the child I once was, small and slight with white-blond hair, light blue eyes and cheap clothes. I see my yellow shoe box of a house and the scraps of overgrown yard with sagging chain-link fencing on three sides that kept nothing out including local cats and dogs and an occasional escaped parrot. I see all of it as if I'm watching a movie or back in time, and then thunder splits the air and lightning illuminates the windows.

"Uh-oh," Desi says as he walks back into the kitchen, and the power has gone out. "The lights in the dining room don't work all of a sudden."

The backup generator has kicked in. But only certain areas of the house will have power. Fortunately the kitchen does, and then someone is pounding on the back door.

"It's Marino," Janet is looking at her phone. "I'm just seeing his text. He was at the front door, now he's in back and needs to see you, Kay."

"I didn't hear him pull up."

"The rain's too loud to hear much of anything," Janet says as I follow the hallway past the pantry, to the back of the house.

When I open the door Marino is standing hunched over in a yellow slicker with the hood up, and he says,

"We need someplace private to talk. The doorbell in front is broke. I rang it trying to be polite for once."

"The doorbell you pressed is original to the house and not connected to anything. Didn't you see the modern little box with the lighted button that's been there as long as we've lived here?"

"It's dark as shit. What about you grab an umbrella or something and we'll talk out here."

"In the pouring rain with thunder and lightning? How about you come inside and I'll pour you a coffee?"

"Nope. Right here." He points next to him. "Really, Doc? I'm not kidding," and I can tell he's not as I grab a waterproof jacket off the coatrack.

I put it on, pulling up the hood, tightening the drawstring. Stepping outside, I close the door and face him in the splashing downpour.

"What is it, Marino? Are you afraid there might be surveillance devices in the house? Is that what the problem is?" I ask because there could be for all I know. "I'm going to have to talk to Page and make sure she's not let someone in, perhaps someone masquerading as a service person."

It's the sort of thing Carrie would do, I explain as the rain coolly taps the top of my covered head. But Marino's hardly listening, and I'm beginning to sense bigger trouble.

"I'm not taking any damn chances, Doc."

"Why are you here? What is it?"

"I don't know how to tell you this," he says, and I feel instantly sick.

"Are Benton and Lucy all right?" I can barely speak as I think of them flying and driving in this weather.

"Huh? I don't know. I guess." Marino's eyes are wild, and he couldn't be more distracted.

"What's the matter with you?" I raise my voice above water spattering pavers and the sound of the wind-rocked canopies of old trees.

Beaten-down flower petals litter the back lawn like tatters of pastel tissue paper, and puddles sizzle as rain splashes the grass and mulch.

"That blue paisley bandanna Desi had on?" Marino says loudly, water streaming down from the peak of his hood. "The DNA's a problem. It's worse than a problem."

Carrie came to my door like anybody else would, standing there smiling, I can only imagine, and Dorothy led her through the house. Then Carrie and the drone appeared in the backyard at precisely the same time, robbing Janet of any opportunity to defend herself or anyone. I realize this probably is why Marino is insisting we talk outside in the middle of a rainstorm.

Carrie Grethen has been inside my house. It's possible she may have planted a device or two as she walked through. Dorothy would have been none the wiser. Apparently she didn't begin to think anything was off until Carrie gave Desi the blue paisley-printed neckerchief, ordering him to put it on and stand by her side as she operated the flight control before turning it over to him so he could destroy his own adopted family.

"Did anyone from the DNA lab call you?" Marino is asking, and I bolster myself for the rest of his bad news.

"Not yet."

"Well I just found out. And maybe they don't want to bother you right now after being in the hospital. But you need to know the truth, and that's why I'm here standing outside in the damn rain with you," as distant thunder cracks.

414

"Who found out what?" Water is splashing over my bedroom slippers, and the hem of my pajamas and robe is already soaked.

"Elisa Vandersteel's DNA is on the neckerchief, which makes sense since it was hers. And we got Carrie's DNA on it and also Temple Gault's."

I'm certain I didn't hear that right. It's so loud and volatile out here, and a part of my brain knows what's coming even as I deny it.

"I'm sorry . . ." I start to say.

"I know what you're thinking. But you heard me," Marino says. "We got a hit on Gault's DNA in the database because he's never been purged due to open cases the Feds are still trying to tie to him. And of course we got a hit on Carrie because she sure as hell's in there."

"This is impossible. How would Temple Gault's DNA get on the neckerchief unless Carrie has some source of it and deliberately contaminated—"

"No." Marino is slowly shaking his head side to side, water dripping, his eyes wide. "No, no, you aren't getting it, Doc."

"What am I supposed to be getting, Marino?" I don't want to believe what he's about to say.

"At first we didn't understand why Desi's DNA wasn't on the bandanna, the neckerchief, whatever you want to call what was tied around his neck. His DNA should be on it," he begins to explain as I get an incredible feeling.

It's like condensation clearing from a window and finally I see what's on the other side. Little Desi with his angular face and mesmeric blue eyes.

"His DNA was on the bandanna after all . . ."

No one is a better fisherman than Carrie. She knows

what to do. She knows how to wait and when to tug the line. Gotcha.

"Do you understand what I'm saying?" Marino asks, and the rain has turned into a roar as I remember what Lucy told me about Natalie's pregnancy.

She used a sperm donor and a surrogate mother she'd carefully selected, but the fact is the process could have been tampered with.

That would be child's play to Carrie, and there would be no reason for Natalie knowing the truth about Desi's DNA. It would have to be run through a criminal database to get a hit on his biological parents, and that wasn't likely to happen. But Carrie has forced the matter to a conclusion, and it's one that I never anticipated.

"She must have saved Temple Gault's sperm, frozen it or whatever." Marino turns as the wind blows, keeping the rain off his face. "You know like these military wives do when their husbands go off to war . . .?"

"I know what she must have done, and I can see her doing it," I reply. "Have we confirmed this with Desi's DNA? He was swabbed for exclusionary purposes."

"Yeah. It's confirmed. Carrie is Desi's mother. Temple's the father."

"Biologically only."

"She was going to take him, Doc. Carrie was going to raise him to be the next monster. A hybrid of her and Gault. Holy shit. How lucky for her that Natalie died and Carrie could then kick her plan into gear," Marino goes on.

He has it all figured out.

"She creates an incident in Maryland, and you, Lucy

416

and Benton haul ass there," he's saying as a gust of wind sweeps a sheet of rain across the yard. "Or she assumed you'd hightail it out of town, leaving only Dorothy, Janet and Desi all by their lonesome. Only you threw a monkey wrench into things by staying here, and then the attack had to be changed to your house . . ."

"I have no idea what was planned or why," I reply. "Only that it's over and all of us are safe."

"Except for Desi. What are we going to tell Lucy and Janet?"

"We'll tell them the truth. Desi can't help who his biological parents are. It's no different than if he'd been adopted and we had no idea who or where he came from. There's no guarantee what anyone gets, Marino. Not even when it's your own biological child."

"But what if he's like them? I mean really. Think about it. He's right here with us. What if he grows up to be like them? I mean as great as the kid is? What if . . .?"

"He won't be raised by them," I reply. "He'll be raised by us. Now let's go inside. Let's get brunch going, and I was thinking of making a pitcher of my bloody marys."

We walk back into the house, taking off our raincoats, and water drips on the mat and the hardwood floor. I kick off my drenched bedroom slippers, and step into a bathroom.

"I think I have what I need in the house to make peanut butter pie." I toss him a towel.

"Since when do you make that?" Marino looks as if he's seen a ghost, and in a way he has.

"It seems like a good day for it with Dorothy here, and she loves peanut butter and chocolate, has quite the sweet tooth." I reset the alarm. "But then you probably know that about her," as we return to the kitchen, where Desi is on a footstool getting plates out of a cabinet.

I look at his thin broad-shouldered frame in the Celtics warm-up suit Marino gave him. Desi isn't going to be very big or tall but already he's graceful and lithe, and he's getting strong. He fixes his wide blue eyes on me as he steps down from the stool with an armload of plates, and I've not really talked to him since it all happened. I take the plates from him.

"I think you know where the napkins are," I say to him.

"Yes, ma'am."

"If you want to get them, please, and I'll help you set the table."

"I already did the mats. I hope the ones I picked out are okay." He grabs my hand.

"As long as they match."

We walk out of the kitchen hand in hand, and take the first left into the dining room.

"How did you learn to fish, Kay-Kay?"

That's what Desi calls me.

"Why do you ask?" I turn on the alabaster chandelier.

"I wondered why you thought of my fishing pole when the bad lady was trying to hurt us with the drone."

I open the side draperies to watch the rain pound the side yard in the early-morning billowing fog. Wind shakes the spruce trees and rhododendrons, and intermittently rain smacks the glass.

"I didn't think of it," Desi then says before I can answer him. "When she kept trying to make me do things, I didn't think of doing what you did. I should have caught it with my fishing pole and stomped it to death."

"It would have been much too dangerous to stomp on it."

"I could have hit it with my baseball bat."

"You wouldn't want to get that close. Think of it as a huge Portuguese man-of-war you see on the beach with its long tentacles. What do you do?"

"Stay far away!"

"That's right."

He follows me around the table, setting down a napkin to the left of each plate I place on a mat.

"But what made you think of my fishing pole?" He's not going to let me evade the question.

"Truthfully? Because I couldn't think of anything else." I open a drawer in the breakfront, and silverware clinks as we gather that next. "When I saw what she was doing I had to do something. I was lucky."

"Why did that lady want to hurt us?"

"There are some people who aren't happy unless they do bad things to others."

"I know, I know. My moms are always telling me that," Desi says, and of late he's started calling Lucy and Janet his moms.

Specifically Mom and Moms. Lucy is the latter.

"But why did she come here and make me try to hurt someone?"

"What matters is that you didn't." I stop and look at him. "You told her no and you wouldn't do what she said. And that makes you the good person, the strong person."

"I guess so," he says, and then he scampers out of the dining room.

I hear the door open that leads into the basement, and his quick feet on the stairs. When I return to the kitchen he's standing near the breakfast table with a fishing pole. Not his because that's been taken by the police as evidence,

419

but he's fetched mine from the basement, and he looks very serious. I recognize the old spinning reel with its graphite-black telescopic rod, and everything is coated in dust.

"Will you show me how you did it?" He offers me the pole.

"I'm not an expert and we can't really do it inside the house." I hold the rod with the reel foot between the middle and ring fingers of my left hand. "But I let out about six inches of line from the tip of the rod just like this. And I tighten it slowly under my index finger."

I show him, and the reel *click-clicks*.

"Then I hold the line and open the bail, and do you know what the most important part is after that?" I ask.

"What?" he says.

"You aim, pointing the rod at where you want to cast. You point at your target. You've got to know what it is. Then bring up the rod and load it using your elbow and wrist. And let her rip," I explain. "Like most things in life, it's all about timing."

"And it's time to make drinks." Marino walks in, and Benton and Lucy are right behind him.

"Tito's, V8, fresh limes. Who's going to help me?" I walk straight to Benton and hug and kiss him.

"I will!" Desi dashes to the pantry where we keep the liquor.

"I've got the V8 and limes." Janet opens a refrigerator.

"Where do you keep your pitchers and glasses?" Dorothy opens cabinets as she asks.

"I'm so glad both of you are back safely in this awful weather." I hug Lucy too, and I can't tell if she knows about Desi.

But I don't intend to get into the discussion now. It shouldn't be important, and if we discover it is, then we'll figure out something.

"Worcestershire, Tabasco, my special seasonings? Who's helping?" I take the bottle of vodka from Desi and tell him he's going to help me wash celery.

"I break off the stalks like this." I show him in the sink as he stands next to me on his stool. "Now we rinse them under cold water, and we pull off the fibers because they're tough and nobody wants to eat them."

"They're like dental floss."

"And all of them come off. Very good. Right there in the garbage disposal."

"Like this?" His hands are in mine as we rinse a stalk under the running water.

"Exactly like that," and we wash celery together, getting every speck of dirt.